ECONOMIC MAN

In Two Volumes: VOLUME ONE

Economic Man

IN RELATION TO HIS
NATURAL ENVIRONMENT

C. Reinold Noyes

VOLUME ONE

Columbia University Press

NEW YORK · MORNINGSIDE HEIGHTS

1948

CONTENTS

VOLUME ONE

INTRODUCTION

Part I: Wants and Means

VOLUME TWO

Part III: Environment

Part IV: Synthesis

Appendices

ECONOMIC MAN

INTRODUCTION

A. THE *CREDO*

THE AIM AND METHOD of this study can hardly be explained without a statement of certain of the articles of my scientific faith. In the first place, I am convinced that, before the "social sciences," so-called, can be developed into true sciences, the apostles of the social sciences will need to have become disciples of the natural sciences. And this in respect of material as well as of methods. It is often remarked that the fields of the several social sciences are not readily distinguished. At the most, they are but different aspects of the same set of data; at the least, they are definitely overlapping. But this is equally true of the social and the biological sciences. Man is one of the organisms, and he cannot be understood unless he is regarded as such. This overlapping is even true, in some respects, of the social and the physical sciences. Man's relation with his environment, which is the background and medium of his social existence, is conditioned by the physical, chemical, geological, and other facts of that environment. Thus an adequate understanding of the biological and physical sciences seems to me to be a prerequisite for sound work in the social sciences.

It is equally essential to adopt and adapt the methods and techniques of the established sciences. Of these there are three, in particular, which it is appropriate to mention here. The first is the most recalcitrant so far as this field is concerned. Perhaps the most fundamental change in attitude produced by the intellectual movement called science has been the change, so far as it has been effected, from attributing to external nature the characteristics of the subjective (animism, anthropomorphism, etc.) to examining external nature in what we define as an objective manner. In essence, objectivity consists in seeing external facts as they are and in permitting them to impress themselves on the mind as free as possible from subjective coloration.[1] Difficult as it is to acquire objectivity with regard to external nature it is, of course, vastly more difficult to do so with regard to human nature.

---

[1] The studies in Part I, below, will offer a physiological basis for the distinction between subjectivity and objectivity.

Nevertheless, it must be done. Either the social scientist must himself become an Olympian, leaving man at his present stature, or, remaining himself a man, he must come to regard *Homo sapiens* as an organism.

The second desirable feature of scientific method can best be suggested indirectly. I should like to substitute the term *analytical economics* for the older term *theoretical economics,* and the substance of analytical economics, as it develops, for the several "theories" of this and that of which theoretical economics has been composed. Theoretical economics has been too largely deductive—logistic—and the connotations of the term "theoretical" have come to suggest a purely abstract if not a purely speculative character. Analytical economics is not speculative, though it uses hypotheses; it is not abstract, though it uses abstractions. This because it is wholly inductive. Its generalizations are never applied outside the range of data from which they were constructed. Analytical economics can follow the lines of analytical chemistry. Its first task is to reduce the data of economic life to manageable classifications or types of entity (analogous to qualitative analysis in terms of atoms). Out of these entities it can construct models representing the various systems of relationship, both static and dynamic, that bind them together in the several varieties of that kind of universe we call an economy (analogous to qualitative analysis of molecules and compounds). The basis and method of such organizing of the data can be of precisely the same order as those utilized by all other sciences for their several universes.[2]

This leads inherently to the third feature that we need to borrow from general scientific method—the reduction of the data to quantitative terms. Again there is some correspondence to quantitative analysis in chemistry. Because the atom has been reduced to a definite magnitude in terms of atomic weight and valences, the structure and composition of each molecule and each compound can be defined unequivocally. It is a waste of time to try to deal quantitatively with entities which have not first been reduced, by qualitative analysis, to terms which represent at least approximate uniformity. Even then, in economics, we face the apparent immeasurability of many of our entities by any method of mensuration known at present. In spite of

[2] As a former chemist, I see the problem in this light. Even better analogies might be derived from biological and geological classification, for, there, the several individuals classed together are never precisely uniform.

this, I believe it is essential so to define our entities that they can be constructed into conceptual magnitudes with definite dimensions that comply with the logic of quantitative thinking. They must not be left vague and uncertain in character; nor must they be conceived in terms of dimensions that are inconsistent.

This study undertakes to practice these preachments. It is chiefly founded upon data, and on constructions from them, that have recently become available in certain of the biological sciences. It aims at complete objectivity—the study of man as an organism. It is an essay in analytical economics,[3] attempting the classification of these data and inductive generalization therefrom. There result certain hypotheses, based partly on inference. An effort is made so to define the entities that they can be conceived as magnitudes with specified dimensions, in the hope that, as such, they may some day become capable of measurement. Nevertheless, in spite of these good intentions, now that the study is concluded, I am impressed chiefly with its shortcomings and its failures. And that introduces the most important tenet of my scientific *credo*—the necessity of patience and perseverance. It will be a long time before analytical economics can show results of a degree of certainty similar to that shown in the physical sciences; we have hardly started; we face perhaps greater difficulties; but we must recognize no bars; and we must accept no substitutes.

B. THE PROJECT

The vast complexity of the subject matter has led to the departmentalizing of economics. It has been divided and subdivided in order to reduce the several fields of specialized study to feasible proportions. The basis of this analytical separation has been chiefly functional or in terms of the relationships between two or more functions. To use a biological analogy, it is as if we had been studying the general principles of organisms, their structures and their functioning—studying the circulation in general, metabolism in general, excitation in general. This division of the subject has served a very useful purpose in that it has made possible an abstract scheme of economic life which makes that life comprehensible. But it is open to two serious objections which appear more and more clearly as knowledge increases. The first is relatively minor, though more frequently mentioned. Car-

[3] That is, it is in no sense "descriptive" economics.

ried on more or less separately from each other, these functional analyses do not always fit together. Concepts and terminology do not always agree; and, even worse, the several universes may not match.[1] The second objection, less often mentioned, is that, to use our analogy again, study of the general principles of organisms, only, does not permit classification of the various forms of life into the several species and genera. But reality is composed of different species and genera; their very differences are of the essence of them; and in hardly any two are the general features of structure the same, or are the general functions performed in the same way. The several—perhaps the innumerable—forms of economic life are subject to the same differences. Their structures and their functionings vary, with the result that the relationships among their functionings may be not only diverse but actually different in kind.

Many years ago it occurred to me that there is available another and supplementary approach to the problem of subdividing or simplifying our subject matter in order to make it manageable, and one which would be more generally useful than the opposite extreme of the present division—namely the descriptive study of each individual form of economic life. This approach would involve, first, a separating out and an analysis of what is necessarily common to all forms of economic life—their uniformities; second, a determination and analysis of the chief factor making for marked differences—division into genera; and, third, determination and analysis of the factors making for differences within the genera—division into species. Obviously this would be a most ambitious project, one far beyond the reach of any single man. But, for three good reasons, I have decided to sketch it out in this Introduction. The first reason is that it is necessary to do so in order to explain what this particular study is directed toward; for this study is a first step in the project. The second reason is that, at my time of life, it does not seem probable that I can myself do much in the way of studies of the second and third steps. Therefore, the third reason is that an explanation of this approach may be suggestive and helpful to other explorers in the field of a science of economics.

The approach involved in this project may serve a purpose larger than the development of "pure" science. The ultimate purpose of all

[1] Not so long ago economists were complaining to themselves that the universe constructed for the theory of money did not accord with the one developed for studies in "real" terms.

science is the benefit of humankind through increased control over the natural and the social environment. To enable such control, it is necessary first to find out how things work and thus to disclose what, under any particular set of conditions, are the limitations set to the possibilities. In the economic field man seems to be subjected to three independent sets of such limitations or conditionings, and these three sets seem to correspond, respectively, to the causes of uniformities in economic life, to the causes of differences between genera, and to the causes of differences within genera. Thus they seem to divide themselves into the several steps of our project. If we can separately analyze each of these three systems of limitation or conditioning, we shall be less likely to confuse them, and thus either to try to disregard them where they cannot be disregarded or to try to apply them where they do not need to be applied.

From this point of view the study of economics would divide itself into three branches. To give these branches names we may call them the biological, the technological, and the sociological or institutional, respectively.

Biological. Man is an organism of a certain constitution living in a natural environment which is subject to certain "laws." The two combined represent the inescapable conditions of man's relations to nature —his habitat. Neither his constitution nor these "natural laws" can be changed by him. They must be accepted as "given." They establish a set of limitations or conditionings which is rigid and final; only within these limitations is there freedom of action. Furthermore, these fundamental relations of man to nature are the data of any form of economic life at any time or anywhere; they are of exactly the same order, scope, and force in the most complex modern form as they were in the simplest and most primitive form.[2]

Technological. Within this rigid primary framework man succeeds in better adapting his environment to himself by adapting his own actions to the "natural laws" of that environment. Thus he develops

[2] These inescapable conditions seem to have been what Marshall had in mind when he said, "The 'strategy' of his [man's] conflict with nature remains nearly the same from age to age, and the lessons drawn from experience of it can be handed down usefully from father to son." What he refers to as "tactics" seems to correspond with our "technique," below (see "Distribution and Exchange," *Econ. J.*, March, 1898, p. 8).

A similar idea is conveyed by Cassel, *74*, vi. (Reference numbers in italics refer to the List of References, preceding the Index.) Cassel says, "The ultimate aim of economic science must be to discover those necessities which are of a purely economic nature and which cannot be arbitrarily mastered by the will of men."

technique. A whole system of technique may be called a technology, or state of the arts. Economics is not directly concerned with the technology itself, but it is intimately concerned with the economics of any technology. It is that which constitutes the technological branch. Each technology beyond the most primitive prescribes a set of differentiated functions which must be performed by some form of human organization—that is, it cannot operate in an institutional vacuum, for it involves more than one man. It also imposes other requirements, some of which will be suggested below. Thus, for any given technology, there is a further set of limitations which are themselves rigid and final; only within these limitations is there freedom of action.

Sociological or Institutional. Within the rigid primary framework (biological), and subject to the limitations and functions prescribed by the technology, there is a third system to which man's life is conditioned. This is his social organization. Ostensibly this is a field in which complete freedom of individual or social action might obtain. True, every form of economic life, from that of the lone individual up to the most complex society, when it is regarded as a whole, is subject to all the limitations imposed by man's constitution and by the "laws" of his environment. True, there is a strictly constraining interaction between the technology and the institutional arrangements. The functions which the technology prescribes may be executed more or less well by different institutional arrangements. But, apart from these, does the fact of social organization itself impose a further set of limitations and conditionings? Are there inherent in the nature of man as a social animal certain dividing lines between what is possible and what is impossible? These questions do not seem to have been asked, at least in economics or at least in any similar form.

It would appear that the data of the biological branch must be accepted as they stand. The facts are unchangeable; the relations between them can be changed only by changing technique. The data of the technological branch do not constitute a *must*, for there are as many technologies as there are stages in the development of the arts. But they probably constitute a *will*. Civilized man could discard modern technology. It is hardly probable that he will do so. If he does not, he must accept its inherent conditions. We cannot yet say as much for the data of the sociological branch. For there are many conceivable institutional systems, and there may be a much wider range of possible variation without an unequivocal preference. But, even there, it is well to regard social human nature as a natural force; for man has always acted far more like such an uncontrollable force than he has like the intelligent human being each of us conceives himself to be.

C. THE METHOD OF ATTACK

The objective unit of study for a science of economics is *an economy*, a *kind* of economy, or *economies* in general—the individual specimen, the species, the genera, or even the order.[1] By an economy we mean an individual, or a group of human beings, viewed in the aspect of making their living—or, more exactly, applying efforts to the satisfaction of their wants. An economy is usually conceived, nowadays, as localized in a circumscribed area. It is projected upon the land.

For analytical purposes an economy must be treated as self-contained. Therefore, any group is only an economy if it is self-contained, or to the extent that it is.[2] Within an economy which is self-contained there may be sub-groups which function as economic units in some respects, but which, in other respects, are not self-contained as to each other (e.g., families, corporations). Such an economy is *compound*. Carried to its extreme that means that no economy can be strictly *simple* unless each of the individuals composing a group is economically self-contained. But, then, each individual composes an economy by himself.

Hence the only economy which is strictly simple, in this analytical sense, is that of an isolated individual. Not only would his economy be self-contained by reason of his having no one else to depend on for the satisfying of his wants, but all his own efforts would be applied to the satisfying of his own wants. Such an economy we are going to call a *direct* economy.[3] It is an analytical abstraction.

To the extent that an economy is not simple, in this sense, and therefore is not direct, it must be compound—that is, the economies

[1] I hope it will be clear to the reader that this concept of the field of a science of economics is as far removed as possible from Wicksteed's declaration of his purpose, his definition of "economy," of "Political Economy," and of "Economics." To him, "economy" is the art of management, not a science. And since "Political Economy" and "Economics" include "economy," they too are arts, or at least are applied sciences. They seem to consist of "oughts," not of "ares" (see *441*, 13–16).

[2] To the extent that it is not self-contained it is part of a larger economy.

[3] According to the definition of compound economies the degree to which any group was self-contained would make of the group as a whole a direct economy to that extent.

of the individuals or groups composing it cannot be self-contained. Therefore, it must be *indirect*. To the extent that it is indirect, the efforts of individual members are applied to the satisfying of the wants of other members, or of members of other economies. And, to that extent, there must be *organization* within or among the economies.[4] The chief functions required of organization in an indirect economy are two-fold. It must provide a system of substitute motivation, since the wants of the individual no longer directly induce his efforts. And it must provide a system of control over the operations of the economy, as well, perhaps, as over its resources. Such control is necessarily vested in persons and exercised over persons and things.[5] In turn, this system of control must perform two subfunctions. First, it must govern the *allocation* of all resources—human efforts and natural resources— among the specific products to be produced. Second, it must either govern the *allotment* of a generalized share in total product among specific persons, leaving to them the *apportionment* of their shares among specific products; or it must govern the *division* of each specific product among specific persons.[6] The second of these two subfunctions of control, performed in either way, may serve more or less adequately to provide the system of substitute motivation. And it may be eked out by other forms of substitute motivation.[7]

[4] As I have demonstrated, I think, in a previous study (see *313*), the economic organization of society is "the property organization with its recent satellite, employment." The proprietary structure includes both private and public property, so-called. Both are private in their ultimate inherence. But public property is held, in the first instance, by political organizations. Political organization may be the guise in which certain private persons appear; or it may be an agency for collective holding by all persons; or it may be something between the two.

[5] This axiom is carefully stated. As stated, it does not preclude the theoretical possibility of separate control by each individual or of joint control by all individuals.

[6] These four common words are arbitrarily assigned, in the terminology we shall use, to these four specific and distinguishable functions. There is nothing particularly appropriate about any of them for its particular use. Any other words or any other assignment for these would do as well. The only important thing is to keep the ideas distinct.

Actually division is almost always present, even if only at a subordinate level. That is, a single *allottee* will usually *divide* among his family. Theoretically, division might be used alone. That is, all of each product might be rationed among all members of the economy without opportunity of choice by them.

[7] The "natural" system of substitute motivation, or incentive, as worked out by classical economics, has been the system of "distribution," so-called. In fact, this identification of the measure of "reward" with performance of economic functions by the individual, at their "market-values," has come to be the basis of what may be called the notion of *economic* justice—to each according to his performance (usually only work). On the other hand, there has always existed and, of late, there has come to be prominent the notion of *social* justice. This involves equal division (or allotment) of

All these functions of motivation and control have their correspondents in a direct economy. There, the motivation is the individual's own wants, which therefore requires no substitute. It is direct. The allocation of his resources and the apportionment to specific products are one and the same process. Strictly, then, his allotment is all to himself and there is no division.

It is clear that the only possible objective unit of study for the biological branch of economics is a direct economy. Only if we limit ourselves to examining the behavior of a single man in relation to his environment as if he were entirely independent and self-dependent can we abstract from the aggregate of actual complexities all those compulsions to which he is subject because of technological or institutional factors. Only if we analyze what would exist in a technological vacuum—in so far as technique requires co-operation of others in developing and applying it—and in a complete social vacuum, can we determine the working of the factors which are absolutely independent of particular technologies or social milieux. Only thus can we separate out the inescapable conditions to which man's life on this planet is submitted—the basic pattern into which all technological and institutional variations must be fitted.

In this strict sense, a direct economy never has, and could not have, existed. No individual man, of record, has ever lived so entirely alone that he acquired nothing from others, past or present.[8] Man lives in society, and has always done so. But by that fact he does not cease to be an individual man.[9] Therefore, the direct economy is an analytical

---

the total output, or even division to each according to his needs. Needless to say, the latter system has always been more or less widely practiced *within* the family. The question needs to be carefully examined whether, or how far, division on the basis of "social justice" would meet the essential requirements of a system of substitute motivation.

In the unsigned article which appeared in the Russian Journal (No. 7-8, 1943) "Under the Banner of Marxism," (Tr. R. Dunayevskaya, as "Teaching of Economics in the Soviet Union," 34 *Am. Econ. Rev.*, 1944, 501) it is stated that "the law of value will be overcome only in the highly developed stage of communism when the productivity of labor will be so advanced and society will have at its disposal such an abundance of products that transition to the distribution of products according to needs will become possible." Is this a possible conjuncture, or is it purely illusory?

[8] The nearest actuality to a direct economy is the family or the isolated farmstead with a single head. For, then, so long as this head allocates the efforts of all according to *his* wants and divides the product according to *his* choices, the economy approaches a single unit. Since "economics" originally meant "the law of the household," in a day when the household was almost self-contained, it is appropriate to think of this type of economy as the nearest exemplar in reality for the study of fundamental economics.

[9] Individualism, in the strict sense, is as imaginary a condition as is socialism, in the strict sense.

abstraction; but it is an abstraction which is not abstract; its components are drawn from life; but they do not exist alone; they are not complete by themselves. The direct economy is what the physicist would call a "virtual" economy. We shall have occasion several times to define our use of the term "virtual." [10] Here it suffices to state that the method of abstraction which it involves is a familiar one in all natural sciences. Both biology and physiology deal largely or wholly with the individual specimen even when they are including consideration of his relations with the environment. His social or group relations usually constitute a separate subject.

The choice of this apparently unrealistic method of approach to the study of biological economics incidentally serves two other useful purposes. The first is that, from the beginning, the development of a science of economics has always included it. In view of the enormous complexity of the subject matter it has often astonished me that, from the effective beginnings with the Physiocrats and Adam Smith, penetration to the basic and fundamental principles—the axioms of man's economic life—should have been so sure and swift. True, many of the simplifications have been but first approximations and well-nigh erroneous. Nevertheless, an insight into these axioms has become the very basis of the thinking of every trained economist. The great difficulty, however, which has arisen from the older method has been that these axioms have tended to become confused with, or distorted by, the extraneous characteristics of the particular technological and institutional background in which they were first, or have been since, studied. It is necessary to separate the axioms—to differentiate the *musts* from the *mays* or the *mights* of economic life. We can do this only by studying a single man as an organism in the environment as his habitat.

The second advantage is more far-reaching. The necessary relations of the relatively unchanging organism, man, as he is, to the relatively unchanging environment, as it is, are more easily perceived by

---

[10] The direct economy is "virtual" in another respect, as well. If we studied an actual isolated man, his specialized economic functions would not be apparent. Only when we lift an individual out of the complex economy of actuality can we analyze with respect to him all the specialized functions of such an economy. The same conditions exist in the study of unicellular *vs.* multicellular organisms. As Semon says (*368, 26*): "When the division of labour amongst cells and tissues is far advanced, and specific organic functions have been evolved, our study of these functions is made more simple and the results of our work are less ambiguous than in those cases where functions are merged in each other, and it seems almost impossible to differentiate them."

abstracting the isolated man—a direct economy. But, taken as a whole, an actual and indirect economy, if it is self-contained, is subject to all the same conditions. As an aggregate, it is a direct economy.[11] There is, however, this difference. In the direct economy—the single-cell organism—these necessary relations would confront the individual human being in an undisguised and unobscured form. In fact, they would stare him in the face. They would be the obvious data of his own experience, given by his own physiological constitution and the unalterable facts of the environment. On the other hand, in a complex, multicellular economic organization—an indirect economy—which is composed of many individuals and even subgroups and whose complexity imports variable relations among individuals and subgroups, the fundamental necessary relations of man to nature confront and compel only the economy as a whole. They are still inescapable; but their incidence may be concealed from many individuals; the incidence may even be shifted, for a time, so that it weighs unevenly on different individuals or subgroups. To that extent the direct relation of man to nature is no longer felt because some men come to mediate between their fellows and nature.[12] And therein lies a danger if the deficit in individual experience is not made good by study and understanding. For the economy as a whole still stands or falls according as it meets the *musts*.

It is true that there is not, and probably never has been, a direct, unorganized economy; it is true that from its origins and in its development economic life has always involved organization. Man actually lives in a society, and it has been man in society who succeeded progressively in adapting his actions to his environment and thus in adapting his environment to himself. Any realistic study of economic life must therefore concern itself as well with the economic effects

[11] That is, in the aggregate, the wants of the members are solely satisfied by their own efforts, and their efforts are wholly devoted to their own wants.

J. B. Clark (*80*, Chapter IV) suggests this approach. He says (*ibid.*, 37), "In particular, it is necessary to know that the primitive law which puts a man face to face with nature and makes him dependent on what he personally can make her yield to him is still, in essence, the law of the most complex economy." "The universal laws of economics depend on relations of mankind to nature . . ." "The picture of an isolated man . . . illustrates a characteristic of modern life which is in danger of being overlooked . . . Think of society as an isolated being, turning its collective energy to the making of one thing till it has enough of it and then making another, and you have the fundamental fact."

[12] This both at the physical level (e.g., the farmer or the ship's officers and crew) and at the economic level (e.g., the businessman).

of man's technological development as well as with the related forms
of his collective organizing—his institutions. To pursue this approach
into the field of the technological branch, which I hope to be able to
undertake, would therefore require the study of economic organization; for none but the most primitive techniques can be made available except by means of organization.[13] That, in turn, would substitute an indirect economy as the objective unit of study. As noted
above, in such an indirect economy certain functions require to be
performed which do not appear, or do not exist as separate functions,
in a direct economy. The actual systems for organizing these functions—substitute motivation and control—are, however, the subject
matter of the institutional branch. Therefore, here again abstraction
would be necessary. For each technology it would be necessary to suppose that there existed an institutional system by means of which
these functions were somehow performed. But all that this technological branch is concerned with is the required functions, not their manner of effectuation. One would assume that men did, as if they were
robots, what was necessary in order to make the particular technology
work. One would examine the ground plan, the mechanics and the
nature and quantitative relations of the magnitudes which were imposed by any particular technology. Such an approach with regard
to the more important technologies—the major stages in the development of the arts—would be serviceable to anthropologists and economic historians. For my part, I would be interested in working it out
only for the modern technology. That is of pressing interest, because
the entire world seems to be in process of adopting, or of attempting
to adopt, that technology.

The ultimate aim of the project would be to superimpose, on the
analysis derived from studies in the two more fundamental branches, a
study of institutional economics. In such a study the prerequisites
determined in the previous studies would be taken as given. The requirements and limitations set by man's life on earth are inescapable;
those established by modern technology are almost equally positive,
if modern technology is to be operative. The scope of variation for
institutional systems under these conditions is presumably limited to a
range in which, within the limitations, the requirements are met more

[13] That is, any technology which involves *concurrent* specialization requires more
than one man; and any that involves more than a small degree of geographical disper-
sion also does so.

or less well. Only one new factor would appear here. That is man as part of his own environment. That factor would introduce modifications from the behavior of the human being when he was considered only by himself. It would influence and perhaps add to his wants. It would bring in the emotional interactions between human beings, the influence of the past—tradition—and that of ideologies—intellectual contagion.[14] As I see it at present there seems to be little scientific basis for a true social psychology, which would be the *sine qua non* for an adequate treatment of this new factor. Perhaps all that would be possible would be certain rough and broad preliminary generalizations, which are commonly accepted. But even without much in the way of effective treatment of that new factor, I am inclined to think that a careful examination of the various chief forms of substitute motivation and of control which we find to have been operative in the past, or to exist in the present, and a careful appraisal of the adequacy of each for an economy composed of human beings as they are, in the world as it is, and for an economy utilizing the modern technology, would help to clarify one of the major issues facing humanity in these times.[15]

[14] Another effect that would appear is worth mentioning here, since we discuss the subject at several points in this study. In economic life the *event* is largely the consequence of men's own actions, constrained, it is true, by the conditioning of the environment. These actions are largely continuing or habitual. Thus the event is apt to have a certain regularity. The event which is solely the consequence of an individual's action can, in time, come to be predicted by him with considerable accuracy. The event which is the consequence of many men's action has far less regularity and, since knowledge of each other's actions is largely lacking, comes to be much less predictable.

The concept of a rational norm for the event resulting from many men's actions, to which the forecasts of individuals fail to conform only because they are irrational is, I am sure, an illusion. Anticipation cannot be "rational," or even correct, until it becomes something else, namely hindsight.

[15] For instance, even without such a study it would seem safe to say that where the institutional arrangements contemplated under "Jeffersonian democracy," or those existing under the patriarchal system, obtain, modern technology is precluded.

On the other hand, only such a study can determine the validity of "historical materialism." In the article on the "Teaching of Economics in the Soviet Union," referred to in note 7, above, it is stated that "the basic law of historical materialism . . . consists in this, that the production relations of man are determined by the character of the productive forces at the disposal of man at a given stage of the development of society" (*ibid.*, 505). It seems proper to identify the "character of the productive forces" with what we are calling technology, and the "production relations" with the subject of "political economy" as defined therein: "The social aspect of production," "the social organization of production," or "those social relations which are formed between people in the sphere of production" (*ibid.*, 503). The supposition seems to be that technology uniquely determines the institutional organization of the economy. Is that true? Modern technology was evolved almost entirely under a single form of institutional organization. Does that fact fix the form unalterably? If not, does the

D. THIS STUDY

The subject of this study is confined to the biological branch of economics, as we have called it, and therefore to a direct economy. That is, as we have said, only the first step in the whole project. Its scope, its self-imposed limitations and its relationship to the other two branches have been sufficiently described in the foregoing. The Table of Contents outlines the organization of the study. But perhaps a word of interpretation is in order. We have taken the direct economy apart, so to speak, along lines similar to those familiar to economic analysis. Part I analyzes the human being as a consumer and therefore deals with his wants, their satisfying, and the means by which they are satisfied. Part II analyzes the human being as a producer and therefore deals with his efforts and sacrifices—"real costs." Part III analyzes the environment in its economic relationship to the human being, chiefly as producer. Part IV undertakes a synthesis of these analyses; that is, it attempts to put the parts together again to see if they will work. Since the parts of the analysis, separated or combined, only exist on paper it is necessarily left to the reader to determine whether, after synthesis, they do work or not.

There are three features of this study as to which I feel I owe to the reader explanations and, in a sense, apologies. They combine to set him an arduous task, if he takes it seriously. The first feature is length. It has always been my belief that, in science, the publication of more or less novel views is unjustifiable unless these views are supported by a thorough assemblage and a careful sifting of the evidence upon which they are based. But evidence, as the law reports show, is necessarily bulky. Furthermore, in a study which covers so diverse a field, mere references are practically useless. The literature is unknown or even unavailable to many who may wish to read critically. But quotations necessarily add much to the bulk. My solution of this problem has been to separate out from the text, so far as possible, my working papers, the details of the evidence and the quotations from my authori-

---

evolved technology uniquely determine a new form different from the one which gave it birth? The answer to these questions does not depend wholly on historical evidence. In fact historical evidence may be equivocal. Adequate analysis of the requirements and the limitations of modern technology and of the manner of performance of the necessary functions under different forms of institutional set-up would at least shed much light on the subject.

ties.[1] As a result, the text itself is not unduly long. That permits each reader to determine for himself how superficially or how deeply to go into the matter. One reader can confine himself to the text. On the other hand, another more particular and interested reader will find, I think, that the footnotes and appendices adequately supply the details and support which he rightly requires. Except for the synopses of the basic data for Part I, the appendices consist, in effect, of footnotes which would be excessively long as such.

The second difficulty with which the reader is faced is one that is inherent in the subject matter. Because of my belief that economics is fundamentally a biological science, this study is written in a number of languages—all English. The babel of scientific terminology is a serious obstacle to intercommunication. Nevertheless, it seems to be an inevitable one. For the essence of scientific expression is precision. I have tried to obviate this difficulty as much as possible by interpreting the special terms for the unfamiliar reader. But there are limits to that, particularly when quotations are necessary in support. These difficulties of language are practically confined to Part I. I hope that economists who find themselves unable or unwilling to follow the inductive studies in the first four—or even the first six—chapters and their supporting appendices will not let that discourage them from reading the rest of the volume. Thereafter, the work consists of economic analysis only, using as a basis the hypothesis derived from the inductive studies. Any competent student and observer can readily follow the analysis and can determine for himself whether the results correspond to reality. If they seem to him to do so, he can tentatively accept the hypothesis even if he does not fully understand how it was developed, or even if he has not fully satisfied himself that the results were correctly derived. An hypothesis that works is worthy of tentative acceptance on that ground alone.

My own contribution to this confusion of tongues—the third "obstacle," as Pareto would have called it—is actually a residue left after as many evasions as I found possible. For my economic terminology I have relied on the standard terms wherever I could. A few special terms have been unavoidable; but for these I have chosen ordinary words,

[1] Sources cited by number, in italics, are identified in the List of References, preceding the Index. My selection of authorities for citation is almost entirely limited to the major *innovators*, during the last fifty or seventy-five years, in the various fields covered. Space forbids anything further.

merely giving them precise and limited meanings in this context. In a few cases standard economic terms will appear in quotation marks. That either signifies that I am using them in the ordinary economic sense without relating them to any category dealt with here; or it signifies that I have had to give a special, precise, and restricted meaning, in this context, to an economic term whose usual sense is broader or looser. Which significance the quotation marks have in each case will be perfectly apparent to the reader because, when I attribute to the term a special meaning in this context, a careful definition is given at its first appearance. I should like to make it quite clear that neither of these methods has been used with any purpose of undertaking, myself, to reform economic terminology, although I agree with the fairly general sentiment in holding that the present unsystematic system is inadequate and unsatisfactory. A new and truly scientific terminology must be the result of a general movement, not of an individual's effort. It is probable that it must consist of a system of coined words, as is the case in all the exact sciences. Such a system will alway be too inconvenient to the reader unless and until it is rather unanimously and more or less simultaneously adopted as a part of a general movement. I feel sure that the time will come when economists will do just this. Before, however, we can be prepared to develop a systematic and specialized nomenclature for our entities, we must determine with far more than present exactitude just what the entities are which we are naming. It is only the struggle with this problem which has forced me to adopt, in part, a new or special, if merely tentative, terminology. Only where it has been necessary for the sake of precision have I done so. But, having analyzed, described, and defined entities which in their nature or limitations (criteria) are in some important respect different from the customary broad or vague ones in use, it is necessary to preserve these results by distinguishing such entities either with a different name or a special definition. It is hoped that this compromise will effect the desired result with not too much inconvenience to the reader and that, in respect of the exact definition and classification of entities, if not of their permanent naming, it will be a step in the right direction.

Part 1

WANTS AND MEANS

I

PRESENT WANTS—THEIR NATURE AND CENTRIPETAL MECHANISMS

THE PROCESS which is assumed to be the occasion for man's economic activities in and vis-à-vis his environment has been termed, in economic literature, *the satisfying of wants*. In this process the motive or driving force has usually been called desire for such satisfaction or for the means which yields it. These naïve and every-day terms and concepts, while they are derived from subjective (introspective) psychology, have in themselves no inherent relation to the categories of objective behavior which are being explored by modern physiologists and scientific psychologists, and which, so far as possible, are being analyzed in terms of the observable physiological processes that underlie them. Since, for effective scientific progress, it is necessary that each branch of science should maintain liaison with the branches on its flanks,[1] it would be desirable, if it should prove possible, to replace the old subjective economic categories with the new objective behavioristic and physiological categories, or at least to identify the one with the other. And since, in all scientific fields, the deeper the level of analysis to which we reach, the more secure the foundation, it is desirable to dig through, wherever we can, to the solid rock of physiological observation of the actual processes occurring in the human body.[2] This is especially desirable in this particular field, for it is certainly true, as Pavlov has said, that "psychology cannot yet claim the status of an exact science,"[3] while physiology, so far as it reaches, can

[1] Moreover, as Pareto puts it (*317*, 40), "La psychologie est évidemment à la base de l'économie politique, et, en général, de toutes les sciences sociales." See also the author's remarks on this subject (*313*, 5–13).

[2] As William James expressed it (*220*, II, 440–449), "the beauty of all truly scientific work is to get to ever deeper levels." The author has elsewhere (*314*, 501–504) discussed the relationship of these "levels" to scientific analysis.

[3] Pavlov, *320*, 3. He also agrees (*loc. cit.*) that "It would be more natural that experimental investigation of the physiological activity of the hemispheres should lay a solid foundation for a future true science of psychology," and that such a procedure is "more likely to lead to the advancement of this branch of natural science."

certainly do so. In fact, it may be that, because of its peculiar nature, psychology will never be able to make this claim, and will always remain *en l'air* except as the processes it studies can be identified with physiological phenomena. Perhaps its subject matter is as unintelligible by itself as that of geology would have been without physics and chemistry. Therefore, our aim in these first chapters will be to develop in terms of physiological phenomena, so far as present knowledge permits, a restatement of the nature and operation of human wants and their satisfying. Beyond those borders we shall have to rely on the more tentative results of observational psychology.

By way of clarifying the issues it will be well to make a brief survey of the course of scientific progress in psychology in the past half-century, so far as it is germane to our subject. Philosophical dualism—mind and matter—has been practically discarded. "After 1850 . . . the hypothesis of a non-physiological mind or soul becomes extremely difficult to hold." [4] The monism which has taken its place is sometimes called "mechanistic." This is a false analogy.[5] We should say

---

[4] Gardner *et al.*, *166, 276*. Rather, the operations of the "mind" have come to be conceived as servants of the basic physiological processes. "While we speak of man as a rational animal, his very reason, his creative intelligence works to the urge of feelings which are deeper than ratiocination and which are the vitality of the stream of life. And the satisfaction of even our most abstract thought comes from this deeper vital urge" (Boodin, *40, 310*). That view does not leave a mystic element either in "mind" or "vital urge" ("vitalism"). For the conviction is prevalent that "it is highly probable that the physiologist will be able to complete his explanation of behavior without bringing in any non-physical or mental factors" (Troland, *408, 10*).

[5] "When we compare organisms to machines . . . we do not imply that the principles of mechanics, alone, are sufficient to account for their behavior" (Troland, *408, 73*). But that is not a sufficient recantation. Nor is mere denial sufficient, even in the picturesque form which MacBride (*279, 1*) ascribes to "Dr. Broad" to the effect that "he who asserts that his brother or his cat is a mere mechanism is either a fool—or a physiologist."

The eminent physiologist, the late J. S. Haldane, went much further. "Organisms are not machines" (*178, 117*). "A living organism has, in truth, little resemblance to an ordinary machine" (*ibid.*, 91). "To me the mechanistic theory of life appears impossible, not merely in connection with the facts of heredity and embryology, but at every point in biology" (*ibid.*, 111). "So far as it is possible to judge, those who seek in physiological phenomena for the same kind of causal explanations as can usually be assigned in connection with inorganic phenomena, have no prospect but to remain seeking indefinitely, unless they cut the knot by relapsing into vitalism" (*ibid.*, 87–88). "To the vitalistic theory itself, however, there are insuperable objections" (*ibid.*, 111). "In the din of the controversy between vitalists and mechanists there was, however, a complete failure to go to the root of the matter" (*ibid.*, 113). When that was undertaken there appeared "a biological conception of life which cannot be reconciled with the mechanistic conceptions" (*ibid.*, 116).

In part, the mechanistic approach failed because, from that viewpoint, the organism was examined "piece by piece" as if it were composed of independent parts instead of constituting a continuum. Today, as Dunbar points out (*122, 8*), there has been a

"organismic"; [6] for it is obvious that, while we may hold to the thesis that the activities of an organism are susceptible of being ultimately stated in terms of physics and of physiological chemistry, nevertheless we must recognize that the differences in degree of complexity and of instability between organisms and mechanisms are so great that they become in effect differences in kind.[7] On the technical side, the method of introspection has been more and more restricted to those phenomena that cannot otherwise be reached, and then only by way of establishing their existence, not their nature and operation. This is not so much on the assumption that its observations are incorrect, as that it is seen to be a very limited,[8] naïve, superficial and, therefore, non-scientific kind of observation. To take its place many objective methods have been devised, some of which we shall have occasion to touch on as we proceed. Finally the central problem has become, or is becoming, *the causation of behavior.* Until, on the one hand, physiologists really set to work on the problem of reflexes and, on the other, Freud began his attack on the problems of abnormal psychology,[9] it

---

"transition from the premise that the whole could be understood by a study of the parts to a new emphasis on the whole." This new viewpoint was based considerably on the work of biologists which we shall discuss later (Chap. 3). But it was also due in no small part to Haldane and his emphasis on the "continuum" which we shall consider in this chapter.

[6] For the noun, Haldane suggested "organicism" (*178*, 3, note 1).

[7] Cannon (*66*, 19) notes, as many chemists have noted, the correlation between the complexity of structure and the instability of a molecule. "Our bodies are made of extraordinarily unstable material." And the macrocosmic structure is as complex and unstable as the microcosmic (that of the cells and molecules). Perhaps this high degree of complexity and instability is at the base of the phenomenon that is called "life."

[8] Because it is limited to the field of consciousness, and "consciousness acts as if it were a section of a much larger system, most of which is hidden from view" (Troland, *408*, 13).

[9] Woodworth (*446*, 4) says "the push from outside that changed the course of psychology came from physiology." But he is referring rather to the German school of the last century. Troland is one who ascribes to Freud—and, politely, to "other psychiatrists"—the beginning of "a scientific discussion of motivation." "Compared with an ideal scientific discussion, Freud's theory is quite vague, but in comparison with previous theories of motivation it is a marvel of lucidity" (*408*, 37). While his influence has been chiefly exerted at this point it is of interest to note, what many must have observed for themselves, that "Freud's dynamic account of fundamental biological processes in the organism lends itself astonishingly well to translation into ordinary physiological terminology" (Gardner *et al.*, *166*, 359) though it is not so expressed. (See also, on this, Brun, *51*, 147). We shall not attempt such a translation, but the close correspondence will appear at many points in our subsequent examination. It is as if Freud, exploring from one side, and the physiologists, exploring from the other, had outlined the same system in two different aspects. Since the Freudian system is—or was, before *Beyond the Pleasure Principle*—based exclusively on psychological hedonism of a special variety, we shall consider its mechanics, rather than its energetics.

may be said that psychology hardly attempted to deal with this sub-ject,[10] and the only answer offered to the question which the popular title formulates as, "Why we behave like human beings," was the theory of psychological hedonism. Since that, in its modern form, de-scended from James Mill,[11] it was natural that it should become the patrimony of Victorian economics. Its influence has been pervasive. Nevertheless, I should say that it is today in such profound difficulties that we must look elsewhere for the firm foothold we are seeking.[12]

During the transition to a scientific basis two psychological schools or methods for attacking the problem of behavior—usually called "reflexology" and "behaviorism"—have been particularly influential, at least in America. They are somewhat allied, and have sprung from the same or similar sources.[13] It was Descartes who "evolved the idea of the reflex. Starting from the assumption that animals behaved simply as machines, he regarded every activity of the organism as a *necessary* reaction to some external stimulus." [14] For three hundred years this has been the basis of the study of the functioning of the nervous system.[15]

[10] As Troland has pointed out (*408*, 1) even modern textbooks of psychology hardly dealt with the subject of the "nature and interplay of human *motives*" at the time he wrote (1928).

[11] So considered by Gardner *et al.*, *166*, 280.

[12] Even when he wrote his classic (*284*) the late Professor McDougall regarded psy-chological hedonism as "now sufficiently exploded."

Troland was the only important "motivationist," with whose work I am familiar, who continued to base motivation on the avoidance of pain and seeking of pleasure. He admits (*408*, 305) that "psychological hedonism is actually a teleological theory . . . which cannot be regarded as lying within the pale of scientific views." And yet he complains that "modern psychologists seem to have a particular aversion to any kind of common sense view, and particularly to the idea that pleasure and displeasure have anything to do with motivation" (to the latter point I would subscribe). There-fore he constructs a "hedonism of the past." McDougall, in his last book (*285*, 325, note 1), says "Troland has made in a series of large volumes heroic efforts to recon-cile hedonism with mechanism." But McDougall was good at calling names and this is not quite fair, since, curiously enough, pure hedonism seems to remain more prevalent —at least as a tacit assumption—among physiologists than among psychologists. We shall have occasion to question their imputations. Of course pleasure and pain—or pleasantness and unpleasantness and so on, *ad infinitum*—exist as phenomena of con-sciousness. No one doubts that. The difficulties have to do with their identification with some certain physiological processes and their interrelations with others. Various current theories are discussed in this and the following chapters, where the evidence is assembled that seems to justify us in omitting these phenomena of consciousness from consideration in our hypothesis.

[13] Gardner *et al.* (*166*, 346) consider them "relatively independent groups."

[14] Pavlov, *320*, 4. Pavlov himself seemed to join in this mechanical view. He says (*321*, 83) that the "idea of reflex action" is a specific and constant "reaction of the organism to the external world."

[15] To such an extent that a biologist, MacBride (*279*, 7) attributes to the "great science of physiology" the "working hypothesis" "that animals are machines."

But the effect on psychological theory is largely due to the work of Sherrington and his school in the field of spinal or unconditioned reflexes, and of Pavlov in that of cortical or conditioned reflexes —which investigations are "closely allied" and "corresponding," as the latter recognizes.[16] We shall have constantly to consider the conclusions of these two eminent physiologists. But at this point we shall confine ourselves to the immediately derived psychological theories. Pure "reflexology," as described by its critics, assumes that all behavior can be explained as a system of reflexes, and that the essence of the reflex is that, "given a nerve arrangement constituted thus and so, it must be set off by a certain stimulus, and, when set off, it must lead to the reaction which is seen to follow"; it is a "mechanical system." [17] Moreover, attention is focused on external stimuli, as if the organism were an apparatus for reacting to "environmental facts" exclusively. Pure "behaviorism," on the other hand, originated as a revulsion from the introspective method. It undertook to confine itself to objective observation. But, since its limited technique enabled it to observe only the external stimulus and the overt response, it came to assume a kind of "reflexology," while tending to overemphasize and thus confine itself too much to causation of behavior by external stimuli. The result was, in both cases, what I have called "penny-in-the-slot machine" psychologies.[18] However, I have yet to find a pure

[16] Pavlov, 320, 378. As Adrian puts it (3, 12) "Sherrington has brought order out of chaos by his work on the simplest reactions of the isolated spinal cord." And Woodworth says (447, 151), "No work on animal learning has awakened as much interest among psychologists as that of the Russian physiologist Pavlov, because his work has seemed to reveal learning at or near its bottom level, and to lay bare the fundamental process in all learning."

[17] Troland, 408, 9. He does not use the term "reflexology." Köhler (243, 98), as another example, describes the "characteristic trait of reflex action" in much the same way. To him it requires "pre-existing arrangement of more or less isolated conductors." And McDougall (285, 323) describes the scheme as the "interpretation of all nervous structures as consisting of reflex arcs; of all nervous activity as the simple conduction of excitation from sensory point to muscle . . . ; and of all mental growth as essentially a complication of pre-existing reflex arcs and systems and of the connexions between them."

As an allied influence from biology, mention should perhaps be made of Loeb's theory of "tropism" (271, and elsewhere). To him (ibid., 15), "animal conduct may be justly designated as consisting of forced movements ("tropisms")"; "tropisms are reactions of the organism as a whole, while reflexes are reactions of isolated segments," while both are "of a pure physico-chemical character," but not confined to the nervous system. On the whole it seems that biologists have accepted this interpretation as of a very limited significance.

[18] Tolman (403, 35) calls them "stimulus-response psychologies." This seems also to be Woodworth's concept of them (446, 36 and 447, 226-230). He calls their formula "S $\rightarrow$ R." Thurstone attacks these points of view in a paper (400) entitled "The

"reflexologist" in this sense; and, for that matter, most behaviorists belong in the group to which we shall refer next.[19] The chief charge against the two tendencies is that they went off at half-cock and became systems on the basis of very partial and insufficient evidence. These systems are now in process of being corrected.[20]

What is now frequently called "motivational psychology" seems to have arisen from perception of the fact that the behavior of an organism is obviously not the result merely of external stimuli.[21] Actually there is great discrimination in response to external stimuli; the nervous energy of the response may be all out of proportion to the

Stimulus-Response Fallacy in Psychology," and refers to the idea as "so general" (*ibid.*, 354). Evidently these—and many others—attribute to the two tendencies an assumption that stimuli are chiefly external.

But this viewpoint has not been confined to psychology. MacBride (*279*, 7) describes the "working hypothesis" of physiology (referred to in note 16, above) with a metaphor similar to mine. "The stimulus proceeding from the environment is compared to the touch on the trigger which releases the stored-up energy of the spring in the jack-in-the-box."

[19] Perhaps Bechterew (*33*) was a pure "reflexologist." Perhaps Watson (*429* and *430*) was a pure behaviorist. But among most psychologists both terms represented merely trends. McDougall (*285*, 324, note 1) identifies the two systems, refers to them as "Behaviorism, which has been until recently so widely taught in America as a substitute for psychology," and attributes "the most thorough-going exposition of the scheme" to Holt (*207*), who, he says, develops it "with an admirable ingenuity and a magnificent contempt for a multitude of facts . . . and for the opinions of 99 % of his scientific colleagues." This is typical of the error in classification usually made by the opponents of these trends. Actually Holt must be included in the next group, though he doubtless overemphasizes the reflex and the external stimulus. Holt has, I think, performed two useful services. He has, in the first place, well stated the case against pre-scientific psychology on the ground of its use of "word-magic" (*207*, 4)—that is, such terms as "will," "instinct," "purpose," etc., which are not explanations of anything, but merely names for the behavior itself which is to be explained. Much the same charge can be made against "instinct psychology," such as, for instance, that of Veblen (*413*, 1–13) and *eminently* that of McDougall himself. On this subject see also note 23, below. Holt has also summarized, from the standpoint of a psychologist, the present stage of what may be called physiological-psychological investigation in a way that is highly informative, if it is also too systematic (i.e., too complete and self-sufficient, considering the limited data on which it can as yet be based). The other perhaps most adequate summary of this work during recent years is contained in Freeman (*152*). But see also Dunbar's fine summary and bibliography (*122*).

[20] Lashley (*260*, 12) believes that the point of view of "reflexology" has been "valuable in counteracting certain trends toward vitalism and mysticism," but is "now becoming an obstacle rather than a help to progress."

[21] The physiologist Herrick says (*190*, 308), "Life in its fullness is more than immediate reaction to stimuli" (perhaps "external" being understood). And he quotes Max Eastman's picturesque statement to the effect that "any rubber ball can react, but it requires life to act." In this respect the new psychology is a reaction against "reflexology," or stimulus-response psychologies in general. But it is perhaps from biology that psychology has received its initial push away from the external stimulus-response viewpoint. We shall examine later Jennings's critique of reflex theory, or his replacement of it. MacBride specifically joins with him in this (*279*, 7).

magnitude of the external stimulus; [22] and frequently there is activity with no apparent external stimulus at all. These facts argue for independent internal sources of activation.[23] Once this is recognized, the investigation of the causation of behavior becomes transposed, and the chief questions which arise concern the physiological sources of this activation and the physiological processes by which they express themselves.[24] If we go as far as the data derived from strictly physiological observation permit us to go, in the examination of these questions, before branching out into hypothesis or depending on external observation, we shall be less likely to have gone astray up to that point. Moreover, it will be better for us to imitate this school of psychology in their direct examination of the physiological data rather than to depend on them for a version which would necessarily be at second-hand. Some of the reasons for this preference are made evident in the following supplementary statement on "The Psychologists' Approach."

The Psychologists' Approach. A composite sample from various psychologists may give an idea of their developing theory of motivation. "The organization is not barren functionally; it is not a box containing conductors each with a special function" (Köhler, *243*, 180). "Behavior, considered as a series of motor reactions to external stimuli . . . leaves out of account the process intervening between the stimulus and the reaction" (Woodworth, *446*, 36). Woodworth (*447*, 226–230) designates what intervenes as O, so that the formula S → R becomes S → O → R. O, then, = the organism as a "stock of activities" given by its "equipment or repertory of possible responses," as "a present organic state" and as a "present activity" in which it is engaged. The external stimulus is "not the full and sufficient cause" of the response. Its action is that of a trigger. "The energy of the response may be much greater than the stimulus." The latter merely releases some of the internal "store" of energy. And, "not only the energy, but the form or character of the response depend on the organism." Therefore response is a compound of structure, condition, and stimulus. Though this takes a somewhat external viewpoint and omits what others call "spontaneous" action, it is an excellent statement of the new approach. Thurstone (*400* and *401*) goes further, in that he conceives the person himself to originate. He considers "the stimuli [restricted to external] as merely the en-

[22] As Sherrington suggests (*378*, 33), "A ghost may be a very weak visual stimulus and yet release a large mental reaction." Every big-game hunter knows how slight a stimulus it takes to start a violent reaction in the animal he is stalking.
[23] See supplementary statement, "The Psychologists' Approach," at the end of this section.
[24] As Woodworth puts it (*446*, 36) the problem divides itself into two parts, "the problem of "drive" and "the problem of mechanism," which would be almost indistinguishable if all behavior consisted of simple reflexes (*ibid.*, 38).

vironmental facts in terms of which he expresses himself" (*400*, 356). "The appearance of the stimulus is one of the *last* events in the expression of impulses in conduct" (*ibid.*, 369), and then it only "determines the detailed manner in which a drive or purpose expresses itself on any particular occasion" (*ibid.*, 356). Tolman (*403*, 20) also recognizes two sources of activation: "The first initiating causes of behavior are environmental stimuli and initiating physiological states"; "Behaviorisms . . . seem largely to have overlooked" the fact that "it is the hungry rat only who is responsive to food-stimuli." Troland (*408*, 7), specifically identifies these internal prime movers—the "physical sources of energy, or of control of response"—as motives. Others, like Thomson (*396*, 20), extends the term "motive" to cover "all the factors that move to conduct" (perhaps because his study far transcends the sources of behavior of which we have any physiological knowledge). To avoid this innate tendency of "motive" to acquire a purely psychical connotation, such terms as "urge" or "drive" have been adopted. For Holt (*207*, 3 and 8), "drive" is, like Troland's "motive," the internal energy, even the prod or lash (*ibid.*, 29), or possibly even both internal and external stimuli (*ibid.*, 233) but not the steering (Troland's control). Holt's "internal stimuli" (*ibid.*, 123) are Bain's "appetites." With Holt's substitution of "internal stimuli" for Woodworth's "O," we come closer to physiology. Thus Freeman (*152*, 399) confines "drive" to inner stimuli and prefers the term "intra-organic excitant." He defines motivation as "variable behavior" (*ibid.* 398) (i.e., as all behavior in which some variable influence intervenes between external S and R). It becomes still more evident that this is the approach which economics is looking for when we find Thorndike (*397*, 3) translating the term "drive" as "wants, interests, attitudes and emotions when these are considered as active forces." A "want" is then at least the first stage of a "drive" or "motive."

I am not referring here to the various earlier works of the late Professor McDougall, though by reason of them, he is usually included among the "motivationists." He was, or became, it seems to me, an adroit but last-stand dualist. His later thesis was not even psychophysical parallelism, which "has been the working scheme of the majority of scientific psychologists since [Leibnitz'] time" (Troland, *408*, 75). Instead, it was "psychophysical interaction" (McDougall, *285*, 8). As I see it, McDougall's chief task, at least in his later life, was to defend the exclusive precincts of psychology from the inroads of the sciences—so much so that he frequently made forays into the enemy's territory. He seemed to conceive it to be the function of the biologist to defend the border between the inorganic and the organic—between dead matter and life—and that of the psychologist, the border between all matter and mind (see *ibid.*, Introduction). His psychological strongholds which he considered irreconcilable with the physical, were "conscious activity" and "goal-seeking" (*ibid.*, 4). As to the first, we do not agree to the limitation that psychology "is concerned with the conscious activities of men" (*ibid.*, 2). The concept "consciousness" is a product of introspection, which, in that form, does not need to be explained objectively. And "goal-seeking," conducted by his "hormic energy" is a kind of animism of the same order as that which was formerly applied in general to all, including what we now call inanimate, objects. On the latter, see below, Section A2.

Unfortunately, much of the psychologists' work in this field suffers from two defects. It is largely vitiated by the use of what Holt (207, 4) calls "word-magic," or what Kempf (233, X) refers to as "fine psychobiological blanket phrases." As Troland puts it (408, 55) ultimately "the physiological analysis of response should provide the theory of motivation with a clear and detailed account of a physical apparatus which operates mechanistically." In the meantime, he says, we might as well avoid "pseudo-psychical entities such as instincts, hormic forces, drives and other hazy conceptions," for we will only have to drop them "in the end." The other defect is well illustrated by Troland himself, whose understanding of physiology was quite imperfect. I would cite particularly his interpretation of Cannon (ibid., 147–149) and his conception of nervous impulses (ibid., 77 and 199). Though there are brilliant exceptions (e.g., Woodworth), this weakness is altogether too common to permit us to rely on psychologists for the presentation and interpretation of the facts.

A. THE ULTIMATE SOURCES OF BEHAVIOR

I. "HOMEOSTASIS" AND PRESENT WANTS

When we abandon the attack on the problem of the causation of behavior from the external angle—external stimulus and overt response—and, instead, look within the organism, the question of the physiological sources is at once answered for us. As to the original causes of at least the simpler and commoner forms of behavior, physiology has been for long quite clear and explicit. We are presented with the view of an organism as a complex structure which, to a large extent, constitutes its own milieu, and which is engaged in carrying on a complex of interacting processes. The structure is built and renewed by means of materials or of elaborations of materials secured from outside. Its functioning—its living—consists in the taking in of solids, of liquids, and of oxygen, their incorporation more or less transiently in the structure, then the oxidation of the solids in the process of living and, finally, the giving off of the oxidized waste—as gas and as liquid (in solution)—and of the unused material from the inflow. Heat is developed in this process and the surplus of that must also be radiated or conveyed away. Sporadically, new organisms are given off by the old.[1]

[1] In fact, it is these processes of which the organism essentially consists. Somewhere, I think, the biologist Jennings says (223), "It is of the very greatest importance for the understanding of the behavior of organisms, to look upon them chiefly as something

In spite of the complexity of this continuous process there is, normally, a comparatively small range of change in the internal states. This "fixity of the *milieu intérieur*," as Claude Bernard expressed it, is due to the fact that "all the vital mechanisms . . . have only one object, that of preserving constant the conditions of life in the internal environment." [2] Comparative constancy is maintained, on the one hand, by compensations for the changes that are occurring internally and, on the other hand, by compensations for differences or changes in the external environment which would, if not compensated, produce internal changes.[3] In the latter respect, this constancy is "the condition of free and independent life," of that "independence of their surroundings" which Cannon notes as "one of the most striking features of the more highly developed organisms." [4] For this constancy Cannon

dynamic—as processes rather than as structures. An animal is something that happens." And the physiologist Haldane says (*178*, 99), "The 'structure' [of an organism] is only the appearance given by what seems at first to be a constant flow of specific material, beginning and ending in the environment." It is the flow which persists, not matter, or energy, or form (*ibid.*, 99–100). Because this flow begins and ends in the environment, "there is no sharp line of demarcation between a living organism and its environment." One can distinguish between the internal and the external environment, but they are not separate (*ibid.*, 98). This states his most useful concept of the continuum, referred to above. Huxley had the same conception. He said, comparing a crayfish to the whirlpool at Niagara Falls, "Now, with all our appliances, we cannot get within a good many miles, so to speak, of the crayfish. If we could, we should see that it was nothing but the constant form of a similar turmoil of material molecules which are constantly flowing into the animal on one side, and streaming out on the other" (*211*, 85).

[2] Quoted and translated by Cannon (*63*, 400, and *64*, 225). Also quoted by Haldane (*178*, 77). This *milieu intérieur*, as Cannon points out, is liquid. We think of ourselves as inhabitants of the air; but "every part of us that is alive is in contact with fluid." Even our surfaces are either dead or moist. The internal environment, or "fluid matrix," in which we live, is the blood (circulation) and the tissue fluid, or lymph (Cannon, *64*, 219).

[3] "External conditions . . . are not the only factors which affect the internal environment. The activity of the body itself may upset homeostasis" (i.e., constancy). (Cannon, *66*, 265.) That is, "from the physico-chemical point of view, the activities of the body consist of a vast number of chemical reactions which take place simultaneously." Therefore this constancy "depends upon a complete proportional and quantitative harmony of the rates at which these innumerable chemical reactions take place" (Barcroft, *17*, 34). Or, "the internal environment is kept constant as the result of a continuous and extraordinarily delicate regulation of the balance between opposing activities" (Haldane, *178*, 89). These activities are opposing because the "function" of an organ is not only "what it does to restore the internal environment" (*ibid.*, 84). The activities which disturb are "no less persistent than the activities which maintain its constancy" (*ibid.*, 83). So that "the internal environment which is maintained so constant is in reality the expression of a balance between activities which disturb and activities which restore it" (*ibid.*, 84).

[4] Cannon, *64*, 225. Elsewhere (*66*, 178), referring to temperature control, he speaks of warm-blooded animals as "freed from the influence of vicissitudes in the external environment" because they can preserve constant their "internal climate" (*ibid.*, 263). "The 'cold-blooded' animals, having the temperature of their surroundings, can act with speed only when the weather is warm" (*ibid.*, 229).

has suggested the term "homeostasis." [5] Viewed in this suggestive light, the totality of the internal conditions and supplies of material may be regarded as being normally maintained in a "mean position" by keeping their "oscillations" "within narrow limits." [6] In this view it is the normal variations, or tendencies toward variation, away from homeostasis which are construed as themselves setting off the activities which tend to re-establish, or maintain, the original condition. [7]

Since, as we proceed, we shall find it immediately possible to identify, as the commoner forms of behavior, those overt activities of the organism which are initiated by these variations—or tendencies to vary—away from homeostasis and which tend to restore it—or main-

[5] Preferring that to "equilibrium" (see Cannon, 66, 24). It is defined as "a condition—a condition which may vary, but which is relatively constant." The term was originally suggested by him in the *Jubilee Volume for Charles Richet*, p. 91, and made familiar particularly in 63, 399. Since these original articles have been expanded into a highly significant book, *The Wisdom of the Body*, our references will be made chiefly to this. Barcroft (17, 1), who refers to the state as the "constancy of the internal medium," recognizes the work of Haldane on respiration and Henderson on the blood as well as that of Cannon, in general, as special contributions to our understanding of homeostasis. On this see also Cannon, 63, 400.

[6] Cannon, 66, 39. In the following pages we are confining ourselves to normal variations from homeostasis and are disregarding pathological states.

[7] As Cannon puts it (66, 299), "Constancy is in itself evidence that agencies are acting, or ready to act, to maintain this constancy." "The more pronounced the disturbance of homeostasis the more intense are the activities of these agencies which resist the change." This is true even when no perceptible change actually occurs, for "any tendency towards change is automatically met by increased effectiveness of the factor or factors which resist the change" (63, 425).

We shall largely follow Cannon's lucid statement of the facts; but it should be understood that this is the general interpretation of physiologists. The life of an organism as a whole and in every detail consists in balancing itself on a tight-rope. And biologists concur. For instance, Child refers to organisms as, "within certain limits, complex dynamic equilibrating systems." And to him also this equilibration depends primarily upon physiological correlation (76, 217). Taken in a larger sense, to include growth and development, this equilibrium is dynamic in that it may be new—may "involve persistent alteration of the living system." So "every equilibration is . . . an alteration, and every regulation is a modification, rather than a return to a pre-existing condition" (*ibid.*, 218). It is also true that the functional regulation may not be "useful"; sometimes it is "injurious," chiefly when it is a reaction to an unusual situation (*ibid.*, 219-221). Cannon cites, for example, the sweating coincident with hypoglycemia and the rise in blood sugar in asphyxia (66, 298). The apparatus is not perfect.

The same concept is particularly well expressed by Rignano (345, 148): "Each organism is a physiological system in a stationary (stable) condition and strives to maintain that condition, or to restore it every time that it is disturbed by a change supervening in either the external or internal environment. This property is the basis of all the most essential organic 'needs' and 'appetites.'" And again (*ibid.*, 142), "If we examine the mode of action or the 'behaviour' of various organisms from the protists to man, we see that a whole series of their actions, including the most essential, may be interpreted as instances of a tendency of the organism to maintain or to return to its 'stationary' physiological state."

tain it—we shall be justified in regarding the variations themselves—
or the tendencies—as the most fundamental causes of such behavior.
If so, we can also at once identify what we call "wants" in economics
with the internal states or tendencies which constitute or threaten
variations away from homeostasis.[8]

There are three general characteristics of the system for maintenance of homeostasis in the organism that it is important to recognize
at the start. In the first place there is provided, generally speaking, a
large margin of safety against too wide departures from homeostasis.[9]
This is secured in two chief ways. The first is illustrated by "numerous instances of compensatory arrangements in the organizing of
bodily processes." [10] That is, for each specific variation, the organism
may have several complementary or supplementary means of initiating and carrying out the corrective process. The second is illustrated
by the storage of surplus supplies of materials available for, but not
yet in, use. As a result of this appears the second characteristic, which
divides the system into two parts. "In the main, stable states for all
parts of the organism are achieved by keeping uniform the material
surroundings of these parts, their internal environment or fluid matrix"
—the "common intermedium," blood, lymph, cerebrospinal fluid. To
that end surplus supplies of materials, beyond those in process of ingestion or absorption, do not remain in the "common intermedium,"
but are reserved elsewhere.[11] This occurs in two ways: Cannon calls
the first of these "inundation" (e.g., the storage of surplus salt and
water in the connective tissue under the skin and elsewhere); and he
calls the second "segregation" (e.g., the storage of glycogen and prob-

[8] See note 23, above. As explained there we are using the term "want" to cover what
psychologists usually mean by the terms "motive," "drive," "prime mover," etc. But
of that more anon. As will be seen from the context this usage will have none of the
usual connotations of the word. It does not mean "wish," "desire," nor even, necessarily, "lack." It has no connection with the "meaning in etymology or common accep-
tation," as Pareto would say (*Mind and Society*, p. 65). And the only excuse for applying the term to this particular class of facts is that it has always and exclusively
been used in economics to denote the fundamental causes of economic behavior—
which these variations are.
[9] See Cannon, *66*, Chap. XV.
[10] Cannon, *66*, 45 and 299. There are usually several successive "lines of defense" (Cannon, *64*, 232), or "adjuvant homeostatic devices" (*66*, 284). Barcroft (*17*, 91) says,
"The body . . . does not put all its 'eggs in one basket.' " The result is his "principle"
of the "duplication of mechanisms." Nature has "more than one way of doing a great
many things"; and "the body is therefore insured against the default of either mechanism" (*ibid.*, 311–312).
[11] As Barcroft points out (*17*, 90), "the combination of a constant internal environment and an intermittent source of supply necessitates a storage of materials."

ably protein in the liver). In the first case, the storage level seems simply to rise or fall [12] by diffusion from the blood of surpluses and diffusion back into the blood to make good deficits. In the second case, the surplus is driven into special organs and again given off by them as needed, under the control of definite neuroglandular processes.[13] In the case of water, intake in excess of requirements or above the water level of storage is disposed of by "overflow" through the kidneys; excesses of other materials are either not absorbed or are promptly burned or washed out through the "spill way"—as Cannon picturesquely describes the kidneys. It is evident, then, that homeostasis of the blood —the first part—is maintained within very narrow limits, while the capacity to prevent wide variations there is insured by a much wider range of variation in the other part—the non-vascular portions of the system. The third characteristic is due to changes in the rate of living. When the bodily processes are near their ebb, what is called "basal metabolism" (oxidation and generation of heat) is at a low rate.[14] In activity this state becomes high.[15] In meeting such rises in activity, the homeostasis of the blood is maintained, in respect of those features of the "steady state" which involve processes rather than stored materials (i.e., temperature regulation, oxygen supply, etc.) by immediately altering the rate of the processes themselves within wide limits. "A noteworthy prime assurance against extensive shifts in the status of the fluid matrix is the provision of sensitive automatic indicators or sentinels" to start corrective measures at the very beginning of a disturbance.[16] But, in addition, since the increased activity also involves the more rapid disappearance from the blood of materials of which supplies are in storage, homeostasis also requires an increase in the rate of supply of these materials to the blood through their "release" from storage. Thus, to maintain homeostasis in the blood, in

[12] Cannon calls it "flow and ebb" (66, 290). But a careful examination of the limited available evidence with reference to this kind of storage suggests the possibility that it, too, is subject to a kind of neuro-endocrine control, not entirely dissimilar to that which controls storage by segregation.

[13] Cannon calls it a "neural or neurohumoral government" (66, 291). As to these two kinds of storage, see ibid., 85, 94–95, 100, 125, 134, 138, and 290–291. Glucose may be temporarily stored by inundation and these stores then gradually segregated (see Cannon, 63, 406).

[14] "Basal metabolism," as a measure, is concerned only with the oxygen consumed and carbon dioxide given off, when at rest and after a fast. That is, "it is the lowest degree of chemical oxidation when the body is at rest" (Cannon, 66, 184).

[15] In great activity the requirements of oxygen may be ten or twelve times the requirements when at rest (Cannon, 66, 147).

[16] Cannon, 66, 288.

these respects, it is upset elsewhere; stores are depleted and, in turn, waste accumulates. So "back of storage, and, indeed, as occasion for storage, are the motivators" which indicate the need of additional supplies of materials.[17] And with the accumulation of waste and refuse other "motivators" indicate the need of their elimination.

The respects in which the warm-blooded organism must maintain homeostasis within narrow limits, because of the lack of storage, are the oxygen [18] and carbon dioxide content of the blood and its neutrality,[19] as well as the body temperature; those respects with regard to which the homeostasis of the blood itself lies within narrow limits, but as to which that of the system as a whole has relatively wide limits (by reason of storage), are water content, and the supply of what we call, in general, food—that is (in the form in which the various constituents exist after ingestion and absorption) glucose and glycogen, protein, fat, salt ($NaCl$), calcium and other salts on a small scale.[20] In all these respects the rate of consumption or loss of the materials and the rate of internal development of heat varies from a minimum (basal metabolism) over a wide range to a much higher maximum in the event of general activity. Therefore, increased activity requires not only that processes be speeded up but also that stores be drawn down. In addition, the framework of our analysis must include homeostasis as to waste products (other than CO_2) either in the system in general or in the organs of excretion, and as to material (food) ingested but not absorbed (refuse)—for both of which we may also use the concept of storage, since these are accumulated before being got rid of. It must also include some complex to which we may at this point give the general name sex, as to which the concept of storage

[17] Ibid., 292.

[18] While there is no storage of oxygen, there are several features of its supply which have somewhat the same effect—modifying the exact correspondence between current need and current behavior. These are, principally, the possibility of incurring what is called an "oxygen debt" (accumulation of lactic acid for later burning) in the muscles and tissues, and the speeding up of transmission by increase of red blood corpuscles and otherwise.

[19] In a sense there is storage in respect of neutrality in that sodium bicarbonate (a buffer salt) acts as an "alkali reserve of the blood" (Cannon, 66, 46).

[20] In all these respects the normal constitution (and quantity) of the blood is remarkably constant, in spite of the change of rate of consumption and therefore of supply from storage. Wide variations from homeostasis, there, constitute pathological states. For instance, the normal concentration of glucose in the blood is 100 mgms. per 100 cc. The kidney threshold (glycosuria) is about 180; at 70 the hypoglycemic reaction (insulin poisoning) is likely to appear. Once the regulating mechanism breaks down the concentration is apt to reach one or the other of these points rather quickly; but normally it hardly varies from 100 (Cannon, 66, 98).

will again be found appropriate.[21] Whether or not it is possible to include under one rubric the several conditions we call "fatigue," [22] it is useful to treat that as well, or its several varieties, as variation from homeostasis in one direction [23] and a condition that we shall call "euphoria," in the corresponding loci, as variation in the opposite direction.[24]

The overt behavior associated with the maintenance of homeostasis does not correspond neatly with this analytical scheme of individual wants. Thus the blood content of oxygen and of carbon dioxide and, to some extent, its temperature and neutrality are all maintained by the one type of behavior called "breathing." The maintenance of the systemic supply of all the solids, and to some extent that of water, is ultimately secured by the one activity "eating"; which is, moreover, by no means a simple process. The water level is chiefly maintained by "drinking," on the intake side, and by overflow (through the kidneys), on the outlet side. The maintenance of homeostasis as regards refuse requires only defecation. So, too, that concerned with the elimination of waste is only micturition, though such elimination is incidentally accomplished in other ways as well. Fatigue and its opposite, euphoria, also have each its single though more complex type of associated behavior, rest and play (one type of induced bodily activity), respectively. At the opposite pole from the first two types of behavior, each of which serves to maintain homeostasis in more than

---

[21] "The activities of the sexual organs may perhaps also be regarded as primarily excretory" (Fulton, *160*, 224).

[22] Sherrington (*375*, 222) refers to "the many phenomena that pass in physiology under the name of fatigue."

[23] Normally only the so-called voluntary neuromuscular system can produce fatigue (Cannon, *66*, 307). In that system it seems to occur in different modes in the muscle and in the nervous system. In the muscle it is definitely a variation from homeostasis in respect of the accumulation of lactic acid (waste). See Bayliss, *27*, 452, and Fulton, *158*, 193, and 195. In the nervous system, since the nerve fibers themselves are practically indefatigable, it seems to occur at the junctions between the several neurons and that between the motor neuron and the muscle (end-plate); see Fulton, *loc. cit.* Apparently the more central this junction the more readily it is fatigued. Sherrington (*375*, 222) thinks this central fatigue may be "nothing but a negative induction" (successive)—that is, "a rebound" phenomenon. If so, that too conforms to the pattern of a variation from homeostasis.

[24] Tolman (*403*, 279) also regards "unspent energy" as due to "physiological disequilibrium." As such we separate it, by reason of its special source (neuromuscular), from what is usually called "random activity," which may arise from any of these disequilibria. This particular variety is illustrated by a child's "fidgets," when he cannot sit still. So Woodworth (*447*, 256–257) says, "We can almost believe in an organic state underlying playfulness"—i.e., "feeling fine" or "euphoria." McDougall (*284*, 110) suggests that the notion of play as the result of a "surplus of nervous energy" is ascribable to the poet Schiller and its development to Herbert Spencer.

one way, are those respects in which maintenance of a particular homeostasis is connected with a compound of several kinds of behavior. Thus the prevention of variation of temperature, in one direction, may lead both to "sweating" and to induced bodily inactivity; and, in the other, both to efforts to insulate the skin—raising of hair or feathers (our gooseflesh)—and to induced bodily activity (shivering or exercise). To some extent for the male, but more particularly for the female, maintenance of homeostasis in respect of "sex" involves a whole complex or series of different kinds of behavior. Thus we have some cases where one type or uniform complex of behavior serves a whole compound of wants, some where there is one type of behavior for each want, and some where there are several alternative or successive types of behavior for each.

Since in most of these cases the process which tends away from homeostasis is continuous and only varies in its rate according as activity ranges between rest (basal metabolism) and some maximum, there is a presumption that (1), where there is no storage, the primary associated behavior must also be continuous or must occur at very brief intervals. In either case its magnitude must vary with the rate of the process it is counteracting; in the latter case its own rate (frequency) may also vary (as with breathing). On the other hand, (2) where there is storage, there is a presumption that the behavior must take place when the store is drawn down, or accumulated, beyond a certain critical point—perhaps variable under different conditions, or perhaps consisting of a series of critical points.[25] Beginning at this minimum or maximum, respectively, the behavior must replenish or exhaust the store to a maximum or minimum, respectively. Therefore, such behavior will be periodic, and the length of the interval will depend upon the frequency with which these critical points, or the effective one of a series of such points, are reached; and that, in turn, will depend, in most instances, upon the current rate of activity. When such periodic behavior commences, its magnitude will depend upon the range between these minima and maxima which has to be made up. Therefore, all behavior resulting from internal causes must have a rate of recurrence varying from no interval—continuity—to consider-

[25] This important point will be developed as we proceed. The organism can lose all reserves of glycogen, all reserves of fat, and half the protein stored or built into the structure, without perishing, but a loss of 20% of the water supply means death (Cannon, 66, 78–79). Obviously, however, these wants develop, and the associated behavior is called for, long before such minima are reached.

able intervals. Also, once we assume that the variation, or tendency toward variation, from homeostasis causes the behavior, we must presume that, without storage, the force with which it acts will vary with its own degree; and that in turn will be determined primarily by the strength of the tendency away from homeostasis and, secondarily, by the failure, if any, in the effectiveness of the behavior to counteract the tendency—that is by an actual variation. On the other hand, where there is storage, we must presume that the force with which the variation will act accumulates proportionately to the degree to which the normal storage is drawn down or accumulated; and that, when the critical point—or one of a series of critical points —is reached in the passage from a maximum to a minimum, or the reverse, the whole latent force so built up becomes active to correct the variation—satisfy the want.

2. THE ADVANTAGES OF THIS APPROACH

There are certain advantages to be derived from the special feature of Cannon's approach, with its single order of cause—variations from homeostasis. But in general, it is otherwise closely similar to the approach of the school of psychology we are following and that of many biologists. However, it goes deeper and is more precise. Among these others the equivalent of "variations"—our wants—take many forms and names. The "appetites," or "drives," or "desires" are sometimes identified with "physiological states," usually not exactly defined but at least corresponding to our "variations"; sometimes with the supposed nervous impulses or other effects which travel centralwards from those internal sources (i.e., the mechanism of centripetal transmission); sometimes with those which travel from the central nervous system to the effector organs; and sometimes, apparently, with the behavior itself (i.e., the result).[26] As a consequence there is both a lack of uni-

---

[26] For instance, Jennings (223, 288) finds that the behavior of the organism depends upon its "physiological state." And (ibid., 339), "Behavior is merely a collective name for the most obvious and most easily studied of the processes of the organism, and it is clear that these processes are closely connected with, and are indeed outgrowths from the more recondite internal processes." Child (76, 258) accepts this. So Woodworth (447, 247) states that "each need is primarily a chemical or physical condition of the organism" which "forms the unlearned core of a whole system of activity." But for Craig (92, 95), while an "appetite" is "dependent upon physiological factors," it is evidently not identical with the state itself. And for Washburn (427, 333), the "drive" is "a state of physiological unrest, due either to a lack or a superfluity of certain physiological substances." Again the "drive" is not the lack, it is the resulting "unrest." To Dunlap "desires" are internal stimuli or the resulting nervous impulses (123,

formity among the various analyses and frequently much vagueness or confusion in the individual analysis.

Certain other weaknesses of a more serious nature are more or less characteristic of some of these other approaches to the causation of behavior. A brief discussion of them will serve to establish the advantages of the special approach we are following. In the first place, it is one thing to permit what Sherrington calls a "kind of natural science teleology" which physiology adopts when it aims at "reasoned accounts of the acts of an organism in respect of their purpose and use to the organism *qua* organism." [27] But it is quite another thing to assign this "purpose" as the *cause* of the behavior. This is unfortunately frequent.[28] In our system of energetics a state of variation from

---

323). To Holt, "appetitive drives" are the latter (*207*, 133). Tolman's "first order drives"—his "appetites and aversions"—are caused by, but are not the same as, the "initiating physiological excitements" (*403*, 28) which, in the case of hunger, he traces back to "disequilibrium" in the "alimentary system" (*ibid.*, 276). Apparently also for Troland "desire or instinct" is not the "physiological state, *per se*," but the "afferent nerve impulses" which normally result (*408*, 138). For Thomson (*396*, 48), "appetites always have an internal stimulus" but are neither identical with this stimulus nor with the "recurring physiochemical cycles" which give rise to them. The agreement is, in a sense, general, only obscured by the failure to differentiate between the causative condition (disequilibrium), the mediating process (mechanism) and the overt result (behavior).

Agreement is, however, more difficult to establish with instinct psychology in general, even in its more modern forms as given by William James and McDougall, for instance.

[27] Sherrington, *376*, 193.

[28] Thomson (*396*, 252) defines a motive as "a drive or urge *to* some realizable end" (italics ours). Tolman (*403*, 28) seems to have difficulty in making up his mind whether the "purpose" is to get "to a final, physiological quiescence or from a final physiological disturbance." So his drives are either "demands for" quiescence or "demands against" disturbance. On the dichotomy underlying this confusion see p. 40, note 33, below. It occurs to us to ask why quiescence and disturbance are alternatives and not merely the end and the beginning, respectively, of a single process. Failure to perceive that fact leads him to the peculiar inconsistency elsewhere (*402*, 354) of defining his drives as "toward hunger-removal, sex-disturbance removal, fatigue-removal, etc.," instead of away from hunger, sex-disturbance, fatigue, etc. His very terminology disproves his notion of the direction. As McDougall has pointed out (*285*, 217, note 1), as Tolman has confessed, and as others have noted (e.g. Troland, *408*, 138-139) Tolman's notion of "purpose" is, like McDougall's "hormic" energy, a teleological conception. Troland (*408*, 303) has made it quite clear that such constructions are intrinsically naive; "for the popular thought it [motive] is usually an effect"; but "for the psychologist or physiologist a motive must be a cause." "Even if we act for the future, we *cannot* act because of the future. Action on behalf of the future must be determined by the past." Skinner (*379*, 376) goes further. To him "a drive is not a teleological force." Approximately equivalent to this "demand for quiescence" in "purposive" psychology is Freud's "death instinct"—"a tendency innate in living organic matter impelling it toward the reinstatement of an earlier condition, one which it had to abandon under the influence of external disturbing forces—a kind of organic elasticity, or . . . inertia . . ." (*156*, 44-45).

homeostasis leads to some form of activity. If and when this activity restores homeostasis, activity ceases.[29] The initial state or tendency is then the cause of this activity, while the end-state, on the other hand, is the cause of inactivity in this respect. One cannot attribute as cause of an activity an end-state which does not arrive until the activity has ceased. We do not ascribe to a clock the "purpose" of running down. It runs because it is wound up; and it ceases to run when it is run down. Nor do we impute to steam, in its action upon a piston, the "intention" of arriving at atmospheric pressure. Of course we still say, picturesquely, that "water *seeks* a level" and that "nature *abhors* a vacuum"; but these are admitted anthropomorphisms.[30] To ascribe "purpose" as the cause of physiological activity is equally so. And, in addition, it is quite superfluous.[31]

The other objectionable feature that is most common to these approaches is a persisting dichotomy which savors of that stage in the evolution of physics when it was held that some things fall because of the "principle of gravity" while others rise because of the "principle of levity." In respect of its relations with specific objects or conditions of its environment an organism is observed to have what Jennings calls positive and negative reactions (i.e., movements of attraction and repulsion, of approach and retreat).[32] But, then, it seems necessary to many to ascribe these contrasting modes of behavior to two opposed forces acting from within the organism—its "appetites"

[29] Subject to the qualification that, when consideration of the mediating mechanism is interposed, the ending of the activity may be due to the cessation of the centripetal transmission and not precisely to the cessation of the originating state.

The same system of energetics can be stated in psychological terms—terms which we will have much occasion to use as we proceed. As Thurstone puts it (*400*, 363), "Behavior starts in dissatisfaction and it terminates in satisfaction."

[30] At least we do not go so far as to say—in terms of Tolman's concepts—that water flows down stream because it has a "sign-gestalt-readiness" to get to a "state of quiescence" in the sea.

[31] The term "purpose" usually connotes consciousness and, therein, a picture of the end-state. Purpose implies "conscious anticipation of the result" of the response (Woodworth, *447*, 293). In this sense both the term and the concept become unnecessary for our system of present wants. The causative factor, for us, may or may not be conscious and, in either case, is associated with the beginning and not with the end of the process. We shall have occasion to discuss the notion of "purpose," particularly in connection with future wants, but there we shall find it necessary to interpret it in terms of homeostasis, not the reverse, and to make of it strictly a *vis a tergo*.

Our objection to the notion is also partly due to its deleterious effect on observation. "Descriptions of animal behavior in terms of purpose may give a superficial sort of understanding of them, but objective study not only leads to a greater increase of information but may also enrich the study of man himself" (Fraenkel and Gunn, *149*, 311).

[32] Jennings, *223*, 265.

and its "aversions." [33] Even in our brief examination of the organism's life processes it was made obvious that certain materials are taken in from, and others given off to, the environment. Breathing accomplishes both. But we did not find it necessary to divide variations from homeostasis into two classes upon this criterion. The direction of movement of materials with relation to the environment seems not to be of the essence of the matter. Nor does the direction of these material movements accord with the direction of movement of the organism as a whole. The organism may "seek" a warm place in order to give off *less* heat, and may "seek" air in order to give off *more* carbon dioxide.

Even when external relations are considered by themselves this dichotomy does not work. When the organism is hungry or thirsty it still has many aversions to specific edible and potable substances.[34] And when it ceases to be hungry or thirsty it acquires an "aversion" for the very substances for which it has just had an "appetite." [35] Of course this effort to divide the causes of behavior into these two classes is a relic of the external stimulus-response viewpoint, which should now be abandoned.[36] Variations from homeostasis are of one order, whether they involve taking in or giving off and whether, in individual instances, the resulting behavior is approach or retreat from some particular selected object which the observer is watching. To some extent the dichotomy is also a relic of hedonism. Thus "behavior may be directed either by movements to get rid of disturbing, annoying stimulation, or by movements to prolong or renew agreeable

[33] These are the common terms. See Tolman (*402*, 357, and *403*, 28, and elsewhere). Thomson's terms are "positive" and "negative" motives (*396*, 274). Lewin (*266*, 94) calls them "positive and negative valences." To Holt (*207*) they are due to "adience" and "abience" (his special "word-magic").

In passing it is interesting to note that Holt explains walking as due, in part, to "abient" reactions to stimuli upon the soles of the feet ("plantar pressure"); see *207*, 54 ff. Yet Head (*183*, 213) finds that "the cat walks when anaesthetic on the soles of all four feet." Moreover, see Chap. 3 for Coghill's conclusion, based on actual observation.

[34] Thus, even if we were to impute two directions to the inner force, a positive and a negative, it would be necessary to accept Kempf's (*233*, 5 and 71) attribution of "ambivalence" to the individual "craving," so that it is "avertive" to ("rejects") some "stimuli" (external objects or conditions) and is "acquisitive" to ("chooses") others.

[35] Craig (*94*) uses the terms. But his "aversion" is usually the third phase (*ibid.*, 103) of a single process, or "type cycle" (*ibid.*, 101). That is, "surfeit" changes an "appetitive stimulus" into a "disturbing" one. He observed this change specifically after the sexual act, with normal or abnormal stimulus (*ibid.*, 102), after a "turn" at brooding (*loc. cit.*) and when a bird was compelled to further drinking after surfeit (*ibid.*, 103).

[36] As soon as the internal causation is admitted, then, as Freeman (*152*, 426) points out, applying Holt's terms, an "adient" response to food becomes also an "abient" response to hunger.

stimulation." [37] Neither is this dualism necessary. We may construe a variation from homeostasis as invariably a disturbance—something which activates the organism until it is got rid of—even when it produces "that unrest which men miscall delight." [38] If, then, behavior turns out to be due to internal excitation by such states, it is all of the first type—it is always directed toward getting rid of this excitation.[39] This conclusion does not dispute the fact of the two possible directions of behavior with reference to external objects and conditions; nor does it dispute the existence in consciousness of the phenomena of pleasure and pain under any of their names—as to which we have so little precise knowledge. It merely treats both classes of fact as diverse effects of a single order of cause—a variation from homeostasis—and therefore as secondary. If the tendency of the organism is to maintain homeostasis, this tendency must take the form of resisting or counteracting all influences, internal or external, which produce variations, and of making use of all those, internal or external, which help to prevent or correct them.[40]

B. THE MECHANISMS FOR CENTRIPETAL TRANSMISSION OF PRESENT WANTS

I. THE INTEGRATING SYSTEMS

The view of the totality of bodily processes which we have briefly indicated in the foregoing makes quite evident, I think, that the ulti-

[37] Cannon, 66, 75. I suppose it would be generally agreed that sex is the type of all "appetites," "positive motives" or "valences" and of "adience," as well as of the incentive to "renew agreeable stimulation." It is therefore amusingly apposite to cite Rignano's interpretation of it in our terms. He says (345, 146–147), "There is a tendency nowadays to regard 'sexual hunger,' like ordinary hunger, as having its seat not in the localised region, such as the genital organs, but in the entire organism, and to suggest as the ultimate cause of the sexual instinct the need experienced of getting rid of the germinal [?] substance." "The impulse to eliminate such a profoundly disturbing substance would subsequently become an impulse towards sexual union as the proper means of effecting this elimination." And see note 21, above, along the same line.
[38] Shelley, "Adonais."
[39] It is refreshing to be able to quote another psychologist in confirmation of this. James Ward says (424, 588), "The term 'appetite' is apt both by its etymology and its later associations to be misleading. What are properly called the 'instinctive' appetites are—when regarded from their active side—movements determined by some uneasy sensation. So far as their earliest manifestation in a particular individual is concerned, this urgency seems to be entirely of the nature of a *vis a tergo*."
[40] In the latter class, according to what seems to me the most plausible explanation of pleasantness and unpleasantness, would belong those corrective external agencies that are purely adjuvant in getting rid of wants and therefore seem to Cannon to produce "agreeable stimulation."

mate causation of the commoner forms of behavior lies in variations from homeostasis—which we shall hereafter, for the sake of brevity and because we are founding our analysis upon their identity, call *wants.* The real problem turns out to be, then, the exact determination of the physiological mechanism by means of which these causes produce the observed results (behavior)—the "how," not the "why." [1] It is typical of the external attack—behaviorism—to hold that "the series of physiological events from the situation to the response is inaccessible." [2] But we shall not be so easily daunted, even though we may admit that there are great gaps in our knowledge of these processes and that what we do know indicates vast complexity. At the start we are cautioned by the physiologist Forbes that the "difficulty arising from the complexity of organisms is due largely to the attempt to make excessively simple explanations fit the behavior of structures whose intricacy should warn us at the outset of the improbability of finding any complete explanation with the means at our disposal." [3]

If we regard mechanism, in general, as a means of transmitting an influence of any kind from one point to another, it is clear that in the higher organisms we have certainly two, and possibly three, orders of mechanism. In physiological terms these are the *integrating* systems. The first, which is apt to be treated as if it were the only one, is the nervous system. This consists of specialized cells, called neurons, anatomically discrete and usually giving off long fibers, which conduct waves of excitation called impulses.[4] Those over which impulses are directed from the body—soma and viscera—are called the "afferent" neurons (*including* the sensory, in our narrow sense).[5] Those

[1] In spite of its unfortunate "mechanistic" connotation we shall be obliged to use the term "mechanism" for the apparatus or instrumentality by means of which physiological effects arise from physiological causes.
[2] Thorndike, *397*, 10.
[3] Forbes, *146*, 161.
[4] Adrian and Lucas prefer the term "propagated disturbance" for the whole neuro-muscular activity. See Forbes (*147*, 164). Forbes says the impulse is dynamically like an explosion or a fuse, not like a sound wave or electric current. Or, in view of the "refractory period which must intervene between each successive impulse," it may be better to say with Adrian (*3*, 27) that these impulses are like "bullets from a machine gun" instead of a continuous stream of water from a hose.
   A nerve—or nerve trunk—such as the sciatic, may contain several thousand fibers (Adrian, *3*, 18), so "neuron" or "fiber" are not merely technical terms for nerve. "Fiber" usually refers to the axone of the neuron, only.
[5] Readers who are physiologists, if there should chance to be such, are hereby put on notice that my usage, in all that follows, of the terms "sensory" and "motor," as applied to elements of the nervous system, will not conform to their common usage. "Sensory" will be confined to those afferent elements only over which impulses travel

which transmit these impulses wholly within the central nervous system—brain and spinal cord—are variously called "central," "internuncial," "adjustors," etc. And those which convey the outgoing impulses from the central nervous system to the muscles—striated (skeletal) or smooth—and the glands are called "efferent" (or "motor," in our narrow sense, *if* to skeletal muscle). The term "center" is applied to groups of cells (nuclei or ganglia) in the central nervous system. "The other great integrating system of the organism" [6] is the circulating blood and tissue fluids (lymph and probably cerebrospinal fluid). It is the blood, of course, which carries to and from the various parts of the entire body all the substances which the cells take in and give off, all the internal secretions and enzymes, as well as much of the heat developed. The blood itself is contained in and circulated through the vascular system, which, like the nervous system, consists of specialized cells and is also anatomically discrete. But it is the lymph, in which most of the cells are bathed, that acts as "the direct intermediator" between cells and blood.[7] The speed of transmission in these two integrating systems is ostensibly quite different. "The nervous impulse . . . travels . . . about 220 miles an hour." [8] Nevertheless, "the circulation [of the blood] is surprisingly rapid; it may take only fifteen seconds for a substance poured into the blood stream by one organ to reach all the other organs." [9] I say "ostensibly" because, while transmission via the blood cannot be stopped nor much slowed down, that via the nervous system may be inhibited or piled up (summated) and thus stopped or delayed at the junctures (synapses) between the

---

which can be appreciated as sensation in the cortex. This, in order not to confuse non-physiologists, who would be apt to suppose that "sensory" connoted sensation. "Motor" will be confined to those efferent elements only over which impulses travel which can lead to activity of skeletal muscles. This, in order not to confuse non-physiologists, who would be apt to suppose that "motor" connoted motion.

However, non-physiologists must also be warned that, in quotations, our authorities often mean merely "afferent" by "sensory" and merely "efferent" by "motor."

The terms "afferent" and "efferent" are also commonly used, imprecisely, to designate those rising toward, and those descending from, the brain, respectively, and even for those coming to, or leaving from, a particular center.

[6] Cannon, *64*, 244.

[7] Cannon, *66*, 30. "The environment of the cell is not really blood but lymph" (Barcroft, *17*, 71). Thus it is strictly this which Sherrington (*375*, 4) calls "the internal environment" in which the multicellular organism is "bathed."

[8] Adrian, *3*, 13. Probably true only of the largest fibers.

[9] Woodworth, *447*, 502. Woodworth is quotable on this since he began his career as a physiologist. Barcroft (*17*, 317) remarks significantly that, "Hitherto we have regarded the nervous function as implying delicacy and quickness while the humoral function is rather crude, slow and massive."

several successive neurons constituting each path. These two systems
depend, as stated, on specialized structures; but, since the integrating
functions they perform—the one "excitatory and transmissive" and
the other "chemical or transportative" [10]—are common to all protoplasm, the possibility must not be excluded that the non-neural and
non-vascular parts of even the higher organisms have retained some
of the original capacity for integration by both means, however de-
graded by specialization of cells in other directions and however limited
spatially and in speed.[11] If any cause, occurring in one part of the organism, is to have an effect in other parts, or in general, it is clear that,

[10] Child, 77, 107; also 76, 214.
[11] "Most biologists are agreed" that the "appearance of a nervous system in protoplasm" does not represent "a new functional activity" (Child, 77, 107). "The qualities
of the nervous system are the general qualities of protoplasm." Therefore "where a
nervous system exists, we are not justified in dogmatically referring all phenomena of
behavior to it." It is probably not the "*exclusive* seat of anything," for "the remainder
of the protoplasm may perform the act in question by its own capabilities" (Jennings,
223, 264). Jennings finds that the "possession of a nervous system brings with it no
observable changes in the nature of behavior" (*ibid.*, 263), for even a unicellular organism shows the same pseudo-neural phenomena (*ibid.*, 262). To Child (77, 78) excitation seems like oxidation (i.e., metabolism) and he calls it the "rate of living" (*ibid.*,
83). His whole theory of the development of the nervous system is based on "physiological gradients" in this rate—Coghill calls them "metabolic gradients" (*89*, 61 ff.).
While these may develop the specialized structures, that does not necessarily remove
the gradient or exhaust the effects outside these structures. "The preneural system of
integration . . . overlaps the neural"; i.e., continues after the nervous system appears
(Coghill, *89*, 78). Coghill (*ibid.*, 40) describes this system as the two opposed "polari-
ties"—the animal and the vegetative, the apical and the basal, oral and aboral, anterior
and posterior, respectively.
   Of course intracellular "chemical or transportative" integration constitutes the basis
of cell life. Then in multicellular organisms it must also continue in inter-cellular ways.
We may not yet know all these ways.
   In Chap. 5 we shall have occasion, in another connection, to examine various, and in
some cases purely speculative, elaborations by certain biologists of what Rignano (*345*,
187) calls Claude Bernard's "conception of the essential identity of all the various
forms of irritability of living substance." "The fact that plants, although completely devoid of a nervous system, manifest the phenomena of irritability, of transmission of stimuli . . . , has lent support to the view that all the somatic nuclei are essentially similar in nature to those of the nerve centres, and that the intercellular bridges
have the same power of transmitting stimuli which is possessed by the nerve fibres"
(*ibid.*, 128). "As Sir Francis Darwin . . . has recognized, the system of intercellular
protoplasmic bridges supplies us . . . with that idioplasmic network penetrating all
recesses of the organism which . . . would allow every local disturbance of the body
to diffuse its echo throughout all other parts of the body . . ." (*ibid.*, 122–123). This
is merely a plausible hypothesis to explain observable facts, though, as MacBride
points out (*ibid.*, Introduction, 12) "it is extremely doubtful" that the cell nuclei are
the origin, since these, both in nerve and other cells, seem to be concerned with the
replacement of the irritable substance rather than its "explosion." However, the possibility of such an undifferentiated "nervous system" must be kept in mind, even
though as yet almost unexplored.

so far as we now know, its influence must be transmitted through one of these three integrating systems.

The transmission of these influences through the integrating systems to the initiating agencies of the "effector" systems have been termed "signals" by Cannon and others. But the use of the term "signal" seems unfortunate, because it suggests false analogies. As stated before, we view the body as a delicately balanced and vastly complex system of states and processes in which the processes tend simultaneously or over time to counteract each other, thus maintaining or restoring balance. The disturbance of equilibrium in any one state or between any processes, which constitutes a variation from homeostasis, may be propagated into this general status over one or more of the integrating systems and in many directions, with different effects in different parts. In any of these parts to which the effect reaches, it may produce changes in chemical or physical conditions. And these in turn may also be regarded as disturbances of homeostasis there. But some of them may also be regarded as means of restoring homeostasis at the first point, since, normally, the disturbance gives rise to or alters the rate of offsetting processes somewhere. At still other points the effects may neutralize each other. Thus only the resultant of all is effective, and this resultant usually tends to maintain or restore the original general status. The analogy of signals is inappropriate even for nervous impulses because these, according to the interpretation of the facts which seems to be coming currently to be accepted, are projected, not along anatomically foreordained arcs to final paths, but into an equally complicated and variegated status of excitation and inhibition which exists throughout an interconnected system and in which the new element adds merely a factor, overbalancing here, reinforcing there, being suppressed elsewhere. Nervous impulses are not like the ripples produced by dropping a single stone into a perfectly calm body of water. Rather they are like the effect of throwing a smaller or greater handful of pebbles upon a surface already disturbed by innumerable other causes.[12]

[12] Sherrington states (375, 152) it as follows: "And this web of conductive channels into which the centripetal impulses of the reflex are thus launched is known to be practically a continuum in the sense that no part of the nervous system is isolated from the rest." This view will prove to be of the essence of many of our later constructions. Since the nervous system, like the rest of the body, is so thoroughly interconnected that it is practically a continuum, what requires explanation is not the spreading of effects throughout, which would be expected, but the canalization of effects to specific

For these reasons and because it better represents the whole process, we shall consider wants as disturbances of homeostasis which may be propagated in many directions and have widespread effects. Among these effects are the specific ones which are transmitted by the several integrating media to the central nervous system—the centripetal transmission of wants. Because "the fixity of the internal environment . . . is controlled by the upper part of the central nervous system," [13] though it is by no means wholly *maintained* there, and because we are interested here chiefly in the effect of these propagated disturbances in producing overt behavior, positive or negative (some form of activity or inactivity), which is almost wholly generated by the central nervous system, we shall give particular attention to the transmission of the disturbance to that system—that is, to centripetal transmission. This mechanism for the centripetal propagation of a want consists, then, of all effects upon the several integrating media which in turn produce effects upon the central nervous system. But it is well to remember that, since "every adaptation [restoration of homeostasis] is an integration"—that is, it results from the "cumulative action of a number of factors" [14]—this mechanism is always complex and these strategic effects are somewhat diffuse.

Even in this limited field, however, the term "signal" has two further connotations which we cannot accept. It suggests that these "propagated disturbances," neural or other, as they are transmitted from the periphery to the nervous centers, are merely informative, leaving the centers free to act or not. We regard them, on the contrary, as the chief factor in the original initiation of corrective measures and consider that they will only be ineffective if they conflict with other stronger influences at the centers or if the apparatus is out of order. In the second place, the term unwarrantably emphasizes, and even begs the question of, the intervention of consciousness or volition. One signals to an intelligent agent; but when the process is automatic we do not think of it as a signal. One *signals* the telephone operator by raising the receiver; one does not signal the motor to start by pressing the self-starter button.

---

parts or connections which is actually observed. We will have much to say about spreading *vs.* localization, particularly with reference to the "bottle neck" which precludes integrated action in more than one mode at one time. But, at this point, it is also worth calling attention to the fact that this structure denies the possibility of foreordained paths from the external stimulus to the response which was so largely the assumption of "reflexology."

[13] Barcroft, *17*, 86.   [14] *Ibid., 17,* 172.

Because the variations, or tendencies toward variation, away from homeostasis vary in the relation between their ultimate sources and these integrating systems we would be ready to expect, as we examine the details, some marked differences in the ways by which the two major classes of wants are centripetally transmitted to the system which is chiefly responsible for such corrective measures as come in the classification of behavior. Our first group of causes of behavior (wants) consists of tendencies toward, or actual variations from, homeostasis in the blood. Since these occur in the blood, they are necessarily almost immediately generalized by means of that integrating system itself. But, since the central nervous system, which initiates the responses we call behavior (i.e., all other than chemical or purely local internal reactions), is everywhere in contact with the lymph (or with the cerebrospinal fluid), it would seem that the need does not exist for another and neural intermediator of any kind to transmit those conditions which will shortly be, if they can be, reflected in these fluids. Such transmission can be direct. On the other hand, all the rest of the causes of behavior (wants) occur originally in the tissues or organs; this we assume to be the case with all materials stored, with sex and, in part, with fatigue and its opposite. In these cases, then, in order to produce behavior other than purely local internal reactions, the want, at least when it reaches a critical point, must be propagated in some indirect way from the point of origin to the central nervous system which produces the behavior. This might conceivably be effected through any or all of the systems of integration; either by way of afferent nerves running centralwards from the particular tissues or organs; or by way of some chemical messenger given off into, or some change in the composition or condition of, the blood stream which thereafter acts on the central nervous system; or by way of some as yet undetected relic of pre-neural and pre-vascular communication between the parts of the whole, such as was suggested above. Thus, while one integrating system seems almost to suffice for the first class of wants, all three seem equally available for the second class.

2. CENTRIPETAL TRANSMISSION OF WANTS FROM THE BLOOD

The homeostasis of the blood—the correction of the aforementioned immediately generalized wants—seems to be managed very largely by that part of the central nervous system which lies between the upper end of the spinal cord and the cerebral cortex (i.e., the subcortical brain).[15] In all but one of those cases which are fairly well understood it may be said that the centers there react directly to the condition of the blood as that is reflected in the fluid in which they are bathed, though these centers are also influenced by afferent nervous impulses from other parts. That is, the majority of these wants are centripetally transmitted by non-neural mechanisms. For example, our first two wants, a deficiency of oxygen and a surplus of carbon dioxide (or perhaps only the latter), will excite the "respiratory center" in the medulla, which is the chief regulator of breathing, even if all afferent impulses are cut off, "so long as normal arterial blood is supplied to it." [16] "We may thus conclude that it is in virtue of changes in the hydrogen-ion pressure of the arterial blood that CO_2 affects the respiratory center." [17] As Cannon puts it "this delicate agency in the brain" operates "by keeping uniform its own status." [18] As to at least one of the purely internal responses to these circulatory wants—the speeding up of the heart rate—"there is evidence that the nerve centers for sympathetic control [of the heart] may be influenced somewhat as the respiratory center is influenced; acidity may develop in them as

[15] Much of the evidence is given incidentally in Appendix II. Since the purpose of that appendix is to assemble the evidence upon which the generalizations of the next chapter are founded, the facts are given there in terms of corrective functions, not variations. However, see especially Appendix II, Sections B, C, and E.

[16] Haldane and Priestley, *179*, 9.

[17] *Ibid.*, *179*, 100. The regulation of breathing is a complicated affair, and this is only the chief influence. Like almost all other physiological theses presented in this study, this one is being constantly amended. At present the explanation of breathing seems to be tending toward "the multiple factor theory" (see J. S. Gray, 103 *Science*, 1946, 739). However, a study of the new evidence leads me to believe that my statements, in the text or notes, are not incorrect, but merely incomplete.

It should be understood that the alternation of inspiration and expiration is a proprioceptive reflex (Hering-Breuer) though mediated via this center in the medulla. That is, "essentially respiration is conducted in the brain" (Barcroft, *17*, 63). Pitts *et al.* (*329*, 689) conclude that there are two centers there, one for inspiration and one for expiration. Weak central stimulation activates the former. Strong stimulation—and thus probably the stronger impulses from "lung stretch"—activates the latter and inhibits the former. But carbon dioxide pressure, directly, or through the hydrogen-ion pressure which accompanies it (disputed), primarily governs the depth and the frequency of this alternating process, breathing.

In addition there are pressure receptors and chemoreceptors "actually (or practically) imbedded in the walls of major arteries" (aortic arch, carotid sinus and aortic and carotid bodies, respectively). The pressure receptors are inhibitory and the chemoreceptors excitatory upon the respiratory center. These latter respond to increases in carbon dioxide tension or hydrogen-ion concentration, but also to decrease in the oxygen tension of the fluid bathing them. Their effect is ordinarily negligible and they are now only useful in emergencies. See Schmidt, *361*, 534 ff. Finally there are several higher controls over rate and depth whose stimuli are of a different order. Many of these are mentioned in Appendix II.

[18] Cannon, *66*, 100.

a consequence of excess of carbon dioxide and the primary result of that may be stimulation." [19] The temperature of the blood seems to be reported directly to "a sensitive thermostat" in the interbrain, which initiates the measures for correcting its variation from "normal." [20] There are many indications that the supply of sugar and probably that of protein and fat—both to the blood from storage and from the blood into storage—as well as the blood content of salts and of water, are also managed from these centers; but the nature of the effects which reach them is as yet not certain, though presumably of the same unmediated character.[21] The one certain exception is the central regulation of blood pressure, the signal for which seems to come, via afferent neurons, from the carotid sinus, located upon the arteries supplying blood to the brain, and lying near the brain.[22] With this exception then, it is probably true of the maintenance of the homeostasis of the blood, that the wants themselves—variations—do not depend on neural means for their propagation—which, where they exist, are compensatory—since they act directly on the centers that are concerned with initiating the counteracting measures. Furthermore, the chain of cause and effect in all these cases seems to be automatic—involuntary, as we call it. These direct effects do not themselves appear as sensations in consciousness, and only the overt behavior they give rise to, as and after it occurs, is known to the organism.[23]

3. CENTRIPETAL TRANSMISSION OF OTHER WANTS—NEURAL

On the other hand, when it comes to the maintenance of homeostasis in all other respects—including the stock of materials which are stored outside the vascular system (either for use or discharge), including those substances which are connected with sexual activities and those

[19] Ibid., 66, 158. Here, too, there are many higher centers which respond to other stimuli.

[20] Ibid., 66, 199. See Appendix II, Section E, for an extensive discussion of the details.

[21] See Appendix I, Sections A and B; Appendix II, Sections B and E.

[22] Cannon, 66, 56. See also Bronk and Stella, 47. Obviously blood pressure does not exist in the immediate surroundings of the nerve centers, but only in the arteries. Therefore, it could not be reported at all elsewhere, nor perhaps accurately after the artery enters the rigid skull space. Pressure receptors are also located in the aortic arch, as described in note 17, above. Afferent impulses to the vasomotor (blood pressure) centers also arise in the heart and the large veins. See Bazett, 28, 458. Finally, vasomotor effects can be produced from higher centers responding to different stimuli.

[23] Of course, the temperature of the skin may be sensed; but it is doubtful whether the temperature of the blood can be. Also radical increases of heart beat, while not overt, may cause sensations which enter consciousness.

substances or deficits which are accumulated outside the circulation in fatigue—explanations of centripetal transmission have, until very recently, emphasized, if they have not given exclusive import to, the neural system of integration. Almost none of the variations have been considered to be transmitted via the blood, and none, so far as I know, are attributed to the third possible means of transmission. Generally speaking, these wants have been supposed to initiate their corrective processes by means of afferent nervous impulses from the parts affected. Furthermore, instead of the automatic or "involuntary" action which seems to result from wants of the first class, these propagated effects have been presumed to appear as sensations in consciousness, and thus to produce "voluntary" action. It is fair to state that these views have been held not only by most psychologists, but also, until very recently at least, by many of those physiologists who have given special attention to the subject.[24]

It is correct to say, I think, that Cannon's theory of the maintenance of the reserve water supply is based on the conscious sensation of thirst,

[24] Among psychologists we may cite Boring (41, 330), who arrives at the general conclusion that thirst, hunger, nausea, the call to, and the act of, defecation, and the call to, and the act of, urination "are all complex experiences reducible . . . to various patterns of pressure and pain" (i.e., sensory). Nevertheless (42, 453) he does not fully accept Carlson's conclusions (below) as to hunger and appetite. Dunlap (123, 105–110) is less specific and therefore somewhat more careful and "safe." Nevertheless (ibid., 324, note), he "speculatively" assigns each of his nine primary desires to the specific part of the organism in which it is supposed to be resident, where it is "initiated by the stimulation of receptors" (ibid., 313). "Receptors" do not necessarily imply sensation, but they do imply neural transmission. Similarly, and in spite of his recognition that there is "astonishingly little of sensation arising" from the internal organs, Woodworth (447, 324) holds that there "can be little doubt" that hunger, thirst, nausea, suffocation, etc., and, in general (ibid., 541) "organic needs," do act "as stimuli to internal sensory nerves." "Internal sensory nerves" probably imply sensation and certainly imply neural transmission. Holt (207, 126–132), while he consistently emphasizes "afferent impulses," ascribes the "afferent impulses," which present his "appetitive drives," to "deficit stimuli" in respect of "chemical substances," presumably in the blood, in the case of the "appetites for oxygen and water" and food, and to stimulation of the proprioceptors by "mechanical pressures" ("distension"), in the case of the appetites for copulation, lactation, defecation and micturition (loc. cit.). Thus he appears to come nearer to the scheme we shall present, except in his division between "deficit stimuli" and "distension." But he doubts that his "chemoceptors" for the "deficit stimuli" are central (ibid., 128–129). In which case they would need to give rise to neural centripetal transmission, of course, if the behavior is initiated centrally.

It is not unreasonable to suppose that the fact that there are no conscious sensations nor "voluntary" actions with reference to the first class of wants (in the blood) has necessitated careful physiological investigation of their mechanisms, whereas the fact that both of these do occur with reference to the second class has concealed the necessity for similar investigations and has left the observers satisfied with the obvious. But perhaps, as with icebergs, the obvious is but a small part. That is indicated by the most recent developments in neurophysiology, discussed in Appendices I and II.

which is "referred to the mucous lining of the mouth and the larynx, and especially to the tongue and palate." [25] This sensation of dryness is due to an insufficiency of salivary secretion. "The importance of this failure of action of the salivary glands . . . lies in the strategic position of these glands in relation to a surface ["the ancient watercourse"] which tends to become dry by the passage of air over it," so that they "serve as indicators of the general bodily need for water." [26] Thus, one may say, his view is that the salivary glands are the "float" so adjusted to the level of water in storage [27] that they cause dryness and the corresponding sensation when that level drops below the proper point; and that they are located "strategically" in the sense that they are at the point of intake of water, at one of the important points of loss, and are located in tissues which may be high in the storage level (i.e., among the first to lose water when it is withdrawn into the blood).[28] Admitting the appropriateness of these features of the specific conscious sensation, dryness of the mouth and throat, nevertheless it appears probable that it is merely a partial explanation of the complex phenomena, and that chief reliance is placed on another and more primary mechanism which not only does not involve sensation but probably does not even depend upon the neural integrative system for its centripetal transmission. We shall therefore defer its consideration to the next subsection.[29]

Cannon's and Carlson's theory of the expression of the need of food (hunger) works out similarly, though it seems to be an even less adequate explanation.[30] In this case, too, the central effect of the condition, hunger, is supposed to be confined to a conscious sensation, de-

[25] Cannon, *59*, 286.

[26] *Ibid.*, *59*, 299-300, and 295.

[27] Not the water in the circulation; for he thinks that "thirst is clearly demonstrable long before any change in the blood is evident" so that "the origin of thirst does not arise in alterations of the blood itself, but in the act of withdrawing water from the tissues" (*59*, 291). He also regards the salivary glands as part of the structures in which the water reserve is held (*66*, 70). Both these points are considered in Appendix I Section A.

[28] This last point is very doubtful, since it appears more probable that the salivary glands, like other glands, secure their water immediately from the arterial supply of blood to them, and not from surrounding tissues.

[29] This thesis is derived from a summary of the evidence and the judgments upon it of qualified physiologists who disagree with Cannon, as presented in Appendix I, Section A.

[30] We shall hereafter follow ordinary terminology in using the word "hunger," or the specific hungers, to mean the need (or want) of food, or for the several necessary food constituents; and we shall use the specific term "hunger pangs" to cover what the physiologist usually means by "hunger," since, to him, all else is "appetite."

scribed as "a disagreeable ache or gnawing pain referred to the lower mid-chest region or the epigastrium." [31] These sensations, according to his own and to Carlson's experiments, are due to contractions of the empty stomach, growing stronger and more frequent to an acme which may be a spasm, and then subsiding for a period, after which the cycle is repeated.[32] It is repeated because it is "a normally recurrent activity of one phase of digestion"—a "wanting something to do." [33] There are many reasons for hesitating to accept "hunger pangs" as the chief or original effect of the want of food. In the first place there is, as yet, no adequate explanation of the cause of this special type of stomach contractions.[34] They may be, usually or largely, a secondary phenomenon. In the second place, this sensation of "hunger" seems to arise from a point which is not at all strategic in the sense that the origin of Cannon's thirst sensation may be regarded as strategic. And this both because it does not come from the point or points where the deficiencies in the stores of food actually exist and also because it is not associated with the point of intake.[35] In the third place, it is entirely undiscriminating as to the kind of nutrition that is needed. It is purely concerned with bulk and occurs in an organ associated with but one of the several types of digestion—and chiefly with one of the food elements only. Like many another physiologist, Cannon seems to relegate "appetite" (for specific foods) to a comparatively minor role and to treat it in an almost purely psychological, even a hedonistic, fashion.[36] Here, again, it seems probable that further investigation is in

[31] Cannon, 59, 286. A. J. Carlson (71) has summarized the previously published work of himself and associates which leads to similar conclusions.

[32] See Cannon, 66, 73, and 58, Chapter 13.

[33] Cannon, 59, 301. Nevertheless, some others hold that the amplitude of these contractions is greater than, and the pattern different from the ordinary peristalsis of digestion. Nafe (310, 1058) regards them as a "particular type of wave movement of the stomach musculature."

[34] The explanation "remains to be discovered" (Cannon, 66, 75). They are clearly not due merely to the absence of contents in the stomach. And the explanation that the contractions themselves are the result of central nervous excitation must not be excluded. At first Cannon (69, 435) seems to adhere to the "local, peripheral origin of hunger"—identified as the contractions or pangs. Later (66, 74–75) he seems not to exclude the possibility of a central cause. There he says that, from certain indications, it "appears that hunger contractions are caused by hypoglycemia acting through vagal [i.e., parasympathetic] influences" (ibid., 74). A center, causing hunger contractions, close to the temperature-regulating center in the diencephalon would account for the stoppage of these contractions in fever. On the other hand, they also stop if the stomach is filled with indigestible material. See Kuntz, 245, 454, and Cannon, 69, 435.

[35] In general, "body need may exist without hunger"—i.e., "hunger-pangs" (Cannon, 58, 242).

[36] He says that "hunger" and "appetite" may each exist without the other (58, 235). Ap-

process of disclosing, behind this conscious sensation, a primary system for transmitting the need of replenishing the requisite food constituents in storage, one that is capable of being specific as to each, that may have its source in the blood or even, ultimately, at some point at which each constituent is stored, and that is also related to the organ of intake (the mouth) and its associated organs of taste and smell (of substances in the mouth), which so largely determine the rejection of the great bulk of external objects as *not food* and the selection among the rest of what precise food is to be taken and when. The probable organization of such a mechanism will be outlined in the next subsection. But here, again, it would appear that the primary system does not depend wholly on sensation nor even wholly on the neural integrating system for its centripetal transmission.[37]

Along similar lines to these "hunger pangs" it has also been customary among psychologists, at least, to assign to "muscle sense" (sensation of distension) in the storage vessels the expression of the need for getting rid of stores of waste and refuse, and even for the origin of sex behavior. But such a simple explanation does not fit the facts. Since the causes of, and controls over, the process of micturition are far better understood than are those of drinking and eating we are in a position to give an established though approximate and incomplete outline of the way the apparatus works. Here the transmission is entirely neural, but the element of sensation is definitely secondary. Fundamentally, micturition is a complex involuntary and autonomic response which certainly can be, and may always be, set in motion by internal stimuli which do not reach consciousness. Superimposed upon this in-

---

petite seems to be "the pleasurable feelings or ["affective states"] which accompany the taste and smell of food during mastication, or which are roused in anticipation of eating when choice morsels are seen or smelled," and which stimulate the largely "psychic" secretion of saliva and gastric juice (*58*, 4 and 8). In this way these appetites become "desires for repetitions of [pleasant] experiences," or a sort of "habitual taking of these provisions" (*69*, 447; see also *63*, 417). This treatment fails, of course, to account in any way for the rise and fall, or the failure, of the appetites. Carlson (*71*, 98) says, "It is obvious that neither the sight, the taste, nor the smell of good food, the memory of these sensations, or salivation and throat kinesthesis can by themselves invariably produce appetite."

Herrick (*190*, 289) takes a broader view. He thinks hunger is a complex of three factors: (1) contractions of stomach, (2) appetite regardless of state of stomach, and (3) malaise from starvation of tissues and weakness. However, he makes no suggestions as to the character or source of the centripetal transmission of the last two.

[37] The reader is referred to Appendix I, Section B, for a brief discussion of some of the pertinent evidence and of the direction in which it is pointing, which is the basis for our tentative outline.

voluntary (and autonomic) process is a learned (not inborn) and voluntary control. This voluntary control is certainly exercised in part through the contraction of the striated muscle of the external sphincter of the bladder which is capable of preventing the consummation of the involuntary act and thus, also, of permitting it by not preventing it. It is probably also exercised in part by contraction or relaxation of other voluntary muscles, which actions have an inhibitory or permissive ("release") effect, respectively, on the autonomic process in general. It is also possible, but not likely, that the autonomic process itself is directly subject to voluntary excitation or inhibition as a whole. The sensations which reach consciousness consist, probably exclusively, of those caused by the fact that the apparatus for the involuntary act is trying to initiate the process (that is, contractions are actually occurring), though it may be prevented from consummation, and also of those caused by the fact that the process is being successfully consummated, because it is permitted. Thus neither of these kinds of sensation can be the cause of the involuntary act. They may constitute merely the cause of the remission of voluntary prevention, when that has been exercised. But what we are interested in is the true causes of the involuntary act, since this is the primary system for correcting the want. It is probable that the actual exciting cause of the involuntary process consists of nervous impulses (analogous to proprioceptive impulses from striated muscle) caused by the stretching of the smooth muscle walls of the bladder at any one of the several degrees of expansion of which these walls are capable. This stretching is due to the tonic contraction of these walls against a non-compressible volume of fluid. These impulses appear to be conveyed to an autonomic center in the brain-stem, rather than to consciousness as a sensation; and there, when they are of sufficient intensity to overcome the inhibition of still higher centers upon this one, or its efferent paths, and to change the tonic into active (phasic) efferent impulses from this center, they initiate the active contraction of the bladder.[38]

While less is known in regard to the neural mechanism which controls defecation, external observation of the process itself and of the conditions under which it does and does not take place argue that it is analogous to the one which controls micturition. And here, whether the sensation which reaches consciousness is active contraction of the rectum only, or also the sense of activity (peristalsis) in the gut (which

[38] For the evidence on which these conclusions are based, see Appendix I, Section C 1.

activity is responsible for filling the rectum and therefore causing the rectal stretch), it is even more certain that the sensations cannot be the cause of anything but voluntary release. For neither activity is subject to voluntary initiation, and one or both must have commenced in order to give rise to the sensation. One infers that, here again, the involuntary underlies the voluntary process and that the latter is wholly a release phenomenon which takes place when the direct response of the smooth muscle to its own stretch—probably reinforced, or even normally replaced, by a long-circuited neural arc reaching to subcortical centers, both of which are unconscious and involuntary —reaches a threshold level of excitation sufficient to convert tonic into phasic contraction. Here, again, there appear to exist relations between this and the voluntary as well as other involuntary muscular systems. Thus the involuntary process may be induced, or reinforced, by voluntary contraction of abdominal muscles and other "associated movements" and suppressed by still other activities which result in its "reciprocal inhibition." [39]

The subject of the causation of sex behavior is too complex for extended discussion here. We need note only the fact that it is probable that all the sensations which occur during the various processes only appear after sexual behavior has actually begun. Therefore it cannot be these which initiate it. This applies to sensations of distension of the glands or organs as well as to other stimuli which produce sensation.[40]

It is perhaps idle to speculate as to the centripetal transmission of fatigue. As noted above, this term covers many and perhaps somewhat independent phenomena. In so far as fatigue is a phenomenon of the central nervous system itself—and this seems to be the region of its earliest and strongest incidence—it obviously requires no transmission from the periphery.[41] We shall find it necessary to consider later the effects that it produces there. In so far as it arises in the motor neurons or their connections with muscle fibers, it is difficult to see how this can itself be transmitted centralwards. Of course, the resulting lesser or different contractions of the muscles must alter the strength or character of the afferent proprioceptive impulses, yielding, if reaching con-

[39] For a résumé of the evidence in this connection see Appendix I, Section C 2.
[40] There is considerable evidence for this conclusion. It is summarized at various points in Appendix II. See also Dercum, *118*, 297, and Kuntz, *245*, 340.
[41] Forbes's results (*148*, 170 and 179) indicate that fatigue is possible with inhibition (central) as well as with excitation. But see Sherrington, *375*, 222.

sciousness, weaker or different kinesthetic sensations, so-called. In so far as fatigue arises in the muscle fibers themselves, presumably due to accumulation of lactic acid, the result is loss of excitability or an inhibition of contractile power. Again the only central effect seems to be less or different kinesthetic sensation, or none at all. Perhaps in all these cases, but certainly in the last, there are, in addition, other sensory reports of resulting muscular conditions, which are sensory in our narrow sense and which we feel as aches and pains, stiffness, etc. In so far as excessive quantities of the products of metabolism in the circulation, on their way to, or beyond the immediate capacity of, the kidneys, may also have a depressing effect on the non-muscular system, that effect would be direct, of course, upon the central nervous system as well. Such a condition would be itself one of the variations from homeostasis of the blood and would be transmitted as the others are. Thus, where any centripetal transmission of fatigue is involved, that via the nervous system would seem to be confined to sensory reports from the periphery to the effect that central excitation had been unable to produce the usual, and therefore "expected," peripheral results, and to "pains" of various kinds; that via the circulation would consist in alterations in the blood (perhaps slight shortage of nutritional substances as well as a surplus of products of metabolism). In this way we assume that fatigue, in its several kinds, may produce sensation; it may also produce other central effects via the neural integrating system which do not constitute sensation; and it may also produce central effects via the circulation which certainly do not constitute sensation.

As to the variation opposite to fatigue, which we have called euphoria, it is not impossible that this condition is an automatic revulsion of the voluntary neuromuscular system, which represents heightened responsiveness to any stimulus—a lower threshold or increased excitability. This would account for the aimlessness of the actions it leads to and the self-regenerative character of the process while it lasts. As Sherrington says,[42] "inhibition of a tissue . . . seems to predispose the tissue to a greater functional activity thereafter." Neurally this is called "successive induction," a rebound phenomenon. While the subsequent rebound, in this case, follows a period of much longer inhibition than in the particular reflexes Sherrington studied, it may

[42] Sherrington, 375, 194.

be of the same general character.[43] If this interpretation is correct, then this want, like certain fatigues, exists in the executory system itself and therefore requires no transmission. Whether or not that is the case, it is quite certain that this phenomenon is non-sensory, in our narrow sense.

However, certain elements both of fatigue and of its opposite, euphoria, may be related to another process, neither sensory nor, on the afferent side, neural. If we construe rest, the behavior induced by fatigue, to be of the same order as sleep,[44] it seems to be a condition of rather general reduction of tone in the sensorimotor and the sympathetic nervous systems. This tone appears to arise as a sort of general fund in certain subcortical centers, which in turn are partially controlled non-neurally by certain substances or changes in the blood. The fund is diminished in sleep and perhaps in some forms of fatigue. It is enhanced in "awakeness" and perhaps in "restedness." Thus euphoria, like such fatigues, may turn out to be ultimately chemical in origin and only proximately neural.[45]

4. CENTRIPETAL TRANSMISSION OF OTHER WANTS—NON-NEURAL

"What energizes the nerves may be the fundamental answer to motivation." [46] But it is not to be supposed that the central nervous system can only be excited (or inhibited) by afferent nervous impulses— that is, it is not to be supposed that centripetal transmission of wants is wholly neural. We have already seen that the contrary is usually the case in the maintenance of homeostasis in the blood. Carbon dioxide in slight excess—or the associated hydrogen-ions—is itself a direct "excitor" of the respiratory center and perhaps also of that sympathetic center which participates in regulating the heart.[47] The temperature of the blood seems directly to affect the "heat center" or centers. It is

[43] At least it appears that something like "chemical modifications . . . induced by long rest, give rise to the impulse to move" (Bianchi, 35, 269).
[44] Gillespie (172, 223) considers fatigue and sleep to be "related but not identical" and agrees (ibid., 222) that "fatigue is still physiologically as intangible as sleep itself."
[45] For a discussion of this subject see Appendix II, Section G 2. As Dott puts it (120, 167), with regard to fatigue specifically, "From analogy with other hypothalamic mechanisms it seems not unreasonable to suggest that it [the hypothalamic sleep mechanism] may receive its normal afferent stimulus [or inhibitory influence] from products of fatigue in the circulating blood."
[46] Troland, 408, 4.
[47] "The regulation of respiration is fundamentally chemical . . ." (Haldane and Priestley, 179, 121). Cannon (63, 421) suggests that "the centers for sympathetic control may be influenced like the respiratory center." Oxygen want or carbonic acid

held that blood sugar directly governs the activity of the paraventricular nuclei in the hypothalamus.[48] But we need not stop there. The
various specific or general effects upon the nervous system of different substances, introduced via the blood, are well known—e.g., strych-
nine, nicotine, atropine, pilocarpine and curare; the anesthetics and
narcotics; the toxins, etc.[49] In some cases, at least, the internal secretions via the bloodstream seem to affect the nerve centers directly.[50]
There is reason to believe that the products of metabolism in the blood
stream may also have direct effects.[51] In respect of all these excitors

excess may develop acidity in them. And he opens the question generally (ibid., 426).
That the effect of changes in pH on the central nervous system is general—though
outside the respiratory and perhaps the cardiac systems it appears to have the opposite
effect—seems to be demonstrated by the changes in activity registered by electroen-
cephalograms. Dusser de Barenne et al. (127) find by this method that, for the brain
and also for lower levels, excitability and the actual response to neural or electrical excitation is decreased by the decrease of pH (acidity) and increased by its increase
(alkalinity). This they construe as an example of the normal effects of the blood condition on the brain as well as a possible explanation of alterations of threshold and of
the states of inhibition and excitation.
[48] See Appendix II, Section B 3.
[49] Some are selective; for instance the toxic action of infections and poisons seems to
affect primarily the nuclei of the interbrain (Dercum, 118, 298). The effect may also
be progressive by reason of decreasing susceptibility. Thus HCN acts from above
downwards (Barcroft, 17, 29).
[50] Cushing (100, 93) proposed the theory that pituitrin (posterior lobe hormone), acting intraventricularly, had a general excitatory effect on the parasympathetic (anterior) centers of the hypothalamus. This has been disputed. Bard (24, 194) discards it.
But something approaching it is now gaining general acceptance. Recently Finley
(140, 305) and Craigie (95, 317) have suggested that the unique vascularity of two of
these nuclei (supraoptic and paraventricular), which is so frequently commented on,
indicates that "their function is closely related to blood chemistry"—in fact that it is
their response to pituitary hormone in the blood stream that enables them to perform
their now recognized function—the regulation of the secretion of this hormone in the
hypophysis. Finley suggests that the cells themselves are chemoreceptors. Kuntz (245,
73) sees reason to believe that this intradiencephalic secretory system is more extensive
than has been recognized and suggests (ibid., 98) that the chemical mediation of autonomic impulses (acetylcholine and sympathin) also operates upon the centers themselves or between neurons. See also Henderson and Wilson, 188. Freeman concludes
that "the glands . . . are much less responsive to neural influences than the reverse"
(152, 400, note 3) and Dercum (118, 295–297) suggests, in line with some of our evidence in Appendices I and II, that "the internal secretions" act directly on the centers.
"In part this action is individual and specific, in part it is general and collective. It is
exceedingly probable that in this way are excited the primitive sensations of hunger,
thirst," etc. We think, however, as outlined below, that it is more probable that it is
the effort of the neuroglandular apparatus to maintain the normal blood composition
which constitutes hunger and thirst.
[51] Freeman (152, 400) regards the products of metabolism as "physico-chemical excitants." Dunbar (122, 13), interpreting the results Coghill reported (53 J. Comp.
Neurol., 1931, 147), attributes to him the belief that his experiments "must mean that
the efferent nerves are stimulated by products of the metabolism of the organism"
(Amblystoma).

or depressors, the facts we have suggest that the old brain—the immediate subcortical centers in the upper brain-stem—which is in the closest proximity to the arterial blood stream of any part of the central nervous system,[52] has retained more of the original undifferentiated "protoplasmic quality of irritability," which, at the periphery, has been specialized into receptors and, at higher centers, has been more confined to dendritic processes for receiving impulses from other neurons. This original capacity of the nerve cell—as of all protoplasm —is a capacity to react to its own immediate environment; that is, it has seemingly the property of quasi-autogenous excitation in that it can propagate nervous impulses without receiving them from any other neural source. It cannot be supposed that this property has everywhere been lost.[53] Nor can we ignore the possibility, noted on p. 44 and note 11, that certain of the states of central excitation, which, if they reach consciousness at all, produce there only vague and entirely general feelings, are the results of some pre-neural and pre-vascular communication, cell to cell, from the soma and viscera to the subcortical central nervous system. Perhaps such centripetal transmission would be confined to cases where variations from homeostasis had reached the point at which they were spreading from their usual locus and avenue of transmission throughout the system.

[52] That is, particularly, the interbrain, which is surrounded by the circle of Willis. The special vascularity of a part of the anterior hypothalamus has been referred to in note 50, above.
[53] There is considerable support in important quarters for this general view. Lashley (260, 23) doubts "the faith that the nervous system is only a conductor having no source of energy within itself." I take it that he holds that this applies to the whole brain. He says, "Within the gray matter the cell bodies and processes are not so protected [unmyelinated]. They are directly exposed in a liquid medium capable of conducting chemical and electrical changes which may readily influence the excitability of the neurons. The arrangement of the gray matter in thin sheets and the projection of the receptor and motor surfaces upon these sheets may have a real functional significance." Hess (192, 646) thinks the "large absorption surfaces of the choroid plexus" have a function and speaks of the "elective sensitivity" of the nervous system to "certain stimulating substances" (ibid., 735). Freud (156, 71) supposes chemical tensions as one kind of "stimulus mass." Pavlov recognizes what he calls "automatic stimulation (and inhibition) of centres" due to the "physical and chemical properties of the blood" (320, 10, 37, 43, and 44) though he does not attempt to explain it (ibid., 386). See also Bayliss, 27, 402, and Dott, 120, 184. See also Dusser de Barenne et al. as cited in note 47, above. Monakow (301, 41–44) outlines the possibilities which are, in his opinion, not "absurd," though "lacking . . . in positive evidence and demonstration." On the other hand, my impression is that this view has not been generally accepted by neurologists—at least that it had not been until the recent intensive studies of hypothalamic mechanisms. Cannon, for instance, holds (69, 435) that "the cells of the brain are relatively insensitive to chemical stimulation." Nevertheless, all would agree, I think, that "it is as a general rule the upper part of the central nervous system which suffers

Not only is there the positive evidence outlined above in favor of the supposition that some of the wants originating outside the blood stream may, nevertheless, be centripetally transmitted, chemically or physically, via the circulation, but there is negative evidence as well. That is, there is evidence against the supposition that, in the case of the more vital wants, chief reliance is placed upon the neural integrating system and, particularly, upon that part of it which is capable of yielding sensation. In disputing—and we think disproving—the so-called James-Lange theory of the visceral origin of emotions, Cannon has relied, in part, upon a supposed inadequacy of the visceral afferent nervous system to produce such states of central excitement.[54] But, if this system is inadequate to constitute emotional states, how can it be adequate to furnish the internal centripetal sources of the powerful "animal drives" we are examining?[55] That would leave only non-neural systems as the means of transmitting both. Moreover, this apparent inconsistency must be faced regardless of whether or not all visceral afferents are capable of arousing sensations in consciousness; for, if any are not, that may simply indicate that emotional states, as well as these drives, are primarily subcortical (i.e., non-sensory) phenomena and do not reach consciousness as sensation. Considering first only the sensory system, in our narrow sense, which is all that is involved in the type of explanation of centripetal transmission referred to in the previous subsection, it seems evident that any general theory that afferent nervous impulses from the viscera, yielding sensations in consciousness, are the exclusive—or even the chief—means of centripetal transmis-

---

if the internal environment alters beyond physiological limits" (Barcroft, 17, 86). But perhaps it has been supposed to "suffer in silence."

[54] See especially Cannon, 68, 266. This is but one of Cannon's objections to the James-Lange theory; it is not even cited by Sherrington in his earlier opposition to that theory, though he agrees to the fact. On this see Sherrington 374 and 375, 251–252, 261–265, and 317–318; Cannon, 58, 267–281, 60, 106, 68, 257–269, and 65, 281. The other points they make will be considered presently.

For the frequently expressed view of anatomical inadequacy see a general physiologist like Bayliss (27, 510–532), or an anatomist such as Villiger (414, 219 and 222–227). A good indication is the fact that when Herrick (190, 102–103) undertakes to describe the visceral afferent nervous system he goes almost completely psychological and lists the "organs" in terms of various conscious sensations ascribed to the viscera, without identifying them anatomically.

[55] Cannon (69, 447) describes hunger pangs as "powerful, persistent, and tormenting stimuli, which imperiously demand the taking of food before they will cease their goading." And (59, 301) he speaks of thirst as "disagreeable sensations which arise and torment us with increasing torment." This dilemma leads Kempf (233, 36–45) to reject Cannon's (and Sherrington's) disproof of the James-Lange theory, but to accept Cannon's apparently sensory theory of the drives, as in accord with his own (see below).

sion of any variations from homeostasis (wants) must depend on proof, first, that such part of the visceral afferent nervous system as is capable of yielding sensations, or such part of its impulses as do so, are sufficient for the purpose, and, second, that this visceral sensory system is directly sensitive to the conditions that constitute such variations. As to the first point, it is generally agreed, upon the basis of the anatomical evidence, that visceral sensibility is far less than is somatic.[56] This has been construed by some to be due to the sparseness of visceral afferent fibers. Of the three usual functional divisions of the peripheral nervous system, the sympathetic (or thoracolumbar) division of the autonomic is now usually treated as if it were confined to the efferent side. The best recognized "visceral afferents" are components of the various nerves belonging to the cranial section of the parasympathetic division of the autonomic, whose impulses are usually held not to reach to levels where they can yield sensations in consciousness. And the rest of the visceral afferents, of uncertain anatomical classification, appear to have their receptors exclusively in smooth muscle (visceral and vascular) and perhaps in mucous membrane (common chemical sense). Moreover, many of these, too, seem to lead into paths which have their highest central ending at subcortical levels and, to that extent, to be incapable of yielding sensation (strictly speaking).[57] There remain,

[56] See, for instance, Cannon, 61, 106, and 58, 281, note; Woodworth, 447, 324; and Nafe, 310, 1057.

[57] Hinsey says (198, 117), "To the best of our knowledge, the primary sensory neurons of the visceral afferent distribution are to be found in the dorsal root ganglia of the spinal nerves or in the ganglia associated with the various cranial nerves." As to the spinal nerves, as Fulton points out (160, 226), "From the point of view of the dorsal root ganglia, however, it is impossible to segregate somatic from autonomic afferents." Nor is it possible to distinguish them anatomically according to the nerves in which they run; for "the thoracolumbar ganglion chain (sympathetic) has large numbers of [apparently] sensory fibres passing along it," while there are apparently "autonomic afferents in cerebrospinal nerves supplying visceral organs" (Fulton, loc. cit.). The only distinction seems to be functional, and that is based largely on whether the impulses can produce sensation (sensory, in our narrow sense) or merely autonomic effects (unsensed)—that is, whether the paths appear to reach to cortical levels or to end at subcortical levels.

Whether the afferents of the spinal nerves, if autonomic, should be included in the sympathetic (peripheral) system is largely a matter of definition. Gaskell (167, 17 and 23) held with Langley that the sympathetic system is wholly efferent. Others continue to take this position. See Appendix II, Section A, and note 51. But Gaskell suggests (ibid., 27) that the "involuntary" system (autonomic) is actually complete but anatomically divided, the efferent part having "left the central nervous system" which thereupon extended its "connectors to keep contact with it," while the "afferent part has remained in the spinal cord with the rest of the 'sensory' nerves."

It should be said that Head's whole theory of "protopathic" sensibility, which has not been generally accepted, is founded on the "adventurous guess" that it is identified

then, but the rest of this last group as the only possible avenues of true visceral sensation.

While this negative evidence radically limits the known possibilities of visceral sensation, the fact remains that something that seems to be visceral sensibility can reach consciousness, as we all know from experience. The only remaining question is whether or to what extent it does so in the form of sensation (strictly speaking) or, on the other hand, chiefly in another form and by another and indirect route outlined in the next chapter. But since we do have the experiences, one way or another, we must, I think, find untenable this one of Cannon's objections to the James-Lange theory of emotions. And, on this ground, in spite of the fact that the paths are largely supposititious, we must admit that the system of sensory "signals" is possible. The real question, then, is whether they are primary.

As to the second point—the question whether the visceral sensory system is directly sensitive to the conditions that constitute variations from homeostasis—it appears that, by a process of elimination, all visceral (and vascular) sensibility—all that which may result in sensation (strictly speaking)—has been reduced approximately to "smooth muscle sense"—including a sense of pressure (or tension) and certainly a sense of pain when spastic contraction exists—and to an uncertain quantity of "common chemical" sense.[58] Even that might be

---

with "the afferent fibres of the sympathetic as they supply the viscera" and perhaps even the vascular system. He asserts that "structurally we know that the viscera are innervated from the sympathetic system" (*182*, 113). However, he also holds (*ibid.*, 113-114) that the viscera are innervated as well by "large afferent fibres connected with the end-organs of Pacini," which "run in conjunction with the motor nerves" and which are "peculiarly associated with impulses of movement and pressure." It may be these fibers which convey "muscle sense" from the viscera, as stated in the text. He also suggests (*183*, 747) that "visceral insensibility is a function of the specific action of receptors, and not the consequence of an absence of afferent impulses" (i.e., the impulses are of a pattern which does not ordinarily permit their reaching consciousness, though, under abnormal conditions, they "can break through" (*ibid.*, 744). Or, as Freeman puts it (*152*, 252), "since the visceral organs are regulated more or less exclusively by the sympathetic [autonomic] nervous system, very few visceral impulses are conveyed to the cerebral cortex" (also *ibid.*, 166, note 5). And this leads us back to the probability explored in Appendix II, Section E 1, where it is suggested that, at the highest central level, most visceral afferent pathways run from the paleothalamus to the hypothalamus only, so that their impulses do not reach the cortex directly as sensation. The difference from Head would be that here the paths determine the route, while with him it is the patterns.

[58] As to "muscle sense" see Nafe, *310*, 1057, and Kuntz, *245*, 466. As Nafe puts it (*310*, 1074), "Visceral sensibility is characterized by rather elaborate patterns, each typical of some movement or system of movements involving either contraction and relaxation of muscle, or the distension or collapse of an organ" (muscular wall). He does not

sufficient for the theory of neural transmission, if we are ready to admit that all these variations from homeostasis consist exclusively of, or produce locally, tonic or phasic contractions of the muscular walls of the visceral and vascular organs or irritations of the mucous linings,[59] and if we are also ready to admit that it is the conscious sensations thus produced which constitute the primary expression of the want. Precisely such contractions seem to be the source of the sensations of need for micturition and defecation. But, as noted above, these contractions themselves seem only to occur when the involuntary process is already trying to get under way. Therefore, they cannot be the original form of centripetal transmission, unless we assume that the contractions are entirely local reflexes without central reflections. The evidence cited in Appendix I, Section C, indicates, on the contrary, that these contractions, in the normal case, are regulated by supraspinal and subcortical centers. Thus we are led to conclude that the primary centripetal transmission in these cases—that which initiates the involuntary processes—reaches only to subcortical centers and does not enter consciousness as sensation; while the "signal" to consciousness is merely secondary and leads only to relaxation of voluntary inhibition. For these functions we accept neural transmission, but regard the primary apparatus as non-sensory, in our narrow sense.

When it comes to the need of water and of food, the sexual complex and peripheral fatigue, however, these limited visceral sensibilities do not seem to suffice as explanations of the system of centripetal transmission. The common chemical sense in the pharynx, etc., doubtless yields the sensation Cannon describes as thirst. "Smooth muscle sense" doubtless yields the sensation which Cannon describes as "hunger pangs." Muscle sense may also enter into the sex complex, at one stage, as labor-pains. And it may register one form of fatigue as muscular aches and pains, stiffness, etc. But in all these cases the "signal" to consciousness seems to be secondary and reinforcing only; this "thirst" and this "hunger" are somewhat unreliable "signals"; and hunger-pangs and labor-pains seem to be the effects of a process which has already been commenced as a result of some underlying and primary centripetal transmission of the want.

---

treat of "common chemical" sense, which is certainly present at some points, and perhaps at all, where mucous membrane exists (chiefly openings).

[59] On that basis the visceral afferent system would suffice for a theory such as Kempf's, *233*, xiv.

The hypothesis with regard to the maintenance of water balance, which seems at present to be most plausible, has been outlined in Appendix I, Section A. Considering here only the probable mechanism of centripetal transmission involved, it appears likely that a decline in the *absolute* water level in storage, being the result of a deficit in the salt (NaCl) in storage, registers as slight *hyposalinity* of the blood, which in turn excites a neuroglandular apparatus in the hypothalamic region to cause the tubular reabsorption of salt in the kidneys (conservation) and perhaps to produce the objective phenomenon appearing as "salt hunger" (replenishing). On the other hand, a decline in the *relative* water level, being the result of a deficit in the water in storage in relation to the salt in storage, registers as slight *hypersalinity* of the blood, which in turn also excites a neuroglandular apparatus in the hypothalamic region to cause the tubular reabsorption of water in the kidneys (conservation) and perhaps to produce the objective phenomenon indicating thirst—that is, drinking (replenishing). In neither condition does the neural system of integration seem to be involved in the centripetal transmission of the want; nor does the resultant central excitation give rise to sensation, strictly speaking, but only to "some vague or general bodily distress."

Even a merely plausible hypothesis with reference to the want of food—or the wants of foods—must needs be far more vague. It appears that there are specific hungers or appetites for the several constituents required as food (Appendix I, Section B). The reserve supply of each of these foods is stored (liver, connective tissue, etc.) by the process Cannon calls "segregation"—that is, "the surplus is driven into special organs and again given off by them as needed, under the control of definite neuroglandular processes," as stated on pp. 32–33. This storing and mobilization is also specific and independent as to each constituent. The specificity of appetites seems to operate through the taste mechanism, but under central control; for the taste threshold can apparently be varied with the need of the constituent.[60] Control of the storage and mobilization of blood sugar, at least, seems to rest in a complex neuroglandular system. The peripheral section is probably excited directly by the processes of digestion to effect storage. One of the central sections is excited by bodily activity or excitement (and perhaps also by deficits) to effect mobilization. But the regula-

[60] At least as to salt this has been demonstrated by experiment. See Appendix I, Section B, note 11.

tion of the peripheral section, and thus the maintenance of blood sugar at a normal level, appears to depend on another central neuroglandular mechanism which responds only to variations in the sugar content of the blood itself (see Appendix II, Section B). Though this center does not produce sensation, its quantitative discriminations appear to be analogous to those of the taste buds in the mouth. There are indications that a similar system is in control of the storage and mobilization of fat; too little is known of the control of protein metabolism to make it possible to include this as more than a probability. However, since the specific hungers, or appetites, appear or disappear as the specific stores are drawn down or replenished, it appears probable that the appetites represent one element in the effect of these central but sub-cortical mechanisms when increasing inaccessibility of stores necessitates increased activity in the mechanisms, in the effort to maintain the normal level of the constituent in the blood.[61] At present that seems to be the most plausible explanation of the specific hungers, as we are calling them. It ascribes them to the source of the higher central control of all metabolism—namely the hypothalamus—and therefore it ascribes the centripetal transmission of these wants to a mechanism, largely non-neural, whose effects do not reach consciousness as sensation.

When it comes to the behavior which maintains homeostasis in respect of food—eating—and to its attendant internal activities—the process of digestion and assimilation—there is, as noted on p. 35, no specificity.[62] And these activities include gastric motility—the source of Cannon's "hunger pangs." All these activities operate as a whole on whatever mixture is selected and ingested. Does this argue that gastric motility—whether utilizing mechanisms that reach consciousness or not—is the ultimate source of eating behavior? Apparently not. For gastric motility itself seems to be largely managed, if not always initi-

---

[61] Using the term "hunger" in its most general sense, Rignano (*345*, 143) asserts that it "is in the final analysis nothing but an impulse to maintain or to restore in the internal nutritive medium the qualitative and quantitative conditions necessary for metabolism to persist in its 'stationary' state [i.e., homeostasis]. This is shown by the fact that once the condition of the internal nutritive medium has become normal, all desire on the part of the animal to seek additional nourishment *ipso facto* disappears." And he cites the "experiments of Schiff" to "prove . . . that the essential nature of hunger is the impoverishment of the supply of histogenetic substances in the blood." Injections of "nutritive substances into the veins of a dog" "not only nourished the dog but they also assuaged his hunger" (*loc. cit.*).
[62] Of course, the digestive juices are specific in their action, but they are not specific in their application.

ated, by a superimposed system of central control analogous to that controlling vesical (bladder) contractions. Again this superimposed system seems to consist of several levels—all supraspinal—the highest subcortical centers for which are also in the hypothalamic region. And at that highest level the co-ordination with the appetites seems to be close, for a low blood sugar concentration in the brain at least promotes gastric motility.[63] This suggests that hunger contractions of the empty stomach may normally be no more than a part of the activity induced by the appetites, or by that one among them which happens to be strongest, and strong enough, when the stomach has ceased dealing with the previous meal. If so, hunger contractions are not primary, and we are left to suppose that the primary way in which the need of food, or foods—specific hungers—expresses itself is through the appetites, which are themselves excited by a largely non-neural mechanism and whose effects, even when they have become neural, do not reach consciousness as sensation, strictly speaking.

It is even more certain that both the original expression and the centripetal transmission of sexual need are non-neural and therefore do not themselves produce sensation. Upon the basis of Bard's experiments, discussed in Appendix II,[64] we can exclude afferent impulses from the genitalia or their surrounding erogenous zones as the original mechanism for the centripetal transmission of the want. Instead, it is evident that the central mechanisms which manage sexual behavior are activated by internal secretions (hormones) from the sex glands, which reach these centers through the blood, and that, without these secretions, sexual behavior does not occur.[65] While the exact locus of these central mechanisms has not been determined, it appears that the

---

[63] See Appendix I, Section B.

[64] See Appendix II, Sections B 1, B 3, E and E 1.

[65] By way of confirming these statements it is worth while to cite Richter's observations on rats (338, 313, 323–328). In the female, the running activity associated with the oestrous cycle begins at puberty. During pregnancy and lactation it declines from 60–95 %; also in pseudo-pregnancy or after sterile copulation it declines similarly for about 15 days. If an ovarian implantation is made on a spayed animal and it "takes," the activity cycle begins almost immediately. If the implantation is removed, activity drops 60–95 %. Extract of pig's follicles has the same effect (on rats). Therefore, the activity is produced by a "substance secreted by the ovaries into the blood stream," and probably by "central stimulation." Obviously, the signal is not the "contraction of a hollow viscus." In the male, the activity is not cyclical but does depend on the sex glands, for transplanted testes increase activity and castration reduces it about 60 %. In general, his males with low running activity took no interest in females, while those with high activity copulated frequently. But, since copulation produced no decrease in the latter's activity, we must conclude that the semen itself is not the source of the internal secretions which arouse the centers.

hypothalamus (especially the mammillary bodies) is the chief but not the only region involved. It is true (see Appendix II, Section B 1) that, "among the long series of acts and activities which constitute sexual behavior," once it is begun, "there are many individual ones which represent short-circuiting of purely spinal—or even intramural—patterns, as well as others which are due to local vascular, not neural, transmission." It is also true that many and different sensations arise during the various processes. But the series of acts and activities are parts of the behavior, not its initiating cause, and the sensations are purely secondary phenomena—by-products of the several processes already under way.

By way of summary of this difficult appraisal of the facts, and of the divergent views based on them, it is worth while to restate certain general points. It seems to be agreed that the homeostasis of the blood is almost wholly managed without the intervention of conscious processes, through an integrating mechanism which is chiefly non-neural, and by means of centripetal transmission directly by the blood supply of the subcortical parts of the brain. In contrast to that, certain of the theories as to the homeostasis of storage, etc., which have been presented, rely on afferent impulses which do enter consciousness, the centripetal transmission of which is wholly neural and which are solely derived from that particular, not always appropriate, part to which the sensation is referred. There is no question, of course, that these latter conscious sensations do occur. But, a priori, it would be surprising, to say the least, if these constituted the primary system of centripetal transmission and if the second group of wants relied upon a mechanism so different from that of the first group and so wholly "voluntary." And, in the second place, it seems impossible to reconcile dependence on the sensory system, in our narrow sense, with the observed fact that some of the behavior appropriate to these wants may occur when consciousness is in abeyance, and that much of it regularly occurs in laboratory animals when the supposed seat of consciousness, the cerebral cortex, has been removed.[66]

It is true that the alternatives we have proposed—neural but non-sensory [67] mechanisms for the primary transmission of the wants of get-

[66] This is also one of the chief difficulties in accepting the pain-pleasure explanation of behavior, in its usual form; for pain and pleasure are, of course, regarded as phenomena of consciousness.

[67] It should be noted that here, as we shall often have to do in accordance with common practice, we are using "sensory" as merely the adjective of "sensation."

ting rid of waste and refuse, and non-neural and therefore non-sensory primary mechanisms for the other wants—are as yet unproved. Nevertheless, the evidence in the case of the sexual want is strong, and the indicia in the other instances seem all to be pointing in that direction. In sum, all these considerations, both negative and positive, lead us to the conclusion that it is probable that the equally imperious wants which originate outside the blood use both the chief systems of integration (and possibly the third), but also that their transmitted effects, whether neural or non-neural, act, like those of the blood, directly upon subcortical centers and, apart from limited and secondary sensations, reach consciousness therefrom in a different, not precisely sensory, way.

2

PRESENT WANTS—THEIR CENTRAL MECHANISMS FOR GENERATING BEHAVIOR

When we come to the question of the central mechanisms to which wants are centripetally transmitted and which, in turn, generate all integrated responses directed toward maintaining or restoring homeostasis, it is hardly too much to say that recent work in the anatomy and physiology of the central nervous system, both experimental and clinical, has discovered what, in respect of its physiological functions, is practically a new and hitherto unknown world. And this is making necessary the fundamental revision of old ideas. This new world is the base of the brain and chiefly its effector branch, the hypothalamus or, more generally, the hypothalamic region. Since the evidence is new it is necessary to cite it in order to justify the various hypotheses which have been built from it; but since it is also voluminous and scattered through a vast literature from which it has to be pieced together, it has been necessary to relegate even the citations to an appendix. The reader who cares to review this evidence will find a synopsis of it in Appendix II. In fact, it may be well for any reader who wishes to follow the argument here, before proceeding further, at least to familiarize himself with Section I of that Appendix, called "Summary and General Inferences." Here, we shall limit ourselves to a brief statement of the hypothetical scheme which results, with merely occasional references to the supporting data.[1]

It should be repeated, at the start, that the management of homeostasis is a general function of the body as a whole, in which all parts participate specifically or generally. In many respects homeostasis is maintained, or even restored, by processes whose basic rates are kept

[1] Aiming for simplicity and for reasonable brevity precludes mention of details, of qualifications and of possible alternatives which would be necessary to make the statement precise. For these the reader is referred to Appendix II.

level by peripheral mechanisms or by centers of the central nervous system in the spinal cord and the lower portions of the brain-stem. But when integrated action is required, these mechanisms and their processes are regulated from higher levels. Since, as we shall see, all behavior (strictly speaking) involves such integrated action, and since we are concerned primarily with the ways in which behavior is produced, we limit ourselves to the consideration of the higher central mechanisms only.

A. THE SUBCORTICAL MECHANISM

I. IN RELATION TO INTERNAL WANTS

Subject to the foregoing limitations the mechanism with which we are here concerned is called the hypothalamus, or, since its functional confines are still uncertain, the hypothalamic region. The hypothalamus itself is very small; it is "well-concealed" in the most protected region of the brain; it is both neural and glandular in character; it is among the most primitive structures in the nervous system; unlike the rest of the basal structures, it has failed to participate in the development of the "new brain" (the hemispheres); it is, therefore, something of a "dead-end" developmentally; in fact it seems to be the surviving relic of the "old brain." [1]

Among the lower animals and among immature primates, this region of the old brain is sufficient to maintain life and to carry on the major types of behavior necessary for the maintenance of homeostasis, even when all new brain (cortex) has been removed. After maturation, this is no longer possible with the primates (including man); there is nevertheless reason to believe that this inability is due chiefly to motor defects only arising from a gradual increase, during maturation, in dependence upon the motor cortex. On the other hand, in the case of all mammals, and birds as well, removal of this particular part of the old brain abolishes all these capacities. This argues that the wants we have considered rely chiefly upon this apparatus for suitable integrated

---

[1] More exactly, it is the highest level of the old brain (i.e., the subcortical brain). But, since it is the only part thereof which has not become subsidiary to the new brain, this usage may be justified for brevity's sake.

Also for the sake of brevity, and because our authorities do so for the most part, we shall use the term "hypothalamus" throughout, though, as noted in the Appendix, it seems hardly likely that the functional entity here described will be found to be confined to the anatomical entity, "almost to be covered by a thumbnail," which has been known as the hypothalamus (see Appendix II, Section B, note 10).

activities to maintain or restore homeostasis. And that, in turn, argues that the primary system of centripetal transmission in all these cases is one which reaches to this apparatus. This is the region of the brain most intimately related to the blood stream and part of it is the region most fully supplied by the blood stream. Thus there is a presumption that it can respond directly to conditions and components conveyed to it in the blood. It is evidently the terminus of a large portion of the visceral and vascular afferent neural paths (non-sensory, in our special sense), which reach it indirectly through centers at this and lower levels. It is also supplied, though sparsely, with afferent paths whose stimuli arise in the external environment; but, as to these, it receives only the crudest and most primitive reports.

Thus, a priori considerations lead us to suppose that both chief integrating systems are used in the centripetal transmission of wants to this mechanism and that it is chiefly concerned with the wants we have already considered. In addition, there is much more definite evidence. Particular centers in this region appear to be excitable by variations from the normal temperature of the blood in either direction, by excessive hydrogen-ion concentration in the blood (partial asphyxia) and by blood-sugar deficits. There is some reason to believe that other centers here respond to deficits in the other food substances, to hypo- and to hypersalinity and to the products of metabolism (fatigue), as suggested in the previous chapter. This appears to be the most strategic point at which the sex hormones operate to initiate sex behavior. All these forms of transmission depend on the integrating system of the blood. But neural transmission supplements some of these and suffices by itself in other cases. Gastric activity certainly affects centers at this level by way of direct or indirect neural paths; and it appears that cutaneous cold and possibly cutaneous heat, reported neurally, serve as excitants here, though also indirectly. It is also probable in the case of man, and certain in the case of lower animals, that vesical and rectal tonic and phasic contraction and perhaps intestinal peristalsis are relayed to centers here by afferent neurons.

Upon the effector side it is equally clear that this neuroglandular system is the chief regulator of all vegetative functions, though, with possibly a few exceptions, it seems to work through lower centers which are in direct control. In other words, it is the source of the integrated internal activities concerned with the maintenance or restoration of homeostasis. It is the "chief ganglion" of the autonomic nervous system, which is the neural means of control over these activities; and it is said to regulate the hypophysis (pituitary), which is "the moderator of the endocrine series." Thus, when they need to be used for general purposes or for maintenance or restoration of homeostasis involving integration, all the vegetative functions may be brought into play by the centers of this system. The several centers here can alter the heart rate and the blood pressure, and can shift the blood to or from the skin, the viscera and the muscular bed, respectively; they can store or mobilize sugar and perhaps fat; they control the resorption by the kidneys of salt and of water; they vary gastric pressure, movement and secretion, intestinal peristalsis and vesical pressure; they can produce salivation, lacrimation, and sweating, general or palmar; they can dilate the pupils, retract the nictitating membrane (cats) and protrude the eyeballs, as well as cause erection of the hair and pigmentation. This almost exhausts the list of vegetative functions; the others may be added as time goes on.

Also upon the effector side, but in respect of those motor activities of the skeletal musculature which constitute overt behavior, it is evident that the old brain has available all of the innate (unlearned) patterns, but only part of the added skill in performing them that comes with growth and practice. These patterns are the stereotyped forms of behavior such as, in quadrupeds, eating and drinking, defecation and micturition (postures, etc.), mating and producing offspring (in respect of motor acts), walking and running, struggle, pursuit of prey, facial expression, and various special forms of breathing and vocalizing. With the gradual development of the cortex, as primates mature, the old brain becomes no longer adequate to perform all of these motor functions by itself. Nevertheless, it is evident that it continues to participate in them in various degrees. The descending paths by which the old brain achieves these motor effects are not precisely known. But it is clear that the movements are entirely executed by way of other (probably lower) subcortical motor centers in which the patterns or parts of patterns are organized—that is, all are indirect. All the old brain does is to combine these stereotyped actions in complexes or in series and produce them in response to excitors which do not reach these lower levels, or in response to a higher degree of the same excitor.

From all the evidence it is concluded that, even in man, internal wants requiring integrated activities and behavior produce these results primarily by means of the hypothalamic mechanism, whose other and far-reaching influences will be considered as we proceed—that is, it is this relic of the old brain which reacts to and primarily manages the integrated maintenance or restoration of homeostasis in respect of *all* bodily wants, not merely of those which originate in the blood.

2. IN RELATION TO EMOTIONS

To a considerable extent the "discovery" of the hypothalamus has been due to the findings which have identified it as the proximate source of what is called emotional expression—expression connoting rage or fear, for instance. This expression is composed of two parts. One part, the "bodily changes" as Cannon called them, consists of various patterns of integrated alterations in vegetative functions such as are available to the old brain, as we have noted. Among these, common observation includes, for example, dry mouth, lacrimation, cold sweat, dilated pupils and the standing of the hair "on end" (piloerection). But the rest can be detected by physiological observation. The other part of emotional expression is behavior, strictly speaking. Stereotyped patterns of facial expression and of special forms of breathing and vocalizing are so identified with particular emotions that they are the usual indices of the several emotions to all of us. But such behavior extends, of course, to struggling, running, biting, and so on. It is now generally agreed that all these expressions of emotion are the direct results of conditions in the hypothalamus. As in the case of the responses produced by the primary apparatus for want behavior, these emotional responses continue practically intact among lower animals and immature primates when the cortex is removed. That proves that the hypothalamus is adequate to produce these responses by itself. In the case of mature primates the hypothalamus alone is adequate to produce the bodily changes associated with emotion. But the hypothalamus cannot alone produce all the motor elements of these responses. Nevertheless, here too, it continues to participate in the behavior in various degrees and ways and contributes what are construed to be the emotional features of such behavior. These conditions in the hypothalamus itself we call "emotional states" in order to differentiate the proximate or central cause from the peripheral results (expression). It is also necessary to distinguish between the various forms of emotional excitement,[2] on the one hand, and the various forms of emo-

[2] *Excitement*, in the ordinary sense, not excitation. As a phenomenon (observable), all excitement is here construed to be evidence of an excited emotional state.

tional depression, on the other. The former are evidently associated with corresponding patterns of more or less general and supernormal excitation in the various centers of the hypothalamus (probably posterior only), and the latter with corresponding patterns consisting of various degrees and kinds of paralysis (loss of excitability, not inhibition), of these same centers. While these patterns, both of excitement and of depression, differ when their degree of intensity is moderate, they evidence a tendency to become almost indistinguishable in intense excitement or great depression, regardless of their origin. This leads to the supposition that each of the several emotional states represents at first a special combination of certain centers only, excited or paralyzed, which, as the degree of intensity increases in either direction, tends to embrace all these centers and thus to become uniform for all excitements or for all depressions.

The identity of the apparatus in which emotional states arise and that through which present wants primarily express themselves as integrated activity or behavior suggests that these emotional states and the primary central effects of wants are one and the same thing.[3] This is proved by the fact that the wants we have considered may result in various kinds of emotional behavior and that, when they rise to great intensity, this behavior is indistinguishable from that ascribable to what are usually called emotions. The emotional character of sexual behavior is obvious; but partial asphyxia, very high blood heat and very low blood sugar also produce great excitement. And, of course, excessive fatigue produces depression. As we shall note later, one of the first forms of behavior evident when a want is beginning to express itself with animals—and perhaps also, but less openly, with man—is "restlessness" (aimless spontaneous activity). This is construed to be a kind of emotional expression. But restlessness and the behavior result-

[3] That is, the "affect," as it is called—our emotional state and emotional experience—is the central condition resulting from any variation or tendency away from homeostasis which requires integrated activities for its correction. On this I think the physiologists are now agreed. Rignano expresses it well (345, 142–143). He says: "If we use the term 'affective' to denote that special category of organic impulses which subjectively appear in our experience as 'desires,' 'appetites' and 'wants,' and which objectively are manifested as non-mechanical movements, either actual or inceptive (i.e. in the nascent state), then we may consider all the principal 'affective tendencies' as examples of the fundamental tendency of the organism to maintain its physiological condition unchanged." And he refers to "the primitive visceral origin of all the most fundamental organic affective tendencies, which constitute the real foundation of all the affective edifice of the psyché" (ibid., 205–206).

ing from euphoria—a small boy's fidgets, for instance—are hardly distinguishable. The evidence clearly indicates that the various stereotyped patterns of vegetative changes and behavior which can be observed and identified are the results of different patterns of excitation or depression produced in the hypothalamic region, and that the emotional quality, so-called, is merely an indication of the degree to which the several wants have varied the normal activity of these centers either in the direction of excitement or depression and, therefore, an indication of the scope of the centers engaged.

When, in utilizing the physiological approach to the causation of behavior, we find that the same central mechanism which produces behavior in response to the bodily wants also produces it in response to other causes, it is proper that we should include these other causes, so far as we can identify them, in our list of wants. We should attempt, therefore, to determine what are the causes of the other stereotyped and automatic reactions generally recognized as common to animals and men and to see whether these too can be ultimately ascribed to analogous mechanisms for the maintenance or restoration of homeostasis. The supplementary list of those for which we can discover any definite, if even only proximate, physiological cause is limited; but all these concern specific and immediate relations of the organism as a whole to the external environment. To distinguish them from the wants which arise directly from conditions in the internal environment only, we shall call them quasi-external wants. We call them quasi-external, rather than external, to discriminate them from the great mass of the external stimulus-response category, because it is evident that each of these wants has available an elaborate and innate mechanism of its own, whose stereotyped pattern is already completely organized at birth and is only touched off by the indication that its particular environmental relation has been disturbed.[4] These additions to our list are as follows: Loud sounds, probably bright light and perhaps any strong somatic stimulus produce the "alert" (i.e., opening eyes, pricking up ears and turning of head); these, when very strong and sudden, produce the "fear" reaction which may include "escape"; loss of equilibrium or support also produces the "fear" reaction, without "escape" but probably with "forced grasping" in primates; restraint and constraint of movement or posture produce the "rage" reaction,

[4] See supplementary statement on "Quasi-external Wants" at the end of this section.

including "attack"; [5] injury by external causes produces "pain" reactions, including "withdrawal" or even "escape." Translating these into terms of our original analysis, we may assume that the necessities of homeostasis in general include also freedom from strong external stimuli of any kind, freedom from loss of equilibrium or support; freedom from restraint or constraint of movement or posture (bodily freedom); and freedom from external injury. [6] Variation from homeostasis in any of these respects leads to stereotyped and automatic behavior patterns suited generally to restore homeostasis—patterns which are analogous in every respect to the types of behavior produced by internal wants. [7]

To place this supplement to our original list of wants on the same basis as the others, it is necessary to establish, so far as we can, what are the means of centripetal transmission by which these quasi-external wants reach the subcortical mechanism in which the expression— vegetative and motor—is organized. Probably all of them use the neural integrating system exclusively. The receptor for sounds is of course the cochlea, that for light the retina, and that for somatic sensory stimuli the cutaneous sensory nerve endings. It appears that certain qualities of sound (loudness and perhaps pitch), of light (brightness), and of contact (heavy touch) can be conveyed to the hypothalamus. There is little spatial organization (localization) there —perhaps only a distinction between the right and the left side— and there is only crude discrimination in terms of strength of stimulus. Nevertheless, the mechanism is adequate to produce the "alert," when stimulation is mild, and to produce the fear reaction, when stimulation is strong and sudden. The receptor for loss of balance or support is the labyrinth (vestibule and semicircular canal). Since the vestibular branch (balance and support) and the cochlear branch (hearing) of the auditory nerve begin together, and since the former also connects indirectly with the thalamus (or the hypothalamus) the vestibular branch is evidently the means of centripetal transmission in this case. While all the other quasi-external wants are due to stimuli whose receptors can be identified, we cannot identify the organic

[5] This is the usual explanation of the reaction called "rage." For a further discussion of "rage," see supplementary statement on "Quasi-external Wants" at the end of this section.
[6] We are disregarding internal injury (i.e., pain from internal causes, digestive, etc.) only because we are limiting ourselves to the physiology of the "normal" animal.
[7] Some other possible respects are mentioned in the supplementary statement on "Quasi-external Wants" at the end of this section.

source of rage. Proprioceptive impulses from the muscles would be a convenient explanation. But, in face of the fact that Sherrington found proprioceptive reflexes at the bottom of the scale in affective tone, while this reaction is at the top, that is a difficult explanation to accept. All we know is that its primary source is below this subcortical mechanism, for the reaction can be provoked even more readily after decortication than before. Also its transmission is probably neural not humoral, for the humoral changes seem to be effects, not causes. Finally, the central effect of external injury has generally been presumed, in the past, to be a sensation which enters consciousness as pain. There is, however, much question whether pain is a sensory modality at all; and, in any case, it is certain that pain impulses reach the hypothalamus unimpaired, or only slightly impaired, even when the cortex is removed. Pain has been much studied, and there are several theories in regard to it. It is clearly a neural phenomenon and is the accompaniment of a process that originates in the part affected, though, in consciousness, it may be "referred" to some other part instead of being correctly localized. Since injury may occur without exciting any afferent impulses,[8] since these may not break through into consciousness as pain,[9] and since pain may soon cease though the injury remains,[10] this particular central effect is not inevitable. Neither, as we shall see, does it continue to serve alone to lead to corrective behavior.[11] Finally, its emotional expression is clearly produced at subcortical levels and therefore in a way which does not involve consciousness or sensation. However, pain itself is of such nature, being obviously capable of producing conscious experience, that we find it necessary to postpone its discussion until we can elaborate the scheme into which it is now presumed to fit.[12]

All the evidence leads us to infer one characteristic of the activity of the central nervous system at this level which we need to emphasize here for future reference. We have seen that each want—internal and quasi-external alike—seems to arise at the periphery independently of

[8] Frogs have been killed by heat so slowly raised that it never gave rise to the normal "escape" movement. A nerve can be crushed so slowly that there is no nervous impulse (Nafe, *310*, 1041).

[9] See Appendix II, Section G, note 82.

[10] "It seems settled that pain adapts from experience that is painful to an experience that is painless and, at least in some cases, adaptation continues until there is no experience at all" (Nafe, *310*, 1064).

[11] See Chapter 3, Section B, note 62.

[12] See pp. 90–91, below.

all others and then to be centripetally transmitted by its own special means. The circulation is the common integrator for some; but the substances or conditions so conveyed are different for each. And, where afferent neurons constitute the integrating system used, even the path for each want seems to be different from that for each other. Moreover, it is believed that each of these several excitors, neural or humoral, which is specific for some particular want, reaches to a specific center (or centers) in this region, a center or group of centers supposedly organized for the particular corrective function required. In such an organization one would expect that each want could lead to its special internal activity or external behavior even while others were independently doing the same, unless, of course, some two required opposite uses of the same agencies. But this appears to be true only to a very limited degree. Very mild wants leading to very limited regulative activity may be able to use this apparatus concurrently.[13] As soon, however, as any one want becomes strong, something which has been called spreading seems to occur.[14] Excitation from the focus of the particular center first reached comes to involve other centers, either by way of excitation or of inhibition and often with seemingly inappropriate results. The greater the degree of excitation from any source, the more centers seem to be involved and the more extensive becomes the pattern of changes in internal activity and of elements in external behavior; that is, the greater becomes the number of effector functions affected. And thus, as noted above, the more intense is the excitation, the more centers are involved and the more ex-

[13] It is a question, even then, whether such regulation is not carried on by still lower and non-integrated centers.

[14] The term "spreading," or irradiation, is used in default of an exact explanation to cover an observed phenomenon. There seem to be three possible explanations. Either (1) the several centers at this level control specific functions though all respond to all the different excitors, but because each center has a different threshold for each excitor the patterns differ at low intensities and yet more are engaged as the intensity of the excitor increases; or (2) the several centers at this level control specific functions and respond each to its own excitor only, but are interconnected in such a way that, as the intensity of excitation at one center increases, it is communicated to the neighboring centers; or (3) each of the centers at this level responds to its own excitor only, but is connected with all or nearly all of the lower centers controlling specific functions, though, because the latter have different thresholds for these various connections, the patterns produced vary from the specific to the general according to the number of centers engaged and differ, in turn, according to the particular higher center which excites them. The subject is discussed in Appendix II, Sections B 3 and D.

As noted in Chapter 1 and repeatedly hereafter, the fact that the nervous system is an interconnected whole—practically a continuum—establishes spreading as the natural assumption. It is canalization, not spreading, that requires explanation.

tensive is the resulting pattern, the more uniform becomes the total expression regardless of the original source. At the extreme it is hardly too much to say that there is one pattern only for intense excitement and one for profound depression for all causes which can produce either. It is a matter of common observation that these two latter conditions are not effective as means for correcting wants. In fact, they are akin to spastic paralysis and atony, respectively. They lead to nothing. It is, therefore, in the intermediate intensities, only, that appropriate corrective behavior of an integrated nature can result. At low intensities there is insufficient integration; at very high intensities there is futility. But between these degrees the phenomenon of spreading connotes a tendency toward the exclusive use of the whole apparatus by one want at a time, which, at any high degree of intensity, becomes a temporary monopoly. This fact of mutual exclusiveness, to the extent that spreading takes place, is of prime importance. It places the several centers of this region on a competitive, more often than on a cooperative, footing. It will prove to be the basis of one of our chief constructions, in Chapter 4, as to the manner of operation of the present want system.

Quasi-external Wants. These have full status as wants because each is a departure from homeostasis in a particular relation between the internal and external environments which produces an innate, integrated, and automatic type of behavior calculated to restore that homeostasis and subserving no other variation nor dependent on the existence of any other. They are only quasi-external because they seem to originate in disturbances of the apparatus for maintaining constant (standard) relations with the environment, rather than in the external stimuli themselves or even in receptors to such (e.g., equilibrium apparatus). The distinction between quasi-external wants and the ordinary external stimulus-response category conforms to that of others. Thus Bianchi (*35*, 269) regards hunger, thirst, etc., as the "fundamental emotions." He defines his "second group of emotions" (fear, anger, etc.), as more "extra-organic" (*ibid.*, 270). In general our class, quasi-external wants, relate to what the biologist means by orientation (see Section C, note 9, below). That includes such relations with the environment as posture, equilibrium, choice of habitat, and such conditions as light, smells, currents, heat, etc. Rignano expresses these relations in much the same terms as ours (*345*, 144 ff.): "For each kind of animal there is an optimum environment as regards the concentration of the solution in which the animal lives, or the temperature of the medium, or the intensity of illumination, above or below the level of which the organism can no longer maintain its normal physiological condition, and which it strives at all costs to maintain." Thus "the tendency to maintain the normal physiological condition [internal homeostasis] is changed into a tendency to maintain the stability of the medium enveloping the organism." "Under the category of stability of environment must be included also the position of the organism in relation to the various forces acting upon it, and above all the force of gravity. From the tendency to maintain this relationship unchanged is derived the effort of the organism to preserve or to re-establish its proper position in space."

That the cause of "rage" is a want in its own right is sometimes questioned. Cannon (68, 257) says that anger is a response to "an inner [note "inner"] stimulus which arises when there is a hampering or checking of motion or an opposition to one or another primary impulse." Tolman (403, 280) calls it "pugnacity," but agrees that the ultimate state to be avoided is "interference with, or blocking of, other activities." So Jennings (223, 299) refers to it as interference "with the normal current of life activities." And McDougall (284, 62) says, "The condition of its excitement is rather any opposition to the free exercise of any impulse, any obstruction to the activity to which the creature is impelled by any one of its other instincts."

It will be noted that these statements all include opposition to other impulses (i.e., other wants) as a cause of rage. So Tolman (403, 282) holds that this "drive" belongs in his classification of "second-order drives" because it is "parasitic upon other drives," or better, because it is "ancillary to the satisfaction of other drives." Its function is "to prevent interference with these other drives," so that, if there are no other drives, there is no "pugnacity." That may come to be true of the experienced organism, since, if there are no other drives there is no motor activity to restrain. But, I think we have to credit bodily freedom with being a want in its own right. And this for several reasons. It appears possible to excite rage by constraint even in a state of inactivity that may denote absence of other wants. But even if another want is present, this one, when excited, does not reinforce that special activity. Rather, it produces its own special response which takes the place of and is usually quite inconsistent with the response to the other want. In fact it appears to compete with and displace other wants rather than reinforce them.

It is true that there may be, at less intense and apparently non-emotional levels, an apparent rise in the energy of response to any want when resistance or force is encountered, though the intensity of the want presumably remains the same. On this see the studies of N. Ach (1), who concludes that "determination" is emotional force ("feeling-tone"), and that the stronger the resistances the greater this energy available for response. That might be construed to mean that "determination" was merely a mild degree of rage. So McDougall: "The first effect of increase of resistance to our effort is to augment our output of energy." This is first felt as "zest" and, as it rises in the scale, as "anger" (285, 141). Nevertheless, it is difficult to combine the ancillary character of determination with the usurping character of rage. Moreover, there is reason to believe that the correct adaptation of energy expended to resistance encountered is a function of the cortex and of the cerebellum, whereas subcortical motor activities are generally marked by the use of excessive force or at least by a degree of force determined by the intensity of the emotional state only.

The limitation of our list of quasi-external wants to those given in the text raises some questions. There are probably also wants for freedom from obnoxious odors and disagreeable tastes, as well as for freedom from bodily discomforts, short of pain. In other words it is possible that all the senses which come in contact with the environment are capable, at times, of directly exciting the subcortical effector centers.

It may be objected that we have omitted those external stimuli, sometimes treated as unconditioned, which are "pleasant." As to certain patterns or degrees of sound it is possible that these also act directly and are sufficient to cause behavior in the absence of other wants. If so, one might conceive a scale for this kind of stimulus varying from pleasant up to unpleasant according to the degree of cacophony, or some other criterion. It is possible that the "pleasant" excitation of "erogenous zones" of the skin may bear some similar relation to the cutaneous pain sense, or it may occur only in the presence of the sexual want. This is another of Watson's "group of emotional reactions" which are unconditioned and belong "to the original and fundamental nature of man" (*429*, 199–201 and *430*, 121–123). The other three, which are due to "sudden loss of support," "loud sounds," and "hampering of . . . movements," have already been mentioned. His list is absurdly incomplete; but we are not inclined to expand our list to include this third—his "love"—until it is evident that it is neither due to internal causes (sex) nor is of the same order as (a mild degree of) pain—the two alternatives. As to the latter, Crile notes (*96*, 101) that tickling, like pain, "compels self-defensive motor acts."

Thus the difference between "pleasant" and "unpleasant" may be a difference in intensity (or some other feature) of stimulus. Since we do not know, we do not go into the matter. Our exclusions are based on ignorance not oversight.

B. THE CORTICAL MECHANISM

I. THE SENSORIMOTOR SYSTEM

Superimposed upon the old brain there has developed from it, in widely different degree according to the phylogenetic scale, a new brain which has relegated most of the centers of the old brain to the function of way stations (relay) for the impulses rising to or descending from the new brain. These relay stations continue to function as elaborators and organizers. Nevertheless, they have become servants of the new brain. Only that part of the old brain which we considered in the previous section appears to have retained its independence—a little, but relatively little, impaired—and to have remained a rival of the new brain for the control of the effector mechanisms of the brain-stem.

The excitors which reach the new brain (the cerebral cortex) seem to be wholly neural,[1] and this neural system appears to be entirely separate from that one which is partially responsible for the excitation of the hypothalamus. Whereas the latter system is non-sensory, the former is wholly sensory, in our non-physiological meaning of these terms. That is, all excitation reaching the new brain from its own afferent system is capable of being appreciated as sensation, whereas none of that reaching the hypothalamus can be so appreciated. Moreover, the two afferent systems subserve different environments, or largely so. The non-sensory afferent nervous system, serving the hypothalamus, arises chiefly in the visceral and vascular organs (smooth muscle) and so represents the internal environment for the most part. The sensory system, serving the cortex, arises chiefly in the skeletal musculature, the skin and the distance-receptors, so-called (sight, hearing, smell), and therefore represents the external environment for the most part. But each environment appears to have some representation as well in the other system. The sensory system, at least so far as sight, hearing and the somatic senses are concerned is organized so as to reproduce the spatial arrangements of the external environment. That organization is almost entirely absent in the non-sensory system. Therefore, appreciation of spatial arrangement, both of the body and of the external environment is practically confined to the cortex. Apparently that is also true to the same degree of temporal arrangement, although the reason for this is not known.

The effector mechanisms of the cortex include a certain degree of control over vegetative functions via the autonomic nervous system. This is attained, in part, through the hypothalamus and, in part, more directly via lower centers in that system. But its exercise by the cortex appears to be not separable from motor activities (behavior). That is, the influence of the cortex on vegetative functions is incidental to specific motor activities in preparation or in process. It is an automatic accompaniment of such patterns. In respect of the operation of the skeletal musculature—that is, the motor system proper—both with regard to posture (tonic) and to movement (phasic), the cortex utilizes

---

[1] Of course the condition and composition of the blood has its effect on the functioning of the cortex, but apparently not by the way of producing specific responses.

the same subcortical centers that are available to the hypothalamus. By this means it can produce the same stereotyped forms of behavior that were mentioned above in connection with wants and emotions. But while these forms of behavior are organized in lower centers which are presumed to be the same for both, there appears to be a difference in their character when engineered by the cortex and when engineered by the hypothalamus. That is, when an established pattern is excited by the latter it evidences the characteristics we associate with the expression of emotion, such as use of excessive force, incoordination, tremor and palsy, and a certain loss of acquired skill. These characteristics do not appear when the cortex is the source. On the other hand, cortical excitation of certain of these lower centers cannot exactly reproduce the effects of hypothalamic excitation. For instance, facial expression and the various uses of the breathing and vocal apparatus are not identical in the two cases. Apparent emotional spontaneity is missing when the cortex is responsible. Finally, we recall that in mature primates the hypothalamus can no longer by itself produce all of these patterns, particularly the more general motor ones. It can only contribute its special characteristics to the actions which the cortex initiates. The cortex, however, remains capable of executing all of them alone.

In respect of another element in the motor system the cortex has a monopoly; for it exclusively controls the pyramidal tracts which run direct to the motor centers in the spinal cord. And it is these tracts which are responsible for all modifications in the stereotyped behavior patterns and for all discrete motor actions, and therefore for all adapted and skilled behavior. It sometimes appears that a chief function of these tracts is to suppress the unnecessary or unsuitable portions of the stereotyped forms. That is, the effect often seems to be obtained by securing a background of inhibition which blots out all parts of a whole synergy except the single act which remains in the foreground, or blots out part and permits the excitation of a modified substitute.[2] Through this apparatus the development of the cortex seems to result in the expansion of behavior forms from a few rather general types of movement, which involve most of the body and which include a varied accompaniment of "associated movements" such as facial ex-

---

[2] For example, as all young pianists know, it is at first very difficult to raise one finger, especially the third, without also raising its neighbors. The acquisition of that skill seems to consist in learning to inhibit the neighbors.

pression, respiratory and vocal expressions, up to a vast variety of specialized movements which have little or no accompaniments. The discrete is derived from the integral, not the reverse.

In addition to the specific vegetative changes and bodily movements which it initiates, the cortex seems to exercise a more or less continuous influence over the rest of the central nervous system. On the efferent side this is in part by way of facilitation—that is, the maintenance of a constant but subliminal excitation in lower, chiefly spinal, effector centers which permits afferent impulses to pass over at these levels. This facilitation is largely responsible for what is called "short-circuiting," and thus for spinal reflexes. In part, this influence is by way of inhibition; that is, the maintenance of a constant but limited inhibition in lower, chiefly subcortical, effector centers which reduces their excitability to afferent impulses reaching them from below. When this inhibition is withdrawn there occur what are known as "release phenomena" (more intense or more continual activity by these lower centers). But such release may also be due to a third element in the influence—to the withdrawal of inhibition upon the afferent side, or rather upon the transit (internuncial neurons) from the afferent to the efferent at lower levels. And this inhibition, while it is exercised, is held to be responsible for the "long-circuiting" of afferent impulses to the cortex itself. Thus selective inhibition, or conversely facilitation, is held to determine which stimuli result in individual spinal reflexes and which result in integrated action. But this afferent inhibition is probably limited to the sensory system and cannot influence the non-sensory afferent system. At least, it appears to be impossible for impulses over the latter to be long-circuited to the cortex.

2. THE REST OF THE CORTEX

While it has been possible to explore in detail the so-called "excitable" region of the cortex—that is, the sensorimotor areas—and thus to determine the character and the localization of its functions, that has not been possible elsewhere. As a result, knowledge of the "inexcitable" regions, which, in the past, have generally been called the "association" areas, is confined to inferences from the effects of their injury or removal. At the start, certain inferences from the morphological peculiarities of the cortex as a whole are in order. "In brute bulk the [human] cortex dwarfs the whole of the rest of the nervous system." [3] The cause of this bulk is its complexity, which differs so greatly in degree from the rest of the system that it becomes practically a difference in kind. It follows that it is not necessary to assume, for the cortex, functions or characteristics different from the rest of the nervous system, but only a development of some of these to such a point as to make them, in effect, exclusive to the cortex. For example, it is probably this complexity which "dilutes" the excitation coming into the cortex into vast patterns which nevertheless remain subliminal, so that they may continue for extended periods without either being drawn off over the effector outlets or suppressed, as they would be at lower levels.

If one examines modern cytoarchitectural charts of the human cortex together with maps showing the regions which have been demonstrated by direct stimulation to be the loci of specific sensory or motor phenomena, it becomes apparent that the association areas comprise the bulk of the surface. The largest part of these areas is distributed around the three chief primary sensory regions, optical, acoustical, and somatic sensory, and between these and their several motor correspondents, the motor eye fields, the motor speech center, and the somatic motor areas. It is natural to suppose, therefore, that this part is concerned with the elaboration and synthesis of those sensorimotor processes whose immediate inlet and outlet is the sensorimotor system described above. It was Hughlings Jackson's judgment that the chief element in thinking consists of what he called "retino-ocular" processes —that is, sensorimotor processes concerned with vision; that the next largest element consists of "audito-articulatory" processes—that is, sensorimotor processes concerned with hearing and speech; and that the smallest consists of tactual (chiefly manual) processes concerned with touch and manipulation. If we accept this scheme, it is evident that such intellectual processes as reading (retino-ocular) and writing (manipulative) are intimately connected with speaking (audito-articulatory), so that at least the intellectual types of thinking argue for elaborate processes in which all these functions participate or to which they are all related. And this, in turn, suggests that what we call thinking is chiefly localized in the regions around and between the narrow areas in which the three sensorimotor processes involved have been demonstrated to be localized. Clinical evidence from injury and ablation goes to support this rather vague conclusion. If, now, we proceed

[3] Fulton and Sherrington, *164*, 262.

to suppose that the sensorimotor processes occurring between these several but not independent pairs of sensory inlets and motor outlets may pass through instanter or may be delayed in transit for extended periods (because they are subliminal as to the motor outlet for any one of several reasons or because they exceed its capacity), we would also suppose that the processes which may be called thinking are exclusively composed of those that are so delayed. Moreover, since the notable characteristic of the whole cortex is its great complexity, with probably a consequent "dilution" of excitation, it may be supposed that, without unusually strong sensory stimulation, or without unusually low motor thresholds (paths worn by habit), or without extrinsic excitation of some kind, the chief activity of the cortex, if it is active at all, consists of processes of the nature we call thinking or revery. We impute these processes, when we observe delayed reactions or no reactions, to the usually mild, general, or even specific, stimulation that is constantly coming in from the external environment over the sensory system.

The remaining part of the inexcitable areas of the cortex is off by itself, so to speak. It comprises the prefrontal areas around the pole of the frontal lobes and anterior to the motor areas. Because the vertical and high forehead is an attribute of man only, and especially of civilized man, this region has been quite generally held to be the seat of those special faculties which man possesses and the beasts do not. Recent work has demonstrated that this is true only in a quite different respect from that supposed. It is true that comparative anatomy shows that the development of this region is very late phylogentically; however, once we understand what this development means, it appears from observation of human kind that it has not as yet progressed very far. After complete ablation of both prefrontal areas no specific faculties are lost. But certain specific faculties are altered and there are noticeable changes in "personality." These changes are "regressive"; that is, the subject becomes more emotional and his behavior in relation to bodily wants becomes more infantile or uncivilized. The alterations of specific faculties consist of an apparent marked reduction in the evincing of "interest" in specific features of the environment—that is, lack of sustained sensory attention—and, probably as a consequence of that, a failure of recent memory and a great reduction in the capacity to learn. The personality changes appear to be release phenomena. That is, it seems that this region of the cortex has some special relation with the subcortical effector mechanism for wants and their emotional states, and that this relation consists both of repression (inhibition) and of elaboration (advance from infantilism and primitivism). The whole of the impairment of faculties seems to be explicable only on the hypothesis that this region is chiefly concerned in the initial establishment of one of the relationships called in the old parlance, "association of ideas." The particular bond in this case appears as "interest." That is evidenced to the observer as orientation. But observation and inference lead to the suggestion that "interest" is a synthesis between a want—an interest of the organism—and some specific fragment of the sensory representation of the external environment, which is only lifted out of the flat background by reason of the fact that experience has taught that it is of special concern to that want. Apparently such syntheses are first constructed chiefly by the prefrontal areas, so that they act as a sort of catalytic agent. In these two ways the prefrontal areas seem to constitute the special representative in the cortex of the want system, or, in other words, the cortical correspondent of the subcortical mechanism (hypothalamus) already touched on.

C. INTERACTION BETWEEN THE TWO MECHANISMS

I. ACTION OF THE HYPOTHALAMUS UPON THE CORTEX

The following hypothesis is still more than usually tentative, though it has wide acceptance and I think it is fair to say that it is becoming general. It is believed that one of the activities of the hypothalamus —the most independent relic of the old brain—is the basic means of keeping the cortex awake. When this particular activity in the hypothalamus declines below a certain point (or ceases), sleep supervenes. Not only that, but it is apparently the same activity of the hypothalamus that maintains the tone of the subcortical centers responsible for posture and for preparedness for movement, so that when this activity declines or ceases the body relaxes. The basic element contributing this "awakeness" to the brain has a diurnal rhythm in the mature. It seems to be tonic and undifferentiated in character and merely to vary in intensity. Apparently it emanates from the most caudal elements in the hypothalamus, the mammillary bodies; but what causes the ebb and flow of excitation there is unknown. By the same route the particular mode of general excitation which happens to engage the hypothalamus at any moment—the emotional state there—is also conveyed to the cortex, and possibly also to the lower centers as well. This reflection of the emotional state is superadded to the basic or tonic element and its intensity increases proportionately the awakeness of the cortex. But the emotional state, as we have seen, is specific and different according to its cause, except as high degrees of intensity are reached. Thus it is usually differentiated. As a result—so it is held—when it reaches the cortex it constitutes there a particular emotion or emotional experience. Other terms for the same thing, derived from psychology, are "affect" or "feeling" or "feeling-tone." Still other terms are "drive," "urge," "instinctive impulse," "mobilization," "preparedness," and the direction of orientation. In accordance with the thesis presented above in Section A, these are merely other terms for emotional states, and, therefore, so far as the cortex is presumed to participate in drives, etc., are again terms for the same thing. Not only does this hypothalamic pattern or mode create the emotional experience in the cortex but, there, it appears to become combined and identified with particular sensorimotor processes so that it adds "feeling" to sensation. And here, at least in the most precise and prompt initiation of such combinations, the prefrontal area appears to play a major role.

According to this hypothesis, the various excitors arising chiefly from the internal and quasi-external wants reaching only the effector portion of the old brain, produce there emotional states of various degrees and modes. In turn, it is supposed that these produce in the cortex, among their other effects in other regions as described above, a corresponding emotion, affect or drive. Independently of this mechanism and via the sensory apparatus only, other patterns, chiefly from the external senses and representing the external environment, reach the sensory cortex. There, or more probably in neighboring association areas where sense impressions have reached the stage of being sensorimotor processes, these processes may become endowed with emotional content. A synthesis may take place between the sensorimotor process and the emotional drive or affect.[1] That is another way of say-

---

[1] The reader should perhaps be put on notice that we are here introducing, for the first time in the text, the basis of our thesis as to the conditioning process. The final reconciliation of this basis with all intervening material is made in Appendix III, Section C.

While we have no knowledge of the exact nature of the process here called "synthesis," it is not mere word-magic. It is the common name for a neural process which is

ing that the sensorimotor process may become invested with "interest" because it has come to be related, on one of the several bases of synthesis or association, with one of the interests of the organism, such as, most fundamentally, the variations from homeostasis we have enumerated and their correction. If all emotional states were excited in the hypothalamus by current and actual variations from homeostasis only, and if all sensorimotor patterns in the cortex were the immediate product of current sensory stimuli only, we would have to assume that simultaneity would be the only basis of association.[2] Then, since only one emotional state can exist in the hypothalamus at any one moment, any concurrent sensation which was to become affectively toned would have to be endowed with that one affect or none at all. That is probably the chief and most fundamental basis of such synthesis. Nevertheless, since neither of the above assumptions completely covers reality—that is, since each represents only the strongest influence in its sphere—we shall see that a much wider field is also available on both sides.[3]

One may establish a rough scale of the relative order of normal intensity of the various processes in the cortex. The evidence indicates that the weakest form of cortical excitation is the subliminal and continuing sensorimotor processes which we have called thinking and which, as they are revived, presumably constitute recall from memory. It is said that this alone, if without emotional effect,[4] cannot maintain the state of awakeness. Next in order come current sensations, or their sensorimotor processes. These too, unless exceptionally strong, are in-

---

evident throughout the nervous system. It has, apparently, two forms—simultaneous and successive. The first (referred to in note 2, below) is evidenced when a complex neural pattern is formed out of simple elements—that is, when there is integration. The second is evident when one pattern follows another without different or even further stimulus. It is not to be supposed that the kind of synthesis called the association of ideas is of any different character, though because it is defined as occurring in the cortex it is doubtless of a vastly greater complexity on account of the vastly greater complexity of the cortex.

[2] The theory of Gestalt psychology supposes simultaneity as the basis of construction of the several elements from any one modality of sensation into a pattern. Evidently the various sense modalities may also frequently combine into a somewhat integrated pattern because of simultaneity. That is a step further. The combination presumed for affective tone and sensation is of the same order, though still a further step and apparently requiring some other agency to facilitate the fusion.

[3] These complications will be introduced step by step as we proceed. They are chiefly, as to the first, the conditioning process, or what we shall call "replicas" of emotional states; and, as to the second, they are the result of conscious memory.

[4] The way in which such processes may have emotional effect is explained below under conditioning.

sufficient to maintain awakeness. The tonic excitation from the hypothalamus is certainly stronger than either of these for, in its diurnal rhythm, it is sufficient by itself to cause, and is primarily responsible for, awakeness.[5] But, potentially, by far the strongest sources of cortical excitation are the emotional drives, for these, at their extremes, are capable of causing what is called "excortication"—that is, a state of confusion in which the cortex becomes so excited that it practically ceases to function. And, even in the strengths at which they frequently occur and are maintained until homeostasis is restored, these drives are capable of absorbing the functioning of the cortex and of excluding all but related sensorimotor processes, new or old.

This hypothesis supposes not only that sensory patterns from the external world can be endowed with particular sorts of affective tone, but that such sensory patterns as arise from the interior of the body itself are equally capable of forming such combinations. To what extent pain is pure affect and merely becomes combined with the various sensory modalities, which are concurrent with it and which thus localize it and identify its character, cannot as yet be stated. But it is supposed that pain is at least largely affect. If so, supplementary sensory signals, such as the "pangs" of hunger, serve only to identify the want and reinforce its demands. They are not indispensable. For the evidence indicates that, with animals, the subcortical apparatus, in the absence of all sensation or emotional experience (decorticate) is sufficient by itself to direct behavior into the channel suitable to the particular emotional state, though such specific behavior is, as we shall see, usually preceded by random restlessness. And, in man, it is apparent that the emotional experience, without supporting sensation, is more or less readily identified, so that it leads to specific behavior, if again only after general restlessness. This seems to be particularly true of the experiences caused by the quasi-external wants (feelings of pain, anger, fear, etc.) but to some extent it must be true also of the internal wants. That is, while they are the vaguest sorts of feeling, the purely affective elements of hunger or thirst or sexual urge (lust, libido) are distinguishable from each other. It is natural to infer, therefore, that, even in man, each emotional state in the hypothalamus consists of a tendency, potential or actual, toward a particular kind of behavior,

[5] We say "it is sufficient by itself." But, since the stream of awakeness contributes no content to consciousness, it may be better to regard its function as "facilitation"—in which case it adds its strength to that of the sensorimotor processes, current or revived. Nevertheless, it remains the strategic factor.

which tendency is reflected in the cortex as a particular drive or urge. When and if this drive becomes combined with a specific and concurrent sensation, it appears that, among human beings, the two are merged and the subject is apt no longer to discriminate them, but rather to attribute the really potent and determining element to the weak and sometimes accidental sensory component. For such combinations are often made erroneously. That is, the cause of the sensation may have nothing to do with the cause of the affect.

As has been indicated above, there is a tendency among neurophysiologists to hold that the recently developed prefrontal areas of the cortex have their own private path from the hypothalamus or from its special neural afferent relay in the thalamus. And by this route it is supposed that these areas receive impressions from the subcortical mechanism which are independent of emotional drive. If so, these impressions are presumably mere samples, without emotional force, and are built up, in a way analogous to the construction of sensation in the sensory cortex out of the cruder material of the cortical relay station in the thalamus. Such an hypothesis would account for a part of the emotional regression which takes place when these cortical areas are removed. It would explain the regression of pattern that connotes a return toward infantilism or primitivism. It would not explain, of course, the purely release phenomena.[6] It is also worth while to suggest that it may be this sampling of the current activity of the hypothalamus which permits these areas to act, as they apparently do, as a sort of catalytic agent in establishing the most precise and prompt combinations of specific affects with specific sensorimotor processes.

2. ACTION OF THE CORTEX UPON THE HYPOTHALAMUS

Consideration of this last relation brings us to the first of the interactions in the opposite direction—that is, from the cortex to the hypothalamus. It is evident that the prefrontal areas exercise some degree of inhibitory control over the subcortical mechanisms in the hypothalamus. The hypothesis which best fits the facts at present known is that this control takes two forms. It is apparently exercised in part by way of a constant but mild inhibitory effect upon the hypothalamus itself or upon its neural afferents. It is also apparently exercised by way of a variable and potentially much stronger inhibitory effect upon the motor outlets from the hypothalamus (but probably not upon its

[6] The hypothesis as to these release phenomena is stated in the following subsection.

autonomic or endocrine outlets). Such a construction fits the fact that removal of the prefrontal areas causes increased excitability of the hypothalamus and free drainage of its excitation into emotional behavior. It also explains the fact that, in the presence of the prefrontal areas, emotional states can exist without emotional behavior, though apparently not without the resultant bodily changes. In fact, it assumes that the intensity of the emotion itself—the cortical reflection—is ordinarily measured by the difference in strength between these two inhibitions—that, except in extreme cases, it is the excitation not suppressed by the first and still denied most of its outlet (the motor part) by the second which, being dammed up so to speak, overflows into the cortex. Even in the extreme cases the same rule would hold good; but then it would be the inability of the motor outlets to drain off the emotional state, rather than their inhibition, which would account for the degree of emotion called "excortication." In summary, it is assumed that the more highly evolved and cortical agency for the want system deals with its subcortical correspondent in a way analogous to that in which the more highly evolved and cortical agency for motor relations with the environment deals with its subcortical correspondents; that is, by way of some degree of direct inhibition at the centers immediately below and by way of a greater but still limited power of discriminating interference with the action of these immediate centers upon still lower levels.[7]

The other chief influence of the cortex upon the hypothalamus is the capacity of the former to excite the latter. Or so the process of conditioning is now coming to be construed. Since we shall devote much of the next chapter to the consideration of this subject it need only be mentioned here. Suffice it to say here that, so far as present evidence goes, this capacity appears to be rigorously limited according to certain definable conditions. The thesis which best fits the facts now known is that sensorimotor processes, once they have become endowed with an emotional content, retain that content. When any one of these processes is revived, even without repetition of the orig-

[7] Because it is not germane to our particular purpose here we are omitting consideration of the additional control evidently exercised by the motor cortex upon the hypothalamus or its outlets, both motor and autonomic. This appears to be of a more specific character and to have the function of co-ordinating this apparatus and particularly the vegetative functions with motor activities preparing or in process. At least its elements are incidental (associated) and inseparable from general patterns.

inal pattern of external stimulus (as in thinking) it evinces some capacity to re-excite the hypothalamus in the particular mode identified with its content. Usually this capacity is weak. When the sensorimotor process is revived by repetition of the original pattern of external stimulus, or when the new and the old are fused by recognition, the effect is the same but much stronger. And still, this cortical capacity to excite the hypothalamus in the appropriate mode varies widely in strength according to the mode—is much greater for some emotional drives than for others—and, for any one mode, seems never to be so great as the capacity of the primary excitor. It is always a secondary and often only a supplementary source of emotional states.

3. JOINT ACTION OF THE TWO MECHANISMS

Out of the details of these functional relationships between the two somewhat independent highest levels of the central nervous system, it becomes possible to build up a schematic statement of the way they co-operate or conflict. Considering for the present only that source of the "motivation" of behavior which consists of variations or tendencies away from homeostasis of the limited number of types we have examined—that is, considering only these *present* wants, internal or quasi-external—it is evident that the primary source for generating the appropriate behavior and the integrated bodily changes is the subcortical mechanism in the hypothalamic region. It is equally evident that the mechanisms for the centripetal transmission of these wants reach first and always chiefly to this same region, and that the specific excitors, neural or humoral, which are effective there are exclusive to that region (and to lower subcortical levels) and do not reach the cortex as such.

While this centripetal transmission is the primary and, for each want, always the strongest excitor (or depressor) in producing emotional states in the hypothalamus, it is now assumed that the same states can be produced there (on a lesser scale) by a secondary apparatus. That is, a cortical sensorimotor process, once it has become endowed with emotional content (that is, related to a particular emotional state) retains, in varying degree, the capacity to recreate that state in the hypothalamus.

The states of excitation (or depression) so established in the hypothalamus are the primary determinants and the primary energizers (or enervators) of behavior.[8] Only one such general state can exist at any moment. The several modes in which such general states can exist are what we have called the emotional states. They might equally well be called drives, or urges, or impulses. More exactly, since the emotional characteristic varies both to the observer and to the subject according to extrinsic influences, they should be called the central states produced by wants requiring integrated action, or by patterns of external stimuli which have become identified with wants.

These states have three avenues of effector action. The first is the downward action over the autonomic nervous and the glandular system, which together control vegetative function and of which the hypothalamus is the chief administrator. Apparently the only influence of the cortex upon this hypothalamic activity is its general and continuous inhibition of the hypothalamus itself. By this means general excitation, there, seems only to be reduced in intensity. But whatever excitation arises in spite of this inhibition, and apparently all depression, registers itself, without further control, in alteration of the rates of various bodily functions. This, then, is the most ready means of detecting the existence of an emotional state; and certain of these vegetative functions, particularly palmar sweating and changes

[8] The evidence for this interpretation is now so strong that I think it must displace alternative explanations which, in any event, have not been able to stand the test. It has long been obvious to observers that, above the level of the spinal reflex, the neural energy of response is, in most instances, wholly disproportionate to the intensity of the particular external stimulus which, from the external viewpoint, has been assumed to be its cause. That disposes of the reflex theory of behavior in its earlier form. The chief explanations offered, prior to this, to account for the extra and variable intensity of response have been two; the first is the "drainage" theory, which supposes that the constant flow of afferent impulses (sensory) from the environment is not inhibited as to its inflow but is canalized to the then dominant "reflex" as to its outflow. On this theory the energy of response would be proportionate, at all times, to total external stimulation. But the phenomenon of rapid "adaptation" in most receptors argues against this constant inflow; and, even if it existed, it could not account for the observed commencement of general motion without apparent change in the intensity of any external stimulus. The second explanation is the "circular reflex"—that is, the supposition that proprioceptive impulses from skeletal muscles furnish the surplus energy. Now, since it is the essence of posture that it is *maintained*, it is quite impossible that postural contraction should itself cause change. If we account for postural tonus by assuming that the state of muscular contraction, once established, gives rise to proprioceptive impulses which act on motor nerves with just sufficient energy to maintain the contraction, there is and can be no surplus. If so this circuit never has a surplus to contribute. Then the cause of phasic muscular contraction must come from outside this circuit. Moreover, as Sherrington and Head have both noted, the circular or proprioceptive reflex has the slightest connection of all reflexes with the emotional processes associated with the chief occasions for the display of great energy of response —have the lowest "affective tone," as they put it.

in blood pressure, have been found to be the most subtle indices of such states.

The second avenue of effector action for these states is downward via the subcortical but supraspinal centers of the motor system—that part which is called the extrapyramidal system. Inhibition by the cortex over the access of the hypothalamus to this system seems to be far stronger than the direct inhibition mentioned above. Nevertheless, this inhibition can be overcome in part (leakage) or as a whole (excortication). And, of course, inhibition does not prevent the spread of depression (the withdrawal of the tonic excitation produced in these lower motor centers by the hypothalamus). To the extent that the emotional state in the hypothalamus produces effects in the extrapyramidal motor system, behavior is described as emotional expression. That is, it then has the characteristics distinguished as use of excessive force, inco-ordination, tremor and palsy, and a certain loss of acquired skill—in other words, primitiveness. The degree to which this emotional component appears in behavior varies according to the intensity, plus or minus, of the emotional state and also according to the extent to which the excitation escapes by this avenue. If the behavior is entirely energized by way of this avenue, it has these characteristics unmixed. In great strength, emotional excitement then evinces itself as a wild outburst or even, *in extremis,* as rigor (excitation of all antagonists). On the other hand, if the emotional state only leaks out and the behavior is only partly energized over this avenue, behavior merely evinces these characteristics in the proportion in which the leakage has been responsible for it.

The third avenue of effector action by which emotional states in the hypothalamus can produce behavior is via the motor cortex. That part of the excitation which is prevented from flowing out over the first or downward motor route, or is beyond its capacity, rises or crosses to the cortex as emotion or affect. Because it must be temperate as long as it is to move via this avenue in order not to produce excortication, because it is tempered by the very organization of the cortex itself, and because the motor cortex has exclusive control of the skilled apparatus for motor activity, behavior—or the component of behavior—which is produced by way of this avenue does not have the apparent characteristics of emotional expression. Nevertheless, the general pattern of the behavior may be determined by the particular emotional state as much by this route as when the outlet is downward; and it is held that, equally in this case as in the last, the behavior may be wholly energized, so far as the central nervous system is concerned, by the emotional state itself.

In short, we are construing behavior in response to present wants requiring integrated activity (or in response to cortical sensorimotor patterns which have acquired the power to excite the same subcortical states) to arise exclusively as, to be determined exclusively by, and frequently to be energized exclusively by, a mode of excitation (or depression) in one source—the highest level of the old brain. Thence the particular mode takes effect, as its related type of behavior, along two channels, both of which may be combined in various degrees, or either of which may be used exclusively, depending upon the intensity of the mode and the capacity and exercise of cortical inhibition. The downward channel originally contributed all the innate patterns of stereotyped behavior which are unadapted, or even without reference, to the external environment. The cortical channel has come to contribute all learned patterns of variable behavior, though of the same types, which are adapted by means of the cortical sensorimotor system to the external environment. The degree to which adequate motor behavior can be and is generated exclusively over the downward channel varies inversely with the development of the cortex, in phylogenetic series and in ontogenetic maturation. For, as the cortex develops, its powers of inhibition over the subcortical mechanisms increase in proportion as the transfer of functions involved in its evolution takes place. The result is that, in mature man, the downward channel becomes inadequate for living. Nevertheless, it still remains an active contributor to behavior. And, so far as the original source, determiner, and energizer of behavior in response to present wants is concerned, that remains the same, after the rerouting of its major outflow, as it was before. By means of this scheme we are able to interpret the part the two highest levels play in joint action. We see that the old brain, almost "blind" in respect of contact with the external environment through its own afferent apparatus, has acquired through its ability to excite and to be excited by the newer apparatus of the precise external senses (the sensorimotor cortex) a means of indirectly "visualizing" that environment. Thus it appears that it is both the primary and the secondary (or conditioned) hypothalamic responses which are chiefly responsible for the discriminations—though not for the capacity to discriminate—of the cortex itself. It is usually such a hypothalamic response that is the ultimate director of orientation. The external environment has a given spatial arrangement, which is reproduced through the spatial organization of the sensorimotor cortex. But in that representation the scene is all background. The director of orientation [9]—the emotional state, whether of primary or of secondary origin—determines the detail of that scene which is of "interest." The determination of the detail toward which to orient is hypothalamic; the particular locus of that detail is given in the environment; the cortical function in this respect is merely to act as compass and rudder, not as navigator.[10]

It will be our thesis in what follows that the old brain—the hypothalamus or hypothalamic region—is the primary source of integrated responses to present wants, both internal and quasi-external, and is therefore the primary source of behavior as a part of such responses. It is, as Harvey Cushing expressed it, "the very main-spring of primitive existence." This general thesis also appears to be confirmed by an examination of the nature of, and relations among, overt responses, which we shall undertake in the next chapter, since these constitute the final links in the process of correcting variations from homeostasis—of satisfying wants.

[9] Our use of the term "orientation" in this narrow sense should be emphasized here, as it is in Appendix II. Orientation to the biologist includes posture, equilibrium, choice of habitat and of other conditions, such as "light, smells, currents, heat and so on" (Fraenkel and Gunn, 149, 3). Here we mean by it only observable attention or motion toward one object in the environment rather than toward another.

[10] It should be noted that this scheme is entirely based on data either proven or definitely indicated by neurophysiological investigation. It certainly disproves the more "mental" theories as well as the more mechanical, such as the external stimulus-response theories. However, it also goes far to regularize certain psychological theories which have been much more speculative because they were largely without physiological basis.

Among these we may cite a few illustrative examples. In respect of the ascription of the cause of behavior, Thorndike, who uses the same term, says of wants, "Thought and action occur largely in their service" (397, 4). In many respects McDougall's instinct theory conforms, though his "hormic energy" seems to us to be mere word-magic. James, though he identifies instinct with the behavior rather than the "drive" and defines the mechanism vaguely if at all, nevertheless presents a scheme which can be grafted upon this one (see 220, II, Chap. XXIV). Kempf constructs his theory on a more definite neurological basis, differing from this one largely in respect of centripetal transmission and of central mechanism (see 233, xii–xiv). He too concludes that "The process of neutralization of the affective disturbance is the dynamic principle underlying all [?] behavior" (ibid., 78).

D. CONSCIOUSNESS AND VOLITION

In the preceding chapter we have criticized one general thesis as
to the maintenance of homeostasis outside the blood itself, partly on
the ground that it is made dependent for its centripetal transmission
upon afferent impulses entering consciousness as sensations. And, in
this chapter, we have presented a different thesis which depends wholly
on kinds of centripetal transmission and resulting patterns of effector
action which do not necessarily engage consciousness and, when they
do so, only do so by way of "reverberations" (emotional experiences).
Thus consciousness has crept into the subject in spite of us.[1] We have
to admit its existence notwithstanding the fact that it is exclusively a
datum of introspective psychology. It would be desirable to discover
its nature. That, physiology cannot do.[2] However, aided by the testimony of the introspectionist,[3] it can with reasonable certainty identify
the locus of consciousness, suggest under what conditions and perhaps
from what causes it appears and disappears, detect what can enter it

[1] Tolman says (403, 204): "If psychology could only be content with the lower animals, and preferably with rats, and not try to mess around with human beings, this
whole question of consciousness and of ideas might well have been omitted." Yet, even
with rats, he does not seem able to evade the issue. Skinner (379, 439) states that "the
property of 'consciousness' is either irrelevant or ineffective in differentiating between
two kinds of behavior." This is an extreme behavioristic statement. Consciousness may
be inexplicable, but it is neither irrelevant nor can it be ignored.

We must agree, however, with Lashley. He states (261, 1) that, for investigations
into the physiology of the nervous system, the validity of the principle cannot be
questioned that "every conscious process must be ruled from consideration unless it can
be translated into objective terms" (based on Bubnoff and Heidenbain, 1881).

In observing this principle we avoid "a flight to psychological terminology" (Walshe,
421, 79). On the other hand, it permits us to escape from the other horn of the dilemma,
which would prevent such translation into objective terms by refusing to consider
anything which requires to be so translated. On that basis Bard denies us even the
right to deal with sensation; for "to consider sensation in an animal is to draw an inference which, however plausible, has no place in objective physiological work" (21,
143). Most scientific hypotheses consist of plausible inferences and are recognized to be
provisional.

[2] In Appendix II we have adopted Hughlings Jackson's attitude on this subject. He
regarded consciousness as an epiphenomenon with a material substrate. That might
permit the position Samuel Butler (55, 67) took when he referred to "the fact that
matter and consciousness are functions one of the other"—that is, each is a dependent
variable of the other and no one knows which is cause and which effect. However,
we have a strong hunch—absolutely unprovable—which is cause.

[3] As Mill says (Comte and Positivism, p. 66), "How is it possible to ascertain the correspondence between two things by observation of only one of them?" The two things
in this case are the states of consciousness, as testified to by the introspectionist, and
the observable external and internal indicia which are found to be concurrent with
them. For a brief discussion of some of the external indicia, see supplementary statement on "Criteria of Consciousness" at the end of this section.

and what cannot, and find for some of its apparent characteristics certain analogies among the activities of the nervous system elsewhere, which have been objectively studied. Admitting, then, that consciousness cannot be excluded as a factor in any hypothesis regarding the causes of behavior, even a purely physiological one, but with these limitations in mind, it will be well to consider what relation it is held, by physiologists and scientific psychologists, to occupy with regard to the rest of the system.[4]

It may be stated with considerable assurance that the locus of consciousness is in the cerebral cortex only,[5] and that, in the cortex, it is rather narrowly localized in a specific area.[6] The process in that area of which consciousness is a concomitant is apparently maintained by the excitation which reaches it from elsewhere, of which the basic and usually necessary element is the "stream of awakeness" already considered—a tonic excitation rising from the subcortical brain and varying only in intensity and according to a diurnal rhythm in the adult. The other sources of the excitation which *can* reach this locus are believed to be: (1) chiefly the "emotional stream" (affect or feeling)—also rising from the subcortical brain and along the same path, but continuously varying both in intensity and kind according to the emotional state which exists at its source; (2) sensorimotor processes (sensation) crossing from the sensory and motor areas of the cortex, which are themselves excited by current stimuli coming almost wholly from the external environment; (3) elaborations of these two processes —emotional and sensorimotor—and of revivals of past processes (memory), which together constitute "thinking" and which reach the locus

---

[4] For a synopsis of the recent work in this field upon which the statements in the text are based, see Appendix II, Sections G, H, and I.

[5] It is worthy of note that this is not only the conclusion of most physiologists. William James said (*220*, I, 66), "We can pretty confidently answer the question . . . by saying that *the cortex is the sole organ of consciousness in man*." Head (*183*, 807) thought that "consciousness for certain elements of sensation" exists in a part of the thalamus (in the subcortical brain). But this view is unusual. It is general to regard the cerebral cortex as the sole field available to consciousness. I should say that Dercum (*118*, 291–293) represents the view that is more usual also among psychologists. Cf. Miller, *299*, 27.

[6] For a discussion of what seems, at present, the most plausible hypothesis as to the locus, see Appendix II, Sect. G 2. Most of the cortex can be removed without preventing the state of consciousness. Thus it appears that Miller's statement (*299*, 113) that "all parts of it can be removed without loss of consciousness" is almost but not quite true, and that the single exception is itself the strategic factor. On the other hand, it also appears, from certain observations, that, if the stream of excitation from the hypothalamus is cut off for any reason, consciousness ceases even if its locus remains unimpaired. The hypothesis we present is built on these two sets of observations.

of consciousness from many or all other regions of the cortex.   Of these three sources the emotional stream is thought to be by far the most potent—the "chief energizer"; the currently originated sensorimotor processes are normally of mild intensity, though the "mechanism of sensory attention" can increase that of some and correspondingly reduce that of all others (by changing the threshold); while the elaborations revived as memories are supposed to be of low, usually subliminal, intensity. All these other excitations contribute, in their widely different degrees of potency, to the maintenance of awakeness and therefore of consciousness; but usually (perhaps always) one of the two forms of excitation from the subcortical regions is necessary to maintain awakeness and therefore consciousness. As either low or high degrees of awakeness are approached, consciousness begins to be dimmed into a state of confusion. Acuity of consciousness therefore accompanies awakeness only along a limited part of its whole range of intensity.

What *does* reach consciousness (besides its basic awakeness) is evidently another matter. It appears that, at any one moment, only one kind of emotion can reach consciousness via the emotional stream, because, in the subcortical brain whence the stream arises, only one emotional state or mode of general excitation can exist at any one time. But such states and consequent emotions may alternate or vacillate rather rapidly and may vary greatly in intensity. On the other hand, it is evident to introspection that very large sensorimotor patterns (*Gestalten*), from different sources, of complex and elaborate organization and either current or revived, may occupy the stage, if not the focus, of consciousness at one time. And, also in contrast to emotional states, it is evident that in respect of these there is continuity, or at least the sequence of a steady stream rather than alternation, either because the focus can move without loss of the background or because, as the patterns pass, they leave some aroma or aftertaste or spoor which remains for a time in consciousness.[7] The essence of the test as to whether any particular element of all this sensorimotor material shall or shall not reach consciousness is probably *delay*. That is, those incoming or re-excited sensorimotor patterns that pass out instanter in the form of motor activities by-pass consciousness. It appears that delay itself may occur under three quite different kinds of condition. As to the first

[7] When we come to consider conscious memory, in Chapter 5, this will not appear so fanciful as it does here.

condition it is probable that the excitation from any or all these sources may be subliminal so far as the motor outlets are concerned. If so, it is confined and never produces an overt reaction. But, while it lasts, it may invade consciousness. If the excitation consists chiefly of sensori-motor patterns, current or revived, that are endowed with emotional content, it may reach consciousness as revery and daydreams; if it consists of these patterns, chiefly revived and non-emotional, it may constitute concentrated thought; if chiefly current sensory, it may result in listening, for instance, or other forms of concentration of sensory attention. From observation it seems that consciousness, even if subliminal, can become so engaged with any one of these three kinds of material that, in the absence of strong excitation from another source, the one in possession may almost exclude the other kinds for the time being. The second condition for the occurrence of delay is that the incoming excitation reaching the cortex—usually emotional but perhaps occasionally sensory—may be so strong that the capacity of the motor outlets is insufficient. It cannot escape rapidly enough, so that the part of the excitation which is dammed up is delayed in producing its effect. Within the limits at which confusion begins, such dammed up excitation may explain certain states of consciousness.[8] The third and most frequent condition appears to be that in which one or more patterns or kinds of incoming excitation—emotional, or current or revived sensorimotor—tend to innervate two or more motor patterns which cannot be combined, with the result that there is mutual reciprocal inhibition—that is, conflict. Whereas, elsewhere in the nervous system, such conflicts tend to be immediately resolved, the structure of the cortex is such that they can here be sustained and remain active indefinitely.[9] In fact, it appears that until a path to a particular motor action has been worn down by repetition (habit) the essential peculiarity of the cortex provides that there is always such conflict. These last excitations (conflicts), inhibited as to their outlet, seem to be the oc-

[8] It is Darrow's theory (102, 573) that "functional excortication" produced by the intracortical conflict resulting from excited emotion does not necessarily result in unconsciousness. It does produce non-voluntary, relatively automatic actions which leave the subject like a "by-stander astonished at his own behavior." Or, as Cannon puts it (61, 123–124): "These powerful impulses originating in a region of the brain not associated with cognitive consciousness [the emotional stream] . . . explain the sense of being seized, possessed, or being controlled by an outside force and made to act without weighing of the consequences."

[9] As noted in Appendix II, the peculiarity of cortical structure is so high a degree of "differentiation" (i.e., a number of somewhat parallel paths each slightly different in its "hook-up") that it becomes incomparable in this respect with subcortical centers.

casion for the most acute states of consciousness, so long as they fall short of producing confusion.

John Dewey has described, in introspective terms, this last-mentioned neural process.[10] He says, "Deliberation is a dramatic rehearsal (in imagination) of various competing possible lines of action. . . . It is an experiment in finding out what the various possible lines of action are really like. . . . Thought runs ahead and foresees outcomes, and thereby avoids having to await the instruction of actual failure and disaster." Precisely this process is imputed by observers to certain animals.[11] It is also called "insight." By many, consciousness is held to be limited to these "deliberations"—subliminal behavior—and to those which accompany the sequence of overt behavior which results—deliberate behavior.[12] We would amend that conclusion only slightly to include the other conditions for delay.

Now, "sensation demands consciousness." [13] Moreover, it is certain that "the most elementary sensation is based on innumerable physiological changes" (integration and differentiation of discrete patterns of impulses),[14] which are probably only completed in the sensory cor-

[10] *Human Nature and Conduct*, p. 190. Rignano (*345*, 209) calls the process "reasoning," but describes it in much the same terms: "Reasoning will appear to us to be nothing more than a series of inter-connected experiments conceived, but not actually performed. In other words, it is made up of experiments . . . which we perform in imagination but do not really carry out, because from the results of similar experiments actually carried out in the past, we know beforehand what the result of each separate experiment will be." "It follows that the logical process is only reality itself, brought into action by the imagination instead of in actual fact" (*ibid.*, 213).

[11] Darwin noted (*106*, 76) that "animals may constantly be seen to pause, deliberate, and resolve."

[12] "Conscious awareness" consists in "the performance of a 'sampling' behavior"; it is "delay" (Tolman, *403*, 205–206). Tolman says "It is primarily in moments of changing behavior, in moments of learning, that consciousness will appear" (in a rat). Hughlings Jackson adopted the view of Herbert Spencer (*Psychology*, I, 496) that, as we pass from compound reflex to imperfectly reflex reactions, we pass from those which take place with extreme rapidity to those which take place "with some deliberation, and therefore consciously" (*216*, I, 111). And Jackson also considered "very important" Fiske's statement (*Destiny of Man*, 46–47) that it is the cortical disturbance which is "reflected back and forth among the cells and fibres of which these highest centres are composed, that affords the physical condition for the manifestation of consciousness" (*216*, I, 375). The notion of *delay* was also the basis of the view of G. J. Romanes (*Mental Evolution in Animals*, New York, 1884), who suggested that consciousness is a matter of time between stimulus and response (motor). The more habituated the response, the less time and the less consciousness; the less habituated, the more time and the more consciousness. The second state Romanes called "indecision" (= deliberation).

[13] Head, *183*, 747. As Hughlings Jackson puts it (*216*, II, 28), the term " 'unconscious sensation' is contradictory" and the term " 'conscious sensation' is tautological."

[14] Head, *183*, 807. This accords with the general view of Gestalt psychology, on the one hand, and, on the other, with the views of Adrian and others on sensation as some-

tex.[15] If the sensory cortex itself is not the locus of consciousness—and it is quite clear that it is not—then sensory impulses do not reach the locus of consciousness directly, but only by way of transcortical paths from the sensory cortex to this locus.[16] Furthermore, if the general assumption is correct that all afferent impulses inherently tend to give rise to efferent impulses,[17] then such completely synthesized patterns of such afferent impulses as succeed in rising to the level where they compose what may become sensations are, in some segment of the arc, at the same time also pieces of the patterns of potential behavior which are forming (i.e., motor). Between the completion of the sensory process and the initiation of the motor process these impulses are neither, or they are both. They merely have two aspects, the whence and the whither. This duality exists equally where the afferent impulse goes over to the efferent without becoming sensation. It exists even as low as in the spinal cord, where but a single internuncial neuron may conduct the impulses of a spinal reflex from an afferent to an efferent neuron. According as the arc reaches to higher and higher centers, so much more of the centripetal path (though central) is purely afferent and so much more of the centrifugal path (though also central) is purely efferent. Nevertheless, even at the highest level there must always be a bridge between the two which is neither or which is both, for this is the almost universal characteristic of the central nervous system. If, as is coming to be believed, the material which reaches consciousness and is called sensation, comes transcortically from this bridge—the jointly functioning region—rather than from the sensory cortex itself, it is more properly to be regarded as sensorimotor material, not merely sensory. And this construction permits us to fit this system with the previous one. If such sensorimotor processes occur instanter—that is, if they pass immediately from inlet to outlet across this bridge—they by-pass consciousness. Only if they are delayed, under such conditions as were described, are they conveyed transcortically to the locus of consciousness. Thus we assume that such part of the afferent sensory material as is short-circuited at lower levels does not reach the sensory cortex at all; and, of that part

---

thing constructed centrally, by a "smoothing" and "integration" of the impulses received (see 3, 118–119).

[15] See Appendix II, Section F 1.

[16] See Appendix II, Section G 2.

[17] As Bianchi puts it, in his own terminology (35, 329), "Every perception [we would say every afferent impulse] contains within itself the rudiment of a motor intuition" (i.e., subliminal or at least wholly central motor impulses).

which does reach this level (is long-circuited because it leads to integration), a large portion does not lead to sensation.[18] It does not do so unless it forms part of the deliberative process in our extended sense of that term.

Just as consciousness has inevitably invaded our field of consideration, the allied distinction between voluntary and involuntary behavior has proved also and equally impossible to ignore. For, like that between the conscious and the unconscious, this one constantly appears in the literature. In the first place, the distinction between voluntary and involuntary behavior does not accord with the distinction between voluntary and involuntary musculature; for while smooth muscle (involuntary) is usually held not to be subject to voluntary control and striated muscle (voluntary) is certainly so subject, nevertheless much of the activity of the voluntary musculature is held to be involuntary. It is not easy to determine the criterion of this behavioral distinction among neurophysiologists.[19] But, fortunately, neither is it necessary. For, since volition is again purely a datum of introspective psychology, observable signs are merely the imputed indicia of its exercise or nonexercise, and the datum itself can only be testified to by that one who has the experience.[20]

Experience implies consciousness. Therefore we must conclude that

[18] It is of course true that consciousness is aware of practically all waking behavior. But this awareness arises from impulses that occur after the fact, not usually from the initiating causes of the behavior, and perhaps generally from material which is not contributing to the behavior.

[19] Without any extended examination of the literature—in fact merely using the notes I have collected for the purposes of Appendix II—I have prepared a rough approximation of the usual criteria of voluntary behavior used by experimental physiologists. This serves the same purpose for volition that the work of Miller (cited in note 3, above) serves for consciousness, though much less adequately. Apparently, to those observers, the voluntariness of a movement is a matter of degree depending (1) upon the degree to which it is variable and therefore adapted to the external situation, rather than stereotyped; (2) upon the degree to which it is spontaneous, rather than a regular consequence of an external stimulus (pure reflex); and (3) upon the degree to which it is construed to be the result of conscious integration because it appears to be "purposeful" and "controllable." For the details, see Appendix II, Section H 3.

[20] The concept of volition would never have arisen, of course, if all our concepts had had to be derived objectively. Nevertheless, the testimony of introspection as to the distinction between voluntary and involuntary acts is by no means so definite or valid as is that with reference to the distinction between conscious and unconscious states. The whole concept of volition might be an illusion, as the determinist believes. But, if the very notion of "free will" proves that it is not all illusion—the thesis that we shall present later—nevertheless it is true that the subject is apt to "feel" that he is exercising volition as much when he acts on a sudden impulse which is consciously appreciated as when he acts on mature deliberation after weighing all available considerations in the balance.

volition is some kind of process, or some feature of processes, which can reach the locus of consciousness, and that it perhaps occurs only when the process does so. On that basis all reactions, motor or autonomic which take place in the absence of a state of consciousness must be involuntary or automatic. Also all such reactions, if they are short-circuited at spinal or subcortical levels, even when a state of consciousness exists, are equally involuntary or automatic. If we accept the thesis that sensorimotor processes which pass through the cortex instanter do not reach the locus of consciousness, even when it is awake, then these too are involuntary. By these successive exclusions we arrive at the conclusion that volition can only occur with reference to processes which form part of deliberation, in its broad sense—that is, volition is a concomitant of delay.

A similar conclusion can be reached from another approach. Volition obviously implies choice—that is, alternatives. The chief basis of choice is differentiation,[21] the degree of which in the cortex is so far greater than it is in the rest of the central nervous system that there is, in effect, a difference in kind. But even differentiation there only provides choice so long as no single pathway among the alternatives has become so worn down by habit that it is, in effect, the only one available—that is, only until the system is "organized," in Hughlings Jackson's sense. Only until then does choice exist. Thus the existence of choice entails conflict—conflict between tendencies toward two or more mutually incompatible forms of behavior, whether these tendencies derive from one or from two or more coexisting sensorimotor processes, or emotions, or combinations of them. And conflict entails delay. Thus volition, as choice between alternatives, is again a concomitant of delay. But each of these alternative and incompatible forms of behavior may consist of an elaborate series of acts, the details of which have become, by practice and habit, almost automatic in their execution (i.e., "organized" among themselves). Volition may occur only with reference to starting, continuing, and stopping the behavior. That is, in so far as the details are unconscious they are involuntary even if they constitute parts of a form of behavior which is, as a whole, voluntary. Thus volition may become restricted to the strategic factors only in patterns or sequences of behavior.

On the basis of both approaches it appears that the definition of

[21] See note 9, above. In a sense the power of inhibition also confers a choice, but only that between an action and inaction.

voluntary behavior should limit it to cover behavior that issues, after delay, from conflict (deliberation) and which has involved consciousness. It is, therefore, presumably the resultant of the resolution of the conflict. If so, is volition the mere fact of the ultimate tipping of the scales toward one or the other course, or is it, rather, the causing and the continuing as well as the resolving of the conflict? And here appears another distinction which can only be suggested because a definite basis is lacking. What is the nature of the forces which cause, continue, and resolve conflicts? We have noted that, so far as present wants are concerned, the probable chief energizer of the cortex and the chief determiner of motor activities generated in the cortex is the current and specific emotion or drive which reaches it from the immediate subcortical brain. On the other hand, we have seen reason to believe that the cortex as a whole, and especially the prefrontal areas, have both a mild and continuous and a strong but variable inhibitory effect on, or as to, the highest level of the old brain. Presumably this inhibition is a by-product of the activity of the cortex itself—that is, of those of its current or revived sensorimotor processes not endowed with the current emotional content and therefore not contributing to the existing subcortical emotional state. Does this argue that conflict, even in the cortex itself, is usually the consequence of incompatibility between the current and revived sensorimotor processes induced in the cortex, on one side, and the current emotional stream entering it, on the other? Does it argue that we have actually two "wills"—one the emotional urge which represents the internal environment and the other which is seen here as the cortical restraint and guidance which represents present and past experience with the external environment? [22] If so, the process of volition itself might consist largely in the causation of conflict by a clashing of the two wills—the cortical influences, on one side, and the current urge, on the other; in the continuance of the conflict and the dilution of the powerful urge during the period it was spreading, by reason of established synthesis, into many alternative and

[22] One recognizes the Freudian "wish" in the emotional urge. There has been a tendency of late either to abandon the older notion of a "will" proper, independent of the "wish"—the cortical kind of "will"—or to merge the two. Thus Rignano (345, 207) concludes that "the will is therefore in essence only an affective tendency of wider vision and one which inhibits other tendencies which aim at more immediate satisfaction; that is why it excites to action like every other affective tendency." In Chapter 6 we examine this notion and find it untenable, both because there is no evidence of affective quality in the purest examples of behavior generated by the "will" proper, and because, if affective quality arises from present wants, no influence toward less immediate satisfaction (non-present wants) could have sufficient of it.

mutually inhibitory channels; and in the ultimate resolution of the conflict when the two wills had finally merged in relation to some single channel or one had overcome the other.

However, this identification of the chief forces which may produce conflict as *the* "will"—or the "wills"—and therefore as the source of volition gets us into difficulties. It is probably true that the naïve introspectionist identifies his "will" with the winner in such a conflict, whichever it is or however the two forces contribute to a joint decision. But we have seen that the emotional state in the hypothalamus produces many involuntary actions, both through its own and even through cortical motor paths. How can the "will" produce involuntary acts? The moral philosopher, on the other hand, would probably, if he understood the physiology of the brain, identify the "will" as the cortical influence only—restraint and even the possible secondary energizing influence which we have not yet considered because it is not directly related to present wants. But that faces difficulties too; for we have seen reason to suppose that cortical processes may pass instanter into motor acts and therefore be involuntary, that these sensorimotor processes may have been endowed with emotional content and therefore represent combinations of the two forces or influences, and that much of the continuing cortical activity may not enter consciousness and therefore cannot contribute to "willing" as a conscious experience. If the subject does not know he is "willing," is he "willing"? These considerations lead us to content ourselves for the present with a tentative definition of what we mean by voluntary behavior (external) and an hypothesis in regard to the corresponding cortical process, volition. We limit the occurrence of volition to occasions when there is an opportunity for choice. We do not identify, or conjecture, or even presume a chooser.[23]

While this little exploration, under the guidance of neurophysiologists, into a field that scientific psychology regards as the forbidden land, has been very tentative and its findings very limited and vague, it has been necessary to go as far as we could with it.[24] And this for

[23] This tentative discussion is introduced here merely to make clear that we recognize a lacuna in our system of energetics as developed to this point. Chapter 6 will be concerned with an attempt, on the basis of much less satisfactory evidence and much more pure inference, to provide the necessary supplement to this system. At least, it will present a rational hypothesis which meets the difficulties mentioned in the text.
[24] As Miller states in the study quoted above (*299*, 38): "Academic psychologists have never been certain what *voluntary* means, and have come to neglect studying the will almost entirely. This in large measure has been because they have assumed determin-

the reason, as we said before, that it is going to be quite impossible
to come to any adequate understanding of the causation of behavior,
even on the most objective basis, unless, on the one hand, the distinction is clearly recognized between physiological events which cannot
or do not reach the arena of consciousness and those which can and
do, and, on the other hand, between those responses which are prompt
and automatic (involuntary) and those which are delayed and deliberate (voluntary). These distinctions can be based on observable
facts or inferences from them and are of strategic importance. Recognition of them does not entail adoption of metaphysical explanations;
for the pragmatic (operational) distinctions may turn out to rest on
differences of degree or of locus rather than of kind. Nor is the undertaking hopeless.[25] In the same way that physics has succeeded in out-
flanking Bishop Berkeley by superseding the direct sensory report of
the external world with an inferred report of quite different tenor, so
physiology must eventually succeed in establishing an inferred report
of consciousness and volition which will reconcile itself with, and
replace, our hitherto almost wholly introspective (quasi-sensory)
accounts of them. However, even the limited report now available
enables us to make three positive assertions: (1) The present want
system does not depend wholly or even chiefly upon sensory "signals"
to consciousness as its means of centripetal transmission: [26] (2) while
the primary mechanism for the generation of behavior in response to
present wants may operate via the motor cortex as well as via its own
paths, the more intense is the want the less deliberate and therefore the
less voluntary is the resulting behavior: [27] and (3) the force of the
drive, or the neural energy of response to present wants, is independent of consciousness or volition; neither is necessary to the existence or strength of the drive and their only relation to it is in connection with its restraint and canalization by the cortex.[28]

ism and so eschewed the investigation of what appears to be 'free will.' " We shall have
something to say about this illusory cul-de-sac later on.
    As a justification of our independent course we may also cite Miller (*ibid.*, 107),
who speaks of "the psychologists' notorious disregard for neurophysiology."
[25] In this connection Poliak (*330*, 216) makes a suggestive remark. He says, "At present
the difficulties in solving the problem of mental-material relations appear, on the whole,
to reside less in the sphere of morphology [i.e., the localization of function] than in
the definition of the localizable elementary cortical processes." That is, we have not
yet analyzed mental processes into suitable empirical categories.
[26] See also Chapter 1, Section B.
[27] And therefore also, the less conscious and, for that reason, the less the result of
sensation.
[28] Therefore, as a whole, we may say that the neuroglandular apparatus concerned in

Criteria of Consciousness. The curious mental trick by which those who undertake to be objective have come to identify the subjective state called "consciousness" with some one or more of its possible external indicia and, at the same time, the difficulty of determining what are the positive indicia are both well illustrated by a recent study by Miller of the usage in the literature of the term "unconsciousness" and its obverse. He finds (*299,* Chap. 1) sixteen general types of definition of unconsciousness. These we shall attempt to convert into definitions of consciousness, identifying them by his numbers. Most, but not all, are in terms of what he calls "outward criteria" (*ibid.,* 294). Two can be discarded at once, one because it is too broad and the other because it is merely verbal magic: (1) animate, and (3) mental.

Some are purely objective, without imputation. These are (2) responsive to external stimuli, (7) noticing, giving attention, and its near equivalent (14) not ignoring (both as to external data). These may exclude states of daydreaming, brown study and concentrated thought which we all know are states of consciousness, and often of acute and absorbed consciousness.

Others involve an imputed psychic process which nevertheless can be somewhat accurately judged by external indicia. These are (11) evidencing capacity to recognize, especially the connection between need and object (our "interest"), (10) evidencing past learning (old conditioning) or even (5) the capacity to learn (new conditioning), (8) exhibiting insight, (9) involving memory, (12) involving volition. In our scheme these are all more or less related, and in some cases are but different aspects of the same process. Each of these would appear to be evidence of a state of consciousness; but we cannot agree that the apparent absence of any one is a positive proof of absence of a state of consciousness.

Another, (13) the ability to communicate, is no indication at all; for one can talk in one's sleep and clinicians would testify that it is possible to be conscious when all means of communication are paralyzed.

The indicium ascribed to behaviorists, (4) evidencing discrimination between external stimuli, while it probably involves several of the foregoing, is perhaps the most useful and prospectively fruitful of the purely objective signs. It is open, of course, to the objections we made to the first group and is thus too narrow. And, in comparison with the corresponding but purely subjective definition, (16) aware of discriminations, it is probably too broad, for there is evidence of discriminations without awareness.

Thus the only definition which seems to be all-inclusive of consciousness and all-exclusive of unconsciousness is (6) a state of awareness, of sensations, ideas, etc., in the seat of awareness. But this is no more than verbal magic, being the mere substitution of the word awareness for that of consciousness. Moreover, it completely evades the question of indicia.

---

the centripetal transmission of, and the generation of behavior for, present wants is more closely related to the apparatus assumed in the psychology of the unconscious than it is to any apparatus whose activities have been assumed in the introspective psychology of the past.

Clinicians rely chiefly upon the negative evidence—that is, upon the absence of what they call "confusion" and its particular type of disorientation, during what they deem to be the state of awakeness, and upon the absence of "alertness to surroundings" as an index of the absence of the state of awakeness. These are, for instance, Alford's terms for the "state of awareness" which is his criterion of consciousness (8, 790). I would think they are fairly typical. But they depend upon the largely intuitive judgment of an expert in the observation of an almost infinite number of minutiae. Miller says (299, 24) "absence of any response or of the normally occurring response [i.e., maintenance of upright posture, etc.] is the index of unconsciousness in the sense most frequently used by the medical profession as well as by the layman." But, of course, this is vastly too broad.

We omit Freud's definition—Miller's (15)—as purely negative (a definition of unconsciousness which merely presupposes consciousness). It is worthy of note that the Latin origin of the term allied it with conscience, or consciousness of guilt, and that, in Latin, its various forms had, or even had chiefly, this sense. Therefore, its use to cover awareness appears to have originated as a peculiar type of wholly subjective awareness which is intimately connected with the Freudian "censor."

A further criterion, not mentioned above, should be included. Whether or not afferent material over the sensory system reaches the sensory cortex at all appears to depend on its intensity and the degree of integration it leads to. It is this last which justifies the frequently proposed partial criterion of material which enters consciousness. Thus Kempf (233, 27) holds that "awareness or consciousness occurs when the body as a unity must adjust itself to the special or dominating activity of one of its parts" (i.e., only in so far as it is integrated). Dunlap (123, 207) also correlates the "vividness" of consciousness, not with the "energy of the reaction," but with the "degree to which the reaction involves the whole organism."

3

BEHAVIOR IN RELATION TO PRESENT WANTS AND TO THE ENVIRONMENT

WHEN WE BEGIN to examine behavior from the standpoint of purely external observation we leave, of course, the special province of physiology. Our method must change. We come to depend upon the observations of animal life by biologists and zoologists, and particularly upon the modern studies of behavior in respect of conditioning and other learning processes by various disciplines, including many experimental psychologists who have devoted themselves to this subject.[1] Yet, since the two fields, internal and external, are but different phases of a single process (i.e., the complete cycle starting with a variation from homeostasis and ending with its correction), one set of observations—the external—must necessarily jibe with the other—the internal. It is of interest, however, to see how far the two approaches have arrived at consonant conclusions without attempt, while they were being worked out, to reconcile them. For, if similar conclusions have been arrived at independently, each is much stronger confirmation of the other. As we proceed we shall indicate how well the two sets of results fit together.

A. BEHAVIOR IN RELATION TO PRESENT WANTS

I. THE DEVELOPMENT OF BEHAVIOR PATTERNS

Recent investigation has necessitated radical modifications in the older "reflex" viewpoint of behavior, with its emphasis on the simple

[1] A curious result of the movement toward behaviorism in psychology—a movement toward objectivity and therefore in itself laudable—is that, to that extent, the field of psychology has become extra-"mental." Thus the chief progress recently made by protagonists of the science of the "mind" has been in the study of behavior, a field which might be regarded as outside their own. By such studies, psychology has developed a large number of problems for a science of the "mind" to solve, but it has not concerned itself particularly with solving them. Instead, exploration in the field of the "mind" itself has been left largely to physiology and its special branch, neurophysiology, and even adequate liaison has not been maintained with these latter.

reflex, on "given" structures and on external stimuli. The first modification concerns the order of development of motility, or motor reactions. In this respect Sherrington seems to represent the older view.[1] While he admits a degree of control by higher centers and evidently does not assume that all "short, simple movements" are necessarily simple or spinal reflexes, nevertheless he seems to hold that the enormous variety of motor responses are largely chains or compounds of those integral elements—the "manoeuvres of ancient heritage"—each of which constitutes a "unit reaction in nervous integration." [2] Pavlov's view is similar but seemingly more positive.[3] To a considerable degree this conclusion is implicit in his special method of investigation. The essence of a conditioned reflex is the production of a piece of behavior (reaction) which is ordinarily associated with a so-called "unconditioned" stimulus, by means of a different, or conditioned stimulus. However, in Pavlov's experiments, it is always the well-recognized and previously established reactions that are induced; and these he treats as reflexes. Unless these sometimes complex reactions are all construed to be integral, and to be given in the structure, there is no explanation of how they arise. And unless all motor responses—all other of the infinite varieties of possible behavior—are conceived to be merely chains or compounds of these integral responses to "unconditioned" stimuli, his results would explain nothing of the way in which modified and better adapted reactions, which constitute so large a part of the process of learning, are acquired.[4]

Upon the basis of biologists' observations, especially, a quite contrary view seems now to be taking the place of this, or at least to be radically modifying it.[5] It begins to appear that, both phylogenetically and ontogenetically, the development of behavior patterns is generally in the opposite direction. As we have remarked, "the discrete is derived from the integral, not the reverse." Instead of building up

[1] Sherrington, 375, 389–391.
[2] Ibid., 375, 7. Elsewhere (378, 10) he takes this position even more strongly. "Motor behavior," in general, "fails to offer anything radically different from that of reflex action."
[3] Pavlov, 320, 9–11.
[4] Woodworth (447, 158) also thinks Pavlov "leaves out of account the organizing of movements into complex action patterns."
[5] Freeman (152, Chapter I), among others, referring to the view that "behavior is primarily compounded out of elementary units such as reflexes," (ibid., 24) summarizes the evidence which indicates that the opposite is true. The reflex "covers only a very limited type of behavior," for only "certain parts of the neuromuscular mechanism have acquired a degree of autonomy" (ibid., 46). Lashley regards the older view as "largely a deduction from the reflex theory" (260, 23).

complex patterns from discrete individual motions (simple reflexes), the latter are only gradually developed by restricting all but individual parts of the original pattern, general motion. While this appears to be almost universally true among the lower animals, it may be somewhat less true of the higher animals. Among the lower animals, the earliest motor pattern—according to Coghill—is general motor activity, beginning at the anterior end and gradually spreading back from there.[6] "Primarily ["the mechanism of the total action pattern"] . . . is strictly motor and its growth establishes the early behavior pattern without the intervention of sensory elements" (i.e., external stimuli) [7] —that is, it is produced by internal excitors only. Later, within this total pattern, partial patterns arise. Still later, though the partial patterns continue to remain part of the whole, they become also capable of independent initiation, first in the form of postural reactions (proprioceptive) and later in the form of reactions to local external stimuli (exteroceptive).[8] Thus "local reflexes . . . emerge as a special feature within a more diffuse but dominant mechanism of integration of the whole organism." There is "no direct evidence for the hypothesis that behavior, in so far as the form of the pattern is concerned, is simply a combination or co-ordination of reflexes. On the contrary, there is conclusive evidence of a dominant organic unity from the beginning.[9]

[6] That is, the development of movement follows the growth of the motor neurons, which are "distributed from the midbrain tailward" (Coghill, 90, 1).

[7] Coghill, 91, 643.

[8] For the information of the reader who skipped Appendix II, these terms should be explained, since we will use them from time to time. They are divisions of the neural "receptive fields," based on those established by Sherrington (375, 130) which have proved so convenient that, in modified form, they have come into general use. "Exteroceptive" signifies the field external to the body; "interoceptive" that within the body excepting the skeletal musculature; and "proprioceptive" that of the skeletal musculature, tendons, and joints. The terms also serve fairly well for a classification of the receptors themselves. The exteroceptive field is served by the "distance receptors" ("projicient" senses) of sight, hearing, and smell, and by the somatic sensory system (cutaneous senses). Though classed by Sherrington as interoceptive we prefer to include here the sense of taste, thus treating the contents of the mouth as a part of the external world, since it can be, and often is, rejected. The interoceptive field is served by the visceral and vascular afferent nerves which are variously classed, peripherally, either as wholly in the sensorimotor system or as partly in one or both of the divisions of the autonomic system. This term was limited by Sherrington to the innervation of the alimentary canal. The proprioceptive, in which he included all else, is conveniently restricted to the elaborate system for reporting posture and motion, of which the cerebellum is the head ganglion (Sherrington, 375, 347).

Cannon applied similar terminology to the effector side. Roughly speaking, "exterofective" signifies motor, and "interofective" signifies autonomic.

[9] Coghill, 89, 89, and see also 90, 1. Child (77, 254) also regards spinal reflexes as a later specialization. This process is described more fully by Coghill (91, 639): "It is well known that, in the development of the reflex, there is a progressive restriction of the

While this "has been demonstrated in the origin of unconditioned reflexes . . . it appears also to apply to the formation of conditioned reflexes, instincts and the so-called process of trial and error." [10] Apparently the first behavior to develop is the general movements of locomotion—in Amblystoma first swimming and then, directly out of that, walking. The limb movements are at first integral parts of the trunk movements; so too, when they develop, are the movements of the gills and, finally, in series, the movements of the jaw and swallowing (the eventual feeding reaction).[11] Gradually these latter all become capable of being, as well, independent or discrete partial patterns of behavior. Even then they are at first "long-circuited" and only gradually does the possibility of "short-circuiting"—the purely segmental or spinal reflex—develop. It seems safer to assume, then, that in the aspect of

stimulogenous zone." At first, stimulation at any sensitive point excites a total reaction; then large zones excite a particular local reflex; then the zone becomes more and more localized. The transition from total to local reaction arises when a stimulus in a certain zone inhibits the total reaction. Then "from a field of total inhibition" the local reflex emerges. Thus the reflex only arises "through restriction both of the field of motor action and the field of adequate [external] stimulation" (ibid., 638). González (174, 442) has studied the appearance of motility in the albino-rat fetus. He too finds the first movement that of the head and that it proceeds from there to involve more and more caudal and more and more distal parts. At first, all movements then available— the primary or basic and the series of secondary movements—are involved together —a mass reaction. The primary movements are thus at first "sovereign." Later there occurs "what at first seems to be a breaking up of the total patterns into individual and specific reflexes." But he is convinced that there is no "disintegration or breaking up"; rather there arises "inhibitory action by means of which the primary or basic movements are in a large measure arrested. In other words, the total-pattern reaction is never abolished completely, nor is the dominance of the primary over the secondary movements lost." This confirms Coghill and coincides with our previous presentation. A similar order of development in the albino-rat fetus has been shown by Swenson (389, 31).

To Coghill the "traditional conception of the chain reflex," as an explanation of reactions in series, is also fallacious (91, 640). Similarly Lashley (262, 381) concludes that the "doctrine of chain reflexes is utterly without foundation," so that "some other explanation of serial acts must be sought" (ibid., 382).

Tracy, whose special views we shall examine shortly, arrives at the same general conclusions as Coghill, whom we are following at this point. He says that, while "current ideas make the reflex arc the functional unit" (407, 347) his own observations lead him to conclude that "segmental reflexes are not the primitive components of behavior" (ibid., 349), but are, instead, the last form of motility to develop (ibid., 350).
[10] Coghill (91, 638). For, as to conditioning, "on the motor side of conditioning, reaction is at first general, approximately a total reaction, at least of a postural nature" (presumably the alert; ibid., 640).
[11] Coghill (89, 5–30). The fact that swimming is the first motion is due to the fact that the motor neurons which develop this motion are the first to appear (ibid., 50). Like this change from swimming to walking, Craig observes that, in birds, flying develops from jumping (94, 99).

development, specialized reactions—or systems of them—usually derive from general movement, not the reverse.[12]

In the second place, we find it necessary to amend the concept of a fixed repertory of built-in reactions which are "given" by the anatomical arrangement of the neuromuscular apparatus in its relation to the skeleton. It is true, of course, that, in all animal life, "in the Protozoa, as in the Metazoa, the structure of the organism plays a large part in the development of behavior." [13] At all times only those actions are permitted which this structure makes possible.[14] But the structure itself—especially so far as the neural part of it is concerned—is a growing thing all through life. This neural growth cannot be either directly or indirectly due to functioning or exercise, for the "neuromuscular structural relations that make the act possible must exist before the act can be performed." [15] It is due rather to what Coghill calls "neural

[12] Carmichael (72, 143) thinks Coghill goes too far, and he accepts Pavlov's view in part—that is, he thinks there are both "individuation" from total patterns and "integration" of these early individuated (specific) patterns into new extensive patterns. Nevertheless, Coghill's generalization seems to hold throughout Carmichael's phylogenetic series up to and including cats; and, though the latter states that the basic pattern of Coghill "may be seen in less typical form in the case of human development than might be supposed" (ibid., 111), it seems to me that this statement is based on the absence of positive evidence rather than on the presence of any disproof. The long period of gestation in human development and the difficulty of detecting and construing fetal movements may merely conceal the first occurrence of the basic pattern. Frolov (157, 85) describes Minkovsky's experiment on living human embryos which showed that stimulation of any one spot of an extremity brought into action all extremities—that is "irradiation" all over. At any rate we may note that Carmichael says also (ibid., 72, 119) that "most writers on the development of fetal behavior agree that locomotion . . . sucking and breathing are three of the earliest essential behavior systems of the new born animal." General movement of the embryo is certainly prenatal in man. Tracy (407, 256) says "sucking or swallowing mechanisms are often active before hatching or birth." But breathing obviously does not begin until birth. Thus the evidence does not preclude their development in the order general to special.

The reader will recall that Hughlings Jackson's hierarchy seems to have assumed that evolution and integration proceed hand in hand from lower to higher levels. (See Appendix II, Section A.) However, that is neither the phylogenetic nor the ontogenetic story. There, integration is the earliest stage—that is, the highest level of the old brain is the first element to develop. But, though evolution does not now appear to follow his anatomical pattern, it does appear to follow his functional one in other respects (i.e., differentiation, etc.).

[13] Jennings, 223, 261.

[14] One of my classmates at Yale, since became the head of a great motor manufacturing works, built himself an automobile in the early days (1900). When it was completed, it was towed out on York Street for the trial trip. It was filled with his friends, a crowd of other freshmen watching. The motor was started, the gear shifted into low speed, the clutch engaged, and off they went—backwards. This has always been my favorite illustration of the limitations of structure on activity. But mechanisms do not grow—organisms do.   [15] Coghill, 89, 83 and 86.

overgrowth"[16] which is believed to be produced by metabolic gradients.[17] That is, the existence of high degrees of excitation in certain regions—a high "rate of living," as Child puts it—leads to the growth of nerve fibers into the regions of lesser excitation—down the gradient. Thus the primary tendency is in the direction of facilitating constantly greater neural development and greater scope to neural control within the "given" limits of the muscular and skeletal systems. For this reason we shall have to assume that, within these possibilities, there is no repertory of "given" motor behavior, but rather that all motor capacities are the result of a continuing neural development under the influence of an increasing variety of excitors which happen to produce results which are, at early stages, more stereotyped, both on repetition and among different individuals, than they are later. And this chiefly because the excitors are themselves more uniform, at early stages, in their reappearances in one individual and in their appearance in different individuals than they are apt to be later.

The third point concerns the relation of behavior—of these systems of reaction—to external stimuli. Biologists seem to be agreed that, developmentally, "the organism acts first on the environment and only later reacts to the environment." And this because, as we noted above, the mechanism is at first solely motor without connections from sensory (external) sources. Furthermore, "the determination of the primary attitude of the organism toward the environment is intrinsic"; and the "initiative of attitude" always remains "primarily within the organism."[18] In this sense action, or motility, is called "spontaneous"— at least if without apparent external stimulation.[19] That is, the term "spontaneous behavior" is used to express the antithesis to behavior of the external stimulus-response type. As such, "action is as spon-

[16] Coghill (89, 92). The "growth of the terminals of axones and dendrites through microscopic dimensions is sufficient to have profound effects in behavior" (ibid., 84).
[17] The same as Child's "physiological gradients" (see 77, and Child's many papers).
[18] Coghill, 91, 642.
[19] Child (76, 253) calls it "modifiable" behavior. It is sometimes called "intrinsic," as by Coghill, above. Skinner (379, 20) discriminates, approximately between external stimulus-response behavior and spontaneous behavior, in other terms. To him "the kind of behavior that is correlated with specific eliciting stimuli may be called respondent behavior," or "a respondent." Behavior that is "not under this kind of control" is "operant behavior" or "an operant." Therefore, "an operant is an identifiable part of behavior of which it may be said . . . that no correlated stimulus can be detected upon occasions when it is observed to occur" (ibid., 21). But, as we shall conclude later, all these distinctions are on the wrong basis—a survival of the old Cartesian viewpoint and therefore rarely true.

taneous in the Protozoa as in man." [20] But, in some sense, all action is spontaneous.[21] Jennings' thesis may be stated briefly: Activity does not require present external stimulation and may change without external cause; such changes are due to changes in physiological states which, in turn, may be due to progressive internal processes (especially metabolism), to the activity itself of the organism, or to the action of external agents; but external agents cause reaction only by producing such changes in physiological states, and the possibility that they can do so may depend, in turn, on the existing physiological state.[22] If conditions are completely favorable—approximately our homeostasis—there is "no need for a change in behavior, for definite reactions of any sort." If not, activity occurs or changes. "When the organism is subjected to an irritating condition, it tries many different conditions or many different ways of ridding itself of this condition, till one is found which is successful." In fact, depending upon the physiological state, "stimulation" may give rise to "all the movements of which the animal is capable." This process of "trial and error" is an indication that "the reactions of organisms are based on the principle, usually correct, that it is the previous behavior [inactivity or particular activity] of the organism that has brought on the present conditions." [23] That is, reactions are initiated by physiological states, and thereafter follow the course which Jennings calls "trial and error," un-

[20] Jennings, *223*, 261.

[21] That is, in the normal organism. "Spinal animals exhibit no spontaneity and seem to be governed almost entirely by external stimulation" (Freeman, *152*, 155). In other words, almost the sole access of the body itself to its motor governing mechanisms is supraspinal, and, as has been suggested, largely subcortical. Because this region is the first part of the central nervous system to develop we would expect spontaneous action and integrated action to be the first to develop, as it is.

[22] Jennings, *223*, 283 ff. This term "physiological state" must be interpreted to include "all physiological factors which determine the excito-motor integration pattern at any particular moment" (Child, *76*, 259).

Even Craig (*94, 95*), who tends toward the external viewpoint, agrees that "probably in every case appetite is dependent upon physiological factors," although he thinks the "immediate excitant" may be an external stimulus. At any rate, "In many cases the rise of appetite is due to internal causes which are highly independent of environmental conditions, and even extremely resistant to environmental interference."

This thesis of a merely indirect effect of external stimuli in producing reactions fits with our previous analysis. Kemp (*233*, 4) agrees that the qualities of stimuli produced by harmful or beneficial agencies and which, in turn, are sometimes supposed to lead to what Jennings calls "negative or positive reactions" are usually not differentiated in the exteroceptor but by the autonomic apparatus through reactions the stimuli produce there.

[23] Jennings, *223*, 301, 263, 280, and 309.

til the "resolution of the physiological state" is attained.[24] Their form is always limited by the "action system" (the repertory of responses then possible to the neuromuscular and skeletal structure) and within these limits by the physiological state.[25]

The relation of these "spontaneous" movements or activities to their source in "physiological states" and to behavior in general is further elaborated by Tracy in a way that supports our previous analysis of the mechanism. He says, "The earliest activity of all the motor mechanisms included in this investigation is of spontaneous origin." [26] These embryonic movements of the larvae arise before the development of an afferent nervous system, and seem, therefore, to be due to "some fundamental activity of protoplasm," similar to that which sets up the activity of the respiratory system. They "may be initiated directly through changes in the nerve cells [of the higher centers] or in conditions around them," "incidental to metabolism," such as hydrogen-ion tension.[27] These "endogenous body movements form a continuous series with the normal progression movements of the free-swimming animal." This "endogenous motility continues throughout the life of the animal and determines its general activity habit." In fact it is not possible to find any line of distinction in this "ontogenetic series" between the embryonic spontaneous movements and what we call "voluntary" movements in the adult.[28] They are all "activated through the same [efferent] neural pathways." [29] Tracy's view, which corresponds in part to that presented by us above, is that, in the mature animal, internal stimuli in general come to work first through internal physiological mechanisms, chiefly by "compensatory adjustments of postural contractions in the visceral musculature (e.g., expansion of the bladder without increase of pressure, adjustment of fluid transport in tempera-

[24] *Ibid.*, *223*, 345. This is a far different view from that of Sherrington (*378*, 7–8), who holds that "the dominant partner in the driving of the brain is the outside world in commerce with the animal." It is the "outer world" which "turns the key" and settles whether to close or open the lock.

[25] Jennings, *223*, 312.

[26] Tracy, *407*, 282, 343. His investigations were made on the toadfish.

[27] Tracy, *407*, 336–341. He cites (*ibid.*, 340) various other authorities in support of the possibility that CO_2 stimulates movements of progression, and suggests (*ibid.*, 383) that "spontaneous body movements" are probably at first due to irregular chemical changes (largely CO_2) around the nerve centers, and that the progressive character of the motility may be due to the "different distances of individual [nerve] cells from the capillaries" (the varying time required for diffusion). At least, (*ibid.*, 335–336) there is "strong evidence that embryonic movements are not stimulated by tension" (i.e., proprioceptive impulses).

[28] *Ibid.*, 336, 342, 344, and 350.   [29] *Ibid.*, 336.

ture regulation, adjustment of stomach contractions to distension); when the physiological limit of compensatory capacity [long before that point, we think] is approached, stimulation through the visceral afferent nerves [and otherwise, we think] takes place and body activity is set up." [30] But, at first, this activity is not oriented to the environment. That only begins when the afferent (sensory) system is developed. Then external stimuli may orient the activity or, in the absence of internal stimuli, even initiate and orient it. But this they do by "asymmetrically" modifying the "primitive progression mechanism" through differential effect on the two sides of the "bilateral motor tract." [31] Thus Tracy concludes that "exogenous activity is oriented activity" but is "essentially the modification of the endogenous activity." [32]

Upon the basis of such evidence we are inclined to accept three general conclusions which seem to be held by many, or most, biologists; that behavior is at first an integrated motor activity of the whole organism and, for the most part, becomes divided into specialized reactions only by a process of restriction (inhibition) and modification; that it is implemented by a continually growing neural apparatus and that its repertory, within the skeletal possibilities, is therefore only limited, at any stage, to the variety of patterns so far produced by the variety of influences which have so far been effective; and finally, that behavior, in its beginnings, is never exogenous (i.e., the result of external stimuli), but is then altogether endogenous (i.e., the result of internal states or influences) and always remains chiefly endogenous— that is, it continues to be almost wholly initiated by internal influences and only to be modified by external stimuli. [33]

These conclusions by biologists are nearly the precise opposites of the hypotheses or assumptions upon which the most mechanistic forms of reflexology have been based, but they fit, confirm, and supplement the conclusions which we arrived at in the previous chapters from recent studies of the internal mechanisms by neurophysiologists. The first conclusion did not appear in our previous examination because we did not consider there the ontogeny of special reactions.

[30] *Ibid.*, 340–341.   [31] *Ibid.*, 346, 349–350.   [32] *Ibid.*, 357.
[33] By way of confirmation of these last two points we may quote from a recent work on orientation. Contrary to Loeb's (*271*) claim that "the conduct of animals consists of forced movements," Fraenkel and Gunn (*149*, 307) state that "neither Loeb nor any one else has ever demonstrated that any animal response is forced or in any way fixed and immutable." That is, they are neither necessary (mechanical) responses to external stimuli nor are they the invariable result of the operation of an unchanging mechanism.

However, it is entirely consistent with the evidence we noted that the old brain—the first part of the brain to develop—represents complete integration and is, therefore, chiefly productive of extensive patterns. Nor did the second conclusion appear in precisely this form. But again it is entirely consistent with the evidence we found for continuing evolution of the central nervous system after birth—i.e., the difference between infantile and mature reactions. The third conclusion precisely conforms to our previous one, that present wants are the chief energizers and determiners of behavior. The "physiological states" referred to here as the causes of endogenous behavior are obviously the same as the internal wants we have already discussed. If our quasi-external wants appear not to fit that category we shall have to consider in what respect they form a class by themselves.

2. THE RELATION OF SPECIFIC TO GENERAL REACTIONS

It is evident from many other observations of animal life that "changes in physiological states," as Jennings calls them, always remain the chief causes of behavior and that, among the lower animals and birds at least, the sequence of reactions to many endogenous causes continues to follow the original order in which they developed.[34] Thus locomotion or merely restlessness continues to be the first form of behavior in many such series.

For instance, Richter found that the cycles of rats' running activity conformed to the periodicity (and the intensity) of hunger contractions and also of the oestrous cycle (in the female); and that, in the first case at least, it began as a "preliminary diffuse activity" which did not immediately lead to eating even if food were present. The animals appeared annoyed, became restless and "moved about" until finally, apparently, the "general discomfort" became "centralized in the hunger sensation." [35] Rogers concluded that the causes of the "walking reflex" in his pigeons were thirst, hunger, and the need of defecation, which he thinks are signaled by visceral impulses, and the last two of which "are connected with hypermotility of the diges-

[34] That even the first stages of this order (rostral to caudal) are due to the original underlying apparatus, which remains intact after decortication, is suggested by observations on dogs. For example, Mettler et al. (297, 1246) found that, "shortly after decortication the origination of somatic movements occurs in a diffuse way and spreads relatively slowly down the spinal cord."

[35] Richter, 338, 313. Apparently the same sequence holds good of the sexual want, for Richter's female rats showed running activity in 4-day cycles with a peak just preceding ovulation; but they would only mate just before or just after the peak (ibid., 322).

tive tract." [36] Craig defined the onset of wants (his appetites and aversions), among his doves, as a "state of agitation" appearing as "increased muscular tension," "static and phasic contractions of many skeletal and dermal muscles," "restlessness," "activity," and "in extreme cases violent activity." But the "active search for satisfaction does not commence until a certain intensity of appetite is attained." [37]

Thus it appears that the initial response to many physiological states which require bodily activity for their correction is a general one—that is, one that is not specific as to the particular state. Neither is it related in any way whatever to an external stimulus. Out of this first pattern of general activity (locomotion or restlessness) there seem to be differentiated, at a certain stage of intensity of these states, special patterns, each of which is related to the correction of a specific state only.[38] But, if we look further, we see that this is not true of the response to all wants. Taking as a basis Carmichael's list of the "seven fundamental acts of behavior in mammals: namely progression, respiration, ingestion, expression [postures, gestures and facies]) excretion, phonation and reproduction," [39] we find a distinction between them. Respiration is continuous and so occurs when no (other) behavior is occurring as well as when any other form of behavior is occurring.[40] Only when normal breathing becomes inadequate—when we are "out of breath"—does breathing preclude other forms of behavior. Expression and phonation, while not continuous, may occur when there is no other behavior or as parts or accompaniments of any other behavior.[41]

[36] Rogers, *351, 567.* This reaction occurred both in normal and in decerebrate pigeons, if the thalamus was intact. It is, therefore, subcortical but requires the highest level of the old brain.

[37] Craig, *94,* 91 and 104. Washburn also says (*427,* 326), "The presence of a desire or drive produces general activity in the animal." Among other observers whose results confirm this may be mentioned Wang (*422*) and Slonaker (*380*).

[38] Coghill (*89,* 33) finds this precedence of the locomotor reaction to exist even ontogenetically in the feeding reaction. In its early development, "the trunk component, consisting of a short quick jump forward, becomes functional first." But he seems to think the feeding reaction develops only as a result of an optical stimulus (*ibid.,* 35). This sounds like Sherrington's precurrent reaction (see p. 125, below).

[39] Carmichael, *72,* 31.

[40] Thus fundamental breathing does not require complete integration. And this because the basic reflex (the Hering-Breuer), engaging only the musculature of the thoracic cage, is mediated in the medulla—the lowest level of the subcortical brain.

[41] All these forms of expression, as well as phonation which is itself another form, and the respiratory expressions alone (sighing, etc.) or combined with phonation (laughter, etc.), are produced (naturally) only in the highest levels of the subcortical brain. That is, they involve levels at which integration is complete. But they are all parts of extensive patterns. That is, they are not exclusive, requiring suppression of all else. When they occur alone it is only because the excitation is too slight to produce the rest of the

But the notable peculiarity of ingestion (eating and drinking), excretion (micturition and defecation), and reproduction (practically all acts of both sexes) is that each of them, when it occurs after maturation, precludes all others and also precludes progression.[42] And yet, as noted above, progression is the initial reaction, among lower animals, to the want which is the cause of each. This fact—that all these special actions, eating and drinking, micturition and defecation and the several sexual acts are not carried on at the same time, that each precludes all others as well as locomotion—is a strong indication that each involves complete integration.[43] Nevertheless, the actual musculature, postural and phasic, engaged in each is only part of the whole, and is for the most part different in each case, so that it is obvious that two or more could, so far as the structure of the body is concerned, be performed concurrently. For this reason it must be assumed that it is the central nervous system that is responsible for the complete integration in all cases where only one special reaction can be performed at a time.

Combining these several approaches it becomes clear that the behavior induced by the particular internal wants we have considered is, or becomes, wholly integrated behavior, and that it remains wholly integrated even after it is converted into the special reaction appropriate to each. It begins as a general reaction involving pretty much the whole of the peripheral motor apparatus (restlessness or locomotion). Thereafter, at some stage in the rise of the intensity of the want, all of the extensive pattern not involved in the special action is in-

---

pattern or, in man, because the rest is cortically inhibited. This is discussed in Appendix II, Section H.

[42] While all of these become exclusive operations in most mature mammals, the reader may object that, with human infants, defecation and micturition are not. Thus we seem to have skipped a stage from the embryo to the mature man during which the order of precedence, general to special, is different. But it must be remembered that we are now talking about motor behavior, not autonomic processes. The human infant's defecation and micturition is wholly what we called, in Appendix I, the "involuntary" (autonomic) process. When these processes come to involve motor behavior (i.e., postures, etc.), they come also to involve complete integration even at subcortical, and therefore wholly automatic, levels. When they come to interfere with the reactions to other wants, they involve integration (inhibitory) both at subcortical and at cortical levels. Then, when they are themselves released, reciprocal inhibition takes place as to all other general activities.

[43] The fact that all of these, except defecation and micturition, are completely integrated as soon as they appear suggests that the centripetal transmission of the wants which cause them is humoral rather than neural, as we have already suspected. On that basis they would begin as completely integrated reactions for the reason that they are transmitted only and directly to the hypothalamus.

hibited and remains inhibited so long as the special action continues.[44] Since general inhibition of this kind is as much an evidence of complete integration in the central nervous system as is general activity, these special acts are as fully integrated as their predecessors. The inference is obvious. If these actions involve complete integration, they must be produced by an effector mechanism at a level in the central nervous system high enough to command complete integration. Thus the necessary inferences from external observation confirm the conclusions we reached in the previous chapter. Even the special forms of behavior adapted to these wants are not produced by segmental or spinal reflexes, nor in the lower brain-stem, though patterns organized there may be used. Instead they are the results of various modes of excitation in the hypothalamus and, through that, of the subcortical or extrapyramidal motor centers.[45] All these modes tend to produce, at first, one general and extensive pattern. Then, out of the background of general inhibition of that pattern, arises the special pattern of each particular mode. If we observe animals and men who do not show general activity prior to these special acts, it is to be presumed that this is because, in the course of time, the special reaction has encroached even further and that the general reaction is then inhibited from the moment the want is strong enough to engage the hypothalamus, as a whole, at all. That is, it is to be presumed that the whole process and the order in which it takes place remains the same, and the *tendency* toward restlessness or general activity continues potentially even though it becomes suppressed and is rarely realized.[46]

Thus we conclude that, in these internal wants, the order of development of reactions, from general to special, remains the order of their sequence thereafter, provided they require integration, and that the special reactions are equally as endogenous as the general one. We

[44] While this process cannot be explained, it can be stated in terms of reciprocal inhibition. We know from physiology that general activity reciprocally inhibits many special vegetative functions and all antagonistic special motor actions. It is equally clear from general observation that these special vegetative functions can reciprocally inhibit general activity and all special motor functions which are antagonistic to the one excited. Apparently, at some stage in the increasing intensity of the want, the balance of reciprocal inhibition vs. excitation is shifted.
[45] We will recall Tower's (*405, 442*) assignment to the extrapyramidal system of "complete synergies involving at least whole extremities and often the whole animal."
[46] This conclusion is in entire conformity with the observations of Coghill, Child, and González (see note 8, above), though they did not attack the problem of the neural machinery.

have as yet no explanation of the way the general-special sequence takes place—how several wants, which at low intensities produce a single uniform and general reaction, come each, at a higher intensity, to convert that into a different and special one.[47] But we have already noted in the previous chapter that all these, and most other wants also, tend to produce one general form of behavior—great excitement—at very high degrees of intensity. This is true even of the need of air which also results in integration and great excitement if the short-circuited reflex does not keep the intensity of the want at a low level. Therefore, it appears that specific behavior, with integration, occurs only in the middle range of intensity—that is, between the lower range, which produces uniform restlessness, and the higher range, which produces more or less uniform excitement.

Can we also apply the three conclusions with reference to the development of behavior patterns to the behavior generated by our quasi-external wants? Apparently these originate as, and always remain, general and integrated motor activity. They are slightly differentiated so that each can be recognized, and yet they also tend toward uniformity at the highest intensity. Therefore, the first conclusion with reference to the order, general-special, does not apply. With reference to the second conclusion, it appears that these reactions are to be included in the repertory of reactions already acquired at birth—in most animals and in man. But, thereafter, they seem to develop more as a result of somatic growth than through any change in the neural pattern. They remain stereotyped. Their development has ended. When it comes to the third conclusion we face an even greater anomaly. These reactions are clearly not endogenous. They take place only

---

[47] That is, we have no explanation of the neural process involved nor of the developmental reason for different special reactions to each want. As to the first point, see note 44, above. As to the second point, which is beyond the scope of our inquiry, two considerations are worth bearing in mind. These particular special reactions are phylogenetically continuous from the earliest forms of animal life. They existed long before the appearance of most of our special organs, including the central nervous system, and they have always been functions of the entrance to and the exit from the gastrointestinal tract, and of the genito-urinary system, which abuts on that exit. The musculature, both smooth and striated, which is involved in each of these special acts is that surrounding or most intimately related to the opening and to the organs which function in relation to the particular want for which the act serves. There is, therefore, nothing inherently different or more remarkable about the development of the mechanism for eating, etc., than there is about the development of that for digestion, etc. While the external activity, perhaps little changed, has come under the control of the later developed system of integration, the central nervous system, so too, to a lesser degree, has the internal activity.

under the influence of external stimuli or of changes in relations with the environment. In this sense they are exogenous. Nevertheless they are not developed under the influence of the environment; they remain largely unchanged by that influence; and they are potential even when no environmental influence has ever caused them. In that sense they are hardly exogenous. That suggests that the antitheses used by our biologist authorities—endogenous *vs.* exogenous, or spontaneous *vs.* external stimulus-responses—may not be the valid ones. But we shall have to wait until we develop the argument further before attempting to clear up this point.[48]

3. CONSUMMATORY *vs.* PRECURRENT REACTIONS TO PRESENT WANTS

Viewing the process almost wholly from the standpoint of external objects and the resulting external stimuli, and distinguishing chiefly according to the class of receptor involved (distance or non-distance), Sherrington divided reactions into two classes, (1) precurrent, or preparatory, or anticipatory, and (2) consummatory.[49] The relationship to the satisfaction of a want is implicit in the terms, but is treated as only incidental. In both cases the cause was conceived to be a stimulus from an external object.[50] The distinction is necessarily somewhat vague. But precurrent reactions "form series much longer"; they "are all steps toward final adjustments, and are not themselves end-points"; whereas "the sequence of action initiated by these non-projicient re-

---

[48] The statements made in this subsection, which are based entirely on external observation, may seem, at first sight, inconsistent with the scheme developed in Chapter 2 and Appendix II on the basis of experimental excitation of various degrees and at various loci in the hypothalamus. Such inconsistencies are always apt to appear when the same set of facts are viewed from two different standpoints. However, one must remember that, there, we were considering the combination of interofective and exterofective reactions. Here we are considering exterofective (behavior) only. The spreading there described was an inference drawn from the successive enlargement of the field of autonomic effects. Only after a considerable amount of spreading has occurred do motor effects appear at all. Then they appear as the motor portions of extensive patterns. Having regard to the exterofective reactions only, the results of the two viewpoints may be rather well reconciled on the following hypothesis. Mild hypothalamic excitation at any center tends to produce a general exterofective pattern (spreading); intermediate hypothalamic excitation tends to produce a special but also exclusive exterofective pattern according to the center stimulated, because, and to the extent that, it incidentally produces inhibition of the rest of the available field; excessive hypothalamic excitation tends to produce the general exterofective pattern of great excitement regardless of the center stimulated—and this because inhibition is then converted into excitation of the rest of the field. This change from inhibition to excitation at great intensity conforms to our interpretation of the process of inhibition as described in Appendix II.
[49] Sherrington, *375*, 326–333.   [50] *Ibid.*, 326.

ceptors is a short one; their reflex leads immediately to another which is consummatory." [51] While it is conceded that this final act (e.g., swallowing) is the only one which is strictly consummatory from the standpoint of the external environment, Sherrington used the term to cover both that and the brief final series. This terminology has come into general use and the distinction is important for our purposes, though we cannot accept the grounds on which it was originally made. Viewed objectively, there is a distinction between reactions which cannot of themselves satisfy a want, though they may lead up to an opportunity for such satisfaction, and those, on the other hand, which constitute the external element—the behavior—in the process of satisfaction. For instance, the reactions we have described as eating, drinking, resting, coition, defecation, and micturition are obviously consummatory in this sense. But the alert, restlessness, and general activity or locomotion are not consummatory except, perhaps, for the want we have called euphoria and for certain of the quasi-external wants. Therefore, we class them, when related to internal wants other than euphoria, as precurrent reactions. The question of the distinction when applied to the reactions to quasi-external wants will be considered in due course.

All of the evidence we have cited up to this point demonstrates that the relationship of external stimuli or external objects to these reactions, consummatory or precurrent, is neither necessary, fundamental, nor original. As to the consummatory, first, it is obvious that defecation and micturition never require at any time an external stimulus or relation to an external object. The need alone is sufficient. The consummatory reaction called eating (or drinking) may appear in the young, if hunger exists, before any external stimulus or object is present, and often does so in the absence of an appropriate external stimulus or object. The same is true of a sex object, if sexual excitement exists. [52] Thus we must construe these consummatory reactions to be spontaneous or endogenous in the sense in which these terms have been used in the foregoing citations. And this is further proved by the

[51] *Ibid.*, 329–330. It is consummatory "because it is calculated of itself to be final" (*ibid.*, 331).

[52] Craig (*94*, 93 and 94–95) notes that, in the first manifestation of the eating reaction, "the animal begins with an incipient consummatory reaction" without the external stimulus. And (*ibid.*, 92) the inexperienced will vent the consummatory reaction upon an abnormal or inadequate external stimulus (also as to sex object and nest). Richter's young rats sucked everything until, by this process of "trial and error" or by the mother's teaching, they found the teat and ate (*338*, 319).

fact that some of them, at least, are "innate," not learned—for they have been observed to occur before contact with the appropriate external object is established.[53] As to precurrent reactions, it is evident from the previous sections that the basic element of these, general activity or locomotion, precedes, both in order of development and in later appearance (at least potentially), the special reactions here called consummatory. This element, too, never requires an external stimulus either through distance or non-distance receptors. It is the very essence of spontaneous behavior. In fact, it is for this reason that it has been described by observers with the external stimulus-response viewpoint as aimless or random. Moreover, until the want reaches a certain intensity and this general reaction is converted into some special one, the behavior is not even specific according to its internal cause. Thus the basic precurrent reaction is at first without direction either from the external or the internal environment.

The term consummatory, as noted before, implies a relationship which has not been made explicit. To us this relationship is to a specific want. Reactions which constitute the external element in the actual satisfaction of a want are consummatory. But this raises difficulties. Precisely the same act may at one time result in satisfaction and, at other times, fail to do so. Presumably such an act would be defined as consummatory if, to the observer, it seemed to be designed to satisfy the want whether or not it succeeded. However, we recall Jennings's description, cited above, of the process of "trial and error." Apparently it is often the case that there is no specific consummatory reaction, and that a want may lead an organism to try its entire repertory of reactions before the want is finally allayed. Therefore, we must not make the conception too definite. There may not be a specific and innate consummatory reaction to each want. This point will recur in Section B 2.

There are also difficulties in distinguishing precurrent from consummatory reactions in certain cases, if the movement is defined in terms of the parts of the body involved and the actual motions made. For instance—among lower animals obviously, and apparently only con-

[53] Craig (94, 92) holds that "the consummatory action is always innate." Tracy says (407, 256): "Some sort of mechanism for securing food is developed and often becomes active before the organism begins its independent existence. Prenatal activity of at least some of these mechanisms appears to exist before the sensory field through which they will later be stimulated is exposed to the environment. Sucking and swallowing mechanisms are often active before hatching or birth."

cealed among the higher ones by inhibition—hunger automatically
initiates general motor activity, at first as locomotion. Ultimately this
culminates in a special reaction, activity at the entrance to the gastro-
intestinal tract—the mouth. This activity is primarily mastication, and
the act, in the young, is observed to commence even before food is
present in the mouth.[54] Obviously, then, it is part of the process set
up by internal causes. Now it is impossible to differentiate mastication
from the getting of food in the case of those animals that do not use
their forelegs, or arms, for the latter purpose. With them, mastication
is merely a continuation of the biting off or killing process. Or, rather,
the same reaction secures the food and then masticates it. And even
with the exceptions—some rodents, the primates, the cat family, and
elephants—there seems to be a tendency among the young to put
everything available into their mouths. Thus we see the possibility
that the consummatory process extends indefinitely into the field of
precurrent reactions. In fact, it becomes difficult to differentiate the
intermediate precurrent reactions either from the initial locomotion
or from the consummatory reaction itself.[55] It has been suggested that
nest-building, burrowing, etc., and even gregariousness, constitute
similar stages in the sequence of reactions which "can be understood
as a part of the heat-regulating mechanism by means of which the
body-temperature is maintained at a constant level." [56] Here the consummatory reaction seems to be "nestling," "huddling," etc., and that,
in the young, is sufficient unto the end. Later the precurrent reactions,
which are adapted to make this possible, seem to develop as a projection backward, so to speak, from this consummatory reaction.

Consideration of these facts leads us to the view that wants first
initiate general activity, as suggested—an activity which is not "random" at all because it has, at the start, no objective whatever.[57] The objective then arises, not by reason (innately) of an external stimulus, but

[54] See note 52, above.
[55] Coghill (91, 640) says that the particular acts of feeding, which appear to be discrete, "are actually only phases of a reaction which is fundamentally unitary." He
uses this as one instance to show the "fallacy of the traditional conception of the chain
reflex," which supposes "that one initial reflex stimulates the next in series."
[56] Richter, 338, 338. He found that this series of reactions increases in low, and decreases in high, temperature, and that their rate is high before puberty, during the inactive dioestrous interval, pregnancy, lactation, and starvation (i.e., periods of low
generation of heat), and low during the oestrous period (i.e., time of high generation
of heat). And he regards them all as an "expression of the same impetus that produces
an increase in fat and hair" (ibid., 340).
[57] It is obvious that the term "random" has only come into use because the organism
had come to be viewed as if it only acted in response to external stimuli. More apt

through the samewhat later initiation of the specific consummatory or special reaction which the particular want causes; that is, also due to wholly internal causes. And this specific reaction thereafter directs, or takes possession of, the general activity. The distinction between consummatory and what appear to be precurrent, or preparatory, reactions is therefore hazy; for the latter may consist of the general activity that is actually aroused first; and later it may be identical with the consummatory reaction, though not an actual consummation (e.g., killing prey).

However, in spite of the fact that the actual consummatory reaction may be fortuitous and the fact that the line between consummatory and precurrent reactions is a vague one, the distinction is convenient and we shall continue to use it as marking two phases of a single process which is only graduated in degree, not in kind. The particular respect in which this graduation is most marked was stated by Sherrington to be the degree of affective tone accompanying the reaction: "To consummatory reactions affective tone seems adjunct more than to the anticipatory, especially the remotely anticipatory." [58] If "affective tone" is produced by a want and is proportionate to the intensity of a want, as has been indicated in the previous chapter, and if, as we found reason to believe in the previous subsection, the consummatory or special reaction is differentiated out of the precurrent or general reaction at a certain stage in the rising intensity of a want, it necessarily follows that the "affective tone" of a consummatory reaction will be greater than that of the precurrent. In fact, we have the key to that difference, which was merely taken as an observed datum by Sherrington. A fuller explanation and a further reason for the gradation in affective tone will appear in Section B 2.

B. BEHAVIOR IN RELATION TO THE ENVIRONMENT

1. CONDITIONING EXTERNAL STIMULI TO WANTS

In the previous chapter and its appendix, where we were analyzing the results of experiments and observation on the brain itself, we con-

---

terms for this behavior are "agitation," "uneasiness," "restlessness," or "general activity," "locomotion," etc.; these are descriptive, and do not beg the question.

[58] Sherrington, 375, 330. He assigns, as the cause of this difference, the fact that "a salient character of most of the reactions of the non-projicient receptors taken as sense-organs is *affective tone*" (*ibid.*, 327), whereas "the affective tone of the reactions of the projicient receptors is less marked" (*ibid.*, 331). This thesis is explained as well as modified by the physiological reports contained in our previous chapters.

sidered the process of conditioning from the inside, so to speak. There we set up a series of inferences as to the neural character of the process. Now we have to consider the same process from the outside—that is, from the viewpoint from which it was first approached. Almost all the generalizations with regard to this subject were first made as a result of external observation of behavior, and still rest on that basis. Their interpretation in neural terms, so far as that has gone, has been by way of inference and imputation. As we proceed we shall endeavor to reconcile and combine the two approaches.[1] That involves a re-interpretation of the data in terms of the newer understanding of the brain—and particularly the old brain. But, since the whole scheme hinges on memory, we shall not be able to effect our final synthesis until we add our examination of that factor in Chapter 5 and Appendix III, Section C.

So soon as the young organism leaves the egg or womb it comes in contact with the external environment. Then begins the process now usually called conditioning—a combination of experience (learning) and, at least in the case of birds and mammals, of demonstration (teaching). The latter seems to work by means of what we call suggestion or imitation, as well as by compulsion and by aid.[2] It seems to involve, therefore, certain factors not present in the process of trial and error alone. Conditioning has two aspects. It includes learning or teaching to relate external objects to specific wants—that is, a conditioning to external stimuli.[3] It also includes the learning or teaching

[1] Only in this way can there be developed a truly physiological theory of learning. So recently as 1932, Dunlap (124, Chapter 4) presented some very pertinent criticisms of Pavlov's as a "physiological" theory of learning, and concluded (ibid., 70) that "a useful physiological theory of learning may be developed at some time in the future." The neurophysiological work on the old brain during the last decade seems to offer a new basis for such a theory.

[2] "Imitation" and its aural counterpart "suggestion" are regarded by Pavlov (320, 406 and 407) as reflexes. The former appears in maturity only as a "long-submerged reflex" of childhood. While we have no alternative explanation to offer, this classification appears to us gratuitous.

The difference between learning by experience and learning by demonstration (teaching) seems sometimes to be overlooked by theory. The former is random, until insight is acquired; the latter is generally not random. Thus the conditioning to specific food objects is not random among young birds and mammals. They are fed. Their untaught consummatory reaction is all that is necessary at first. The rest is taught them. In immaturity the "polymorphous perverse" manifestations of the budding sex want are doubtless also untaught. Whether the ultimate consummatory reaction, after puberty and with an appropriate sex object, is wholly untaught or not is difficult to determine.

[3] Pavlov states that "we recognize them [conditioned reflexes] in ourselves and other people under such names as 'education,' 'habits,' and 'training'" (320, 26). They are "acquired" (ibid., 25).

of reactions, especially the so-called adapted precurrent reactions—
that is, reactions adjusted to the environment and suited to deal with
the objects which have become related to the specific wants. These
latter reactions are, for the greater part, modifications of, or special
patterns within (fractions), the unlearned but developing pattern of
general activity (primarily locomotion). The two aspects of conditioning should be distinguished, for the first would be conceivable
even if the organism never went beyond its innate repertory of general
activity (locomotion) and of special reactions. It will be noted that
both these definitions introduce, at least far more explicitly than is
usual, the connection of wants with conditioning. The justification
for that will be brought out as we proceed.

Let us consider the first of these processes—conditioning to external
stimuli. The experiments of Pavlov were usually conducted on mature
dogs who had presumably already acquired the full complement of
conditioning to external stimuli which learning and teaching develops
in the normal animal. Therefore, his was an "artificial conditioning,"
as he calls it. But his results seemed to him to demonstrate, as well,
how the original and "natural" conditioning took place; so much so
that he decided to abandon this distinction.[4] In his scheme, an unconditioned stimulus is such a one as food in the mouth, in which case "the
physical and chemical properties of the food itself acting upon receptors in the mucous membrane of the mouth and tongue" produce
salivary secretion by means of what he considers a pure reflex process,[5]
and which he assumes to be "innate"—that is, unlearned. Thereafter,
under the right conditions, a "conditioned" stimulus may come to
produce the same result, though usually on a smaller scale.[6] For this
subsequent conditioning the following were found to be the chief
requirements: (1) That the to-be-conditioned stimulus shall "begin
to operate before the unconditioned stimulus comes into action"; [7] that
it shall "overlap in point of time with the action of the unconditioned
stimulus"; [8] and, so far as the salivary "reflex" is concerned, that hunger
should exist at the time.[9] After the "conditioned reflex" becomes thus
established it will come gradually to be inhibited (experimental ex-

[4] Pavlov, *320*, 50.   [5] *Ibid.,* 23.
[6] As Fraenkel and Gunn (*149*, 303) state it, "This kind of learning always starts with
a reflex response to a given stimulus, the unconditioned stimulus; the training consists
in substituting a different stimulus, the conditioned stimulus, for the unconditioned
one in such a way as to lead to the same response."
[7] Pavlov, *320*, 27.   [8] *Ibid.,* 26.   [9] *Ibid.,* 31–32.

tinction),[10] if the conditioned stimulus (artificial) is not "reinforced" by the arrival, as the animal has learned to expect, of what Pavlov regards as the unconditioned stimulus, in this case food in the mouth.[11] Thus the first "association" [12] is established on the irrational principle of *post hoc et cum hoc ergo propter hoc*,[13] and rationality only enters when experience either establishes or refutes ("dissociation") this supposed causal relation.[14] We see, then, that when the condition of hunger is actually present [15] and the animal is in readiness,[16] that part of the consummatory reaction which consists of the flow of saliva and which is supposed to occur "innately" only when food is in the mouth, can be initiated, not only by the "naturally" conditioned external stimulus of the sight or smell of food,[17] but gradually by many other external stimuli which prove to be signs of the near presence of food.[18] It is almost wholly by means of such conditioning that the distance receptors, or "projicient senses" as Sherrington calls them, come to initiate reactions.[19]

[10] *Ibid.*, 49 and 68.

[11] *Ibid.* This is approximately and eventually true, though a more cautious statement would be that "the strength of a conditioned response is increased by reinforcement and decreased by non-reinforcement" (Hilgard and Marquis, *197*, 75).

[12] Pavlov (*320*, 110 and elsewhere) calls this "integration," after Sherrington. For an interpretation of "integration," see supplementary statement, "Requirements for Conditioning," at the end of this subsection.

[13] The reader will, I hope, excuse this specious Latin.

[14] This is called "reinforcement." See supplementary statement, "Requirements for Conditioning," at the end of this subsection.

[15] See Pavlov, *320*, 31–32. Or, as Frolov puts it (*157*, 93), it is necessary to have the "food centre" in "a state of average excitability." And he interprets this in much the same way that we did in Chapter 1: "The further the exhaustion of the blood proceeds, the higher becomes the 'charge' [excitation] of the food centre" (*ibid.*, 95). For the details, see supplementary statement, "Requirements for Conditioning," at the end of this subsection.

[16] For this and other requirements, see supplementary statement, "Requirements for Conditioning," at the end of this subsection.

[17] One of Pavlov's experiments (*320*, 22–23) demonstrated quite definitely that these stimuli are conditioned. Nevertheless, as Skinner says (*379*, 353), "The behavior of approaching and picking up a bit of food is so common in the behavior of an adult rat and so uniform from one rat to another than it is apt to be looked upon (mistakenly) as unconditioned."

[18] Such other stimuli may be "any environmental change to which the organism is sensitive" (Hilgard and Marquis, *197*, 35), even including the passage of time. For even "time [duration] can be an exciting agent" (Frolov, *157*, 126). Or, as Pavlov himself stated it (*320*, 43), "innumerable individual fluctuations in the external and internal environment of the organism may, each and all of them, singly or collectively, being reflected in definite changes in the cells of the cerebral cortex, acquire the properties of a conditioned stimulus."

[19] Of course, this fact proves the fallacious ground of Sherrington's distinction between precurrent and consummatory reactions, for here the distance receptors are giving rise to a part of a consummatory reaction.

This statement of the conditioning process, while it correctly represents Pavlov's conclusions, is not satisfactory for our purposes in two respects. In the first place, it is not entirely consistent with the facts brought out in our discussion of the development of behavior patterns in the previous section. To that extent it must be modified. In the second place, it does not make evident the essential part that wants play in this process. To that extent it needs to be restated in terms of the neurophysiological facts which underlie it and which we have outlined in the previous chapter and in Appendix II. As to the first point, all these "dependable" unconditioned responses are the general and the several special forms of behavior (plus some internal activities) which are primarily caused by present wants. Most of those utilized by Pavlov were the special responses to the particular internal and quasi-external wants we have considered. These responses originate as the spontaneous or endogenous and unlearned reactions discussed in the previous section; and the special activities would, for the most part, be defined as consummatory reactions or parts of them. These reactions constitute the repertory of reactions available directly to the subcortical brain, chiefly the hypothalamus. They occur, in series from general to special, or even as general or as special alone, when the hypothalamus is excited in the appropriate mode. In turn, the primary excitors of the hypothalamus are the several wants, centripetally transmitted thereto from the regions where they arise. These responses, then, can occur without other, or external, stimulus [20] in the case of internal wants, and without other than the specific quasi-external stimulus, or relation to the environment, in the case of quasi-external wants. They are among the unlearned and unmodified synergies inherent in the subcortical brain.

Primarily, the unconditioned stimulus, so-called, is therefore the present want itself. Existence of the want at the time is always necessary to establish a conditioned stimulus; [21] but its existence is not always adequate by itself to produce the response. Whether or not it is

[20] This statement applies strictly only to the external activities. Internal activities which are excited before the actual process of satisfaction begins are of a different order from those attending the process itself. Thus digestion—even gastric motility of the type accompanying digestion—does not start until there is something to digest. Nor does the mere existence of the want start such a process as digestive salivation—at least, in maturity.

[21] See above, note 15. A more precise, but complicated, statement is this: Existence of the want *during all, or before the end of,* the period of application of the to-be-conditioned stimulus is necessary in order to establish it as such.

adequate alone depends, in part, on the relative intensity of the want in comparison with other existing wants—that is, whether or not it is capable of exciting the hypothalamus generally in its own mode in competition with other existing wants. The quasi-external wants, if aroused at all, are usually adequate immediately and alone; the internal wants, normally of a lower intensity,[22] only gradually come to the point at which they can excite the hypothalamus generally, as the variation from homeostasis increases. Even then, as we shall see, many of the internal wants are hardly ever adequate, after maturation, to produce their consummatory responses alone.

In the case of the quasi-external wants the only stimulus that is ever called the unconditioned stimulus is the want itself. The experimentor can cause all such wants by his manipulations. That is in fact exactly what he does when he produces his so-called unconditioned stimulus; for these stimuli are loud noise, loss of equilibrium, restraint, injury, etc. But, even in these cases, the stimuli are not truly unconditioned unless they are confined to those that are capable of reaching directly to the hypothalamus.[23] That is, they must be stimuli capable of being centripetally transmitted by the purely subcortical afferent mechanisms without recourse to the strictly sensory mechanisms of the cortex. At any rate, it is in this way that the experimentor produces at will the corresponding unconditioned responses to quasi-external wants. On the other hand, in the case of the internal wants, the want itself has not usually been called the unconditioned stimulus. Instead, the want has been regarded only as a necessary condition precedent. This is chiefly because the experimentor cannot cause the internal wants by his manipulations; or does not proceed in the right way to cause them.[24] Therefore, he has to wait until these latter wants exist before he can induce the corresponding unlearned response. That is, he has to wait until hunger, thirst, sexual desire, etc., exist in some considerable degree before he can induce the response. However, he does not need to wait until the response occurs of itself (spontaneously). In fact, with mature animals, he would often wait a long time for that. For mature animals have learned to suppress the consummatory reaction to any internal want which requires an external object for satisfaction

[22] See Chapter 2, p. 93 and Appendix II, Section G 4.
[23] Or, in some cases, to lower centers.
[24] He can of course cause asphyxia or changes in body heat and, ultimately, hunger and thirst by external manipulation; and these are internal wants. But he cannot cause them by external stimuli.

until that object is present (e.g., food in the mouth). As we noted above, the existence, in very young animals, of an internal want of sufficient intensity produces the special or consummatory reaction in the absence of the appropriate external object.[25] This soon disappears. Evidently the young learn early to suppress (inhibit) such reactions —presumably because such aimless reactions do not lead to satisfaction;[26] and this inhibition persists throughout life. But this suppression does not occur if the appropriate object is present. That is, the external stimulus arising from the appropriate external object releases the inhibition.[27] Discrimination of the crudest order—presence or absence of external stimulus—has then been learned. The food object in the mouth has become a conditioned external stimulus.[28] Or, more exactly, discrimination has been established between the sole stimulus of hunger and that combined with the stimulus of food in the mouth. For the latter is only a supplement which cannot act alone to produce the reaction. Hunger alone has become an inhibitory stimulus leading to the suppression of the consummatory reaction. Hunger plus food in the mouth have become an excitatory combination for the same reaction, because the external stimulus (food in the mouth) releases the central inhibition set up against the internal stimulus (hunger). It follows that, in the case of the internal as well as that of the quasi-external wants, the only unconditioned stimulus is the want itself. But, with the internal wants, the corresponding reaction is automatic only for a short time, if this unconditioned stimulus arises alone. Thereafter the internal want continues to be the necessary unconditioned stimulus, but it is only active if its conditioned inhibition is released by the conditioned stimulus. In fine, the only relation of external objects to internal

[25] Thus young infants drool (salivate) merely because they are hungry.
[26] That is, they are not reinforced. This seems to be an example of negative conditioning which we shall consider below.
[27] It must be in part a release phenomenon, not one of excitation, because the existence of the want continues to be the necessary basis for the reaction. However, it remains probable that some part is due to the excitation of a replica (see below).
[28] Thus, in reality, Pavlov's conditioning of other external stimuli to the conditioned reflex—food in the mouth-salivation—was the building of one conditioned stimulus on another—what he calls a "secondary" conditioned reflex, or conditioned reflex of the second order.
Pavlov's experiment on a decorticate dog with what he called the "water reflex" seems to class this as subcortical conditioning and to indicate that, with cortical discrimination gone, anything in the mouth serves to release the inhibition of hunger. But, in spite of the behavior produced, it is possible that this was a subcortically conditioned stimulus to rejectable substances in the mouth—in this case acid. That it required 500 injections to establish is certainly evidence of its subcortical nature, however differently Pavlov interpreted it (see 320, 328-330).

wants—even objects in the mouth—is that of a conditioned stimulus.[29]

It is quite evident that both the early negative and positive conditioning processes with reference to internal wants are wholly subcortical. In the first place, they remain undisturbed in the decorticate animal below primates. His consummatory reactions do not appear in the absence of an appropriate external stimulus. On the other hand, he eats if he is presented with food in such a way that his subcortical afferent apparatus is adequate to receive the stimulus. So, too, with drinking and with such sexual behavior as has been observed. In the second place, both this negative and the corresponding positive conditioning occur, with animals and human infants, before the cortical apparatus has developed sufficiently to play any part. It may take the infant a long time to learn the futility of sucking an inappropriate object, but he soon ceases to suck the air.[30]

This analysis of the true unconditioned stimulus also suggests that the quoted statements as to reinforcement are incorrect. As a matter of fact the reinforcement is always and only the satisfaction, or partial satisfaction, of the want—that is, in our view, the partial or complete disappearance of the unconditioned stimulus. That is obvious with the quasi-internal wants. The reinforcement is the cessation of the stimulus producing the want and therefore the cessation (satisfaction) of the want. All experiments prove that. But it is not so obvious with the internal wants, largely because of the external stimulus-response viewpoint. There the reinforcement has been identified with what has been called the unconditioned stimulus (e.g., food in the mouth). But, if that stimulus is, in reality, merely the earliest and subcortically conditioned stimulus, how could it have been, in turn, conditioned without reinforcement? There, as we have suggested, the reinforcement was certainly the fact that food in the mouth was found to satisfy, or partially satisfy, the want so that the want was reduced or ceased. Probably this continues to be the case with all subsequently conditioned stimuli. They, too, only become established and continue as

[29] See note 17, above.
[30] William James regarded such "instincts" as sucking by mammals to be transitory and only prolonged by habit. The instinct is gone quickly. The habit may remain (220, II, 398-399). As noted elsewhere, our system of energetics requires no such difficultly explicable "self-starting" mechanism for habit. We know now that the sucking reflex becomes suppressed in time by cortical inhibition. But it requires more or less time before hunger fails to excite this, its original, reaction if an object yielding a stimulus similar to the original food-in-the-mouth stimulus, whose absence produced the original negative conditioning, releases the subcortical inhibition.

such if they lead to satisfaction of the want with which they have become associated.[31] The observer has merely noted the superficial rather than the fundamental essential for reinforcement. We conclude that all reinforcement is partial or complete satisfaction of the activating want.

So much, at this point, for the strictly unconditioned stimulus, for the unlearned response, and for reinforcement. Let us now consider what relation the conditioned stimulus has with the system of wants and how it produces its effect. It used to be supposed that conditioning is an exclusively cortical phenomenon; [32] but "recent experimentation . . . demonstrates . . . that conditioning is possible at a subcortical level"—perhaps even at a spinal level.[33] The facts we have cited above with reference to conditioning to food in the mouth, etc., are also evidence that subcortical conditioning is possible—nay, that it is the ontogentically earliest form.[34] However, the importance of the cortex in conditioning "increases throughout the phylogenetic series to man" —in other words, in proportion to the relative development of the cortex.[35] If this is true phylogenetically, it is doubtless also true onto-

[31] I know of no experiments bearing on this question. The test would be to discover how long the reinforcing effect of food or water in the mouth continued if satisfaction were prevented—e.g., by an esophageal fistula or stomach pump. Of course, long experience of the correctness of the association would probably mean a long time in breaking down the association after it was made to be incorrect.

[32] "When an originally indifferent stimulus becomes an emotional stimulus, that is to say, when it acquires the property of eliciting diencephalic discharge, it does so by the discriminative powers of the cortex" (Bard, 20, 307). Or, as Cannon put it (61, 120), the response to external stimulation, initiated in the cortex, may be in a "certain mode or figure" which stimulates [hypo]thalamic processes. For Pavlov, the processes are at least cerebral (320, 16 and 361), but are usually referred to as if they were cortical (ibid., 43, 234, etc.).

[33] Hilgard and Marquis, 197, 313.

[34] For our purposes it is unnecessary to discuss most of the details of subcortical conditioning or of such remnants of originally chiefly cortical conditioning as persist after decortication. But we should make clear, in passing, that we do not suppose conditioning to be a process of synthesis of nervous impulses radically different from any other such synthesis. Anything that occurs in the brain is, or was, probably possible in some degree throughout the nervous system. On that basis, even the hypothalamic region would be supposed to be necessary only if a want requiring an integrated response were necessary. Hence, it may be possible to condition a suitable stimulus to a purely spinal reflex and even in a spinal animal.

[35] Hilgard and Marquis, 197, 335 and 317. Miller (299, 100) states that "the experimental data dealing with conditioning . . . show: (a) That conditioning can take place in other parts of the nervous system—even in the spinal cord," and "(c) That it may be possible to develop conditioning . . . at more than one level at the same time." "Animals are conditionable even when anesthetized" (loc. cit.), as well as when decorticated (Hilgard and Marquis, 197, 314).

Bard says more recently (24, 235) that conditioned reflexes can be established in decorticate dogs and cats, but are, in higher animals, predominantly cortical.

genetically. We should expect then that subcortical mechanisms play a larger part in conditioning among the lower than the higher animals and among infants than among the mature. Moreover, at its best, subcortical is definitely limited in comparison with cortical conditioning.[36] This would naturally follow from the fact that the exteroceptive apparatus reaching to the hypothalamus, etc., is both much less precise and much less complete than that developed in connection with the cortex, and the fact that, when the latter is removed or before it matures, sole reliance for reports from the external world must be placed on the former.[37]

All this is entirely consonant with, and is explained by, the assumption that the development of the cortex, both phylogenetically and ontogenetically, consists in the gradual withdrawal and further evolution of neural functions that already existed subcortically. We have no direct neurophysiological knowledge of the process of subcortical conditioning; but considerable light has been shed on that process as it occurs in the cortex. Until proved otherwise we naturally assume that the former is analogous to the latter. As we developed the scheme of cortical conditioning in the previous chapter and in Appendix II, it is one form of the general type of synthesis of neural patterns which is based on simultaneity (here succession plus simultaneity). This type of synthesis also occurs in building many other cortical patterns (Gestalten). But in this particular form, though that basis is essential, it is not enough. Not all simultaneous stimuli are synthesized in this way. In conditioning the process is or becomes, selective. The cortex, repre-

[36] It requires intense stimuli and long training (Hilgard and Marquis, *197*, 316); but it can be done with decorticate dogs even in response to visual and auditory stimuli; and salivation can be taught from the metronome. Obviously, the subcortical external senses of the dog are superior to those of man; and yet subcortical vision and hearing are very limited even with dogs.

[37] For instance decorticate dogs do not respond to the sight of food (Frolov, *157*, 44) though previously naturally conditioned to it. "A decorticate dog . . . never shows anger" in response to any particular visual or auditory stimulus" (Bard, *24*, 197), though there is apt to be previous natural conditioning to such stimuli. Of course, in both cases, this is because the afferent apparatus appreciating such stimuli is cortical and has been removed by decortication. On the other hand, a decorticate dog will show fear to a loud sound (Bard, *loc. cit.*) because that can be appreciated subcortically.

Though conditioning to stimuli appreciable after decortication is possible (Frolov, *157*, 44), the arc of the conditioned reflex is usually through the cortex, while that of the unconditioned is always through lower centers (*ibid.*, 39). Thus, when the conditioned stimulus alone is not sufficient, as in the case of internal wants, "when the *food* centre is stimulated by hunger" (unconditioned stimulus), the conditioned stimulus via the cortex follows the "*well-beaten track* between the point of the conditioned reflex in the cortex and the point of unconditioned stimulation in the lower lying centres" (*ibid.*, 75).

senting chiefly the external environment, is, by itself, presented with a scene which is usually all background. The hypothalamus, representing chiefly the internal environment, is presented at one moment with but a single mode of general excitation, if any—the mode determined by the prepotent want. In accordance with the hypothesis already outlined, the process of cortical conditioning consists in the investment of some portion of the external scene with "interest"—that is, such sensory representation becomes endowed with an emotional content—because it is found to be related to the then prevalent bodily interest.[38] Thereafter, re-excitation of the same representation in the cortex, either by repetition or by association of likes, or even to a slight extent by recurrence of the representation in memory only, can, by reason of the emotional endowment, continue to re-excite the hypothalamus in the same mode—that is, establish there the corresponding emotional state. In other words, cortical conditioning means that an external stimulus, capable of causing sensation but incapable of directly exciting the hypothalamus, comes to be able, by means of this synthesis, to excite the hypothalamus over corticohypothalamic paths. But it can do so only if the emotional endowment is strong enough. And here the quasi-external and the internal wants differ, apparently because of a difference in their relative normal strength. A cortically conditioned stimulus can by itself excite the reaction called rage, fear, etc.; though, if it reappears in memory only, it can do so only with less intensity.[39] But a cortically conditioned stimulus cannot by itself excite hunger, thirst, sexual urge, etc. It can only raise to threshold the excitation which already exists at somewhat subliminal intensity due to the unconditioned stimulus—that is, to hunger, etc. The distinction may go deeper than that. While the effects are summative in respect of intensity, it may be that the hypothalamus discriminates between its own stimuli from below and those set up by

[38] In other words, as Frolov says (157, 124), Pavlov's "analyzers" are "rather organs of analysis and synthesis." At first the whole scene is invested with "interest"—is weakly conditioned. Gradually with repetition of, and reinforcement by, the single essential factor, that alone becomes conditioned, but strongly. The process is a combination of association and discrimination—or "differentiation," as Pavlov called it.

[39] William James makes a sharp distinction here. "The revivability in memory of the emotions . . . is very small." But memory can produce, not remembrances of the old grief or rapture, but new griefs and raptures, by summoning up a lively thought of their exciting cause" (220, II, 474). Or, in our language, the emotional content of a memory is itself very faint, so much so that it hardly yields an experience of the emotion itself. But, to the extent that it succeeds in producing an emotional state in the hypothalamus—a new emotion—it may produce an intense one, though probably never as intense as the original stimulus produces.

the cortex, so that the consequent felt emotion transmitted to the cortex is different in the two cases. Thus the "feeling" excited by an external stimulus which is of "interest" may be distinguishable from that excited by the want itself. The sight of food which makes one's mouth water may cause a feeling which is different from, or only a part of, hunger. Some think that fear is largely a conditioned precursor to pain. If so, the two certainly remain distinguishable.[40]

This analysis makes it clear that a conditioned stimulus never causes the corresponding want. It merely causes an emotional state in the hypothalamus that is similar to, though weaker than, the emotional state produced there by the want upon which the conditioning has been established. After conditioning, the two processes always remain independent and their sources are never the same. For the sake of clarity in our further analysis we must therefore distinguish between the primary excitation of the hypothalamus in response to wants and the secondary excitation of the hypothalamus in response to conditioned stimuli.[41] Though the two kinds may be distinguishable and though the secondary may reproduce only part of the primary excitation, these secondary states will be referred to as "replicas" of wants, because they are purely central states having similar effects.[42]

The importance of this distinction is greater in regard to the quasi-external than it is in regard to the internal wants, because, as we have noted, in the former case the conditioned stimulus can cause the appropriate reaction alone while in the latter case it cannot.[43] We have already discussed those relations with the environment which constitute quasi-external wants, the stimuli from which are the unconditioned stimuli to the corresponding reactions. Thus injuries and consequent pain cause pain reactions; sudden loud noise and bright light and

[40] On the other hand, dizziness in high places is almost the same as the sensation of falling, as I can testify.
[41] Presumably the latter class should include subcortical conditioning when that is excitatory (e.g., food in the mouth) but when the stimulus is probably received directly by the hypothalamus.
[42] In psychological terms such responses to non-existent wants are sometimes said to be due to the "principle of expectancy" (e.g., Hilgard and Marquis, 197, 87 ff.). But this is pure verbal magic. Such responses are due to the neural facts we have cited.
[43] This difference in capacity, probably due to a difference in usual intensity, is also a justification for our distinguishing quasi-external wants from the old external stimulus-response category. If the degree of affectivity depends, as we suggest in Chapter 5, upon the generality of the peripheral excitation, then quasi-external wants derive their force, not from the stimulus, but from a generalized bodily reaction to it. If so, sensation results from the canalized impulses from a specialized receptor—while the affect results from the generalized response of a part or whole of the body.

their consequent stimuli—perhaps including all other very strong stimuli—cause fear reactions; so does loss of equilibrium through its vestibular consequences; and restraint or constraint, producing some unknown stimuli, cause the rage reaction.[44] Unlike the internal wants, these are normally entirely absent, do not regularly recur, but only occur fortuitously.[45] Without conditioning, all other external conditions and stimuli are indifferent so far as these emotional states are concerned. Gradually, in the course of learning and teaching, many other external stimuli which are originally emotionally indifferent— particularly those via the distance receptors—become conditioned stimuli because they prove to be signs of the coming of some quasi-external want and its unconditioned stimuli, having regularly preceded and overlapped the latter. Thus fear-objects become conditioned to injury and pain; [46] the signs of an explosion become conditioned to a loud noise; looking over a declivity becomes conditioned to loss of equilibrium; signs of the threat of restraint become conditioned to actual restraint.[47] In each case, the resulting reaction is the one ap-

[44] Some have regarded these too as conditioned stimuli, since they can be "unconditioned." Thus pain to the masochist or flagellant, or to the soldier who, in the heat of battle, does not know he is wounded; or loud noise to the boilermaker or Woodworth's spider (447, 161), etc. But these processes seem not to be similar to "unconditioning." They are, rather, a miscellany of other and different processes, which we shall undertake to account for as we proceed.

[45] These facts lead Tolman (403, 274) to the curious conclusion that such wants—his aversions—are "relatively continuous."

[46] "Fear has been defined as the premonition of pain" (Cannon, 66, 229). "In fear there is then a negative reaction to a representative stimulus—one that *stands* for a really injurious stimulation" (Jennings, 223, 332). "Fear arose from injury" (Crile, 96, 59). "The ultimate state to be avoided in fright is pain" (Tolman, 403, 280). And (420, 353) Tolman holds that avoidance is ultimately not of the fear-object but of the injury threatened by that object. This may be true in part. But, as we have noted, there seems to be a subcortical fear reaction which is an innate response to certain unconditioned stimuli other than pain—loss of equilibrium or support and very loud noises or sudden bright lights. McDougall agrees that fear is "capable of being excited by any sudden loud noise," and even construes flight as the consummatory reaction to noise (284, 35). It can be conditioned to signs by what he calls "association in virtue of temporal contiguity" (*ibid.*, 39) (i.e., conditioning) and can be unconditioned by absence of hurtful effects (*ibid.*, 35). Also there seems to be some as yet unexplained relation between fear and rage. Jackson (216, II, 107) said "fear is anger 'broken down' prematurely." But, even in the case of rage, the reaction to "to-be-fought objects" is because of the implication of resultant interference. In the case of fear, as well as rage (see above), Tolman holds (403, 282) that it "tends at times to combine with the other drives. It tends to fasten on to and wax fat on the appetites."

[47] We permit ourselves only this very limited expansion of our cause of rage, because we are dealing only with emotions that are primarily excited by explorable peripheral causes. It is admitted, of course, that inability to accomplish what one aims at, because of internal not external hindrances, is a frequent cause of rage (e.g., the golfer smashing his clubs, or the pianist's tantrum). But we recall that Jacobson's apes without pre-

propriate to the want itself—the unconditioned stimulus. But, though the whole response may be similar, the fact that it takes place as the result of a surrogate stimulus may involve this difference. Whereas, if the want itself arises, the reaction, if successful, is reinforced by getting rid of the want, in this case the reaction usually operates in such a way that the want itself never arises and its unconditioned stimulus never arrives. In fact, these are "avoided." [48] Strictly speaking, then, the response to a stimulus conditioned to a quasi-external want helps to prevent the true want from arising, instead of helping to satisfy it after it arises, as is the case where the reaction is to the want itself. And, strictly speaking, all reactions that can be called "avoidance" are reactions to conditioned stimuli.[49] The effect of a replica is thus dif-

---

frontal areas had no such tantrums (Appendix II). That introduces a factor—other than conditioning to external stimulus—with which we are unable to cope.

[48] As Tolman puts it, "that which is avoided is ultimately not the fear-object *qua* object, but an injury 'threatened' by that object" (*402*, 353). In the same manner a secondary conditioned stimulus may arise. For, as Freud suggests (*155*, 342 and *156*, 37), a forewarning of "fright" (*Shreck*) leads to "apprehension" or "anxiety" (*Angst*), which is itself a preparation against, or protection from, the shock of "fright"—a preparatory inhibition which corresponds to adaptation of receptors (raising of the threshold).

[49] I am inclined to think that all of the great variety of responses to prevent injury are usually set off by conditioned stimuli. Even the so-called pain reflex of the laboratory —withdrawal of a limb, etc.—while it is doubtless the inherent pain reaction, seems to have often become too quick to be due directly to pain. Other cutaneous receptors, whose thresholds are lower, or impulses from which travel faster, are therefore able to convey their signal to the exterofective agency and even to consciousness earlier. Herrick (*190*, 309) says that pain is often delayed as compared to "tactile" stimuli; for "painful stimuli pass through a mechanism of slower reaction time." And see note 62, below. These senses report a stimulus of an intensity which the organism has learned to associate with injury (usually to be accompanied by pain). They identify or localize the peripheral source in a way which is impossible by means of the pain impulses alone. Localization is probably always cortical and perhaps always learned. Nafe says (*310*, 1039), "localization appears to be learned." And it is particularly poor for pain. The reaction is immediate to these conditioned stimuli, and the pain, if it is nevertheless produced, is at least not felt until momentarily later. Similarly may arise other so-called "protective reflexes" such as blinking. For this purpose the projicient senses are, of course, particularly well adapted, but the somatic may also serve. If these reactions are successful, they may prevent the injury and pain altogether—and this becomes the more possible the more projicient the source of the warning signal.

However, if both the want (injury) and its "signal" (pain) were as yet absent and therefore no consummatory reaction set in motion by them was active, how did these stimuli originally become conditioned; how did they lead to learning such skilled responses of avoidance? In the same way as salivation in Pavlov's dogs; that is, the to-be-conditioned stimulus must have first preceded and overlapped the unconditioned stimulus (injury) which aroused the pain reaction. So, "the burnt child dreads the fire."

Just as with the salivary reaction, the intensity of the reaction produced by a conditioned stimulus is less than that produced by the unconditioned one—in this case so much less that we do not "feel" pain by reason of the conditioned stimulus, but only fear, which "feels" different in kind though it may be only different in degree. In this

ferent from that of the quasi-internal want on which it is based. And the reinforcement necessary to cause and maintain the condition must be either the fact that the want does not arise—is prevented—or that the ultimate disappearance of the replica itself constitutes its own reinforcement.[50]

The replica, if it can be called such, which arises as a result of stimuli conditioned to internal wants behaves quite differently, perhaps because it is much weaker. It is doubtful whether it is ever effective in the complete absence of the want itself, though the intensity of the want requisite to make the replica effective and produce the reaction may vary through a wide range. In this respect subcortically conditioned stimuli—e.g., food in the mouth—appear to be more effective than cortically conditioned stimuli—e.g., the sight or smell of food. And here, certainly in the case of the cortically conditioned and probably also in that of the subcortically conditioned stimulus, the necessary reinforcement is always ultimately the cessation or reduction of

way, too, the successive overt reactions which ordinarily follow upon the pain reaction come also to follow upon the milder fear reaction. This interpretation can also be applied to conditioned stimuli built upon the other quasi-external wants.

[50] The fact that the failure of the unconditioned stimulus (the quasi-external want) to appear, because it is thus avoided, strengthens rather than extinguishes the conditioned response has been held to be evidence of "a secondary or learned motive" (Hilgard and Marquis, *197*, 87). This is unnecessary, for, after a time, the opposite is apt to be the case. Familiarity breeds contempt. If, after many repetitions, the conditioned stimulus fails to result in injury, say, it loses its power to excite the replica—fear. As Frolov puts it (*157*, 54), "if the signal [conditioned] ceases to be the herald of approaching prey or threatening danger, it ceases to be a signal and becomes a neutral phenomenon." Proximately, reinforcement in these cases probably consists in the disappearance of a replica, due to the reaction it has produced, and is thus exactly analogous to disappearance of the want which constitutes reinforcement in the case of internal wants. But the capacity of the conditioned stimulus to excite a replica may also disappear (i.e., it becomes unconditioned); in which case the recurrence of the want itself, preceded and accompanied by this stimulus, can recondition it. Thus "avoidance" is probably never the ultimate reinforcement, and we do not have to rely, mystically, on the absence of the cause as an explanation of the effect.

Freeman (*152*, 421) holds that all conditioned external stimuli come to have an increasing potency in arousing activity; so much so that the activity tends to divorce itself from the internal state and to respond to the external stimulus whether the state is present or not. He seems to have had chiefly in mind the quasi-external wants. William James took a similar position (*220*, II, 395). "A habit once grafted on an instinctive tendency" at least restricts that tendency to the first object upon which it fastens itself. And McDougall went further. He construes (*284*, 356) one of the functions of habits to be a "tendency to convert means into ends." In my judgment this "transference," as Rignano calls it (see below) is, in most cases, no more than the strengthening of a conditioning by long experience. And this because the conditioned external stimuli can equally well come to have a decreasing potency if they are not reinforced. On the other hand, there are other cases where what we shall call ancillary wants develop with reference to the reactions produced by other wants (see Chapter 4).

the want. For, since the conditioned stimulus and its replica are inadequate to produce the reaction alone, the question of the reinforcement of the replica cannot arise. In fact, it is doubtful if, in the absence of the want, the conditioned stimulus can produce a replica at all—that is, excite the hypothalamus in its particular mode. So far as external observation goes, one would judge that, in the absence of the want, the organism had no "interest" in the appropriate object. At least it evinces no emotion, not even the alert.

While the foregoing discussion has been almost wholly in terms of positive conditioning—that is, of the excitation of the appropriate responses to various wants by conditioned stimuli—it is clear that negative conditioning is equally prevalent—that is, the inhibition of the appropriate responses to various wants. So far as I recall, Pavlov did not consider negative conditioning, but only treated of a somewhat different process which he called "internal inhibition" and which we will consider in the next paragraph. This had four forms all of which consisted ultimately, not in negative conditioning, but in unconditioning a conditioned stimulus by failure to reinforce it.[51] But failure to reinforce will, in time, inhibit the regular response to all wants or their replicas, which is the same as saying all unconditioned as well as all conditioned stimuli. This is negative conditioning. Negative conditioning appears to be as capable of being produced subcortically as it is cortically, though, there, probably only after a much longer period of non-reinforcement. We have construed the early inhibition of the consummatory reaction to hunger, when the food object, etc., is lacking, to be a case of subcortical negative conditioning. In the next subsection we shall find it proper to construe the whole field of unsuccessful reactions, which are gradually discarded in the process of trial and error only because they are not reinforced by a cessation of the want, to be also negative conditioning; and in many cases these also appear to be subcortical.[52] But even the more general cortical conditioning leads as extensively to the suppression of reactions to wants as it does to their excitation. In fact, as noted in the previous chapter and in Ap-

[51] His four forms were experimental extinction (320, 49), conditioned inhibition (*ibid.*, 68)—as distinguished (*ibid.*, 87)—inhibition of delay (*ibid.*, 88), and differential inhibition (*ibid.*, 125).

[52] Of course, reactions to internal wants which are repressed because they are found, under certain conditions, to cause quasi-external wants are not cases of negative conditioning. These are cases of positive conditioning to the particular stimuli through the appearance of replicas of these quasi-external wants, which in turn suppress the internal wants.

pendix II, this form of inhibition is one of the chief functions of the cortex in its relation to the subcortical brain.

In much of the literature, negative conditioning seems to be confused with unconditioning. But the processes are quite different. What has come to be called unconditioning is covered by the four forms of Pavlov's internal inhibition. As he put it, "when a positive conditioned stimulus repeatedly remains unreinforced, it acquires inhibitory properties." [53] But it was his thesis that this occurs in the cortex itself. In accordance with our interpretation of his internal inhibition it consists of loss of "interest"—that is, the emotional divestment of a previously endowed cortical pattern. By that step the power of the pattern to excite the hypothalamus (produce a replica) is lost. The stimulus, the resulting pattern and its revivals have become unconditioned. The relationship to the want is broken. Obviously this can only be true of conditioned stimuli, though perhaps of subcortical as well as of cortical. It is never true of the want itself—the unconditioned stimulus—for what that excites in the hypothalamus is not a replica (secondary) but the real thing (primary). But negative conditioning works differently from unconditioning. With negative conditioning also, the appropriate reaction comes to be repressed if it is not reinforced by the cessation of the want which gives rise to the unconditioned stimulus or upon which the conditioned stimuli have been established. That is the only similarity, however. When the negative conditioning has been cortical, the cortical pattern has become emotionally endowed and its endowment remains intact. It excites the hypothalamus and produces a replica. But its effect is to suppress the appropriate reaction—to counter the ordinary effect of its own replica. It is not itself inhibited, nor is its emotional relation lost; but it inhibits the subcortical motor mechanisms. For example, mature carnivora have learned to suppress the spring or chase when they first see or scent their prey. Too often those actions did not result in reinforcement. Instead they wait and crouch or stalk until the right moment.[54] That process has resulted in more frequent reinforcement. But in the meantime the replica exists. In fact, because the motor outlets of the

[53] Pavlov, *320*, 234.
[54] "Thus, the savage animal which sees its prey approaching it in ignorance of danger, does not at once spring upon its victim, but, though excited by the most ardent desire, waits motionless, with all the muscles which will be used in the future spring in tension, until the poor animal approaches still nearer and comes within its reach" (Rignano, *345*, 208).

hypothalamus are inhibited, there are more signs of emotional excitement than attend the original and the still ultimate reaction. It may be possible for a subcortical conditioned stimulus to be conditioned negatively as well as positively, though I have been unable to find a certain case. However, though a want itself can probably never be unconditioned—that is, lose its power to excite the hypothalamus—it can certainly be negatively conditioned. As we have just noted, if the want does not achieve reinforcement by means of its original special reaction, that reaction is suppressed (inhibited). However, the hypothalamic effect appears to remain the same and merely to be diverted into some other and uninhibited reaction, which then, if reinforced, becomes the new but learned special reaction to that want. Is it not clear that this is the way in which the sucking reaction, for instance, comes permanently to be suppressed and the talking or the eating reaction comes to take its place? Is not this, as suggested below, the process of all trial and error learning?

Requirements for Conditioning. What Pavlov calls "integration" goes by various other names as well. In Appendix II we call it both "integration" and "synthesis," terms common in neurology. It is one of the types of synthesis which, in psychology, have been called "association of ideas." This particular type is the association based on simultaneity. That, in turn, allies it with the narrower concept of "Gestalt." It is, as we shall see in Chapter 5, Semon's "association," in his restricted meaning of that term. That is, it is the relation between two engrams entering into a single engram-complex.

This "association" is at first undiscriminating. "When conditioned reflexes are being established in dogs for the first time, it is found that the whole experimental environment, beginning with the introduction of the animal into the experimental room, acquires at first conditioned properties" (Pavlov, *320*, 115). Then, gradually, "differentiation" occurs by "contrasting the single definite conditioned stimulus, which was always accompanied by reinforcement, with different neighboring stimuli which were never reinforced" (*ibid.*, 117). Thus discrimination among all concurrent stimuli and the narrowing down of the "association" to the single to-be-conditioned stimulus (or Gestalt) is only the end-result of the process and is only established by reinforcement.

The usual psychological terms for reinforcement are "reward" and "punishment." Washburn says that "an animal will not learn without reward, except through punishment" (*427*, 325). Rewards and punishments are Pavlov's "unconditioned" stimuli. Thus Hilgard and Marquis (*197*, 70) assume that, in Pavlov's conditioning process, what he calls the "unconditioned" stimulus is the original stimulus which not only determines the form of the conditioned response but also constitutes the source of the reinforcement. As is shown in the following subsection, "instrumental conditioning" is an exception to the first statement, since, in that, the learned response is not the natural response to the "unconditioned" stimulus. And the second statement requires elaboration. Reinforcement, either by "reward" or by "punishment," is one and the same thing. "Reward," or reinforcement, is the partial or complete satisfaction of a naturally occurring want. When the want is imposed—usually quasi-external—as "punishment," it is the cessation of the want which constitutes the reinforcement. And that, too, is a "reward."

The requirement that the want—the "unconditioned" stimulus—should exist at the time applies to all internal wants. "With the conditioning of food reactions and some others, it is known that a certain emotional tension (related to hunger, pain or sex) is necessary for the formation of the conditioned reflex" (Gantt, *165*, 857). Or, more generally, "the most important of all conditions governing learning is the *motive* or *drive*" (Washburn, *427*, 323). Conditioning depends, in part, on "the nature of the cravings at the time of stimulation" (Kempf, *233*, 58). However, this requirement only applies to quasi-external wants when these are actual, unless one construes the existence of a surrogate quasi-external want, due to the threat of an actual one, to come to the same thing. While the following is stated in terms of reinforcement, it also furnishes evidence of the necessity of the existence of the want in order to establish or even to repeat conditioned responses: "Experimental results have shown that acts are reinforced if followed by presentation of food when the animal is hungry, by water when the animal is thirsty, by moderate temperatures when the animal is hot or cold, by a sex object when the animal is in heat, by infant offspring following parturition, by a free situation when the animal has been confined, and by escape from electric shock and other powerful or uncomfortable situations" (Hilgard and Marquis, *197*, 81). Note that, in the last two cases, it is the cessation of the imposed want that constitutes reinforcement.

There are two other minor, though essential, requirements for conditioning. These are readiness, or "an alert state of the nervous system" (Pavlov, *320*, 28), and freedom from distraction, either due to "any other nervous activity" (*ibid.*, 28), or by reason of the fact that the to-be-conditioned stimulus is so strong or unusual that it gives rise to a reaction of its own (*ibid.*, 29). Even after conditioning, any strong or unusual stimulus may inhibit the reaction by producing Pavlov's "investigatory reflex" (positive) or his "caution reflex" (negative), which supersede and therefore "externally inhibit" others (*ibid.*, 312). This matter of "interference" (our term for this supersession) will be discussed fully in the next chapter.

The "salivary reflex" (or "psychic secretion") was Pavlov's favorite. Bard (*19*, 299) refers to it as the *type* of "inborn, stereotyped, emotional reactions." In order, therefore, to generalize the foregoing statements to other responses we should add the qualification that it is always necessary to discover "some dependable unconditioned response on which to base the conditioning" (Hilgard and Marquis, *197*, 32).

2. LEARNING REACTIONS ADAPTED TO THE ENVIRONMENT

While, from the standpoint of exposition, it is convenient to differentiate the basic kind of learning—conditioning a particular external stimulus to a particular want—from that kind of learning which alters the nature or form of the response to a want, as a result of experience with the environment, it is already evident that the two are but different phases of the same process. For we have already had to consider several of these alterations of response.

The first type of learned alteration of response is the suppression of the primitive subcortical reaction due to failure of reinforcement. Thus, as noted above (pp. 134–135), hunger, the unconditioned stimulus to the sucking reaction, soon becomes an inhibitory conditioned stimulus in the absence of food in the mouth because, in such absence, hunger is not satisfied. Doubtless this negative conditioning is wholly subcortical. An example of cortical conditioning of the same type is the suppression of the spring or chase reactions cited above. In both these cases the suppression is temporary—that is, the subcortical reaction is later released (inhibition removed) by a conditioned stimulus. In other similar cases the suppression is practically permanent, though it always remains due to inhibition, not to absence of excitation; for it may always be released under certain conditions. It is doubtless in this way that the primitive sucking and grasp reflexes disappear among human beings after infancy—only to be restored when cortical restraint is removed.

This first type of alteration of reaction—negative conditioning—can work very fast, or is built upon a process that can work very fast; for the so-called method of trial and error involves at least the same underlying process. In that case the first reaction—presumably the primitive response to the want—ceases very quickly if it is unsuccessful, and some other reaction is tried. As Jennings expresses it, this process may give rise to "all the movements of which the animal is capable," "till one is found which is successful." [55] Without inhibition of the first reaction another could not be tried. But it does not follow that, with inhibition of the first reaction, another need be tried. Therefore these further trials require explanation. It appears that the nervous

[55] See p. 117, above. Presumably conditioning is not truly established until the repetition of the want leads regularly to the suppression of the primitive reaction. If so, negative conditioning builds upon a process as "innate" as does positive conditioning. That is, the failure of a reaction to secure prompt reinforcement produces its inhibition as "innately" as the appearance of the want originally produced its excitation.

energy of response developed in the subcortical centers, when it is inhibited as to its regular outlet by the first process, is *diverted* into some
other outlet or into a succession of other outlets. So far as I know we
have no neurophysiological explanation of this. The explanation is
therefore no more than an inference from external observation; but,
until a better one is available, it will have to stand as the hypothesis.

In the course of repetition the successful (reinforced) reaction in
such a series of trials becomes conditioned to the want.[56] This is the
second type of learned alteration of response. Unlike the first, it is positive; but it cannot occur until the first alteration has preceded it, for
it consists of the substitution of a different reaction for the primitive
reaction, or its successor, which has been suppressed. Exactly as in
the case of the conditioning of an external stimulus to a particular want
by overlapping in time and by reinforcement, in this case "the effective
factor in determining the selection of the 'correct' response is its
proximity in time to the reinforcement. The last response which occurs
prior to the reward [reinforcement] is the one most strongly reinforced." [57]

This process of establishment of conditioned (learned) reactions
by reinforcement has been used to explain, not, as here, the substitution
of one reaction for another, both of which may be consummatory,
but the "backward" development of the whole series of precurrent
reactions that may be necessary to permit a successful consummatory
reaction. As Washburn states it,[58] "The drive itself is a condition of
unrest produced by too little or too much of some substance of physio-

---

[56] Thus arises what Jennings calls (*223*, 312) the "readier resolution of physiological
states after repetition" of the successful reaction. It is his objective category, "memory
or habit" (*ibid.*, 333).

[57] Hilgard and Marquis, *197*, 84.

[58] Washburn, *427*, 333–335. Engell (*137*, 8) attributes the origin of this thesis to Watson,
who ascribes the gradual selection of the successful reaction and the suppression of all
others to "frequency and recency" on much the same basis (see *430*, 165–166). Rignano
uses much the same construction (*345*). An "affective tendency" is non-specific as to
ways and means but is specific as to "the point it strives to reach"—our objective, or
homeostasis. It is this which gives it the appearance of a *vis a fronte* and creates its unforeseen, anti-mechanistic character, as compared with the "pre-determined and mechanical behavior of the reflex" which "only admits of a single solution" (*ibid.*, 170).
"It is only when a series of movements has succeeded by chance better than others in
restoring the organism to the desired environmental conditions, that from that time on
it will be preferred to the others"; "that the affectivity will become . . . an impulsion
towards a given series of movements which bring about the desired end"; "that these
movements will be constantly repeated, under the influence of the affective tendency,
until they are 'mechanised' in the form of reflexes." Until then, "the affective tendency
is not impelled to discharge itself in one way rather than another" (*ibid.*, 169–170).

logical importance." It "is not a momentary stimulus . . . but a persistent physiological state that is present through the whole system of reaction." It "sets in readiness those movements which have habitually followed it and put an end to it; as for example the stomach movements and the flow of saliva, or chewing movements, in the case of hunger [consummatory reactions]. If these do not put an end to it, because some further stimulus [object] such as food is lacking, the physiological state sets in readiness those movements which have on former occasions occurred just before it came to an end"; and so on back, "step by step to those at the beginning of the earlier series." Thus it "may set in readiness any movements which occurred while it lasted on a previous occasion." [59] But it will energize most strongly those which "immediately preceded its resolution" and the "gradient of excitation" will descend from the last to the first, both by reason of the greater recency of the later reactions and because the want was presumably strongest just before the previous consummatory reaction occurred.[60]

While this process may account in part for the gradual conditioning of the members of a series of precurrent reactions according as they are found to be more or less conducive to making the consummatory reaction successful, the generalization must certainly be qualified. In the first place, it is entirely inconsistent with the order of development and the continuing order of activation of reactions from general to special, and therefore cannot apply to the original series of primitive and unlearned reactions. The evidence cited in the previous section showed that, among these, the general reaction (locomotion, etc.), which is not precisely the consummatory reaction even in the case of

[59] Woodworth has a similar view of the process. Precurrent reactions with specific objectives are evoked "when the mechanism for a consummatory reaction has been and is in activity," so that they are "driven" by the "inner tendency towards the consummatory reaction" (446, 40-41). The general tenor of this seems to be the same as that of Washburn's statement, but it cannot be true that the mechanism is specific as to a particular consummatory reaction; for this may change. Rather it is specific as to the want, and the only "inner tendency" is continuing central excitation in some particular mode until, by some means, the want is corrected and the resulting excitation ceases.

[60] These conclusions of Washburn's were directly derived as inferences from external observation. The analysis of the drive and its effect conforms to ours and to the essentials of the conditioning process. There is no explanation of the reason why other movements should have occurred on previous occasions. But our "diversion of nervous energy of response" hypothesis seems to supply the deficiency, so far as it goes. Finally, the "gradient of excitation" from the consummatory back to the first precurrent reaction conforms to Sherrington's observation as to the gradient of affective tone (see p. 129, above).

quasi-external wants, not only develops first but probably always precedes the special reaction, even if only potentially (inhibited). That is, these primitive and subcortical general reactions are the first responses to wants and only give place to special (consummatory) reactions when the want arrives at a sufficient state of intensity. The first part of this primitive general reaction we have described as the "alert"; the second part, as "restlessness" or locomotion. It is evident that these are originally and directly excited by the want and occur before the want has excited its corresponding primitive special or consummatory reaction. In the case of defecation (and probably micturition), the consummatory reaction may follow in due course. But the precurrent reaction is evidently one phase of the whole process and does not in any respect depend on the consummatory one. In the case of internal wants requiring an external object for satisfaction (hunger, thirst, sex), the several parts of this general reaction are inherently qualified to enable the organism to stumble upon the necessary object. If this external object has been conditioned to the want (probably always necessary), the consummatory reaction (e.g., killing, mastication and swallowing) [61] follows, again in due course. Again the precurrent reaction does not depend on the consummatory one. It precedes the latter and is excited independently of it. Only if the precurrent reaction is unsuccessful or unnecessary would it have to become conditioned, and then negatively—learning not to do. If it is successful, it is continually reinforced and thus remains the first reaction to the want— the first phase of the whole process. In the case of the quasi-external wants, as noted on p. 124, it is difficult to divide precurrent from consummatory reactions. All the reactions are of general (locomotion) rather than special nature—righting and the fear reaction from loss of equilibrium or support, escape and the fear reaction from loud noise, etc., attack and the rage reaction from restraint, and escape or withdrawal from the source of injury (pain). The primitive response may turn out to be successful (and thus consummatory) or it may not.[62]

[61] See pp. 127–128, above.
[62] For instance, the reaction to bodily injury is not of a single nature—in the simple thesis of the reflexologist, "withdrawal" or "escape." When an injury is actually suffered, the resulting pain may lead to general or special movement which in turn may result in escape from the causing agency. But, even then, the pain may persist. The next reaction is apt to be immobility—what Hess (192, 726) calls the "reflex of rest." Adrian (3, 101) takes the same view. He says the first reaction may be "withdrawal," the second, rest, because further movements "renew or reinforce the excitation." In the case of visceral injury the "reflex of rest" is the first reaction. In both cases it is probably

But, even if it does not, it is unlearned with the greatest difficulty. What needs to be explained is why the failure of reinforcement tends so slowly, or not at all, to lead to negative conditioning—in Washburn's terms, why the primitive reaction continues to be energized so strongly in spite of the fact that it did not immediately precede the resolution of the state; and this cannot be explained on Washburn's basis.

It is evident, then, that the primitive precurrent reactions stand on their own feet. They are not dependencies or outgrowths of the consummatory reactions. Moreover, they are unconditioned and sometimes they do not submit readily to negative conditioning. On the other hand, substitution can take place rather quickly. Trial and error shows that the primitive precurrent reaction can be suppressed, if it fails, and that this may in time turn into permanent negative conditioning. Perhaps its successor is selected and conditioned on the basis Washburn outlines. Even then, however, it is equally possible that it is nervously energized by the process we have described as "diversion" and thus by the nervous energy formerly going to the primitive precurrent reaction rather than by courtesy of its time relationship to the successful consummatory reaction. That is, the relation of the new to the old precurrent reaction may be direct. It is also possible that the selected reaction is not positively conditioned at all. Instead, it may be that its competitors become gradually negatively conditioned, leaving it the sole beneficiary of "diversion." Thus either construction can be placed on the evidence available now, and it is necessary to await further experimentation directed at this question before it can be settled.

What is called "instrumental conditioning" consists primarily of this second type of learned alteration of response. The subject has been confused by the persisting external stimulus-response viewpoint. In their recent résumé of the whole subject of conditioning, Hilgard and Marquis say that, while in this type the conditioned response is instrumental in bringing about the reinforcement, it "may be entirely unlike

---

a tonic rigidity, not relaxation. Finally, if the pain persists in spite of immobility—that is, if the first or second reactions do not cause the pain to stop—a third reaction, general motion, writhing, etc., may result—and in the alimentary tract, "even a retrograde removal of the content" (Hess, *192*, 309), which is an extraordinarily complex operation (Cannon, *66*, 216). These may all be regarded as constituting a repertory of innate reactions. But only that one is consummatory which happens to stop the pain. Which of these is to be conceived to be "in activity," even subliminally, to provide the "drive" or "inner tendency" for preparatory reactions?

the response to the reinforcing stimulus" and therefore cannot be accounted for by the latter. Instead, the response is "determined by the drive," which may be regarded as "a conditioned stimulus evoking specific behavior." [63] This precisely reverses the relationship as we have construed it above. The drive or want is the unconditioned stimulus, and is always and only that except in negative conditioning. The reinforcement is the partial or complete satisfaction of that want. The primary conditioning process here consists in teaching the suppression of the primitive reaction by means of negative conditioning and the substitution of any other reaction desired by means of positive conditioning (i.e., by reinforcement with reward, escape, avoidance, or token of reward). If this substitution is the result of experience (natural conditioning) it forms the basis of insight and of what is called "purposive behavior." But, since in a laboratory experiment the response does not have to be really responsible for the reinforcement, the insight such teaching may lead to is insight into the arbitrary mental vagaries of the experimentor rather than into the "laws of nature." [64] Upon such a primary instrumental conditioning may be superimposed a secondary one. But this secondary conditioning is no other than the conditioning of external stimuli to wants which we considered above. Any suitable external stimulus which is the adequate unconditioned stimulus (want) of a primitive response, or which has become the conditioned stimulus to any want and its response, can be "instrumentally" conditioned, along with its response, to a second want the satisfaction of which is to provide the reinforcement, provided only that this second want is "physiologically stronger," as Pavlov put it, than is the first.[65] That is, a dog, for instance, can be trained to lie down when told to do so (conditioned stimulus to lying down) by a reward of food (reinforcement) when he does so. In so far as this process becomes conditioned to hunger—and not to fear, etc.—it will gradually become unconditioned if it is not reinforced with food. Ultimately, therefore, the external stimulus has become conditioned to the hunger want and the new response has become substituted for the primitive

[63] Hilgard and Marquis, 197, 65–66.
[64] Such substitutions, both when natural and also when artificial, if not coached, are what Hilgard and Marquis (197, 66) call self-initiated acts, not really random or spontaneous, and not due to external stimuli.
[65] Substitutions of this kind, dependent on some special stimulus, are of the type Hilgard and Marquis refer to (197, 70) where the original stimulus determines the form of response, though both stimulus and response are entirely distinct from the reinforcement. Nevertheless, failure of the reinforcement extinguishes the conditioning.

one, but only in the presence of the conditioned external stimulus.[66] Similar transpositions are seen in what, in Appendix II, we called "the remarkable dislocations of the normal relation between stimulus and response which Pavlov produced in his conditioning experiments." His conditioning of nocuous stimuli to the alimentary reflex [67]—completely eliminated the ordinary defense reaction to the former and substituted all the behavior of the alimentary reflex. Again this could only be done because hunger was physiologically stronger than these pains. While such examples are not strictly "instrumental," since no new reaction to the dominant unconditioned stimulus is substituted, they are allied because, in both cases, the unconditioned stimulus to one want may become a conditioned stimulus to another and stronger want. And, in both cases, the dominant want is proved by the nature of the required reinforcement.

The third type of learned alteration of response consists of changes in the form of movements themselves away from the primitive synergies. It is the fractionating or modification of these synergies into discrete and adapted or skillful movements. Since, among primates, the pyramidal tract is entirely responsible for effecting all such alterations, as we noted in the preceding chapter, it is necessarily true that this process is with them wholly cortical. This is also evident from the fact that, since the modifications are fine adaptations to the environment, the means by which the external data upon which they are based are appreciated must be sensory and therefore also cortical.[68] While, in certain respects, the process is analogous to conditioning and is always a vital and principal element in learning, the exteroceptive circuit runs directly from the sensory to the motor cortex and, so far as the proprioceptive guidance is concerned, is probably afferent directly to the motor cortex itself. Thus, this conditioning, if it may be called that, does not involve the subcortical brain so far as the improvement of the motion is concerned, even though the motion itself

[66] Learning of both these types is common in the natural state—without training. A dog learns, when hot, to dig down to damp earth and lie with his belly on it. This is not the primitive heat response. It is a learned substitute. He also learns to leave his calling card where other dogs have done so; but the conditioned stimulus here (smell) and its response (micturition) appear to have become conditioned to another want, rage, to judge by the growling and clawing that usually follow.

[67] Pavlov, 320, 29–30.

[68] Functions which have become wholly cortical at the highest phylogenetic level are less exclusively so among lower animals. This must be borne in mind, and subsequent statements must be qualified according to the zoölogical order the reader happens to have in mind.

may be driven by a want and the want may have been aroused or reinforced by a conditioned stimulus. It is this distinction that has led us to differentiate the two elements in all motions. The one, the basic synergies which are available both to the subcortical and cortical brain, come to be fractionated or modified by the second element, the effects of the motor cortex proper. But what the second element contributes by its selective excitation and inhibition is the change rather than the motion. It is the driver rather than the drive. It merely canalizes and directs the drive. Thus what it is controlling—the impulse—may continue to take the form of the original synergy, though more or less inhibited. In this way motion comes to be a mixture, in widely varying degrees, of these two elements, the skillful, or adapted, or cortical, and the emotional, or random, or subcortical. Since almost all the primitive synergies come to be modified and split up after this fashion —except when they reappear in their pure form in the wildest outbursts of emotional behavior—these more or less adapted and more or less modified movements come in time to compose almost the whole repertory of motions of a mature animal. Therefore, they come to be the normal responses to wants, varying somewhat in the strength of their emotional component; then all the other forms of learning we have described come to deal with the members of this enlarged repertory. Thereafter, the response to any conditioned external stimulus may be such a skilled action; it may be these which are suppressed by the first type of alteration of response, and it may be these which are substituted for the primitive synergies as well as among themselves.[69] But the test for all this learning, whether skilled or primitive (usually mixed), remains reinforcement. That is, a fractionated or modified motion also. becomes positively conditioned only when it proves successful, or more successful, in leading to the satisfaction of the want which has neurally energized it.[70] Or conversely, to the extent that all other

[69] It is because all these learning processes have been and are concurrent in the experimental animal that Hilgard and Marquis (*197*, 36–39) can say that the conditioned response is "very complex and not often identical with the unconditioned." What they call redintegrative responses (Pavlov's type, because he chose to work with them) are practically the same for conditioned as for unconditioned stimuli. "Fractional responses" constitute parts only, and "preparatory responses" are different because the "subject is getting ready." But the difference all depends on the extent of previous alteration of responses.

[70] It might be said that it then becomes "habitual." But this is a large term covering many different processes. I have preferred to reserve this term for one special technical sense, confining it to cortical motor behavior. An habitual action is different from an automatic one (i.e., subcortical or uncontrolled cortical). It is an adapted action (py-

and failing attempts, however skillful, become negatively conditioned, the successful one remains the beneficiary of "diversion," though here of "diversion" via the cortical motor system.

Though they come to be much modified—in the absence of great excitement—in the course of the development of this second element in behavior—the canalizing and directive element—the original synergies remain still recognizable and continue to fix the general character of most motions. The least specific and usually first response to any want, which we have called the alert, is little changed; however, it comes to be set off by innumerable conditioned stimuli which reach only the cortex, though it also continues to be the first effect of those unconditioned but external stimuli which are conveyed to the subcortical brain direct. Restlessness may be repressed so that it leaks out only as "fidgets" and other innumerable "nervous habits" which connote restrained excitement. Locomotion retains its original form and its automatic grace; but the capacity suddenly to change direction, to alternate with it the leaping over obstacles, and to spring from a crouching start are all learned. So, too, are probably most of the hundred and one habits which arise to modify the form of the various special reactions—eating, drinking, sexual acts, defecation, micturition, etc.—and which differentiate mature from infant behavior.

C. BEHAVIOR AS THE RESULTANT OF INTERNAL AND EXTERNAL INFLUENCES

Having erected this construction as to behavior with reference to the internal and external environments and having reconciled it with the neurological scheme already developed, it is now necessary, for the sake of clarification, to tear down some of the scaffolding with the aid of which it was built. The first scaffolds we need to get rid of are the dichotomies we have borrowed from the authorities cited in this chapter. Behavior among mature higher animals cannot be divided into two kinds according to any of these criteria. There are not, on the one hand, kinds of actions which are responses to external stimuli and, on the other, kinds of actions which are spontaneous—that is, actions cannot be classified as exogenous or endogenous. Almost all actions are

ramidal) which no longer requires deliberation and therefore consciousness, in its performance. It can be deliberately, or voluntarily, or consciously started, stopped, and even modified, but the rest of the performance takes care of itself. In fact, when it is left to do so, the performance is far better.

both.[1] Apart from the most excited responses to quasi-external wants, which are somewhat anomalous, all are endogenous. But they also have an exogenous feature, orientation, which is "essentially the modification of the endogenous activity." [2] Thus the energizing of such behavior is endogenous or spontaneous, but its orientation and modification are exogenous. It is generated from the internal environment, but it is guided and adapted by, and to, the facts of the external environment. Neither are there kinds of actions which are precurrent and kinds which are consummatory. Instead, reactions to a present want take place in series during the existence of the want. Some may appear toward the beginning of the series, when the want first becomes effective, and some may appear toward the end, when it is about to be satisfied. But there is no definite line between; in many cases, there is no uniform consummatory (final) reaction; in others, the whole series may be repeated several or many times before satisfaction is achieved and the want ceases to be active.[3] All are parts of one process from general to special; the process is always continuous and often variable. Neither is it possible to identify certain reactions as unlearned and certain others as learned. There is a process called learning. It comes to suppress some of the primitive reactions; to substitute some for others; and to modify the form of almost all. To that extent all are learned. Nevertheless all the primitive reactions continue potential and continue as the basis of the modified system. To that extent all are unlearned.

Furthermore all these dichotomies, even if they are converted into terms of the two component elements of actions in which they exist as mixtures in various proportions, seem to fail to serve the purpose. For the distinction which best interprets the facts and which seems to underlie these others is a different one. That distinction is between the two components in behavior which we have called the subcortical and the cortical components. These two are definite, recognizable, and traceable; but they do not precisely conform to those classifications which have risen from external observation only. It is true that the subcortical brain represents chiefly the internal environment, while the cortex represents chiefly the external environment.[4] But the subcortical brain may be directly excited by the quasi-external wants, whose

[1] Cf. Jennings, p. 117, above, and Tracy, p. 118, above.
[2] See Tracy, quoted above, p. 119.
[3] E.g., drinking, eating, and even the sexual act.
[4] The cortex is "the immediate projection of the external world" (Frolov, 177, 78).

stimuli are relations with the external world; or, for that matter by any external stimuli capable of reaching it directly; and, on the other hand, the cortical activities are to a large extent dominated and driven by present wants acting upon the cortex through the subcortical mechanisms. Therefore, neither component is wholly endogenous nor wholly exogenous. It is true that the subcortical system develops, from the egg, almost wholly under internal influences and is almost unaffected by external influences; but it can be directly excited by a few kinds of crude stimuli from the external world, though it has but the grossest appreciation of the environment. It is also true, on the other hand, that the cortical system develops, chiefly after birth, almost wholly under external influences; but these have their effect chiefly through their relation to the internal. It is under the spur of this latter relation that the cortical system acquires its finesse. Nor does one system have charge of precurrent (distance receptors) and the other of consummatory (interoceptive) reactions, as Sherrington described them. The first precurrent reaction, in many cases, is the alert, which is wholly subcortical, though it may also become conditioned to a stimulus that can only be appreciated in the cortex. And the last or most consummatory reaction may come to be one of the most skillful and adapted modifications of a primitive synergy that is to be observed—for example, walking the tightrope as a means of preventing loss of equilibrium and of support and as a reaction excited by a replica of this want. Again, one cannot say that subcortical reactions are "innate" and cortical reactions are learned. We have seen that learning may affect both systems, though its chief field is doubtless the cortex. It is true that the subcortical component in behavior is largely governed by the growth of the individual along lines which are stereotyped for a species. It is not true, however, that this component does not change during maturation, even before birth; [5] nor is it wholly invariable within a species, even among

[5] At this point we may raise another question which the term "innate" evades or begs. As Haldane pointed out, it is not possible strictly to separate the internal from the external environment. The two constitute a continuum. The same difficulty arises as to temporal division. Is the embryo, during its intra-uterine life, to be regarded as being in contact with an external environment? If so, at what stage does it become so—as the egg, as the fertilized egg, as the fetus, or only as the embryo? Are its reactions, then, in part reactions to its maternal environment—external rather than internal? At birth there occurs a marked change, and the infant is suddenly exposed to a new and wholly different external environment (the trauma of birth, Freud). Is this to be regarded as a first exposure or only as a sharp step-up in an expanding series of external influences? If the latter, why should we treat the effects of the maternal environment as innate and

normal specimens. Individuals vary in their subcortical make-up.

Perhaps we should differentiate between maturation, developing disposition (temperament or idiosyncrasy), and learning in the subcortical component. Perhaps we should limit subcortical learning to negative conditioning (suppression of primitive responses). Perhaps we should assign to maturation all the gradual perfecting of the primitive synergies that comes about with muscular development and with the blending of the various influences into what we call co-ordination. Perhaps we should allow for some variation on the score of different dispositions. If so, we should have to include in the inherent or innate category all those modifications and variations deemed to be due to maturation or disposition and reserve for the learned category only those which were certainly adaptations to the environment.[6] Even then it would be difficult, if not impossible, actually to distinguish in a particular case how much and what details of any mature synergy were the result of each of these factors. Nor could we be sure that such part of these alterations in the primitive synergies as we decided to assign to learning was actually subcortical.[7] On the other hand, the cortical element in behavior is not wholly the result of experience with the external environment (learning). It, too, has certain stereotyped features laid down in the germ and which develop along definitely established lines, for each species, from the embryo to death. Finally, we must remind the reader that even this distinction between the subcortical and the cortical components in behavior is not a hard and fast one and never applies in the same way to two different species. For the cortex is morphologically an outgrowth of the subcortical brain,

---

those of the new world as learned? Is it not all of it one continually expanding process? Innate, or inborn, is the wrong term. Inherent or hereditary would be better, since what we mean to designate are those features which are the results of the internal tendencies of growth.

Dunlap makes a nice distinction in this matter. He says (*123*, 210, note 98); "The actual meanings of the terms 'acquired' and 'innate' are liable to serious confusion. Innate predispositions are not necessarily operative at birth; many of them appear much later, and some are operative before birth. Predispositions acquired by the process of growth, and general reactions, and not dependent on the animal's previous reactions of the same type, are not 'acquired' in the sense in which the term is technically used. *Inherent* and *learned* are much better terms."

[6] With these qualifications, our statement of the case on p. 96 is approximately correct.

[7] At the earliest stages the whole might be assigned to subcortical learning by a process of elimination, because the cortex would be assumed to be there undeveloped. Frolov (*157*, 86–87) interprets the change in a newborn babe's sucking, from a crude to a skillful performance, as the effect of conditioning to external stimuli. Presumably this conditioning is, at that stage, subcortical.

and its degree of development depends on the phylogenetic and ontogenetic stage; moreover it is concerned with the elaboration of functions which were, and to some extent remain, operative in a cruder form in the subcortical brain.[8]

Nevertheless, the distinction between the subcortical and the cortical components in behavior is the basic one and does furnish the key to the exceptions as well as to the rules. The subcortical component does determine the nature of the response, if a present want is dominating, and the cortical element does determine the relation of the orientation so directed to the proximate, if not to the ultimate, facts of the environment. The subcortical component represents and contributes the emotional or affective attributes of the response, while the cortical represents the attributes of restraint and of skill. Thus, in the early stages of a series (precurrent), when the facts of the external world are non-co-operating, the second component must usually predominate if the series is to be successful, while in the later stages (consummatory), when these facts have succumbed to treatment, the first component is usually adequate and can be released. Again it is true that the first component represents, almost wholly, neural operations which are inherent in the organism, while the second comes to represent almost wholly those that are acquired (i.e., modified by experience with the external environment).

However, the two components are rarely seen separately. That is, when behavior is dictated by present wants these two components are almost always combined, though in widely varying proportions. Under such conditions, behavior is rarely subcortical only (excited emotion), and never cortical only. The repertory of primitive synergies is subcortical. These are perhaps unmodifiable subcortically, but they can be conditioned negatively and perhaps positively through subcortical conditioning. It is this repertory which is used and modified by the cortex. Through its power to excite the subcortical brain (cortically conditioned stimulus) it can arouse these reactions. Through

---

[8] Phylogenetic position is the chief determinant of the relative development of the two components. As Hering said (*189*, 84), "the brain [cortex] of man at birth is much farther from its highest development than is the brain of an animal." "Man's brain, and indeed his whole body, affords greater scope for individuality, inasmuch as a relatively greater part of it is of post-natal growth. It develops under the influence of impressions made by the environment upon its senses, and thus makes its acquisitions in a more special and individual manner, whereas the animal receives them ready made [inherited] and of a more final, stereotyped character."

its power to inhibit that brain it can suppress these reactions or canalize their neural energy into its own adaptations of the same. Thus the ultimate repertory of usual behavior in response to present wants consists of cortically modified subcortical reactions, neurally energized both directly (leakage) and indirectly (the emotional stream). On the other hand, this cortical component is always limited, not only according to the degree of maturation (ontogenetic development), but also by the position of the species in the phylogenetic scale. The latter limit is roughly fixed; the former continually widens with the development of the individual and with experience, chiefly the experience of successfully relating the subcortical component to the external world.

Interpreted in this light, all of the distinctions considered in this chapter fall away into characteristics which blend together into a single scheme. We have concluded that the evidencing of "interest" by an organism in any particular element of the external scene is the indicium, most of the time, of a conditioning process toward that element (conditioned stimulus). That is, conditioning of this kind is the process of connecting such an external element with a present want. And it is the want which, through this connection, confers the "interest" and leads to the phenomena of "conscious attention" and of orientation directed toward this element.[9] True, certain elements in the external scene are of "interest" without conditioning, if one includes those stimuli which are the causes of quasi-external wants and of the inherent responses to them. But we conceive the difference between a conditioned and an unconditioned stimulus not to be a hard and fast one. Rather we think of the development of the organism as being

[9] While in his day, of course, the process of conditioning had not yet been "discovered" and therefore his terminology is different, it is remarkable to note the close correspondence, to these statements, of William James's statements in regard to "passive immediate sensorial attention." He says (220, I, 416–417) that the required stimulus for such attention is a "sense impression, either very intense, voluminous or sudden,—in which case it makes no difference what its nature may be, whether sight, sound, smell, blow, or inner pain,—or else it is an *instinctive* stimulus, a perception which, by reason of its nature rather than its mere force, appeals to some one of our normal congenital impulses and has a directly exciting quality." The first class includes the causes of our quasi-external wants whose effects are directly appreciable in the hypothalamus, are not strictly sense impressions at all, and which are unconditioned stimuli. The second, related to all of our list of wants, includes, we think, only conditioned stimuli, though James thought that some are "innate" and only the rest are "derived." Their effects are only appreciable in the cortex; but, by means of synthesis (endowment with emotion = instinctive impulse), they become capable of indirectly exciting the hypothalamus.

continuous from the egg to death. Those influences which govern its early development are chiefly internal, few, powerful, regular, and frequently recurring, as well as nearly uniform among the individuals of a species in a single habitat. Gradually there come to be superimposed on these a vast multitude of chiefly external, less powerful or even weak influences which are highly variable and irregular in their recurrence, as well as heterogeneous for different individuals according to slightly different circumstances. As this complex comes to bear it requires and develops a much more facile apparatus for appreciating it and for responding to it.[10] But the process is not then fundamentally different. The conditioning mechanism is not fundamentally different from the mechanism of the so-called inherent responses. The differences are in degree of complication; and, in the last analysis, complication is merely the result of the complexity of influence.

Thus the point at which one draws the line between unconditioned and conditioned stimuli and between inherent and learned responses is a necessarily arbitrary division in a continuum—a process of development which proceeds in the individual from conception to maturation, and even thereafter, and which is only limited in each instance to the inherent possibilities and by the inherent impossibilities which are fixed for that species at that age in rough accord with its position in the phylogenetic scale.[11]

It may be well, before passing on, to relate this scheme of the internal mechanisms and their external activities (behavior) to the more tenable forms of instinct psychology as it still appears among psychologists and to some extent among zoölogists. In the first place, the term, instinct, is generally applied both to actions of a certain kind and to the imputed causes of these actions.[12] In this second sense the term is practically pure word-magic. "To call an action instinctive is merely to cover our ignorance."[13] But, on the basis of observation, to classify actions of certain uniform types as instincts may be useful, because it may lead to discovery of some uniformity in their causa-

[10] In certain respects the distinction between these two classes of influence conforms, or is analogous, to the distinction Langmuir makes between *convergent vs. divergent* phenomena (*249, 3*). For a further discussion, see Appendix III F.

[11] Or, conversely; for the concept of a phylogenetic scale is, to a large extent, the result of an arrangement according to these limits.

[12] Having described certain kinds of actions which are technically called instincts (see below), Fraenkel and Gunn (*149, 314*) state that "even technically the word 'instinct' has the second quite distinct meaning of drive or urge."

[13] As Fraenkel and Gunn put it (*149, 314*). They say that "Loeb was very vigorous in pointing out that to call an action instinctive is merely to cover our ignorance,"

tion or mechanisms and thus justify the practice. In technical usage, the term is applied to actions which are unhesitating, inherent, complex, and stereotyped.[14] Under the first criterion it is intended to exclude all actions that are deliberate; under the second all that are learned; under the third all autonomic activities, all spinal reflexes and most single actions not component parts of extensive patterns or series; under the fourth all those that vary considerably upon repetition or among different members of a species.[15] In other words, instincts, or instinctive actions, are approximately what we have been calling primitive synergies and the sequences into which these regularly enter. Since we have found that such synergies are the integrated subcortical reactions which prevail in their original form, both phylogenetically and ontogenetically, in inverse proportion to the development of the cortex, it does not surprise us to learn that instinctive actions play a much smaller part among mammals than among arthropods or even among birds, that "the more variable kinds of reaction involving learning take a larger part" among mammals, and that, so far as reactions at the opposite pole are concerned (deliberate behavior and its preparatory deliberation or insight), there is "no reliable evidence at all of its occurrence outside the Mammalia." [16] The gradual diminution in the relative importance of the repertory of instinctive behavior, as we proceed along the phylogenetic scale, seems to follow closely the gradations in adequacy for the maintenance of life of the subcortical brain when it is deprived of the cortex. We have already noted that this varies from absolute inadequacy in the case of mature primates, through impaired competence in the case of two carnivorous species, down to

[14] Fraenkl and Gunn use the method of successive elimination in their definition (*149*, 314). Actions "without hesitation or taking thought" may be "acquired automatisms" or "inborn reflexes." The latter may be simple or complex. "Only those which are both inborn and complex are technically called instincts." And (*ibid.*, 301), "Instincts—that is to say, complex behavior patterns as distinct from the basic urges or drives—are generally regarded as very fixed."

Two of these features are well brought out by Rogers's description (*352*, 24): "The instinctive activities of birds exhibit a great series of complex reactions to internal and environmental stimuli. ["The mating and nesting behavior of the pigeon comprises a series of at least a dozen separate types of activity each following the other in definite sequence" (*ibid.*, 25).] As a whole, these 'cycles' of reactions are stereotyped in character."

[15] McDougall seems to regard this last point as the crucial one. He says the criterion for instinctive behavior now is that it is "common to all members of any one species" (*284*, 23).

[16] Fraenkel and Gunn, *149*, 303–304. What we have called deliberation or insight they call "intelligence," which is evidenced by the fact that "new responses to new situations may occur at the first trial.

apparently complete competence in the case of birds (pigeons).[17] But that parallel may prove too much. Among the lower orders of animal life all subcortical behavior may not be instinctive. If the cortex develops and gradually takes over a function—learning, conditioning, or synthesis—which is nevertheless originally subcortical, it may be that the animal with relatively little cortex learns, within much narrower limits, subcortically. Perhaps what has been called instinctive behavior is very largely learned, but only appears stereotyped because the influences which produce it are very limited in number and very uniform, both upon repetition in a single individual and among different individuals of the same species in a uniform habitat.[18] At any rate, for mature man who is our subject, one has to conclude that instinctive behavior, precisely defined, hardly appears as such except in fragmentary form, and that, though it constitutes the basis of behavior, it has become so overlayed with modification and fractionation that it is hardly any longer to be recognized in complete specimens of behavior.

The instinctive quality in behavior is, then, the integrated subcortical component in that behavior. Upon that basis it becomes possible for us to eliminate the other use of the term instinct—the imputed cause of such components—and thus to substitute for its vague and somewhat mystical connotations precise and observable phenomena. Since we have devoted the first two chapters to detailed examination of the neurophysiological evidence as to the causation of many of these synergies, it is not necessary to repeat the analysis here. Suffice it to say that this component of behavior has its original source in present wants—that is, it is a part of the effect of a variation, or tendency,

[17] Among pigeons, "Loss of all but traces of the cerebral cortex but leaving the major part of the hyperstriatum intact is followed by no characteristic behavior deficiencies" —that is, "feeding, drinking, mating, nesting, incubation and rearing of young go on much as before" (Rogers, 352, 50). The hyperstriatum is a relatively large area between the corpus striatum and the cortex (ibid., 22). Its precise homology is undetermined, but, if it can be identified with Elliott Smith's hypopallium (birds), it is at least subcortical. In birds, however, the "true cortex" is small and primitive in type and of unknown functional value (ibid., 22). And, in birds, the hyperstriatum can carry out a simple association or learning process (ibid., 50).

[18] Though he continues to call them instinctive actions, Frolov (157, 37) agrees that it is difficult to separate "inborn from acquired" parts of them. Craig found, even with pigeons, that the series of mating reactions are "dependent on preliminary association with other birds" and therefore involve "a certain degree of learning" (cited by Rogers, 352, 32). Since it is probable that so-called instinctive behavior is very largely learned, wherever the evidence does not prove that it is an inherent primitive reaction to an unconditioned stimulus, it is safer to describe the behavior as learned. That does not mean that it is not a response to a present want.

away from homeostasis in some respect. In so far as such an upset in the balance of bodily processes is propagated to the highest level of the subcortical brain, it produces there what we have called an emotional state (i.e., generalized central excitation or depression). From that point onward the course followed is divided. That part which proceeds directly to the motor apparatus (chiefly) is what is usually called emotional expression. But this expression consists of the primitive synergies. That part which proceeds to the cortex sets up there the emotional experience or emotion, proper. But this second part provides also the neural energy which is cortically directed, with fractionation, modification, and orientation, into the primitive synergy. Shall the whole of this process be called instinct? If so, why distinguish, as accompaniments, the emotional expression or the emotional experience which are no more than stages or phases of the process? And how appropriate are the connotations of the term to the wants themselves, when these are recognized to include such phenomena as, for example, the osmotic effects of hypersalinity (the need of water)? If the whole of this process is not to be defined as instinct, then what part can be appropriately so called? Is it the want? Is it the centripetal transmission of the want? Is it the subcortical central state (emotional state) so established? Is it the cortical effect of this state (emotion proper)? Or is instinct, in this sense, merely a term for an attribute of the process—the inveterate regularity which seems to be characteristic of them all?

The Question of Instinct. This is no place for a discussion of instinct psychology. But it may clarify matters if we consider two samples of it, William James's and William McDougall's, and show in what respects they differ from or confuse the elements of our scheme.

To James (*220*, II, 383) instincts are certain faculties of acting which are "the functional correlatives of structure," all of which "conform to the general reflex type" (*ibid.*, II, 384) and are "blind, automatic and untaught" (*ibid.*, II, 437). The nervous system is to a great extent a preorganized bundle of such reactions (*loc. cit.*). But the instincts are not, or are not only, the actions; they are also the "definite tendencies to act" (*ibid.*, II, 383) or impulses; so that "every instinct is an impulse. Whether we shall call such impulses as blushing, sneezing, coughing, smiling or dodging, or keeping time to music, instincts or not, is a mere matter of terminology. The process is the same throughout" (*ibid.*, II, 385). He speaks of his analysis as physiological (*ibid.*, II, 440, note). However, all his instincts (human) are described in terms of external behavior and are limited to responses to external stimuli (*ibid.*, II, 403–440); he does not include the "vegetative physiological functions" (*ibid.*, II, 440, note), except perhaps the sexual one (*ibid.*, II, 437); and "kinds of activity" are called instinctive, so far as they "may be *naturally* provoked by the presence of specific sorts of outward fact" (*ibid.*, II, 403); "they are called forth by determinate sensory stimuli in contact with the animal's body, or at a distance in his environment" (*ibid.*, II, 384). Finally, though "every object that excites an instinct excites an emotion as well," "instinctive reactions and emotional expressions" are different in that "the emotional reaction usually terminates in the subject's own body, whilst the instinctive reaction is apt to go farther and enter into practical relations with the exciting object" (*ibid.*, II, 442).

From our viewpoint such a classification serves no useful purpose and, in many cases, cannot be carried through. Behavior in response to present wants is a part of emotional expression, though one may, if one chooses, differentiate the motor effects from the autonomic effects. There is a repertory of inherent motor acts (primitive synergies), both general and special, available as direct outlets for the central excitation produced subcortically by these wants. But in so far as these acts are provoked by "specific sorts of outward fact" the provocation is chiefly the result of conditioning or learning and, according to age and position in the phylogenetic scale, the effect is that the acts themselves become more and more modified by learning.

Take one example of the difficulty, if not impossibility, of distinguishing certain acts as instinctive and others as learned. We say the child "learns" to walk. James holds (*ibid.*, II, 406–407) that what occurs is the "mere ripening of his nerve-centres." But is not all learning such a "ripening"? (See Coghill, above.) Is not the difference between the relative uniformity of the gait and the wide divergences in capacity to dance or walk the tightrope due chiefly to the fairly homogeneous and uniform influences which affect walking and the much more heterogeneous and divergent influences that affect the other locomotor activities? Can one draw the line, except by determining experimentally how much of the influences are internal and how much external? But, even then, that is not the distinction drawn between instinctive and learned actions. The whole classification seems to be an attempt to distinguish between the effects of heredity and those of environment, as if each influence determined whole actions independently of the other, instead of working together upon the organism from the beginning.

McDougall's analysis runs into much the same difficulties. He says (*284, 30*) that instinct is "an inherited or innate psychophysical disposition which determines its possessor to perceive, and to pay attention to, objects of a certain class, to experience an emotional excitement of a particular quality upon perceiving such an object and to act in regard to it in a particular manner, or, at least, to experience an impulse to such action." In almost all respects this is a description of the conditioning process and its effects. Even more so is his statement of the four "complications of instinctive processes" (*ibid.*, 33). In fact, he holds that some "instincts" "remain inexcitable except during the prevalence of some temporary bodily state." Such states "determine the stimulation of sense organs within the body" and maintain "the psychophysical dispositions" "in an excitable condition." This is precisely the conclusion we have arrived at with regard to the conditioning of external stimuli to internal wants. While his physiology of the emotions does not conform to more recent views (*ibid.*, 34, note 1) he, unlike James, identifies emotions with instincts. "Each kind of emotional excitement is always an indication of, and the most constant feature of, some instinctive process" (*ibid.*, 35). Thus, while his terms do not always conform, instinct is the action or attitude or its impulse, and emotion is its accompanying feeling or experience (see *ibid.*, Chapter III). In this respect his analysis approaches ours. And, when he disregards external objects, his statements conform, at least verbally or superficially, to ours. Thus his "instinct" keeps "unchanged its essential and permanent nucleus . . . the central part of the innate disposition, the excitement of which determines an affective state or emotion of specific quality and a native impulse towards some specific end" (*ibid.*, 93). Again, among human beings, "a few only of the simple instincts that ripen soon after birth are displayed in movements determined by the innate dispositions," such as sucking, wailing, crawling, winking, and (?) shrinking from a blow. Most ripen later, and thus have at their command a motor system already guided by intelligence and imitation. That is, they are not restricted to native movements. Reactions may be modified, controlled, or even suppressed (*ibid.*, 42). To all these statements visceral or interofective reactions are exceptions (*ibid.*, 43). In almost all respects, though in less physiological terms, these statements conform to ours. However, if this is so, what becomes of instincts? They can no longer be the actions (now learned) in terms of which they are usually stated; nor the emotions, for these are aspects or by-products. They are the "psycho-physical dispositions," whatever that means. Does that mean the processes through which wants cause certain modes of central and subcortical (i.e., non-psychic) excitation? Does it mean the functional canalization of that excitation? Or does it mean the wants themselves? It seems better to pin this course of events down to physiological fact, so far as we can, instead of leaving it *en l'air*, as the term instinct, or the translation of that term into "psycho-physical disposition," does.

We are going to leave this question of instinct without further debate. Suffice it to say that to find a difference of more than degree between the complex reaction of the digestive system when food enters it or even the complicated patterns of growth, on the one hand, (cf. Semon, *368*, 61) and, on the other, the truly stereotyped parts of the reaction of a bird when mating seems to be one way of preventing any future explanation of so-called instinctive actions.

D. OTHER WANTS DEFINED ONLY AS TYPES OF BEHAVIOR

It is, of course, obvious that, in limiting ourselves to the list of internal and quasi-external wants that have been treated in these first three chapters, we have attempted to deal only with the beginnings of a physiological analysis of human motivation. There are a great number of other more or less stereotyped and therefore recognizable systems of reaction to which names are commonly given. But the difficulty which has prevented our investigating these systems is that it is as yet impossible to assign to them even a plausible cause in the nature of a variation of homeostasis analogous to the causes of those we have included. Perhaps that argues that these other systems of reaction belong in the external stimulus-response category and have no independent internal causation. However, our success in tracing to internal causation so many of the basic forms of behavior leads to skepticism as to this possibility. At least we will not be ready to accept such an explanation without having exhausted the possibility of internal causation. Perhaps, on the other hand, the difficulty in uncovering internal causes for these forms of behavior is due to the fact that they have no special or individual cause of their own at all—that they are merely highly specialized and adapted reactions for dealing with external objects in the interests of the basic wants we have established. Thus among "motivational" psychologists there is a frequent disposition to treat the "drives" we have listed as the "primordial basis for all behavior" and to regard the rest of motivation as "refinements, modifications or elaborations" of these.[1] Nevertheless, as Thorndike notes, while the "action of original wants" may be the "seed," the "tree" is far different;[2] so different, in fact, that one naturally questions the direct relation.

There may be value in cataloguing the more standardized of these other forms of human and animal behavior, the causation of which is as yet unexplained, since to do so sharpens the point of the problem to be attacked.[3] When that is done, however, it seems better to limit the terminology to one which is descriptive of the behavior itself, including its accompanying emotional expression, and to forgo the use of

[1] Tolman, *403*, 271—a doctrine that he ascribes to Craig.
[2] Thorndike, *397*, 16.
[3] Partly for this reason, apparently, Knight (*240*, 332) holds that such lists, while usually "superficial in the highest degree," do represent "progress in comparison with the naive psychologizing of conventional economics."

pseudo-explanatory terms such as "instinct," "desire," "drive," etc., which are mere word-magic substitutes for the unknown causes. And this for the reason that the latter terms dull rather than sharpen the point of the problem, since they give the appearance of solving it. Among the forms of behavior that seem to be most nearly within the reach of neurophysiological investigation are those which Tolman includes in his "second-order drives," [4] and which he defines entirely in objective terms. As he states them, these are curiosity (a tendency to get more of a distant or unfamiliar stimulus), gregariousness (to seek, or stay in, the presence of others), self-assertion (to dominate or control others), self-abasement (to submit to others), and imitativeness (to copy the ends pursued by others).

Of these the only one, so far as I know, upon which any extensive experimental work has been done by neurophysiologists is curiosity. Curiosity is a general characteristic of all the mammalian world, at least, and is a dominant one among the primates. As Clarence Day said, in *This Simian World*, "Many animals have some curiosity, but 'some' is not enough; and in but few is it one of the master passions. By a master passion I mean a passion that is really your master; some appetite which habitually, day in, day out, makes its subjects forget fatigue or danger, and sacrifice their ease to its gratification. That is the kind of hold that curiosity has on the monkeys." "Being of simian stock, we had simian traits. Our development naturally bore the marks of our origin." [5] Thus he accounts for what he regards as the most striking attribute of human civilization (and perhaps the cause of its progress); and he contrasts this attribute to the dignity which might have been our most conspicuous trait if instead we had come from feline stock, or the devoted affection if from canine stock. This comment by our great, kindly satirist is not so far from Pavlov's remarks on the same subject. The latter's correctly objective name for curiosity is the "investigatory reflex," with which should perhaps be included the allied "caution reflex." "In man this reflex has been greatly developed with far-reaching results, being represented in its highest form by inquisitiveness—the parent of that scientific method through which we may hope one day to come to a true orientation of the world around us." [6]

The "investigatory reflex" itself is not definable in terms of specific

[4] Tolman, *402*, 357.
[5] Day, *112*, 37 and 4. Romanes says (*354*, 477), "Curiosity is more strongly pronounced in monkeys than in any other animals."
[6] Pavlov, *320*, 12.

motions except as to its first component, which we have called the "alert"; [7] thereafter, the motions involved are almost infinitely variable.[8] Instead, it must be defined in terms of the manner of orientation of the subject to some external object or other source of stimulus. It is "an immediate response in man and animals to the slightest changes in the world around them, so that they immediately orient their appropriate receptor organ in accordance with the perceptible quality in the agent bringing about the change, making full investigation of it." [9] But, "Of course in the case of a new, even small, change in the environment, two reflexes appear—a positive one, the investigatory reflex, and a negative one, which might be described as a reflex of caution or restraint. Whether these two reflexes are independent, or whether the second is a sequence to the first and results from external inhibition or negative induction, cannot be settled at present. The second supposition seems to me the more probable." [10] On the basis of Pavlov's ex-

[7] Frolov says the investigatory reflex is the "physiological basis of *attention*" (*157*, 65). By that we assume he means the alert. We should say, rather, that the alert is the first phase of the reflex. We have reserved the term attention for "conscious attention," and we hold that the basis for that is "interest"—a different part of the process. On the other hand, we are not inclined to admit that the alert is confined to the investigatory reflex. We have included it, along with the usual second component, restlessness or locomotion, as the *general* reaction to all wants. We have noted that any excitation of the posterior hypothalamus produces, first, the alert and, second, restlessness (Appendix II). "Coming to attention" is Woodworth's first kind of generalized preparatory reaction (*446*, 40–41). It is to Washburn "a state of suspended reaction" (*427*, 344). Perhaps both were thinking of external stimuli only, but the context makes it appear otherwise. It should be noted in this connection that Pavlov found that "an alert state of the nervous system is absolutely essential for the formation of a new conditioned reflex" (*320*, 28). If we may identify this "alert state" with a hypothalamic condition which is, at least potentially, the alert, then it would appear that such a state is the result of *any* stimulation, external or internal, that is capable of reaching the hypothalamus, and is a preliminary to any motor activity, not solely the "investigatory reflex."

[8] Frolov holds (*157*, 66) that the investigatory reflex is a "weak form of the reflex of grasping objects." This does not hold water. The grasp reflex in primates is a primordial and subcortical postural reflex. In the course of time it becomes suppressed by the development of cortically directed manipulation of objects—one of the finest developments of pyramidal expertness. At the most, we can say that the investigatory reflex may proceed into such manipulations among its infinite variety of other possibilities. The term reflex is entirely inappropriate to such deliberate activities.

[9] Pavlov, *320*, 12. "The slightest alteration in the environment—even the very slightest sound or faintest odour, or the smallest change in intensity of illumination" arouses it (*ibid.*, 29).

[10] Pavlov, *320*, 312. If we interpret the caution reflex as the first signs of fear, this connection coincides with the observations of psychologists. McDougall says (*284*, 60) that it is "not easy to distinguish in general terms between the excitants of curiosity and those of fear," for fear also arises from the "unfamiliar and strange as such" (*ibid.*, 56–57). Perhaps the degree of unfamiliarity differentiates (*ibid.*, 60); but perhaps the two are related (*ibid.*, 56–57). James also pointed out that strangeness causes both forms of behavior (*220*, II, 417, 429). But he assumed that they were independent "instincts"

periments, Frolov says that this, or these, reflexes are "inborn" [11] and that the investigatory, at least, is subcortical, for it remains after decortication though, of course, within a more limited range of stimulation.[12] But here there appears a marked difference. Whereas in both the normal and in the decorticate dog the "investigatory reflex" inhibits all other reflexes and first and foremost the acquired ones, so that old ones may be inhibited only slightly while new ones disappear entirely,[13] the effect of repetition of the stimulus is precisely the opposite in the case of the normal animal and the decorticate. In the normal dog this reflex has been called a reflex to novelty,[14] for, upon repetition of the stimulus, the reflex is extinguished and this extinction inhibits all other reflexes and eventually results in "general limpness and sleep." [15] In the decorticate dog, on the other hand, the repetition of a stimulus which can be appreciated at all calls forth "an investigatory reflex in a stereotyped manner and for an unlimited number of times." [16]

This difference conforms to and confirms our reading of the process of conditioning. It is apparent that the subcortical process consists of an increase in the state of excitation in the hypothalamus—at least a greater degree of awakeness—by reason of some change in external stimulation appreciable there. The first motor effect of that, as we have noted, is the "alert"; thereafter this may develop into the general reaction, locomotion. This is the behavior of the investigatory reflex. Eventually either the stimulus ceases or adaptation of receptors sets in. In either case the hypothalamic excitation also ceases. Upon successive repetitions of the stimulus, the process is repeated without change, being an automatic increase of awakeness. Therefore, the subcortical or unconditioned response is not one to novelty, strictly speaking; it is a response to any detectable change in the environment, however often that may recur, so long as it is only intermittent. When the

and used them as an example of successive ripening (ibid., II, 395–397). We should say, rather, that the investigatory reflex comes to be conditioned to the quasi-external want called fear, how quickly in the experience of each organism being dependent on how harmless changes in stimulation prove to be (i.e., how tame or how wild the environment).

As to the stress on strangeness or novelty, see below.
[11] Frolov, 157, 64.   [12] Ibid., 63.   [13] Ibid., 64.
[14] James says (220, II, 429) curiosity is evinced only for objects that are novel. Tolman (above) stresses the "unfamiliar" stimulus. So does McDougall. But it is evident from Pavlov's experiments that this is not the basis of the unconditional reaction.
[15] Frolov, 157, 66. See also Pavlov, 320, 258–259.
[16] Ibid., 259.

cortical circuit is included, however, the process is altered. Then, co-incidently, the sensory cortex is presented with an independent report of the same change in the environment. Coincidently, the enhanced awakeness of the hypothalamus communicates itself to the cortex and the sensory representation becomes enlivened by this non-specific form of emotional excitement. Probably this is the basis of the "conscious attention" aroused. But, if thereafter there appears no actual correspondence between some interest of the organism and this change in external stimulation—if no want appears as a result of it or no existing want is relieved by reason of it—then no "interest" attaches to the sensory representation. It does not become conditioned to any want. Apparently it may even become definitely unconditioned, so that it is inhibitory to awakeness.[17] Having no "interest" (specific emotional endowment), when the memory is re-excited by repetition the cortex rejects it. Why, it may be asked, does not the original process then repeat itself? The explanation must be cortical inhibition. At first this occurs only in respect of the enlivenment of the sensory representation by the stream of awakeness, for the hypothalamus is still preoccupied, as is proved by concurrent inhibition of other conditioned reflexes. But eventually this inhibition must increase to a point where corticohypothalamic tracts are involved, for suppression of hypothalamic awakeness and even sleep may supervene upon sufficient repetition.

If, now, we have interpreted these facts correctly, it is evident that the requirement of novelty is cortical only; that the investigatory reflex, so-called, is no more than the alert, developing into locomotion; that it has the subcortical character of the responses to quasi-external wants, being an automatic response to appreciable changes in external stimulation; that its internal cause has the hypothalamic character of an enhanced condition of awakeness, being non-specific (no special mode); and that, therefore, so far as the cortex is concerned, its internal cause does not of and in itself reflect a want—for, unless the change in external stimulation as cortically reflected becomes associated with some want, the effect of repetition of this stimulation does not become conditioned to the response. Rather, in some way, it becomes unconditioned or even negatively conditioned to the response. Finally, this interpretation fits the fact that curiosity is most con-

[17] That is, internal inhibition, loss of "interest," and even sleep supervene. See quotation from Frolov, above.

spicuous, by far, in the primates. Among them the greater degree of cortical development admits a much wider range of more subtly discriminated stimuli from the external world—at least through sight and hearing. Along with this goes a far broader protection from the uninteresting (cortical inhibition). Nevertheless, what sifts through the latter—the novel which may prove to be interesting—is, because of the far greater fineness of the sensory data, a much more arousing contact with the environment, calling for far more thorough investigation. Curiosity, then, seems not to be itself precisely a want. Rather it appears to be an external stimulus-response system, cortically limited to novel stimulation, which, along with the cortical mechanism of sensory attention and of emotional endowment (conditioning), serves the purpose of establishing the relation of external objects to the several wants.

With regard to the rest of Tolman's list of second-order drives we know even less. It is possible that gregariousness is a reaction sometimes to cold and sometimes to fear. Both have been suggested. It is possible that self-assertion is related to rage and self-abasement to fear. There is disagreement whether imitativeness is even an "instinct"— let alone a want—in its own right.[18] Many lists include other types of observed behavior patterns, more often under names given by past psychology to the various instincts, emotions, and feelings; and, frequently, brave but purely speculative attempts are made to relate these to the primary "drives" (our wants) or to some other organic source.[19] However, since it is as yet impossible to extend the relatively secure physiological foundations which we have established under our list of wants to any of these other forms of behavior, we choose to stop short of them, while recognizing that they still remain an open problem. We shall proceed instead to attempt to build up certain generalizations as to the relations between present wants, on the basis of the evidence derived from the limited number of want-behavior patterns which we have analyzed and as to the course of which, from the variation from homeostasis clear through to the consummatory reaction, we do have some definite, if very incomplete, understanding. We are justified in proceeding from so limited a basis for two reasons. In the first place, it is generally "conceded that it is

[18] See McDougall's interpretation of imitativeness in the supplementary statement.
[19] For some sample lists of "drives," see supplementary statement, "Various Lists of Drives," at the end of this section.

necessary to explain the commonest forms of behavior first, just because they are more universal." [20] In the second place, there is a reasonable presumption that generalizations in regard to interrelations that are found to apply to this limited list will, in the course of further investigation, prove to be correct also as to all others.

Various Lists of Drives. A few samples of these lists may justify the self-imposed limitations of our own list.

William James (*220*, II, 404–440) presents a list largely borrowed from, and sufficiently representative of, the older school. It is completely unco-ordinated, running from simple motions to complex feelings and even objectives. The movements are sucking, biting, clasping, and pointing, carrying to mouth, crying and smiling, turning the head aside, holding head erect, sitting up, standing, locomotion, and vocalization. Other "tendencies which are worthy of being called instinctive" (*ibid.*, II, 440) are imitation, emulation or rivalry, pugnacity or anger, sympathy, hunting instinct, fear of the strange, of black or dark, of height, of the supernatural and of the agora, acquisitiveness and kleptomania, constructiveness, play, curiosity, sociability and shyness, secretiveness, cleanliness, modesty or shame, love, jealousy, and parental love. Most of our wants are not included; a few of these are among our wants; most of the rest are neither integral nor unlearned.

McDougall (*284*, Chapter III) improves this list in all three directions. He includes more of the wants, reduces the number of unanalyzed and dependent systems of reaction, and defines those he accepts in more objective terms. The principal "instincts" are flight, repulsion, curiosity, pugnacity, self-abasement, self-assertion and the parental. Those with "less well-defined emotional tendencies" are the sexual, the desire for food (described in terms of the precurrent and consummatory reactions), gregariousness, hoarding, constructiveness, and perhaps crawling and walking (i.e., locomotion). Self-abasement is expressed in low muscular tone (*ibid.*, 67); the basis of gregariousness is "a mere uneasiness in isolation and satisfaction in being one of a herd" (*ibid.*, 87). He rejects the religious instinct and those of imitation, of sympathy, of play, and of emulation. Suggestion, imitation, and sympathy are pseudo-instincts because they involve mental interaction between at least two individuals; if the effect is to produce a similar presentation, we call it suggestion; if a similar affective excitement, sympathy; if similar bodily movements, imitation (*ibid.*, 93–94). Play, while a "native tendency of the mind" [*sic*] is, from his approach, not classifiable as an instinct because "no one of the many varieties of playful activities can properly be ascribed to an instinct of play" (*ibid.*, 110); i.e., the action is not stereotyped. Moreover, "the motives of play are various and often complex, and they cannot be characterized in any brief formula" (*ibid.*, 115–116). As James says (*220*, II, 427), "Simple active

[20] Troland, *408*, 3.

games . . . involve imitation, hunting, fighting, rivalry, acquisitiveness and construction." We agree; but what we have called euphoria is not play, though it may be one of the bases of the active forms of play. Emulation is a compound of pugnacity and self-assertion (*ibid.*, 92). Still another "tendency" is the "tendency to repetition" or habit, which is not in itself an instinct (*ibid.*, 119) nor one of our wants. It is, rather a general characteristic of the nervous system.

Dunlap's list conforms much more closely to ours. He includes (*123*, 323–324) desires (1) for aliment (food and drink); (2) for excretion (to be rid of disturbing things); (3) for rest; (4) for activity; (5) for shelter (protection from disagreeable factors in the environment)—and these cover some of the ground of our wants; (6) for conformity (doing as others do, or as a leader does); (7) for pre-eminence (leadership); (8) for progeny (parental desire); (9) for sex gratification (amatory desire; *ibid.*, 324). His fifth is only omitted from our list because we cannot explain it fully as a product of the heat mechanism. His sixth and seventh seem to parallel McDougall's self-abasement and self-assertion but on a less integral basis. Dunlap also goes further in our direction, though without adequate physiological proof, when he "speculatively" assigns these desires as follows: 1 and 2 to the alimentary canal and urinary system; 3 and 4 to the striped muscles; 5 to the skin, mucous membrane and connective tissue; 6 and 7 to the circulatory and respiratory systems, and 8 and 9 to the sexual organs (*ibid.*, 324, note). Troland (*408*, 137) cites Dunlap's list but offers a somewhat different list of his own, consisting of eight "desires or instincts."

At the opposite extreme is Thomson (*396*, 89–104), who works up the system of motives into reflexes, appetites, emotions, sentiments, moods and temperaments, gives four primary emotions and then produces a list of 54 compound or secondary emotions—each of which is quite familiar to all of us—with synonyms or special names for different degrees of intensity of each and with an analysis of the chief component (primary emotion) in each. He undertakes no physiological analysis whatever. But this mere list evidences the complexity of the problem. So, too, does the recapitulation of the various proposals by different authors as to classes of instincts, given by Bernard (*Instinct*, Chapter VIII). However, all such classifications on such bases remind one of William James's remark. He said (*220*, II, 448): "the merely descriptive literature of the emotions 'makes' you feel that its subdivisions are to a great extent either fictitious or unimportant, and that its pretenses to accuracy are a sham."

4

THE ANALYTICAL SCHEME FOR
PRESENT WANTS

WE HAVE NOW fulfilled, so far as seems to be at present possible, the requirement we set ourselves in the very beginning. We
have borrowed from physiology a "restatement of the nature and operation of human wants and their satisfying" and have found that objective studies of behavior confirm, and conform to, the principal
conclusions thus derived. However, the general tenor of this restatement turns out to be so different from that of the hedonistic psychology
upon which economic theory, so far as it deals with these subjects,
has been chiefly based, that we seem to be compelled to undertake a
reconstruction of the analytical scheme of present wants and the process
of satisfying them, as this has been developed in economic theory—
particularly in what we shall call, generically, marginal utility theory
and its developments. Evidently it will not be sufficient merely to relate the new terminology to the old categories; for the categories themselves are too widely different. If human wants are still to be regarded,
in economics, as the motivating causes of human behavior, then, in the
first place, we must redefine the nature of wants themselves; and this
because physiology demonstrates quite clearly, as far as it now goes,
that the ultimate and primary causation of the fundamental forms of
behavior lies in states of, or tendencies toward, variation from homeostasis in the various respects in which it is necessary that the organism
should maintain this homeostasis. We therefore start with the definition of a present want as such a state or tendency.

However, before proceeding to work out this analytical scheme, it
is proper that we give notice of two changes of method at this point.
Hitherto, we have developed certain limited and hypothetical generalizations from certain specific data by the use of the inductive method.
But the reduction of these generalizations to an analytical scheme involves something more than induction. If these generalizations are

correct, certain inferences from them are permissible—that is, certain other and dependent hypotheses derive from these, and hypotheses incompatible with these conclusions are to be rejected. Our analytical scheme will include some such dependent hypotheses and will attempt to expose some that are incompatible. Furthermore, we have now clearly entered the field of the virtual [1] and must make that step explicit. This scheme is a presentation of the way the forces we are dealing with *would work*, if they were the only forces at play. They are not the only forces at play, as we shall attempt to make clear in the following chapters. Nevertheless, they can only be analyzed at all, if they are analyzed on a virtual, not an actual, basis. And when this scheme is combined with those of the other forces which are to be developed later, we will come, at least more nearly, to a representation of the actual in so far as the major and fundamental forces and resistances embraced in our energetic scheme suffice to account for actuality.

A. THE HOMOLOGY OF ALL PRESENT WANTS AND OF THEIR SATISFYING

Development of our analytical scheme upon the basis of the particular form of causative relation between wants and behavior that has been worked out in the preceding chapters requires, first, the clarification and final formulation of one of our early conclusions. It is clear that the mechanisms for the restoration or the maintenance of homeostasis are primarily set in operation by variations or tendencies away from homeostasis. Apparently those which manage the homeostasis of the blood may become effective upon so slight a variation that they may be said to prevent rather than to correct the variation. They usually counteract a tendency instead of correcting a condition. They change the rate of a continuous process which maintains a balance

---

[1] Borrowing the notion of physics to describe the essential analytical method by which tendencies, actually in part or in whole merely potential, are projected *as if* they were fully realized. This is related to the common analytical method of economics, called *ceteris paribus*. It does not cover quite the same ground, however. *Ceteris paribus* accepts all other factors and conditions, merely keeping them the same. The virtual is an isolation of a single factor *in vacuo*, so to speak. *Ceteris paribus* is a condition which might exist—a "controlled" experiment. The virtual is one which cannot exist—an abstraction. The virtual is usually constructed from—purified out of—*ceteris paribus*. But, as a means of testing the validity of the construction, it is a further step. For the net of the projected or virtual effects of all factors combined must conform to reality. If they do not, then either the factors dealt with have not been pure and homogeneous or other factors have entered which were not taken account of. It is our intention to use the virtual method to test the validity both of our own analytical scheme and that of marginal utility theory with its corollaries in the theory of demand.

with other continuous processes. Only when they become considerable variations (asphyxia, etc.) do they become definable as states instead of mere tendencies. On the other hand, those mechanisms which control inflow or outflow of stored material only operate within much wider limits and are only called into action periodically. Then they generate movements *en masse*. They eliminate deficits or surpluses and restore parities. Finally, those which manage homeostasis in respect of the continuous relations with the environment are not only capable of being brought into action by sporadic variations (actual wants) but also—and in the main unlike the others—by a conditioned process which forewarns of, and thus enables the mechanism to prevent, the actual variation before it occurs.[2] In a sense we may say that the mechanisms for the second class operate to get rid of a want when it recurs and that those for the first, almost, and those for the third class, usually, operate to prevent the want.[3] But, to some extent, this distinction is one of degree only; for wants of the first class may become actual variations from homeostasis, in which event their mechanisms have not prevented them; the mechanisms for those even of the second class prevent further variation when they begin to correct the existing ones; and, in the case of the third class, we have assumed the existence of a milder or surrogate central replica of the want, which is aroused cortically and which is itself not prevented—is, in fact, the cause of the behavior. For this reason it is impossible accurately to classify wants according to the favorite dichotomy which, in our terminology, would be expressed as "wants to be got rid of" and "wants to be prevented." Nevertheless, we shall find it desirable to treat the two types separately, classifying under the first type all actual present wants and under the second all merely potential present wants that give rise to surrogates whose only existence is a central replica of the want itself. And this although we recognize that some of the wants to be got rid of consist merely of potential tendencies and that those to be prevented are only prevented by central replicas of the wants themselves.

The value of having looked beneath this somewhat superficial and not wholly valid distinction arises from the fact that it makes evident that the relative magnitudes of all these present wants, actual or surrogate,

[2] This conditioned process was described on p. 92. In Chapter 3, Section B 1, it was covered more fully and its hypothalamic effect was referred to as a "replica" of that of the want itself.

[3] The nature of this prevention has already been described for the first class in Chapter 1 and for the third class in Chapter 3.

are only comparable at one point. On pp. 36 to 37 we used the phrase "the force with which a want acts" and the term "magnitude" of the corrective activity to express our quantitative categories. But it is clear that such categories are only comparable in terms of each want and its corrective activity separately. There is no common denominator here. However, as will be fully developed later in this chapter, when we transfer the point of measurement to the hypothalamic region and determine the force or magnitude in terms of the intensity of the emotional state (plus or minus) which is produced there, our scale becomes a single one, whether this magnitude reflects a tendency, a state, or only a surrogate for either. All present wants or their replicas then become comparable in quantitative terms.[4] For, though these emotional states differ in kind, they are all commensurable in terms of intensity (plus or minus).[5]

We must now relate these several types of process to the ordinary economic notion of the satisfying of wants. For us, the process of satisfying the want has, in this way, come to consist of the corrective measures—the system of reactions—which are set up in the organism to compensate for the tendency or to get rid of the state. Some of these measures do not reach the level of overt behavior. But, for our general purposes, we shall usually confine ourselves to the consideration of those which do; and, therefore, our type will be a want which requires overt behavior to satisfy it.[6] Furthermore, the process of satis-

---

[4] The notion one frequently meets with in economic literature that the terms "quantitative" and "scale" connote measurement in terms of a standard and objective unit—usually deposited in the U.S. Bureau of Standards—is quite foreign to mathematics, whose numbers are "abstract symbols" connoting only relationships among themselves. This subject will be dealt with further as we proceed.

[5] The reader is put on notice that, at this point, we are beginning the development of our scheme of economic energetics, which will be gradually completed as we proceed. Offhand, there appear to be three dimensions in which one might measure the force of wants and the magnitude of the consequent behavior.

  1) the intensity of the want;
  2) the duration of the process of satisfying;
  3) the quantity of material ingested or eliminated.

As we shall make clear at the end of this chapter, the duration of the process has nothing to do with the question. A single want of usual intensity may at one time be satisfied slowly and at another rapidly. Nor is the third dimension usable. In the first place, many wants do not deal with material. In the second place, as we shall demonstrate in the next chapter, many materials are objectively incommensurable and all are subjectively incommensurable. Thus, by default, we are left with the dimension intensity as the only possible common measure either of the force of the want or of the magnitude of the resulting behavior.

[6] Some of these measures can hardly be said to constitute a part of the process of satisfying. We found the distinction between precurrent and consummatory reactions one

fying must usually be conceived to include only the consummatory reactions, however difficult it may be to discriminate these. Analytically,
the terminology of economics, if reduced to its most precise formulations, has indicated that the *satisfying* of a want is a process; *satisfaction* is the degree to which the want is satisfied; *satiation* is the process
of satisfying it completely; and *satiety* is the end-state, complete satisfaction.[7] These terms and the distinctions they convey are readily
applicable and useful in regard to those wants which consist of states,
and for which the corrective behavior is periodic—the storage cases
above. In these cases we may consider the initial state to be homeostasis;
gradually the want develops through a range of variation away from
the initial state; at some point the corrective behavior begins; if it is
completed, it restores homeostasis. Therefore, homeostasis is the state
of satiety, or that of absence of the want, according as it is regarded
as the end-state or as the initial state of the whole process; that is, the
end and the beginning are the same.

These distinctions are not so obvious, however, nor the terms apparently so applicable, in regard to those wants which usually consist
of tendencies only, and whose corrective behavior is therefore continuous, or nearly so. For them, the want being continuous, the process
of satisfying must also be continuous. In one sense, the state, satiety,
seems never to be reached even temporarily in these cases, since the
want always exists. Such, for instance, are the processes of heat regulation (continuous) and breathing (nearly so). On the other hand,
in another sense, the state of satiety is continuously maintained in these
cases, in so far as the corrective behavior succeeds in confining the
want to a tendency toward variation without any actual variation—
that is, in so far as the rate of the corrective process varies with, and

which is difficult to apply in many cases and the identification of a consummatory reaction a matter of doubt in others. Nevertheless, there is some relation between the
process of consummation and the process of satisfying; and we must regard the precurrent reactions, in certain cases, as occurring prior to the beginning of satisfaction.
That rough statement will suffice at this stage of our analysis. It calls attention to a
difference with which we shall have to deal fully later on (see Chapter 5).

[7] Perhaps we are attributing too much precision even to economic usage. To excuse,
to the meticulous, this somewhat unsystematic distinction between forms, we may call
attention to the fact that the verbal noun in -ing, from the verb "satisfy," has no other
sense than that of process. The verbal noun in -tion has several senses—is, in fact,
synonymous with all these definitions. Nevertheless, it is built on a past participle of
"satisfy," which makes it more suitable for use in the sense of quantity of process accomplished. The difference in sense between the verbs "satisfy" and "satiate" makes
the distinction here justifiable.

fully equalizes, the changing rate of the process it is compensating. For these wants, we may regard satiation as any satisfying which is entirely adequate to offset the tendency to variation and which results, therefore, in a current degree of satisfaction which is complete—a continuing state of satiety.[8] If, among these wants, an actual variation takes place, we may regard the state and its correction as analogous to those of the first group. Nor do these terms and distinctions seem at first to be entirely appropriate to what we have called the quasi-external wants. Nevertheless, they may be conveniently applied even there. When the actual wants occur, as a result of external injury, sudden loud noise, or bright light, loss of equilibrium and restraint or constraint, the resulting overt behavior may or may not correct the condition. If it does not, the want may nevertheless quickly or gradually disappear because of cessation of its external cause. Only if the behavior does correct the condition—and this is only possible for the last two wants—can the restoration of the normal state be said to be satiation and the state itself, satiety. Otherwise, we must consider that a limit is merely set to the want, because of escape from its source, or that it subsides, because of the healing of the injury, or the cessation of the noise or light. While, in either case, the final result is a restoration of homeostasis, it is better to confine the term satiation to the result accomplished by the corrective process only. On the other hand, when only replicas of such quasi-external wants appear we may always apply these distinctions and terms; for then, if the replicas of fear or anger, for instance, set up reactions which are successful in preventing the true states, the very success itself, at the end of the process of satisfying, may be said to be a state of satiety; and this for the reason that the replica of the want has then ceased because of the behavior, with the consequence that the true want has never occurred at all. It has been necessary to go into some detail to clarify this point because we shall find that the satisfying of many of the common wants, beyond the range of those we have been able to establish on physiological foundations, shows more nearly the characteristics of these last two

[8] It may be objected that we cannot regard a want and its state of satiety as coexisting. But, of course, that apparent inconsistency lies in the facts, not in our analysis of them. If these wants normally exist only as tendencies away from homeostasis which are continuously compensated for, both the state of want and the state of satiety actually do coexist. The behavior—or other activity—being concurrent, never permits an actual variation to occur; yet the tendency to do so persists. Thus we must regard these wants as continuous ones which are nevertheless normally kept satisfied.

groups—continuous processes and surrogates (preventions of actual) —than those of the first—corrections after the fact.[9]

B. OCCURRENCE OF PRESENT WANTS

Since, in the first chapter, we have already outlined the characteristics of the various wants in respect of their periodicity, it is only necessary at this point to summarize these details in order to lay a basis for our systematic scheme. For this purpose we may classify the wants we have discussed as follows:

I. Internal wants; that is, wants which arise wholly by reason of internal processes.

    a. Continuous tendencies, without storage. These vary in strength according to the degree of general activity. They relate to homeostasis of the blood in respect of oxygen, carbon dioxide, neutrality, and temperature. When these tendencies are not fully compensated and become states, they become analogous to the next class, except that their occurrence is sporadic, not periodic.

    b. Periodic states of deficit or surplus in storage. These are also the consequences of continuous tendencies; but, by reason of storage, they are not, as to the system as a whole, concurrently compensated, and are therefore cumulative. The want itself is continuous, like the first group, but does not lead to behavior until the store has reached some one of a series of critical points in the direction of a minimum or maximum.

        1. Those which accumulate more rapidly by reason of activity, so that the interval during which they increase from homeostasis (zero) to their critical points is thus shortened, are variations in systemic content of water, sugar, protein, fat, sodium chloride, waste, and the several phenomena of fatigue.

        2. Those whose periodicity is dependent on other internal criteria are systemic content of calcium salts, refuse, sex and "euphoria."

II. Quasi-external wants; that is, wants which arise internally by reason of relations with the environment.

[9] We are not using the term "avoidance" in this particular sense. That should be clearly understood. We have reserved that term for the kind of avoidance which consists of a relation with some object in the environment, not for the *prevention* of an actual variation from homeostasis.

a. Actual.

    1. Sporadic tendencies. These are loss of equilibrium, and restraint or constraint (loss of physical freedom) or resistance in general. Perhaps we should include here again the regulation of body temperature, in so far as tendencies to such variations in temperature are induced by environmental causes.

    2. Sporadic states. These are external injury and the effect of sudden loud noise or bright light, etc.

b. Surrogate. The milder central replicas of the foregoing, produced by conditioned stimuli to these wants.

This tabulation makes it clear that, so far as these examples are typical of all present wants, we must conceive wants to divide themselves into the following classes: (1) The continuous and non-cumulative,[1] which therefore induce continuous corrective behavior; (2) the continuous but cumulative, which therefore induce only intermittent corrective behavior; (3) the sporadic actual, which induce simultaneous corrective behavior;[2] (4) the sporadic surrogate, which induce prior behavior preventive of the sporadic actual. While further analysis may somewhat alter it, we will carry forward, for the present, this classification of wants, according to their temporal effect on the appropriate forms of behavior, as *continuous*, *recurrent*, and *sporadic*. In the main, this division seems to accord with the usual economic treatment. However, its development upon this different basis will turn out, as we proceed, to involve also somewhat different results.

C. CONSTELLATIONS OF PRESENT WANTS

In two instances which we have already found [1]—and we shall find many more—the same behavior, or system of reactions, is caused by —and, in turn, is a corrective for—several different wants. Thus breathing and eating each serve, or may serve, to satisfy what we may call a *constellation* of wants. Without going into the technical details it seems safe to say that the rate and depth of breathing may be affected by a need for more or less oxygen as well as by the need to get rid of more or less carbon dioxide; and, at any rate, it is certain that, under some circumstances, such breathing as suffices for one purpose may

[1] Or that part of such wants as does not go over into states.
[2] Including the continuous and non-cumulative (1) when these tendencies sporadically go over into states.
[1] See p. 35.

not suffice for the other.[2] Moreover temperature regulation, as well as the homeostasis of neutrality (via CO_2) must also be partially included in this constellation. With respect to eating, this grouping is even more evident. The want for each particular systemic constituent is a separate and independent want. Yet all are normally corrected by the single system of reactions which constitute eating. As far as sugar, fat, and protein are concerned, while the first two are capable of being internally converted into each other to a certain extent, nevertheless chief reliance for them and entire reliance for protein seems to be placed on their ingestion as such, or in those forms which the processes of digestion are able to convert into the blood constituents. Certainly the needed salts (and the vitamins) must be ingested as such, for they cannot be manufactured or converted into each other internally. In view of the uncertainty surrounding "hunger" or "hungers," and "appetite," we cannot make too definite statements on this subject. Nevertheless, the evidence cited in Appendix I, Section B, indicates that there are "specific hungers" or "appetites" for most, if not all, of these individual constituents; so that it is probable that each of these wants may express itself and may lead to eating, independently of the others. The fact remains, however, that usually the requirements of each constituent are more or less well supplied by some approximation to a "balanced diet," which is incidentally achieved in the course of satisfying the most pressing of these wants or, possibly, in taking in the bulk needed to produce the sense of repletion; and only if the less pressing become very intense, do they succeed in directing the system of reactions to the particular ingestion of their specific requirement.

It is evident that, in these two examples of jointly served groups of wants, the usual economic treatment is defective. Because this treatment has construed wants to be "desires" for external objects—since it has assumed such "desires" to be the cause of economic activities—it has led frequently to the classification of wants according to conglomerate objects. Thus among the chief wants have been the want for "air" and the want for "food." But the wants that relate to these

[2] See p. 48 and note 17.

Cannon (66, 153) seems to construe an oxygen deficit as having no direct influence, but to be corrected only incidentally along with an excess of CO_2. But I judge that Haldane considers both oxygen deficiency and body temperature to have independent access to the complex mechanism for control of respiration (see 179, 99). And the chemoreceptors in the aortic and carotid bodies still seem to respond to a deficit of oxygen, which is effective at least in emergencies.

objects are no more integral than are the objects. Therefore, the next necessary modification in the ordinary economic concept of a want is that, in such cases, the single "want," in the old sense, must be subdivided into a constellation of different and largely independent wants which may, but do not necessarily, exist or have their effect on behavior at the same time, and the true connection between which is the fact that the satisfaction of any or all of them can only be secured by a single system of reactions (e.g., breathing or eating).

D. PREPOTENCE AMONG PRESENT WANTS

1. THE DETERMINANT OF PREPOTENCE AMONG MUTUALLY EXCLUSIVE REFLEXES

By far the most important modification in the economic theory of wants and the process of satisfying them—especially for marginal utility theory—which our physiological approach has made necessary, has to do with the operation of the system of preferences established by the competition among present wants, a system based on the fact that all such wants are homologous. While we have, in the preceding chapters, laid the foundations for this part of our analytical scheme, it will be desirable here to go into considerable detail in order to introduce certain new physiological evidence which outlines more clearly the quantitative operation of this system.[1]

It is necessarily true by definition that an organism cannot conduct two bodily activities at the same time, if they require two different uses of one set of muscles. But, as we remarked in the previous chapter (p. 122), it is a conclusion from common observation that this limitation actually reaches much further. As a matter of fact, with a few exceptions, an organism does not do two different things simultaneously even if they involve entirely different sets of muscles. It walks and breathes at the same time; but it does not swallow and breathe at the same time;[2] neither does it, usually, carry out any of the other

[1] The several points that have been made, in all of which the scheme we are now developing is implicit, are as follows:
1) the unitary character of the central nervous system;
2) the concept of integration;
3) the tendency toward spreading, opposed by the development of inhibition and therefore canalization;
4) the development from general of special and therefore differentiated integrated reactions;
5) the separation of non-integrated reactions, including spinal reflexes, from the original general reactions.
[2] "Respiration is always inhibited during deglutition" (Kuntz, *245*, 241).

common systems of reactions, such as eating or drinking, the sexual acts, defecation, micturition, etc., while it is performing any of the others.[3]

One reason for this mutual exclusiveness of systems of reaction seems to be the limitations established by a structural feature of the central nervous system which Sherrington, considering primarily spinal re-flexes, has termed "the principle of the final common path." [4] Since there are approximately five times as many afferent as there are efferent neurons, it is necessarily true that, on the average, at least five afferent arcs must be in competition for the use of each efferent arc. But, in addition, by reason of the interposition of a vast system of "internun-cial" neurons, between the afferent and the efferent, each afferent arc may have access to many different "final common paths"; and this, in turn, multiplies many times over the number of afferent arcs that may compete for the use of each efferent arc. The result is that, in so far as the various afferents lead "to a different or opposed effect" in the efferents, since any "final common path" is "adapted to serve but one purpose at a time," [5] it is necessary that the afferents have only "suc-cessive and not simultaneous use of" each final common path. Count-ing the possible ("simple") reflexes as equal to the total number of afferent neurons (receptive points), Sherrington then classes them as "allied," to the extent that the afferent arcs use the efferent to the same purpose ("reinforcing") or combine in using one or many "final common paths" to one or more effector organs in a co-ordinated move-ment; as "antagonistic," if they conflict in purpose so that one, to se-cure the use of this, or these, paths, must inhibit the other; and as "neu-tral" or "indifferent," if, because they use final common paths which are independent of each other, they may both occur at the same time. Conceivably, all these last, the neutral reflexes, could occur simul-taneously. But he finds that neutrality between two reflexes is corre-lated with their weakness, so that "the stronger two reflexes are, the less do they remain neutral one to another." [6] It appears from this last observation that, among the "simple," [7] or even the usual reflexes, if

3 This point has already been made on pp. 121–122. It is repeated here because we are approaching the subject from a different angle.
4 Sherrington, 375, 115, quoted from Pres. Address, 1904 Brit. Assn. Advancement of Science, Sect. Physiol., Report, p. 728.
5 Sherrington, 375, 115–117 and 233.
6 Ibid., 114–147.
7 Sherrington regards the "simple reflex" of this analysis as a "convenient but arti-ficial abstraction" (375, 114).

one is of sufficient strength, it is capable of inhibiting not only those which use the same "final common paths" or effector organs to different effect, but also *all* other reflexes which may be stimulated at the same time. This argues for the "long-circuiting" of all stimuli when they are of sufficient strength. It suggests the conclusion that this "long-circuit" leads through some single system of "internuncial paths," which is potentially common to all reflexes and which, if it is engaged at all, permits only one species of reflex to be innervated at a time. In fact, it suggests as well that the distinction between "allied" and "antagonistic" reflexes is not only one between similar or opposed uses of final common paths, but also depends on the capacity for coordination in this single "internuncial" system, so that those elements of reflexes which come within this capacity are "allied" and those beyond it are "antagonistic." There appears to be a "bottleneck" for all "strong" reflexes which is a far more effective limitation upon their concurrence than is the relative paucity of "final common paths."

If this is true of simple reflexes, which Sherrington particularly studies, how much more likely it is to be true of elaborate integrated patterns of behavior such as the systems of reactions that we are particularly considering. The very complexity and all-inclusiveness of the co-ordination evident in such responses argues a temporary dominance in some such "bottleneck" over nearly the whole of the exterofective neuromuscular apparatus. And that in turn would involve the complete exclusion for the time being of all other activities if, according to some as yet unknown criterion, their patterns of response are not included within the limits of "co-ordination." [8] Thus we are led to the supposition that the fact that the organism does not ordinarily do two things simultaneously cannot be accounted for only by that structural feature of the central nervous system which Sherrington calls "the principle of the final common path." Instead, it appears that all complex motor activities, as well as all simple ones of sufficient intensity, must engage some single central system, or group of centers acting as a whole, which ultimately and potentially controls all effectors, and which, when involved, is capable of only a single activity at a time.

[8] For the moment we leave *en l'air* the nature of the competing stimuli. Head speaks of the "constant struggle for physiological dominance" upon the afferent side (*183*, 748). And Tracy (*407*, 351) says, "Since only one set of impulses can possess the common motor outlet at any given time, a 'conflict' ensues until the impulses from some one system reach a sufficient intensity to establish an activity gradient in the nervous system and dominate impulses from other sources." These quotations illustrate the way the problem is envisaged.

Our problem, then, is not only to find the "bottleneck" but also to find a criterion by which we can define "a single activity"—since some of those we are considering are simple, while others are highly complex. What is the elastic principle of co-ordination that unifies and makes compatible the parts of which such complex activities are composed and can still exclude all but one simple reflex? [9]

Adhering for the moment to the antagonistic reflexes, since Sherrington's studies in that field have been so precise, let us inquire what factors are found to give to one reflex this temporary dominance over others along the "final common path" or over the effector organ. "Whatever be the nature of the physiological process occurring between the competing reflexes for dominance over the common path, the issue of their competition . . . is largely conditioned by four factors. These are 'spinal induction,' relative intensity of stimulus, relative fatigue, and the functional species of the reflex." [10] These four factors "all resolve themselves ultimately into *intensity of reaction*." [11] The first and third factors, being fortuitous, are not of interest to us in this connection. But it is of great interest to consider what Sherrington means by the "functional species of the reflex," since this seems to modify, in important ways, the effect of the second and, in nature, also fortuitous factor which he calls "intensity" of stimulus. It is this fourth factor which, in his terminology, gives "prepotence" to the reflex.[12] In turn he ascribes this "prepotence" to the relative strength of the "affective tone" which is found to be an accompaniment of the

---

[9] This has already been discussed in the previous chapter. But, again, we are now approaching the question from a different angle.

[10] Sherrington, *375*, 206.　　　　[11] *Ibid.*, 231.

[12] Sherrington, *375*, 228 and thereafter. Others have come to use the term "prepotence" for all the causes which lead to one response rather than another and thus, in fact, for Sherrington's "intensity of reaction" (see below). So for Woodworth it is the whole of his "law of advantage." The "strongest stimulus is apt to prevail," but "protective reflexes prevail over all others, and postural reflexes yield to all others" (*447*, 233). Only the governing factor in the second case, which is based on Sherrington (*375*, 229 and 231) would be treated by the latter as "prepotence." Washburn has taken over this term from Sherrington, but accounts for the determination on a different ground (*427*, 273–276 and 407–409).

While Pavlov seems occasionally to hold that intensity of stimulus is the governing factor (e.g., *320*, 142, 269, 383, etc.), nevertheless he concludes that there is a "hierarchy of reflexes" (*ibid.*, 31), position in which is determined by the "physiological strength" of the stimuli (*ibid.*, 30 and 98), or even of the centers (*ibid.*, 37); later the latter seems to be denied on "reinvestigation" (*ibid.*, 383). Nevertheless, the "physiological strength" is something different from intensity, for it belongs to the nature of the reflex, not merely to the stimulus. And it is this physiological strength of the strongest reflex which produces what he calls the "external inhibition" of all other reflexes while it remains dominant (i.e., prepotent).

reflex, and which seems to vary over a wide range according to the "functional species." [13] Sherrington defines what he means by "affective tone." It is "physical pain or physical pleasure." [14] At first sight the introduction of these terms appears to be a piece of pure psychological hedonism. However, it is obviously impossible for Sherrington, or anyone else, to observe pain or pleasure in his laboratory subjects or preparations, since these are exclusively experiences in consciousness to be reached only by introspection. Let us discover, therefore, what are the *phenomena* that he has observed and to which he imputes these experiences. [15] As a first step we may note that he also identifies "affective tone" with emotion ("feeling"), the difference between them being one of degree. [16] But we have previously concluded [17] that, usually, what "the experimentor takes as the signs of emotion" are the many special forms of motor activity (behavior) which we have regarded as one part of the *expression* of emotion—the exterofective part—the other part being "bodily changes" resulting from autonomic (interofective) or endocrine causes. It is safe to assume, then, that what Sherrington has actually observed is that spinal reflexes, upon their motor side, vary in the degree to which they are accompanied by certain other concomitant motor activities (such as facies) and in the degree in which the primary motor activities have certain characteristics (such as the use of excessive force), both of which signs are construed to be the external expression of the various emotions; the "liveliness" of this expression is then construed to represent the degree of "affective tone"; and this degree, in turn, is held to determine the "prepotence" of the reflex it accompanies. [18]

[13] Sherrington, 375, 231.   [14] *Ibid.*, 327.

[15] That he only imputes the experiences is obvious from his statements elsewhere (375, 266–267) in reference to "animals reduced to merely spinal condition" where, in response to "stimuli calculated to produce pain," "the motor reaction occurs and is expressive of emotion; but it is probably the reaction of an organic machine which can be started working, though the mutilation precludes the psychosis" (experience).

[16] "The development of [sensations rich in affective tone] . . . is closely connected with the origin of the coarser emotions" (375, 255). "Emotion may be regarded almost *as* a feeling—a feeling excited, not by a simple little elaborated sensation, but by a group or train of ideas" (*ibid.*, 256). "Even the primitive emotions seem to involve perception—seem little other than sense-perceptions richly suffused with affective tone" (*ibid.*, 262). "Feeling is implicit in the emotional state; the state is an affective state" (*ibid.*, 266). Cannon also holds that "dominant emotions are states into which many other commonly milder affective states may be suddenly transformed" (58, 275). This view is, of course, quite general.

[17] See Appendix II, Section D.

[18] For his actual *observations*, see Sherrington (375, pages indexed under "Affective Tone").

2. THE LOCUS AND NATURE OF THE DETERMINANT OF PREPOTENCE

It is already quite evident that we are again dealing here with the same system around which we constructed, in Chapter 2 and Appendix II, our hypothesis as to the primary proximate source of integrated behavior.[19] The term "affective tone," when used by physiologists and experimental psychologists, is but another and unlocalized name for what we have been calling emotional states—that is, general excitation in the posterior hypothalamus—with its two kinds of manifestation, interofective (psychogalvanic reflex, etc.) and exterofective (facies, etc.), and its effect in consciousness (the emotional stream).[20] To be sure, Sherrington's gauges of the degree of this tone were necessarily very imperfect. On the one hand, to the extent that he imputed it on the ground of his own introspective knowledge of its occurrence in himself in similar reactions, he was, according to our thesis, considering only that portion which had a cortical effect by reason of its damming up (cortical inhibition or insufficiency of the

[19] In two respects our two approaches do not match. But we are using Sherrington's observations as proof and are therefore confining ourselves to his results, merely adding our own interpretation.

The first point is that Sherrington considers only the neural integrating system on the afferent side. We hold that the hypothalamus can also be excited by humoral excitors.

The second point is that when we call the hypothalamus the "bottleneck," we are ignoring all Sherrington's observations of less integrated reflexes. We are warranted in this because of his emphasis on "affective tone." Our evidence indicates that no reflex produces "affective tone" if it is not long-circuited to the hypothalamus. Thus any of his reflexes that are actually wholly short-circuited at the mid-brain level or below would have none. That may explain why proprioceptive reflexes were at the bottom of his list in respect of affective tone. In fact, they may have none if they reach only to the cerebellar region.

[20] The term "affective tone," when used by physiologists, is either identical with our "emotional stream" or with the imputed source of the emotional expression—our "emotional state." For instance, the physiologist Herrick states that "affective tone" is not "to be regarded as essentially an attribute or quality of sensation." "Each has its own mechanism." "Affective tone" is integrated centrally in the [hypo-]thalamus" (*190*, 313–314). Even psychologists, while they have not localized the apparatus, have come to analogous conclusions. For instance, Marston (*292*, 143) concludes that "our awareness of our reaction *as it occurs* is the emotion." He says that it is "exceedingly difficult to correlate such emotional states with sensations or with the conscious relationships between sensations." Instead, they should be connected with "simple units of motor consciousness and their interrelations in the primary motor pattern" (*ibid.*, 147). His argument and citations supporting this conclusion are given (*ibid.*, 147). The difference between this and James's supposition—presumably in Marston's case and certainly in ours—is that James treated the "felt" reaction as bodily (peripheral); we treat it as purely central. Woodworth also holds that "feeling is inextricably bound up with doing" (*447*, 280). It is "internal rather than overt activity" (*ibid.*, 283). Nevertheless, he thinks it is in some way "both sensory and motor" (*ibid.*, 285).

motor outlets of the hypothalamus);[21] and when he imputed it on the ground of observation of emotional motor expression (facies, etc.), he was, according to our thesis, considering only that portion which had a motor effect by reason of leakage (overflow of the cortical inhibition of the motor outlets of the hypothalamus).[22] Obviously these are but rough measures of the degree of affective tone. More precise measures have been used by others, though not for the purpose of determining prepotence. Such measures deal with the far more subtle and uncontrollable signs of emotion which compose the other, the interofective part of its expression. Two of these, which we have described,[23] are palmar sweating (the psychogalvanic reflex) and changes in blood pressure. The degree of the first, usually, and that of the second, frequently, is held to be proportionate to the degree of affective tone accompanying the reaction. Both are subject to refined quantitative measurement so that narrow differences in degree of affective tone can be gauged. And, as stated in Appendix II, both are found to vary, not directly according to strength of stimulus, but according to intensity of emotional experience (introspective), and in the same direction and in rough accord with the intensity of the exterofective signs. Nevertheless, even though rough, Sherrington's measures of affective tone showed to him a definite correlation with the prepotence of various "functional species" of reflex; and they sufficed for him, since they led him to make more than usually positive statements in regard to the determination of the prepotence of his various classes of reflex. Furthermore, the evidence we have indicates that it is probable that the finer measures, at least at low intensity, of the psychogalvanic reflex or of blood pressure would yield a far more exact correlation and thus confirm, even more positively, his view of the determinant of prepotence. Finally, we are the readier to accept Sherrington's correlation since our hypothesis, framed from the results of many attacks on the whole subject from other angles, closely conforms to it. It was our conclusion that the primary "nervous energy of response" is a function of general hypothalamic excitation. It is his conclusion that the "intensity of reaction" is, in large part at least, a function of the accompanying "affective tone," which in turn, in his case, is judged by phenomena which we have found good reason to believe are partial indices of such general hypothalamic excitation.

If now we re-read Sherrington's observations in the light of this

[21] See p. 95.   [22] See p. 95.   [23] See p. 94.

identification, we are led to the following interpretations.

1. The single system of "internuncial paths" (or group of centers acting as a whole)—the "bottleneck" already referred to—is apparently the hypothalamus (posterior). It is the capacity for co-ordination in this region which determines whether compound reflexes are "allied" or "antagonistic"; and it is the fact that simple reflexes, when sufficiently intense, are "long-circuited" to it that prevents them from being any longer "neutral" among each other if they, too, cannot be co-ordinated here into a compound reflex.[24]

2. When there is general excitation in these centers from any one "source," the pattern of the resulting interofective activities is so similar in kind as when it is from any other "source," that the "source" is frequently not distinguishable, the only difference being one of intensity according to the degree of excitation; the resulting exterofective activities are, however, sufficiently different in pattern, at least in the median range of intensities, so that it is possible to recognize the different "functional species of reflex" even among the complex and therefore always "long-circuited" systems of reaction which can only be produced at this level, and to assign each to its own "source." A fortiori, it is possible to distinguish among the several "simple reflexes" which only engage this level when they are of sufficient "strength."

3. When there is general excitation in these centers from any one "source," all other "sources" of excitation are for the time being excluded from access.[25] And, at least in the median range of intensities, when any one "source" thus dominates, all exterofective activities not included in the specific pattern are inhibited.

4. Which among the several "sources" shall obtain this temporarily exclusive access to the hypothalamic region is determined by the then relative capacity of each "source" to cause general excitation in these

[24] This identification of the hypothalamus with the "bottleneck," which we have read into Sherrington's observations, does not depend exclusively upon the fact that we have found it to be the source of affective tone. It is also supported by the facts shown in Appendix II, Sections B 3 and C 3, indicating that this is the first level in the series from lowest to highest at which there is potentially complete integration, in the intact nervous system, of both autonomic and motor activities. As we shall show in Section D 4 below, it is the degree of integration involved that determines whether reflexes are neutral or antagonistic. The elimination of all neutral reflexes and their conversion into antagonistic reflexes cannot, therefore, occur except by reason of the involvement of this level.

[25] In so far as this derives from our own conclusions, we made the generalization (p. 94 that "only one such general state [emotional state] can exist at any moment." See also references cited below in p. 197, note 37. In so far as it is based on Sherrington, it is inherent in his definition of prepotence among antagonistic reflexes.

centers, a capacity which is indicated by the evidences of degree of "affective tone" resulting. That "source" which has the potential capacity of creating the highest degree of general excitation there obtains exclusive access, for the time being, to these centers.

These conclusions arise from Sherrington's observations when they are interpreted in terms of the hypothesis as to the central mechanism which we have previously developed. But there are two respects in which, superficially considered, the two do not fit together. The first is that Sherrington has defined his exterofective evidences of "affective tone" as signs of pleasure and pain, as if affective tone had a double scale. But this difficulty is only apparent, not real. For, in the first place, only a single scale would fit Sherrington's observations and his deductions from them. The quantity, not the "quality," of tone must be determining. And, in the second place, he seems to treat the difference in "quality," so-called, as actually one of quantity, in line with one of the common forms of psychological hedonism.[26] This suggests that it is possible that the symptoms here ascribed to degree of "affective tone" may be evidences only of what Wundt treated as a quite different dimension of feeling—that is, "excitement." Somewhat confirming this interpretation we find Beebe-Center concluding

[26] Thus "in the competition between reflexes the noci-ceptive [with pain] as a rule dominate with peculiar certainty and facility"; (375, 229) while "those concerned with sexual functions," "with sensations similarly of intense affective quality [but pleasure]," are nevertheless less prepotent (ibid., 230). We may perhaps infer that a single scale was in his mind from the following: He says (ibid., 255): "No region of the cortex cerebri has been assigned to pain. Such negative evidence gives perhaps extraneous interest to the ancient view, represented in modern times by Schopenhauer, that pleasure is the absence of pain."

In this particular form of psychological hedonism the common mental diagram of a double polarization according to an algebraic scale, running, from zero, in the minus direction for "pain" and in the plus direction for "pleasure" (or the reverse) gives place to a single polarization, the scale of which runs from zero through what is perhaps a pleasant part, up to what is perhaps an unpleasant part, as it approaches some maximum. In this latter form the physiologically unknown quantitites, "pleasure" and "pain," come to be regarded as mere differences in degree of intensity of "affective tone." That may be an interesting explanation of these experiences; but it does not concern us otherwise than to suggest the possibility that the organism responds differently to affective tone of different degrees, being led, so to speak, to reactions whose tone is mild, and driven, so to speak, to those whose tone is severe, though in both cases the ostensible end-result of the reaction is to get rid of the want and thus to cause all tone —pleasant or unpleasant—to disappear. At any rate it is evident that differences of "quality" of tone are entirely aside from the issue for us.

Another single scale, so far as comparability is concerned, but one that does not eliminate the distinction of "quality," is commonly derived from the interofective evidence. So, in the case of the psychogalvanic reflex, it is said that affective tone is "the same for a given degree of either pleasantness or unpleasantness" (Beebe-Center, 34, 329). This conclusion is based on such points as Wechsler makes (435, 147).

that "the energy of voluntary musculature"—which is probably much the same thing as our "neural energy of response" or Sherrington's "intensity of reaction"—is "related not to hedonic tone [pleasure or pain], but to presence or absence of excitement."[27] Similarly when Hess makes the shrewd observation that "the waking condition reaches its highest degree in the affect," it seems clear that his "affect" is excitement, not pleasure or pain.[28] At any rate it is evident that differences in "quality" of tone are entirely aside from the issue for us. The fact of the matter is that we do not need any hedonic theory to interpret these data. Signs of pleasure or signs of pain seem merely to be variable symptoms—whose differentiation is due to an as yet unknown factor—arising from a cause which varies according to a single scale.

The second difficulty in reconciling Sherrington's inferences with our hypothesis is more serious.[29] It is, or was,[30] his view that affective tone is a "quality" of sensation which is determined by the particular "species of receptors considered as sense-organs."[31] We have previously seen excellent reasons to question both the theory of the specificity of receptors for somatic and visceral sensation and the supposition that pain, at least, is a sensory phenomenon at all.[32] On the contrary, it would appear that differences in character among somatic and visceral sensations may equally well be due to as yet obscure differences in the "pattern" of the impulses and that many, if not all, these "patterns" may arise from any and all of the somatic and visceral receptors. Also it seems more likely that pain is a cortical reflection of an effector reaction organized in the hypothalamus, which is only associated with sensation (and therefore localized) because and if it is "felt" simultaneously. As such, it would belong with the other so-

[27] Beebe-Center, 34, 336. In this view, degree of "affective tone" may represent the intensity rather than the mode of our emotional states.

[28] Hess, 192, 734.

[29] That is, his expressed inferences only; for it will be noted that it is consistent with his statements of fact to treat "affective tone" as an accompaniment of the reflex as a whole. In fact (375, 252) he says specifically that "pain is the psychical adjunct of a protective reflex."

[30] The basis for attributing "views" to Sherrington on this subject is his magnum opus, first published in 1906. I have found no reconsideration of these views in such of his contributions to scientific journals, since that time, as I have examined. Nevertheless, the results of others' investigations in the field of sensation, which have so radically revised the general theory, may lead us into error in attributing the same views to him now. However, this should be pardoned, for we are not undertaking a critique of Sherrington, but only undertaking to reconcile his observations with those of others in a way that will permit us legitimately to use his explicit and precise inferences as the basis of our construction.

[31] Sherrington, 375, 231.   [32] See Appendix II, Sections E 2 and G 3.

called "feelings" (affective tone), all of which we construe to be reflections of the direct excitation of effector reactions in the hypothalamus, produced without the intervention of the sensory apparatus and
frequently without any concurrent sensation appearing in consciousness. But even disregarding these positive objections, there is an insuperable negative objection to the assumption that the sense organ determines the affective tone. For it is notorious that one and the same
kind of external stimulus will at times give rise to "adient" behavior,
at other times to "abient" behavior and at still other times to no behavior at all, depending upon the "physiological state" of the organism.
Along the same lines, there is also ample evidence for the rejection of
such a thesis, based on the study of reflexes themselves. If affective tone
were actually a "quality" of sensation, its effect in securing the prepotence of a reflex would needs be operative at all times whenever the
associated sensation was produced by the appropriate external stimulus of adequate intensity. But this is not the case. Both the "unconditioned" and the conditioned stimuli had small effect in producing the
alimentary reflex and its evidences of tone among Pavlov's dogs when
the dogs were not hungry. On the other hand, a differential inhibition
established against a once conditioned stimulus was rendered "wholly
inadequate" when the animal was very hungry or when the "general excitability of the central nervous system" had been increased (e.g., by
caffeine)—that is, both the reaction and the tone appeared in spite of
the negative conditioning of the stimulus.[33] Again, if differences in
kind of affective tone were actually determined by the particular system of receptors stimulated, as Sherrington seems to think, the evident
signs would be appropriate to the nature of the stimulus or the receptor. Neither is this necessarily the case. Pavlov was able to condition a strong nocuous (pain) stimulus to an alimentary reflex. Since all
the symptoms of the alimentary reaction appeared and none of those of
the defense reaction, he was convinced that the resulting affective tone
was attributable to the alimentary reaction, not to the pain stimulus.
Again the, in themselves, non-affective preliminaries to the injection
of morphine were conditioned so that, without the injection, all the
symptoms—nausea, secretion of saliva, vomiting and sleep—were produced with, presumably, the appropriate affective tone.[34] Finally, it
must be obvious that, in the case of all (even "natural") conditioned
stimuli (visual, aural, etc.), it cannot be the nature of the stimulus or

[33] Pavlov, *320*, 31–32 and 127.   [34] *Ibid.*, 29–30 and 35.

of the receptor that determines the kind of affective tone, if any; for these can be directed to any number of different responses and only take their tone from the nature of the response.[35] And, if these responses fix the kind, they must also, apart from the influence of strength of stimulus, fix the degree.

3. THE MUTUALLY EXCLUSIVE "SOURCES" COMPETING FOR PREPOTENCE

Up to this point in our identification of Sherrington's inferences with the scheme we have previously developed, we have been using the indefinite term "source" of excitation to cover that which has or attains prepotence by reason of its relative capacity to produce general excitation in the hypothalamus. In Sherrington's scheme, degree of prepotence is an attribute of the several "functional species" of reflex. It is determined by the relative intensity of the associated affective tone which, in turn, is a "quality" of sensation whose intensity, presumably, as well as whose kind depends on the particular "species of receptors considered as sense-organs." Upon this basis, his classification of "functional species" of reflex, also, would depend upon the species of receptor at which the reflex arc originates. However, in the light of the points we raised in the preceding subsection, this seems to be an impossible basis for such a classification; for we have seen that neither the kind nor the intensity—except in respect of the indecisive factor of variable intensity of stimulus—of affective tone can be fixed at the level of the receptor. Actually, though Sherrington appears to have attributed the differentiation of the various kinds of reflex to this anomalous afferent source—calling them "noci-ceptive" (rather than "noci-fensor"), etc.—his classification was stated in terms of the motor reactions he observed. But it is equally clear that prepotence cannot be an attribute of activities in the motor section of the reflex arc, for there are no such activities in the case of the weaker and inhibited antagonistic reflex. Prepotence is therefore certainly determined before that stage is reached. If so, kinds of reflex in respect of their prepotence can no better be defined in terms of motor activities. Apparently the actual differentiation which is related to prepotence is based on something much more internal and central (internuncial) and something

---

[35] Even "such external stimuli which have been from the very birth of the animal transmitted to a definite centre, can, notwithstanding, be diverted and made to follow another route . . . provided always that this second centre is physiologically more powerful than the first" (Pavlov, *320*, 37). Thus the determination of the tone and of the prepotence must be central, not peripheral.

much less obvious from the external stimulus-response viewpoint.

If the determinant of prepotence is affective tone and that, in turn, consists of, or arises from, an emotional state in the hypothalamus, then any excitor capable of causing such a state there must be a "source" and must be among the entities to which prepotence attaches. If so, the criterion of classification among these excitors, in terms of which they are homogeneous in respect of prepotence, must be the kind and the degree (or some range of degrees) of emotional excitement they customarily produce. We have already made a careful examination of the recent evidence as to what are the excitors of the hypothalamus. Ultimately they are the bodily wants—internal and quasi-external. Proximately they are the final effects of the several mechanisms of centripetal transmission of these wants (and their conditioned stimuli). No reconciliation is required to adapt Sherrington's observations upon prepotence or Pavlov's upon the "physiological strength" of stimulus (or center) to this scheme of ours. In fact, both only clarify and confirm the analysis of the competition among these wants which we have been developing in the previous chapters. We have found that affective tone, in whatever aspect it is defined, is, or is the consequence of, an emotional state (general excitation or depression) produced in the hypothalamus by those bodily wants requiring integrated activities for their correction.[36] We have found it necessary to recognize the mutually exclusive character of these wants when it comes to producing such general states of excitation (or depression) in the hypothalamus.[37] We have supposed that it is the strongest (i.e., most intense) which succeeds in the competition.[38] We have explained the rapidity of the determination of prepotence on the ground that the resolution of conflicts (i.e., determination of prepotence) takes place very rapidly in the subcortical nervous system, unlike the cortical, and probably by reason of the relatively slight degree of differentiation at that level.[39] Thus all of Sherrington's inferences apply specifically and precisely to our scheme; and all of his observations can be interpreted in terms of it. In fact, when so interpreted, they are more satisfactorily explained. Prepotence cannot attach to the afferent patterns from the

[36] See Chapter 2, Section A, and Appendix II, Sections D and E.
[37] See pp. 77–79 and Appendix II (see Index).
Psychological observation of emotional expression confirms this mutual exclusiveness. For instance, William James says (219, 18) inhibition among the emotions takes place on a large scale. "Witness the evaporation of manifestations of disgust in the presence of fear, of lust in the presence of respect, etc." (loc. cit., note 3).
[38] See p. 101.   [39] See Appendix II.

different species of sense organs; it can attach to the potential excitation set up by the several wants. The competing entities cannot be stated in terms of external stimuli or their receptors; they are largely physiological states. True, the origin of the reflexes Sherrington studied were always regarded by him as somatic. But were they? Of those requiring integration some were what we have called quasi-external wants (e.g., the "noci-ceptive"). These are somatic in a sense, but not in the external stimulus-response sense. Some were what we have called internal wants, for which the somatic stimulus is inadequate (or does not occur in nature) in the absence of the want (e.g., the sexual). These cannot be called somatic. Those which he concluded had least prepotence (e.g., the proprioceptive or postural) lacked it, in our interpretation, because the degree of integration required does not reach to the hypothalamic level; that is, they produce no affective tone. Whether or not these last are to be called wants is a mere matter of terminology. They do not participate in the determination or orientation of integrated behavior. They are not "motives." They are adaptations to, or "associated movements" with, other governing activities.[40] Thus our previous analysis prevents us from accepting Sherrington's interpretation. On the other hand, there was nothing in our previous analysis which gave us the precise basis upon which the competition

[40] Lest it seem that we are assigning "sources" too far dissimilar to the external stimuli with which Sherrington usually deals, it is worth while to note what he and others assign as "sources" of those sensations which are affectively toned. In an older work he stated that "affective tone is an attribute of all sensation." Later he qualified this: "some sensations are neutral or devoid of affective tone, while others are rich in affective tone." At one point he says that "all sensations referred to the body itself rather than interpreted as qualities of objects in the external world, tend to be tinged with 'feeling.'" Yet later, when he is arguing against the James-Lange theory of the emotions, he seems to slip into the same sort of inconsistency with which we have charged Cannon; for he says there that "visceral and organic sensations" are merely contributory, "reinforcing rather than initiating the psychosis" in the primitive emotions. (Quoted from Contribution to Schafer's Physiology, 1900, II, 1000; 375, 255, 266, 267–268). The class of sensations which are "referred to the body itself" and which are nevertheless not "visceral" or "organic," seems to be a very limited one to which to confine this phenomenon. Nor is this exclusion accepted by others. Dunlap, for instance, regards "affects," including the simple feelings and more complex emotions, as "organic, or bodily sentienda" which are "initiated by the stimulation of receptors just as [external] sentienda" are. And "the visceral organs are the most important sources of feeling" (123, 313–314). Tracy (407, 351) treats "visceral activity" and "emotional states" as equivalents. Herrick agrees that "affective tone is intimately bound up with the visceral reactions peripherally" (190, 312). Thus we see that Sherrington, somewhat grudgingly, but others quite freely, are attributing the phenomenon of affective tone almost exclusively to excitors arising from the viscera (i.e., the internal organs). Our only disagreement with them is that they assign all, while we only assign a part, to the afferent neural integrating system.

and conflict between the several wants are resolved—that is, what it is that makes one rather than another, at any time, capable of seizing control of the single agency in which "emotional drive" is developed and in whose behalf it is cortically directed. These "economic" aspects of the way the apparatus works have only appeared as a consequence of our examination of Sherrington's inferences, which, in the large, are so readily confirmed by common observation, as we have noted.

To complete our interpretation, one further point must be made. We have stated that the determinant of prepotence is the *potential* capacity of creating general excitation in the hypothalamus. This assumes that the determinant is not the actual state of excitation and, therefore, that the determination is made either at the point of access to the hypothalamus itself, or at some prior point in the mechanism for centripetal transmission. This necessarily follows, since the only effective tone produced and therefore the only general excitation there, is that appropriate to the prepotent want—the one which does gain access—and since all of Sherrington's concurrent but antagonistic reflexes, which are inhibited, and all of our wants which lose in the competition, fail to produce any of their appropriate form of affective tone as well as any of their motor affects. Determination cannot be made at a point where one of the competitors does not appear. But the point at which the determination is made can be narrowed down still further. Sherrington did not experiment with conditioned reflexes. But we have seen that conditioned stimuli can also influence the determination of prepotence among the competitors (or "sources") for exclusive control of the motor apparatus.[41] Stimuli conditioned to the quasi-external wants can gain prepotence alone (i.e., in the absence of the corresponding want). These surrogate wants cause what we have called replicas. But stimuli conditioned to the internal wants can only do so if the corresponding want already exists. This indicates that the potential hypothalamic effect, in these internal cases at least, must be the result of a summation from two separate "sources." We have come to the conclusion that the effect of almost all conditioned stimuli upon the hypothalamus cannot be transmitted directly, since the afferent systems over which most of them are centripetally transmitted run only to the sensory cortex, not to the hypothalamus.[42] Their hypothalamic effect, then, must come over a corticohypothalamic path. From

[41] See Chapter 3, Section B 1 and Appendix II, Section G 4 c.
[42] See Appendix II, Sections E, F, and G.

this it appears that, if conditioned stimuli are ever summated with unconditioned stimuli (wants) in determining prepotence, that determination must be made at or after the point at which the paths conducting the conditioned and those conducting the unconditioned stimuli, meet or merge. So far as the quasi-external wants are concerned it is anatomically possible that these paths should meet in the thalamus or in the hypothalamus or anywhere between. But with respect to the internal wants—other than waste and refuse—it appears that the integrating mechanism chiefly used for centripetal transmission of the actual want is the circulation (blood). In their case, the unconditioned stimulus (the want) and the conditioned one can only meet at the point of access to the hypothalamic centers. And it is these wants only that give positive evidence of summation. Thus we must conclude that the determination of prepotence is made at this point for all, since only at this point do all these factors, simple and summated, come into play.[43]

To put our conclusions at this stage of the argument in more precise form we may summarize them as follows:

(1) The entities to which prepotence attaches are the various conglomerates of excitors associated with the several wants.

(2) The determination of prepotence among them rests on the sum of the capacity of each want and of stimuli conditioned to it to produce an emotional state in the hypothalamus.

(3) The conglomerate excitors so summated which are capable of producing the highest degree of general excitation (or depression) there become prepotent.

(4) The determination is made at the point of access of such summated excitors to the hypothalamus and therefore as a result of their potential, not their actual, effect.

4. THE SPECIFIC AND MUTUALLY EXCLUSIVE MODES OF THESE "SOURCES"

The conclusion heretofore reached that the conglomerate of excitors related to any want must, in order to obtain access to the single central agency, exclude the conglomerates of all others involves the corollary that, at least under certain circumstances, the posterior hypothalamus acts, and can only act, as an integrated unit. This raises

---

[43] Again it is evident that conditioned stimuli cannot make their contribution to the determination of prepotence in the effector system beyond the hypothalamus because then they could not contribute to affective tone, as they do.

a problem. There are certainly specific functions, autonomic and motor, which can be controlled or regulated in this region of the brain independently of each other. This argues for a large number of anatomically separate and functionally different centers. We know that many, if not all, of the autonomic centers are in a constant, if mild, state of excitation; that is, they are functioning independently but concurrently and continuously, each in its own way, with only a variation in degree. Presumably this means that each center, or group of centers, is activated by its own excitor only and that, at low intensity, the effect of each excitor is limited to its own center and is also specific. Nevertheless, it is also apparent that, beyond some critical level of intensity, excitation in any one of these centers involves others so that the excitation may become general. What is the explanation of this initial specificity and later generality? We have already discussed this question a number of times.[44] The answer is not definitely known, and we have been obliged to use the indefinite term "spreading" to cover the phenomenon. Three possible ways in which this spreading might take place, all conformable to the functional and structural characteristics of the central nervous system, have been suggested. But, in default of conclusive evidence as to which is the actual one, we confine ourselves to the general notion that the anatomical substrate in the hypothalamus is such that excitors, when at low intensities, reach only to their own centers and therefore have only specific effects, while, at higher intensities, they reach more and more centers, either directly or indirectly, and have more and more general effects. Here a distinction must be noted between the vegetative and the motor effects. For the former seem to conform precisely to this rule; but the latter, at least when they are the results of many of the excitors, are already general and undifferentiated when they first appear at all (e.g., the alert and restlessness); they only become specific (special reactions) in the median range of intensity; and they go over again to general and hardly differentiated reactions when the intensity is so high as to produce great excitement. However, this difference between the motor and vegetative effects may be limited to the range in which the vegetative effects have already become general. For we have noted the usual occurrence of what we have called "extensive patterns"—largely autonomic—whenever motor behavior results from hypothalamic excitation at all.[45] Thus the real problem is to explain the appearance of

[44] See Appendix II, Sections B 3 and D.   [45] Appendix II, Sections B 3, D, and E.

"special" motor reactions at a level of excitation which is already producing chiefly general autonomic reactions. The problem needs to be stated; but we cannot solve it as yet.

It is evident, then, that each excitor originally excites but one center (or group of centers), and that the conglomerate of excitors representing a single want, while it may excite several centers simultaneously or successively, nevertheless initially establishes thereby what we may call a different "mode" of excitation from each other conglomerate. This is certainly true when only the several appropriate centers are directly excited; but it is apparently also true that the character of the special mode remains, at least so far as the motor effects are concerned, when the excitation increases and becomes general, and presumably by reason of the fact that it is spreading from a certain center or centers.[46] Only in this way, can we account for the specificity of special reactions which are produced only after the excitation has become general. Whether this "mode" of general excitation is established in the form of topographical differences because of the dominance of one center or group of centers over all others, or whether it takes the form of some special character in the pattern of impulses from each conglomerate, the result, as we know from general observation, is that, for the time being, all other conglomerates of excitors, whose resulting "modes" are different and whose capacity to cause general excitation is less, are prevented from interfering.

This construction of a "mode" of general central excitation in this region, while necessarily indefinite, is a useful hypothesis. For upon it one can hang the facts each in its place. In the first place, whenever there is a condition of hypothalamic excitation which has become general, it must be in some one "mode"; that is, some one want is dominating through its centers. At such time the excitors of all other wants are ineffective. But also, at such time, it appears that external stimuli are almost excluded from access to consciousness (via the mechanism of sensory attention) and are certainly excluded from access via the cortex to the hypothalamus unless they are being or have been conditioned to the particular want then holding sway. Thus they are "of interest" only if appropriate—only if they fit the then "mode." Being "of interest," and therefore admitted to sensory attention, their only

---

[46] Whether this difference in "mode" is fixed directly by the pattern of the fibers excited, or indirectly by the pattern of impulses set up, we do not know. Nor is an assumption of either necessary for our purpose.

effect may be to modify the direction of the cortical control of the emotional energy of response. But, being "of interest" they may also themselves reach the hypothalamus and thus add their weight to this energy.[47]

As we noted above, if conditioned external stimuli are capable of adding to the general hypothalamic excitation, they must also be capable of participating in the determination of the particular "mode" of excitation which is to hold sway; that is, if they can reach the hypothalamus at all, then they are on the same footing as the excitors of the wants in general. Now we have previously found that conditioned stimuli to the quasi-external wants are capable alone of producing their own "modes" of excitation (fear, etc.)—that is, of competing with and securing prepotence as against others. But we have regarded the "modes" thus produced as milder replicas only of the central effects of the actual quasi-external wants themselves. That is, while potent enough to secure prepotence alone, they are far less potent than the actual wants for which they are surrogates. On the other hand, conditioned stimuli to the internal wants—food-objects, sex-objects, etc.— have this power to a much less degree, if at all.[48] To produce their specific mode, they require also concurrent, though not yet prepotent, excitors rising via the mechanism of centripetal transmission as a result of the existence of the want itself. The difference in contribution to prepotence between stimuli conditioned to these two classes of wants cannot be due to differences in the strength of the stimuli, for the optical stimulus which can alone produce the violent fear reaction is, in itself, no more intense than the optical stimulus which cannot, alone, produce the hunger reaction.

Undoubtedly, as already outlined,[49] this difference is due to the

[47] All this is obvious to the crudest external observation. When an animal is very hungry it will usually not respond to the smell of the female, but only to the smell of food, etc. Its behavior is conjoined with the central pattern of eating which has perhaps already started, though not overtly. So Craig (94, 95) admits that "In many cases the rise of appetite is due to internal causes which are highly independent of environmental conditions, and even extremely resistant to environmental interference."

However, these several statements are based more particularly on the analysis of the mechanism that we have already made. Selectivity among external stimuli in respect of their effects has been dealt with in the discussions of "interest," of the mechanism of sensory attention, of resultant orientation, and of course throughout that of conditioning to external stimuli. See particularly Chapter 3, Section B 1, and Appendix II, Section G.

[48] That is, food objects cannot make a satiated animal hungry. Nor can the revival of a sensorimotor pattern representing food produce a replica of hunger of sufficient intensity to give rise to an emotional experience which "feels" the same as hunger does.

[49] See Chapter 2, pp. 92–93, Chapter 3, Section B 1, and Appendix II, Section G.

relative intensity of the emotional endowments of the sensorimotor patterns that are produced by these several conditioned stimuli—or rather of the sensorimotor patterns in memory which become fused with the new impressions by recognition. It is not the weak external stimulus itself that can produce the hypothalamic effect; it is only the emotional endowment than can do so. And these emotional endowments vary greatly in intensity as well as in kind. In fact, the particular kinds derived from the emotional states produced by quasi-external wants seem always to be of a higher degree of intensity than those derived from the internal wants. This seems to be the explanation of the fact that stimuli conditioned to the former produce replicas of the corresponding emotional states in the hypothalamus while those conditioned to the latter can do so little, if at all. Which is another way of saying that stimuli conditioned to the former are adequate alone to gain prepotence, while those conditioned to the latter can only contribute to gaining prepotence when they happen to be summated with the unconditioned stimulus—the want itself.

So much for the specificity of excitors on the incoming side. Each conglomerate of excitors—the combination of those produced from below by the centripetal transmission of the want and those produced from above by reason of conditioned stimuli—results in a mode different from and mutually exclusive of all others. But, so far in the argument, each conglomerate (or "source") might conceivably result in the same patterns of activity as every other. Let us see. On the outgoing side (effector) the difference between the effect of the different "modes" of excitation is not always so great as Sherrington's term "functional species of reflex" would lead one to expect; that is, not so great when it comes to the behavior produced by these general excitations, as distinguished from the short-circuited and strictly spinal reflex, or the effect of mild excitation in a single center. We have already noted frequently that the interofective effects of the sympathetic system, while its several functions may be performed separately if the excitation is low (one center or group), tend to become indiscriminate and uniform if the excitation is high (general). On the exterofective side we have also noted that the first motor effect, the alert, and the second, restlessness or locomotion, seem to be common to many of the "modes," or activating wants. Again we have noted that in extreme intensity of general excitation (states of great excitement or emotional outbursts) there is a very considerable similarity in the behavior produced whatever be the cause. Apparently the difference in "mode" shows itself in behavior, in a definite way, only when the degree of general excitation is in the intermediate range between a low and a high intensity. But in this range the specificity is perfectly definite.[50] For instance, sexual excitement does not produce hunger behavior; thirst does not produce the rage reaction. However, it is only in this limited range, to this extent and in this somewhat vague way that we can define what we referred to above as "a single activity," so far as the primary energizing of the motor apparatus is concerned. As we said in the previous chapter, a "single activity" is any group or series of motor responses which its structure permits the organism to carry on simultaneously and which are "unified" by reason of the fact that they are capable of being simultaneously energized by a single "mode" of central hypothalamic excitation—a single want.

This definition of a "single activity" brings out exactly what is meant by the term integration. It is a fundamental characteristic of the intact central nervous system that the higher the level involved up to the two highest levels—the hypothalamus and the cortex—the greater the degree of integration, and therefore the less is it possible to produce, on the motor side, two simultaneous activities which do not fall within the limits of co-ordination.[51] The level reached in the intact system depends in part on the intensity of stimulus. Thus even Sherrington's "neutral" spinal reflexes become "antagonistic" if the stimulus is strong enough. But the level reached also depends on the character of the afferent or other integrating system stimulated. Thus all our wants, when they become actual variations from homeostasis, reach to this highest level as soon as they are centripetally transmitted at all. For this reason they always produce mutually "antagonistic" systems of reaction. Primarily, then, it is the degree of integration involved that determines whether "reflexes" and all other reactions are "neutral" or "antagonistic." But integration is evidenced as much by the scope of the reciprocal inhibitions that result as it is by the scope of the excitations.[52] In fact, when integration is complete, the whole central nervous system is always involved in one way or the other. This brings in a

[50] We may say with Craig (94, 93), "While an appetite is accompanied by readiness for certain actions, it may be accompanied by a distinct *unreadiness* for certain other actions." He suggests that this may be due to inhibition, internal secretions or "incompatibility of their motor components." The prime reason seems to be this business of prepotence in gaining access to a single apparatus.

[51] See Appendix II, Section A.   [52] See Appendix II, Section A.

different element. And it is this element that determines whether "reflexes" and all other reactions are "allied" or "antagonistic." They are "allied" if they come within the limits of co-ordination; they are "antagonistic" if they do not. But the limits of co-ordination vary. Even at the highest levels, if the central excitation is strong enough, the limits of co-ordination may include the whole musculature. This was Hughlings Jackson's explanation of the epileptic convulsion in which all, even antagonistic, muscles are contracted.[53] Thus, at these levels, the limits of co-ordination are only restricted at all by the creation of a background of inhibition against which some particular movement only is excited. If there is no such background, or if the inhibition is overcome, the limits of co-ordination embrace the whole system. It is this inhibition, therefore, that delimits the scope of co-ordination, in the ordinary narrow sense. In part, the extent of such a background of inhibition is in inverse proportion to the degree of central excitation; but, in large part, it depends directly upon the degree to which the cortex is involved, or, inversely, upon the degree to which the central excitation is short-circuited at subcortical levels. For, as we have seen, the essence of all skilled and adapted and thereby differentiated movements is cortical inhibition. How, then, can we define a "single activity" and its determinant, the limits of co-ordination? We can only do so by saying, "That depends." [54]

However, lest all these qualifications leave a wrong impression, it is well to emphasize again how specific to the prepotent want reactions are within this, the usual, range of intensity. As shown in the previous chapter,[55] there are only two classes of activity which are not subject to the rule of mutual exclusiveness when, in this range, some want is prepotent and is causing behavior. The first exception consists of activities which do not require complete integration; for instance, breathing

---

[53] "Convulsion . . . is a development of many movements at once" (*216*, II, 33). It "is nothing other than the sum of the contentions of different movements" (*ibid.*, II, 31), or "the 'running up' of very many movements into a fight" (*ibid.*, II, 89).

[54] According to the story, after the first J. P. Morgan had discussed with President Cleveland the means of saving the Treasury from the necessity of suspending specie payment, a little pile of tobacco dust was found on the floor beneath the arm of the chair on which his hand had rested. It was the remains of an unlit cigar which he had, reputedly, reduced to powder with his little finger while he talked. Under the stress of internal excitement, and yet against the background of almost complete inhibition imposed by his powerful self-control, all the intense neural energy that escaped was focused upon a single activity of minute proportions and one, at that, that could only have been effected via the cortical motor area proper and its pyramidal tracts. This, if true, is an instance of the extreme minimum limits of co-ordination under great stress.

[55] Chapter 3, Section A 2.

or, among infants, involuntary micturition and defecation. The second consists of activities which may appear as extraneous parts of many extensive patterns; for instance, facial or thoracic expression, associated movements, etc. Otherwise, activity, so far as it results from present wants, is limited to that of the dominant want. We have inferred [56] that each emotional state in the hypothalamus consists of a tendency, potential or actual, toward a particular kind of behavior. But, as we have repeatedly stated, that tendency takes as much the form of inhibition as it does of excitation. It may be inhibition of all else—a background of inhibition. But it may also be inhibition of the special inherent reaction, itself, or of any of its successors. And this may lead to what we have called diversion (i.e., the trial and eventual substitution of a new special reaction). Thus we come back to the conclusion reached in the previous chapter,[57] that the specificity of these special reactions is not their particular motor character; their specificity is due to the fact that they are the inherent or learned responses to the several wants—responses which have maintained that relation because they have been reinforced by leading to the partial or complete satisfaction of these wants.

To add these considerations to what has gone before, the hypothesis that seems best to accord with the facts—though of course it leaves the details of the mechanism largely unexplained—is as follows:

1. The excitors resulting from the various present wants we have examined, and probably those from all others, reach directly each to its own "center" or group of "centers" in the subcortical regions— particularly and ultimately the hypothalamus. It is probable that all stimuli conditioned to each want also reach the same center to which go the excitors from below resulting from that want. However, the capacity of conditioned (external) stimuli of given strength to contribute to the excitation of these hypothalamic centers varies widely. Apparently this variation is due entirely to the intensity of emotional endowment of the sensorimotor process, which the stimulus re-excites, and hardly at all to the relative strength of the stimulus.

2. The determining factor which governs the prepotence of one conglomerate of excitors over all others is its relative aggregate capacity, at the moment, to produce general hypothalamic excitation by means of the phenomenon we have had to call by the vague term "spreading."

[56] See pp. 90–91.   [57] Chapter 3, Section B, 1 and 2.

3. Therefore this dominance may depend on either of two elements or on their sum:

a. the intensity of the excitors resulting from the transmission of the actual want;

b. the intensity of the emotional endowment in the sensorimotor process aroused by conditioned external stimuli.

4. Because each conglomerate of excitors reaches initially only to its own center or group of centers and spreads thence, if and when it attains prepotence and produces general hypothalamic excitation, the "mode" of general excitation differs in each case up to the point at which all centers are embraced. Judging by observable effects, the range of excitation during which the modes differ ends at a lower point for the autonomic than it does for the motor system.

5. Since, at this level, integration is complete, differentiation in the motor and autonomic effects of the several modes is the result as much of what is blotted out by the background of inhibition as it is of the remaining pattern of excitation. Thus the scope of this background determines the limits of co-ordination and therefore what are "single activities." Furthermore, through the processes of negative conditioning and of "diversion," differentiation of motor effects may show itself in different forms of special reactions (different "single activities") for each want at different stages of learning.

6. If, then, we combine the effects of the wants themselves with the effects of conditioned stimuli, including the capacity to produce what we have called "replicas" of wants, we may say that the relative intensity of the conglomerate of excitors associated with the several wants, in so far as it is potentially effective at their respective centers, is the ultimate factor which determines which shall have exclusive access for the time being to the whole unified subcortical region which primarily initiates and energizes, though it does not usually direct, all overt behavior.[58] Prepotence attaches, then, not precisely to the wants

[58] In our use of the terms "access" and "exclusion" we have deliberately side-stepped the, at present, undeterminable question of the exact point at which one want excludes others, and, therefore, the question of what happens to the excluded excitors. This is the crucial question for abnormal psychology. As Kempf expresses it (233, 100): "Out of the affective conflict between the cravings of the organism as a unity and the cravings of an individual part for control of the final common motor path of adjustment, arises the mechanism of suppression, repression, the summation of allied cravings, and the summation of the antagonistic cravings, dissociation of the personality and affective compensation with satisfaction giving compromises as sublimations." Obviously the competition between wants is a highly complex process. Nevertheless, it appears that its general characteristics are not misrepresented in the oversimplified scheme which we have set forth.

themselves, but to the conglomerate of hypothalamic excitors associated with them. And these several conglomerates become the several
"sources" with which we started.

7. By this avenue we have arrived at a concept of *effective* intensity
of present wants which is at least at one remove from the variation
from homeostasis with which we started, for it depends not only upon
the actual states or tendencies, either peripheral or central (as centripetally transmitted), but also upon the capacity of conditioned stimuli
to arouse or contribute to emotional states, whether by themselves (i.e.,
the replicas of the quasi-external wants produced by what we have
called surrogate wants) or only when summated with the effect of
the corresponding want (i.e., the internal wants).[59]

5. LATENT AND EFFECTIVE INTENSITIES OF PRESENT WANTS

Upon this plan, then, we may lay out the scheme which represents
the way in which the intensity of the several classes of present wants
rises and falls, the way in which this intensity expresses itself at each
of the series of steps in the process of becoming effective, and the way
it is added to from extrinsic causes, until finally the stage is reached at
which prepotence among wants is determined. For this purpose we
must discriminate between our previous measure of *latent* intensity,
which we conceive to be determined for each want—and for actual
wants only—by the degree of variation or tendency away from the
state of homeostasis, and the *effective* intensity, which corresponds
to the degree of general hypothalamic excitation when the want or its
surrogate secures prepotence. In the case of what we have called the
continuous internal wants, so long as the corrective process successfully maintains homeostasis by varying its rate, the rate of this process
corresponds to the latent intensity of the want—the strength of the
tendency away from homeostasis. But, under those conditions, the
want has no effective intensity, for it arouses no general central excitation. And, by reason of that fact, it does not foreclose access by other
systems of excitors to their respective centers. So soon, however, as
the corrective process in these cases fails to an appreciable extent to
maintain homeostasis—so soon, that is, as a mere tendency toward variation gives place to an actual state of variation—the latent intensity of

[59] Effective intensity is equivalent to "the force with which the want acts" as used in
our first approximation on pp. 36–37. It is also the measure of magnitude according
to which all wants are comparable upon a single scale, as outlined at the beginning of
this chapter.

the want rises rapidly, and effective intensity may appear, which is capable of producing general hypothalamic excitation and obtaining exclusive access there. In the former condition we say the want is continuously satiated; in the latter it is not satiated until the actual state of variation has been restored to a mere tendency. Thus there are, among these continuous internal wants, two ranges of change in latent intensity—one, the lower one, in which satiety is maintained and there is no effective intensity, and another, higher and very steeply rising, in which effective intensity appears. These two ranges have profoundly different relations to the scheme. So far as I know, no external stimuli have been conditioned to these wants. In default of such evidence we are obliged to assume that their effective intensities, like their latent intensities, are always limited to the effect of the actual wants themselves.

The intensity of the rest of the internal wants, which we have found to be continuous but cumulative and have called recurrent, behaves very differently. In these cases, it is more difficult to discover what is the latent as distinguished from the effective intensity. If we regard the condition of homeostasis as repletion in storage, where the storage is on the inflow side, and emptiness (or depletion) in storage where it is on the outflow side, then it is natural to suppose that the latent intensity of the want rises continuously as withdrawal decreases, or accumulation increases, these stores toward their physiological minima and maxima respectively. However, the gradations of intensity of neural excitors, perhaps secondary, seem to correspond only very roughly to this pattern. For these neural excitors generally show periodic cycles of rise and fall in intensity which repeat themselves, with intervals between them, during the increasing phase of the want.[60]

[60] In the case of those animals whose wants are few and far between this pattern of the excitors makes itself apparent in the overt behavior. Thus we have noted that Richter (338, 308) found that "spontaneous motility" (due in this case to hunger) is rhythmic (among rats), that periods of activity alternate with periods of quiescence (even without eating), and that activity at the start of the recurring period is slight and increases to a maximum near the end.

This rhythmic quality in the effect on behavior conforms also to the periodicity in the associated gastric contractions and sensations which have been demonstrated by Cannon's (58, 244–245 and 255–263) and by Carlson's (71) studies of hunger-pangs.

In the case of one internal want specifically—waste—we found, in Appendix I, Sec. C 1, that the detrusor muscle adjusts itself to, and therefore compensates for, increases in bladder contents, by step-like adaptations of its stretch. Thus there is a series of points in the filling of the bladder, up to some limit, at each of which tonic contraction may give place to phasic (involuntary micturition), which is probably the cause of

Nevertheless, there is good reason to believe that, as these cycles succeed each other, each peak is usually higher than the last, corresponding in some degree to the presumed rise in latent intensity of the want during the interval. A similar disparity between the latent intensity of the want and its central effects may also exist, in some cases at least, when the centripetal transmission, probably primary, is circulatory and the excitors are humoral (or conditions of the blood). Without going into the details,[61] the most probable thesis as to the expressions of the need of water, of salt, and of other food requirements is that not until the shortage of these materials in storage begins to register in a slight change in the composition of the blood, due to reduced availability of stores, does general central excitation from the corresponding special regulatory centers begin. This would account for the periodicity in the appearance of thirst and of the hungers. It is these periodic central appearances or re-appearances that represent what we have heretofore described as "critical points" or "series of critical points," and it appears that it is only at these stages or points that the centripetal transmission occurs which seems to be capable of causing general hypothalamic excitation.

Thus, in the case of many of these wants, it appears that there is something which, for lack of a better term to describe such manifold phenomena, we may call inertia.[62] And this, up to a certain level or during certain intervals, prevents the latent intensity from becoming effective even in the absence of competing wants. But, when the latent intensity of the want reaches a point where it has overcome such inertia and its excitors exceed in intensity those of any other want, it becomes

---

neural centripetal transmission, but which, if inhibited, may lead instead to adaptation to the increased volume. Here, again, the neural transmission to the highest levels seems to be intermittent.

[61] See Appendix I, Sections A and B.

[62] For the sake of inclusiveness under this purposely indefinite term we may describe the absence of effective intensity of the continuous internal wants, until they become actual variations, as also due to inertia.

This term includes neural thresholds; it includes the possibility that certain of the storage wants are not centripetally transmitted until the blood itself suffers a slight change. It may even be stretched to include subcortical negative conditioning, as suggested in the previous chapter, where, for instance, behavior of eating seems to be suppressed until there is food in the mouth. On the other hand, we do not know that such suppression takes place at the gate of the hypothalamus. It may be purely motor inhibition. But, for such cases, we may have to modify our concept of summation of conditioned with unconditioned stimulus. The former may merely "release" the latter.

At any rate the term is intended to cover any gap between the peripheral state of the want and its potential force as a claim for prepotence at the "bottleneck."

effective intensity by causing general hypothalamic excitation; that is, by gaining prepotence. Even then we have noted that behavior (exterofective) does not become immediately specific as to that want, but must pass through a period of general activity until, perhaps, the effective intensity has risen to the still higher level required.[63] It is also possible for the effective intensity of some, at least, of these internal wants to be increased somewhat, without any change in their presumed latent intensity, by the added effect of allied unconditioned or of appropriate conditioned external stimuli.[64] This summation may occur before the want has gained prepotence and help it to gain prepotence by increasing its effective intensity; or it may occur while the want is prepotent and thus enhance its already effective intensity.

In the case of the sporadic wants, only the actual have latent intensity at all. But with them, unlike the others, it seems usually to be near its maximum immediately at the onset of the want. In some cases it may be difficult to determine what the latent intensity actually is; for, if there is warning, the effective intensity may be largely given by the emotional endowment of the sensorimotor processes which conditioned stimuli arouse before the onset of the actual want. Thus the latent intensity of these wants can probably only be judged when they appear without warning, in which case, presumably, the effective intensity is a measure of, because it arises exclusively from, the latent intensity. In the case of all the actual sporadic wants, in so far as their effective intensity is the result of latent intensity, there appears to be no question of inertia or delay of any kind in bringing this latent intensity to bear upon the hypothalamic region and the determination of prepotence there. Finally, the question of this discrepancy cannot arise in the case of the surrogate wants; for these have no latent, but only effective—that is, central—intensity.

Certain qualifications remain to be made before we proceed. The foregoing scheme is seen to embrace only those wants which produce general central and subcortical excitation (hypothalamic) because

[63] This was the general explanation given in Chapter 3, Section A, 2 and 3, for the original and continuing order of succession of motor reactions—general first, special later. One of the clearest instances of it was also presented in the description of "sham rage" in Appendix II, Section D.

[64] In this respect the basic sexual want seems to differ from other internal wants, in that suitable external stimuli, both unconditioned and conditioned, make a far larger contribution to the rapidly rising hypothalamic excitation during the act. Nevertheless, it would appear that even here the steepness of this rise as well as its maximum are largely functions of the initial state of the want.

they require general activity for their satisfaction. We must emphasize, first, that among the continuous internal wants, in so far as the corrective process is adequate to keep the want in the stage at which it constitutes only a tendency to variation, no general hypothalamic excitation occurs, and therefore the want does not need to compete with others for exclusive access to, and control of, the whole system. But once these wants come to represent an actual variation—i.e., once we are "out of breath," or chilled, or overheated—then they too compete, and compete with great force and effectiveness. We must note, second, that there are also wants which require inactivity for their satisfaction—most typically, fatigue. Obviously these wants do not compete for access to the hypothalamic centers on the ground of their capacity to excite these centers—that is, on the ground of the kind of prepotence we have analyzed. Quite the contrary. Their prepotence depends, rather, on their ability to suppress such excitation of these centers as might arise from other sources. What that involves and how it is accomplished we do not know. The most plausible explanation seems to be something in the nature of functional paralysis, referred to in the second chapter. But it will be convenient to include this special negative (not inhibitory) type of prepotence in our general scheme, with the understanding that it involves only the one aspect of prepotence in general—that is the power to exclude and not the power to excite.

E. THE ORDER OF PRIORITY AMONG PRESENT WANTS

Implicit in Sherrington's observation that certain functional species of reflex prevail over others, by reason of what he calls prepotence, is the assumption of some sort of customary order of potency among them. As he expresses it, in his different concepts, "If various species of reflex are arranged . . . in their order of potency in regard to the power to interrupt one another, the reflexes initiated in receptors which considered as sense-organs excite sensations of strong affective quality lie at the upper end of the scale, and the reflexes that are answerable for the postural tonus of skeletal muscle lie at the lower end of the scale"; among the former, those initiated in the noci-ceptive receptors "appear to particularly dominate." [1] If, in accordance with our pre-

[1] Sherrington, 375, 231 and 226. Or, as Woodworth puts it (447, 233), "Protective reflexes prevail over all others, and postural reflexes yield to all others." Jennings (223,

vious analysis, we discard his association of prepotence with particular systems of receptors, and instead we attribute prepotence to the wants which give rise to these reflexes or systems of reaction, it necessarily follows that there must be some order of priority among these wants; that is, a protocol according to which each takes precedence over some others.[2] And this conclusion conforms to many observations.[3] At once two major difficulties confront us. In the first place, how can we reconcile the supposition that any definite customary position in this order of priority can be assigned to each want with the evidence that the latent intensity of the several actual wants seems to be constantly changing—that is, rising as they recur, regularly or sporadically, gradually or suddenly, and falling as, or when, they are satisfied. In other words, what is the particular phase in these successive cycles the degree of latent intensity of which is assumed to be thus characteris-

---

150) notes that the reaction of infusoria to gravity gives way easily to other reactions. Sherrington explains all strictly postural tonus as anti-gravity reactions (see *375*, 340 and *376*, 208).

The general idea of an "order of potency" is also implicit in Pavlov's concept of a "hierarchy of reflexes" referred to above, Section D, note 12.

[2] Thorndike (*397*, 14), approaching the subject from a wholly external angle, arrives at the same conclusion. He suggests that differences in "strength or intensity of wants" may be conceived "in terms of relative position only or in relative position plus some crude or vague specification in units of some scale." Of that scale, more later.

[3] In general, "If various reactions were arranged as to their prepotency, those to pain, hunger, and thirst would head the list" (Freeman, *152*, 300). Warden, in his experiments, (*425*, 378, 393) found the order of purely internal drives among male rats to be (1) thirst, (2) hunger, (3) sex, (4) exploratory; among female rats (1) maternal, (2) thirst, (3) hunger, and (4) sex. Moss (*308*, 183) found "vast individual differences." But, after 72 hours without food, hunger was stronger among rats than sex; the latter was as strong in the female as in the male and varied most widely of all among individuals, while the maternal drive in the female was relatively weak. He attributes a good deal of the difference to the choice of the lesser of two evils (i.e., the lesser resistance, or "repelling forces in the situation which stimulate the animal to negative reactions"). This concept of resistances is, however, equivocal. Richter's rat (*338*, 341) defecated in his water hole. If the water was not changed, the rat covered the hole. But, after three days, thirst conquered disgust at the odor of the water. This we would construe as one want rising to an intensity sufficient to overcome another want —the latter a want to be prevented, not a resistance. We reserve the term resistance for those elements in the environment which require force to overcome. Among male seals and salmon, on the contrary, during the breeding season, sex takes precedence over hunger, and difficulties (resistances, in our terminology) only seem to act as an incitement.

Cannon discusses the resolution of the antagonism between the various "emotions" (*58*, Chap. XIV). He does not attempt a system, but notes many instances indicating an order of priority. The best actual examples from Pavlov's work arise from his inability to procure an experimental conditioned reflex (presumably alimentary) when some external stimulus caused the "freedom reflex" (*320*, 28), the "investigatory reflex" (*ibid.*, 29), or even the "caution reflex" (*ibid.*, 312). In fact, it was this that made the elaborately insulated rooms so necessary for his experiments and led to the provision of a special building for his purposes (*ibid.*, 20–21).

tic of each want and to govern in their competition? In the second place, how can we reconcile the supposition that position in the order of priority is regular and inherent in the want, because it depends on relative latent intensity during some phase in its periodic or sporadic changes, with the fact that prepotence is given by the effective intensity of the want, not by its latent intensity? Effective intensity includes the effect of extrinsic and accidental factors such as conditioned stimuli from the environment. Moreover, it appears in the case of the surrogate wants as a result only of such factors and without any latent intensity.

The resolution of the first difficulty seems to rest partly on what we have called inertia. As we have noted, the continuous internal wants do not require integrated behavior and therefore their latent intensity does not rise to a level where it can become effective intensity until the tendency toward variation from homeostasis become an actual variation. For somewhat different reasons the same discrepancy appears to exist with reference to many—perhaps all—of the other internal wants. That is, as long as water or food supplies in storage continue to be readily available for absorption into the blood, or as long as the accumulation of waste can be accommodated by expansion of storage space, these local processes of drawing down or increasing stores do not require integrated behavior. Only when the processes of depletion or repletion in storage arrive at their critical points—or their series of critical points—do the integration mechanisms become involved so that latent may become effective intensity. Inertia seems to exist only in the case of the internal wants. But they are also the only wants that seem to show the characteristic of a slowly rising phase. The others rise sharply and at once when they occur. We may conclude, then, that the particular phases in the fortuitous or successive cycles of the continuous or recurring wants at which the increasing latent intensities of the wants may become effective are the critical points or series of the same already described. Thus, so far as the rising phases are concerned, the claim for prepotence is not made until a level of intensity is reached which is somewhere near the peak. So far as the declining phase (satisfaction) is concerned, there is only one possible resolution of this dilemma which we will proceed to elaborate in the following subsection.

The resolution of the second difficulty—the introduction of conditioned stimuli—requires some new constructions. In the first place, so far as the phase of rising (latent) intensity is concerned, it is necessary to assume that the respective maximum intensities which the various wants customarily attain during normal living vary over a considerable range. These normal maxima are the levels which the internal wants must approximately attain before their latent intensity becomes effective and thus before the opportunity arises of their gaining exclusive access: and these normal maxima are the levels which the actual quasi-external wants ordinarily attain sharply and at once when they occur at all, so that their opportunity of gaining exclusive access usually comes immediately. What we start with, then, is the scheme of an order of priority according to which the several actual wants are arranged in the order of the normal maxima of latent intensity to which they approximately rise before even laying claim to prepotence. It would follow that, to the extent that several wants reached their maxima at the same time, they would attain prepotence in his order; and, when no want had approximately reached this level, no behavior would be produced by present wants.[4]

[4] This concept of a declining series of peaks along the order of priority which, if all present wants co-existed, would determine the temporal order in which they would be satisfied is a useful analytical tool. It must be slightly modified and complicated in two ways to fit reality, especially with reference to the recurring internal wants. First, the actual maximum of each want is not fixed. If any internal want is not satisfied, it may rise to an abnormal intensity. The periodic satisfaction of all—or almost all—of our fundamental physiological wants is indispensable. Therefore, if left long enough unsatisfied, each will rise to an intensity which will make it prepotent. We must recognize, of course, that among the internal wants we are considering there is no fundamental difference in importance; the satisfaction of all is essential. Nevertheless, their relative urgency differs. "A man may live 30 or 40 days without taking food, 1½ to 3 (once even 7) days without water, but "lack of oxygen for only a brief period may result in unconsciousness and even death" (Cannon, 59, 283). On the other hand, even when coexisting, there is still a difference in the maximum intensities possible to each want as well as in the time required to reach these peaks. Thus Warden (425, 393) found the peaks at maximum intensity among his rats to be as follows: Males—thirst (highest), 2d day; hunger (second), 4th day; sex (third), 1st day. Females—maternal (highest) at standard age; thirst (second), 1st day; hunger (third), 3d day; and sex (weakest), only during oestrum.

Second, when we confine ourselves to this limited list of fundamental wants, we find that, according to their periodicities, they are all normally satisfied in due course (i.e., their normal maxima are sufficient to give them prepotence at some time). And this is explained because, among animals and many men, it is not true that some other want is always occupying the field. But that, in turn, requires an explanation of the necessity of rising to a maximum at all. The reason, then, that minor wants are not usually satisfied as soon as they have any latent intensity at all seems to be due either to the various phenomena of inertia already referred to, or to the fact, already noted, that many of the excitors do not lead to the specific corrective behavior, even if they occupy the field, until they arrive at a certain level of intensity. Nevertheless, competition is usually a factor. Even for the rat, Richter (338, 341) found that, in a cage

We may now modify this scheme to include the effect of unconditioned stimuli (other than the want itself) or of conditioned stimuli. All of these contribute to effective intensity without themselves representing the want and therefore without themselves involving any latent intensity. Consider first the effect of unconditioned stimuli in connection with the want we have called sex. When, under natural conditions, the sexual act has commenced, many unconditioned stimuli contribute greatly to the excitement (effective intensity), though presumably the want itself, and therefore its latent intensity, remains at the same level. But this is a phenomenon of the process of satisfying, not of that of securing prepotence. For prepotence must have been already gained, since the act had commenced. It is doubtful whether extraneous unconditioned stimuli, under normal conditions, ever contribute to the determination of prepotence. However, conditioned stimuli certainly do so and unconditioned stimuli may possibly do so. When they make such a contribution we assume that their central effect is added to that of the latent intensity of the want. That latent intensity, therefore, must have already risen to a level at which it has overcome inertia, but must not yet have risen to the level at which it has achieved prepotence. In other words, the central effect of these extraneous factors helps to secure prepotence by making up the deficit in effective intensity between the customary maximum and the existing latent intensity of the want itself. If so, there is no reason to assume that, when this occurs, the customary maximum is different than when prepotence is secured by the want itself without such extraneous influences. In other words, the effect of what we have called summation does not seem necessarily to involve any change in the first scheme for an order of priority. But we have seen no evidence that summation occurs in the case of the quasi-external wants. It may be exclusively a phenomenon of stimuli conditioned to the internal wants—or at least only observable with such.

The second modification must deal, therefore, with the effect on the order of priority of stimuli conditioned to quasi-external wants. Now we have continuously assumed that the hypothalamic effect of conditioned stimuli is derived from the emotional endowment with which

---

"offering many diversions, the frequency of its eating period is greatly reduced." It becomes once in 5 to 6 hours instead of about 2 hours. Thus, when competition is increased, a higher maximum is required.

the associated sensorimotor process is invested; and we have also assumed that this emotional endowment is a reflection not only of the kind but also of the intensity of the emotional state from which it originally arose. If, now, the several wants have different customary maxima of latent intensity which, in the absence of any other influences, determine their position in the order of priority, the several corresponding emotional endowments will also vary in the same order and to the same degree in their capacity to contribute effective intensity. But, presumably, this capacity will in all cases be much less than that of the want itself. Thus, except in the case of the most potent wants, the quasi-external, the effect of a conditioned stimulus alone will not be adequate to secure prepotence for its corresponding system. It can only contribute to that result by summation. That inference, here, conforms precisely to the generalization we have previously made from the observations of the conditioning process. Stimuli conditioned to internal wants cannot produce central replicas of these wants. They have no central effect unless summated with that of the want itself.

On the other hand, stimuli conditioned to quasi-external wants can produce replicas. They are adequate to secure prepotence alone. Their emotional endowments are more intense because the emotional states produced by the quasi-external wants are more intense. It is for this reason we have given them the status of surrogate wants. By means of these several constructions we have reconciled the fact that the position in the order of priority is given by the customary maximum of latent intensity of the want while actual prepotence is gained by relative effective intensity. The reconciliation rests on the apparent fact that the effective intensity contributed by conditioned excitors (and any extraneous unconditioned excitors) for any want, in so far as the competition for prepotence is concerned, is proportionate to the customary maximum of latent intensity of that want. Thus, when such customary maxima are low in the scale, the associated conditioned excitors are weak—inadequate to become prepotent by themselves— and, because their effect is merely supplementary, they do not change the order of priority. On the other hand, when the customary maxima are high in the scale, the associated conditioned excitors are strong; they are therefore adequate to become prepotent by themselves and thus appear as surrogate wants with positions of their own in the order of priority, though these positions are considerably subordinate to the wants of which they are replicas.[5]

This schematic statement of the order of priority does not mean, of course, that each want is satisfied according to its position in the order of priority without regard to its then degree of latent (or effective) intensity, but only that the process of satisfying does not usually begin at all until that intensity secures prepotence by reaching approximately its normal maximum. Considering our several classes, we are led, then, to the conclusion that the actual sporadic wants, whose maximum intensity is reached suddenly at the onset, usually come first in the order of priority because this customary maximum intensity is normally highest; [6] that, as a general rule, the surrogate sporadic wants follow next in the order; [7] that the continuous internal wants, if they become actual variations, are apt to take precedence over the other internal wants, and that at great intensity they may even interrupt the quasi-external wants; and finally, that the recurrent internal wants, while in ordinary life they are usually satisfied in turn as and when they rise to their normal maxima, have nevertheless maxima which are comparatively so low that, even at them, all the previously mentioned classes of wants, if they occur at all, retain the power to interrupt.[8] However, it is the fact of an arrangement of wants in an

[5] Since, according to this modified scheme, the surrogate wants are the only ones whose positions in the order of priority are given by their effective intensity, because they themselves have no latent intensity, we will insert "(or effective)" in our subsequent statements on this matter, to cover these exceptions to the rule.

[6] Though external injury (and the emotional state called pain) is usually put at the head of the list, it may be suppressed by greater excitement from other causes—though probably always also quasi-external. "The soldier who does not feel the pain of a wound during the excitement of battle, feels it later" (Dercum, *118*, 294). The want (injury) persists in a latent state until the then prepotent want is satisfied or subsides.

[7] Among Rogers's pigeons (*351*, *565*), when normal, conditions arousing fear or surprise (i.e., conditioned stimuli) inhibited the hyperactivity of the crop (i.e., the sporadic surrogate wants were prepotent over hunger). But with decerebrate birds, though with the thalamic region intact, this was not the case. Since, in both conditions, painful stimuli or lesions of the equilibratory apparatus (equivalent to our "loss of balance") superseded hunger, this is further evidence for our conclusion that the excitors from actual quasi-external wants reach the hypothalamus directly from the thalamus while corresponding surrogate wants reach it only via the cortex.

[8] Even so rough a statement as that would seem to be contradicted by some experimental results. But one must remember that, in the laboratory, the natural customary order is not free to operate. We must agree with Frolov (*157*, 98) that there is no unchanging "hierarchy." Pavlov (*321*, 260) says, "Generally the food centre is much more energetic than the guarding centre." But sometimes the heavily charged weak center will predominate over the small charge in the strong. On the other hand, Frolov thinks Yerofeyeva's experiments showed that it was only when hunger gets strong

order of priority in which we are interested and not the exact assignment of a particular place to each.[9]

A necessary complication arises in this order of priority due to the fact that many wants are also members of constellations. It does not follow that, because certain wants are satisfied by the same system of reactions, they also occupy contiguous positions in the order of priority. In fact our subsequent examples will show that such is far from being the actual arrangement. Thus there are major and minor members of a constellation—a sub-order of priority among its several members. The normal maximum of latent (or effective) intensity of the first may be far higher than that of the last. It is necessarily true, then, either (1) that the latent (or effective) intensity of all members of a constellation will be summated in arriving at the effective intensity which determines prepotence, or (2) that it will be the prior want of any constellation which will normally determine prepotence and produce the system of reactions appropriate to all. Both our analysis of the mechanism and observation of the resulting behavior indicates clearly that it is the second alternative which accords with the facts; [10] that is, the particular system of reactions which will exclusively hold the field at any moment is determined, so far as constellations are concerned,

---

enough that unconditioned defense stimuli could be conditioned to it, and then only within some limit of strength of the latter (*157, 97*). All this shows that it is a question of relative strength—strengths that can be artificially manipulated.

[9] What we are considering here is purely the objective evidence of the relative force of present wants. This force may be assumed to operate automatically so far as the primary system is concerned. The subject himself has two ways of knowing about it. The first is the experience of the intensity (emotion). This may be a poor gauge if the emotion is reduced irregularly by leakage and is only a by-product of the degree to which the emotional state is dammed up. Thus wholly involuntary and immediate reactions might cause little "felt" emotion.

On the other hand, the capacity for interference (see Section F 2) can be observed by the subject himself, even without considering the emotional experience. Thus, by insight, each present want can be placed in its relative position in the order by observing what other wants it is capable of displacing. I am inclined to think this very extensive but indirect experience of the order of priority comes to constitute a considerable part of learning to "know thyself," and thus even automatic or unconscious choices come to form the basis of a system of preferences of which the subject is well aware.

[10] For instance, a deficiency of salt in the diet, which presumably causes "salt-hunger," does not, however, increase either the frequency or magnitude of eating in general. Only when "salt-hunger" becomes so intense that it is the prepotent member of its constellation does it govern eating; and then the diet chosen is the nearest thing to pure salt available. The same is true of any other dietary deficiency in so far as the necessary elements give rise to specific hungers. This conclusion will be even more apparent when we come to consider other examples of wants which form constellations.

See also Haldane's studies of breathing.

by the comparative latent (or effective) intensity of the most intense member of each competing constellation.[11]

It should not be understood from any statement above that the order of priority of wants is conceived to be a temporal order. Far from it. The very term "sporadic" indicates that wants of this class do not exist continuously or occur regularly; and we have noted that the continuous internal wants only enter into competition with others when they develop actual variations due to hyperactivity or to special external conditions; only the recurrent wants can be conceived to exist as potential competitors regularly and continuously, and then only at different stages in the phase of rising latent intensity. Nor is the determination of prepotence among concurrent competing wants as definite and clear-cut as might be assumed from our oversimplified statement. If at any time several are somewhat evenly balanced, we may note, for a time, a rather rapid alternation in control, evidenced by tentative essays toward different kinds of specific behavior.[12] But, when only the influence of present wants is at play, and when the determination of the conflict is entirely subcortical, in a very short time this competition is resolved in favor of one want and the rapid alternation ceases. Usually this decision conforms to the order of priority.[13]

F. THE SATIATION OF PRESENT WANTS

I. TENDENCY TO SATIATION

So far as the rising phase of all these wants is concerned we conclude, then, that the latent (or effective) intensity of each has a normal maxi-

[11] This would follow from the evidence for the generalization that the central effects of all wants are mutually exclusive. Even when the system of reactions for all is the same, the "mode" of central excitation of each must be somewhat different from that of every other. This conclusion seems to be so directly contrary to Sherrington's that a reconciliation is necessary. He states that "allied reflexes"—that is, reflexes arising from stimuli within a single "receptive field"—reinforce each other because they are to the same effect (375, Lecture IV). On that analogy we might expect that members of a constellation, because they lead to the same behavior, would also reinforce each other. Nevertheless, the observations referred to in note 10, above, and in Section F, note 19, certainly indicate that they do not. Perhaps the explanation lies in different central organization—the various hungers, for instance, reaching different centers whose modes compete, so that the strongest inhibits the weaker, even though the apparent behavior is the same for all.
[12] As Craig puts it (94, 94–95) one can watch the appetites compete because "expressive signs (consisting partly of the incipient consummatory reaction) show which is gaining control."
[13] That is, it does so unless the latent intensity of some minor want has risen above its normal maximum.

mum (as well as some absolute limit) which establishes its place in the order of priority; that it needs to rise approximately to that maximum in order to gain exclusive access, when other lesser wants are coexisting; that it needs to rise to some point near that maximum, even when no other wants are coexisting, in order that it shall be of sufficient latent intensity to overcome inertia and become effective; and that, even after becoming prepotent, its effective intensity must increase still further in order to bring the effector centers to a state of excitation such as will convert the initial general activity into the requisite special corrective behavior. There remains to be resolved the second portion of the above-mentioned dilemma—that dealing with the declining phase of the want. Once the corrective process is commenced and the consummatory reactions occur, or are occurring, it might be supposed that either the latent or the effective intensity or both would decline abruptly or gradually. But this does not seem to be the case. On the contrary, it seems that not only the condition of satiety—the return of the latent intensity of the want to zero—is sometimes only indirectly related to the termination of the corrective behavior, but that the pattern of decline in intensity of want is quite different from the usual negatively inclined curve of marginal utility theory.[1]

Let us first present the purely logical difficulty with such a supposed curve. If prepotence is secured in accordance with position in the order of priority—and by that of the major want of a constellation—and only during a phase in the cycle at which the normal maximum is neared, how does it come to be maintained while the corrective process proceeds? If we assume that the effective intensity of the then prepotent want declines gradually during the process of satisfaction (corrective behavior), we must conclude that: (1) If there are other wants coexisting whose latent intensity is less, the then prepotent want will lose its prepotence as soon as its effective intensity declines below the level of the latent intensity of the next in order, and its appropriate corrective behavior will then cease; under these conditions, no single want could ever be satiated; (2) if there are no other wants at the moment whose latent intensity is sufficient to overcome inertia, etc., the then prepotent want will nevertheless cease to produce the cor-

[1] The negatively inclined curve of the earlier forms of marginal utility theory, which is also implicit in the indifference curve systems, usually refers to quantities of means larger than those necessary for the single satisfaction of a want. However, it seems to assume that such a decline also takes place within a single satisfaction. For a full discussion of this matter see Chapter 7, Section D 2.

rective behavior so soon as its effective intensity declines below the level initially required to overcome inertia, or even so soon as this effective intensity ceases to be of sufficient strength to maintain the specific behavior; under these conditions, as well, no single want could ever be satiated.

Not only does there arise this logical difficulty with the supposition of gradually declining intensity during the process of satisfaction, but in several different ways observation seems to contradict such an hypothesis. There is, first, the observed fact that "an activity in progress" tends "to complete itself," as Woodworth puts it.[2] Thus he treats such activities as "motives" in themselves, in the sense that "what you are doing in toto [i.e., the "purpose" or goal] determines what you do piecemeal."[3] A drive "is itself a mechanism which, once aroused, persists for a time in activity, and is able in turn to arouse other mechanisms."[4] This "automatic" persistence is observed, but not explained. Some, like Freeman, undertake to explain it on the ground of "compensatory reinforcement" (i.e., the tendency of all stimuli to flow into the path already active).[5] While this remains a possibility, it is inconsistent with our entire conclusion that access of one conglomerate of excitors to the hypothalamus is exclusive for the time being, that only external stimuli which are appropriate to this mode engage the mechanism of sensory attention, and that these probably add to hypothalamic excitation only in respect of emotional endowment in the same mode. Nevertheless, even if it is unexplained, there remains this observed persistence in a reaction. Another approach, which involves a rising gradient of intensity, has been used to explain this continuity of a system of reactions. As we have already noted, Sherrington distinguishes, within such a compound series—which may be regarded as a single activity, and which we regard as the corrective behavior for a single want—between precurrent and consummatory reactions. In such a series he finds that the degree of excitement (or affective tone) increases from the beginning until the final consummation.[6]

But exactly what, we may ask, is the consummatory reaction in all these cases; does it actually differ in form from the so-called precurrent

---

[2] Woodworth, 447, 542.   [3] Ibid., 265 and 238.   [4] Ibid., 446, 157.
[5] Freeman, 152, 354–355.
[6] "To consummatory reactions affective tone seems adjunct much more than to anticipatory," though, by conditioning, "a tinge of the affective tone of the consummatory reactions may suffuse the anticipatory" (375, 330–331). This fits, but is not an essential element in, Washburn's explanation of a series of reactions. See above, pp. 149-150.

reactions; and what relation has it to the satisfaction of the want? We found difficulty in identifying the consummatory reaction in the case of external injury except as that one, if any, in an experimental series which happened to stop the pain.[7] So, too, with the surrogate wants, consummation can only be construed as successful escape from an external relation which would cause the actual want. Apparently Sherrington identifies swallowing as the consummatory reaction in the feeding series.[8] But this seems to be due to his viewing the transaction from the standpoint of the external object. Eating actually consists in a continuous repetition, for a period, of a series of reactions— biting (which may include procuring), chewing, swallowing. From the standpoint of the want, swallowing is still far from satisfaction (replenishment of stores). Nor does swallowing the first mouthful satisfy the want and stop the behavior. Not even cessation of the secondary signal—hunger-pangs—does that. At an early stage the pangs of hunger may stop; nevertheless the behavior continues. Considering other wants, what is the consummatory reaction in the sexual act, or defecation or micturition? Is it the whole act, or only its final part—its completion? We have already seen reason to hold that in the whole sexual act, regarded as a single reaction, the curve of excitation is positively inclined and then drops sharply; nevertheless it may be repeated several times in succession.[9] And, in the case of defecation and micturition the curve seems at least not to be negatively inclined, for these are processes which, once commenced, are normally completed. As a matter of fact the actual consummation in all these repetitive or continuous processes seems to be something quite different from the partial act which Sherrington has identified as such. Thus we must consider the behavior connected with the process of satisfying, in the case of a number of wants at least, to be a repetition of a considerable sequence of precurrent and consummatory reactions, so-called. And any expla-

[7] Sherrington takes the view that "the reaction initiated by a *noci-ceptor* . . . is to be regarded as consummatory" (*375*, 320). But see Chapter 3, especially p. 151, note 62.
[8] "Once through the maw the morsel is, we know by introspection, under normal circumstances lost for consciousness." Affective tone then usually ceases, for "no *effort* can help us incorporate the food further. Conation has done its all" (*375*, 333). "Mind loses touch with this suite of motor behavior exactly at that point where the brain's executive can influence that behavior no longer" (*378*, 30).
[9] Richter (*338*, 328) found that his male rats with high running activity would, if given the opportunity, copulate frequently. But even repetition did not produce a decrease in the running activity. Craig noted the same frequent repetition among house sparrows (*94*, 103).

nation which involves only a rise in the level of intensity through a single sequence, and then a decline, fails entirely to explain the fact of repetition.

If we account for the initiation of corrective behavior on the ground of the effective intensity of the then prepotent want, we must also account for the continuation of that behavior, in spite, perhaps, of the coexistence of other wants, as well as for the eventual cessation of that behavior, even if no other wants coexist, by the temporal pattern (curve) of that effective intensity during the process of satisfaction. Now, in their normal living, most organisms succeed in maintaining homeostasis—that is, their corrective behavior, does suffice to prevent or periodically correct actual variations. Not only as to this result but as to the process itself, what we observe is that, as a general rule, in the absence of interruption by a want which has precedence in the order of priority, the then prepotent want holds the field until it is satisfied.[10] In the case of the continuous internal and the quasi-external wants the point of satiety has already been defined as a restoration of the state to a mere tendency, and as cessation of the want or of its replica, respectively. Either form of satiation results in discontinuance of effective intensity (i.e., ostensibly in satiation).

In the case of the recurrent internal wants the matter is not so simple. Previously (p. 180, above) we went no further into this question than to define their satiation as the restoration of homeostasis. But when the process of satisfying is correlated with the behavior which accompanies it, a discrepancy appears in some cases. Those whose satisfaction consists in the depletion of stores—sex, waste, and refuse—show a cessation of behavior when the depletion is completed, and usually not until then. Thus they seem to conform to the simple rule. But those whose satisfaction consists in the replenishment of stores do not seem to follow this rule.[11] That is, the behavior, eating or drinking, ceases long before the ingested food or water can possibly reach the

[10] So general is this assumption that Craig can say (94, 93) that when "the appetitive behavior ceases," "we say the animal is satisfied."

All we are saying here, of course, is that there is no tendency in the emotional (automatic) response to a present want to terminate before satiety is reached. The restraint, if any, short of that mark, comes from non-emotional sources. In fact, among men if not among animals, the very existence of four of the "Seven Deadly Sins" shows an inherent tendency to reach beyond normal satiation. Surely, among them, gluttony argues that, when abundance first became available, the practice of overeating and overdrinking must have been a "natural."

[11] This matter is discussed more fully in Appendix I, Sections A and B.

ultimate storage reservoirs and thus long before homeostasis is actually restored.[12] Nevertheless, the behavior stops when the quantity ingested is sufficient to accomplish that result—that is, it stops when homeostasis is potentially restored. This has led to the suggestion that there are, in these cases, independent "signals" arising from the stretch of the gastro-intestinal tract and yielding the "sense" of repletion. While such signals doubtless occur, we have seen reason to doubt that they are the agencies which terminate the behavior. Rather we have guessed that the same agency—the blood—which initiates the centripetal transmission of these wants when they have risen to a latent intensity that slightly alters the composition of the blood is also the cause of the cessation of this transmission and of the corresponding behavior, when the process of absorption (of water) or of digestion and absorption (of food) has restored the normal composition of the blood.[13] Obviously this point would be reached long before absorption was completed; in fact, it would probably be reached just as the blood, having replenished its own stores, began to dispose of the surplus into the various storage reservoirs. If this is correct, then, in these two instances, behavior would be presumed to cease because the want thus lost its effective intensity and that, in turn, because its latent intensity, though continuing for a time, sank below the level necessary to overcome inertia. The state of repletion or satiety would not exist at the ultimate locus of the stores but at a locus more proximate to the central apparatus.

But, whether repletion occurs in the blood or in the gastro-intestinal tract, at any rate we must recognize the fact that it is these states of repletion (somewhere) or of depletion which constitute the end-point of the systems of reaction to the recurrent internal wants, and that they are customarily reached. If that is so, even in these cases, we are led inevitably to the conclusion that the effective intensity of all classes of wants does not and cannot decline gradually during the process of satisfying, but that, instead, once a want becomes prepotent, its effective intensity must and normally does remain sufficient to maintain

[12] Sherrington (375, 333) thinks "the naïve notion that when we have eaten and drunken we have *fed* is justified practically," since, thereafter, " 'conation' is no longer of advantage." But we cannot accept an explanation which is no more than the imputation of providential design. The fact of discontinuance of eating and drinking by decorticate animals shows that this is an automatic affair. According to our analysis it must be due to the disappearance of the cause—the state of general excitation in the hypothalamus.
[13] See Appendix I, Sections A and B.

that prepotence—that is, practically unabated—through the process of satisfying, in order that it may continue to exclude the less intense wants that it excluded at the outset and in order that it may continue to overcome inertia; and that, then, it must and does drop quite sharply to zero—satiety. That is the only pattern which can be fitted to the facts of the competition between wants. Thus we resolve the second part of the dilemma presented above. In that view, then, consummation is the point at which the behavior normally stops—it is the end-point of satisfaction or the point of satiety. And, conversely, behavior does not normally stop until satiety is reached. It is impossible to reconcile this self-evident conclusion with the basic postulate of marginal utility theory.[14]

2. FAILURES TO SATIATE PRESENT WANTS

While the normal course of behavior seems to be to satiate each present want by a continuous or repetitive process, once it arrives at prepotence, there are three general causes or occasions which may interrupt or even prevent such a consummation. And these exceptions to the general rule are of sufficiently frequent occurrence to make it necessary for us to incorporate them in our scheme.

[14] The foregoing argument seems to the writer so conclusive that it is not necessary to labor the point. Nevertheless, for doubters, two other considerations may be introduced. In the first chapter (pp. 38 to 39), we disputed the necessity of introducing the purely subjective concept of "purpose"—i.e., a future end—into the explanation of behavior. We said, "In our system of energetics a state of variation from homeostasis leads to [energizes] some form of activity. If and when this activity restores homeostasis, activity ceases [is no longer energized]." How, we may ask, could the human mind ever have conceived the subjective notion of "purpose" from the self-contemplation of this process, which is undoubtedly its source, if the thing felt—the "drive"—was continually running down during the process? On that basis the "ends" of our ultimate purposive actions would actually be their "beginnings" only, for only the beginnings would be strongly felt.

The other consideration is the matter of the reinforcement needed to condition stimuli to wants. In Chapter 3, Section B, we construed reinforcement to be always and only the partial or complete satisfaction of the want to which the stimulus is conditioned. One has only to glance through the records of Pavlov's experiments to note many instances in which conditioned stimuli to the salivary reaction (hunger) were repeated at intervals of a few minutes in a considerable series and were each time reinforced with a "morsel of food" or a "few seconds" of eating. The saliva produced continues to be the same throughout such series—though with some irregularity. That proves that the want remains at the same intensity, even though, at each repetition, it is partially satisfied. When the want is satiated the conditioned stimulus no longer produces the reflex at all. Other experiments by psychologists with their "rewards" prove the same point. It would be hardly possible to conduct such experiments, using storage wants as the basis, were it not for the fact that modicums of the reward continue to work with approximately the same effectiveness throughout a series.

The first of these we may term "interference." [15] If all present wants coexisted, they would, according to our scheme, be satisfied in the order of priority. And this process could only be completed if, before the least want was satisfied, the one which is first in that order had not arrived again at an intensity sufficient to give it prepotence. But all wants do not coexist. Instead, the occurrence of some is quite irregular and the recurrence of others takes place after different intervals. Since the wants which occur irregularly (sporadic) have also normal maxima which place them at the head of the list in respect of prepotence, and since their phase of increasing intensity is usually short and sharp, it is especially true of these that, when they occur, they are apt to interrupt the current behavior; that is, interfere with and suppress the want then holding the field. Among the internal wants this interference is less likely, chiefly because their latent intensities increase slowly, so that there is apt to be no change sufficient to make another of them prepotent during the process of satisfaction of any one want. Nevertheless, interference does occur even here, especially when the continuous internal wants develop an actual variation from homeostasis. For instance, becoming completely "winded" or excessively overheated will suppress even the excitement of the chase. And these, or fatigue, may reach points at which even fear loses its prepotence. Therefore, we may say, in general, that if, during the dominance of any one system of reactions, some other want, alone or as part of another constellation, arrives at a latent (or effective) intensity greater than that of the then prepotent want, this newly prepotent want will suppress by "interference" the reactions of the former one.[16]

[15] This is Sherrington's term (see 375). But, whereas he used it to cover all interference between reflexes, however local, it should be understood that we are applying it here to the highest subcortical level only. To him interference depends on opposed use of the same muscles and then on relative intensity. To us it depends only on relative intensity (though not of the stimulus only); for that determines the reach of the long-circuiting and therefore the extent of the integration (level reached). At the hypothalamic level, where integration is practically complete, an excitor sufficiently intense to spread will involve excitation or reciprocal inhibition of the whole effector field available there.

[16] As stated on p. 147, note 16, what we are here calling interference occurs or is prevented by reason of the phenomenon that Pavlov calls "external inhibition" (see 320, 44–47). He regarded this as "indirect" inhibition—that is, what is now more usually called "reciprocal" inhibition—the inhibition of certain activities or patterns produced as an incident of the excitation of other activities or patterns. Our views of inhibition were discussed in Appendix II, Section G 4. "External inhibition" is one of the two phenomena upon which Pavlov bases his notion of a "hierarchy of reflexes" arranged in the order of their "physiological strength"—the other phenomenon being the possibility of conditioning the stimulus of a weaker reflex so that it produces the

When a want is interfered with in this way, before the normal process of satiation is completed, so that its remaining intensity becomes again merely latent, at what level, we may ask, does this latent intensity stand; does it remain at the level it had while effective; is it reduced from that level by reason of the partial satisfaction already accomplished; or does it behave as if the partial satisfaction was a complete one for the time being (i.e., as if satiated)? In this regard it appears that the different classes of wants act differently. The sporadic actual wants—at least external injury—resume prepotence at the same intensity once the interruption is over. Pain is no less because some other excitement has caused one temporarily not to feel it. The continuous internal wants, if their intensity has been determined by an actual variation, seem to resume at a new level corresponding to the degree of satisfaction accomplished before the interruption (i.e., there is a discontinuous change). After a panting dog is startled, his panting (cooling) is resumed with less intensity.[17] But the internal recurrent (storage) wants seem temporarily to be obliterated by interference. And apparently this is for the reason that, some part of the stores having been replaced or discharged, latent intensity, under these circum-

---

reaction of a stronger one.

Among Pavlov's examples of external inhibition, two illustrate the occurrence or prevention of interference most clearly. "In the season when the females are in heat," "if the males have been housed near the females before the experiment, it is found that all their conditioned reflexes are inhibited in greater or less degree" (ibid., 47). That is, when the powerful sexual want has become prepotent—or is at a high level of latent intensity—it is difficult or impossible to distract the dog's attention even temporarily by arousing lesser wants or their replicas or by summation (i.e., by interference). This makes it plain that it is the central effect of the prepotent want that causes the inhibition (prevents interference); for, at the time, no conditioned external sexual stimuli and possibly no unconditioned external stimuli were being received and, at least, no sexual reaction was under way. Another example is more complex. "An experiment may be running quite smoothly, and suddenly all conditioned reflexes begin to fail, and finally disappear altogether. The dog is taken out [of the stand], allowed to urinate, and then all the reflexes return to normal" (ibid., 47). At first sight one would say that, here, the latent intensity of the want we call waste had risen to a point at which it became prepotent and thus interfered with the lesser wants being experimentally aroused or brought to prepotence. But that is not all; micturition is "a most unusual occurrence for dogs while in the stand" (ibid., 46). This shows that the dog was subject to a still stronger want, which was the one that actually became prepotent. The inhibition of micturition while on the stand was the "naturally" conditioned response to this still stronger want—not one of those we have listed. Thus the prepotent want may assert itself solely in the form of inhibition and, so long as it remains prepotent (i.e., no other becomes strong enough) all other wants are prevented from interfering and no general activity can occur at all.

[17] I do not feel at all sure of this observation. Neither, as a matter of fact, am I certain that these particular wants, when they become actual variations, do not show a declining curve of intensity while still prepotent. Perhaps they constitute an exception to our general rule.

stances, falls below the level necessary to overcome inertia, so that the only effect has been to shorten the period before the next recurrence of the normal maximum.

What often appear to be instances of the phenomenon referred to above as preliminary indecision must be mentioned here, since they are actually instances of interference. One example will have to serve. Those wants which require inactivity for their satisfaction (fatigue, etc.) cannot attain or maintain prepotence in the presence of another want capable of overcoming the then degree of hypothalamic depression and thus of causing hypothalamic excitation. In terms of his own concepts, Craig has a nice description of this common phenomenon. He says:

In some cases the seeking of a certain situation involves both appetences and aversions in considerable number. Thus, when the day draws to a close, each dove seeks as its roosting-place a perch that is high up, with free space below it and above it, with no enemies near, with friendly companions by its side, but these companions not too close, not touching (except in certain cases of mate, nest mate, or parent). The endeavor to achieve this complex situation, to secure the appeted stimuli and to avoid the disturbing ones, keeps the birds busy every evening, often for an hour or more.[18]

We would interpret his observations as follows: Driven by the want which requires rest or sleep, the doves nevertheless cannot begin to secure this satisfaction so long as other activating wants, arising from stimuli from the environment, and chiefly conditioned ones, continue to interrupt. As each interruption ceases, because the activating want ceases or is satisfied, the want for inactivity resumes prepotence, only to be interrupted again. Finally all interruptions are successfully ended by the proper adjustments to the environment and rest ensues. The same phenomena are often observed with dogs who wheel or scratch until their "lie" is comfortable. It is only because the inactivating wants leading to rest are normally of a low potency and therefore, at most times, far down in the order of priority, that the phenomenon of interference becomes an almost regular one in their case. And it is only because such interrupting wants are usually minor ones, which cease or are satisfied rather easily and quickly with some change in the relation to the environment, that the inactivating want is permitted to resume its prepotence so readily. Evidently, then, the inactivating wants, like the sporadic actual, usually resume their prepotence at the same level

[18] Craig, 94, 101.

of intensity. Nevertheless, too long-continued interruption, even without satisfaction, may cause a marked reduction in intensity and a loss of prepotence for a considerable period (e.g., sleeplessness).

The second type of failure to satiate we may call "incidental failure." This occurs when, in the course of carrying through a system of reactions at the behest, and to the point of satiation, of the major member of a constellation, some minor member remains unsatiated. Using again as our example the food constellation, it appears that as a general rule we may say that: (1) If the minor member is completely unsatisfied it may then come to determine the prepotence of the constellation so that, if its intensity is sufficient to maintain exclusive access against competition, it will continue the series of reactions after the major want is satiated. (2) If the minor member is partially satisfied, its latent intensity will probably drop to zero for a time and, when it recurs earlier than the major member of the constellation—because of its incomplete satisfaction—its latent intensity will still be insufficient to secure prepotence by itself, because of its subordinate position in the order of priority. (3) But, whether completely or partially unsatisfied, if there results from recurring deficits in satisfaction of the minor want a cumulative effect on its latent intensity, this intensity may rise to a level which makes the minor want prepotent in the constellation until it is satiated.[19]

The third type of failure to satiate is due to the premature cessation of the behavior because of imposed external conditions. Under this rubric it is convenient to include all deficiencies which do not result

[19] This scheme seems best to cover the spontaneous dietary habits of animals and men. It seems to be the only explanation of unfelt partial dietary deficiencies, on the one hand, and of the occasional outburst of the specific hungers, on the other. There seems to be no doubt that, among men, overeating is frequently, if not usually, due to the insufficiency of some needed constituent in a meal which has sufficed for the major want. And surely the special character of between-meal eating usually indicates a specific hunger—not merely a "sweet tooth."

The most precise evidence along this line is offered by the experimental feeding of animals. Incidentally, that goes also to confirm our distinction between the different hungers as independent phenomena. For instance, Young (450, 34) cites his earlier experiments as warranting the assumption that "food preferences change during a period of eating." Among his white rats the normal preference for sugar over wheat was reversed by 15 minutes or more of pre-feeding of sugar. The result was a preference for wheat which disappeared only gradually when the pre-feeding of sugar was stopped. "Because the amount of glycogen stored in the rats' bodies became excessive it took several days to reduce it." "The fact that the preference of sugar to wheat can be reversed implies that the organic conditions which regulate the appetitive demand for sugar and for wheat are, at least to some extent, functionally independent" (ibid., 63). Other observations bearing on the same subject were cited in Appendix I, Section B.

from factors operative within the organism itself. Thus we include failure to escape and the inability to compensate for, or to correct, shortage of oxygen, extreme heat or extreme cold. But chiefly we are concerned here with the fact that when all available firewood, or water, or food is consumed, a want may still remain unsatiated. In general, we may say here what we said above in regard to the effect on the remaining intensity in connection with the first type of failure. In this case, too, the effect is different for the three general classes of wants, and for each class it is the same as it was in the case of the first type of failure. The impotence of rage does not diminish it; the cessation of external warmth leaves one warmed but cooling; but the incomplete satisfaction of a recurring (storage) want leaves the want suppressed for the time being and only causes it to recur again the sooner.

Thus we find that what has been treated in economics as a continuous reduction in intensity in the course of the satisfaction of a want, which, in the competition between wants, would always have to terminate short of satiation, must be, instead, regarded, in almost all cases, as a discontinuous reduction occurring only at the end of the process of satisfying. And this end, if it is not satiety (reduction to zero), must be construed to fall short of that only because of "interference," or because of the "incidental failure" to satisfy some of the minor components which participate in a co-operative system of reactions, or because of the premature cessation of the process due to imposed external conditions—chiefly an insufficiency of some external object.

G. SUMMARY AND INFERENCES

While it is not now possible, and perhaps will never be necessary, for economic analysis to translate each of the present wants it must consider into terms of the physiological substratum of behavior upon which we have based our analysis, it is certainly desirable that its conceptual model or ideal type of wants and the process of satisfying them, as a whole, should accord with the general features of the analytical scheme developed from that substratum, or at least should not conflict with that inductive scheme in any respect without good and sufficient reason. With that in mind, we shall proceed briefly to summarize the results of this analysis and will then undertake to enumerate the several respects in which it seems necessary to modify the usual conceptual model in order to eliminate those inconsistencies which seem at present indefensible.

We have identified wants as internal tendencies or states, resulting from internal processes or relations with the environment, among whose effects are some that compensate for, or correct, these states and which give rise to overt behavior suited to accomplish that result; that is, to satisfy the want. These wants we originally divided into three classes—continuous, regularly recurring, and sporadic—according to the appearance over time of their appropriate behavior. But we have found that the continuous wants, so long as they remain tendencies only, give rise to special activities which are not incompatible with other simultaneous general activities. In their aspect as states requiring general activities—that is, in their competition with other wants—we may therefore regard even the continuous wants as recurring, though irregularly so, or as sporadic, as we prefer. Thus, so far as general behavior is concerned, we may treat all wants either as recurring regularly or as occurring irregularly.

Since but one system of integrated reactions can hold the field at one time, the whole gamut of wants must compete for control of the single apparatus. The basic element in this competition is, in general, the comparative latent intensity of the want. It is this which *primarily* determines prepotence. During the phase of latency the intensity of some wants seems to rise suddenly and sharply while that of others rises gradually or even intermittently. But, on account of the necessity of overcoming inertia, of attaining a sufficient intensity to direct behavior into a specific pattern, and of securing prepotence against the nearly continuous competition of other wants, it is usually necessary for each want to attain a considerable intensity in order to become effective. The point to which it usually does rise before becoming prepotent we have termed the customary maximum of latent intensity. These maxima seem to vary over a considerable range. If all wants were at their respective maxima of intensity at one moment, they would thereafter become prepotent and be satisfied in the order of their intensities. These maxima, then, determine the potential order of priority. But, in their actual occurrence, since the interval before the regular wants recur varies and that before the irregular wants occur is fortuitous, the intensities of the former may, at any moment, be at various stages of the rising phase below the maximum and that of the latter may be at zero (i.e., non-existent). Thus the actual order of priority, at any moment, depends on the then relative intensity of existing wants. However, taken over a long enough period, the potential order of priority does show the relative potency of wants.

All these generalizations have then had to be modified to include the effect of stimuli conditioned to these wants and, possibly, of unconditioned stimuli not arising from any want itself. And this by reason of the fact that these stimuli may, according to the extent of their emotional endowment, be included in, or even constitute, the conglomerate of excitors producing the mode of the several wants. Thus, in determining effective intensity, they may be added to, or substitute for, those excitors which result from the latent intensity of the want itself—i.e., the effective intensity of the want. In this way they become *secondary* influences in the determination of prepotence. The influence of such stimuli, when they are conditioned or related to internal wants, seems to be confined to the *timing* of the arrival of the want at prepotence. This because they are inadequate to secure prepotence by themselves. They can only contribute by being summated with the effect of a sufficient latent intensity of the want. Thus they may make their corresponding want prepotent sooner by bringing its effective intensity to its customary maximum; but they do not alter the position of the want in the order of priority; for the customary maximum, which fixes that, remains the same. The influence of such stimuli, when they are conditioned or related to quasi-external wants, is different. Being then adequate to secure prepotence by themselves, and usually occurring in the absence of the corresponding want, they attain a position of their own in the order of priority, as surrogate wants. But since the effective intensity in each case is less than that of the corresponding actual want—producing a mere replica—their several positions in the order of priority are subordinate to that of the corresponding actual wants, respectively. The phenomenon of summation does not seem to take place with the quasi-external wants, and the phenomenon of conditioning does not seem to take place with the continuous internal wants. Therefore no further modifications are required.

If it is necessary that the latent intensity of a want should rise approximately to its customary maximum and become effective alone, or that its effective intensity should be brought to that level by the addition or substitution of the effect of conditioned (and possibly other unconditioned) stimuli in order that it may become prepotent in its turn, it is evident that its effective intensity must be maintained at approximately this level during the process of satisfying, if that process is to be completed and satiation is to result, as it usually does. It follows that effective intensity does not change markedly until the process ceases for any one of several causes.

Many wants are subject to a dual arrangement. According to the customary maxima of their latent (or effective) intensities they have their places in the order of priority; according as they participate in a joint system of reactions and are therefore non-competitive among themselves in this respect, they are grouped in constellations. Wants which are included in a constellation may have all sorts of different maximum intensities. Thus the arrangement by constellations does not accord with the arrangement by priorities. The prepotence of any constellation at any moment is determined by the component want whose latent (or effective) intensity is greatest. If, in the course of the appropriate reactions the most intense component of a constellation is satiated and some other less intense component is not, the latter thereafter determines the remaining intensity of the constellation, provided it retains any effective intensity at all.

The several reasons for which a want may be left wholly or partially unsatisfied are: (1) That neither it nor its constellation ever secures prepotence, so that its corrective behavior is never initiated; (2) that the corrective behavior is prematurely suppressed, (2a) because of the "interference" of another want which rises to prepotent intensity during the process, (2b) because of the "incidental failure" to satiate some minor member of a constellation, whose intensity is insufficient to secure prepotence by itself, before the satiation of the major member ends the process, (2c) because imposed external conditions make completion of the process impossible. When premature suppression occurs for any of these reasons the latent intensity of the unsatisfied want may continue unchanged, may drop proportionately to the partial satisfaction, or may drop to zero, according to the particular type of want concerned.

In regard to those respects in which modification seems necessary in the currently accepted conceptual model of wants and the process of satisfying them, we have perhaps already sufficiently emphasized the matter of the "shape" of the curve of intensity of a want. We have found it to be positively inclined—steep or gradual or even serrated —during the phase of latency, then approximately level during the process of satisfaction, and finally declining vertically to zero at the normal end of that process, satiety,[1] or in the same direction, but not necessarily to zero, if the process is prematurely suppressed. There remain the following points which require to be made, but which have not previously risen.

1. A present want is, if actual, always a tendency to be curbed or a state to be got rid of, or, if surrogate, a central replica, leading to the prevention of the corresponding actual want. In this scheme of present wants, an economic want in the form of a state which the subject wishes to attain or to continue to enjoy becomes an anomaly. Such a state would consist in the absence of any want and the result would be *no* behavior—not even inactivity. Therefore, it could not be among the causes of behavior, nor play a part in any physiological system of motivation.

2. The list of present wants which we have found it possible to examine is merely a tentative and preliminary one. We have confined our attention to it because it has proved impossible as yet to expand it while continuing upon the same objective physiological basis. However, we may presume, at least until the contrary is proved, that all other present wants operate in the same way. Therefore, our definition, if not our list, of present wants covers all such causes of behavior. It follows that, in applying this scheme to the examination of economic life, we must not let some sort of sense of intellectual symmetry lead us into excluding from the category of wants any recognizable present causes whatever so long as they lead to attempts toward satisfaction which, according to the pragmatic criterion to be developed later, are comprised in the activities of economic life. This pragmatic criterion concerns the nature of the attempts—the behavior—and not the character of the wants. We do not have economic and non-economic wants. We merely satisfy our wants in economic and non-economic ways. The more extraneous wants, which we find it especially important to include, are particularly of three kinds.

a. The first kind of extraneous present wants are those which are

---

[1] This "shape" does not seem to be characteristic of intensity during the sexual act, in which the curve apparently rises during satisfaction. But it is normally characteristic of any succession of such acts which eventually result in satiation. On the other hand, it is not characteristic, even in this way, of certain abnormalities—wants that "feed on their satisfactions," such as alcoholism, priapism, vanity, love of power, miserliness, etc. In fact, these seem often to be *insatiable*. Nevertheless, the normal type of actual want remains our recurrent hunger with its periodic appeasement to the point of satiety.

themselves satisfied by features or aspects of what is or has been the process of satisfying other wants. We have already noted that the members of a constellation are to a large extent satisfied incidentally to the satisfaction of the chief member. But that is not the relationship referred to here. Rather, those we now refer to act as if originally they had no independent origin. They give the impression of being dependent outgrowths of behavior which was originally energized by other wants but which has come to be, on some occasions or in some phases, energized by secondary wants to which it is consummatory. Behavior, so taken over, always consists of the precurrent, never the consummatory, reactions to those other wants.[2] For instance, the savage may originally hunt to satisfy his hunger. But the want of hunting per se then appears, and continues into civilized times. So, in more advanced stages, we have many cases where some feature of the activity involved in providing for, or the accumulation of means to provide for, one want comes to constitute directly and for its own sake the satisfaction of another, or of other wants.[3] At any rate, when this condition develops, it is clear that the activity which was, or still is, precurrent to the satisfying of one want has come to be at least partially energized by another, or by other wants, to which it is consummatory. These we may distinguish, for future reference, as *ancillary* wants. They are satisfied, originally at least, by features of the precurrent reactions to other wants, as contrasted with the independent wants that

[2] For further discussion of this type of want, see supplementary statement on "Ancillary Wants" at the end of this section.

[3] In connection with satisfaction through some feature of an activity, it is not a realistic view of economic or social psychology to conceive that the business leader works only for his compensation; nor the foreman, nor the artist, nor many "artisans," nor the politician. The instinct of workmanship is a bad term for this want, both because it is not an "instinct" (many do not have it) and because it is not for "workmanship." It seems to have several components, an urge to activity, a satisfaction in having performed "well"—particularly if confirmed by others—and, at times, the want to exercise power over men and things for its own sake.

In connection with satisfaction through accumulation, as Knight says (*240, 319*), "The increase in wealth is to a large extent an end in itself as well as a means to the increase of income, and this also again to a rapidly increasing degree as the standards of life are advanced. Men work 'to get rich' in a large proportion of cases, not merely in addition to, but in place of, consuming larger amounts of goods. It is a grave error to assume that in a modern industrial nation production takes place only in order to consumption." Of course the truth of that statement depends on the definition of consumption. If consumption is the satisfying of wants, then it is not true to that extent; for to that extent production would then yield some consumption while it was in process.

The relation of accumulation to the so-called instinct of hoarding, or acquisitiveness, as a want in itself will be examined more closely in Appendix V, Section B.

we have dealt with, which are satisfied only by their own consummatory reactions.[4]

b. The second kind of extraneous present wants is usually confined to those that are among the more subordinate in the order of priority. Though they are recognized as forcible "motives," they seem particularly intangible and subjective, so much so that it is difficult to conceive that they have a physiological (peripheral) basis at all. Thus, from the standpoint of our approach, they are the most remote and inaccessible of all, lying far beyond those apparently physical wants which we mentioned at the end of the previous chapter, but which we admitted are still beyond our reach. Merely for example we may mention, "keeping up with the Jones's"; fads and fashions; love of power, success, admiration, prominence and publicity; family loyalty; sense of duty, patriotism, generosity; belief in a cause.[5] It is obvious that this particular list comprises wants that could not arise in a direct economy, since they involve reactions to other men. However, we must not adhere to our self-imposed limitation too closely.

c. Finally, we are going to find it useful in this study, and necessary as a foundation for later studies, to define another type of extraneous wants. These we shall call *imposed* wants. Here the distinction is not grounded on a difference in the character of the want, but on a difference in the way the want arises and in the resulting behavior. Imposed wants consist largely of our quasi-external wants when they are deliberately provoked in some men or organisms by other men or

[4] Knight (*240*, 331) says, "It would be hard to overestimate the error involved in the psychological interpretation of economic motive as desire to consume goods alone." On the other hand, Schumpeter (*364*, 92) takes the, to me, untenable position that, to give "meaning" to the term "wants," it must be restricted "to such wants as are capable of being satisfied by the consumption of goods." I fear he confuses mere symmetry with "meaning."

In Chapter 9 we shall regard these ancillary wants in the aspect of the activity which satisfies them, as the element of "play" in the processes of production.

[5] There are some wants still more emulative than those at the head of the above list. There is, for instance, the want which lasts only so long as "the general" cannot secure the means which ostensibly satisfies it. Marginal utility theorists (e.g., Böhm-Bawerk, *38*, 153) usually ascribe the value, for example, of pearls and diamonds to the fact that the quantities are, or were, insufficient to satisfy more than the most intense wants. Actually it is, in these and other cases, very considerably the rarity—the fact that everyone cannot possess them—which is the cause of the intensity of the want. Some British economist has suggested that, if the price of silk hats were greatly lowered, so that "the general" could afford them, the "consumer's surplus" of the few who can now afford them would disappear.

organisms in order to procure the satisfying of the latters' wants. When this object is accomplished by means of the reactions so induced, reinforcement of the imposed want takes place by discontinuing its imposition. Through conditioning, the surrogate quasi-external wants also come to be used in the same way. Thus, imposed wants may be regarded as those which do not occur spontaneously. When we come, later, to consider indirect economies, we shall find that such imposition of wants constitutes some part of all systems of control—i.e., the use by some of power over others. We shall also find that imposed wants shade into many other forms of inducement such as persuasion, praise, honors. At some point in this series we shall find it useful to draw the line. That line is defined as the point where reciprocity becomes predominant—i.e., where the process becomes mutual and therefore spontaneous. As we shall see, it is not easy to assess such reciprocity. Obviously, this class of wants could also not occur, so far as man is concerned, in a direct economy. However, it is an important class to establish.

3. The determination of prepotence among present wants is, as we have seen, based exclusively on a single quantitative difference in terms of a common and uniform measure—that is, their latent or their effective intensity. Therefore present wants have but one dimension —intensity. Their actual or surrogate recurrence is, for all alike, a movement in a single direction—the increase in their magnitude in terms of this single dimension—and their satisfaction, as a result of a single process, is similarly a movement in a single and opposite direction—the decrease in their magnitude in terms of this single dimension —which seems to take the form of a discontinuous or step-like reduction of intensity, and usually only at the end of the process. In no respect, then, can time be said to be a dimension of a present want or of the process of satisfying it. It is true that changes of the dimension intensity, in either direction, can only occur with the passage of time. But, if the intensity of a present want is unchanged, the magnitude of the want cannot be said to grow greater in any respect merely because time passes; if the intensity of a present want is rising, its magnitude is not affected by the fact that it is rising more or less slowly in the course of time; nor is the process of satisfying a want of a definite intensity a greater or smaller magnitude according as the satisfying is spread over a longer or shorter period of time. The notion of time as

a dimension of present wants and their satisfactions, derived from pain-pleasure psychology, must therefore be eliminated.[6]

4. One of the important effects upon the conceptual model, arising from the analysis of present wants as physiological states or tendencies, instead of as "desires" for objects, and resulting in the break-down of their classification in terms of such objects—usually compound—is the grouping of wants in constellations. But it will be more convenient to defer examination of the modifications this necessitates until, in Chapter 7, we have examined the effect of this analysis upon the whole relation of wants to external objects.

5. Several implications of our scheme in respect of the order of priority and of the tendency to satiation need to be brought out for future consideration, since they suggest modifications of, if they do not actually contradict, the usual view.[7] These implications are the logical corollaries of our scheme and will be carried forward tentatively for our final synthesis in Part IV.

a. Among the lower animals we observe periods of quiescence, apparently not due to fatigue or the want of rest, but to the fact that all wants are temporarily satisfied or are below the level required to overcome inertia. On the contrary, among men (at least civilized men) this is rare. Usually, with them, there are unsatisfied wants which are beyond their "capacity"—as we shall later define it—to satisfy.[8] Thus we conceive that capacity fixes the reach of satisfactions along the descending series of wants in their order of priority, if that is governing.

[6] This notion is to be ascribed particularly to Jevons (*224*, Chapter 11, and 64–69). He is followed by Edgeworth (for instance, *133*, 54, note 2). Perhaps its economic application originally derived from Bentham, for whom, it will be remembered, pleasure had *seven* dimensions.

[7] All the following statements deal with present wants only. When we have examined the system of future wants, this scheme will have to include them. That will modify the statements, but it will not alter the scheme.

[8] At this stage of our analysis the concept of "capacity" must remain a purely abstract category—i.e., some limit on the satisfaction of a practically unlimited set of wants. This suffices for its use as an analytical tool. By conceptually moving the limit from an initially small scope to a larger and larger one, and thus supposing successive as well as simultaneous sets of choices, we are enabled, in Chapters 7 and 8, to develop the scheme of virtual orders of preference among means for different wants. Conversely, through the development of the actual order of preference, we will find ourselves able to define the notion of capacity with precision—and in no other way. But this cannot be completed until Part IV, for this is one of the chief goals and tasks of our entire analysis.

We should say, however, at this point, that one of the chief reasons why civilized man is distinguished from the savage, in respect of having many unsatisfied wants, is that with him, future wants compete with present wants, and that greatly enlarges the number of wants that he is pressed to satisfy.

b. If the order of priority, alone, governed the order in which present wants are satisfied, it would be safe to assume that all prior present wants have recently been satisfied or are then non-existent whenever man proceeds to apply himself at all to the satisfaction of his subordinate present wants.

c. If the order of priority, alone, governed the order in which present wants are satisfied, it would be safe to assume that an increase in the capacity of the individual to satisfy his wants would never be exercised in a greater satisfaction of prior present wants, since these would have been completely satisfied (satiated) in the order of their priority up to the limits of the previous capacity.[9]

6. In the further development of this scheme, we shall make certain other assumptions which seem reasonable in and of themselves, as a matter of observation.

a. Since the capacity of the individual to satisfy his wants is presumably dependent in large part on the kind of economic organization and on the stage of technique that exist, we would expect the expansion of capacity to have occurred, and the more subordinate wants in the long series to have evolved (and to be continuing to evolve), to a large extent as the development of organization and of technique has permitted, and as the discovery of new means has made possible (see b below).[10]

b. It is safe to assume that the nature of wants and their positions in the order of priority do not change greatly over short periods—only evolving gradually at the subordinate end—and that they do not vary from person to person to nearly so great a degree as is frequently supposed.[11] It is probable that this evolution takes place chiefly in the

[9] Mill says, "The rich man consumes no more food than his poor neighbor." "The desire for food is limited in every man by the narrow capacity of the human stomach" (298, I, 164-165). Mill's differences of quality and preparation which the rich man requires, are to us wants subordinate in the order of priority but of the same constellation; his "desire for the conveniences and ornaments of building, dress, equipage and household furniture" is to us a complex of the elements of other constellations, of various and subordinate positions in the order of priority. These questions will be considered later.

[10] The pithecanthropus, it may be presumed, devoted himself to getting food and only sought natural shelter when he had eaten enough. The effort to obtain a mate may have been prepotent, for a time, in season. General Walker (418, 294-308) seems to me to have made an exceedingly plausible summary of this probable evolution; first, mere subsistence; second, "diversified diet"; third (at least in temperate zones), shelter and clothing; fourth, decencies "prescribed or required by public opinion" (Sumner's all-inclusive "vanity").

[11] The first statement is made on the ground that most apparent changes in wants turn out to be, when analyzed, changes in the means of satisfaction or in the terms of sub-

sense that, most subordinate wants being wants that are prevented rather than got rid of, man does not know that he can prevent these wants until he has discovered the way of doing so. After that, not doing so involves a choice; before that he had no option but to suffer the want.

c. At least after the major and fundamental wants are passed, there is no reason to suppose that, in most cases, the decline of the customary maximum intensities is sharp as we move from one want to the next along the order of priority.[12] Neither is there evidence to indicate that this maximum is low in the case of the last wants in the order of priority which are within the limit of capacity, nor in the case of those immediately beyond that limit.[13]

d. It is generally agreed that economics accepts as its data the wants of human beings as these exist. It does not question their wisdom, nor attempt to appraise their beneficent or harmful effects except, perhaps, as these effects interfere with the efficiency of the economic process. Nor does it dispute their arrangement in each individual's order of

---

stitution between the various means for the same want, as we shall note later. As to the second statement I may quote Mises. He says (*300*, 126) that, "while satisfaction is subjective [therefore among different persons incommensurable], there is a tendency to forget that the physiological structure of mankind and the unity of outlook and emotion arising from tradition create a far-reaching similarity of views regarding wants and the means to satisfy them." This caution is worthy of emphasis.

[12] Of course there must be a decline in maximum intensity along the order of priority. But this evident fact seems to have led certain economists to a false conclusion. They have argued from this that, as a man's capacity to satisfy his wants expands, the maximum intensity of the marginal want will show a marked decline from that of the prior want—that the rate of decline along the order of priority is steep. Cf., for instance, the assumption lying behind the "flexibility of the marginal utility of money." Edgeworth (*130*, App. V, 108) goes so far as to assume that the "marginal utility" of one "sort of wealth" diminishes with the increase in quantity of other sorts of "wealth." Pareto also seems to have this notion. Neither is there reason to suppose that the subordinate wants "bob up" in intensity as the prior wants are satisfied. This seems to have been the idea of Banfield (quoted by Jevons, *224*, 41–43), which Jevons corrects (*ibid.*, 54). Veblen (*413*, 86–87) treats "idle curiosity" and "the instinct of workmanship" in precisely this manner, as if they were the results of "surplus energy." But see our comment under (b, above).

[13] On the contrary, common observation would lead us to assume that the rate of decline is so slight that, in effect, the greater the reach the greater the grasp.

Henry George says that "Man is the unsatisfied animal. He has but begun to explore, and the universe lies before him. Each step that he takes opens new vistas and kindles new desires. He is the constructive animal; he builds, he improves, he invents, and puts together, and the greater the thing he does, the greater the thing he wants to do" (*169*, 330). Marco Polo relates the fact that the Great Khan, hearing of a ruby larger and finer than any other, as a matter of course wanted it and sent a special mission to India to secure it. Did Napoleon's conquests satiate him? As power expands men come to want everything in sight. It may be true, however, that only those whose wants are unlimited are driven to acquire great power.

priority. Such evaluations belong to other and more speculative fields of investigation.[14]

Ancillary Wants. We doubt that the apparent dependence of these wants on the wants whose precurrent reactions they adopt as their own consummatory reactions is a real dependence. Instead it seems to us more likely that these are obscure but original and independent wants—that they are the wants which may make of activity a "game." They are present wants; each produces its emotional state, like the others; they even have the capacity of becoming prepotent; they always take over the whole behavior, or some phase of it, and may do so even in the absence of the original want. But usually, as we shall conclude in Chapter 9, they contribute only their own emotional component to, and thus only partially energize, behavior that is principally energized in another and non-emotional manner.

It will be noted that this category is not inconsistent with our general scheme. Here we are not supposing the reinforcement by one want of the behavior still partially energized by another, in a way analogous to Sherrington's "allied" reflexes. Instead, we are assuming that the secondary want becomes prepotent over, or in the absence of, the primary want during the precurrent phase. There is no reinforcement, but only prepotence for the strongest.

There has been a disposition among psychologists to explain the influence of habit upon behavior in a way that would trench on the field we have assigned to these dependent (?) wants—would, in fact, define many of them as no more than habits. If we examine, for instance, William James's treatment of habit (*220*, I, 110–114), we find that he regards it approximately as a greater readiness for a more standardized response. It is the fact of grooving a well-worn path. It "simplifies the movements required to achieve a given result, makes them more accurate and diminishes fatigue"; and it "diminishes the conscious attention with which our acts are performed." To all that we agree. But then, he goes on to say that "*Many instincts ripen at a certain age and then fade away* . . . if, during the time of such an instinct's vivacity, objects adequate to arouse it are met with, a *habit* of acting on them is formed, which remains when the original instinct has passed away" (*ibid.*, II, 398). In terms of the conditioning process that means that if, while the "instinct" is active, an external stimulus is conditioned to it, that stimulus retains the power to excite the habitual action even after the original "instinct" has faded. But such a thesis is directly controverted by our demonstration of the necessity of reinforcement. If the original impulse (instinctive) had actually disappeared, the external stimulus would have become unconditioned by reason of the fact that it could no longer be reinforced. This proves to us that, in the cases he considered, either what he called the "instinct" (the impulse or our want) did

[14] For further mention of this question, see the second supplementary statement, entitled "Evaluation of Wants," at the end of this section.

not fade, or, if it did, some other "instinct" had taken over the habitual action and the external stimulus had become conditioned to that in turn. Perhaps this is the explanation of the continuance of hunting.

If it is hardly possible for an habitual action to continue long to be energized by a conditioned stimulus alone, it is still less possible that the habitual action should be self-energized. That is what McDougall seems to assert. "Habits are formed only in the service of instincts"; but then they can themselves become a weaker "source of impulse or motive power" (*284*, *44*). From the standpoint of a system of energetics this seems to us preposterous. In fact, it seems to deny the need of such a system. Habits of this order would seem to belong in the category of perpetual motion. Both these explanations of the continuance of habits are impossible. And the worst feature of them is that they close the door to further investigation by seeming to explain. Our hypothesis that the want must continue, or some other want must take over, however unproved, at least does not close the door.

Rignano's concept of "transference," taken from Ribot, explains the connection on mnemonic grounds, which we discuss in Chapter 6. But his examples serve as illustrations of what we mean by ancillary wants, even though the explanation is pure verbal magic. "The 'conquest of the opposite sex,' which is indispensable for the satisfaction of 'sexual hunger,' eventually becomes in certain people an end in itself; the delight in seduction for the sake of seduction, the sexual vanity of the male as well as the female, and other similar affectivities are further derivations of the sexual appetite." "As a result of further 'transference,' in the case of man, this struggle for life gave rise to the desire of victory for its own sake, the lust of domination, the greed of power, the passion of glory and renown, and the ambition to excel above one's equals." So too, "arms, originally invented by man as a means of self-preservation, have attracted an 'affective tendency' to themselves, typical of the warrior and the hunter; similarly the soil, the culture of which has been the principal means of obtaining food, has engendered that intense love of it, for its own sake, which is found among peasants" (*345*, 163–164).

Evaluation of Wants. Wieser, among many others, has well stated the case against evaluation, so far as economists are concerned (see *442*, 6). To Pareto, "L'individu est seul juge de ce qui lui plaît ou lui deplaît" (*317*, 62); for such discrimination of sensation "est un fait primitif, qui ne peut être déduit par la raisonnement" (*ibid.*, 61). On the other hand, Edgeworth undertook in his *Mathematical Psychics*—without success, as it seems to me—to establish a common standard of wants and satisfactions among all men. Pigou (*325*), while he barely manages to stay on the preserve, has, in his treatment of welfare, confined himself largely to "interferences with the efficiency of the economic process" and has included judgments of other's "state of consciousness" only so far as normal human "sympathy" makes these reasonably safe.

Older economists had their categories in terms of what they deemed to be essentiality—e.g., Cantillon's (*Essay*, pp. 1–2) *nourriture, commodités* and *agréments*. There have been distinctions as to "mere material wants" and the "higher wants"—e.g., Banfield (cited above) and many others. So Senior, in true Victorian fashion, discriminated between the uneducated motive—"appetite"—and the educated motive—"vanity," or "the desire of distinction" (371, 67). On the other hand, there have been many critics of society who have mixed economic analysis with appraisals in terms of their own tastes. Of these I think one of the most "awful examples" is Veblen. His otherwise excellent analysis of the priority of wants (see 411, Chapter V) seems to me considerably vitiated by his "invidious" (in spite of many denials) terminology and the imputation of unworthy motives (*The Theory of the Leisure Class*, in general). To impute practically the whole application of surplus economic power, beyond that required for the simplest and most essential requirements for the satisfaction of the animal wants, to the spirit of emulation (*ibid.*, 154), and to name it "conspicuous waste," "conspicuous leisure," "vicarious consumption," etc., is as crude and incorrect as to deny altogether this apparently partial and minor influence! This is social satire, not objective scientific study. It is based on some ideal, which he does not describe, but which is evidently in his mind as the criterion of his value judgment.

In this study we will not go back of the expression of demand. We accept that as a datum, whatever it is and whoever expresses it. Nevertheless, it is wholesome, even here, to bear in mind Veblen's critique, because it forces us to recognize for what a short distance the satisfaction of his basic material wants serves as explanation, in any advanced economy, of man's actual selections and valuations of the "goods and services" among which his power to demand is distributed.

We may derive a certain amusement from the observation that the constant change in fashions seems to result from the fact that most people want to be exactly the same as the people who want to be different. We may rise to Olympus and note with philosophic detachment that the progress of civilization in one aspect seems to consist of eight steps: (1) Inserting a dish between the food and the ground, (2) inserting a rug between the dish and the ground, (3) inserting a floor between the rug and the ground, (4) inserting a table between the dish and the rug, (5) inserting a space (basement) between the floor and the ground, (6) inserting a cloth between the table and the dish, (7) inserting another dish between the first dish and the cloth, (8) inserting a doily between the two dishes. But such observations have no scientific importance.

On the other hand it is of scientific importance to note that it was the articles or materials of personal adornment, the "food of vanity," that ultimately became the treasures which served as store of wealth, as measure of value, and as medium of exchange; that the second function was, as a matter of fact, a by-product of the first. Also it is of scientific importance to note that the "consumer's surplus" involved in a rare product may disappear when it ceases to be rare because it no longer satisfies the want of rarity for itself (see note 5, above).

5

FUTURE WANTS—THEIR NATURE

A. FUTURE WANTS AND BEHAVIOR

I. AN UNTOWARD INCIDENT

As I LOOK from my study window across the fields that roll away into the distance under the misty sunlight of this early autumn morning I observe a neighboring farmer plowing his field. He *drives* a pair of draught horses, and they, in turn, *draw* a plow. Presently he drops the reins, walks over to the fence and engages someone in conversation. As soon as he leaves them the plow and the horses stop; in fact they stand quite still until he returns; when he takes up the reins again the process is resumed.

This simple and familiar bucolic scene intrigues me. As soon as I begin to reflect on it I see that it is of quite different character from the phenomena we have been examining under the guidance of neurophysiology and biology. It seems at once to present a new and fundamentally different problem. Let us consider it. That degree of god-like omniscience with which the scientific and objective observer is permitted to credit himself, without crediting the like to the animal or man he observes, allows me to know certain facts not at present observable and to draw certain rather obvious but important inferences from these facts as well as from my observations. In the first place, I infer that I need not look to the plow for the source of the motivation of this process. I know that the plow is inert; it is not now moving under its own power and cannot do so; it is being *drawn* by the horses. On the other hand, I see that the horses are moving under their own power; while they are being guided by the farmer by means of the reins, they are not being *driven* by him in the sense that a motor drives a car. Clearly, then, some motivation within the horses is responsible for their movement. But, I noted that when the farmer left them the horses stood still; their motivation ceased; they did not plow. Therefore, I conclude that the ultimate source of the motivation for the whole process, plowing, must be looked for in the farmer.[1] Evidently this ultimate source is responsible not only for the process but for the fact that the plow and the horses are there at all. I know that plows do not grow on trees; nor are they found ready-made. They have to be made by man. I know, too, that horses are naturally wild, so that they require to be domesticated—that is, tamed, "broken," fed, and stabled before they will draw a plow. That, too, has been done by man. From these considerations I argue that this process, plowing, did not begin here, but that preparations for it began in the more or less distant past. And that, in turn, means that the motivation has been operative for a long time.

However, having regard now only to the process going on before me, I am permitted to know what this farmer is doing. He is preparing the ground for the growing of food, perhaps for his own consumption. On the other hand, I also know this farmer; I know that he has already had his breakfast, and I know his breakfast. I am sure that he cannot be hungry. If not, what is impelling him to begin the preparation of food? Moreover, here is going on a precurrent reaction suited to be preparatory to the consummatory reaction of eating when he does become hungry. And yet I know that this precurrent reaction cannot result in food, and therefore permit the corresponding consummatory reaction, for nearly a year. If, much before that time, the farmer should begin to be hungry, my physiology tells me that he would die of hunger before he could gather in his crop. From all of which knowledge and inferences I conclude that this farmer friend of mine is not now motivated by hunger, that he was not motivated by hunger when he "prepared" the horses and the plow, and that he will not be motivated by hunger during the successive processes of food production that will follow this one. If he is not driven by hunger and yet is preparing food, it seems reasonable to conclude that he is not driven by a present want at all. This phenomenon, then, is evidently entirely outside or beyond the system of energetics we have been examining previously. If he had heeded the admonition, "Consider the lilies of the field; they toil not neither do they spin," he would have been lying in bed at home at this early hour. If he had listened to the advice, "Lay not up for tomorrow," he would be eating, drinking, and making merry on the theory that tomorrow he would die. In-

[1] We will consider later, in connection with imposed wants, the particular form of motivation of the horses, which may be regarded here as auxiliary motivation.

stead, he is quite shamelessly and publicly "providing for the future," as we say.

This incident, intruding itself at a point so well along in a scientific exploration of human behavior in the economic field, is most disconcerting. For, when I reflect on it and upon my inferences from it, I am forced to the conclusion that it is a sample of an extensive class and, therefore, that all the careful analysis which has gone into the previous four chapters and their supporting appendices fails to explain a very large, if not the major, sector of such behavior. Seen in this new light, it is apparent that *present wants* are only the beginning of the subject.

2. CLASSIFICATION OF BEHAVIOR SPECIMENS—PRESENT WANTS OR BORDER-LINE CASES

Before attempting to attack this new problem, it may serve to keep our exploration on an objective level if we establish at once the extent to which behavior analogous to that of our farmer friend can be found in the animal world below the phylogenetic level of man. In Appendix III-A we have taken samples from the observations of natural historians of many types of animal behavior that might be construed to come in this category. Referring the reader to that source for the data, we shall here attempt only to sift out from these several types those that seem to present the characteristics of the plowing incident by means of excluding those that seem more likely, or even possibly, to be motivated by present wants. However, while we are about it, we may as well make this exclusion complete. Some other forms of behavior which have been already dealt with are readily confused with, and must therefore be definitely distinguished from, these new types if we are clearly to comprehend the characteristic marks of the new types. For the sake of convenience in future reference we shall classify these exceptions in terms of their probable or possible origin as present wants and of the resulting peculiarities of behavior. All the following may be classified as present wants, though some of the later ones seem to be border-line cases.

1. Surrogate Present Wants. In the previous chapters we have found it necessary to suppose that external stimuli conditioned to quasi-external wants become capable of exciting subcortically a central replica of their corresponding wants. The actual wants do not exist peripherally; but the central conditions produced are the same, though milder. In the case of internal wants it appears that conditioned stimuli can only *add* to the central excitation if the want already exists in a latent state peripherally; they cannot alone create a surrogate. In a strict sense surrogate wants are not present wants. Nevertheless, since the central and behavioral effects are similar, each to its corresponding actual want, since the same central apparatus is involved, since the competition for prepotence is at the same point, and since the emotional quality is of the same order, these seem to belong, as a special case, in the category of what we are calling present wants.

2. *Imposed Present Wants.* This class was introduced briefly, under the rubric extraneous wants, at the end of the previous chapter. When we discussed "instrumental conditioning" in the third chapter we omitted one term that is much used in connection with "reward" among the experimental psychologists who work in this field. That term is "punishment." Punishment is a form of imposed want that can be used in the negative conditioning of the primitive reaction to itself or to any other present want and in the positive conditioning of any other reaction desired. In the process the subject learns to substitute inaction or the new reaction for the old because in that way he secures the cessation of the imposed want—punishment. And this cessation of the imposed want constitutes the reinforcement. Punishment almost always consists of one of the quasi-external wants because practically only these can be immediately caused by artificial external means and because these are the "physiologically strongest" wants. That being the case the imposed wants behave like naturally excited quasi-external ones. The evidence or means of punishment becomes itself conditioned, so that its appearance comes to excite the corresponding surrogate want with its central replica. Thereafter the mere "threat" of punishment may suffice. When that point is reached, the actual want may no longer occur and reinforcement consists either of the fact that it does not, in spite of the "threat," or in the fact that the "threat" is withdrawn—we do not know which. In either case, the surrogate want ceases and the replica disappears; and that cessation or disappearance constitutes the reinforcement.

When we referred above to the behavior of the horses in the plowing incident we noted that, while their movement was obviously due to their own motivation, nevertheless that motivation ceased when the farmer left them. We were also permitted to know that this indirect motivation was due to the fact that they had been tamed and "broken."

But this is a good example of motivation by imposed wants. The process of taming and breaking is one of "instrumental conditioning." With the horses observed, it had arrived at the point where the stimuli conditioned to the originally excited external want sufficed to lead to plowing, though in the absence of these stimuli the horses stood still. It is clear, then, that imposed wants belong in the category either of quasi-external wants or of their surrogates. As such they are present wants in our classification. We shall have occasion to examine this sub-class more fully as we proceed and shall see that it represents a common phenomenon among men, between men and animals, and even between animals. It is not always easy to distinguish it from symbiosis in its pure form.[2] For there seems almost always to be some element of reciprocity about it—e.g., the feeding and stabling of the horses in the plowing incident. The element of mutual back-scratching does not rest on imposed wants. It rests on a conditioning process by which each partner learns that the other is a means, or makes available the means, for the satisfaction of many of his internal wants and for the prevention of the causation by third parties of many of his quasi-external wants. But, however much imposed wants may be mixed with symbiosis, they constitute an independent element of a different nature.

3. *Ancillary Present Wants.* The present wants we described in Chapter 4 and included under this rubric are those "which are themselves satisfied by features or aspects of what is or has been the process of satisfying other wants" (p. 236). This definition is, strictly speaking, too broad, for it includes all members of the same constellation. Ancillary wants are distinguished, therefore, because they are "dependent outgrowths" of precurrent reactions only, so that "the activity which was, or still is, precurrent to the satisfying of one want has come to be, at least on some occasions or in some phases, energized by another want to which it is consummatory" (p. 237). The example we cited was hunting. A want for that activity may become self-standing, among animals as well as men, in the absence of, or even becoming prepotent over, the original want, hunger, that first developed the precurrent reaction.

It is quite possible that many ancillary wants are developments out

[2] Nor, for that matter, is it ever possible to determine by observation, in the absence of punishment, the extent to which symbiosis exists. That could only be determined by the testimony of the horse, ant, etc., who asserted that he felt he was getting a "square deal."

of the original present internal want which we have called, for lack of a better name, euphoria. In the first chapter we were not able to assign to this want any certain physiological peripheral origin. Nor are we able to circumscribe the activities to which it gives rise. It is quite possible, as already suggested, that all activities we call "play" and all the element of play in other activities are the means of drawing off surplus energy and thus restoring homeostasis in this respect. From rather a "purposive" viewpoint. Thomson says, "It has been said that play is a good safety-valve for overflowing energy and exuberant spirits." It "is the young form of work—a rehearsal without too great responsibilities, when mistakes can be made without too severe punishment." [3] Thus it provides "an apprenticeship to the serious business of life . . . an opportunity for learning the alphabet of nature . . . elbowroom for new departures (behavior-variations) which may form part of the raw materials of progress." Hence its marked "experimental character." [4] Construed in this way, euphoria or surplus energy may continue to be the source of certain phenomena of adult activity. Thorndike points out that the dog or cat has "specialized, definitely aroused, utilitarian activities." "If nothing that appeals to his special organization comes up, he does nothing." That is, in our terminology, he has limited wants, which, when all are satisfied, leave him inert. On the other hand, in the case of the monkey, "everything appeals to him. He likes to be active for the sake of the activity." That holds true "of mental activity as well." "The fact of mental life is its own reward." It is this that is responsible for his marked development. For "the only demonstrable intellectual advance of the monkeys over mammals in general is the change from a few, narrowly confined, practical associations, to a multitude of all sorts." [5] In some part, this peculiarity may be due to what is called "curiosity," as to which we have found no physiological basis; but, in some part, it seems to be due to surplus energy seeking an outlet. Later on, we shall find it helpful to construe much of the emotional element in chiefly non-emotional behavior as due to this behavioral development and perhaps from the source of the "play-instinct."

The so-called acquisitive instinct, however, does not seem to derive from this source. And yet, where it leads to acquisition merely for the sake of acquisition, it appears to belong among the ancillary wants. The propensity, characteristic of jackdaws and small boys, to collect

[3] Thomson, *393*, II, 490–491. [4] *Ibid.*, I, 231. [5] Thorndike, *398*, 55–57.

things that, to the observer, seem to have no present or future usefulness is by that very fact comic. That indicates the prevalent supposition that collection is usually done only when the things are or will be useful—that they should have a definite correlation with some definitely anticipated need. The instances of this type of behavior that are cited in Appendix III, Section A, are commonly observed. They may be arranged in order from those in which the collecting and hoarding is most certainly useless to those in which they are least certainly useless. At one extreme, according to our authorities, we find jackdaws and ravens; next wolverines; next rats and mice (bank voles); next foxes; and finally squirrels, as to which there is considerable disagreement whether surplus nuts are really cached for future use or merely buried and forgotten. We find no available explanation of this type of behavior, in so far as it is non-utilitarian as to hunger, etc., and therefore belongs among the ancillary present wants. To treat it as if it were motivated by hunger is, of course, impossible, since these pre-current reactions, even without interference, are not followed by the appropriate consummatory reaction—eating. To explain it as habit is no better; for, to treat an action become habitual—that is, canalized—as if it thereby acquired a self-starter is, to us, to deny not only the kind of system of energetics that we have worked out, but the need of any system of energetics whatever. It is an action without a cause; and to assume that a stimulus become conditioned can set off an habitual action appropriate to an internal want in the absence of that want, goes quite contrary to all the evidence we have assembled with regard to the process of conditioning. Finally, to call such an action instinctive is merely to use word-magic and shut the door to further investigation. There must be an originating cause for such behavior; we suspect it is a present ancillary want; we do not know the peripheral origin or the mechanism of such a want.

4. *Present Wants Satisfied by Deliberate Reactions.* The mere fact that behavior is delayed, skilled, adapted, and evidences "insight" does not, of course, prove that it is not a response to a present want. Our system of energetics envisages the subcortical central mechanism as energizing a large part of behavior via the cortex. Provided there is evidence that the appropriate present want is prepotent, *and* provided the deliberate behavior is calculated to permit the satisfaction of that present want while it is still prepotent, such behavior should, it seems,

be construed as one kind among the several kinds induced by present wants.

A number of remarkable instances, serving to illustrate this class, are cited in Appendix III, Section A. In respect of "insight" leading to the use of tools found ready to hand monkeys and apes clearly head the list. We have Yerkes's word for it that they also *produce* apparatus by way of attaining otherwise impossible effects in adapting the environment. As to this we find no evidence. Several instances more or less of the latter kind are, however, attributed to mice. We note a considerable number of examples among the more civilized ants where feats impossible for their unaided powers are accomplished by indirect means—that is, by first providing artificial ways of making them possible. Several examples are also given of artificial improvements of their habitat by ants to make it more favorable for their living or pursuits. One case of the use of a tool by a sphex wasp is cited. Finally bees have been observed to bite through the corolla in order to get at the nectar more readily. While all of these types of behavior evidence insight and can only be first produced after deliberation, it is quite possible that all of them are the result of present wants. In other words, the mere demonstration of intelligence in behavior is not sufficient to bring it within the class we are endeavoring to segregate.

5. Present Wants Leading to Stereotyped, Often Complex, but Apparently Unlearned Behavior. We are now arriving near the border line and are therefore making no positive assertions. The phenomena we are placing in this class may be wholly due to present wants, or may be due to them only in part. At any rate we have to recognize that there may be such a class of behavior, whose motivation is as yet unexplained and which consists of a number of phenomena attributed to "instinct." The chief type is the *making* of residences. The burrow is the simplest and commonest form both among insects, rodents and even carnivorous mammals. In Appendix III, Section A, we cite only the beaver's burrow in the bank of a stream and the ant's burrow (hill). The burrow is artificial only in the sense that it is excavated. The chief difficulty in assigning burrowing to a present want is the length of time the process takes. That is hard to reconcile with the requirement, mentioned above, that the behavior should be calculated to permit the satisfaction of the want while it is still prepotent. However, if the activity is a product of the heat-conservation mechanism, it may be that even the beginnings of a burrow are enough to satisfy the want. That would suppose, nevertheless, that consummation would begin at this stage, and would leave the continued burrowing thereafter unexplained. Possibly fear (a surrogate want) might be adduced as a sufficient supplementary cause. Cases occur where the animal is satisfied by finding and utilizing an old burrow. Clearly that is due to a present want. But here we run into a difficulty in regard to the notion of instinctive behavior. If burrowing is instinctive, it should always occur, when the time is ripe, and in its stereotyped pattern. Theoretically the process, the activity, could not be short-circuited by the discovery of a means of satisfying the want without going through the process.

The building of nests by birds is an even more difficult case.[6] Here the true nest is always wholly artificial, since it is built from assembled materials. Here it takes a number of days of intermittent labor. And here we have the additional difficulty that it is only built (and used) in preparation for and during the period of incubation (i.e., during the mating period). Possibly this timing of the process may be due to the low generation of heat during pregnancy, as with rodents, and thus the originating cause, as with burrowing, may have to do with the heat regulating mechanism. In support of this or some other feature of the sexual process as the initiating cause we may note that nest-building does not occur among castrated birds. But the greatest difficulty is described in Appendix III. Nest-building seems to be largely unlearned, for it is performed even by artificially incubated birds more or less according to the hereditary pattern of the variety. On the other hand, nests of a single variety may be placed in different situations and be appropriately modified both in design and materials (i.e., the process is not fixedly stereotyped). Finally, the process is governed by the product, not the reverse, so that, like the use of old burrows, it is not an automatic reaction to its originating cause. If the nest is removed, the process may be repeated again and again until successful; but, if an old or even a man-made nest is supplied, the process is suppressed, or the only building is rebuilding to make the nest "right," if that is possible. How is all this to be reconciled with the usual conception of unlearned and therefore automatic behavior? If the bird has not learned

[6] Of course nest-building is not confined to birds. In Appendix III we cite two species of ants who build globular nests of loam on stalks of grass, and of scales worked up from cow-dung on trees, respectively. These are as wholly artificial as the most artificial bird nest. The honeycomb of bees and the wasp's nest may be analogous.

how nests are made by observing the one in which it found itself when it emerged from the shell—and the artificially incubated bird has no such opportunity—how does it "know" in what respects the old or man-made nest is not "right"?

An even subtler and more difficult problem arises when we consider the care and feeding of the young by others than their mothers, instances of which are also given in the appendix for ants, for bees, and for wasps. The explanation of this activity by the "workers" may be that the sterile females retain this want for nursing among their secondary sex characters and take it out on the generality of the young in the hill or nest.[7] Or the explanation may be, in whole or in part, "reciprocal feeding," which is a form of symbiosis to which we referred in the discussion of imposed wants above. If the eggs, larvae, pupae, and even the young insects provide delicacies of various kinds for the workers and thus satisfy some of the workers' wants in return for the care and feeding lavished on them, this could be construed as a case of "insight" on the part of the workers (i.e., a series of learned reactions dealing with an object indirectly because it is found by observation and experience to satisfy a want). However, an examination of the data cited in Appendix III, Section A, will perhaps leave the reader as doubtful as I am myself that these elaborate processes can be wholly accounted for as responses to present wants of any kind.

6. Present Wants Leading to Apparently Unlearned Behavior Which Certainly Terminates before the Consummatory Reaction. Here we seem to be right on the line of demarcation. These so-called instinctive reactions, however much they may be unlearned, seem almost impossible to account for on the theory that they are energized by present wants. We refer to what entomologists call "mass-provisioning." The workers among the stingless bees and all solitary bees or wasps never see the young. Nevertheless, they provide supplies of food for the eggs or larvae to live on until they hatch out. This provision is exactly adjusted to the requirements of the species; discrimination is made in favor of the queen-cells by the stingless bee; and

[7] While we do not know the basis among ants, bees, and wasps, we would assume it to be analogous to the present want that is supposed to lie at the root of the so-called maternal instinct among mammals.

As Rignano expresses it (*345*, 157–158), "That the need of being suckled is the origin of maternal love we see quite plainly from the fact that if a mother is deprived of her offspring, she feels the need of replacing them by other nurselings." " 'Maternal affection,' observes Girard, 'does not usually survive the causes which have brought it into being, and only obscure traces of it can be found once lactation has ceased.' "

the sphex wasp may even leave its provision in the form of prey, paralyzed by stinging, but alive and therefore preserved fresh through the winter. Here the process of collecting food—the precurrent re-action—is the same as for self; but by no stretch of the imagination can one conceive of any consummatory reaction following. The food is bequeathed to the young, in carefully measured doses, by a worker or a mother who is about to die.

3. CLASSIFICATION OF BEHAVIOR SPECIMENS—NON-PRESENT WANTS

At this point we leave the borders of behavior that can by any possibility be accounted for as the result of present wants and begin the consideration of the two major classes that are analogous to the behavior of our farmer friend. Perhaps we have already left those borders far behind. The old line of demarcation is well stated by Lloyd Morgan.

One marked characteristic of many of the habits and instincts of the lower animals is the large amount of blind prevision (if one may be allowed the expression) which they display. By blind prevision I mean that preparation for the future which, if performed through intelligence and reason, we should term "foresight," but which, since it is performed prior to any individual experience of the results, is done, we must suppose, in blind obedience to the internal impulse. . . . Instances of such blind prevision might be quoted by the score. . . . Thus where a motive emerges at all into consciousness, that from which we may presume that instinctive activities are performed is not any foreknowledge of their end and purpose, but the gratification of an immediate and pressing need, the satisfaction of a felt want."[8]

We are going to suggest later another criterion for the distinction that might place the line of demarcation much further back in our series above.[9] But, at least, Morgan's line is at this point. His thesis seems to be untenable in so far as the specimens we are now consider-ing are concerned. For the fact that all the cases we cite below con-cern *social* animals who live more than one season together, and whose group may therefore be continuous, is an indication that all the fol-lowing activities may be learned by teaching. Therefore, whatever "prevision" they involve is not necessarily, at least since the original Prometheus, blind. And by no manner of means can any of those we select be construed as the "gratification of an immediate and pressing need." In fact, in so far as they can be so construed, they will be ex-

<hr />

[8] Morgan, *302*, 429–431.   [9] Under our analysis of mnemic phenomena.

cluded on the ground that they belong among types of behavior incited by present wants.

The common characteristic of all these sifted samples of animal behavior is their *futurity*—that is, none of them yield results that are of immediate advantage. An additional characteristic common to some of them is their indirection—that is, one thing is done now in order that, in the future, some other thing can be done. Still a third characteristic is seen in some. One thing is done now in order that, in the future, some other thing can be done more easily or in shorter time. And yet all of these activities, or those parts of them we are considering, stop short of anything that could be construed as the consummatory reaction to a present want. Those which have only the first, or the first and second, characteristics we shall call *provision;* those that have also the third we shall call *labor-saving provision.*

Provision. The beaver is clearly the most capitalistic of all animals except civilized man.[10] In respect of provision for his comfort and security in winter (against cold, and injury or fear) he builds himself an artificial and elaborately contrived hillock or mound into which to burrow (beaver lodge). In part for the security of that lodge and particularly of the submarine entrance to it, and in part to permit him a safe and convenient depth of water for his swimmings to and fro, he builds a dam below his lodge and thus raises the water level in the stream, making an artificial pond. Dams may also be built above the pond to control flood waters, and below the main dam, apparently to balance some of the pressure of water and ice against it. Either for security or for rapid transit or both, slides and tunnels are constructed where the river banks are high and steep. Finally, the systems of canals with their dams are doubtless also in part provisions for security during the working operations of the late summer and fall. All this is done, so far as new work and additions are concerned, in that same season; and all this is done solely by way of preparation for the winter. None of the advantages from it develops until then. Present wants cannot account for any of it.

In respect of provision of the winter's food supply the beaver, during this season, fells and cuts up his food-trees, transports the pieces overland to the pond or canal, floats them thence to a point near the lodge entrance and there submerges them in a pile, anchored to the bed of the stream, in order to keep them fresh (undried) for winter

[10] What follows is abstracted from the evidence cited in Appendix III, Section A.

consumption. In the process of harvesting, the working beaver satisfies his hunger on the spot before transporting his food supply; but the harvesting process is intermittent, is only done at night, and does not commence until the autumn. Hunger cannot be the motivation; nor is the motivation continuous. Other rodents reported to store food (chiefly for the winter) are the prairie dog and the rat-hare.

Among the social insects, provision is in some instances even more indirect and elaborate. The truly artificial residences are those of bees (honey comb) and of wasps (nests of paper). In so far as these are arranged for incubating the young we might class the behavior as the result of present wants under type 5 above. But they are also built for storage of food for current and perhaps for winter use. This is also true of the natural burrows of many ants (ant hills). In respect of that objective it does not seem possible to attribute the behavior to present wants. Most social insects seem to store food for feeding their young and for themselves; and those whose colonies survive the winter frequently store also their winter's supply. The food so stored is honey or insects among the wasps, honey and beebread among the bees, and honey and almost anything else that is edible among the ants. But there are also remarkable cases of indirection where anticipatory work precedes the storing and makes it possible. Of these we cite the Texas harvesting ants (so-called agricultural) and the leaf-cutting ants (horticultural): both prepare the soil for the crop they want; the latter grow their indoor food on that soil placed in their burrows. The extreme instance of provision of food is the practice common to many species of ants of raising the eggs of aphides during the winter, pasturing and stabling them in the spring, all for the sake of the sweet secretion which the developed insect yields and of which they are milked. This, like certain of the cases cited under type 6 above, may have certain elements of symbiosis about it from the standpoint of the aphides. That is true, also, of man's dairy cattle. Nevertheless, from the standpoint of the ants, the prolonged period of preparation for the final product cannot be attributed to present wants.

Labor-Saving Provision. This characterization may seem to the reader to be gratuitous. Therefore its basis must be explained. Behavior cannot be described as labor-saving provision when it merely evidences skill or insight into doing things in the easiest or quickest way. Many animals naturally take the shortest distance between two points. The labor-saving method of the bee is merely a short cut. That of the wasp has somewhat more the character of futurity. The domestication of slaves by two species of ants has also this character. Here the ants capture the young of the species and raise them as domestics to do their work for them—so much so that *F. rufescens* has become parasitic in important respects. The leaf-cutting ants are said to use certain leaf-bugs as beasts of burden. While these instances may represent symbiosis upon the side of the slaves and draught animals, it is clear that, upon the side of the predatory ants, they involve futurity as well as indirection, however much the practices may have been discovered accidentally. Nevertheless, the essential point may be lacking; for the preparatory activities—the raids, etc.—may be carried out for themselves (i.e., for present wants).

In the most perfect case the preparatory activities can serve no purpose and satisfy no want in themselves. They represent heightened or prolonged own activity now which can be explained only on the ground that it will permit attaining the objective with easier or briefer own activity in the future. In fact, in order to incite such behavior, the gain in the future must apparently be greater than the cost now. Of this calculated behavior the leaf-cutting ant and the beaver seem to afford our only examples. The only conceivable reason for the ants' road-building is to avoid the difficulties of transporting bulky pieces of leaves through the thick grass. The many devices of the beaver are even more unequivocal. He economizes his current labor, it is true. His tree-felling and cutting is done the easiest way and with considerable calculation. The tree is felled toward the stream; sometimes it is left for the wind to finish the job; if the tree is right on the bank, it is felled into the stream and left there, as well preserved as if it had been transported to the winter store near the lodge. The branches are always gnawed through one side and then turned over before gnawing through the other. But in the following cases current labor is not economized; in fact it is heavily invested for the saving of future time and effort as well as for the sake of future security. That is true when beaver slides or tunnels are excavated in the high river banks. The whole system of canals and dams to permit water transportation of the cuttings is the product of even greater labor. Aside from the security it may offer, which is minor, almost its whole advantage is the great reduction of time and effort needed for transportation as against pushing, rolling, carrying, or dragging the cuttings overland. But the latter is the method preferred when the trees are being harvested near enough to the stream so that the investment in canals is not worth while. Finally, of the traveling canals cited, the first two types might be construed to be in part means for security; but the last one is no more than a short cut. The first two, in part, and the last, entirely, are the result of prolonged activities now to make for ease and speed of movement (less activity) in the future.

4. CHARACTERISTICS OF BEHAVIOR DUE TO FUTURE WANTS

It is clear that we have found a residue of two behavior types, with numerous examples of each, which conform in pattern and characteristics to that of the plowing incident and which cannot be motivated by present wants. We conclude that behavior which cannot be accounted for as the result of present wants extends at least some distance, among a few species of a few orders, into the animal world and that these species include several that are usually considered the most highly developed forms of animal life. Finally, we already see the possibility of characterizing such behavior by objective criteria and perhaps of analyzing it by means of inferences based on observation and not by means of mere anthropomorphic intuitions. For the sake of defining as clearly as possible the types of behavior we are now seeking to explain, if we can—since our previous explanations of responses to present wants are here inapplicable—it will be well to summarize the distinguishing characteristics that we found in the sifting process. That will not only aid the reader to envisage the problem, but consideration of the characteristics gives us a lead as to the direction in which to explore. The proof of some of these dicta will only appear as we proceed.

1. The present want does not exist peripherally when the behavior appropriate to it begins.[11]

    a. The reaction cannot be explained as symbiotic or reciprocal— that is, the reaction appropriate to one want that is not present is not excited by some other present want to which the reaction is inappropriate, but which the reaction has been found indirectly to satisfy.

2. No replica of a present (surrogate) want, excited by a conditioned stimulus, exists centrally. There is no sign of a sufficient emotional state to account for the reaction. Nor is either an unconditioned

---

[11] With human beings we have for this the added testimony of introspection. The plowing farmer will tell us that he is not hungry.

or a conditioned external stimulus necessary, as it is for a surrogate want.[12]

    a. Nor is there an imposed present want, which is usually merely an artificially produced replica.

3. The behavior is confined to precurrent reactions appropriate to some present want, but it ends before the appropriate consummatory reaction, in spite of the fact that the latter could quite well take place immediately—thus supporting (1) above. But the precurrent reactions serve the same purpose ultimately, and the effect of the behavior is merely delayed; for the proper consummatory reaction does take place with reference to this effect after a considerable interval (perhaps months).[13]

4. These precurrent reactions have not been taken over by ancillary wants, as their own consummatory reactions, on a sufficient scale to account for the energizing.

    a. Nor are they due to euphoria whether in the young form (play) or in the adult form (seen in monkeys), where the activity is carried on apparently for itself.

    b. Nor can they be explained as self-generating habitual activities or as self-generating instinctive activities—this, since we do not admit that activities can take place without a cause and since we define the only cause to be wants (i.e., our "instinct," as impulse, must be based on a recognizable want).

The proof of these statements is that, as noted under (3), these precurrent reactions ultimately result in a suitable consummatory reaction. This demonstrates that they were preparatory for (precurrent to) the corresponding want, not due to another kind of want.

5. These precurrent reactions always have the characteristics of skill and adaptation, and, at first, of delay (deliberation and insight), while the reactions to present wants may or may not have these characteristics. This evidences that these actions are all intelligent, not blind, and suggests that they may be in large part taught.

6. These precurrent reactions are not performed to the extent that

[12] In fact, one of the notable characteristics is that there may be apparent a seeking for objects or acts when no external stimulus can indicate their presence. That can occur as well with present wants. But here it occurs in the absence of the present want also.
[13] Of course, in many cases of behavior excited by present wants, the satisfaction, if ever obtained, is long deferred—e.g., a swain courting his sweetheart. But, there, the delay is not of the swain's choosing. It is due to external causes. The consummatory reaction cannot "quite well take place immediately" because his sweetheart keeps him dangling.

the effect they would produce is found ready-made and is "right." This, too, is true of some reactions to present wants. But it is proof that they cannot be mere habitual or instinctive activities (4b) automatically carried out when the initiating internal condition (want) appears.

All these characteristics evidence the element of futurity we have mentioned, or leave that element as a necessary implication.

As to certain of these types of behavior we have two other distinguishing characteristics which require an explanation.

7. Many of these precurrent reactions show indirection. That is also true of many precurrent reactions to present wants. But here, if the effect is by indirection, it must take a sufficiently permanent form to remain until the ultimate consummatory reaction takes place.

8. Some of these precurrent reactions evidence what we have called the labor-saving element. But they do so in a different way from that in which this element appears in reactions to present wants. There, the labor-saving is immediate and present—present labor is reduced; [14] here present labor is increased, but only so that future labor may be decreased. This is evidence that these particular precurrent reactions are not carried on for their own sake (4a). It is also evidence that there is some sort of internal resistance to carrying them on at all; and that marks their fundamental difference from all consummatory reactions and from most precurrent reactions incited by present wants.

These then are the differentiating characteristics of this phenomenon. Precurrent reactions suitable to a certain want are performed in the absence of that want, in the absence of anything that could cause that want, and even in the absence of an external conditioned stimulus that could cause a replica of it. Though the appropriate consummatory reactions could be carried out then, they are not. However, after a considerable lag they are carried out, proving that the precurrent reactions were not done for themselves (ancillary wants). The force behind these precurrent reactions is not a present want of any kind. What then can it be? Are we to suppose that a want which is going to arise in the future can act in advance? But this is to suppose that a force becomes effective before it exists. We know of no cases in which causes follow their results. The only alternative supposition is that

[14] It is a notable characteristic of this labor-saving in respect of present wants that it consists chiefly of making the activity briefer and only incidentally and through the utilization of acquired skills (cortical) of making it easier.

some other kind of present force, not the result of existing present wants, energizes now but in behalf of a want that does not exist now. In order to avoid any unwarranted semi-explanatory term we shall simply call such a present force a *future want*. That term may cause some trouble because it seems to imply that the future want acts in the future. It does not; it acts now. We might call it "anticipated" or "potential," or some other term. But all other terms are subject to equal, if different, objections. Moreover, this term has the advantage of forming an antithesis as well as an analogy with the present want. Whatever a future want may be now, it is not a present want; and this is the point to emphasize. Nevertheless, it does act in much the same way as a present want. As yet "future want" stands for us as the equivalent of an unknown quantity. It denotes a purely hypothetical cause of behavior which must be introduced into our scheme to supplement the explanation of the causation of observed behavior beyond the range at which present wants have left off.

Having distinguished future from present wants we must now bring out the relationships of similarity between them. The behavior (precurrent reactions) produced by each of the several future wants is the same as that produced by some present want. We naturally infer from that fact, and shall see it proved as we proceed, that there is a future want corresponding to each present want—that the list of both is the same.[15] Such close correspondence argues that one derives from the other. It will be evident that, actually, future wants derive from present wants, not the reverse. Thus it will be our thesis that only the present-want system is original. The future-want system is wholly an after-effect or by-product of the present-want system and contains only duplicates of that system.[16] It follows that the wants we have studied hitherto are the only ultimate causes of behavior. But the

[15] I have carefully gone through the list of the basic wants as to which we have some physiological evidence of source, etc.,—those that we found it possible to examine in the first chapter—in order to determine whether *all* of them have corresponding future wants. I find that there are no exceptions. This being the case, on the general tentative presumption we are using throughout, we shall suppose that all other present wants, even those at present unanalyzable ones mentioned at the ends of Chapters 3 and 4, have also corresponding future wants.

[16] On the other hand, though the future want is a consequent of its corresponding present want in point of development, it is thereafter an antecedent in point of another relationship. The future want that causes only the appropriate precurrent reactions, now, is succeeded after some interval by the corresponding present want which finishes the process with the appropriate consummatory reactions. It seems that something that acts in part like, but is not, a present want, is in a manner of speaking the herald or omen of something that both acts like and is a present want.

mechanism we have previously analyzed and to which we have allocated what we have called "primary nervous energy of response" cannot be the only mechanism. For we find in these few species of a few orders that the same behavior, or behavior adapted to the same end, takes place when the corresponding present want is non-existent. Therefore, there must be some other mechanism as well—the mechanism of the future-want system—to which we shall have to ascribe "secondary nervous energy of response." In other words, we are not imputing to the future-want system a different set of wants in any respect; we are only imputing to it a different proximate source, different energizing, and a different apparatus.[17]

B. THE NATURE OF FUTURE WANTS

I. ON METHOD

In the earlier chapters we outlined a scheme which represents the most probable hypothesis, based on modern physiological analysis, in regard to what we have called the present-want system. This analysis demonstrated quite clearly that the organism does not behave in response to external stimuli to any very large extent. The peripheral stimuli that excite its behavior are chiefly internal—its wants—and the penny-in-the-slot-machine psychology, the simplest form of reflexology, is certainly fallacious. But, when we come to examine man, and for that matter a few of the higher branches of lower animal orders, we find that much of the behavior of these particular organisms is not response to current peripheral stimuli of any kind, either internal or external. Since the concepts and observations of neurophysiology have been almost wholly limited to peripheral stimulation and to its central effects, it would appear that for our further explorations any sure physiological footing has slipped from beneath our feet. Of necessity we must adopt a different method of approach to this problem, but not necessarily a less scientific method. Instead of starting at the beginning of the process of causation and tracing it through its successive steps, as we were able to do before, we are now compelled to

---

[17] As we have proceeded through the previous chapters I have preferred not to qualify and therefore to confuse our presentation of present wants. Nevertheless, though it was called the primary one, at no point did I say that it was the only system or that it accounted for all behavior. Moreover, I wanted it to stand on its own feet unqualified; for in the case of most animals it appears to be the exclusive system, while in the case of a vast majority of the rest of the animal world, including a considerable part of mankind, it is the chief system.

start at the end of the process and work back. And, if we find it impossible to work back very far, we will be compelled to impute some unknown and purely hypothetical agency to account for the observed results. But this is nothing new.[1] This is and always has been the primary method of physics, the most "exact" of sciences. My schoolboy textbook on physics (Ganot) says of "natural forces," gravitation, etc., "Since these physical agents are disclosed to us only by their effects, their intimate nature is completely unknown." Nevertheless, the characteristics of these agencies can be determined by careful observation. Newton could develop his law that the attraction between two material particles is directly proportional to the product of their masses and inversely proportional to the square of their distances asunder. By such means the unknown, the x, can be clothed with its attributes until our knowledge of it becomes more complete and dependable than is our knowledge, say, of a mysterious woman up to her tricks right before our eyes.

Freud developed his metapsychology [2] in this manner. He closed his eyes to preconceived notions, and even to other sources of evidence, and worked out a scheme which *would* account for the details, the distinctions, and the variations that he collected from his vast series of observations. And this scheme proved to be a revelation in many respects. This method is, in fact, that of the "virtual," to which we referred at the beginning of the previous chapter; but it is that method in reverse. According to the "virtual" method we construct an imaginary system on the basis of induction, and we determine how it *would* work if it existed and were left to itself—that is, if it were operating *in vacuo.* Then we compare the results with reality to learn whether such a system does exist and, if so, how far it is actually left to itself— that is, we compare virtual with actual behavior. When we operate this method in reverse, we first examine and measure the effects observed; then we set up the model of a system that *would* work that way—that is, we infer a virtual cause from actual behavior.[3] Just as

[1] As Semon says, "Neither science nor philosophy has yet explained the 'real nature' of any phenomenon whatever" (*368*, 275). We are always confined to dealing with relations, not with relata; and our explorations deal only with differences (analysis) and with resemblances (synthesis). It is more satisfactory when we can analyze to deeper levels; but that is not an argument against dealing with the levels nearer the surface of things when we have as yet found no means of going beneath them.
[2] Ucs-Pcs-Cs, or Id, Ego, and Super-ego.
[3] That great master of inference, Sherlock Holmes, describes it as "reasoning backward" (see "Conclusion," *A Study in Scarlet*).

we do not expect the virtual behavior to conform precisely to the actual, in the first case, unless and until we can allow for all interfering factors (i.e., the effects of all the confluent causes), so we do not expect, in the second case, that we shall ultimately find an actual cause (or system) that precisely conforms to our virtual one. For, again, the deeper down we succeed in getting, the more complex things appear to be—the more likely we are to find many systems, only the resultant of which has appeared on the surface, or many of the effects of which have appeared elsewhere in phenomena we did not recognize to be related at all.[4] The virtual method is the method of physics. We shall use it directly in later pages. Here we shall use it in reverse.

Nevertheless, however much we shall make this method the core of our investigation, it is not necessary to deny ourselves any available sources of information, or side lights, which will enable us to relate the mechanism of future wants to other known fields. Freud almost excluded such other sources. It was this for which his system was chiefly criticized by psychologists. True, it was that very exclusiveness which enabled him to escape the prepossessions inherent in these other bodies of knowledge and so, in fact, to discover something new.[5] However, we have no hope of discovering something new and shall therefore seek help wherever we can find it.

We proceed, then, to set up a system of hypothetical and virtual forces and their relationships which *would* account for the characteristics of the observed behavior, on the ground of which we are imputing this future-want system. We shall attempt to uncover the relations of this system with the other forces at work. We shall assume that it has a physiological basis of some kind, obviously quite different from that of present wants. Therefore, we shall, as far as we can, locate and identify this system in the physiological scheme and work

[4] Hence we should here repeat Freud's caution (*154*, 424): "We may give free rein to our own assumptions provided we at the same time preserve our cool judgment and do not take the scaffolding for the building."

In fact, this point should be emphasized. Our inferred entities are solely *named constructions*, whose existence is entirely hypothetical. We must be careful not to deceive ourselves into thinking that we know what these entities are just because, for the sake of convenience, we give them names. They are no more than imputed causes of observed effects.

[5] Freud said himself (*154*, 424), "We shall entirely ignore the fact that the psychic apparatus with which we are here dealing is also familiar to us as an anatomical specimen, and we shall carefully avoid the temptation to determine the psychic locality in any way anatomically. We shall remain on psychological ground. . . ." He describes his method as an "attempt to make clear the complication of the psychic activity by breaking up this activity and referring the single activities to the single component parts of the apparatus." That is precisely what we shall try to do in the following pages.

out its relations to that other objectively determined system of present wants which has already been outlined. Furthermore, we shall not hesitate to use the terminology of introspective psychology where we see reason to identify our entities with those that have been derived from personal experience only.[6] In that course, we continue to follow the neurophysiologists who are not afraid, as some scientific psychologists seem to be, to impute consciousness, volition, etc., on the ground of purely external observation. But, though we admit these subjective entities as matters of experience, we prefer to continue to look upon them solely from the outside, objectively, and therefore to limit ourselves to the kind of analysis of their causes and effects that can be made by the observer rather than to depend on that of the experiencer. On account of the risks of this method and the danger of contaminating our simon-pure hypothetical and virtual system, we must warn the reader in advance that what he knows or thinks he knows about physiology and psychology must not be allowed to intrude on this exploration. We infer nothing from either source as to our system. Our system is inferred wholly and directly from behavior. Physiological and psychological entities appear here only as possible stamping grounds and backgrounds for our system. Their data cannot alter its character.

So much for the method—the virtual method in reverse—by which this hypothetical system came to be established. I have come to the conclusion, however, that, for the convenience of the reader, the method of exposition should follow a different order. The actual and logical order of development would make of this and the following chapter something like a single sentence, in the style of German syntax, with the verb only at the end. After reading, I hope that will be the form which the whole takes in the reader's mind. But, during reading, such a structure would certainly overtax the powers of any mind. Therefore, I have chosen the less abstract method of carrying along, in parallel lines, our three approaches—the analysis of the behavior, the inferences as to virtual causes and the possible relationship

[6] And this for the reason that the substitute terms are no better, since they refer exclusively to the same data. As Dunlap well says in connection with the use of substitute terms as explanations, "Such explanations are merely restatements of the problem in figurative language" (124, 51). Or, in Freud's phrase (154, 431), "We have done nothing more than give a name to an inexplicable phenomenon." Lotka (275, 4) suggests that these introspective terms may be merely "subjects for such verbs as to think, to feel, etc." much as the "ether of the physicist of the 19th century may have been nothing more than the subject for the verb to undulate." As such, they may be "relatively harmless. But they may also cause confusion, or worse, a sort of pseudo-scientific ponderosity."

of these to other entities. This procedure is made possible and still more convenient by the very fact that our hypothetical system turns out to be complex, not simple. We have to take it up one step at a time. But this is notice that the last step, the capstone, will not be in place until we have finished Section B of Chapter 6. Only then will we have completed our analysis of the behavior to be accounted for, and, as a result, only then will we have a coherent, if hypothetical, system. In the meantime, the reader will not be kept in suspense, awaiting the "verb." But I hope he will remain in suspense as to his verdict.

2. FUTURE WANTS AS MNEMONIC PHENOMENA

At the end of the previous section we concluded that the behavior described cannot be due to wants existing in the present or, directly, to wants that are going to exist in the future. If, then, they are due to wants at all—and this seems to be the only possible conclusion—the third alternative is that they are due to wants that existed in the past. But how, we may ask, can that which has existed but has now ceased to exist constitute a present force? Obviously it cannot, unless its apparent cessation was not real—that is, unless it remains potent, or at least latent and potential and capable of revival from some cause which is not itself a want. But these are precisely the characteristics of that entity to which we refer by the term memory, with its retention (remaining) and its recall (reviving). This consideration suggests that future wants are mnemonic phenomena. Does the exploration of such a possibility take us out of the field of objective science into that of introspective psychology? Not at all. It was not possible for us to deal with the objective data in our neurophysiological chapters and appendix without constant allusion to memory. Moreover, many of the particulars which were not specifically ascribed there to memory were, as we shall see, also phenomena of the same order. All physiology and biology presupposes something corresponding to the psychological concept of memory, and usually does so explicitly. Sherrington speaks of the "redistribution of so-to-say stored stimuli by *associative recall*," [7]

[7] Sherrington (375, 352). This is the natural inference of psychology, even that which avoids the use of the term memory. As Thurstone says (400, 354), "If we cannot find a stimulus which is obviously responsible for the present mental state, or for the present overt act, we rest convinced nevertheless that some stimulus in our past is now finding expression in us." In fact, according to Holt (206, 169–170), "It is here that behavior [as distinguished from "plain reflex action"] begins." "Since the immediate stimulus does not account for the reflex movement," "the response in question is a response to a past event, it is describable only in terms of (as a function of) this past event."

and uses the term memory as well. Parker regards the nervous centers as "a storehouse for the nervous experiences of the individual." [8] Jennings says, "The objective side of *memory* and what is called *habit* is shown when the behavior of an organism is modified in accordance with past stimuli received or past reactions given." [9] And Child calls these "the stability of protoplasmic records of behavior" and the "persistence of the new effective integration." [10] As Bertrand Russell puts it,[11] the phenomena of this order are "those responses of an organism, which so far as hitherto observed facts are concerned can only be brought under causal laws by including past occurrences in the history of the organism as part of the causes of the present response"; and this because they depend "not merely upon the stimulus and the hitherto discoverable present state of the organism." [12]

As these references already begin to suggest, the objective view of memory, in the strict sense, makes clear that it is but one of a very large class of natural phenomena with certain common characteristics, some of which extend even into the inorganic world. If then we are to obtain the most objective viewpoint possible of memory in the narrow field, we would better proceed by working up from the simplest and least evolved representatives of this class rather than by starting at our own experienced memory and working down. Not only is the latter method apt to lead us to impute to the lower forms in this class the characteristics of memory as we know it—which may be quite wrong—but it is apt to make us overlook in the familiar case characteristics which are made obvious by first looking at the unfamiliar. To be brief we shall have to be abstract.

First, a word as to the class itself. It was Ewald Hering's paper, delivered at a meeting of the Imperial Academy of Science at Vienna in 1870, which "made Memory a biological problem, and such it has remained." [13] The title of the paper was, "On Memory as a Universal Function of Organized Matter." [14] His "lineal successor," Richard

[8] Parker, *318*, 217.   [9] Jennings, *223*, 333.   [10] Child, 76, 263.   [11] Russell, *357*, 78.
[12] Russell (*357*, 75). It is to be assumed that "hitherto discoverable" is inserted to indicate that the real cause is not past, but some effect of the past that remains potential in the "present state."
[13] Engel, *137*, 5.
[14] "Über das Gedächtnis als eine allgemeine Funktion der organisierten Materie." Samuel Butler translated it (*55*) with the title given as in our text. So does Engel (*137, 5*). Curiously enough, Vernon Lee, in his introduction to the translation of Semon's *Mnemic Psychology*, substitutes the term "organic" for "organized." And Rignano (*345*, 34) paraphrases it as "living substance." But these seem to restrict Hering's meaning, however much he may have confined his attention to its appearances in the organic

Semon,[15] first gave the name "Mneme," or "mnemic phenomena," to the whole class of phenomena referred to in the preceding paragraph, thus avoiding the implicit inference that these phenomena resemble memory, rather than the reverse. In fact, "Mneme is not another word for memory, nor synonymous with the act of remembering." [16] For two good reasons we shall adopt Semon's special terminology, which applies to the whole class of phenomena rather than to memory alone.[17] In the first place, the value of his viewpoint lies in the fact that thereby the single familiar instance becomes but one representative of a general and previously unrecognized class, newly synthesized. In the second place, his viewpoint enables us to argue from the general to the particular, from the objectively known to the objectively unknown and from the primitive to the highly evolved, rather than the reverse.[18] The title of his first book defines mneme as "being the principle of conservation in the mutability of organic happenings." [19] Objectively regarded, it is the totality of mnemic potentialities.[20] What these potentialities are we shall see as we proceed. The mneme is not only neural. Semon "insisted upon the unity of the process of building up the mneme whether in simple engraphic effect upon the simplest form of stimulable cell protoplasm or in the action upon the highly specialized nervous substance." [21] And his theory "is that all the organic phenomena of reproduction, repetition of bodily form or of dynamic experiences, are expressions of one and the same energetic process." [22]

---

world. It will be noted that Semon confined his attention to "organic happenings." Whether it is quite proper to ascribe to biologists such as Hering and Semon "the position of regarding memory as the most general and fundamental function of all living matter" (Rignano, *345*, 90), I leave to the reader to judge. At least "mneme," if not "memory," is a "fundamental property of all living matter" (*ibid.*, 94).

[15] Engel, *137*, 8.

[16] Vernon Lee, in Semon (*369*, 53).

[17] We shall use his terms, mnemic and mnemic phenomena, for the whole class and the terms memory and mnemonic phenomena for the sub-class—conscious memory (memory proper) and its components.

[18] See the end of Appendix III, Section B, for further remarks on my use here of this so-called biological theory of memory.

[19] "Die Mneme, als erhaltendes Prinzip in Wechsel des organischen Geschehens," which Lee (*369*) translates as in the text. Elsewhere (*368*, 14), Semon defines it as "the conserving principle necessary for the maintenance of alterations produced by a constantly changing environment."

[20] Semon, *368*, 24.   [21] Jelliffe, *222*, 338.

[22] *Ibid.*, 333. "My purpose has been to furnish evidence of a common physiological foundation for the apparently heterogeneous organic phenomena of reproduction" (*368*, 273). That was his "citadel" (*368*, 278). Reproduction is his term for Jelliffe's "repetition of bodily form or of organic experiences." He does not mean "reproduction," in the sexual sense, only.

He aimed to "replace as far as possible such unknown quantities as memory in the restricted sense, heredity, capacity for regeneration and periodicity, etc., by the function of one single factor—'the mnemic excitation.'" [23] He says, "In this way I have tried to deduce from a common property of all irritable organic substance—namely, that of retaining revivable traces or engrams—a number of mnemic laws, equally valid for the reproductions commonly grouped under memory, habit, or training, and also for those which come under the head of ontogenetic development, inherited periodicity, and regeneration— laws common, in fact, to every kind of organic reproduction." [24] Thus his "two main mnemic propositions" are good for all mnemic phenomena, not merely for those of "higher memory." [25]

In fact, this viewpoint, once gained, makes it somewhat difficult to distinguish memory, as we have come to think of it, from other members of the class. As we note elsewhere,[26] it is not really distinguishable from all other canalization of stimuli, including current stimuli. Vernon Lee attributes to Bertrand Russell the view that the definition of mnemic phenomena includes memory, but "includes it as one of a class of phenomena which embrace all that is characteristic in the subject matter of psychology," so that psychology comes to be the dealing with mnemic phenomena.[27] Even when the limits of memory proper

[23] Semon, *368*, 276.

[24] *Ibid.*, *368*, 13. The principles underlying these cases are identical, not analogous, even though the manifestations are diverse (*ibid.*, 279).

Hering had already stated that "one and the same primary force of organized matter —namely its memory or power of reproduction," appeared not only in the voluntary or involuntary reproduction of "ideas," but in "other phases of organized matter," though "in simple guise." Thus "muscle becomes stronger the more we use it"; there is "reproduction of the cells themselves" (growth); there is heritage of acquisitions from the lifetime of the parent and heritage of congenital resemblances. "An organized being, therefore, stands before us as a product of the unconscious memory of organized matter" (*189*, 68 and 75).

Rignano's list (*345*, 82) of the class is somewhat similar: "Cellular specialization in virtue of which each cell gives its proper and characteristic response even when excited by stimuli of a different character from those to which it is usually subjected; the great law of the acquisition of habit to which all living substance is subjected; the development of organisms; the fundamental law of biogenetics or the recapitulation of phylogeny in ontogeny; the transmissability of acquired characters; the inborn instincts of animals; all these phenomena which suggest vaguely that they have a common basis, more or less analogous to memory, are seen . . . to be clearly and definitely nothing but so many manifestations or so many direct results of one and the same elementary phenomenon. . . ."

Most of those we are quoting on this subject hold to the doctrine of the heritability of acquired characters. At present most biologists reject that doctrine altogether. But this one possible defect or error should not cause rejection of the whole of this useful synthesis.

[25] *Ibid.*, *368*, 324.   [26] Appendix II, Section I.   [27] Lee, in *369*, 15–16.

are strictly defined, it remains fundamental. "Without memory indeed no conscious life is conceivable." [28] However, Butler seems to have gone a bit far when he said, "Life is that property of matter whereby it can remember—matter which can remember is living." [29] As Rignano points out, this is neither true of memory nor of mneme, "for ordinary psychic memory belongs to a category of phenomena [mnemic] of a less general order and more complex than ordinary vital phenomena, since every manifestation of psychic memory [or of mneme] is certainly a vital phenomenon, whilst the contrary is not true." [30]

Since Semon's synthesis, as far as we are here concerned, serves only as a basis for our analysis of conscious memory, we have relegated to Appendix III, Section B, our synopsis of his generalizations. There we have organized it in terms of our whole study of present and future wants and have added much of Rignano's frequently illuminating, if less scientific, elaborations. The interested reader should consult this appendix. Nevertheless, the text which follows will stand on its own feet and can be understood by itself as soon as Semon's technical terms, which we adopt, are clearly comprehended.

3. THE CHARACTERISTICS OF CONSCIOUS MEMORY

If we were to deduce, a priori, the characteristics of conscious memory from our examination of mnemic phenomena in Appendix III, Section B, and from Semon's generalizations as to the whole class, on the assumption that such memory is a phenomenon of the same order without fundamental differences, we would piece together its design somewhat as follows: [31] The physical substrate of conscious

---

[28] MacBride, *279*, 1.   [29] Butler, *55*, 272.   [30] Rignano, *345*, 80.

[31] Except in the generalization of mnemic phenomena and in the fact that the characteristics of conscious memory are then based upon these generalizations, Semon's analysis does not differ widely from that of neurophysiologists and psychologists. As an example of the former we may cite the basic concept of our leading authority Hughlings Jackson. He said (*216*, I, 43) "What is recollection but a revivification of such processes," i.e., sensorimotor processes "representing certain impressions of surface and particular *muscular adjustments?*" Furthermore (*ibid.* I, 240): "After seeing the brick the modification (or, we might say, education) in a certain nervous arrangement is an actual part of our body. But the excitation or discharge of this modified nervous arrangement have ceased with the removal of the brick; the idea becomes latent; the adjustment is potential. For when at any time afterwards the more central parts of that arrangement are re-excited even but slightly, an idea or vision of the brick is roused, although in a faint form; and as there is a more limited (only a central) excitation, the idea is less vividly referred to the environment." Thus the impression or modification (effect) "remain as the physical substratum of all we can ever after know of the brick in its absence"; for "ideas are acquired [only] during the correspondences between the

memory, so long as it is a *tabula rasa*, exhibits a high degree of plasticity ("engraphic susceptibility"). This permits a ready alteration of the status to which it will be restored after an excitation and therefore the modification of its initial reaction. Thereafter, plasticity completely disappears as to each element impressed, so that, after each subsequent repetition of its modified reaction, there is self-restoration to this altered status, and again the repetition only of the modified reaction. But neither is it any longer necessary that the whole original influence should be repeated in order to reproduce this modified reaction. In fact, but an infinitesimal part, a mere reminder, is necessary. Finally, since, in each element impressed, plasticity has completely disappeared, the succession of experiences must produce separate memories in series, which thereafter coexist and are to a degree separately reproducible.

According to Semon, while the individual details of an experience are separate in memory, they form a complex, for they represent *in toto* the whole system of excitation that was simultaneous. These complexes are connected in series because the "acoluthic" phase of declining after-excitation, in one, subsists during the current ("synchronous") excitation of the next. That and that only is, to him, the basis of "association." Thus the recall ("ecphory") of any part of one complex tends to recall the rest of it, and thence, because of the connection in series, its successors and even its predecessors. But the process of recall is, according to Semon, most usually started by similarity ("homophony"). That is, when the current experience contains a stimulus which creates an excitation related to (like) one that has already established a memory, the latter is recalled, and it is this second cause which more often starts the chain of recall. Thus similarity (homophony) and association together create what might be called a cross-

---

organism and its environment—the innate forms are then developed and filled up." His "innate forms" are "sensori-motor arrangements."

As an example of a physiologically minded psychologist, we may cite the fundamental concept of another great authority, William James. He reserves the term "memory for the conscious phenomenon" (220, I, 646). The exercise of memory presupposes "retention" and "recollection," or "recall." "Now the cause of retention and recollection is the law of habit in the nervous system, working as it does in the 'association of ideas'" (*ibid.*, I, 653). "The machinery of recall is thus the same as the machinery of association" (*ibid.*, I, 654). It is "the brain-paths which *associate* the experience with the occasion and cue of the recall." "When slumbering, these paths are the condition of retention; when active they are the condition of recall." "Retention is a purely physical phenomenon, a morphological feature, the presence of these paths." "It is not a fact of the mental order at all." On the other hand recall is, physically, "the functional excitement of the tracts and paths in question," but also, psychologically, the conscious vision and its pastness" (*ibid.*, I, 655).

indexing system in memory—the one based on the criterion of resemblance, the other on the criterion of simultaneity.[32] The former permits recognition and the perception of differences in detail; the latter permits the relation of parts to whole experiences and thence to the entire succession of experiences.[33]

In so far as the detail of experience is discontinuous, each detail that registers in the conscious memory at all creates a separate memory, no matter how nearly identical it is to some previous one. When some new experience contains a similar detail it tends to revive as a mass all detailed memories which were recognized as similar (homophonous) to each other as each occurred. But by means of some particular association (i.e., cross-indexing) it is also possible to recall a single instance only. The perception of an incongruity between a detail of current experience and any thoroughly well-established mass of similar (homophonous) memories seems to be an activating force in itself, and produces a tendency to react in such a way as to make the current experience congruous with the old, if that is possible.

In most respects conscious memory evidences no notable differences as compared with other mnemic phenomena, such as homeostasis, the successive stages of homeostasis marking ontogeny, the re-enactment of an old stage of homeostasis marking regeneration, the alteration of homeostasis marking adaptation (learning and conditioning) and, if it occurs, the inheritance of such alterations of homeostasis (the inheritance of acquired characters). The chief differences seem to be due to the fact that conscious memory is the latest arrival and the most highly evolved of all the mnemic potentialities. These differences reduce to two. Of these the first relates to time, a subject to which we shall devote the next section. The second is that the physical subtrate of conscious memory exhibits by far the greatest degree of original plasticity (susceptibility) of any part of the body and even of any part of the nervous system, and therefore of all mnemic potentialities —that is, memories can be established from single excitations and even when these are weak. As a corollary of this it seems to follow that the induced repetitions of the original excitations are far less potent than

[32] These are what Frazer (*150*, I, 221–222) calls "two great fundamental laws of thought, namely, the association of ideas by similarity and the association of ideas by contiguity in space or time."
[33] Hughlings Jackson held (*216*, II, 228) that "there is, at least often—always, I imagine —involuntary prior to voluntary revival of perceptions" (i.e., involuntary association). He also held that association is always stronger between memories and between perceptions than it is between perceptions and memories (*ibid.*, II, 212).

those of the rest of the system. This may be due to the fact that conscious memory has been differentiated as a very delicate instrument for the recording of the experiences of the individual. Because the individual's history is short and varied, similar (homophonous) engrams are far less massive than those which represent the accretion of racial history and which are inherited, or than those acquired from long habit. Conscious memories have not originated from a sufficient number and persistence of experiences to have much potency.[34] Correspondingly they are, in themselves, non-affective. Affectivity appears, then, to be a concomitant of excitations, whether mnemic or original, that have become generalized throughout the system, where all parts participate to some extent in the reactions because it results from a condition so extensive that it is called a physiological state—the distinction between which and a slight localized excitation is, of course, only one of degree. The reactions of conscious memory correspond to the words of a single person or a small group; affective reactions correspond to the *vox populi*. Only as the words (reactions) of conscious memory have that demagogic appeal which makes them capable of stirring the crowd are they capable of exploiting its monopoly of affective reactions. We shall remind ourselves as we proceed that it is the lack of generalization of effects of stimulation confined to conscious memory which distinguishes them in degree from excitations which connote affectivity.[35]

[34] But the degree of their potency in comparison with the accretions of racial history increases rapidly as one ascends the phylogenetic scale. One would assume, in line with Semon's analysis, that conscious memory represents not only the most irritable and therefore the most mnemically susceptible substance, but also that which is most accessible to current experience. He cites (*368*, 107) Fabre's experiment with the sphex wasp. This wasp always drops her paralyzed prey at the entrance to her hole and goes in to investigate before dragging the prey in. Forty times in succession Fabre removed the prey a short distance while the wasp was inside; and forty times the wasp dragged the prey back to the entrance and then repeated the performance. The experiment demonstrates that what is called "instinctive behavior" or "racial habit" is relatively unmodifiable compared with behavior guided by individual memory. If so, it must take a long time to create instinctive habits and only a short time to create mnemonic habits, though "in the Hymenoptera as well as the Vertebrates, we meet with many cases where inherited series of engrams are liable to become transformed by new individually acquired engrams" (*loc. cit.*).

As William James pointed out (*220*, II, 390), "It is obvious that every instinctive act, in an animal with memory, must cease to be 'blind' after being once repeated." That is true if the result of the act has been noticed and attributed to the act as cause, and if the causative relation has been "remembered." Then "instincts combine with experience." Thus the readiness with which instinctive (blind) behavior can be modified by experience is largely a mark of the degree to which conscious memory is developed.

[35] We have, of course, found that a stimulus conditioned to a want—at least a quasi-external one—can arouse a central replica of that want which corresponds to the emo-

However, this matter of the strength of excitation involved in the recall of memories, both as compared with the original excitation that laid them down and also as compared among themselves, requires further examination. Semon refers to "such a faint sensation as a mnemic one usually is." [36] Hughlings Jackson says: "In thinking of objects (faint ideation) the central discharge is (1) slight, and (2) limited to the centre. In actually seeing them (vivid ideation) it is (1) strong, and (2) spreads from the periphery to the centre, and from the centre to the periphery." Thus "an idea is only a faint external perception, and an external perception is only a vivid idea." In the former the externality also is "faint," in the latter "vivid." [37] As compared with actual sensation, sensations in memory, then, seem to be conceded to be less "vivid"—that is, more "faint." Presumably the same thing holds true of all mnemic excitation (recall) as compared with its corresponding "original" excitation (i.e., the excitation that laid down the engram). But, though they are all in this lower range of "vividness," these mnemic sensations (recall), and presumably all mnemic excitations, also vary widely among themselves in point of "vividness."

This serves as a beginning. But then we find that Semon attributes two dimensions to mnemic excitations. They vary in intensity as well

tional state the want itself produces, though much weaker. But that is different. The memory of that stimulus can hardly do so. As William James says (*220*, II, 474), "The revivability in memory of the emotions . . . is very small." He does believe, however, that "we can produce . . . new griefs and raptures, by summoning up a lively thought of their exciting cause. The cause is now only an idea" (a memory). It is possible, therefore, that with certain wants and under certain conditions the mere memory of a conditioned stimulus is sufficient to excite a replica. However, that does not seem to apply to any great extent to the kind of wants we are chiefly concerned with.

[36] Semon, *369*, 337.

[37] Jackson, *216*, I, 56 and 246. Elsewhere (*ibid.*, II, 211) he defines externality as "regarded as outside." Both may be "regarded as outside"; but the idea is "indefinitely 'projected,'" while the precept is "definitely 'projected.'" James Ward says (*424*, 591), so far as memory is limited to revived percepts (i.e., apart from abstraction) "reproductive imagination is so far but a faint rehearsal of actual percepts, and constructive imagination but a faint anticipation of possible percepts." William James seems to treat externality and vividness as concordant. He says (*220*, II, 70): "There is between imagined objects and felt objects a difference of conscious quality which may be called almost absolute. It is hardly possible to confound the liveliest image of fancy with the weakest real sensation." Nevertheless, the evidence of hallucination (and I should say the observation of savages and children) leads him to the conclusion (*ibid.*, I, 72) that the difference is "less absolute than has been claimed" and that the two processes "are not quite as discrete as one at first is tempted to suppose." The discrimination between the subjective and the objective (Jackson's externality) is, I suspect, a learned discrimination, not wholly dependent on relative vividness. Nevertheless, the difference in vividness, as a normal thing, seems to be well established.

as in vividness. In fact, the foregoing statements, making no such discrimination, seem to combine the two dimensions of the magnitude under the one term "vividness." Thus it appears that memories are both less intense and less vivid than their corresponding "original" excitations.[38] In the first place, for all mnemic phenomena, the "engraphic effect is in a definite relation to the strength of the synchronous excitation." [39] Also there is a fundamental difference, in this respect, between the engraphic effect of the repetition of many stimuli and that of a single strong stimulus. This difference "lies in the fact that repetition of a stimulus does not strengthen an already existing engram, but generates a new engram, and the mnemic excitations resulting from any subsequent ecphory of these engrams are homophony." [40] Therefore, the first, the strength of the single stimulus and its resulting excitation, determines in a definite ratio the intensity of a sensation and so, presumably, the intensity of the memory when revived.[41] But the second, repetition and its resulting homophony, work in the opposite way; for the "homophonous congruence of sensation is accompanied by a notable rise in vividness but with little or none in intensity." [42] Thus, the intensity of mnemic excitation is predetermined by the intensity of stimulus, while the vividness is not. The latter depends, in part, on the number of similar memories recalled along with it and, in part, on the degree of conscious attention accompanying the recall.[43] We should assume, then, that it is the strength of the stimulus—intensity of the experience—which is responsible for the potency of memories in one respect—their intensity—while it is repetition—frequency of the experience—and therefore homophony, which is partially responsible for the potency of memories in another respect—their vividness. The other determining factor of vividness is said to be the degree of conscious attention to the memory. Let us see what that signifies.

In Appendix III, Section C, we have undertaken to elaborate Semon's mnemic hypothesis with reference to the conditioning process and

[38] Nevertheless, he also says (369, 336) that the chief difference between mnemic and original sensations "regarded as direct processes in consciousness" lies in "their usually very different degrees of vividness, not of their intensity." I find it very difficult to interpret Semon's meaning in the use of these terms, vividness and intensity. Nor do I find any exact definition of them.
[39] Semon, 368, 123. [40] Ibid., 169. [41] Ibid., 369, 335. [42] Ibid., 336.
[43] Ibid., 369, 336. All this seems to be a correct interpretation of Semon. But, as noted above one cannot be too sure, for Semon did not define these terms, and he makes certain statements in regard to the phenomena that seem contradictory.

Pavlov's constructions from his experiments, in so far as both require an emotional (affective) element as the strategic factor. As a result, we conclude there that conscious attention to revived memories is, primarily, like conscious attention to current sensorimotor processes, a function of the "interest" attached to them—in other words, that it depends on their emotional endowment.[44] The degree of such endowment depends, in part, upon the intensity of the several emotions—which follow the order of priority of the wants that give rise to them —and, for the rest, upon the intimacy of the union of emotion and sensation when the memory was laid down—which, in turn, seems to be related to the process of focusing conscious attention. That is, the nearer to the focus, the greater the intimacy. Thus vividness of memories, in Semon's sense, would be construed to be determined by the character of the emotion directing conscious attention during the experience, by the nearness to the focus of this attention that the particular detail of the experience attained, and by the frequency with which such homophonous details occurred and were endowed with one and the same emotion. However, when so analyzed, it would seem that Semon's distinction between intensity and vividness may not be wholly valid. For, if the intensity of memories varies according to the intensity of the original excitation, both intensity and vividness will have been chiefly determined by the degree of the concurrent emotional excitement. Thus it may suffice to suppose that intensity of memories varies *only* in proportion to the intensity of the individual experience, while the vividness of memories varies in proportion to the intensity of the individual experience *and* the frequency of its repetition. All memories would be much less intense than their respective experiences, but the effect of very frequent repetition might be to make them almost as vivid as a current sensation.

4. CONSCIOUS MEMORY AND TIME

We may assume, I think, that the passage of time registers in experience, both conscious and unconscious, as a result of the fact that it is a fundamental dimension in the occurrence of events—an external phenomenon—and is not, therefore, a mere "categorical imperative," or a mere dimension of "mental" processes. However, it does not fol-

[44] This is true only of involuntary conscious attention. Voluntary conscious attention, as we shall see in the next chapter, is of a different order.

low that the reflection of time in experience is a precise one; nor does the reflection in experience prove that an exactly corresponding one exists, as a result, in memory. Therefore, let us examine first the reflection of time in experience and develop from that, so far as we can, the characteristics and defects of the temporal organization of memory. The fundamental element in the passage of time is duration. In fact, that is the only dimension of time. Now duration can be roughly measured by animals.[45] Darwin asserted that "animals can certainly by some means judge of the intervals of time between recurrent events."[46] The means by which they do so has been assumed to be some regular physiological periodicity. Hughlings Jackson was positive that neither the heart, in its three known representations at the highest level, because it varies in rate, nor the highest nervous centers which cause these variations in the heart rate, can be the standard for this "idea of time." Instead "nervous elements which are independent, and which do not vary, and cannot be made to vary in their rate of activity, can alone be a standard to all else which is varying, can alone be the physical basis of the Time Constant." And he supposed that the original representation of the regular systole, having lost control of the heart's rate, remains as the physical basis of this constant.[47] While the effects of the passage of time are universal throughout organic systems, it may well be that any basis for measurement of it, such as this, is confined to consciousness. Perhaps Freud went too far when he speculated that "unconscious mental processes are in themselves 'timeless' . . . they

[45] In respect of ecphory, Semon does not distinguish sharply between the passage of time and the interval before the arrival of a phase which requires the passage of time to develop—that is, between chronogeneous and phasogeneous ecphory. In fact, speaking of time as an ecphoric agent, he says (368, 50), "In all periodical phenomena in the animal and vegetable kingdom, whether acquired or inherited, time is commonly supposed to determine and regulate the appearance and disappearance of reactions." Actually the only time period ecphorizer (chronogeneous) occurs in the course of change, when "at the end of a definite series of metabolic or other life processes, a state of the organism results which partially or altogether corresponds to the state which ruled it at the time of the production of a definite engram, and by the repetition of which state this engram becomes now ecphorized" (ibid., 54). Perhaps this is the only measure of the passage of time in all organisms; but in at least the higher vertebrates there is a more accurate and regular one against which other experiences can be measured.
[46] Darwin, 106, 75. Romanes (354, 314–315) recounts the tale of a correspondent about tame geese who came regularly every other Sunday morning to pick up corn left after the corn market on every other Saturday. They came whether or not the corn market had been held.
[47] Jackson, 216, II, 111 and 113. His speculations on time (ibid., II, 98–118) are well worth study. They demonstrate how much this subject intrigues the more deep-thinking physiologists.

are not arranged chronologically, time alters nothing in them, nor
can the idea of time be applied to them." [48] But he hardly went too far
when he continued, "Our abstract conception of time seems rather
to be derived wholly from the mode of functioning of the system
W—Bw. [perceptual consciousness], and to correspond with a self-
perception of it." [49] Combined with Jackson's plausible supposition,
that means that the duration of successive experiences in consciousness
can be roughly measured against a time-scale, the unit of which is furnished by a neural event that recurs at short intervals and with perfect
regularity.

Is that all there is to it? Apparently not; for we have the testimony
of introspectionists that the actual experience of duration varies from
this perfect measurement. In the first place, there seems to be another
unit—a unit of experience—which can distract from and thereby confuse the unit of duration or its summations. William James says, "The
unit of composition of our perception of time is a duration, with a
bow and a stern, as it were—a rearward- and a forward-looking end
. . . we seem to feel the interval of time [this unit] as a whole, with
its two ends embedded in it." [50] This, I take it, is not strictly a unit of
duration. It is, or may become, the unit of experience; and then it
seems to be identical with the unit of engraphy as analyzed by Semon.
According to Semon, a continuous stimulus may produce but one engram. Discontinuous stimuli, provided the intervals between them are

[48] To the extent that Semon's observations apply generally to mnemic phenomena, all,
not merely conscious memory, are at least arranged chronologically. That is our interpretation of the successive stages of ontogeny and of the revivals responsible for regeneration.

[49] Freud, 156, 32.

[50] James (220, I, 609–610). He shows that this has its logical basis too. Thus it is impossible to identify the "conterminous of the past and future" (an infinitesimal instant)
with (quoting Clay) the "specious present" (the present or unit of duration in experience). For, since the instant has no duration it must be beyond experience. If successive
elements of experience have duration, "then one must make duration, otherwise duration must be made up of parts which have no duration, which is impossible" (quoting
Reid; ibid., I, 609). That eliminates the infinitesimal. Marcus Aurelius exaggerated
when he spoke of "this present, as't were but a hair's-breadth of time" (Meditations,
iii. 10, Tr. M. H. Morgan). But there is a minimum set by physiological test—the
minimum sensibile. "To be conscious of a time interval at all is one thing; to tell
whether it be shorter or longer than another interval is a different thing." There can
be no measurement more accurate than that in terms of a unit which can vary undetected by anything less than the "smallest difference between two times which we can
perceive" (ibid., I, 615). On the other hand, James cites the experiments of Wundt
and others to the effect that this second unit of duration cannot be greater than twelve
seconds (ibid., I, 612–613). Perhaps; but it may vary widely, as we are suggesting in the
text.

longer than their acoluthic phases, produce separate engrams for each recurrence. But each engram-complex is composed of all the simultaneously formed engrams. If perception corresponds in this respect to engraphy, the unit of experience in perception would correspond to the period during which all stimuli were continuous, or, if discontinuous, were divided by intervals less than their acoluthic phases. Thus any discontinuity anywhere, corresponding to a change in the engram-complex (whether followed by a repetition of the same or by a new stimulus), would, perhaps only if registering in conscious attention, put an end to that unit of experience and commence a new one. Hence this unit of experience would vary in absolute duration according as the motion picture remained unchanged (a still) or moved across the screen more and more rapidly. This seems to coincide with the testimony of introspectionists. When the succession of experiences is rapid, each one is brief in actual duration as measured upon the time-scale. If, then, consciousness does not automatically do addition or multiplication of the many brief intervals, the whole series would seem brief because each member was; or, if we are hardly conscious of the passage of time at all during the rush of experience and only join its severed ends together without measurement of the missing interval when the experiences are finished, then the interval as a whole seems brief. When single experiences are prolonged they also seem long against the time-scale, either because they are correctly measured and cumulated or because we are only then conscious of the passing of time. At any rate, duration seems short when events are moving rapidly, and long when they are moving slowly.[51] The basis of our perception of time would then be elastic. When crowded with experience engaging conscious attention, the unit of experience would expand—the whole series seeming to be composed of units either fewer or briefer than they really were; when containing but a single experience so that conscious attention relaxed, the unit of experience would contract

[51] William James, for instance, says, "In general a time filled with varied and interesting experiences seems short in passing. . . . On the other hand a tract of time empty of experiences seems long in passing" (220, I, 624). He interprets this to mean that these tracts of time seem to shorten "whenever we are so fully occupied with their content as not to note the actual time itself." But periods of "waiting, of unsatisfied desire for change" are long. Boredom and ennui (well-named *Langweile*) arise "from the relative emptiness of content of a tract of time," because then "we grow attentive to the passage of time itself" and that "is susceptible of such fine-grained successive subdivisions" (*ibid.*, I, 625). But emptiness of a tract of time is different from fullness of disagreeable experiences. What we feel during a night of pain "is the long time of suffering, not the suffering of the long time per se" (*ibid.*, I, 630).

to terms of the units of our absolute neural time-scale—being then correctly measured and cumulated.

Can these hypotheses as to the sense of duration in experience be transposed unchanged and as a whole over to that of memory? Perhaps they can, in so far as the individual experience and its revival in memory are concerned. Semon says "the mnemic state of excitation reproduces the original excitation in all its proper proportions, inclusive of time values," so that the "temporal limitation of the mnemic excitation is therefore, in a sense, predetermined." [52] Hence the dimension, duration, in memory, is basically a reflection of external fact, like that in perception. But the transposition does not seem to work when we come to a succession of experiences revived in memory. Then, again according to the testimony of introspectionists, the departure of the sense of duration from actual duration is in the opposite direction from that of perception. Then "a time filled with varied and interesting experiences seems . . . long, as we look back"; while "a tract of time empty of experiences seems . . . in retrospect short." [53] If this is true, we would have to conclude, at least whenever a succession of experiences is concerned, that the unit of duration in memory is only the unit of experience (above) not that of time (duration in the strict sense). The more of these units appeared in retrospect, the longer would seem the time, and vice versa. In fact, it would then appear that the true physiological sense and measure of duration does not carry over into memory. True, memory is also an experience; and our sense of duration might well be applied to the period during which it was revived; but that revival would not carry with it its own sense of duration except in terms of units of experience.

There is another relation of memory to time which may be built upon, but which must be distinguished from, the one we have just considered—duration. So far as we can ever know, it is, even more definitely than the first, confined to conscious memory. It is the sense of "pastness." According to the introspectionists, we grasp the whole of a unit of duration or experience as being the present, with no more than a sense of the direction of its movement—that is, as James said, that it has a bow and a stern. If so, there cannot be inherent in such

---

[52] Semon, *368*, 149–150.
[53] William James, *220*, I, 624. This is supported by the observation that the more habitual, the less novel, the experience, the more tracts of time seem to shorten in retrospect; and, because all experience is then less novel, they also shorten for the older as compared with the younger (*ibid.*, I, 625).

experience the sense of pastness. According to Semon there supervenes, after the synchronous (during stimulation) phase of each original excitation, an acoluthic phase, during which the excitation previously aroused dies out—more or less slowly. It is conceivable, then, that the very dying out of the excitation in the acoluthic phase, or the contrast between that and the synchronous phase, which is perceived at the same time, might represent to us the sign of *becoming* past. But, against that supposition, we have the general impression that the excitation of the acoluthic phase always seems to us a part of the present, not of the past—in fact, it is just that which gives it its peculiar and deceptive character.[54] By this process of elimination we conclude that the sense of pastness can attach only to, and arise from, true mnemic excitations. Semon holds that between the acoluthic phase and the occurrence of a mnemic excitation there must always intervene a phase of "secondary indifference." But the mnemic excitation is not only separated from the new excitation (present) which recalls it, by reason of this interval of time; it is not only contrasted because it is fainter than this new excitation, being mnemic; but it is also evidently separate physiologically; it is laid down in a region somewhat apart from that in which the original excitation—the current experience— takes place.[55] But even these several separations or contrasts do not satisfy the requirements of a basis for the sense of pastness. If we assume that the "mind" is furnished only with current sensorimotor processes and with memories, together with the constructions and reconstructions made from these, then it is obvious that many mnemic excitations are free from the sense of pastness. In fact, in large part, the mental processes, ranging from day-dreaming to intellectual activities, including all that we call imagination, while all of them must be reworking these old materials, having nothing else to work, nevertheless do so without the connotation of pastness.[56]

[54] William James distinguished "primary memory," which corresponds quite well to Semon's "acoluthic phase." It contains objects "belonging to the rearward portion of the present space of time, and not to the genuine past." It is "hauntings of consciousness by the impression." These "form the transition [with a break, we think] to that more peculiar and proper phenomenon of memory"—"memory proper, or secondary memory" (*220*, I, 646–648).

[55] This is implicit in Semon's thesis as described above. William James also held that "the brain-tracts excited by the event proper, and those excited by its recall, are in part different from each other" (*220*, I, 657).

[56] William James admits this, though apparently with some hesitation. He says "wherever, in fact, the recalled event does appear without a definite setting, it is hard to distinguish it from a mere creation of the fancy," so that, if we could recall it entirely

Apparently the occurrences which are most regularly accompanied by the sense of pastness are certain instances of the reaction of recognition and its congener, the reaction of the perception of differences. These, it will be remembered, are called forth when homophony exists between elements of the current original excitation and those among themselves homophonous mnemic excitations which, as a result, it recalls (ecphorizes). When the mnemic excitations so revived arise from single memories (engrams) they are always felt as past. It seems possible, then, that the sense of pastness consists of some unknown contrast which single details of memory (single engrams) may evidence when they are recalled by and confronted with a current experience that is homophonous. Doubtless this contrast would be reinforced if, within narrow limits, there were some perception of difference within the homophonous detail. And doubtless it would be still further reinforced when the single detail (engram) is able to recall by association all or any part of its own *mise en scène* (engram-complex), and thus extend the area of differences and their perception without disturbing the homophony. It appears, nevertheless, that the mere reaction of recognition may suffice by itself to establish pastness in certain cases. However, we face another difficulty here. We have seen that Semon supposed that abstractions are formed by the superimposition of innumerable homophonous memory details (engrams) upon each other. When the reaction of recognition results from the recall of such a highly composite photograph, this abstraction no longer yields the sense of pastness when confronted with the current homophonous excitation. We recognize any horse as a horse when we see one; but we are not thereby deceived into thinking that we have seen this one before, if we have not. On the other hand, a certain horse that we have seen before, even if at several different times and places, may be recognized as one that we have seen *before* (i.e., in the past). This difference suggests that the more composite the homophonous engrams called up, the less they give rise to the sense of pastness; and the less composite, the more the sense of pastness. And this regardless of the

---

separately, we would "simply dream that we were undergoing the experience as if for the first time" (*220*, I, 657–658). He goes so far as to say that "no memory is involved in the mere fact of recurrence" (revival). Memory requires that "the fact imaged be *expressly referred to the past*." It must be thought with some point of reference. In fact it must even be "my past" (*ibid.*, I, 649). This is, of course, a very narrow definition of conscious memory. In our definition, memory includes all revivals. But James's statements are apt to our present purpose because we are here considering only those which are related to time.

precision of homophony (i.e., the individuation of the homophonous memories); for a person whom we see constantly is recognized with at least much less sense of pastness than one seen rarely, while the sense of pastness is most vivid when we see again one whom we have only seen once before.

By means of this discrimination between those particular memory details which approach the simplex, and are accompanied by the sense of pastness, and those which approach the multiplex, and have it not, we seem to have arrived at the most probable key to the sense of pastness as well as furnishing ourselves with a likely hypothesis as to the organization, or order, of pastness in memory. There must be such an order; for, as between two memories, we can tell with some degree of accuracy which is the older and which the newer—that is, which was laid down earlier and which later. Now, according to Semon's thesis, the successive strata of experience, each stratum of which constitutes one of the aforementioned units of experience, are laid down separately in the conscious memory in such a way that each simultaneous complex of continuous stimulation is a related whole, but that each related whole is connected with the next preceding and the next succeeding in some respect discontinuous complex through the simultaneity of the acoluthic phase of the earlier with the synchronous phase of the later. These relations (simultaneous) and connections (successive) are held to be the only basis of what Semon calls "association."

If we suppose that the continued operation in memory of the processes of association, both simultaneous and successive, is simply due to the fact that the order in which these successive strata of experience (engram-complexes) were laid down is preserved thereafter, then the whole of the sense of pastness and the order of pastness would be the result of the mechanism of association.[57] The mechanism of simultaneous association—constituting in memory a cross-section of time—would yield the sense of contemporaneousness in memory; that of successive association—constituting in memory the transition from one cross-section to the next—would give the sense of before and after, there. From this might develop the sense of the approximate distance into the past of the position that any particular complex—cross-

[57] It will be recalled that Lashley states (262, 382) that "the temporal aspects of experience must . . . have a spatial basis" in the brain, though not an individual locus (ibid., 373). This was quotd in Appendix II, Section F 1.

section—occupied in the order, at least in terms of more-or-less—some sort of rough dating. But each cross-section (complex) would be composed of many details (single engrams) and, as we have suggested, each of these details is "cross-indexed" according to another classification the criterion of which is homophony. Homophony is not concerned with the cross-section of time; it parallels the movement of time; it cuts through all intermediate cross-sections; it penetrates, so to speak, to the cross-section or sections where homophonous details are stored.[58] If, now, the current excitation should recall by homophony some detail which composed a part in one or several complexes, the question whether or not it would be dated would depend on whether or not it could be dated. If it composed part of one complex only, it could be definitely dated by simultaneous association according to the place of that complex in the order; if it composed part of several, the dating would at least be blurred—since the several complexes could not all be recalled by association at one and the same time—and thus only some sense of pastness might remain; but if it composed part of innumerable complexes, either individualized or abstracted, no associations could take place, no dating could be made at all and, in fact, even the sense of pastness would be lost.

We would summarize these assumptions as follows: Under this construction homophony alone yields no sense of pastness; that comes only when homophony can call to its aid association; association in turn can only occur when homophony recalls but one, or, in succession and separately, a series of specific homophonous instances (engrams). When the instances are many, homophony does not or can not arouse association; it becomes abstract, or at least composite, because the instances are not then recalled separately, but rather in the mass (superimposed). Thus the sense of pastness consists in the identification of a specific instance with a certain cross-section of time (engram-complex)—or a few of them—through simultaneous association; in turn, the order in which these cross-sections are laid down yields, through successive association, the order of pastness and the ability to discriminate in pastness, with some accuracy, between the

---

[58] The working mechanism suggested in this hypothesis is somewhat on the model of the Hollerith machine, but in reverse. Here the apparatus of homophony penetrates the cards of association, while they are still stacked, until it reaches one that is "not punched" (i.e., contains a homophonous detail). Even—and here the analogy falls down—it can reach many or all the "not punched," in series, and bring them up together. But the more it does this last, the more the cross-indexing—that is, the rest of the details on each card—are lost to view.

earlier and the later—to locate, in fact, the point in a long series at which the record of an experience exists and thus roughly to gauge its degree of pastness.[59]

Out of the self-perception of the way these processes work might well begin to arise what William James distinguished as "conceived time." [60] But this self-perception would form the basis only of even the most primitive concepts of time—that part derived from the way the "mind" works, or the way it seems to the early introspectionist to work. Soon there would commence, and with civilized man there would develop, another process—including analogy between the organization of time and other categories as well as abstraction of its

[59] Our thesis that pastness and the order of pastness are given by the order of the successive strata laid down in memory is not unlike that of certain psychologists. Thus James Ward (424, 577) says that there is probably, in memory, some trace or residue "of that movement of attention of which we are aware in passing from one presentation to another" (i.e., our discontinuities). "These residua are our temporal signs, and, together with the representations connected by them, constitute the memory-continuum."

However, Ward then attempts to add to this the "time-perspective"—a position in which William James coincides (see 220, I, 629–630). The "pictorial exactness of the time-perspective" is due to "the working of oblivescence," which, "by insuring a progressive variation in intensity and distinctness as we pass from one member of the series to another, yields the effect which we call time-distance. By themselves such variations would leave us liable to confound more vivid representations in the distance with fainter ones near the present, but from this mistake the temporal signs save us." At a far distance there is "no such distinct appreciation of comparative distance in time as we have nearer the present when these perspective effects are considerable." So, too, James says, "There is thus a sort of *perspective projection* of past objects upon present consciousness, similar to that of wide landscapes upon a camera-screen" (*ibid.*, I, 630).

The serious difficulty with this supposed additional basis for judging the order of pastness is that it most certainly does not exist. There is no reason to think that old memories are fainter than new. In fact, it is well recognized that, as one ages, childhood memories remain among the most vivid. We say, "I remember that as if it happened only yesterday." As Hughlings Jackson says (216, II, 191): "In failing memory recent events are soon forgotten, whilst old events are remembered; but this is not without qualification; the *most* recent events are remembered as well as the old; on the physical side, nervous arrangements just discharged remain for a short time in a state of slight independent organization, rivalling that of nervous arrangements discharged when the person was young and vigorous, or that of nervous arrangements often discharged."

If, then, old memories are not fainter than new, they cannot grow fainter due to *their* age. Thus the actual vividness cannot be a measure of time, and the time-scale must be something independent of the vividness or fading of memories.

[60] The intuition of time is "limited to intervals of considerably less than a minute. Beyond its borders extends the immense region of *conceived* time, past and future, into one direction or the other of which we mentally project all the events which we think of as real, and form a systematic order of them by giving each a date. The relation of conceived to intuited time is just like that of the fictitious space pictured on the flat back-scene of a theatre to the actual space of the stage" (James, 220, I, 643). Our thesis would separate "intuited" (experienced) time from "conceived" time by a much longer evolution. Intervening would be the whole experience of the memory system in its relations to time.

internal relationships. For "conceived" time is also the product of observation of the phases of all natural processes which change through time, as well as of their accurate mensuration—including astronomy, with its calendars and chronometers. Even the most highly evolved concepts of time seem, however, to retain the prepossessions of the earliest concepts. These fundamental prepossessions of conceived time, as outlined in Appendix III, Section D, are pure analogies and are not given as direct experiences, either from perception or memory. One is spatial; events pass in review before a stationary beholder, *coming* from the future and *going* into the past (literally "the passed"). Another is based on aging; events grow old as they recede into the past. Out of the first analogy arises the concept of "time perspective," discussed above,[61] in which events are *conceived* to be arranged in something resembling spatial order according to their "distance" in the past or even in the future, and are even *conceived* to grow smaller or dimmer, or both, according to the degree of this distance, in spite of the fact that the actual memories do neither. Time perspective is a purely conceptual analogy, derived neither from temporal perception of experience nor from that of memory.

Futurity and the order of futurity are secondary derivatives from pastness and the order of pastness. The facts with regard to the future are inescapable. Unlike the present it does not exist; unlike the past it has not existed. Therefore, since it is not a reality, either present or past, it cannot be directly apprehended by any apparatus whatever; one cannot "peer" into it. Neither is it, as some poet has said, a dark curtain drawn across the face of oncoming events. For there is nothing behind it. Events do not "come from" the future; they occur successively for the first time in the present. Instead, the future is counterfeit; it is only a mirror—a mirror of the past—in which memory is reflected back at us in more or less successful disguises—a mirror from which events, as they occur, emerge into the present with considerable divergence from, and confusion of, the reflected patterns we have let ourselves see there. What is reflected in this mirror and the way that material is organized there are, in part, a direct result of experience and the memories it has laid down and, in part, a more indirect result, one which the processes of abstraction and analogy have greatly elaborated. Experience combined with memory must directly teach all organisms that new events that have not previously happened are

[61] See note 59, above.

always arriving in the present in a continuous series. Thus is established the category of succession in time, which, as we saw in Chapter 3, seems to be the basic element in the naïve category of causation—*post hoc ergo propter hoc*. If, in the experience of an organism, a series of several successive events have usually or always followed one another, upon the appearance of the earlier members of the series the organism, by successive association, recalls the later members of the series and tends to take it for granted that they will follow as usual. They are projected upon the mirror, so to speak, while the former are still occurring. They are "expected," as we say. Even their temporal order in succession may be preserved in the reflections. In this way, the "future," to all organisms with conscious memory of individual experience, may well consist of "unfinished business." Perhaps the apprehension of the counterfeit future is confined to this experience of the perpetual succession of events, to the attitude of habitual expectation to which that might well lead, and to the specific expectation of certain normal successions of events once a series begins.

In part, the mirror we call the future reflects also "conceived" time, which, though it has been elaborated from the past by abstractions and analogies, is also, as we have seen, projected into the future. Hence the notion of flow or procession of coming events constructed on the analogy of spatial flows or processions that we can observe. Hence also the illusion of time perspective under which prospective events are supposed to contract or become dim the greater their futurity.[62] But, in addition to these figurative beginnings, observation and mensuration yield a purely abstract order of futurity—though this again is wholly a reflection of the past. It suffices to space out along an accurate scale, compound of chronometers and calendars, those recurrent events the intervals between which are extended or are dependent on phases in slow and even irregular processes—days, months, seasons, years, and even "business cycles."

Wholly out of the data of memory, as reflected in the mirror of the future and projected along this accurate scale of "conceived" time, arise two forms of calculation.[63] The first, concerning itself with

[62] Premonitions of the future may be presented with great vividness. But, of course, that cannot have any proportionality to their degree of futurity.
[63] Calculation, as a mental process, is of course common to many animals as well as man. For instance, your dog calculates when he catches a ball. The wolves cited by Romanes (*354, 433*) calculated. This business of projecting—spatially and temporally—the past and present into the future had already been reduced to a fine art before *Homo sapiens* graduated from the class of anthropoids. Nor has man changed its funda-

regularly recurring phenomena, we may call *periodicity* over time. It is conceived in terms of the interval of time between regular recurrences. The second, concerning itself with irregularly recurring phenomena, we may call *contingency*. The periodicity of a contingency cannot be calculated; for there is no possibility of assigning to its recurrences any definite dates. The only calculation of contingency that is possible as to a phenomenon whose causation is very complex or is unknown—that is, a "chance" phenomenon, as we say—is its frequency over periods of time sufficiently long to give it some degree of regularity.[64] That is, the evidence of past experience of its recurrences over time can be used to form a conclusion that the contingency is likely to occur with a frequency of once, or more, times during such certain period. Considering the incident by itself, recurrence is a contingency; considering it with respect to the time-scale, recurrence has no certain periodicity, but it has a somewhat definite and uniform frequency during successive periods of time. Winter is a periodic phenomenon; drought is a contingency.

To summarize: It would appear that regularly recurring experiences would give rise to a series of homophonous details in memory, which, by way of simultaneous and successive association would be evenly spaced in the rough order of pastness in memory. Then, as they became more accurately located in the past by means of "conceived" time, the intervals between their recurrence would be calculated. And thence, in turn, the whole scheme would be projected into the counterfeit future. Recurrence would come to be expected at a certain point ahead, along the scale of time, and its constantly nearer approach would be calculated by the passing of time—duration since, or order of pastness of, its last appearance—also measured along the scale. Irregularly recurring experiences would likewise give rise to a series of homophonous details in memory; but here the spacing would be more difficult. Even in terms of "conceived" time and its scale each interval would be different from each other. When such a scheme was projected into the counterfeit future the only expectation would be that the experience would recur "sometime." However, as observations of its recurrence increased and longer periods were included in the scale

mental character. What the dog does when he catches a ball is now called extrapolation by our most sapient *homines*. If extrapolation is a sign of smartness, then the dog belongs to the smart set among organisms.
[64] Gamblers bet on the contingency of *rouge* or *noir*. Actuaries estimate the contingency of a conflagration or an epidemic.

of time, the probability of its recurrence *any* time might be reduced to a probability that it would recur at *some* time within a limited period. While that period was passing it would be constantly expected; and, as more of the period became past it would be felt to be increasingly imminent.

5. CONSCIOUS MEMORY AND FUTURE WANTS

The foregoing brief analysis of certain features of conscious memory, based in part upon deduction (assuming that it has the characteristics common to mnemic phenomena in general) and in part upon inference (the assignment to it of certain special and different characteristics inferred from observation and introspection) suffices for our purpose. It enables us to interpret future wants in detail as if they were functions of conscious memory, and thus to test the suggestion advanced earlier. But, before proceeding to do so, it may be advisable to clear up one issue that might cause confusion. In the course of our examination of mnemic phenomena it appeared that most of the processes we have examined in connection with present wants—the restoration of homeostasis, conditioned stimuli, learned behavior, etc.—are, in some respects at least, to be included in that classification. If, then, the phenomena connected with present wants are also, in part, mnemic, in what respect are future different from present wants? They are not different in respect of the activities or behavior that result from them, for both these are largely regulated by mnemic phenomena, inherited or acquired (habits). They are not different in the relations they establish with the environment in respect of the extensive conditioning of external stimuli that relate to them. The fundamental distinction lies only in this: All present wants are actual variations from homeostasis, or they are central replicas of the effects of such variations produced by external conditioned stimuli. No future want is an actual variation from homeostasis; neither, when it exists, is there a central replica of the corresponding present want, nor, for that matter, the necessity of an external conditioned stimulus. The actual present want is peripheral; the surrogate present want is central but subcortical. Neither exists in the arena of consciousness in the cortex, though either may invade that arena as sensation or as emotion or both. The future want, on the other hand, if it is a function of conscious memory, has no existence either peripherally or subcortically. It must then be purely cortical and conscious. Thus the essence of the difference lies in the locus, and perhaps in the timing, of the cause and the initiation of behavior, and not at all in the behavior itself.[65] We have preserved that distinction intact by means of the order of our investigation. For we have postponed the examination of conscious memory until we come to deal with phenomena that would be incapable of being explained at all without memory, if memory is responsible for their very existence rather than merely for the guidance of the behavior to which they give rise, which is also true of present wants.

This distinction, we conclude, is one of degree only in respect of the mnemic character of conscious memory. For such memory, being the product of individual experience only, is merely the latest evolved and the most exposed—the strategic front line—in a long series of mnemic phenomena and apparatus. It differs in degree, as a result, in being the most susceptible or plastic and, correspondingly, in being the least potent—least intense—and therefore the least affective, or actually non-affective. It also differs, perhaps only in degree, in being the one mnemic phenomenon which contains the precise record of the passing of time and therefore which gives rise to the experience of duration, pastness, and the order of pastness.[66] Out of that, in some way, is derived the projection of a counterfeit future with the same system of mensuration. Certainly all animals and perhaps most organisms show signs of such projection (i.e., exhibit expectation). But in whatever degree this counterfeit future may have a place in the mental life of all animals, it is clear from our examination of capitalism in the animal world (Appendix III, Section A) that only a few species

[65] We may present this distinction from a somewhat different angle. (1) There is no question that the internal stimulus of a specific "physiological state" (present want) will ecphorize an engram-complex that includes the engram of a learned reaction and thus, by association, lead to procuring an object required to correct that state, even when the object is not present (i.e., no external stimulus). (2) There is also no question that an external stimulus that has become associated (simultaneously) with such a state (conditioned) will ecphorize the engram-complex, inherited or acquired, which that state has left in the central but subcortical mneme, and do so without internal stimulus. Whether it then leads to a learned reaction dealing with the stimulating object appears to depend on whether the replica suffices by itself or not. (3) But there is also no question that, among man and certain animals, learned reactions are initiated when the state is non-existent and the object is not present (neither internal nor external stimulus). We are suggesting an imputed cause for the third phenomenon in the memory system —that is, a system in which the effect of previous stimuli (internal or external) is stored up so that corresponding excitations can be revived to activate the motor apparatus.
[66] Of course growth is arranged in a phasogeneous order, and some behavior managed from below the level of conscious memory seems to be chronogeneous (i.e., the shedding of leaves by beech trees regardless of climatic conditions or variation in the seasons.

besides man *act* on the energizing of future wants. Thus, at the best, future wants could only be construed as a particular class of futurized memories and we would have to search further for their *raison d'être* as activating wants. We would have a legitimate hypothesis as to their futurity, but none as yet as to their ostensible character as wants, as generators of behavior.

In our differentiation of behavior specimens (Section A 2 above) we set up future wants as hypothetical forces that also operate in the present and are obviously related to present wants, since, up to a point, the resulting behavior is similar. If they are actually derived from present wants they can, conceivably, only be derived from present wants that have occurred in the past—whether the racial or the individual past. But they are distinguished from present wants by reason of the fact that, when they give rise to behavior, the corresponding present want is non-existent peripherally, and no conditioned external stimulus needs to be taking its place, with the result that there is no evidence of an emotional state. They are further distinguished by the fact that the resulting behavior does not include the later part of the series of reactions—the consummatory part. These distinctions apply equally well when "expectation" is introduced. The fact that all animals exhibit "expectation" does not argue that they are also driven by future wants. When the dog extrapolates the course of the thrown ball or the wolf that of his prey, the one is motivated by the present want, play, and the other by the present want, hunger. Memory projected into the counterfeit future is merely a guide to behavior initiated and energized by present wants. In the absence of such a want, the behavior is not initiated, however available the memories. Thus if future wants are futurized memories of a particular class, they are particular in the special respect that, unlike all other futurized memories, they are adequate to initiate and not merely to guide behavior.

Recognizing the deficiencies of the hypothesis, let us proceed to interpret future wants as if they were functions of conscious memory. That, at least, might explain their relationship to present wants and their futurity. As memories of past wants they would appear in consciousness when revived. The intensity, though not the vividness, of such revivals would be derived from, and therefore proportional to, the intensity of the individual occurrence of the present want. Therefore, the more intense was the former present want—at least at its normal maximum—the more intense its revival, the future want. But since all memories are much less intense than the "original excitation" which laid them down, all future wants would be much less intense than their corresponding present wants. Since frequently recurring present wants would lay down long series of homophonous memories they would tend to become, in memory, composites or even abstractions. They would thus tend to lose their dates and even their sense of pastness. Correspondingly they would accumulate vividness without change in intensity. Out of the past these memories, individual and dated or composites and abstractions undated, would be projected into the counterfeit future. This future would be organized in the same way as the past; it would have an order, corresponding to the perceived temporal order of memory, and a time-scale, more or less accurate according to the degree of development of conceived time. If the present wants had been found by experience to be regularly recurring, that definite periodicity would become part of the abstraction even if the precise datings were lost. Derived future wants would then be projected along the time-scale of the future at regular intervals. If the present wants had been found by experience to be irregular in their occurrence, the individual instances might remain dated, or more nearly dated, and the abstractions, if formed at all, would not contain periodicity but only contingency. Then the future wants would be projected along the time-scale of the future according to frequency (i.e., so many recurrences at *any* time in a period).

In three respects this interpretation does not account for the observable characteristics of future wants. The first respect is this. It will appear in due course that there is some sort of rough correlation between the effectiveness of future wants in initiating behavior and the nearness of the position in the future into which they are projected. This cannot be accounted for on any mnemic basis. In the first place, as we have seen, there is no necessary diminution in intensity of memories merely according to their degree of pastness. In the second place, even if there were, there is no reversal in the projection by which the more past becomes the more future. If anything, projection continues the same order of events as that of the past. As between two different events recurring at equal intervals, that one which occurred first, and therefore more past, would be projected to occur first in the future, and therefore with less futurity. For both reasons the intensity of memories projected into the future cannot be less intense the greater the futurity given them. In fact, it appears that all memories of one kind (homophonous), if projected at all, are projected with the same intensity into an indefinitely prolonged future.[67] The second respect, perhaps due only to our ignorance of the workings of futurized memories, is the apparent absence of any adequate ecphorizing influence in the case of future wants. The sight of the ball to the dog who wants to play is enough to ecphorize by recognition and association, and even to project, the memories of this series of events from the past. The sight or scent of prey, or even his own hunger, is enough to do the same for the wolf who "expects." But since neither the want nor a conditioned stimulus exists in the case of future wants, what can it be that calls up these memories and projects them? Finally, there is the apparent deficiency as an energizer of behavior of mere memories even if projected. Not only must they be inadequate, if they occur at all, in the whole range of the animal world outside a few species, since there they never lead to behavior, but we have recognized their marked lack of intensity as compared with the "original" excitation of such experiences as present wants. If, then, we are to supply the deficiencies of this mnemonic hypothesis, it is apparent that we must look elsewhere for supplementary forces or mechanisms or both. These questions, in reverse order, will engage our attention in the following chapter.

[67] It is evident that the property of this system which projects future wants along a scale of time with different degrees of futurity is not itself affected by that futurity. In that sense it is a timeless property. Like a filing clerk, it can recognize the dimension A to Z; but it has no less inclination, or finds it no more difficult, to file under Z than under A.

6

FUTURE WANTS—THEIR MECHANISMS
AND ANALYTICAL SCHEME

A. THE ENERGIZING MECHANISM OF FUTURE WANTS

1. MEMORY AND THE MISSING LINK

PERHAPS the best cue as to a region to explore for the supplementary forces or mechanisms that would account for those characteristics of future wants which memory and its counterfeit future seem unable to explain is given to us by the fact that we have already had to confine our hypothesis to *conscious* memory. In Appendix II [1] we arrived at the conclusion that consciousness is a concomitant of neural excitation when communicated to a certain region of the brain.[2] The experiences that can occur only in consciousness are there stated to be emotion (the experience), sensation, and volition. Furthermore, "since memory, in its strict sense of recall, implies recall to consciousness, it too can occur only where consciousness occurs." The characteristic of the neural processes that produce consciousness in its locus, and therefore may become part of its content, appears to be deliberation or delay—that is, consciousness occurs when incoming excitations

[1] Consciousness was discussed from as nearly as possible an objective basis in Chapter 2, Section D, and the evidence therefor was assembled in Appendix II, Sections G, H and I.
[2] Hughlings Jackson said (*216*, II, 85): "I take consciousness and mind to be synonymous terms." That shows that he was thinking of content and not locus. Tending more to the distinction of locus was Hering's remark (*189*, 70): "Our ideas tread but for a moment upon the stage of consciousness, and then go back again behind the scenes." But, like Jackson, he considered them to be ideas only when recognized (i.e., conscious). It is clear that access to consciousness is limited. Consciousness, at any one time or during one process of deliberation, does not embrace more than a small portion of existing or actual cortical excitations and a far smaller portion of potential excitations. The study of abnormal psychology seems to indicate that, in addition to this functional concentration, the whole of the "association" areas of the cortex may become divided so that parts may become temporarily or permanently shut off from access to consciousness, or that consciousness may move from one to another divided part and be accessible for that one exclusively for long periods. That means to us that interassociation between the parts is broken at the border between them. Even normally there must be restrictions such as Freud presupposes in repression.

are not immediately drawn off into outgoing channels (chiefly motor), and is usually restricted to containing them. The conditions
in which this characteristic emerges seem to be, (1) when the
incoming excitation is below the threshold of the motor outlets (daydreaming, reminiscing, reflection of certain kinds, etc.), (2) when
the incoming excitation (pain, fear, etc.), is beyond the capacity of
the motor outlets immediately to draw off, and (3) when the incoming
excitation produces conflict—that is, when the several motor tendencies of its various elements are antagonistic to each other so that
mutual inhibition of their several outlets results.[3]

As we analyzed the probable sources of the excitations that contribute to the production of consciousness in its locus and may therefore give it its content, they were as follows: (1) The stream of emotion, (2) the stream of awakeness, (3) incoming sensory excitation,
(4) the memory-system. The second is regular (continuous when
awake) and is non-specific (i.e., without pattern and therefore unable
to contribute content—of the nature of tonic excitation). The other
three are irregular, constantly changing, and specific (i.e., each has a
pattern and therefore may contribute a content to consciousness). But
the point in which we are specially interested here is their relative
strength. The stream of awakeness is sufficient by itself to produce
consciousness when it raises the state of awakeness to its median range.[4]
Not only can the stream of emotion by itself raise awakeness to its
median range and thus produce consciousness, but it is capable, when
very intense, of raising awakeness to a point beyond that range and thus
of producing confusion or unconsciousness.[5] It is doubtful whether
incoming sensory excitation by itself, if devoid of emotional accompaniment, is capable of causing awakeness and, therefore, of producing
consciousness. But perhaps it is. It is certain that the memory-system
by itself cannot cause awakeness and is therefore incapable of producing consciousness. Thus we rank the four sources in the order of their
potency as we named them above.[6] And we assume that in the absence

[3] For further discussion of this condition for consciousness, see supplementary statement on "Conflict and Consciousness" at the end of this subsection.
[4] However, it may do this only by way of "facilitation" of the incoming sensory stream
and of the memory-system.
[5] This is in accord with the interpretation of the facts in Appendix II, Section G. It is
also confirmed by Hughlings Jackson (216, II, 89). He says, "Although consciousness
arises during slight sequent discharges of nervous arrangements of the highest centres,
it ceases during the sudden, etc., discharges thereof."
[6] Since we have previously acknowledged the affective tendencies to be also mnemic
phenomena, it will be well to clarify this statement in that respect. The distinction in

of excitation from one of the first two sources—the streams of emotion and awakeness—or both, the third may be, and the fourth is certainly, inadequate to produce consciousness.[7]

The ultimate sources of the excitation coming from these proximate sources into consciousness are different in the four cases. That of the emotional stream arises, as we have seen, in the hypothalamus, where it is, in turn, excited either by a peripheral condition transmitted there or by a conditioned stimulus. That of the stream of awakeness arises also in the hypothalamus as a result of some rhythmic process that is not understood. That of the incoming sensory excitation comes, of course, ultimately from external or even internal stimuli through the afferent sensory apparatus, peripheral, subcortical, and cortical. It

strength between mnemic phenomena is a matter of degree of ingrainedness (or engravedness). Of the ones considered here those most frequently repeated and most continuous in the phylogenetic past (inherited) have become affective, or, in other words, strongest. Those acquired during the ontogenetic past are weaker; and, of these, the cortical (most recent) are usually, by reason of less repetition and continuity, weaker than the subcortical and the somatic.

[7] This statement, so far as external (sensory) stimuli are concerned, is radically opposed to the external stimulus-response viewpoint. For, according to that view, the organism is a machine merely reacting to such stimuli. But, in the first place, we have previously assembled the evidence to show that the really powerful elements in producing behavior are the internal "drives." True, these may be aroused by external stimuli (quasi-external wants). But, when they are, it is not the sensory apparatus that gives them their force. That is merely the detonator. The force comes from the primary source of neural energy of response. Failing to arouse such "drives," or in their absence, the sensory apparatus produces excitation of the mildest.

The organism has been pictured as being under constant and heavy bombardment by innumerable stimuli from the outer world. This needs much qualification. In the first place, there is "adaptation" at the receptors and perhaps in the fibers. In the second place, the central thresholds must be high, so that, unless conscious attention lowers them, what comes through is of the mildest intensity. In the third place, even the most acute conscious attention focused on some element of the external scene does not yield sensory excitation of a high order. Excitement, then, is the product of the emotion which causes and directs the sensory attention, not of the sensations themselves. In fact, the greatest acuity of consciousness of external facts is reserved largely for those which deliver the most subtle and mild stimuli—e.g., the *pianissimo* passage in a concerto, the delicate shadings in a painting, the bouquet of a wine.

So far as mnemonic excitations are concerned, it is generally conceded that all memories are weaker even than the original excitations that formed them. Here are some more statements in support. "The mnemic reproduction is usually weaker than the original excitations were at the time when they created the engrams" (Semon, *368*, 92). "The presence of such engrams . . . suffices . . . to reproduce completely, although with much diminished liveliness, the previous group of phenomena" (Semon, *369*, 323). An engram is a "faithful, if somewhat weakened, image" (Semon, *368*, 94). Hering thought that memory sensations of qualities (i.e., Semon's homophonous abstractions) "arising from within," are "feeble repetitions," although he believed that recent memories can "return suddenly to our consciousness with all the force and freshness of the original sensation" (*189*). Whether this is true of anything but the acoluthic phase is doubtful.

probably reaches consciousness from the sensorimotor cortex. But the memory-system seems, at first sight, to have no independent origin of its own. Memories may be ecphorized, as we have seen, by reason of the homophony of current sensation. If they were, when laid down, strongly endowed with emotion, they can, under such an ecphorizing influence, produce a replica of a quasi-external want or raise the latent intensity of an internal want so that it becomes prepotent in the hypothalamus. If not so endowed, memories are weak. They may also be ecphorized by other memories by way either of association or even of purely mnemic homophony. When that occurs they are always weak. And, in that case, there remains the question as to the source of their revival, their re-excitation; for we have seen no reason to suppose that their re-excitation is autogenous. If they must always be ecphorized by some other agency, what constitutes the original excitor of a chain of memories? Does such a chain always start with a sensation? [8]

Let us now apply these considerations of energetics to the three conditions named above in which the characteristic called deliberation or delay emerges. Provided the subject is awake, it is easy to see that memory alone, revived by some ecphorizing influence other than current sensation and therefore very weak, might still be responsible for the merely subliminal excitations in consciousness which we experience as reminiscing, day dreaming, or some kinds of reflection. Again provided the subject is awake, it is evident that current sensation without emotional content ("interest"), though considerably stronger, still might cause only similar subliminal excitations such as mere awareness of the current scene. On the other hand, it is clear that only the emotional stream is capable of arousing those degrees of excitation in consciousness that are beyond the capacity of the motor outlets immediately to draw off, though they may still be below the level at which consciousness would give way to confusion.

However, when we come to the question of the sources that contribute to the third condition, conflict, we find ourselves in difficulties —difficulties that have not been faced at any previous stage in our entire investigation, simply because we were not yet ready to deal with them. On the one hand, we are obliged to establish a rational

[8] We have not, as yet, considered what this other ultimate source might be. One memory can revive another by association or homophony. But is there always, at the origin of the series, some current sensation; or is there some other ecphorizing influence capable of initially energizing these chains? This matter is discussed in Section A 6 below.

scheme of energetics and one that complies with the known neurophysiological facts. On the other hand, it is now time to recognize
that the relationship between the cortex and the subcortical brain, as
that has been developed from the neurophysiological data, does not
furnish us alone with such a rational scheme—in fact, presents us with
one that cannot, as it stands, be reconciled in many respects with any
scheme that would be rational. A scheme of energetics to be rational
must not suppose that a weaker force can overcome a stronger. Fundamentally, all our neurophysiological interpretations rest on the notion
of comparative strengths of forces. But neurophysiology has constructed an edifice in which, in one region, weaker forces are treated
as if they could overcome stronger forces. We do not suggest, of
course, that this structure has been misrepresented in gross ways. The
evidence for it is too strong to permit that inference. We only suggest
that some feature must have been omitted from the energetic picture—
omitted, of course, because it was unobserved and unknown. We proceed, therefore, to infer another energetic element that we must suppose to exist if we are to account for the observed facts. We may be
permitted the hope that this element, inferred as the planet Neptune
had at first to be inferred because of the necessity of imputing some
other body as the source of observed action upon the planet Uranus,
will ultimately be confirmed by neurophysiological observation as was
that at one time purely hypothetical entity. Until then, however, the
best we can do is to suggest a possible but wholly speculative neural
basis. And, if that turns out to be an untenable hypothesis, we are still
under the necessity of supposing something to fill the evident gap.

It will clarify matters to list at the start the chief deficiencies in the
system of energetics as hitherto presented in our study.

1. We have inferred that there can be conflict in the cortex and
that this conflict is one of the chief conditions producing consciousness.
In respect of this possibility of continuing unresolved conflict the
cortex seems to be different from all the rest of the nervous system
including the immediately subcortical regions. For, there, a conflict
can also occur; but, there, it is almost immediately resolved and in
favor of the strongest influence.[9] On this basis we have concluded that

9 McDougall holds that the mutual exclusiveness of drives is purely motor, so that two
or more may be present in consciousness. In fact, if the system of reactions of two
drives are not incompatible, the one may support or modify the other. Therefore, we
may observe not "merely a rapid alternation of these two states [what we have called
preliminary indecision], but rather an imperfect fusion of the two for which we have

conflict between the causes of emotional states (subcortical) is settled at the threshold of the hypothalamus and that, once settled, but one emotional state, and that the then strongest, can exist at any moment.[10] If the emotional stream always reflects that one state, it is obvious that cortical conflict cannot arise by reason of the presence of two current emotions, or "drives," in the cortex at one time. We have concluded that a conditioned external stimulus, through arousing emotionally endowed memories, can reproduce or aid in reproducing an emotional state in the hypothalamus; but, of course, this occurs only if its effective intensity is potentially greater than that of the state then prepotent (i.e., only if it can win the subcortical conflict). We have inferred that all other sensorimotor processes and memories may also become endowed with any of the several emotions. But these endowments, when incapable of producing a replica, have been conceded to be weak. If so, they would appear to be too weak to conflict effectively with the dominant cortical emotion by reason of their own force. The dominance of a single incoming emotion and the weakness of all cortical emotional endowments would seem to preclude the possibility of cortical conflict between two different "drives" with different objectives.

2. We have concluded that it is the emotional stream that furnishes the "drive" behind behavior (at least the primary neural energy of response) and that the cortex functions largely as a servant of that drive by relating it effectively to the external world—in other words, that the organism is oriented by its "drive," which is determined subcortically, but that it is oriented to specific features of the environ-

---

no name" (284, 183). We do not believe this is ever true of subcortical drives (emotional states) when they are strong enough to give rise to behavior, and suspect that what he is talking about is the resultant of conflict in consciousness in which volition may be participating.

[10] It is true that, in seeming contradiction to this thesis, we have followed Hughlings Jackson in interpreting convulsion as "the 'running up' of very many movements into a fight" (216, II, 89); "the sum of the contentions of different movements" (ibid., II, 31); or "the development of many movements at once" (ibid., II, 33). Perhaps decerebrate rigidity might be construed as similar in nature. But the degree and kind of conflict assumed in such abnormally intense excitation and the degree and kind here assumed are different. In those cases it is a single source of very intense excitation that spreads everywhere (uncanalized) and creates no inhibition. In the cases we are considering now, the conflicts are between different sources, no one of which presents such irresistible and all-invading force. From Sherrington's external stimulus viewpoint (375, 177–178), the organism is usually "acted on by many stimuli concurrently" but is only "driven reflexly by some group of stimuli which is at any particular moment prepotent in action on it."

ment by means of its cortical sensorimotor apparatus and its memories (conditioning). Such co-operation might permit another kind of conflict—that is, a conflict between various methods of reaching a single objective. But this raises another difficulty. We have seen evidence that the energy of each different "drive" is specific and that the energy of one cannot be diverted to the objectives (behavior) of another. If so, how can it be directed at all, even to its own objectives (behavior) by influences that are conceded to be so much weaker?

3. We have accepted the evidence that seems to prove that the cortex is capable of inhibiting, in various degrees, the subcortical source of emotion (the hypothalamus) as well as its direct motor outlets. This inhibition has been conceded to be complete at times and has even been found to include excitation of antagonist muscles. If inhibition is only a by-product of excitation, as seems to be the case, how can the cortex obtain such inhibitory power to use against its own chief source of excitation and in view of the weakness of the rest of its sources of excitation?

4. Finally, as we shall find much reason to believe, it is possible for a future want, which we have concluded to be a mnemonic phenomenon and thus to be formed essentially by memories, to overcome and annul a present want, which is an emotional phenomenon, so that the resulting action serves the future instead of the present want. How can it be that the weaker should thus completely overcome, and substitute itself for, the stronger?

It appears, from this recital of the several instances, that conflict in the cortex must be confined (1) to cases in which only parts of the conglomerate of current sensation and revived memories, or the latter alone, conflict with other parts, so that, in the absence of any strong dominant emotion, they are on an approximate parity so far as strength is concerned, or (2) to cases in which parts or wholes of such conglomerates, or memories alone, conflict with the single then dominant emotion. On purely rational grounds it follows that, in these latter cases, there must be some other source of neural energy or some energetic condition available to the cortex which reinforces the weaker partner to the conflict and enables it to direct, control, repress, or even substitute itself for the stronger.

Conflict and Consciousness. That cortical conflict is one of the conditions producing consciousness is pretty well agreed upon by physiologists. Psychologists usually concur. "Consciousness is the presence of impulses that have been more or less defined and which conflict with each other and thus arrest their own expression" (Thurstone, *401*, 49). Or, as I would express it, consciousness is attendant upon neural sequences that have as yet neither been excluded nor resolved into the action or inaction which is to be their resultant. I speak of them as sequences, for it it is true that ideas seem to follow each other in series. Nevertheless, the whole chain seems to remain in some sense in the field, as the background remains in the visual field even when the focus is at one point. For example, I feel that the idea I am now having is inconsistent with a previous one. Thus it must be possible to compare the two. But this argues that three things can be simultaneously in consciousness—the new idea and the old idea, plus the idea of inconsistency.

But the field of consciousness seems to be larger than conflict in its strict sense. It may be the result of the interplay of any simultaneous cortical activities remaining as yet central. Hughlings Jackson's basis is broader. "The middle and lowest centres are not only 'reservoirs of energy' but are also 'resisting positions' " (*211*, II, 67). "When there is discharge of part of a higher centre giving rise to currents not strong enough to overcome the resistance of the next lower centre, the currents ["are boxed up in" and] spread more widely in the higher centre" (*ibid.*, II, 30). "Thanks to the protection of the highest sensory centres by the lower sensory centres (which are 'resisting positions' as well as 'reservoirs of energy'), they can energize uninterfered with by the present environment. Again, thanks to the resistance of the lower motor centres, the sister higher motor centres can act without producing peripheral reactions; the muscular periphery is 'protected' from the highest motor centres. Here we have the physical conditions answering to the differences between vivid and faint states of object consciousness." And, "thanks to the 'protections,' there occurs internal evolution in our highest centres; we can have combinations never actually experienced ('ideal combinations'), as indeed we obviously have when dreaming, and certainly during much of our waking lives" (*ibid.*, II, 117, and see *ibid.*, II, 81).

Thus with internal as against external speech. "Speech is a part of thought —a part which we may or may not exteriorize." "The *same* nervous processes are concerned" in both. One spreads to the articulatory and vocal muscles; the other does not. Nevertheless, "it is not well to say that thought is internal speech, for the man who is speechless (the man who has no internal speech) can think." He cannot express himself in speech or writing, but he can understand the words of others. Jackson supposed this is due to the fact that understanding of what comes in occurs in the right hemisphere and is "entirely automatic" (*ibid.*, II, 131).

Whether such subliminal excitations extend to unobservable muscular activities, or are exclusively central, or vary between the two, we do not know. But the most likely hypothesis as to all concentrated thinking (verbal, visual, or tactual) is that it is a rehearsal, at this subliminal level, of associated chains of past experience in which we explore the processes and their end-results. Nor does this hypothesis exclude diffuse thinking of so low an intensity that it involves no inhibition and is merely a wandering around of excitation below the level of the sills to the doors of the motor system. Neither does it preclude the possibility that some other simultaneous impulse which knows its way and is unopposed (habitual) may pass through or even be initiated in the cortex without consciousness.

2. VOLITION AND SECONDARY NEURAL ENERGY OF RESPONSE

In the beginning of this section we mentioned volition as one of the experiences that occur in consciousness. This is the only one there mentioned which has not been referred to since. On the principle of Occam's razor it is therefore advisable to examine volition first in order to see whether, by any chance, it meets the requirements—that is, whether it might produce the effects which we must attribute to this reinforcing agency.[11]

What is volition? In our examination of this subject in Appendix II and Chapter 2 [12] we concluded that the term voluntary in reference to movements, as used by physiologists, connotes (1) an action adapted to the external data and therefore contrasted to stereotyped actions, (2) one not the result of observable external stimuli and therefore spontaneous, and (3) one which is, as a consequence, "purposeful" and controlled or inhibitable and therefore consciously integrated. In accordance with our analysis of the neural conditions necessary for such actions we supposed the foregoing to indicate that choice must be possible—that is, that there must exist, in order that actions should be voluntary, (1) a considerable degree of differentiation, in Hughlings Jackson's sense, (2) delay [13] and (3) the particular cause of delay that we have called conflict.[14] To meet these requirements, action, to be voluntary, (1) must have its proximate origin in the motor cortex (non-stereotyped); (2) it must be energized chiefly by

[11] "The traditional description and organization of behavior represented by the concepts of 'will' etc. . . . cannot be accepted so long as it pretends to be dealing with a mental world, but the behavior to which these terms apply is naturally part of the subject matter of a science of behavior" (Skinner, 379, 441). Observing this distinction we approach the question from the starting-point of behavior and the distinction between voluntary and involuntary behavior.

[12] See Appendix II, Section H 3, and Chapter 2, p. 104 ff.

[13] When a habit groove has been formed even in a highly differentiated system it has become "organized," in Hughlings Jackson's sense and thereafter delay and therefore consciousness are no longer attendant upon it.

[14] In discussing voluntary *actions* we are obviously not concerned with the two types of delay or deliberation which do not produce conflict. The one, subliminal excitation, does not produce action; neither does the surplus of the other, excessive excitation, which is the only part delayed.

an internal cause, not an external stimulus (spontaneous); (3) it must be oriented *by* such a cause but oriented *to* the environment through the influences of the sensory cortex and the store of memories ("purposeful," controlled, inhibitable); and (4) it must be conscious—that is, these several influences must produce delay and conflict (conscious integration). These requirements exclude all short-circuited reflexes or other behavior that does not involve the motor cortex; all behavior that is unadjusted to the environment because it is uncontrolled by any of the solely cortical influences, even though it may utilize the motor cortex; and all behavior (or elements of behavior) that eludes consciousness because it has become habitual, however much its organization is confined to the motor cortex. This last exclusion is made because, as we have repeatedly noted, the voluntary element in behavior that is composed in any part of actions become habitual is limited to that extent to the strategic factors only—that is, the starting, continuing, and stopping of the behavior. On the other hand the hesitancy that attends the learning of new movements—the breaking of new motor paths—is the sign of conflict, of conscious integration, and therefore the very hall-mark of the voluntary.[15]

Within the precincts of the voluntary so defined we have found three recognized sets of specific forces operating: (1) sensation, or current sensorimotor processes reaching consciousness, (2) recall from the memory-system, and (3) the current emotion. As to the last we have recognized that the subcortical emotional state that produces it may be short-circuited and thus produce typical involuntary behavior; that even the cortical emotion itself, if excessive, may seize on the motor cortex and produce behavior that seems to the subject involun-

---

[15] The notion we have presented that consciousness contains only the excitations that are "backed up," so to speak, implies this. As Hughlings Jackson says (*216*, I, 111), if the connection between an impression and a motion is "organized," the action is reflex, simple, or compound and is not conscious. If not "organized," "then the psychical changes which come between the impressions and motions are conscious ones." Semon interpreted this "organization" as a mnemic phenomenon—motor habit formation. He said (*368*, 44) it is objectively notable that reactions frequently become quicker and stronger on repetition. "By the repeated action of stimuli it is possible, therefore, to lower their stimulation threshold. Most frequently, these are instances of ecphoric action on engrams" (*ibid.*, 45). In other words, as Hering put it (*189*, 74) the "motor nerve system" has "also its memory"—"the force of habit"—which is the "power of recollecting earlier performances."

Of course, "an act may be learned, and yet be [or, rather, "become"] involuntary" (Hilgard and Marquis, *197*, 259). "By far the greater number of our movements are the result of long and arduous practice." Over them "the will need exercise a supervising control only" (Hering, *189*, 73).

tary, however much it may retain some of the external earmarks of the voluntary; and that this force or "drive" undoubtedly energizes many of the elements in behavior that have become habitual and to that extent involuntary. It follows that the participation of emotion in energizing and directing behavior, since much of the behavior so energized is defined as involuntary, cannot constitute the criterion for defining behavior as voluntary. The element of volition must be contributed by some other source or condition. Nor, if volition implies the initiation, maintenance, and cessation of cortical conflict, can it be a concomitant of two competing emotions, since we have agreed that two emotions cannot exist at the same time. The only other cortical influences we have found available as conflicting agencies are the current sensory impressions and the memory-system. In this connection we may resolve these two into a compound. Since behavior adjusted to the environment only appears after conditioning, and conditioning is itself a process of relating current sensation to the memory-system, it is the memory-system, merely re-excited by current sensation, that is responsible for the guidance of adapted behavior. Moreover, so far as cortical conflict is concerned, it must be that the memory-system contributes more effectively than the sensory. For, once the acoluthic phase of a current sensation is passed, its only possible contribution is through the memory it has created. Thus a past event, even if only just experienced, must already be only a memory by the time the conflict into which it enters can be resolved. Nevertheless, however much the energy of these two, sensation and memory, may be combined, we have conceded that they cannot constitute a sufficient force by themselves to cause conflict with an emotion of any considerable force whatever.[16]

[16] It must be evident that the old kinesthetic—or Wundt's "feeling of innervation"—theory of voluntary action does not fulfill the requirements. As stated, for instance, by William James (219, 19), an "accidental" reflex first excites the (? proprioceptive) sensory. Thereafter it works both ways. "As the motor originally aroused the sensory, so the sensory may now arouse the motor." "Voluntary acts *are* in fact nothing but acts whose motor centres are so constituted that they *can* be aroused by these sensorial centres, whose excitement was originally their effect." This is all very well, but it does not account for the arousal of the sensorial (presumably proprioceptive) centers. Frolov's (157, 72–77) interpretation of "voluntary" is based on "*reciprocal* connections in the cerebral cortex," of a different kind. In his view "the *well-beaten* track between the point of the conditioned reflex in the cortex and the point of unconditiond stimulation in the lower lying centres . . . may function in the reverse direction also." We have accepted this thesis, but not as a definition of "voluntary." For this limits the voluntary act to what we have called the arousal of a replica or the raising of effective intensity in the subcortical regions. We should say that, to the degree this occurred, to that extent the act became involuntary (i.e., emotional).

We are thus left in a dilemma. The only occasion which is decisive for the use of the term voluntary in connection with behavior is that in which the memory-system, perhaps incited and perhaps reinforced by the sensory, conflicts within itself or with the current emotion. But, then, we face the other horn. For the memory-system, even with the aid of the sensory, is incapable alone of competing with current emotion in point of strength. Almost by default we are compelled to assume that what makes an act voluntary is the entry of another influence to supplement the force of the memory and sensory systems alone. We may as well call this something "volition." Volition, then, must be a function of the memory-system when that system operates under certain conditions. But it must be a source of neural energy or an energetic condition apart from the memory-system itself, for it is only available to the memory-system when that system is in conflict either within itself or with the current emotion or when, the conflict having been resolved, it is giving rise to current behavior. At other times, even when the memory-system occupies consciousness, as during daydreaming, etc., volition is absent or quiescent, for no conflict results. The exact definition of the term voluntary implies, then, the supposition of some process independent of the energizer of involuntary or automatic behavior. And it must be the participation of this secondary energizer which forms the criterion for voluntary behavior. Or, to be more precise, the term volition and its participation in behavior—the volitional element—should probably be reserved for this energizer and its effects, while the term voluntary can also be applied to behavior energized through the motor cortex by the primary source of neural energy of response—emotional states and emotion—provided the memory-system is not in conflict and therefore "consents" without calling on its reinforcing agency to guide, control or repress such behavior or to substitute some other.[17] Under this terminology, behavior would be in large part a compound effect of two energizers—emotion, the primary

---

[17] This particular case has been generalized, in one view, to cover all voluntary activity —that is, the view "that voluntary activity is little more than a 'release' phenomenon" (158, 489). But all release phenomena are not voluntary. Cortical inhibition may be overpowered. And, in the modern view of inhibition, it appears impossible to suppose that volitional activity occurs merely through the withdrawal of inhibition, like the opening of "stops" to organ pipes. It appears, rather, that the very fact of inhibition is a by-product of excitation and is co-ordinate in degree. It is withdrawn in one sector when there is no excitation in an antagonistic sector, and only then. Even the tonic tendon reflexes in the anti-gravity (extensor) muscles are only inhibited when the flexor muscles are excited. Even the subcortical inhibition by the cortex is withdrawn when the cortex is asleep—i.e. unexcited.

one, and volition, the secondary one. According to its composition it would range from subcortically short-circuited response (wholly emotional), through cortical responses energized wholly by emotion because volition was overcome or not aroused, through mixtures in which volition participated—or lent itself—in guiding, controlling, or almost suppressing emotion, and thence up to the extreme where volition repressed emotion so that no behavior resulted, or even where volition energized behavior without the intervention of emotion at all or against its opposition. The last should include the cases of conflict already mentioned where, no emotion existing, the conflict is between elements of the memory-system alone. Thus actions vary from those in which volition plays no part to those in which it is almost sole player. And conversely with emotion.[18]

At once we recognize the possibility already suggested in the second chapter (p. 106). This thesis supposes two "wills" competing with each other. The one is the drive of present wants from the source of the primary neural energy of response, and the other is an agency connected with the memory-system and therefore with future wants and one that represents a secondary source of neural energy of response or a condition in which excitation from sources already recognized can be marshaled to make it more effective. We might be tempted to call the first "will" the "wish," as Freud did, and only the second the "will" proper.[19] But, if we were to do so, we would need to recognize that common usage does not support this terminology. To the naïve, his "will" is always the winner in this conflict, whichever it be; to the "willful" his "will" is no more or other than his "wish." On the other hand, introspective psychologists have often reserved the term "will" for the repository of their "moral" motives. There is no connotation of that in our interpretation. All we are saying is that the "wish" is an essentially involuntary impulse, while the "will" is developed in consciousness out of the memory-system when it arouses another

---

[18] This concept of degree of automaticity, if not of compounding, coincides with Hughlings Jackson. He conceived "evolution" of the nervous system as being in the direction of the voluntary, while "dissolution" reduces to more automatic (*216*, I, 173). And, for instance, "There are three degrees of the use of the word 'no.' It is used most voluntarily (as speech) when the patient can 'say' it when told. It is used more automatically when the patient can 'utter' it in reply correctly, and it is used most automatically when it only comes out like an ordinary interjection with states of feeling" (*ibid.*, II, 134).

[19] Thus we would be differentiating volition from conation, in the terminology of introspective psychology, just as many introspective psychologists have done.

source of neural energy or causes another condition of neural energy which is the critical participant in volitional action. Our position is clear. We have been dealing with the now rather well-understood mechanism of present wants; we are now endeavoring to arrive at some definite, if hypothetical, conclusions as to the mechanism of future wants. The latter, so far as we are concerned, are wants that correspond to the former; they are no better and no worse. In fact, they are the same wants in the status in which these persist when they are non-existent peripherally or subcortically. We are merely saying that present wants give rise to emotional energy of response, while future wants give rise only to non-emotional energy of response, or, at least, to an energy tinged so slightly with emotion that it cannot become prepotent by force of emotion.

3. A NEURAL BASIS FOR VOLITION AND ITS ENERGY

Although the hypothesis of the existence of this inferred force or condition we are calling volition has been the result only of our effort to supplement the purely neurophysiological scheme of energetics in order that it shall meet the requirements of a rational one, the mere use of the term has already trenched on an area thoroughly explored, from their several standpoints, by many psychologists. It may assist us, therefore, in discovering the further conditions that our hypothesis must meet—the kind of process this has been conceived to be when examined from the psychological approach—if, before we consider its possible neural substrate, we consider a few selected samples of psychological analyses of volition or "will," or what occupies an analogous position in particular schemes. For that purpose we have briefly examined, in Appendix III, Section E, the constructions of William James and of William McDougall, as well as both the earlier and later constructions of Sigmund Freud. There are certain characteristics more or less common to all these metapsychologies—or, at least, metaphysiological psychologies—which may prove suggestive, and even to some extent corroborative, as we proceed to consider the neurological possibilities. In all these versions the process we are calling volition is a conflict or repression that takes place at or before the entry to the motor outlets and involves their inhibition. In three versions, specifically, the process is determined by, or involves, conscious attention—or concentration, which seems to be the same thing. In three versions there is supposed an independent agency capable of directing neural energy—McDougall's Self and Freud's Preconscious and his later Super-ego (with the Ego, perhaps). In two versions the neural energy subject to such independent direction is definitely assigned to its source. McDougall says it is the "free energy" in the brain at the moment. Freud says it is the "mobile energy" available to the Preconscious, of which attention constitutes only a portion. James avoids this issue, and Freud, in his later formulations, does not seem to account for the energy available to the Super-ego. Finally, in two versions—James's and Freud's first—the process is merely the means by which the cortex acts as the "servant," as we have called it, of the instincts, drives, or emotions. In the other two the process is directed by other and contending motives—McDougall's Self and Freud's Super-ego.

Let us now proceed to consider the four aspects of what we are calling volition in respect of the possible identifications with known neural phenomena which might be made, and in the light of these psychological analogies. The first aspect is the condition in which volition appears (i.e., cortical conflict); the second is the hypothetical extra neural energy that we have inferred must be available to or in volition, together with its possible source; the third is the possible nature of the neural process itself (i.e., what volition does); and the fourth is the question of whether there is a specific agency outside consciousness which mobilizes the energy and gives rise to and controls the process.

In his description of allied *vs.* antagonistic reflexes Sherrington has furnished us with a conceptual basis for what we have called one kind of deliberation—conflict—and one that he himself says "may serve as a paradigm of the correlation of reflexes about every final common path." [20] The mechanism is that of spatial summation and immediate induction, on the one hand, and of interference on the other. The nodal point of the former is, in his opinion, the perikaryon with its converging dendrites. That of the latter may be the synapse. [21] For he presumes that the synapses between each of the dendrites of one neuron and the several axones of prior neurons, with which they respectively connect, suffer a change of states by reason of the excitation or inhibition passing through or created at any one. [22] Summation operates both by the successive summation of subliminal stimuli from one point, if separated by the proper intervals, and by the spatial summation of subliminal stimuli from several points whose reflexes are allied. Both tend ultimately to provoke a reflex. [23] Interference operates chiefly

[20] Sherrington, *375*, 140.   [21] *Ibid.*, 141.   [22] *Ibid.*, 143.   [23] *Ibid.*, 37 and 123–124.

by reason of the fact that, between reflexes which are antagonistic because they use one common path to different effect (i.e., each excites
"it in a manner very different") [24] the stronger prevents the weaker.[25]
Moreover, on the efferent side, "the spatial field of response of a reflex
increases with its intensity. Two reflexes may be neutral to each other
when both are weak, but may interfere when either or both are strong;
when weak they remain 'local.' " [26] However, not only strength, but
also long-circuiting counts in determining antagonism, so that, "in
presence of the arcs of the great *projicient receptors* . . . and the *brain*
there can be few receptive points in the body whose activities are
totally indifferent one to another" (i.e., neutral).[27] "In the presence
of the brain the knitting together [integration] of the whole nervous
network is probably much greater than in its absence." [28] Finally, in
Sherrington's interpretation, a motor reflex is "referable to a constellation of congruous stimuli of which one is prepotent" (determining);
that "gives the nervous intercommunications of the central organ a
certain pattern, which pattern may ramify through a great extent of
the central organ . . . its positive side traceable as active discharge
. . . and its negative side symmetrically opposed to its positive and
traceable conversely by check, depression, or absence of nervous discharge." [29]

All that we are assuming for cortical conflict reaching consciousness
is that precisely these same processes may occur when the excitations
remain subliminal as to the motor outlets and when, therefore, they
would have no overt motor effect even if unopposed; that the complexity (differentiation) in the cortex is such that summation up to the
threshold is slower and more apt to fail there, and that interference
is much more general than at lower levels; and finally, that cortical
excitations which are subliminal, or become so by reason of conflict
(mutual inhibition), may still reach consciousness from the rest of the
cortex,[30] whereas when and if they occur elsewhere they cannot. Thus,
if volition is a participant in cortical conflict reaching consciousness
and is capable of initiating, maintaining, and resolving such conflict,
with one exception it need only act as all other effects of stimulation

[24] *Ibid.,* 147.
[25] "The term 'interference' as applied to reflexes would mean simply the interaction between antagonistic reflexes, that is, reflexes that are incapable of simultaneous combination" (Sherrington, *375,* 199).
[26] Sherrington, *375,* 146–147.   [27] *Ibid.,* 147.   [28] *Ibid.,* 179.   [29] *Ibid.,* 179.
[30] The locus of consciousness, being itself a region of the cortex, is within the walls, so
to speak.

act.[31] The exception is this. If at any prior point on the afferent side of the so-called reflex arc excitations are in conflict, those which lose in the competition are suppressed and therefore cannot reach consciousness. Probably such suppression or repression also continues in the cortex as to much of its excitation. But there, at least, conflict between subliminal excitations does not preclude access of all of them to consciousness, at least successively, during the conflict.

The second aspect of volition as a neural phenomenon that we wish to consider is the possible neural energy that it may represent or have available. Hughlings Jackson said, "Our highest sensory and motor centres (together the organ of mind) can energize to a large extent, independently of the lower, out of which they have been evolved, and by aid of which they have developed." [32] One can hardly suppose, however, that this is auto-excitation. The neuron of the central nervous system *reacts* to many physical and chemical influences which reach it from its surroundings, by no means all of which are themselves neural. But its autogenous changes seem to be confined to the metabolic restoration of the *status quo*. Moreover, in sleep there are no such energizings as Jackson supposed. That indicates that the cortex has no sources of excitation within itself. But it also suggests that these seemingly independent excitations may in reality be ascribable to what we have called the stream of awakeness. This is the only one of the sources of excitation that can produce consciousness which we have not hitherto used in our scheme of cortical conflict. It is the only one that probably could not of itself produce conflict, since it seems in itself

[31] The conflict would originate presumably between antagonistic excitations which were already, or which made each other, subliminal; it would be maintained by the development of summations and of further interferences; and it would be resolved when one pattern of excitation, as the central core, became prepotent in a constellation of congruous excitations.

As to the resolution, one other point from Sherrington is worth suggesting. We may suppose that, for a time, the algebraic sum of excitatory and inhibitory effect from the antagonists keeps them all subliminal—that is, the thresholds are raised against each other as fast as each is summated by continuous excitation of itself or by the addition of congruous patterns. Irradiation is proceeding (they being "boxed up in themselves"— Hughlings Jackson). More and different excitations are coming into play. Finally, a single pattern of motor excitation becomes supraliminal. It starts. All contrary patterns are now inhibited. But, by a process of rebound similar to "successive induction," the minus portions of the algebraic summations (the inhibitions) upon the winner, being now withdrawn, might give an extra plus (excitatory) force. This could "feel" like decision.

[32] Jackson, *216*, II, 117. The same statement is made elsewhere (*ibid.*, I, 375). Apparently energize is equivalent to "discharge" or "liberation of energy by nervous elements" (*ibid.*, II, 412).

to be a tonic, non-specific, non-patterned excitation that contributes no content to consciousness, but which merely revives memories and enlivens sensations—that is, one that merely lends itself to (facilitates) other and specific excitations. In the second place, it seems by its nature to be diffuse and correspondingly weak at any particular point or pattern except when reinforced by its specific congener, the stream of emotion.[33] In the third place, the fact that the capacity for volition seems to vary with the degree of awakeness, being nil when sleep intervenes and apparently at its highest level in the most awake state, if nonemotional—that is, when consciousness is most acute—gives us an important correlation.

This possible identification offers an advantageous possible simplification. We have already concluded that volition must be a function of the memory-system when that system is operating under certain conditions. But it must be that the stream of awakeness is also peculiarly allied with the memory-system. The stream of awakeness seems to have no content of its own. Yet the consciousness it produces always has a content. Whence does that content arise? In the absence of emotion and of emotionally conditioned sensation, we are apt to drift into a state we have called revery. We are awake; we are conscious; the content of consciousness consists then largely or even exclusively of revived memories; yet the memory-system alone cannot produce consciousness. Does it not seem to follow that the memory-system is, in this case, energized by the stream of awakeness and that such states of consciousness are themselves the results of this energizing? The stream of awakeness may facilitate the incoming sensory stream; it is unnecessary for the incoming emotional stream. Is not its chief effect, then,

[33] On the other hand, it is not necessary to suppose that this diffusion and consequent low intensity are always a complete bar to the effectiveness of the stream of awakeness in creating cortical conflict. For the stream of emotion itself, although it is specific, may nevertheless also be diffuse when it has not been canalized by the process of conditioning. In fact, this may be the very reason that confusion and consequent loss of consciousness result when the stream of emotion is of high intensity. Thus the acuity of consciousness may be only secondarily a result of a middle range of intensity of excitation; it may be primarily a result of the fact that only in this middle range of intensity can a single pattern of excitation remain in the focus of consciousness for some little time. Confusion may be due primarily to rapidity of change of content (diffusion), which, in turn, may be due secondarily to intensity of emotion. On this basis, it might be supposed that, at more usual intensities of emotion and when the stream of emotion is not too definitely canalized (conditioned), its own diffusion brings it down to a level of potency in any particular patterns of excitation (contents of consciousness) at which the particular patterns excited by the stream of awakeness are adequately energized to compete.

the excitation of the memory-system? In turn, is it not peculiarly a fund of neural energy available to the memory-system? Is it not responsible for the continuous chain of revived memories entering consciousness, each ecphorized by the previous one, but none capable of self-energizing? Is it not the explanation of all but the first in any series of reappearing memories, in so far as these are not ecphorized by new experiences? Is it possible, even, that its recent canalizations may be responsible for the revival also of the first of any series that arises on awakening or on lapsing into a state of mere awakeness? On the principle of economy of entities we have, therefore, some reason to carry along into our further examination this possibility—that the energy of volition is the stream of awakeness—without, at the same time, excluding the possibility that there is some other cortical source of neural energy which is in itself specific and potent and which has not yet entered our scheme at all.

As to the third aspect—the neural nature of the process of volition—we have noted that the judgments of our three somewhat diverse psychologists agree in making conscious attention at least an element if not the whole of it. In ordinary terminology we *concentrate* our attention. This has two aspects. On the analogy of the visual field attention is focused on the center of the field, its periphery remains also in consciousness but not in the focal center, and all else is excluded. The other aspect relates to the persistence of this content. It is *held* in consciousness, either by continuity or repetition of excitation, for some considerable time. As to the first aspect, when dealing with sensory attention we interpreted the concentration of this attention to mean that the focus of the field is facilitated by directing into it corticofugal subliminal excitation, so that the threshold for incoming excitation is lowered. The exclusion is provided in part by the mere occupation of consciousness which this increased intensity yields and in part, perhaps, by the resulting reciprocal inhibition of other parts of the sensory apparatus. As to the second aspect, the persistence can only be provided by continuance of the facilitation. We have supposed that sensory attention can be directed by "interest"—that is, that an external stimulus once conditioned to some present want (emotion) revives memories or even replicas of that want, whose emotional endowment or newly aroused emotion then act automatically as the facilitating agency. Correspondingly, we would now assume that the process of volition consists in the prolonged facilitation of certain elements of the whole system capable of reaching consciousness—i.e., both memory and current sensation—so that the content of consciousness for a time consisted of certain elements at the focus and certain other elements in the peripheral field, while all other parts of the system were temporarily excluded. We would also assume that the agency producing such facilitation in this case is not emotion and therefore not automatic, at least in the same sense.

We have used here the terms diffusion *vs.* concentration of attention. These terms, so far as consciousness itself is concerned, connote respectively the entry of a rapid succession of not specially facilitated and therefore background excitations of low intensity *vs.* a sustained and single specially facilitated and therefore more intense excitation occupying the focus. Assuming that what enters consciousness is always the most intense of the subliminal excitations, this distinction would correspond to the distinction, in the cortex outside consciousness, between diffuse and therefore somewhat evenly spread excitation *vs.* concentrated and therefore unevenly spread excitation. This suggests a possible relationship to two neural phenomena considered independently both by Sherrington and by Pavlov. The first is irradiation; the second is concentration. The two are, of course, different degrees of the same thing, though the process that expands the area of excitation or inhibition and that which contracts it may be, as Pavlov suspected, opposed influences. "The centrifugal discharge elicited by any reflex seems as regards its spatial distribution to be focussed about a center round which its irradiation varies according to circumstance" —"especially according to intensity of stimulation." [34] However, it occurs "along certain lines and not along others"; and it extends "rather *per saltum* than *gradatim*." [35] Pavlov assumed that such peripheral irradiation corresponded, in the case of long-circuited impulses, to cortical irradiation, as to all motor and at least as to those sensory mechanisms that are spatially organized. Frolov interprets Pavlov's results to indicate, in general, that there is, first, irradiation in all directions over "definite elements of the brain" and then subsequent concentration.[36] Inhibition irradiates rather slowly; excitation from weak or very strong stimuli irradiates much faster, the latter producing "affective" reactions. Average strength stimuli produce the least irradiation or the most effective concentration; and that represents "optimal functioning." Considering the concentration of inhibition, or "the nature of

[34] Sherrington, *375*, 150–152.   [35] *Ibid.*, 154 and 168.   [36] Frolov, *157*, 133–134.

the recession of inhibition from those cortical points into which it was irradiated," Pavlov says,

Does this represent a destruction or waning of the inhibition in these places, or is it some kind of return of active concentration of the inhibition to its starting-point due to some antagonistic process? In face of the constant fact that strengthening of differentiation by repeated contrasts is accompanied by a corresponding shortening of the duration and extent of irradiation of the inhibitory after-effect, we are naturally more inclined to accept the second hypothesis, namely that we deal with the reverse of irradiation, i.e. "concentration" of the inhibition toward its initial point of origin in the cortex.[37]

Thus Pavlov supposes an independent process, opposing irradiation or producing concentration, which seems to be identical with the more slowly aroused process usually called discrimination. He concludes that, "It is, indeed, our experience that conditioned reflexes in which the phase of initial generalization [irradiation] has not been succeeded by sufficient specialization [concentration], as well as reflexes of small intensity of excitation, become very easily disturbed, both by external and by internal inhibition"—that is, in our terms, both by interference and by loss of "interest." [38]

Three inferences arise from Pavlov's conclusions. The first follows from the fact that he allies the "phase of initial generalization" (irradiation) of any reflex, however potent, with "reflexes of small intensity of excitation," in respect of their readiness to succumb to interference. It is as if, for any given strength of excitation (stimuli), irradiation leads to a lowering of intensity throughout the area excited —a sort of dilution of the given energy—while subsequent concentration leads to a heightening of intensity, as if the given energy were then concentrated in a narrower field. We may suppose that these phenomena of irradiation and concentration are general characteristics of excitation and inhibition and thus apply as well to all regions and functions of the cortex. If so, we may also suppose that the process of concentration of conscious attention is like all other processes of neural concentration; that it is the process of contracting the area excited (or inhibited); and, finally, that concentration, whatever it is due to, raises the level of excitation when it takes place, not by the application of more neural energy in toto but by narrowing the field over which it is spread.[39]

---

[37] Pavlov, 320, 156.   [38] Ibid., 176.
[39] In discussing inhibition in Appendix II, we saw reason to believe that the inhibition the cortex exerts on the subcortical brain is proportionate in strength to the concentra-

The second inference arises from the fact that Pavlov allies the process of concentration with that one which is called discrimination. He says (quoted above) that concentration takes place more rapidly as a result of the "strengthening of differentiation by repeated contrasts." Considering, first, emotional concentration due to present wants,[40] we note that differentiation follows a "period of generalization." It results from discrimination, or what we have called the "recognition of differences." At first such recognition of differences leads to an exploration of the "different" stimulus (i.e., the "investigatory reflex" or our alert), since that presents another and its own "interest." But, as that dies down, there follows a gradual strengthening of differentiation in the form of "differential inhibition" of all but the reinforced stimulus. This is his fourth type of internal inhibition, and we have construed all his internal inhibitions to be loss of "interest" (i.e., disconnection from emotion). The ultimate effect is "extinction," or what we have called unconditioning, of all but the reinforced stimulus.

This fits in with, and offers an explanation of, much of our previous analysis of conditioning and learning. On the afferent side the first conditioning is the "whole experimental environment."[41] Gradually the process is concentrated on the single incoming stimulus or group, which experience proves to be causally related (i.e., which is reinforced). Stimuli from all other parts of the scene are gradually inhibited and then extinguished. Similarly on the efferent side. At first a single stimulus, or the stimulation from the whole scene, irradiates and produces what we have called general responses. Learning consists in the narrowing down, or concentration, into a special response that experience proves will produce the appropriate results (i.e., which is reinforced). All other parts of the whole general response are gradually inhibited and then extinguished.

In turn, this suggests the third inference, at least as a possibility. Is volition a process similar to this emotional concentration, distinguished only (1) because it takes place at a vastly higher rate of speed, (2) because its specific elements, being chiefly memories, constitute an enormously greater complex, (3) because its specific elements are at subliminal intensities, and (4) because its whole process can reach consciousness? If so, we might conceive the ultimately available force to be derived from the gradual elimination of alternatives by reason (1)

---

tion of cortical excitation, not to the quantity of that excitation. If inhibition is a by-product of excitation, we now have a rationale for the previous observation.
[40] See Pavlov, *320*, Lecture VII.   [41] *Ibid.*, 115.

of their loss of something corresponding in this field to what constitutes "interest" in the emotional field, (2) the consequent narrowing of the field of excitation and, therefore, (3) the concentration of the available energy in that focus. This suggestion that volition is a process of the same type as conditioning and learning will give rise, further in our discussion,[42] to consideration of its possible implications. Volition may be related to the initiation of conditioning and learning—may, in fact, be their initial stage, before they become automatic (emotionalized or habitual), or may be a development of that stage that continues and elaborates it, in so far as it does not become either emotional or habitual.

Along these lines it would be possible to conceive that the tonic excitation of the stream of awakeness, or any other cortical excitation from an as yet unknown source, could, in the process of concentration, become sufficiently potent (of sufficient intensity) to cause conflict even with such formidable forces as canalized incoming emotion. The ultimate question of agency—the fourth aspect—would then be placed at one further remove. We could conceive the energy being available from a source other than such agency; we could conceive that energy, ordinarily diffuse, being concentrated to a higher pitch; but the question would then be what is the cause of concentration. Is concentration an automatic characteristic of the neural process; or is it the effect of a concentrating agency? If volition is one of the concentrations of neural energy (awakeness or other) which can hold the field of conscious attention against other competing concentrations (emotion and perhaps even current sensation), is it as automatic as these competing concentrations seem to be, or is it controlled and directed? That is, is volition the effect of the forces at play (the content of consciousness) or is it peculiarly something that "I" do? Examination of this second alternative will have to wait until we have considered the first one. It is clear that the neural energy supplied by the stream of awakeness, being non-specific, could not of itself determine the outcome of conflict. Only the content of consciousness at the time could be responsible for mobilizing (concentrating) and for controlling and directing such energy. Therefore, the gist of the question whether the whole process of volition, so defined, is the automatic result of the forces at play at its level, in the same way that emotional concentration, once established by conditioning, seems to be at its level, depends on the question whether the nature of the content of consciousness during volition,

[42] See Section C 2, below.

or of some critical features of it, or of some critical interrelations within it, is such as automatically to determine the outcome of the conflict.

4. THE CONTENT OF CONSCIOUSNESS DURING VOLITION

It is often said that every excitation, afferent or central, is a motor tendency, so that all the content of consciousness is inherently such, and is so as much when volition is taking place as when it is not.[43] This broad generalization, based on reflexology, appears to be true of present wants—the emotional drives—and of all excitation caused by adequate stimuli of the simple reflexes. However, it may well be limited to these kinds of excitation. It is doubtful in the case of consciousness; and it is definitely not true of the conscious memory-system—the major portion of the whole field of potential excitation available to consciousness. In fact, there the opposite is true in large part. It would seem to follow that, since volition is a function of the conscious memory-system, volition cannot consist of, or fill consciousness with, motor tendencies to any great extent, if at all.

Thinking, both that which does not call volition to its aid (daydreaming) and that which does (conflict), consists chiefly of the re-

[43] Statements of William James will serve as a sample. All neural activity "is already on its way to instigate a movement." Its "essential consequence is motion" (*220*, II, 526). "Movement is the natural immediate effect of feeling, irrespective of what the quality of the feeling may be. It is so in reflex action, it is so in emotional expression, it is so in the voluntary life" (*ibid.*, II, 527). "Consciousness is *in its very nature impulsive*," though "it must be sufficiently intense" to be so (*ibid.*, II, 535). In spite of this qualification, "we do not have to add something dynamic to it to get a movement" (*ibid.*, II, 526). Thus the fourth of his "inevitable" assumptions as to the manner in which processes come to be organized in the hemispheres is this: "Every idea tends ultimately either to produce a movement or to check one which otherwise would be produced" (*ibid.*, I, 24). Or, interpreting the "idea" more specifically, "every representation of a motion awakens the actual motion which is its object, unless inhibited by some antagonistic representation simultaneously in the mind" (*219*, 17). On this basis he supposed that the fact that "we have so many ideas which *do not* result in action" is wholly due to the fact that "other ideas simultaneously present rob them of their impulsive power" (*220*, II, 525). Or, again interpreting the "idea," "Every representation of a movement awakens in some degree the actual movement which is its object; and awakens it in a maximum degree whenever it is not kept from doing so by an antagonistic representation present simultaneously in the mind. The express fiat, or act of mental consent to the movement, comes in when the neutralization of the antagonistic and inhibitory idea is required." If there is no antagonistic idea, no fiat is required (*ibid.*, II, 526).

We accept this description as to every excitation up to memory, and therefore up to the volitional process, and therefore up to the content of consciousness furnished by memory and volition. It should be noted that when the memory-system alone occupies consciousness excitations are of low intensity. Therefore, even to James, they might not be impulsive. Also volition, dealing only with mnemonic materials, cannot add to them a *quality* they do not have.

vival of memories in consciousness and their manipulation. We have accepted Hughlings Jackson's judgment that these memories ("ideas") consist most largely of retino-ocular sensorimotor processes (visual "ideas"), considerably of audito-articulatory processes (verbal "ideas"), and to a small extent of tactile processes (tactual "ideas").[44] The only motor content possible to such ideas are movements of the eyes, of the lips, etc., and of the hands, respectively. These movements are not action at all, in the usual sense.[45] Nor do the "ideas" include impulses to action in that sense. In the unskilled, the "ideas" alone may result in movements of the eyes; they often result in movements of the lips; occasionally they may cause motion of the fingers. It is also true that when these "ideas" are being aroused by current sensation they may give rise to a directing of conscious attention. That is chiefly cortical and non-motor, though it may include the ocular, auditory, and tactile movements above, and even some adaptation of posture— all of which are for purposes of facilitating reception only. But when these "ideas" are but chains of memories there is no motor element whatever involved in conscious attention. Then conscious attention is directed from within and to within the cortex itself. In spite of the fact that none of these "ideas" seems to contain in itself a motor tendency to a course of action, it is just such "ideas" as these of which the material for deliberation, conflict, and the volitional process is composed and from which may result behavior in the broad sense—i.e., a course of action.

In the second place, we have had to recognize that the motor side of memory works in precisely the opposite way from the sensory side. On the one hand, as the sensory aspect of a particular memory becomes more familiar by repetition, it becomes more easily recalled to, and more vivid in, consciousness (homophony); on the other hand, as the motor aspect becomes more familiar by repetition, it becomes more

[44] Jackson, 216, II, 139 and elsewhere.
[45] It is interesting to note the distinction that Hughlings Jackson makes (216, II, 91). He divides the "lowest level" centers into four groups, one for the simplest reactions of the eyes, one for those of the hands, one for those of the tongue, palate, lips, etc., used in swallowing, etc., and one for the simplest movements of the limbs. At the highest level the first three of these become evolved, respectively, into the physical basis of visual ideas, of tactual ideas, and of words (verbal ideas). Only the last is said to be evolved into the "physical basis of volition." This does not mean, of course, that "looking," "touching," and "speaking" are not often volitional, nor that dealing with these three classes of ideas is not also often volitional. I take it to mean that "volition," to him, corresponds to these "ideas" and is therefore as detached from the motor aspect as they are.

readily repeated but also more completely excluded from consciousness (habit). Even when new, the motor aspect of the memory of
any sensorimotor process is peculiarly invisible to consciousness. We
have the testimony of introspection as to this. If the motor aspect exists
in memory, it is only as the implicit and unseen obverse of the sensory.
It is as if, when the memories of sensorimotor processes were projected
into consciousness, they were projected hind-end-to, with the front
end—the motor end—not showing. We have also the observation of
learning of skilled actions. The child learns by observing himself objectively as others do. He must *watch* his hands in order to acquire the
ability to do scales on the piano, and his feet in order to learn to dance.
He must "try" again and again until he *sees* that his action conforms
to the pattern of the example or the instructions, both of which are
given him in purely objective terms.[46] Then the action may become
habitual, so that his chief attention during playing becomes listening,
and his dancing becomes an almost automatic accompaniment of con-
versing with his partner.[47] Skilled motor actions are learned in terms
of results not causes. And when they become habitual, the only parts
volition plays in them, and therefore the only parts that enter consciousness, are the strategic factors—chiefly starting, continuing, and
stopping.

In the third place, we meet another fundamental difficulty. We have
necessarily assumed that volition "takes place at or before the entry to
the motor outlets and involves their inhibition." If there are motor
association areas, and that seems to be a necessary assumption for the
formation of motor memory or habit, volition must take place at or
before the entry to such areas. For volition is conscious, and we have
seen that these areas are peculiarly unavailable to consciousness. Moreover, the locus of volition must be at one still further remove. If the
final act of volition, decision, is the same when the decision is executory
or contingent, to use James's expression, as when it is immediately carried out, there must be some intervening region where it can be put in
cold storage, so to speak, until released. And this region cannot be one

[46] If so, acquisition of skill would seem to consist as much in learning *what* to do as in
learning *how* to do it. In fact, consciousness and volition may have little to do with
the latter. They may only be concerned with the question whether the "what" that
was done was the right one or not.
[47] That is, they become so habitual that, aside from starting, continuing, and stopping
them, volition is not required. With some minor actions that do not conflict with other
activity it may even be that they become like "associated movements," so that "many
acts now involuntary began as voluntary action" (Rignano, *345*, 132–133).

inaccessible to consciousness, and therefore to volition, like the motor association area. Quite the contrary; it must be part of the memory-system, for the executory decision requires to be recalled before it can be put into execution.[48]

Conscious memories consist of experiences as these have impinged upon consciousness, together with the constructions subsequently made with them.[49] If experiences as registered in consciousness appear chiefly as sensory (and emotional) and only very slightly as motor —and this seems to be the case particularly when the action component is habitual—we cannot expect the memories to contain much of a motor element. If so, since volition is a process that deals chiefly with, or is produced chiefly by, memories, its elements cannot consist largely of motor tendencies. Like conscious memory, it is not actions, nor does it deal considerably with them; it is, or it deals chiefly with, experiences. Volition is concerned with situations, with scenes and the objects in them, with auditions and the sounds in them, with contacts and the "feel" of them. Its dynamic aspect is concerned with changes in a present situation or the return of a past one. In this sense it attends to ends, not means—at least not motor means.[50] In this sense it seems to be contrasted with emotion. For emotions—the drives or present wants —seem to consist of blind urges (inherently motor) that have to achieve their ends by accident or have to be guided toward them by cortical relations with the environment and by conscious memory. Volition seems to deal with clearly seen ends (inherently non-motor) to which it needs to add the necessary impelling force, although the guidance of that force comes in the same way as with the emotions. In both cases this guidance may be a part of the volitional process, but only before the action has become habitual. In the second case, only, does volition cover the energizing.[51]

[48] I may decide today to go downtown on a mission day after tomorrow. If, then, I do not forget—that is, if, then, I remember—the memory suffices. No further deliberation is necessary. The memory already contains, or can at once arouse, the reinforcement. I go.
[49] William James went so far as to say that "all the mind's materials without exception are derived from passive sensibility" (219, 25). It will be recalled that he held that the "motor idea" is the sensory record of the action and of its result.
[50] For a further discussion, see supplementary statement on "Volition and Purpose," at the end of this subsection.
[51] One point needs to be clarified. We have assumed that memories may be endowed with specific emotions. In so far as that occurs we would judge that the emotional endowment behaved like emotion, though weakly. Thus what we say of memories, in the text, applies only to their non-emotional sensorimotor aspects.

However, in spite of the difficulty raised by this examination of the content of consciousness during volition and the apparent lack in it of a motor element, it seems necessary to assume that, in some unknown way,[52] volition forms, or initiates, the missing link between the conscious memory-system, which is weak and which has little motor content, on the one hand, and motor action, on the other. The process of volition seems, at least, to establish the potential which, when released, leads almost automatically into action.[53] But conscious memories themselves do not seem to specify the form of any action.[54] Thus it appears that, until conflicts are resolved into actions to which the conscious memories concerned may refer but which they do not contain (and which cannot be implicit in them), they do not result in behavior. When that behavior does occur it seems to be strictly the automatic result of the victory in conflict. That conflict, in turn, was not between motor tendencies. It was between memories of experiences, sensory and emotional, which have been more or less abstracted or even futurized.

On the basis of this evidence it seems necessary to classify the motor components even of volitional behavior as automatic in the same sense that unguided emotional behavior is automatic. There remains the question whether, prior to the beginning of motor behavior, the process of volition and of conflict is also aroused, maintained, and resolved as the automatic result of the forces at play—namely the memories of experiences which then form the content of conscious-

[52] William James, admitting the "notorious fact" that the will seems concerned only with results and not with the muscular details of execution (*219*, 6), held that "an anticipatory image of the sensorial consequences of a movement, hard or easy, *plus the fiat* that these consequences shall become actual, ought to be able to discharge *directly* the special movement with which in our past experience the particular consequences were combined as effects." This scheme would rely on association within an engram-complex of which the motor elements were not available to consciousness. Or, as he put it without this last qualification, there would be a "connection by association" between the "end conceived" and the "proper motor idea" represented by "an exclusive nerve tract," so that the idea would be itself directly the stimulus to the special tract (*ibid.*, 5).

[53] To quote James again: The motor effect of decision (the victory of one idea) is "certain bodily effects automatically consequent thereon" (i.e., not a definite motor idea; *219*, 23).

[54] We must recall that Hughlings Jackson said of all higher motor centers that they "do not represent muscles but movements of muscles" (*216*, II, 83). We would therefore not expect them to harbor anything of the nature of kinesthetic sensation. But the curious thing is that those centers that are available to conscious memory do not seem even to harbor movements. The memory of a movement seems to be that of its objective effects. We see our arms stretched out; we feel them stretched out; and that remains the sole content of the "idea" of stretching them out.

ness. If it is, we must conceive it to consist in the bringing to bear (ecphorizing) of many diverse but related memories which conflict with each other or with the current drive, of some sort of organization of these memories into a consolidated pattern, and of the presentation of their resultant (positive or negative) which would correspond to the notion of decision.[55] We would assume that the automatic part of the process of bringing memories to bear on the conflict would be due to homophony, with its recognition of likenesses and differences, and to association with previous similar situations. There would remain, in that connection, the question of whether there can also be non-automatic ecphory of memories—that is, what is called "voluntary" recall. That will engage our attention in the last subsection. We would assume that the process of organization would require a period of gestation and would be the result of the appearance of these memories successively in the focus of conscious attention, and thereafter the relegation of them or of residues of them (their detected relation to the matter in hand, analogous to "interest") into the field of consciousness outside of the focus, in such a way that the resultant would be built up out of an accumulation of these memories or residues. We would assume that memories coming to bear but found unrelated, or perhaps even to be rejected, would be excluded (inhibited) so that they would not form part of this accumulation of effective factors. We would assume that, finally, either the "allied" influences would arrive at a preponderance (positive) or that the "antagonistic" influences (not necessarily "allied" among themselves) would arrive at a preponderance (negative), so that the process would be concluded.[56]

[55] If memories and current sensations are included with emotions on the positive as well as on the negative sides, we can agree with Bianchi's statement that conduct is "the resultant of impulsive and inhibitory forces" (35, 311). "Will, after all, is only a compromise in the individual consciousness, a resultant of impulsions and inhibitions." Ultimately, it may also be true that "both impulsive and inhibitory forces are directed to the motor field of the cerebral mantle, where all sensory and intellectual representations resolve themselves into motor intuitions and subsequently into movements and, as a whole, into conduct" (ibid., 329).

[56] It is not necessary here to limit alliance and antagonism to their motor counterparts. They may be constituted by an analogue to "interest" in the emotional field—a sort of sense of pragmatic right and wrong, what will work and what will not—yielding a harmonizing of experience.

This is close to William James's version, if stated in more physiological terms. To him (220, I, 142), "Consciousness is only intense when nerve processes are hesitant." And (ibid., I, 139), it is "primarily a selecting agency." It "emphasizes and accentuates" "one out of several of the materials presented to its notice" and suppresses "as far as possible the rest." The one emphasized is closely connected with an "interest felt by consciousness to be paramount at the time."

Whether the active agent is, at the point of decision, another force which, after the period of gestation, closes the debate and permits or enables the initiation of the action, under the direction of the resultant, or whether it is the resultant itself, we do not know and perhaps cannot know.[57] If the latter, volition is so far automatic, in the sense that the stronger party wins, and it becomes a merely very elaborate and prolonged counterpart of the resolution of conflict at lower levels.[58]

There would still remain, however, to be explained—perhaps to increase the complexity and thus to reduce the automatic simplicity—why certain memories are more potent than others in concentrating the stream of awakeness. The conflict would not necessarily have been determined by the relative intensity of the memories themselves. We have assumed that the reason these memories have appeared and remained in consciousness during conflict is that there has been concentrated in them a large portion of the excitation derived from the stream of awakeness.[59] We have assumed that it is this volitional analogue of emotional "interest"—this potency—which gives them their strength in the conflict. We have assumed that all the allied influences have by summation and induction combined their force, at least to the extent that they have added to the energy and supported the special pattern of the prepotent influence which ends up by occupying the focus of consciousness and acting as the strategic factor in determining the outcome. Are we also to assume that the potency of memories throughout this reinforcing process is proportionate to their unfortified intensity? This would be the simplest assumption. On a comparative

[57] This suggests one of the difficulties with the thesis of automaticity which we are exploring. Some people who deliberate are prone to be unable to "make up their minds." Why should such irresolution be chronic in some persons, if the resultant acts by itself? That is, why should it occur so frequently in some cases that the negative and positive factors happen to remain in balance, while among the "resolute" a resultant always occurs and is effected.

Another difficulty lies in what we know as "determination"—when we say one acts with "determination." "Determination" seems to have an emotional quality. Nor can we find a place for it in our scheme because it seems to be just as characteristic of emotional as it is of non-emotional behavior.

[58] Different also, in that conflict at lower levels is on the basis of either-or, while here it is on the basis of compounding innumerable influences into a resultant.

[59] The stream of awakeness seems to be incapable of intense excitation when irradiated. But its concentration might bring excitation up from a weak level (diffusion) to that of optimal functioning. Conversely, concentration seems to be required for optimal functioning and, in turn, takes place most readily under medium excitation.

Moreover, this notion of the concentration of the stream of awakeness seems to conform to Pavlov's thesis that internal inhibition (i.e., what occurs outside the area of concentration of excitation) is equivalent to sleep (i.e., withdrawal of the stream of awakeness).

basis, we could then ignore the capacity in each memory to step up the excitation available to it—i.e., its potency in mobilizing the stream of awakeness. But we do not know, and we are merely evading a possible additional complexity by making the assumption. That acknowledgment will suffice, however. In default of any knowledge, we shall proceed hereafter on the assumption that the intensity of memories determines their power in conflict. On that assumption each memory participating in conflict can multiply its available energy proportionately to its intensity. The result is the algebraic sum of "allied" and of "antagonistic" memories, gradually accruing so long as the net plus energy does not become supraliminal. When it does so, the conflict is resolved and decision, resulting in present or potential action, supervenes. Volitional action, when it was produced, would always and only be "single-minded," in this sense. This would then be a reasonable hypothesis, as a supplement to our single possible emotional drive, to explain the outstanding characteristic of all behavior, emotional and non-emotional alike—"that concentration of the whole organism upon one action at any one moment which characterizes all the higher organisms, and is the essential mark of individuality or complete integration of the vital unit." [60]

Having now delved somewhat deep but still only into the most accessible complexities of the volitional process, on the basis of inference and rational hypothesis, what do we find has become of the question as to whether or not it is automatic? Even so far as we think we can see, does it not already appear that the term is a travesty on the facts? If this be automatism it is only because we live in a deterministic universe. Whether we do or not I leave to the physicists. But so far as we are concerned here we have only two interests in the question. The first is this: What could "I" possibly be other than the multifarious forces at play in this enormously complex process? If that is all "I" am, does it follow, from the assumption that the process of volition may be automatic in these respects, that man does not have "free will" in the only respect in which that notion makes sense? The respect in which that notion has meaning is discussed in Appendix III, Section F. Here we propose only to present the conclusion. It is obvious that vis-à-vis the environment man has only a limited "free will." He must perforce conform to its so-called laws, and he is confined in his freedom of action to what they make possible. Even vis-à-vis himself he is not fully free.

[60] McDougall, *282*, 381.

For instance, he cannot choose both to live and not to eat. But within these limits of what is possible he is free to choose in the only meaningful sense of that term—that is, to choose between such alternatives as are actually presented. These alternatives—the physiological basis of choice—we have found to exist on an either-or basis wherever inhibition is possible—that is, where there is choice between activating or not activating some effector agency—and to exist on any one of several bases wherever there is as yet "unorganized" "differentiation" in the central nervous system, in Hughlings Jackson's sense—that is, where there is choice between activating one of several different effector agencies or of activating any one of them in one of several different ways or degrees. What then determines the choice? According to our hypothesis it is either automatic at this point—that is, it is determined by the most potent party among the many influences brought to bear in consciousness—or it is subject to some reinforcing agency, coming from outside consciousness, which lends its strength to one side or the other. But even that agency cannot exist outside of the human system. Thus, in either event, choice is automatic as to the system as a whole, in the sense that it is determined by the most potent party to the conflict; and the only question that remains is the question where or how this prepotency arises.

Such a conclusion does not make of man an automaton. For, in so far as his behavior is determined at this, the volitional level, his whole memory-system including his own idea of his "free will"—if he has that idea—provides the great bulk of the influences brought to bear. If he identifies his "self" with this memory-system, and if this memory-system determines the choice,[61] then the process is potentially as ideal a form of self-government as any democracy could aspire to.[62] All it requires is the extension of the franchise in each case to every pertinent memory—that is, to all qualified voters—giving each an opportunity to express itself—that is, through deliberation.

[61] These two postulated conditions seem to fulfill the requirements of what Hilgard and Marquis (*197, 276*) call "self-commands." "It is the self-commands which can be made relatively independent of present environmental stimuli—often in the presence of great obstacles, and in line with remote goals and purposes—which constitute the essential problem in volition."
[62] It is not necessary, here, to pursue the alternatives. If one identifies one's "self" with one's "wishes," one's emotional system, one's behavior will be automatic in a different sense, because it will not be deliberate. If, to one's consciousness, the "self" seems to be the reinforcing agency from outside consciousness that steps in to decide conflicts, one's behavior would be automatic in still a third sense, because it would depend wholly on the, so far as we can see, arbitrary action of this other cortical agency.

Our second and remaining interest is the question which we shall take up in Section C 2 of this chapter. That is the alternative possibility that the process of volition in consciousness is not self-governing (automatic) there, because there is, outside consciousness, another cortical agency or source, which directs or supplies (or both) the extra neural energy—in that case probably specific—that seems to be required as an assumption for any rational hypothetical scheme of energetics in this field.

Volition and Purpose. We have said that volition seems to attend to ends, not to means. William James says much the same thing (*220*, II, 487). "Voluntary movements," being results of memory "with full prevision," "must be secondary not primary functions of our organism." The real question is, however, of what this prevision consists. We are saying that it consists, not of movements, but of the effects of movements, or of the completed movement. In this we are at variance with Hughlings Jackson (*216*, II, 199–200): "In the voluntary operation there is preconception; the operation is nascently done before it is actually done; there is a 'dream' of an operation as formally done before the operation; there is dual action." "The difference betwixt thinking of now doing and now actually doing" is that the first is a faint and the second a vivid discharge. The first is "knowing" or "intending" or "trying" or "remembering." Then he concludes that the faint discharge must be both sensory and motor because it entails a relation between the sense of movement and its initiation (*ibid.*, II, 201). It could not otherwise be identified. We have no explanation of this identification; but we cannot accept the supposition that it is due to a "sense of movement."

Thurstone (*401*, 97) presents more nearly our view: "Rational behavior differs from instinctive behavior mainly in that rational behavior is subject to more deliberate trial-and-error choice by *anticipating the consequences of overt fulfilment of the impulse*" (italics ours). Our difference from him is that, whereas Thurstone holds that "both rational and instinctive behavior are instinctively driven," we hold that his "rational behavior" may be "instinctively driven," but that it may also be purely volitional and thus wholly non- or anti-instinctive.

We also disagree with his motor interpretation. To him "every momentary mental state should then be interpreted as an unfinished act with the overt completion of the act as a basis of interpretation" (*ibid.*, 47), so that "the intelligence of any particular psychological act is a function of the incomplete stage of the act at which it is the subject of trial-and-error choice" (*ibid.*, 159). Omitting the motor features, we can agree that the intelligence of any act is measured by the degree of deliberation involved, which is somewhat the same thing.

The essence of our concept of the nature of the presentation is well stated by Hilgard and Marquis (*197*, 255): "In common language 'voluntary' refers to acts which are preceded by an idea or intention, acts of which the individual foresees the consequences." That, we think, is all he sees, or "foresees."

This seems to be the appropriate point at which to make our final distinction between apparent "purposeful" action and true "purposeful" action in this limited sense. True "purposeful" action is limited to action which is solely the result of memories revived in consciousness which picture a *situation to be reached*. Even then, the driving force, or its detonator, is solely memories, not something which has not existed or does not yet exist; but it is memories projected into the counterfeit future. All other driving forces not wholly due to external stimuli may also be mnemic. But their drive is unconscious; it is the tendency to restore the *status quo ante* or after modification, a new status. Thus we reserve "purpose" as a term for one element in *some* behavior.

Rignano lumps together all actions that are apparently "purposeful"— that is, all that arrive at an equilibrium, a status of homeostasis. Nevertheless, he gives the source of all of them as a *vis a tergo*. "The purposeful nature of certain vital phenomena only becomes apparent in the relation between actual phenomena and certain future phenomena, separated from each other by a certain interval of time, as, for instance, between the formation of the baby's eye in the darkness of the mother's womb, and its future use when it will be exposed to the light of the outer world, between the present behavior of the swallow which builds its nest and the future use of the nest when the same swallow will lay its eggs in it, between the present act of a man who is making a machine and the future use he will make of the machine" (*345*, 197).

However, after accepting the mnemic thesis, "Now we see that the final result of the action is really present from the beginning in the form of a mnemonic accumulation; the medium, or the environmental relations towards which the animal strives, operates now like a *vis a fronte* solely because they have formerly been a *vis a tergo*, and because the physiological activities which they have then aroused in the organism have left behind them a mnemonic deposit, which now acts like a veritable *vis a tergo* in moving the living being. . . . Thus the same explanation is seen to be valid for all the finalism of life." And we see "every manifestation of purposefulness . . . as so many manifestations of mnemonic nature" (*ibid.*, 171–172). Or, if we prefer other terminology, mnemic phenomena are the tendencies toward the restoration of homeostasis, old or modified. And that definition in other terms doubtless includes the phenomena of conscious memory, though it is particularly difficult for us to conceive them in that light.

5. VOLUNTARY ECPHORY

At the end of the previous chapter we left, as one of the characteristics of future wants which did not seem to be adequately explained by their mere classification as mnemonic phenomena, the question of what revives (ecphorizes) them, in view of the fact that the ordinary ecphorizing influences do not seem necessarily to appear in connection with them. That question appeared again in the course of our examination of the matter of automaticity in the volitional process. It is possible to suppose, on the basis of penny-in-the-slot psychology, that memories are only aroused—excitation caused in the memory-system—by a *reminder*. On this supposition, while memories might ecphorize each other in series when once started, the original member would always have to be aroused by, and all excitation in the memory-system would be ascribed to, current stimuli. We have already seen reason to question the completeness of this supposition and have assumed the existence of a source of excitation—the stream of awakeness—which, while it does not make excitation in the memory-system autogenous, nevertheless furnishes a possible and perhaps at first somewhat haphazard source for it. Nor is it easy to fit into this supposition the distinction we make between "voluntary" and "involuntary" recall. What "voluntary" recall is we cannot even imagine. How can we identify and "try" to recall an idea that is not present in consciousness? Nevertheless, it seems to be a fact that we do.[63] If so, "voluntary" ecphory is also an essential part of the process of volition, and volition involves the bringing to bear of memories that are not automatically ecphorized through homophony or association. That is, the content of consciousness during volition is, partly at least, determined by volition itself.

There seems to be another kind of ecphory for which it is even harder to conceive an explanation, but which seems even more certainly to be connected with volition. We have noted that the dog when catching a ball is extrapolating. That is, on the basis of his experience that certain events follow in series, he assumes that those members of the series that have not as yet occurred will follow in due course, and he places himself accordingly. That may not involve the counterfeit future, and it may be automatic or involuntary recall. However, when I deliberately place myself somewhere along my scale of time into the counterfeit future—say a year hence—and then furnish the scene or situation with the features that are automatically aroused by

---

[63] Hughlings Jackson made a suggestion that I have not seen followed up by his successors—and curiously so, for they seem to have developed all his other suggestions. Speaking of retino-ocular images (visual ideas), at least, he said (*216*, II, 141–142), "I submit that one half of the brain is for the automatic revival of images and one for their voluntary revival." The posterior part of the left occipital lobe, he held was "for the automatic revival of images, and the right side for their voluntary revival—for recognition,"

association (the background of a past experience, or of many homophonous past experiences) *but also* with features that I deliberately
choose to place there, both the placing of myself and of the chosen
furniture seem to be the work of volition.[64] True, daydreams may also
enter the counterfeit future and may be tinged with emotion—"wish-
ful thinking." But that wayward process is far different from the controlled process of cold-blooded planning or calculating, particularly if
the latter involves conflict, as it usually does. This kind of thinking—
planning—seems to require, not only voluntary ecphory of memories
but also the capacity on the part of the process of volition to substitute
for the sense of pastness and actuality, inherent in the materials it uses,
a sense of futurity and potentiality, and even to place these futurized
materials at a definite point somewhere along the conceived scale of
time.

Here, in these two ecphoric influences, we see the surface of still
deeper complexities in the volitional process—complexities as yet
wholly inaccessible to our understanding. That should lead to an even
greater degree of intellectual humility in venturing to apply the notions of automaticity and determinism.

6. VOLITION AND FUTURE WANTS

In order to establish a rational scheme of energetics, both to escape
from the inconsistencies now apparent in the neurophysiological
scheme as hitherto presented and to offer a reasonable postulate as to the causation of other behavior which is not accounted
for in that scheme, we have now been obliged to infer what we have
called a secondary source of neural energy of response. As to the
locus of this source and the course its excitation takes in reaching the locus of consciousness we remain quite uncertain. We have
suggested that it may be the non-specific (tonic) excitation that we
have called the stream of awakeness, the ultimate source of which appears to be the mammillary bodies in the hypothalamus. On the other
hand, it might be derived from some other region of the cortex, as we
shall suggest later. Even there, or anywhere in the cortex, it is not
probable that it is autogenous. The condition in which this neural
energy becomes effective, or perhaps the condition which it produces,
seems to be one of concentration of excitation or inhibition. The

[64] Clearly one can even run back and forth along the time-scale in the counterfeit
future.

neural aspect of such concentration would seem to correspond to the physiological concepts of concentration of reflex fields. The psychic or subjective aspect would seem to correspond to sustained concentration of conscious attention. But, as distinguished from reflex concentration in the first aspect, and from the direction of conscious attention by emotional "interest" in the second, this appears to be an independent and somewhat different process. It is what we are calling the volitional process, strictly defined. The only occasion when this condition arises and when, therefore, the secondary neural energy of response becomes mobilized is when the memory-system is in conflict within itself or with the current excitations in consciousness produced by the emotional stream—the primary neural energy of response. Then the condition of concentration of otherwise diffuse excitation, or possibly the advent of excitation from some other cortical source, may act as a reinforcing agency to the in itself weak memory-system; it is this condition or added energy that initiates, maintains, and resolves the conflict and sustains the resulting course of action in so far as it is not habitual, or when the old conflict recurs, or when new ones with regard to it arise. In the process of volition the actual neural energy that is mobilized, or that appears on the scene, varies greatly in degree of intensity; it may produce inhibition as well as excitation in any or all its outlets; and it may participate with the primary neural energy of response in all proportions in behavior. Thus it may direct, control or repress the primary neural energy; it may even substitute itself *in toto*, whether in the absence, or against the resistance, of the latter.[65]

This inference leads us to identify future wants also as volitional phenomena; that is, we assume that the behavior, or any component of behavior, that is instigated by a future want is almost wholly energized by secondary neural energy of response as a result of the re-

[65] We must clarify one point here. We have already concluded that there are two components in behavior—the cortical and the subcortical. This applies to apparatus used, not to the source of energy. Thus behavior energized entirely by emotion may, nevertheless, consist to a varying degree of a component produced via the cortex. Only the component that is produced by leakage—subcortical short-circuiting—appears to be emotional. That is, when the apparatus used is subcortical, the behavior appears to be emotional; when the apparatus used is cortical, it does not. What we are discussing here, on the contrary, is behavior, or the component of behavior, *energized* by the cortex.

We are assuming that what we are calling primary neural energy of response is the subcortical effect of conditions existing only in the periphery or of subcortical replicas of the same, and we are assuming that what we are calling secondary neural energy of response (or its concentration) is the cortical effect of conditions existing only in the cortex.

inforcing of the future want in or by the process of volition. Combining the two analyses of future wants as mnemonic and as volitional phenomena, a more precise statement is as follows: Future wants are, as we have already concluded, mnemonic phenomena; that is, they are memories, or abstractions of memories, of "present wants" that have been experienced in the past; that correspond respectively to the several members of the list of present wants; that may be recalled to consciousness when the corresponding present want does not exist; that vary in intensity according to the same order of priority which is produced among the corresponding present wants by reason of the latters' several maximum intensities, but at a much lower level of intensity in each case; and that are projected along a time-scale into a counterfeit future which is organized temporally like the past so that, if regularly recurring, they are regarded as periodic and, if irregularly recurring, they are regarded as contingencies and arranged according to frequency per time period.

In certain other aspects, future wants are also volitional phenomena. In the first place, their revival as conscious memories—their ecphory—seems to be largely a matter of volition. The change of attitude in which the subject projects himself into the counterfeit future and gives the quality of futurity to his memories of the past seems to be essentially volitional. Furthermore, a large part of the furnishing of this future scene is a result, not of association, but of what is called "voluntary recall." These statements do not explain the ecphory of future wants—one of the inadequacies we found in treating such wants as mnemonic phenomena. They merely classify ecphory of this type as a part of the volitional process, rather than of the nature of automatic ecphory by homophony or association. When the volitional process itself can be explained, this type of ecphory can be explained—and not until then. In the second place, future wants are volitional phenomena in respect of the energizing of the behavior to which they give rise. Only in that way have we been able to supply the second deficiency in the previous hypothesis—that future wants are mnemonic phenomena—to which we called attention at the end of the previous section.

However, even after this rounding out, which gives us at least a plausible objective basis for identifying the nature of, and the energizing mechanisms for, future wants, we are still left with certain deficiencies. These are concerned with the question of what we are

going to call their limiting mechanisms. The problem of what it is
that prevents or stops activities in response to future wants has hitherto
only been mentioned in connection with one of its aspects (p. 294)
—the necessity for an explanation of the observable fact, evidence for
which will be cited in due course, that future wants of any single
kind diminish in their effectiveness in producing behavior somewhat
according to their degree of futurity, that is, the distance of projection
along the time-scale into the counterfeit future. But the problem is
much more extensive than that. Our next undertaking, therefore, will
be to seek a rational basis for an hypothesis with regard to the limiting mechanisms, in general, and one that is consistent with neurological possibilities and the observation of behavior. In the course of
this undertaking we shall find that the question is exceedingly complex
—that it opens up, in fact, a whole new field which it is necessary to
explore.

B. THE LIMITING MECHANISMS OF FUTURE WANTS

I. THE LIMITATIONS ON BEHAVIOR IN RESPONSE TO FUTURE WANTS

The energetic scheme that we presented in the first four chapters
for the system of present wants and the energizing of its behavior
mechanism—primary neural energy of response—was, so far as it was
self-contained, entirely rational, quite simple and complete. It supposed that variations or tendencies away from homeostasis produce
effects upon the several integrating systems. If, in their centripetal
course, these effects are short-circuited (neurally or humorally), some
sort of corrective activity not requiring complete integration is initiated. If this activity then corrects the variation or tendency, the effects
cease at their source and thus their result, the corrective activity, also
ceases, since its energizing stops at the source. If such short-circuited
activities are inadequate to correct the variation or tendency, the
effects of the latter "rise," become long-circuited (neurally or humorally), may attain prepotence at the subcortical level where complete integration is available, and a general reaction results. When and
if that general reaction or its successor, some special reaction, succeeds
in restoring homeostasis, or gives rise to some counteracting condition
such as the sense of repletion, the transmission of effects again ceases at
the source and the energizing of the behavior terminates. We have
called the end condition, in both cases, satiety. Satiety, being the same

as the initial condition, is equivalent to homeostasis. Thus, in the absence of one of the three causes of failure to satiate, or of exhaustion, the only influence that puts an end to a behavior series composed of precurrent and consummatory reactions to a present want is the satiation of the want—that is to say, cessation of the excitation that produced the behavior. In other words, primary neural energy of response consists, as we have said before, of blind impulses leading to actions which may put an end to its generation. This offers a satisfactory scheme. It explains the initiation and continuation of the generation of this energy. But, let us emphasize at this point that it also suffices to explain how the process is brought to a stop.[1]

There is another feature of the duration of these reactions that requires a different explanation—one that we have already presented in Chapter 3. It has all the appearance of a tendency to the shortening of the period of activity, as if there existed a sort of principle of least activity—as if the reactions were, by economic analogy, directed toward economizing of activity, or as if they were, by physical analogy, subject to a sort of contractility. This tendency shows itself only as a result of the process of learning of adapted reactions, as a result of which some span in the series of precurrent reactions, consisting at first of a long process of aimless trial and error, is succeeded by a short single special reaction.[2] A reasonable explanation of this substitution is offered by Washburn's hypothesis (cited in Chapter 3) that the particular precurrent reaction making the consummatory reaction possible is necessarily the immediate predecessor of the latter, is therefore most recently and most closely associated with it, and thus tends to survive. This hypothesis also explains away the appearance of short-

---

[1] Freud describes the same scheme in hedonistic, animistic, and picturesque terms which are quite unnecessary in face of the simple physical explanation. He says (*154*, 474-475) his first system, "the primitive psychic apparatus," is "directed to the free outflow of the quantities of excitement." That is, its "work is regulated by the efforts to avoid accumulation of excitement and as far as possible to maintain itself free from excitement." For "accumulation of excitement . . . is perceived as pain and sets the apparatus in motion in order to reproduce a feeling of gratification in which the diminution of the excitement is perceived as pleasure." One could describe the scheme in still other and economic or accounting terms. Viewed externally, the animal economy operates as if the restoration of homeostasis were compensation or reward for the activity. All reactions—other than those which are produced by fatigue and its opposite, euphoria, which are concerned only with the reaction—appear to be directed toward an ulterior result. The reaction is necessary to secure the result. The result balances the reaction.
[2] Thus it may be said that, in this aspect, the cortex seems to be an apparatus for economizing the response by canalizing it into those channels which will most readily put an end to its generation.

ening or economizing. The apparent tendencies are merely the by-products of a cause which operates along quite different lines. The shortening is really due only to the fact that the precurrent series stops when and because it succeeds—that is, it leads at once to consummation which, in turn, ends the energizing. Nevertheless, viewed objectively, the phenomenon is a remarkable one. Economizing of activity is probably a biologically necessary function. The existence of the want seems to produce a condition of tensity, of excitation. That, in turn, produces a state of activity. But the state of activity itself, to judge by introspection and observation, seems like a release of such tensity and excitation. Therefore, in itself, the latter gives the appearance of containing no tendency to shortening. But the existence of the want leads to learning the briefest way to get rid of it, by directing reactions into those channels which will soonest put an end to the state of excitation. Thus it is the fact of association (learning) that evinces the apparent tendency to shorten the state of want and, quite incidentally, insures that the quickest way to do so—the briefest reaction —will be selected. It should be noted, however, that only the quickest way, not the easiest way, is selected by this process. And that proves the source of the influence. For, though briefer, the selected reaction may involve the use of greater energy. It does not evince economizing in that dimension.[3]

Now it is equally evident that the behavior to which future wants give rise is also subject to limitations. Something equivalent to satiation must stop it, for it does not go on forever. We have already conceded that there is an order of priority among future as among present wants—that is, a prior want takes precedence over a subordinate want in producing behavior. We shall see evidence that this behavior shows a tendency to the shortening of activity much as does that due to present wants. In these three respects the behavior due to future wants seems to conform to that due to present wants. But our observations do not permit us to stop there. The limitations on behavior in response to future wants appear to be a much more complex matter. There is, first, the fact that behavior in response to future wants may be stopped and then resumed after an interval. There is, second, an inability on the part of certain future wants ever to give rise to behavior, which

---

[3] Carnivora do not stalk prey, or lie in wait for it, because it is the easiest way, but because experience shows that, in terms of minutes spent per successful denouement, it is the quickest. Fighting for a female is not the easiest way to secure one, if there are others elsewhere; but it is the quickest way if it is successful.

inability seems to apply to all future wants at certain times. There is, third, an evident tendency toward the facilitating as well as toward the shortening of activity. There is, fourth, the tendency we have already mentioned, toward labor-saving provision—that is, to lengthen the period of activity now if it will shorten such periods in the future by a greater amount. There is, fifth, the previously noted apparent diminishing ability to produce behavior the greater the distance along the time-scale into the counterfeit future to which the future want is projected—its degree of futurity. And this, in turn, seems to be related to the previous one, for the same influence diminishes the effectiveness of time-saving or activity-saving in the future, proportionate to its futurity.

Hitherto, in this chapter, we have only provided an hypothesis as to the energizing of behavior in response to future wants. This may account for starting it and continuing it, but it does not account at all for stopping it or for limiting it in any of the above ways. We have now to seek, therefore, for adequate explanations of these phenomena. Because our inquiry must necessarily proceed step by step, much of the evidence proving the fact of the several limitations described above, particularly the evidence derived from the observation of human beings, will be left for Part II, where it is most appropriate. There is no existing literature on this subject which we can cite here. However, this is the point at which we are examining future wants from as nearly as possible a neurological and biological standpoint, so that this seems to be the point for a limited examination of the question. We shall confine ourselves, therefore, to the above dicta as to these limitations, which will be supported here by the few examples available in the animal world. The several limitations will be considered in the order named above.

1. The behavior in response to a single specific future want projected to some specific time stops if it reaches a certain point. That is, there is some equivalent, here, to satiety, which is the normal end of behavior in response to present wants. In this case cessation cannot be due to satiation, for the very definition of future wants is that they produce only precurrent reactions, and of course consummatory reactions are necessary in any process of satisfaction. Moreover, in no sense does the future want cease when the behavior stops. It remains potentially as lively and intense a memory as ever. Furthermore, our criterion for the feature of futurity, which is characteristic of all the

behavior we are now considering, is that it secures no immediate advantage. Nevertheless, there is here again a regular correlation between the magnitude of the want and the magnitude of the behavior analogous to that we found for present wants (pp. 36 to 37 and 178).

Aside from the fact that it would be manifestly impossible that such behavior should not be stopped at some time, we have sufficient proof among our examples from the animal world that it is stopped, by some influence and at some point. Nor is it necessary to confine ourselves here to cases which are certainly due to future wants. For it is quite evident, even in certain cases which may be due to present wants, that the influence stopping the behavior and the point at which it is stopped is neither satiety nor any internal sense of repletion. Instead, it is something that can only be effective with the aid of the exteroceptive apparatus—in fact, the distance receptors. In cases which we construed as future wants, we saw that the beaver provides only one winter's food supply during one season. It is adequate but not excessive. When it is adequate the harvesting stops. The same is true of the prairie dog and of the rat hare. In a case which might be construed as a present want we noted that some bees and wasps, who provide winter food for the young, adjust this nicely to the requirements of the species and favor the queen-cells. Another instance is even more positive. Hens and ducks usually lay a certain number of eggs before setting. If the eggs are removed as laid, the bird will continue to lay. When they are no longer removed, the bird will lay up to the requisite number and then stop.[4]

Thus there must be such a thing as a visual sign of "enough." And, though we shall be able to rely, so far as our future discussion of human behavior is concerned, on the probability that this is a result of experience—a quantitative memory—it appears from the insect and poultry examples, above, that it may also be unlearned, however difficult that may be to explain. Moreover, it is clear that "enough is enough." For the activity does not overshoot the mark. Neither does

---

[4] William James quotes Schneider (*Die thierische Wille*) to this effect. He translates (*220*, II, 388) as follows: "The perception of the empty nest, or of a single egg, seems in birds to stand in such close relation to the physiological functions of oviparation, that it serves as a direct stimulus to those functions, while the perception of a sufficient number of eggs has just the opposite effect. It is well known that hens and ducks lay more eggs if we keep removing them than if we leave them in the nest. The impulse to sit arises, as a rule, when a bird sees a certain number of eggs in her nest. If this number is not yet to be seen there, the ducks continue to lay, although they perhaps have laid twice as many eggs as they are accustomed to sit upon."

it simply run down. Something enters at that point to stop it short. That something starts as an external phenomenon and is, in no other sense, an experience as yet. This appears to give rise to a phenomenon of recognition—a revival of homophonous memories—which proceeds to counteract the further effects of the memory constituting the future want—or, if it occurs as an unlearned reaction with present wants, it appears to be a mnemic phenomenon. We used the term "provision" on p. 257, as applying to all the behavior produced by future wants. In those terms this first limitation may be called, in its purely objective aspect, adequacy of provision.[5]

2. Even within the limitation set by adequacy of provision the behavior in response to a single specific future want projected to some specific time is apt to be intermittent on a regular basis, if it is long continued, and is also subject to erratic interruptions. We noted that the beaver's construction, excavation, and harvesting operations are conducted only at night. Furthermore, if his enemies are sensed as approaching—even when his tree falls and makes a noise that might attract them—he stops these operations and flops into the water of his canals or channels. Even in the case of behavior not certainly due to future wants it was apparent that there is some time limit per day. For bees collect honey, etc., only during daylight, some thirteen hours a day, and wasps limit their activities to some sixteen hours a day. Nevertheless, both the beavers and the insects resume the same activity the following night or day, or after an interruption, showing that the limitation by reason of adequate provision has not yet become effective. This phenomenon parallels and therefore reminds us of the phenomenon of interference which we considered in reference to present wants in Chapter 4. There it was explained as loss of prepotence by one want to another more intense want which becomes prepotent in its stead. While the apparatus in which prepotence is determined is not involved here, since by definition future wants do not engage it, this phenomenon appears to be of the same order. It may also be the result of conflict which differs only in that it occurs and is settled in a different apparatus. This second form of limitation might then be called, in terms of a somewhat less objective aspect than the first, interference. But, to maintain the distinction from the interference of one present

[5] The term provision, and now the term adequate provision, have had to creep into this chapter, without any consideration or real definition. This because we are postponing such consideration until we treat the whole matter of "means" in the next chapter.

want by another with which it is certainly not identical, let us call it interruption, regular or fortuitous. That merely suggests the resemblance.

3. A third form of limitation, one which cannot be observed but only inferred, must also be included. If we are to assume that for each present want that we have considered there is a corresponding future want, we might expect that we would be able to observe behavior attributable to each future want in the list—that is, we might do so except in those cases when the present want produces no precurrent reactions at all; for the corresponding future want, which produces only precurrent reactions, would then have no precurrent reactions to produce. Now, even eliminating the exceptions, this is very definitely what we *do not* find. At all times, many probably existing future wants produce no behavior at all; at some times, even for whole seasons, no future wants produce any behavior; and, in general, adequate provision seems to be completed for certain future wants before the behavior appropriate to others appears at all. As to the first, animal examples would involve too much imputation. We will have to depend on the testimony of all men save only the apostles of the simple life. As to the second, it is sufficient to cite the beaver, who takes a summer-long vacation from behavior in response to future wants. As to the third, we may again use the beaver. Beavers always work in families. Their harvesting, their excavating, their dam-building, and the repair of their lodge engage the attention of the whole family. We do not know the precise order in which this program is undertaken.[6] But evidently first things are put first. All this simply signifies, in the first place, that there is an order of priority among future as among present wants. We have already suggested that it corresponds to the order among present wants and is due to the fact that future wants differ in intensity according to the normal maximum intensity of the experiences (present wants) from which they were derived, though each is at a much lower level of intensity than its progenitor. Those certain future wants which produce no behavior might then be the ones which are subordinate in this respect. But this imports the notion of capacity which we introduced in Chapter 4. It introduces a limitation

---

[6] Judging by reports, harvesting begins in late summer and appears to be the first part of the program. However, this may not be wholly due to priority, in our sense, but to the fact that cuttings are required for some of the other parts. Or the fact that canals are required before harvesting can begin may enforce canal-building as first in order. Repairs on the lodge seem to come last.

on the total quantity of behavior in response to future wants and assumes that this will exclude certain wants altogether. In the case of present wants, taken alone, that exclusion required the supposition that, at all times, some prior want would be prepotent. That theory will not serve here, at least as applying to future wants alone, for we stated above that, at certain times or seasons, no future wants are effective. That also makes it necessary to assume that the limitation here, which is analogous to capacity there, is a variable one. At all events, our third limitation turns out to be based on an order of priority, so that prior future wants exclude subordinate ones [7] until their limitation of adequate provision has been reached, with the addition of some variable critical limit to the total amount of behavior in response to future wants that will be produced. For this last feature we may well retain the term capacity, since it will turn out that capacity applies, among men, almost wholly to behavior in response to future wants.

4. Behavior in response to future wants often evinces a tendency not only to substitute shorter processes, as with that resulting from present wants, but to substitute easier processes, and that even if they are somewhat longer. However, though somewhat analogous, this cannot be explained in the same way as it was for present wants. There we noted that the underlying tendency is toward the abbreviation of the state of want and that any apparent abbreviation of the system of reactions is purely incidental—a by-product of that. Here, on the contrary, since the tendency takes the form either of a shortening of the duration or of a reduction of the intensity of the system of reactions, whichever reduces the total neural energy used in the reaction to the greatest extent, it is clear that it derives directly from, and applies directly to, the processes of activity themselves. It does not appear as a running out or cessation of the energy, as in the first case, but as a deliberate economizing of it. Even it might be said that in the case of behavior due to present wants it appears as if the organism were trying to get rid of the want, while in the case of behavior due to future wants it appears as if he were trying to get rid of the activity only.[8]

[7] This is subject to the exception, outlined below and applicable only to future wants, that future wants of the same constellation are not necessarily mutually exclusive.
[8] In the case of future wants the limitation by reason of adequacy of provision applies. This, and not the quantity of behavior, is the magnitude that is directly related to that of the want. But this remains the same whether the activity is brief or prolonged, easy or hard. Therefore short cuts and easy methods cannot be due to the want. They must be due to a feature of the behavior.

A few instances, taken from the behavior of the beaver as described in Appendix III, Section A, will serve to illustrate this point. Beavers fell their trees toward the water to reduce the distance of transport. It has even been asserted that they notch the tree as little as necessary and leave the wind to do the rest. They go to the extra work of cutting the branches into short lengths to make transport easier. If they can fell a tree near the bank of the stream, so that its branches are submerged, they leave it there and come and eat the thus preserved branches during the winter. The first two and the last are devices to shorten the process; the third lengthens the process, since more cuts and more trips are necessary, but makes the transport easier. This limitation may be stated as an apparent tendency to economize energy used, in the two-dimensional aspect of the product of intensity into duration of activity.

5. Behavior in response to future wants often evinces a tendency to lengthen activities now—or even to make them more arduous—if the effect will be to shorten or make easier activities in the future, directed to the same end, by a greater amount. This characteristic shades into the previous one. Like that, it is a direct relation between two forms of activity, neither between a want and activity nor even intermediated by a want. But its distinguishing mark is the fact that there is always a considerable interval, sometimes a very long one, between the expenditure and the subsequent economizing. It is therefore a relation between present and future behavior, not one between two forms of present behavior. Moreover, this type of behavior usually produces its ultimate effect through what we have called indirection —that is, "one thing is done now in order that, in the future, some other thing can be done." The relation is between two forms of behavior whose immediate courses and objectives are different. It is clear that this limitation has no correspondent whatever in the case of behavior due to present wants. It could not have, since the more or less distant future enters into it. It is, therefore, entirely a new phenomenon. Nor is the nature of the limitation so simple as it was in the preceding cases. Here it operates solely on a reciprocal basis. Here it seems to induce a retraction of many of the foregoing limitations, in the present, provided that, in the future, there will be a better than corresponding extension of the limitation set by the tendency to economize energy—or, at least, that there shall be a greater quantity of such economizing. Thus the only time when this economizing—this

extension of the limitation—becomes actually effective is in the future, and its present influence can only be a reflection of that. In fact, its direct present influence is merely to make other limitations less effective now. The more certain examples of this type of limitation that we cited from animal behavior on pp. 258 ff. were the roads built by leaf-cutting ants in order to reduce the later difficulties in transporting the leaf-cuttings to their nests; and the canal and dam systems for transportation, as well as the slides, tunnels, and canals for traveling, which the beaver constructs. All these involve prolonged and intense labor of clearing and excavation at the time they are made. The chief or only benefit of all is the easing and expediting of other processes later in the season or in subsequent years. It will be convenient to refer to this limitation hereafter as *future* labor-saving in order to differentiate it from the previous one.

6. At the end of our list we may place the limitation already several times mentioned, which is intimately related to the one just described. The effectiveness of a future want in producing behavior appears to diminish in rough proportion to the degree of futurity that has been conferred upon it. Thus, at first sight, this limitation would seem to derive from the side of the want rather than from the side of the activity. In that respect it would appear to be more of the order of the limitations on behavior in response to present wants. But, on closer examination, it is clear that is not true. For, here, it is neither the magnitude of the want, nor its cessation (satiation) that is the determining factor. Instead, that factor would have to be chiefly the position of the want as projected along a wholly conceptual time-scale into a wholly counterfeit future.

This preliminary analysis leaves us *en l'air* so far as any correspondence to what has gone before is concerned. This last limitation is *sui generis*, though we shall find that the preceding one, in respect of the necessary magnitude of the net labor-saving, is related to it. At any rate it is clear that the solution of the problem of all the preceding limitations in terms of a rational, if hypothetical, system of energetics will not, at the same time, solve this sixth problem. We will therefore leave this to the last in our further investigations. Nor is it easy to support the assertion, above, as to even a rough proportionality between this limitation and the degree of futurity of the want upon the basis of any evidence of animal behavior. That assertion will have to wait for more precise proof when we come to consider man's behavior in Part II.

However, animal instances do prove the existence of the limitation. Let us approach the question from a purely logical standpoint. In the first place, if the degree of futurity offered no impediment whatever to behavior we would have to suppose that the most intense future want would, within the foregoing limitations, monopolize all behavior producible by future wants at all. Provision for this one want would extend over successive instances into the indefinite future. And this regardless of whether it happened to be a want which experience had shown to be a regularly recurring one, so that its instances would be projected at regular intervals along the time-scale of the counterfeit future, or whether it happened to have been irregular, so that it would be projected as a contingency according to its frequency per time period (see pp. 289–290). In the second place, if the degree of futurity were not an influence, an organism which could not at one time make provision for two expected occasions for a single future want, would be just as likely to make provision for the more distant rather than for the nearer one. The law of probability would lead, then, to an equal number of cases of each procedure. Observation shows clearly that neither of these conditions obtains. Beavers and other rodents who store their winter food only accumulate for the next winter. When that is done, beavers, at least, turn to provision for other and presumably lesser future wants—security, comfort, ease of transport and travel, etc. Nor, for these, do they prepare separate provisions for more than one season and never for the season after the next one instead of the next season. One does not read of dams for the future protection of as yet non-existent lodges, of canals for ready access to wood that is not yet to be harvested, etc. Beavers take thought for "the morrow"; but they leave some future day, after "the morrow," to "take thought for the things of itself." All this might be explained by the supposition that the effectiveness of future wants in producing behavior reached to some definite point in the counterfeit future and was then completely lost. But the observation of man leads us to believe, instead, that this effectiveness continues more or less indefinitely into the future, but declines more or less exactly as that degree extends. We shall proceed on such an assumption. This final limitation, then, will be termed the degree of futurity.

2. THE SENSE OF VOLITIONAL EFFORT

Having found nothing, either in our hypothesis as to their nature or in that with regard to their energizing mechanisms, that would account for any such limitations on behavior in response to future wants, let us proceed to investigate further to see whether or not we can find any recognized psychological entity to which it would be plausible to attribute the characteristics which we have found it necessary to infer for the limiting mechanisms of future wants. Classic economic terminology suggests at once where to look. There is another and well-attested characteristic of the volitional process not mentioned hitherto, which, as we proceed with our consideration of future wants, will serve even more effectively to identify them, or the behavior to which they give rise, as volitional phenomena, and which offers the possibility of eliminating the remaining deficiency in our hypothesis. As Hilgard and Marquis put it,[9] "Introspective studies have discovered feelings of effort, kinesthetic sensations, determining tendencies, and so on, as correlates of voluntary activity." Since, then, we have to rely wholly on such introspective studies, we choose those of William James as a particularly usable basis for our purpose. He distinguished sharply between the first of these two categories, both of which bear the same name in common usage. "Muscular effort . . . and mental effort . . . must be distinguished." [10] And he speaks of "the unfortunateness of their being confounded under the same generic name." [11] The kinesthetic sensations, the sense of muscular effort, are exclusively afferent from the periphery and only occur as muscular activity is effected.[12] To preserve this distinction we shall hereafter use the term "exertion" for muscular effort. What, then, "is the volitional

9 Hilgard and Marquis, *197*, 256.
10 James, *219*, 31. He cites instances where volitional effort and muscular exertion are entirely disproportionate (e.g., getting out of bed on a cold morning; *220*, II, 562).
11 James, *219*, 25.
12 James, *219*, 31, and *220*, II, 562. See also, on this, Chapter 6, Section A 4. In making this distinction James starts with the thesis, "That we *have* a feeling of effort there can be no doubt." Admitting such "feelings of active energy," "of what nervous processes are they the concomitants?" (*219*, 3). He then discusses the views of Johannes Müller, who held that the feeling of muscular exertion arises from a "discharge from the motor centre to the motor nerve" (i.e., a felt efferent impulse), and the similar views of Bain, Hughlings Jackson and Wundt, the last of whom distinguished the felt efferent from the feeling of an effected movement. His own conclusion is that the "feeling of *muscular* energy put forth is solely due to a complex of afferent impulses from the muscle" (*ibid.*, 4). That is, "consciousness of muscular exertion, being impossible without movement *effected somewhere*, must be an afferent and not an efferent sensation, a consequence, and not an antecedent of the movement itself." In other words, only when the motor impulse "discharges by the preappointed mechanism into the right muscles" does "motor sensation" accrue and "muscular effort as distinguished from volitional effort begin" (*ibid.*, 24). Even the idea of such exertion is an anticipatory image of the movement's effects (*ibid.*, 10). With this we entirely concur, for we have found (in the text above) no reason to believe that conscious memories contain a motor element.

effort proper?" [13] In the first place, "the ideational nerve tracts alone are the seat of the feeling of mental effort." [14] For "volition with effort" is "incidental to the conflict" of ideas. Or, better, "Effort is felt only where there is a conflict of interests in the mind." [15] Conflicts "are subserved by the ideational centres exclusively and involve no downward irradiation into lower parts." Such irradiation only occurs after the conflict is resolved and the process of volition is completed.[16] Even then, either inhibition or excitation of movement may be the result, and both may, but do not need to, involve effort.[17] He then discusses the so-called "effect-theory" (what we have called automatism above). On the supposition that "the only resistance which the force of consciousness feels or can feel, is the resistance which the idea makes to being consented to as real," this theory holds that such a "sense of reality" is "a simple resultant of the victory which was a foregone conclusion decided by the intrinsic strength of the conflicting ideas alone," so that "choice and decision" are nothing but the "resultant of different ideas failing to neutralize each other exactly." [18] Now this might go, in his opinion, for the first four of his types of decision consequent upon deliberation or conflict. For "the immense majority of human decisions are decisions without effort" (i.e., "the sense of inward effort").[19] These seem even to our consciousness to settle themselves. But, in decisions of his fifth type, when the decision is made against the resistance of "some inhibitory agency, whether of intrinsic unpleasantness in the doing, or of represented odiousness in the doing's fruits," then volition "comes hand in hand with the sentiment of effort." [20] In other words, here, his resistance, if it is proximately resistance to consent as real, is ultimately resistance arising from "disagreeableness." [21] The effort involved is proportionate to these resistances. Thus he derives an antithesis founded on common language and impressions. Sensual impulses are strongest and can only be suppressed by a force that involves effort; but "moral motives per se can be annulled without energy or effort." Therefore, when the two conflict, the moral motive, being the weaker, must be "artificially reinforced." "Effort is what reinforces it." So construed, moral action is "action in the line of greatest resistance." [22] Thus he construes

[13] James, 219, 15.
[14] James, 219, 32. "Volitional effort" and "mental effort" are one and the same (ibid., 31).
[15] Ibid., 220, I, 451.　　[16] Ibid., 219, 23.　　[17] Ibid., 220, II, 527.
[18] Ibid., 219, 31 and 27.　[19] Ibid., 220, II, 531–535.　[20] Ibid., 219, 22.
[21] Ibid., 23.　　　　　　　[22] Ibid., 28.

"effort" to be "purely moral." Nevertheless, it seems to be involved in a much wider field than purely moral decisions; for it is "identical with the effort to remember, with the effort to make a decision, or to attend to a disagreeable task." [23] The essence of the process of decision, in his opinion (as we noted above), consists in the sustained concentration of attention. "Mental effort may . . . accompany" the maintenance of an idea in "vivid and stable consciousness," for "to sustain a representation, to think, is what requires the effort." [24] The effort, then, is something apart from the idea; its strength can be varied.[25] We feel that the effort is peculiarly something exerted by the self.[26] Hence, perhaps, "the strange intimateness of the feeling of effort to our personality." [27]

[23] *Ibid.*, 4. Thus, "the impression which the facts spontaneously produce upon us" is that the ideal impulse is *per se* weaker than the native propensity, but that this impulse, when reinforced by effort, is stronger than the propensity, as if effort were "an active force adding its strength to that of the motives which ultimately prevail." "Our spontaneous language never speaks of volition with effort" as if it were exercised in the line of least resistance, like other forces, but as "action in the line of greatest resistance." It supports "the ideal impulse . . . a still small voice which must be artificially enforced to prevail." It compensates for the deficiency in strength of this impulse as compared with that of the propensity and, therefore, it is quantitatively determined by this deficiency and must vary with the strength of the propensity (James, *220*, II, 548–549). "The normal . . . sphere of effort is thus found wherever non-instinctive motives of behavior are to rule the day" (*ibid.*, II, 536). Or, in more physical terms, "Effort complicates volition . . . whenever a rarer and more ideal impulse is called upon to neutralize others of a more instinctive and habitual kind . . . whenever strongly explosive tendencies are checked, or strongly obstructive conditions overcome" (*ibid.*, II, 548).
[24] James, *219*, 31 and 23. At least this is true of a representation which is not "intrinsically exciting," which will not, therefore, "keep going of its own accord," but "needs incessant pulses of voluntary reinforcement" (*220*, I, 451). When such a representation is in conflict with one which is "intrinsically exciting," "both alternatives are steadily held in view, and in the very act of murdering the vanquished possibility the chooser realizes how much in that instant he is making himself lose" (*ibid.*, II, 534). Evidently James conceives the moral ideas to be those which are not intrinsically exciting, while the "inclinations" or instinctive motives must be adequate by themselves, for they do not require the support of effort. But effort is evidently extrinsically exciting, for it accomplishes the same result of sustaining a representation. "In short, one does not see any case in which the steadfast occupancy of consciousness does not appear to be the prime condition of impulsive power. It is still more obviously the prime condition of inhibitive power." All impulsiveness is the "urgency . . . with which it [the idea] is able to compel attention and dominate in consciousness" (*ibid.*, II, 559).
[25] James, *219*, 28.
[26] "But the E [effort] does not seem to form an integral part of the I [idea]. It appears adventitious and indeterminate in advance. We can make more or less as we please, and *if* we make enough we can convert the greatest mental resistance into the least" (*220*, II, 549). James admits that, while "we have the feeling of voluntary reinforcement (or effort)," "the feeling of effort *may* be an inert accompaniment and not the active element which it seems." Nevertheless, he does not subscribe to the "effect-theory" (*220*, II, 451–452)—our automatism.
[27] James, *219*, 31. As if effort were an attribute of the sense of self and its assertion—of self-assertiveness within.

In three respects this analysis appears to set too narrow limits on the sphere of effort. In the first place, while we can accept James's dictum that the "sphere of effort is thus found wherever non-instinctive motives to behavior are to rule the day," [28] we cannot accept his conclusion that it is only involved when it is necessary to overpower instinctive impulses. Rather, even in the absence of these, it seems to be a concomitant of the effectiveness of all non-instinctive (non-emotional) motives; it seems potentially to accompany all activating of such motives, which in themselves are too weak to produce overt behavior. In the second place, we cannot accept his limitation of its sphere to "moral action" nor even his simple antithesis between "moral action" and "instinctive" action, as if these two rubrics covered all actions. Non-instinctive (non-emotional) motives may include all that he means by moral motives, but we shall see as we proceed that they include a vast deal besides. In fact, we shall conclude that effort may be a concomitant of all behavior which is activated by, or to the extent that it is activated by, the memory-system. In the third place, one might gather from James that the sphere of effort was limited to decision only.[29] We have considered the several steps in conflict to be its initiation, its maintenance, and its resolution. Only the last is decision proper. Yet effort may be involved throughout. Furthermore, after the thus-determined course of behavior is begun, effort may still be involved. It is true that the execution of such a course of behavior will be "easy" to the extent that its details have become habitual. Then "the only impulse which the centres of idea or perception need send down is the initial impulse, the command to *start*." [30] That is to say, "habit diminishes the conscious attention with which our acts are performed," and "habit . . . diminishes fatigue." [31] Conscious attention is the occasion for effort, according to James, and fatigability is one of its measures according to Waller (see below). On the other hand, the execution of the several steps will be "hard" to the extent that they are new (unaccustomed) and have, therefore, to be consciously integrated. For such conscious integration requires a concentration of conscious attention which can, then, be attained only with effort. It is as if effort were involved in breaking the new paths. Furthermore,

[28] James, *220*, II, 536.
[29] A careful study of all that he says on the subject would make it clear that this was not his view. Nevertheless, he emphasizes this one occasion so much that one runs the risk of forgetting the rest.
[30] James, *220*, I, 116.   [31] *Ibid.*, I, 114 and 112.

if the course of action is a prolonged one, the original conflict may recur (*voluntas invita*), or a new one may arise to contend with it. That is what happens, apparently, when hesitancy develops during its course. Thus, while the appearance of effort may be intermittent, being only notable in the interstices between habitual actions and during the recurrences of old or the occurrences of new conflicts, it nevertheless reappears usually and frequently after the decision is settled and as long as the course of action lasts.

We have as yet no basis for assigning a neural substrate to the sense of effort. In Appendix III, Section G, we outline Waller's theory, derived from experimentation on the voluntary contraction of muscle. But that concerns directly only what we are calling the sense of muscular exertion. He suggests that it is the current effect of the same process of which fatigue is the after-effect. Since fatigability—and therefore presumably the sense of exertion also—seems to increase by degrees from the peripheral to the highest nervous centers, the feeling of volitional effort above the highest levels of the motor system may be of the same order and only different in degree from the feeling of muscular exertion in the motor system itself. Moreover, since fatigue increases with the continuance of excitation, so presumably would the sense of effort. And we have noted that James's criterion for effort is *sustained* concentration of attention. Against Waller's theory as applied to volitional effort is the fact that "effortless attention is the rule." [32] We would have to assume that the levels at which such effortless attention is innervated—which we have assumed to be derived from emotional "interest"—are of a different order—lower than—those concerned with effortful concentration of attention. What we have been assuming is that the levels or tracts involved in attention itself, are the same in both cases—the difference being rather in the source of the facilitating excitation. Thus to fit Waller's theory into our scheme it would be necessary to locate the sense of effort at the external source from which the field of conscious attention was excited, not in that field itself.

Judging from the occasions when the sense of volitional effort is said to appear, it seems likely that it pertains to some feature of the contest of weaker excitation against stronger, or of the raising of subliminal excitation to the point at which it is capable of producing overt action. In other words, it appears to accompany a reinforcing process

[32] *Ibid.*, I, 451.

of some kind which only develops as it is needed. As we have already suggested, this reinforcing process may take either of two forms. It may be concentration in Pavlov's sense—a building up of the intensity of excitation by concentration of its field. If we assume that the "natural state" of weak excitation is irradiation, it is not impossible that concentration of this excitation itself would yield a "peculiar feeling of effort, difficulty or strain." [33] We still would have no explanation of why concentration takes place—whether by reason of some characteristic of the excitation patterns or by reason of the influence of some external agency. Alternatively, the reinforcing process may consist of an access of strength from some other cortical source, the generation of excitation in which is felt in consciousness as the sense of effort.[34] As a matter of fact, however, these three alternative possibilities as to a neural basis for the sense of effort are not mutually exclusive. That sense may be a correlate of the extreme fatigability of a certain region which has the capacity of concentrating weak excitations [35] in the substrate of consciousness and whose own neural energy is derived either from the non-specific excitation of awakeness, or from some other particular cortical source, as we shall suggest later, or which, finally, is autogenous. Since there is no evidence to indicate that the last is possible, on other than a metabolic basis, it seems very unlikely.

Thus again, as in the case of the process of volition, we find ourselves unable to identify any neural process as the basis of the sense of effort, strictly defined. We can do no more in this case than in the other— that is, to suggest in what ways it might be neurally possible. But, as a result of our consideration, I think we have achieved one definite result. Our examinations of the process of volition and of the sense of effort have turned out to indicate that the two are absolutely parallel. When, as finally and narrowly defined, the process of volition takes place, it is always accompanied by the sense of effort. Neither occurs without the other. We conclude that the sense of effort is what James called it, "volitional effort," pure and simple. But, since we have modified his boundaries of volition, we have also modified his boundaries of effort.

[33] *Ibid.*, I, 451.
[34] It is this alternative which reminds us of the intuitive aspect that William James presents and which he seems to favor (see *220*, II, 549).
[35] And the fact that concentration due to emotion is not so subject to fatigue might be due to the fact that the emotional excitation is already strong, or even to the fact that emotions do not actually persist for a great length of time. This latter fits the requirement that, as we shall see, actions due to present wants frequently tire if the satisfaction is too long delayed and then effort is required to supplement the diminishing drive.

Both occur whenever some unknown reinforcing process or agency comes to the aid of the memory-system and enables it to produce, maintain, and resolve conflict in consciousness with the emotional system; or whenever this agency contributes to produce, maintain, and resolve conflict in consciousness, even when that conflict is solely between elements of the memory-system itself, to the extent that these are raised to a level of excitation which, when the inhibitory effect of one element on the other can be overcome, is capable of producing overt action. Both volition and effort continue or recur thereafter, to the extent that the course of action so commenced does not consist of habitual movements or to the extent that either the previously resolved conflict or a new one due to newly aroused emotions reappears, or attempts to reappear, in consciousness.[36] In other words, the sense of effort is a concomitant of the generation or concentration of secondary neural energy of response. It occurs when that is going on, and it is proportionate in degree to the intensity (potency) of that energy. On the other hand, it is quite clear that there is no sense of effort in so far as any process is energized by primary neural energy of response.

3. HYPOTHESIS AS TO LIMITING MECHANISMS

Utilizing the three identifications we have now built up in these two chapters—that future wants are mnemonic phenomena, that the behavior they give rise to consists of volitional phenomena, and that the volitional process has as a concomitant the sense of effort—we shall now proceed to construct out of these bricks and mortar a purely hypothetical scheme of energetics for future wants. Its only requirements are (1) that it shall be rational, (2) that it shall use no other entities than these, nor attribute any characteristics to these that we have not found other reason to assign to them, and (3) that it shall account for all the limitations described above in a way that is not neurologically impossible, that is consistent with our neurological thesis as to present wants, and that fits, and so far explains, observed behavior. Whether it also conforms to an actual neurological substrate there is, at present, no means of knowing. It is, thus, pure inference. But—it should be noted—when and if a plausible neurological substrate is uncovered, it, too, will have to meet the first and third requirements above, though not necessarily the second.

[36] That is, both occur and persist whenever, and as long as, any concentration of conscious attention exists that is not due to "interest" (emotion).

The structure of our hypothesis—the design in which our bricks and mortar are placed—consists of the following suppositions.

1. There is a multiplex of future wants (memories), whose varying intensities arrange them in an order of priority and produce a tendency for the strongest, at any one moment, to be dominant.[37]

2. All are too weak by themselves to resist any active emotional drive (primary energy)[38] or to produce supraliminal motor activity.

3. Any conflict between the memory-system and emotional drive is capable of arousing secondary energy on the side of the former. So, too, is any conflict wholly within the memory-system itself. In the latter case, until the conflict is settled, secondary energy takes no sides. It merely sustains or heightens the conflict—that is, it raises the energy potential of the conflicting memories, though these continue to neutralize each other. When one memory, or allied group,[39] gains preponderance, the conflict is decided and the secondary energy comes to be at the disposal of the winner—which, in our instances, is the dominant future want or constellation.[40]

4. It is, then, this secondary energy which energizes not only the conflict but all the subsequent effects. It does so only at the instigation of the memory-system; in turn, the memory-system does little more than instigate it.

5. Secondary energy may vary widely in intensity; its generation (or concentration) is accompanied by a sense of strain (effort) proportionate to this intensity.

6. Once aroused, so long as the intensity of secondary energy remains adequate it enables a continuance of conflict in consciousness. Once the conflict is resolved in favor of some future want or constellation, secondary energy enables this dominant want to maintain itself exclusively in consciousness (sustained conscious attention), unless and until it is interrupted (see supposition 11 below).

7. During conflict with emotional drive the entire secondary energy

[37] Again, as noted above, this is subject to a certain qualification in the case of future wants belonging to the same constellation.
[38] The precise terms for primary and secondary energy are primary and secondary neural energy of response. With that connotation, the shorter terms will be used hereafter.
[39] Including ultimately, in the "allied group," a whole constellation of future wants.
[40] We have noted that conflict seems to be the only occasion arousing secondary energy (or concentrating it). But, once aroused, it seems to be capable of continuing under the limiting conditions outlined below. Were this not true, we would have no reinforcing agency to continue the volitional process into, nor to energize, the subsequent phase of resulting behavior.

may be absorbed in resisting such drive. Then secondary energy must equal primary energy at this point.

8. Or, after the resolution of conflict with emotional drive or of conflict within the memory-system, the secondary energy may be absorbed in producing volitional activity (motor excitation). To do this, secondary energy must exceed motor resistance. In general, the more muscular exertion is required the greater the motor resistance. But, on the other hand, this is greatly modified by the fact that the more habitual the actions, the less is the motor resistance. Therefore, the more habitual the actions the less secondary energy is required.

9. Or, during conflict with emotional drive or after the resolution of conflict within the memory-system, the application of secondary energy may take both directions (suppositions 7 and 8). It can do so, however, only if it exceeds the primary energy exhibited at this point, and only that excess is available to energize volitional activity. Thus, for any given intensity of secondary energy, the greater the primary energy opposed to it, the less will be the portion of it that is available for volitional activity.

10. The intensity of secondary energy seems to vary principally according to the requirements placed upon it. That is, no more is generated than is needed. It is never excessive. But this is true only up to some limit. Up to that limit it rises in response to the intensity of emotional drive in order to maintain the inhibition.[41] Also, up to that limit, it rises in proportion to increased motor resistance, whether that be due to a briefly strenuous action or to a gradual rise (as under supposition 19 below).

This limit, in turn, varies in proportion to the intensity of the future want, though at a much higher level. That is, the stronger the future want, the greater is the maximum potential of secondary energy it can arouse.

Whether there is still another cause of variation in the intensity of secondary energy—something of the nature of a "voluntary accession" of energy—we cannot say. Nor is the supposition necessary for our scheme.

11. If at any time motor resistance exceeds the limit of secondary energy, volitional activity stops. But, then, the dominant future want and the existing secondary energy (excitation) seem to remain in the

---

[41] This seems to be notably the case for short periods. For instance, when an emotion succeeds in breaking through into consciousness for a moment, secondary energy rises, conflicts with it, and may eject it.

field of consciousness and, just as with a present want, to seek another way of arriving at the objective. There is evidence, in these circumstances, of a high state of cortical excitation, supraliminal but unable to flow off. The effects are similar to those of an emotion, but are not due to one (i.e., are not subcortical and need not spread to that level).

12. If at any time emotional drive exceeds secondary energy, inhibition is overcome and consciousness is invaded. The dominant future want is then ousted from conscious attention, secondary energy may subside, and volitional activity may cease.

13. Within these limits (suppositions 11 and 12) there may be a mixture of volitional and emotional behavior. That is, the memory-system may arouse secondary energy sufficient only partially to inhibit the drive from access to cortical motor outlets. This selective inhibition may control and direct the drive into channels chosen by the memory-system, so that the activity is actually energized by primary energy, though it is guided by secondary energy under the influence of the memory-system. This only occurs when the dominant elements in the memory-system are concordant with the prepotent present want (not opposed) or when they yield to it "voluntarily." That is, the behavior is then a release phenomenon; and yet to the extent that release is not due to overpowering of the secondary energy, it is volitional.[42] This phenomenon of mixing or co-operation also frequently involves some degree of energizing of activity by secondary energy. If primary energy flags—usually due to prolonged inability to satisfy the present want and to resulting fatigue—the corresponding future want is ecphorized and may supplement and support the weakening present want. Or, put in another way, when satisfaction of a present want is deferred too long, the present want loses effectiveness; its satisfaction becomes projected into the future. The future satisfaction then corresponds to a future as well as to a present want and the corresponding future want thus comes to participate in the behavior.

14. The sense of effort, being an experience, leaves memories, and

---

[42] This enables us to include in our scheme the whole of our previous analysis of the function of the cortex as a "servant" (guide, director, controller) of the subcortical want system. To the extent that the cortex is not merely overpowered—that is, to the extent that selective inhibition takes place—it can only be because secondary opposes primary energy in detail, if not *in toto*. It canalizes the latter. To the extent that secondary energy operates at all, even only in these selective inhibitory ways, to that extent the form of the behavior is due to the volitional process though its actual energizing may be wholly emotional. Moreover, in the second series of cases given in the text below, secondary energy may even participate in the energizing, going to reinforce failing primary energy.

these become an integral part of the process of conflict in the memory-system. But the sense of effort is the only experience in connection with the generation of secondary energy.

a. The intensity of each of these memories is determined in part by the intensity of the experience and, in part, by the duration of the experience. Moreover, the intensity of the memory may apparently be unduly affected by the fortuitous or gradual increases in intensity which occurred during the experience, so that intensity in memory is overly weighted by these high points.[43]

b. If there are several or many different forms of activity simultaneously or successively available for a single future want, the intensity of the memory of effort for each will be different from that of the others.

15. When any future want has become dominant in consciousness, association will bring up the memory of the sense of effort incurred in the corresponding activity.

a. If the memory of the corresponding sense of effort is more intense than is the future want, then, since the two conflict, the former will be dominant and the future want will be unable to arouse secondary energy and cause behavior.

b. If there are several memories of different forms of activity suitable to the future want, that one which is least intense,[44] and thus offers the least resistance in conflict, will be the first to yield (or be overcome) and thus to resolve the conflict. The others will remain potentially in conflict.

c. By the process of insight (subliminal experiment with various sequences of activity and their results), such forms of activity involving least effort may be composed anew.[45]

16. Adequate provision, being an experience, leaves memories and

[43] This sounds as if it meant that the magnitude (intensity) of the memory is the product of a two-dimensional experience. But, as we shall see, a two-dimensional experience is probably impossible, and a magnitude with two different direct dimensions is probably an illusion. In actual fact, the memory itself may preserve the separate effects of these two dimensions. Thus the memory created during an experience may accumulate over time (become a greater magnitude) whether the intensity of the experience changes or not. Changes in intensity of the experience would merely alter the rate at which the magnitude of the memory is accumulating. We seem to separate the time dimension from the intensity, or rate, dimension. We recall a long or short period of action involving more or less intense effort.
[44] It would be less intense if the experience were less intense for a given duration or were shorter for a given intensity.
[45] That is, insight, while it deals only with actually experienced individual motions, may always compound them into new systems of reactions.

these, too, become an integral part of the process of conflict in the memory system.

a. When, in the course of current experience, adequate provision is reached, this memory is ecphorized by recognition and conflict arises.[46] The memory of adequate provision balances the future want and behavior stops. Or, rather, the memory of effort, having no longer any force to overcome it, comes into play and leads to a clean-cut ending of the activity.

b. Since adequate provision sets the limit upon the duration and intensity of the activity necessary to secure it and so upon the duration and intensity of the sense of effort in each case, it is ultimately this which determines the magnitude of the sense of effort under 14 and 15 above, in so far as that is determined by the dimension, duration.

17. When, under supposition 15a above, the dominant future want is barred from producing effects by reason of a more potent memory of effort for even the shortest and easiest way to secure adequate provision, or when, under 16a above, the recognition of adequate provision has put an end to its activity, the dominance of that future want is lost and the next most potential future want is free to become dominant in its place. This might seem to argue that it is only the excess intensity of a future want over the concomitant memory of effort or the resulting memory of adequate provision which is effective in the competition between future wants. Nevertheless, we shall see reason to believe that is not the case. Apparently the competition between future wants is settled first, and only if it is thereafter taken out of the lists by one of these fully off-setting memories—effort or adequate provision—does any future want fail to exercise its full intensity in competition with the rest. Each is presented in turn in the order of priority, and, unless it is refused an opportunity by reason of a more potent memory of effort or until it ceases to be effective by reason of a counteracting memory of adequate provision, the next in order has no chance to become dominant.[47] An exception to this orderly procedure is, of course, the sudden rise of an especially potent future want due to ecphory by some current experience.

18. During any prolonged activity, or series of actions energized by secondary energy, the level of primary energy changes both regularly and irregularly. Regular changes result chiefly from the recur-

[46] How the measure of adequate provision is originally determined will be set forth in the next chapter.
[47] With the exception of "allied" wants that are members of the same constellation.

ring present wants (hunger, thirst, etc.). Irregular changes are fortuitous and are chiefly due to the quasi-external wants (injury, fear, etc.,
but also watching the circus parade, appearance of beloved, etc.).

a. When the primary energy rises, from any one of these causes,
more secondary energy is required to repress it. If secondary energy is
not thereupon increased, the result is that there is less secondary energy,
for the time being, available to energize the current volitional activity.
The activity flags without ceasing, or signs of hesitancy appear.

b. When and if the primary energy rises to a point above the limit
of secondary energy set by the then dominant future want, the secondary is unable longer to resist the primary and volitional activity
ceases, as under 12 above.

19. During any prolonged activity, or series of actions, there is a
gradual but usually steady rise in the present want we have called
fatigue. While the effect of this is to diminish primary energy and
therefore the amount of secondary energy necessary to repress it, that
is more than offset by the increased resistance due to the fatigue of the
motor outlets and even of the volitional process itself. For, it will be remembered, we have found some reason to believe that the regions of
the central nervous system in which this process takes place are the
most readily fatigable of all.[48] Gradually the net difference between
this declining demand (against emotion) and this rising demand
(against fatigue) for secondary energy increases to such a point that,
though the intensity of secondary energy may also be increased up
to the limit set by the then dominant future want, the latter becomes
inadequate to overcome the former, and volitional activity ceases.[49]

We shall leave the reader to satisfy himself that this purely inferen-

[48] Nevertheless, distinction should be made between the present want, fatigue, whether
its locus is peripheral or central, and the particular form of central fatigue which may
constitute the basis, or be a correlate, of the sense of effort. The former seems to oppose secondary energy; the latter seems only to oppose the instigator of secondary
energy.

[49] For the sake of future reference we may well clarify here the scheme of energetics
as it relates to secondary energy and its two applications, the inhibition of emotion
(primary energy) and the excitation of the motor system. We regard inhibition as a
by-product of excitation. Excitation produced by secondary energy just sufficient to
inhibit primary energy remains subliminal (blocked) so far as the motor system is concerned. This is self-restraint. Even during mental operations (conflict), additional
secondary energy may be required to inhibit (shut out) distractions (sensations endowed with emotional interest). On the other hand, when there is great concentration
(secondary energy) upon a new activity, since excitation produces inhibition as a by-
product, this inhibition is normally adequate, below the level of consciousness, to prevent interruption. But, when the same activity becomes habitual, it requires less secondary energy, which thus produces less by-product inhibition, and interruption will occur

tial hypothesis meets all of the several requirements that we set for it, except the single requirement that it should account for the observed limitations on behavior in response to future wants. As to that single requirement, it will help to clarify matters if we review these limitations here and show how they are explained by the hypothesis.

Adequacy of Provision. Supposition 16 seems to cover this. We assume that, when the current perception of provision recognizes it as equal to the memory of adequate provision, that memory, being recalled, conflicts with and offsets the future want. Behavior then stops short because the memory of effort remains with nothing to overcome it.[50]

Interruption. Intermittent limitations that arise before adequacy of provision has become effective, so that the same activity may be resumed later, may be explained, under our hypothesis, in several ways. The first was mentioned at the end of supposition 17. It is the accidental ecphory of a future want of higher rank in the order of priority, which becomes temporarily dominant, but is soon provided for (for instance, the muezzin is heard). The second was contained in supposition 11. When motor resistance proves greater than secondary energy available and until an easier way is found, action is temporarily

---

more readily unless secondary energy is increased to raise this inhibitory level.

It is probable that these predominantly inhibitory or predominantly excitatory conditions are distinguished in consciousness. One seems to be passive (resisting), and other active (doing).

[50] In this and in several other cases below, the sense of effort, or its memory, seems to function in somewhat the same way that physicists and chemists assume for the resistance which is at the basis of all aperiodic processes. Thus

motion is expressed as $\dfrac{\text{Force}}{\text{Inertia}}$;

electrical current as $\dfrac{\text{E.M.F. (in volts)}}{\text{Resistance (in ohms)}}$;

a chemical reaction is $\dfrac{\text{Chemical Force}}{\text{Chemical Resistance}}$.

As Bayliss puts it (27, 41), "chemical reactions arrive at their point of equilibrium and stop dead at it without overshooting. They are, in fact, aperiodic, like processes in general taking place against a large resistance. This being so, a formula like Ohm's law [above] in electricity must hold."

However, there seems to be a difference in one respect. Whereas all these resistances (denominators above) are independent of the forces (numerators), in our case the resistance seems to be dependent upon and proportionate to the force. Moreover, our resistance does not work against the force itself; rather it works against the instigator of the force only. It is as if the instigator opened a valve which permitted the force to be released or concentrated, as if the counterpressure against the opening of this valve increased the further it was opened (the greater the force released) and as if, when this counterpressure came to exceed the force of the instigator, or the instigator stopped operating, the counterpressure closed it.

suspended. The third was outlined in supposition 12, merely as the rise of primary to a level above secondary energy. As a likely incident in any prolonged activity, that was elaborated under supposition 18 (18a). There it was noted that the interruption may occur fortuitously—as it always does if it occurs in the first two ways mentioned above—when it is the result of the rise of a quasi-external present want or of a conditioned stimulus capable of bringing to prepotence either a quasi-external or an internal want. Or it may occur regularly as a result of the arrival at prepotence of some recurring internal want. The final way was given in supposition 19. It is the fairly regular and absolutely certain interruption as a result of increasing fatigue—in itself a present want, but with an effect opposite to that of the other present wants included in our list.[51]

Priority and Capacity. Supposition 1 adds nothing to our previous conclusion as to an order of priority. That followed from the fact that future wants are mnemonic phenomena and that, as such, the intensities of the memories should bear the same ratio among themselves that was borne by the intensities of the original experiences. However, supposition 17 elaborates that conclusion. It assumes that future wants become dominant in their order of priority, and that, after they have become dominant, they may then "get the hook" if the memory of corresponding effort is more potent, or may be "blacked out" if and when the memory of adequate provision arises. The former case supplies one feature in our general limitation of capacity.[52] It supplies one possible reason why certain future wants never produce behavior. That applies, however, only upon the basis of an individual instance. But that is all we can do at this point; for any collective view of the limitation of capacity must wait until we have completed our full array of competitors—that is, until we have included the effect of peopling the counterfeit future with a long series of instances of each future want projected at different points along the scale of time. That also necessitates the postponement of consideration of those radical changes in capacity which may, for long or short seasons, eliminate practically all behavior in response to present wants.

Economy of Energy. According to several of our suppositions the intensity of the memory of effort is measured by the intensity and

[51] That is, fatigue abstracts rather than presents primary energy.
[52] That is, it does so if these exceptional wants are not members of a constellation. If they are members, as we shall see below, behavior may be adapted to them even if they, by themselves, are incapable of becoming dominant.

duration of the experience (14a); the intensity of the experience, in turn, is proportionate to that of the secondary energy (5) which is required to overcome primary energy and motor resistance (10); the duration of the experience is largely determined by the limitation called adequate provision (16b). Thus the intensity of the memory of effort associated with each form of activity available for a single future want will vary (14b). As a result, and since the memory of effort conflicts with the future want, that program which involves the least effort will be followed (15b), and shorter or easier activities will be devised by insight (15c).[53] As presented in our hypothesis this is no more than saying that, in this as in all other operations of forces, the line of least resistance is followed. When a future want becomes dominant, being faced with several alternative outlets which conflict with it in varying degrees, action will take place through that one which can most readily be overcome.[54]

[53] Both memory and its elaboration, insight, will choose the shortest and easiest ways, not merely the shortest, as in the case of present wants. This for the reason that the memory of effort has, or its intensity is determined by, the rate of the experience (intensity) and its duration. Thus, between two activities involving equal duration, that causing the least intense sense of effort will be chosen, and, between two involving equal intensity of effort, the shortest will be chosen. Any easing process will be chosen if it involves less than compensatory lengthening; any shortening process will be chosen if it involves less than compensatory dis-easing.

We are not suggesting that nature has supplied us with a kindly economizing agency in the form of a sense of effort. It operates only upon the generation of the volitional process. In point of fact, it would doubtless be more kindly if it were a less potent bar to volitional behavior. Neither, in reality, are we introducing a piece of hedonism in disguise. That only appears to be so because we have to accept it as an entity solely on introspective grounds. Even though it appears in this guise and thus suggests hedonism, we have no doubt that, if we understood the neural character of the phenomenon underlying the sense of effort, this aroma of hedonism would prove as entirely inappropriate (or unnecessary) as it did in the case of primary energy of response.

[54] There is one potential discrepancy in this energetic scheme which needs to be cleared up. We are treating the memory of effort as a kind of resistance to the memory of a want (future wants). We are treating primary energy and motor inertia as kinds of resistance to the secondary energy which the dominant future want can arouse if it overpowers the resistance of its concordant memory of effort. Thus the two conflicts are treated as if they took place on different planes and independently of each other. Why, it may be asked, does not the current sense of effort, once the volitional process is commenced, override the mere memory of a want? We have conceded that all memories are much less intense than the corresponding experiences. If so, that must also be true of the memory of the sense of effort. That, as a memory, may fail to disbar the future want as a memory. But, when the new experience of effort begins, that, being much stronger than the memory, would certainly put a stop to the process if it had any intensity to speak of.

This does not occur. If it did, then the volitional process would always stop almost as soon as it started. But that does not prove our energetic scheme rational. It may disclose a flaw in it.

A possible explanation, and one that seems to correspond to the evidence, is this:

Future Labor-saving. While this appears to be related to the preceding in respect of the fact that it also evinces a tendency to the economizing of energy, in this case, as noted above, the tendency only works back from the future. The economy that *will* result leads to an increase of activity now, provided only that such economy exceeds the increased activity now by a sufficient margin. Since, as we shall see, it also appears that the margin of net economy must also grow greater the longer into the future is projected the realization of the net economy, this limitation becomes also related to the next one—to the effect of futurity.

Degree of Futurity. So far as this limitation is concerned, our hypothesis, so far as it has now been developed, seems to furnish no explanation whatever.

4. THE INFLUENCE OF FUTURITY

This appraisal seems to indicate that the several identifications worked out in this chapter furnish an adequate, if wholly inferential, scheme to explain the existence of future wants, their relative excitatory powers, and most of the limitations upon the behavior to which they give rise. The system of limitations turns out to be a complex, not a simple affair, due to several influences rather than to one. As memories, future wants are capable of arousing secondary energy of response which, in turn, is capable up to some limit, of competing with primary energy of response and of energizing the motor apparatus in spite of

---

We have already suggested that the magnitude of the memory of effort depends on the two magnitudes of the experience, its duration and its intensity, or rate. Since the intensity of the experience seems to vary widely during the concomitant volitional process, we may conclude that the intensity of the memory is determined by the average intensity of the experience, or that it is determined by the peak intensity of the experience. But the experience itself, as it proceeds, can represent only one magnitude, intensity or rate. As fast as it passes through the present it becomes a memory only. We may suppose that the intensity of the experience of effort is much less than that of the experience of a want. If so, the memory of effort achieves its power of resisting the memory of a want largely in proportion to its duration and only slightly in proportion to its intensity, whether average or peak. This duration is cumulative, of course, but it is only cumulative in memory.

On that basis, the accumulating memory of effort involved in a current activity being produced by a future want might be conceived ultimately to rise to a magnitude at which it overcame the future want. But why? If it accumulates to a magnitude no greater than it had on previous occasions, and if the memory of that previous occasion did not suffice to disbar the future want, why should it do so now? If it does accumulate to a magnitude that is greater, I am inclined to think it often does have the effect of shutting off the behavior. On the other hand, I believe the behavior is more usually ended by reason of the incapacity of the secondary energy any longer to compete with regular rises in primary energy or gradually rising fatigue.

the inertia of the latter. The limitations we have called interruptions are due chiefly to this competition and this inertia. In part, the limitation called priority and that called capacity are due to the varying potential of the memories in arousing secondary energy in so far as that determines the limit of that energy and therefore the point at which it may no longer be adequate. This secondary energy has, as a concomitant, the sense of effort, and the memory of this experience of effort conflicts with the future wants, both being mnemonic phenomena. The limitation called capacity is, for the rest, due to this feature. So too are those called economy of energy and, so far as it is due to the same cause, future labor-saving. Further, the limitation by reason of adequacy of provision is similar, since it too is due to one memory working against another—first that of adequate provision, then that of effort. However, the hypothesis furnishes us with no explanation of the last limitation, degree of futurity, nor any of the effect of futurity on future labor-saving.

Let us proceed, then, to re-examine this matter of futurity in order to see whether we can determine at least the precise effects of the influence that produces this remaining limitation and thus complete our hypothesis, if only with a wholly inferential entity. First, by way of clarifying the problem, let us recall the conclusions we reached in the previous chapter as to this matter of projection. The future is counterfeit, being no more than a mirror of the past. Nevertheless, it has transferred to it something of the automatic temporal order of memory together with a more or less developed conceptual time-scale. The memories of past wants, when futurity is conferred upon them, are projected along this time-scale. If they were regularly recurring wants in the past, they are projected into the future as regular occurrences and thus at regular intervals of the same length as in the past. Each single kind of future want of this recurrent variety will thus give rise to as many instances as there are intervals in the period of future time considered. Such wants as were found in the past to occur irregularly are, if they are projected at all, projected only as contingencies. They are not projected as regular occurrences, but according to the experience of their frequency per time period, and so as being imminent once or more times at some time during such time period. Each single kind of future want of this contingent variety will thus give rise to as many instances as its frequency requires. However, each instance will tend to be placed at some point—at the beginning or at the middle, or at some actuarily determined stage of the period during which it is apt to occur once—at which provision for it should be ready, if at all. Thus we may visualize an imaginary diagram representing the way projection works. The several future wants are arranged in a plane (two dimensions) in their order of priority. Each is projected in the third dimension along the time-scale into the counterfeit future. Along that scale each is represented by a varying number of dated instances. An instance of each daily recurring want would appear daily on this time-scale. There would be as many instances as there were days as far ahead as the time-scale reached. An instance of each contingent want would appear once for each period during which it was recalled as occurring once. There would be as many instances as there were such periods in the total distance the time-scale reached.

Now, we have accepted the postulate that the effectiveness of future wants in producing behavior diminishes in some way the further into the future they are projected. That is, each of these instances seems to be less effective than its fellow which is placed nearer the present. But, now, as a result of our association of futurity as an influence on future labor-saving—which will be fully confirmed as we proceed—it becomes necessary to suppose that the memory of effort derived from the activity involved in providing for each of these wants also has futurity conferred upon it and is also projected along the time-scale—that, in fact, each instance of a future want has, or may have, an instance of the corresponding memory of effort associated with it. Moreover, it will become increasingly evident that these instances of futurized memories of the sense of effort associated with any particular activity also undergo a similar diminution in effectiveness the further into the future they are projected. Instances of future economizing of effort, like instances of future wants, appear to be less potent to produce behavior *now*, the greater the degree of futurity. Or, we can match the effect of the apparent diminution on these two—the force and the resistance. Since the memory of the sense of effort, when that is projected to a year hence, evidences a tendency to diminish the effectiveness of its resistance in somewhat the same proportion that the effectiveness of the force of the future want projected to a year hence diminishes, the tendency is exhibited to act on the theory, "Sufficient unto the day is the evil thereof." The present resistance of an activity to be conducted *then* seems to be less than the present resistance of the same activity to be conducted *now*, so that the line of least resistance always shows itself as a tendency to defer the activity until *then*.

How can this effect of futurity be explained? We have already agreed that memories cannot lose any of their intensity merely because they are projected further along a purely conceptual time-scale into a counterfeit future. That being true of all memories, it must be true of futurized memories of effort as well as of future wants. If, nevertheless, both do lose effectiveness—the future want, as a force, and the future effort, as a resistance—in rough proportion to their degree of futurity, there must be some other explanation. Let us analyze the problem further. The present effectiveness of a future want in producing activity *now* varies, in the first place, according to its intensity and therefore according to its place in the order of priority. Nevertheless, if the intensity of the memory of the sense of effort experienced during that activity exceeds the intensity of the future want, no activity results; and the activity that offers the least resistance in this respect is always the one produced. Thus the actual working of the system is the result of a set of forces *vs.* a set of resistances. If now, we find it difficult to impute to future wants diminishing intensity proportionate to futurity—that is, to explain the diminution by a decline in the force per time interval—the alternative suggests itself that this diminution, like the selectivity in those cases referred to above, may be explicable by a change in the resistance—that is, by a rise in the resistance per time interval. But it is immediately apparent that the resistance due to the memory of the sense of effort during the activity [55] cannot be responsible here; for an adequate provision for any instance of a particular future want requires no more activity because that instance is projected two years hence than if it is projected one year hence. Moreover, we have already observed that this diminution of present effectiveness affects the memory of the sense of effort as well. That, by self, becomes a continuously lessening line of least resistance the further it is projected. Finally, this secondary resistance, if such it is, must accrue during the interval between the present activity and the date of the instance of the future want, since the diminution in both cases is at least roughly proportionate to that interval.[56] But that is just the

[55] For the sake of brevity, we shall use the phrase duration effort, hereafter, to cover this memory. But both here and there it should be understood to include such volitional effort ("thinking") preliminary to activity as is not merely concerned with determining the dominant future want.

[56] It is like gravity in ballistics. For a given muzzle-velocity, etc., the longer the range the greater will be the effect of gravity in deflecting the projectile from its original aim.

period during which there could be no sense of effort of the kind we have established, since the activity is then finished.

While precise evidence is only available in connection with the most highly evolved forms of behavior in response to future wants and that evidence will not be presented until we come to study these forms in Part II, we are at liberty to use here, on the basis of proof there, certain measurable characteristics of that behavior in order to determine what is the factor responsible for this apparent diminution in the present force of future wants and in the present resistance of future effort. The simplest demonstration can be made with the former. Let us suppose that there become successively available for provision for some future want, four different activities whose respective durations conform to the ratio $5:4:3:2$ units of time. For the sake of simplicity we will also suppose that the intensity of all four is the same. Then the memory of effort involved in the four activities will have the same ratio as above, and this will measure the resistance they offer now to present provision for a future want. We cannot measure these resistances against the force of the want, for we do not know by how much the latter exceeds the former in any particular case. But we can determine the several strategic points at which each ceases to do so.[57] Now, if it were the force of the want that declined with futurity, it would, presumably, do so at some constant fraction of the original force per unit of time projected. If, then, it were found that the first form of activity reached to an instance at a certain distance along the time-scale, while the second form, offering less resistance, reached to an instance further along that scale by a certain number of time units, we would have to assume on the basis of a uniform rate of decline in the force of the want—a constant fraction of the original force per time unit—that the third and fourth forms of activity, since they reduce the present resistance by the same amount as the second does, would reach to instances further along the time-scale by exactly the same number of time units or exactly double the number, respectively.

[57] It has been implicit throughout our analysis that if, for any instance of a future want at a certain degree of futurity the corresponding activity offered too great resistance to permit provision, nevertheless the discovery of a new activity for the same objective by means of experience or insight—which new activity offered less than critical resistance—might permit this want to remain dominant. And this is a matter of common observation. For instance, in medieval times—which seem to us benighted and yet in which human nature was scarcely different from the present—it was notorious that men, unwilling to pay the price of abstinence from sin in order to insure their salvation in the hereafter, were nevertheless quite willing to buy penances on the assurance that these would accomplish the same result.

What we do find is something quite different from that. Each activity, in turn, which offers a resistance less by a uniform amount than its predecessor, extends its reach by a greater distance along the time-scale than did its predecessor. Attempting many formulae and considering all the possible relations to each of the variables, we find one solution which fits, at least as a first approximation. This solution discards the assumption of a diminution in the force of future wants proportionate to the futurity of their instances. Instead, it assumes them to remain of constant force no matter how far they are projected. And this assumption seems to accord with their mnemonic character. In place of this assumption of diminution of force there is substituted one of accretion of resistance. The rate of accrual of this resistance turns out to be a constant fraction of the initial resistance per unit of time. Therefore the quantity of this accrued resistance is measured by the initial resistance, multiplied by this fraction and by the number of units of time in the interval between the present activity and the date of the instance of future want. It is obvious that this explains the discrepancy in our example above. The initial resistance being smaller for each of the activities successively applied, the *rate* of accrual will also be smaller. Therefore, it will take a proportionately longer time interval for each of these activities, successively, to offer sufficient resistance to the uniform force of the future want, to exclude further instances.

This is the first piece of evidence that the diminution in effectiveness we are examining is due, not to a subtraction from the present force of the future want, but to an addition to the present resistance to provision for it.[58] Nevertheless, the additional resistance here imputed cannot arise from an increase in the memory of the sense of effort incurred in experiencing the activity itself. This must be a different form of resistance, even if it is also due to a memory of a sense of some other kind of effort incurred in experience. The intensity of the memory of effort of the first kind accrues during the activity at a certain rate per unit of time (inverse time dimension)—the duration of the initial activity is a direct time dimension, whence can be derived the quantity accrued. The intensity of the memory of effort of the second kind— if it is such—begins to accrue only after the initial activity is finished and again at a certain rate per unit of time (inverse time dimen-

[58] A considerable amount of additional evidence will appear in Chapter 10 and Appendix V, Section A.

sion)—the interval between conclusion of the activity and the date of the instance of future want is a direct time dimension, whence can be derived the quantity accrued. It becomes necessary to assume, therefore, that this second form of resistance is something different from the first.

While we are here clambering around the borders of the unknown and have gone beyond the reach of the psychological scaffolding erected earlier in this chapter, it appears that we have demonstrated here another influence, a Pluto, which must be imputed in order to account for certain vagaries in the behavior of our Neptune—another unidentified entity whose description, at this stage of our knowledge, must be confined to a statement of its effects—an abstraction to which we can only attribute dimensions, because these, like those of the force of gravity, can be inferred from careful observation of the effects.

Nevertheless, we have some hints as to the identification of this entity which, however little positive they are, should not be overlooked. The second kind of resistance must be related to the first kind, for it has as one of its dimensions the magnitude of that first kind. We recall that the first kind is the memory of the sense of effort experienced during (and before) an activity. But, once derived from such an experience, this memory offers resistance *in advance of* a repetition—before the new experience begins. So does the second kind, as we have just seen. The second must offer this resistance in the memory-system —that is, in the same milieu as the first—for it opposes future wants which are solely memories. If so, it must itself be a memory. Nor could it be anything but a memory for, as we have seen, the only psychical entities that accrue over time are memories. If it is a memory, it must derive from experience. But the only experience it could derive from is an experience which takes place in the interval between an activity and the date at which provision for an instance of a future want turns out to be provision for a present want—i.e., the date at which the provision comes to fruition. Finally, we have some faint introspective testimony identifying the only experience that always and only takes place during this interval with the exercise of patience or with volitional processes overcoming impatience. For all these reasons I think we are justified in tentatively classifying this new inferred entity as the memory of an experienced sense of effort of another kind. To summarize and clarify: Instances of future wants have no less force because of greater futurity. They merely meet greater resistance from memories of effort. The effort involved in the activity, duration effort, is no greater because the activity is to be applied to an instance in the distant future than if it were to be applied to one near by. But to this duration effort is added what we may call interval effort. Since that accrues at a rate per unit of time which is some constant fraction of the duration effort, the longer the interval the greater it will be. This has the effect of diminishing the effectiveness of future wants in producing present behavior the greater their futurity. But it does not do so in proportion to the intensity of the future want; rather it does so in proportion to the concomitant duration effort.

This supposition that we are really dealing with memories of two forms or occasions for effort—one arising during the activity (duration effort) and the other arising during the subsequent interval (interval effort)—also greatly simplifies our treatment of the effect of futurity on the memory of duration effort. Future activity offers less resistance now to future wants than does present activity. And, apparently the further the activity is projected into the future, the less resistance does it offer. Yet there is, as we saw, no reason to suppose that the memory of duration effort, nor any other memory, is lessened in intensity because of the degree of futurity to which it is projected. When we introduce interval effort, however, this difficulty is overcome, because the apparent diminution in the resistance of future effort for future wants turns out actually to be an accumulation in total resistance to present effort for future wants. The following statements will make that clear. When a present activity is finished and the sense of effort experienced is laid down in memory at a certain intensity, the experience of interval effort begins. It accrues per unit of time at a rate which is some fraction of the memory of the duration effort. At the end of the interval the accumulation from the experience of interval effort terminates and it becomes a memory of proportionate intensity. Thereafter the memories of the two forms are combined as resistances to repetitions of present activities for future wants. On this basis we can construe the resistance offered by future activity— the duration effort—to be actually precisely the same as that offered by present activity, just as we did with the force exerted by distant future *vs.* near future wants. As in that case, the difference is not due to the lessening resistance of future activity, but to the fact that present activity has added to it the interval effort, so that it presents the sum of both. Future activity offers less resistance than present activity, not because its resistance is decreased in proportion to the interval, but because the resistance of present activity is increased by a supplement proportionate to the interval. This construction also explains the fact that future labor-saving must offer not merely a reduction of activity, *then,* just more than the increase of activity, *now,* but one sufficiently greater to more than offset the addition to the activity *now* of an increment covering the intervening interval effort.

5. SYNTHESIS OF THE LIMITING MECHANISMS

It will be well, at this point, to draw together successively the several influences which our hypothesis supposes to be at work in the system of future wants, both in order to summarize our investigation and to demonstrate the necessity of introducing each of these influences, or some equivalent, if the facts of behavior are to be accounted for. In the first place, our representation assumes a series of future wants decreasing in their intensity as one passes along their order of priority. According to our imaginary diagram, referred to on p. 363, we conceive this series as descending from left to right across a plane (two dimensions). In the third dimension we conceive the several instances of each future want to be projected along the scale of time to definite dates, and at regular intervals or as contingencies. All instances of each want we now assume to be of equal intensity, regardless of their futurity—that is, however far they are actually projected into the counterfeit future. If this were all there were to it, any provision that would be made at all would all be made for the prior want; for, when one of its instances was met by adequate provision, another instance would assume dominance, and so on indefinitely.

However, in the second place, we assume that duration effort is associated with each of these future wants in their descending order of priority. Its intensity is not determined by the want, but by the duration and intensity of the activity required to secure adequate provision for one instance of the want. There is no correlation, then, between the force (intensity) of the several wants and the resistance of the effort associated, respectively, with each of them. In some cases the force may far exceed the effort (resistance); in others the effort (resistance) may exceed the force so that the future want cannot produce behavior. Duration effort is also projected in the third dimension —along the scale of time—so that each instance of each future want has associated with it an instance of the corresponding duration effort to be applied at that time. The addition of this second influence would have no effect, for the instances of the prior want would always be dominant, if we supposed, as above, that the time-scale extended into the indefinite future. Even if, for some reason, it did not, the effect of this second influence would enter to exclude those future wants from producing behavior whose duration effort exceeded their intensity; but, even then, this cause of exclusion would be the effective one only if the available behavior time (capacity) sufficed to reach them in the descending order of priority.

Even with both these influences at play the operation would be entirely hit or miss. Since each instance of each future want would have the same force as each other, and each instance of its corresponding future duration effort would offer the same resistance as each other, there would be no basis for determining which instance would become dominant first. According to the laws of probability, along a scale extending for two years, for instance, individual adequate provisions for a few instances out of many would be apt to be distributed half in each year, and then at irregular intervals.

When, in the third place, we introduce interval effort the picture changes in an unexpected way. We then suppose that to any instance of duration effort whose date is prior to the instance of the want, there is added interval effort, and that this increases the longer the interval between the date of the instance of duration effort (the date when interval effort begins) and the date of the instance of the future want (the date when interval effort ends). But to include this we require a new imaginary diagram; for, now, we are comparing, not the force of instances of want and the resistance of instances of duration effort, both projected to the same point along the time-scale, but instances of duration effort projected not so far as the instances of want, so that there is an interval between them. While the same phenomenon of accrual in total resistance may be conceived to begin wherever we choose to start—that is, at an activity say ten units of time hence for a want twenty units of time hence—it will simplify the presentation if we consider only the relation of immediate duration effort (an activity *now*) to the several instances of future want at greater intervals from *now*. That will make clear that the total resistance offered *now* is based upon present duration effort, but that it contains an increment of interval effort proportionate to that and also to the interval between the present and the date of the instance of future want. Thus the total resistance offered for an activity *now* will increase at a uniform rate the further along the time-scale is the instance of future want for which this activity is providing.

The third influence explains why the most intense future want does not monopolize all present behavior in response to future wants. Just as the duration effort (the second influence) may offer too great resistance and so exclude any behavior in response, *then* or *now*, so the addition of interval effort will necessarily exclude provision *now* for all instances of even the prior future want that lie beyond some point in the time-scale. But, though the first exclusion is fortuitous (i.e., depends upon the duration effort involved in an adequate provision), this second one is certain and invariable. This always cuts off the indefinite future and thus permits the appearance of the phenomenon of exclusion by reason of position in the order of priority, described above, where subordinate wants have insufficient force to overcome the resistance of even an almost simultaneous activity. This also makes it possible for subordinate future wants to become dominant and effective in turn, if aggregate behavior (capacity) suffices to reach down that far in the order of priority.

If, now, we compare the two imaginary diagrams, we see that for each instance of a future want, the resistance offered for activity *now* is greater than that offered for activity *then*, and is greater by exactly the increment due to the interval effort. Activity *then* has no interval effort imposed on it. Activity *now* has a little or much, according as it precedes the date of the future want by a little or by a long time. Since this will also be true, though to a continually lessening extent, of activity at any intervening date prior to that of the instance of the future want, activity at the date of that instance will always show the least total resistance. In other words, the line of least resistance will always be to defer the activity until at least just before the date of the want. Again, if that were all there were to it, we would have arrived at a curious conclusion. For, then, having studied the mechanism that produces behavior in response to future wants, we should have found, in the end, that there can be no such behavior—at least until just before the date of the want. The last of our influences would have completely negatived all the preceding ones. If it operated at all, it would preclude the possibility that the whole mechanism, however elaborate, however capable and however ready, should ever go into action.[59]

Obviously, since there is behavior in response to future wants, there must be still one more factor at play. We are going to investigate that factor in detail in Part II.[60] Suffice it to say here that it consists in the discovery by experience or insight that, when the date of the instance of the future want arrives, the activity will either be impossible or will be greater than it need be by more than enough to cover the interval effort in the meantime. In the first case, activity *then* is no longer the line of least resistance, simply because it has disappeared as an alternative. The choice is either now or never. In the second case, activity *then* is no longer the line of least resistance because a new combination of some activity *now* with some activity *then* offers less total resistance, in spite of the increment of interval effort in the former, than does the old activity *then* by itself. The choice is either both *now* and *then* and easier, or only *then* and harder. Thus the effect of this final factor is selectively to handicap the usual line of least resistance so that it becomes no longer effective as a competitor. Whenever that particular factor comes into play it negatives the negativing. Then behavior in response to future wants does occur—and only then. When it does occur, it conforms precisely to the pattern that would be produced by our hypothetical apparatus, with its several influences, as that has been outlined heretofore.

To use a simile, we have been analyzing an organ. We have examined its several ranks of pipes, its stops, its bellows, etc. We have even found that the air pressure is sufficient. But, as we would expect with an organ, since all the keys are up, it does not sound. The whole apparatus is at a standstill—neutralizing itself, as it were. All that is needed, however, is an organist who will press down the keys in order to *release* the organ. Then it will play whatever tune the organist chooses. But,

[59] The analysis up to this *impasse* also shows, however, what a large portion of the apparatus and operation may be general in the animal world and still have no overt effects. It makes out of the influence which we are now going to consider the critical point. Animals, or men, not subject to that influence would evince no behavior in response to future wants, no matter how completely they were furnished with the apparatus and subject to all the other influences.

[60] For only then will we be in position to build a complete analysis of the competition in the whole field. This competition includes that between present and future wants, between future wants of different position in the order of priority but of the same degree of futurity, between instances of the same future want with different degrees of futurity, and finally between activities now with different duration effort as well as between those of the same duration effort but with different increments of interval effort.

though it plays his tune, it does it in its own way, strictly according to the laws of its internal organization. So our final factor, like the organist, only releases the mechanism of future wants. It sets the pattern; the mechanism determines what behavior is released within that pattern.

The introduction of the second form of effort—interval effort—completes our scheme so far as we can go with it at this stage of our inquiry. The scheme is rational in the sense that it outlines a system of energetics which would work in the way the broad aspects of observed behavior indicate the mechanisms do work—subject only to the condition that some part of it be released to work at all. The identifications and the entities—forces and resistances—which entered one by one as we proceeded, had each a less secure foundation in physiological evidence than the previous one until we came, at the end, to one which is, at the present, almost wholly inferential. Nevertheless, none of the scheme is incompatible with what we do know of the central nervous system. In order to clinch this last statement, and particularly to show that the scheme here drawn is not inconsistent with—in fact, dovetails into—the scheme of present wants in its neurophysiological aspect, and in order to suggest certain other possible or probable neurophysiological bases for the scheme of future wants, we shall, in the following section, undertake a brief restatement of the future want system in its relation to the present want system in terms of the anatomy and physiology of the brain.

C. THE NEUROPHYSIOLOGY OF FUTURE *vs.* PRESENT WANTS

I. THE LOCUS OF THE FUTURE WANT MECHANISMS

Implicit in our entire examination of future wants, their nature and their mechanisms, as it has developed in this and the preceding chapter, is the fact that they are exclusively cortical phenomena, having no existence outside that region and involving no other apparatus unless and until they result in overt behavior. That completely and sharply differentiates future wants from present wants; for the latter are, on the contrary, primarily peripheral (somatic) and subcortical, if they are actual, and primarily subcortical, if they are surrogate. However, the differentiation is not so sharp when it comes to the apparatus used by present wants; for, though the subcortical and peripheral mechanisms suffice for present wants among lower animals, the highest mammals require, and all animals utilize, the cortical apparatus as part of the exterofective mechanism for present wants, if overt behavior is required; and it is the same cortical system in which future wants exist that produces surrogate present wants. Thus present wants trench on the mechanisms of future wants (cortical); but future wants do not trench at all on the mechanisms of present wants (peripheral and subcortical). In spite of this overlapping as to apparatus used, so far as locus is concerned future wants are exclusively cortical and present wants exclusively subcortical.

Throughout our study we have repeatedly called attention to the fact that there is no special function in the cortex that is wholly absent elsewhere in the central nervous system. The cortex is entirely a product of the evolution of that system.[1] It is possible that, in those species in which it has become highly evolved it now monopolizes certain functions that were formerly general. Such, for instance, may be consciousness.[2] But, for the most part, the differences between this highest level and all lower levels are differences in degree. The cortex is far more "differentiated" (Hughlings Jackson), far less "organized" (Jackson) and far more accessible to the effects of external fact.[3] However, though these differences are almost wholly differences in degree, the future want system only arises, as a product of such differences, when they are reaching their maximum development. For it is a fact that, when the cortex is inoperative, the future want system does not operate either; and it is also a fact that the evidence of the existence of such a system, as we proceed up the phylogenetic scale to man, is roughly proportionate to the development of the cortex, rather than to any other criterion such as size, strength, energy, etc.[4]

The exclusively cortical character of future wants helps to confirm our identification of them as mnemonic phenomena. In the extensive

[1] We must not assume that the lowest animals operate without the functions of the cortex, but only that they have a less functionally developed cortex or its homologue. Nor has the anthropoid, with his new brain, something which is functionally new, but only one which is greatly developed as compared with his old brain.

[2] The fact that, in man, the new brain and the old brain have different functions now does not argue that, at the phylogenetic stage in which the old brain was the only brain, it did not include all the functions now carried on by the new brain.

[3] Sherrington says (375, 352), "in the higher [animal] types there is based upon the 'distance-receptors' a relatively enormous neural superstructure possessing million-sided connections with multitudinous other nervous arcs." As we have noted, Hughlings Jackson held that it is these "distance-receptors" (chiefly sight and hearing), which are almost exclusively cortical, that constitute the two principal bases for the neural processes we call thinking. Thus it is chiefly this extraordinary accessibility to external fact that makes the brain of Homo sapiens sapient—that is, "discerning."

[4] It is also notable that behavior in response to future wants seems to be confined to animals who sit up, or even stand up, and use their forelegs for manipulation.

class of mnemic phenomena, as outlined by Semon, we have distinguished those engrams that are "individually acquired." He says that "a strictly definite localization of the individually acquired engrams" is generally imputed to the cerebral cortex.[5] But this is not quite true. Instead, in warm-blooded animals, "the individually acquired memory is predominantly, though by no means exclusively, localized in the cerebrum" (cortex), for he thinks that complex acts, become habitual, "are localized in subcortical portions of the central nervous system."[6] So far as conscious memory is concerned, however, this involves no exception, since such acts, though individually acquired, have, when they became habitual, passed out of conscious memory. It is true, then, that conscious memory is an exclusively cortical phenomenon. Its contents consist of the effects of experiences in forms which are not appreciable at lower levels, though these effects seem to be colored by the reactions of lower levels to these experiences (emotional endowment).

By assuming that the cortex of the cerebrum in the Vertebrata gradually evolved into a kind of "multiplicator" of the excitations, we can best understand the exclusive position which, according to the findings of comparative anatomy, of physiology, and of pathology, it occupies in relation both to consciousness and to the individually acquired engram-stock. For it is to those excitations which have entered into the cerebral cortex and have reached their maximum strength there that, from the point of view of introspection, conscious sensations correspond.[7]

Since the development of the cortex takes the form of increase of stimulus-receptivity and of engraphic power, which determines the increase of "intelligence," it follows that it is the locus of the most pronounced and most ecphorable engrams—that is, of conscious memory. Within the cortex, the fact that the incoming paths are definite implies a certain degree of localization.[8] But, at most, the localization of individual memories is only graduated outward from a central focus for each.[9]

[5] Semon, 368, 119. This because of loss of memory as a result of cortical degeneration.
[6] Ibid., 127–128. He says (ibid., 128) that, among decorticate animals, hearing and vision and all acquired habitual motions such as flying and running are "practically unimpaired." This shows that these "complicated reactions of flying and running" have become localized subcortically because of frequent recurrence. However, we have seen good reason to doubt that this is true in the case of man, all of whose acquired skillful acts require the cortical motor mechanism. But it is unnecessary to debate the matter since we have Semon's support for the next point.
[7] Semon, 368, 126–127.   [8] Ibid., 120.
[9] Ibid., 128. "The notion that . . . engrams are so localized in the brain that each cerebral cell represents, so to speak, a drawer for each single 'memory-image' " has been "re-

When the cortex is removed, animals lose "recognition," because the ability to compare the present with homophonous past objects (stimuli) is gone.[10] For the same reason, the difference between the whole animal and the hemisphereless one is "that the one obeys absent, the other only present, objects." [11] As a result, futurity disappears. "An animal with hemispheres acts in anticipation of future things"— "from consideration of distant good and ill." An animal without them does not.[12] So, too, the effects of conditioning disappear in so far as the reception of the conditioned stimulus is dependent on cortical sensory apparatus or in so far as the conditioning has failed as yet to create a subcortical engram or habit. It follows, then, that all the dependencies of conscious memory—recognition, effectiveness *in absentia*, futurizing, and almost all the conditioning process—are equally as exclusively cortical phenomena.

The exclusively cortical character of future wants also helps to confirm our identification of them as volitional phenomena. All "voluntary contraction [of muscles] involves *the setting up* of *impulses* in the cortex of the brain." [13] Moreover, when the cerebrum "is removed, though coördinated locomotor activities are still possible, the power of 'voluntary' inhibition of these activities is lost, and with this is lost the power of 'voluntary' excitation of them." [14] That is, as we concluded in Appendix II, Sect. F 1, "whatever it may mean and whatever it may involve, action of any kind which is regarded as volitional, as opposed to automatic, most certainly can take its efferent origin in the cortex alone." [15] The same is true of the part of the volitional process

linquished as absolutely untenable," "discarded by every scientific man who specializes in the localisation of cerebral function," and is "completely obsolete"—i.e., among the "mythological views" and "antiquated notions" now discarded (*ibid.*, 284).

[10] *Ibid.*, 128.

[11] William James (*220*, I, 20): "The hemispheres would then seem to be the seat of memory."

[12] William James, *220*, I, 26.

[13] Fulton (*158*, 483) quoting H. Piper (*Arch. Anat. u. Physiol.* 1909, 491-498).

[14] Fulton, *158*, 528.

[15] If Hughlings Jackson's supposition turns out to be correct, it may be necessary to refine this down still further—that is, to localize the volitional process in the cortex of the left hemisphere only, for the right-handed. He opined (*216*, II, 73-74) that, since "the higher in the scale of intellectual life the less of a duplicate are the two halves" of the cortex in respect of unsymmetricalness of convolutions, the two halves are not mere duplicates. There is a difference in the quality of representation in each hemisphere of the other side of the body (contralateral), for the left side suffers later than the right from injury to either hemisphere. He thought this indicated a different "order of representation," the right running from voluntary to automatic and the left from automatic to voluntary. Even in speech he held that the right hemisphere contained the automatic mechanism, for the loss of the left hemisphere seems to leave this intact (*ibid.*, I, 65).

that precedes action. "No animal without it [the cortex] can deliberate, pause, postpone, nicely weigh one motive against another, or compare." [16] Finally, the exclusively cortical character of future wants helps to confirm our identification of them, or their behavior, as effortful phenomena. That is, it does so if, as Waller supposed, the sense of effort as part of the volitional process is related to an exceptionally high degree of fatigability. "There is ample evidence for believing that the process by which nervous impulses are controlled at the higher levels of integration [the cortex] is one eminently susceptible of fatigue.[17]

All this, being interpreted, signifies that the neural processes of which future wants consist, or to which they are directly related, are cortical processes only and that the evidence for their exclusive cortical character is derived independently of, and is not dependent on, the evidence that future wants themselves are wholly cortical.

2. THE PREFRONTAL AREAS AND FUTURE WANTS

At many stages since the beginning of this study we have been led by suggestive points into intriguing speculations about the function of the prefrontal areas of the cortex—that formation which has lain behind and has produced "the godlike forehead" of every "rapt" and "heaven-eyed creature," whether he were poet, philosopher, or scientist. The most plausible interpretation of the very limited set of facts we have about these areas led us to a highly tentative and rather vague hypothesis—a mere groping in the direction that seems to be indicated.

According to this hypothesis the prefrontal areas constitute the cortical correspondent (almost homologue) of the subcortical hypothalamus. As such, they act as the local representative in the cortex of the internal milieu, though that milieu is also represented by mobs of intruding and vociferous delegates from the hypothalamus who invade the sacred precincts and are difficult to control. Being far more highly evolved than their primitive subcortical correspondent the prefrontal areas become, so to speak, the *educated* hypothalamus. That suggests a resemblance to Freud's metapsychological Super-ego—the repository of the end-products of infantile relations with the parents.

[16] William James, *220*, I, 21.
[17] Fulton, *158*, 483. Probably this, the voluntary, effect is to smooth out the contractions, for the voluntary system fatigues soonest, and voluntary fatigue admits clonus or "fatigue tremor" (i.e., by reason of the "partial removal of the higher influence"; *ibid.*, 490).

The prefrontal areas have private lines of communication, both ways, direct to the hypothalamus. Over the incoming lines, they appear to keep in touch with the internal milieu, at least indirectly through the hypothalamus. Over the outgoing lines they appear to be able to control (inhibit), within limits, the excitation of the hypothalamus and therefore to be the only cortical agency capable of suppressing emotion at its source. In view of this fact we suggested [18] that the prefrontal areas may play some part in initiating and maintaining deliberative conflict in the cortex in so far as that requires the temporary reduction or suppression of excitement in the hypothalamus in order that emotion may not immediately carry the day. Thus we guessed [19] that these areas may be the "educable focus of deliberate behavior."

Being intimately connected with all the rest of the cortex—or at least with all so-called association areas—the prefrontal areas are far closer to the external milieu than is the hypothalamus. Whereas the latter must depend for its external impressions upon a crude subcortical exteroceptive system, or upon blind re-excitations produced by cortically received stimuli that have become conditioned, the former are directly accessible not only to the subtlest impressions of external facts as registered in the sensory cortex but also to the vast store of conscious memories laid down by past experiences of these facts and to all the orderings and elaborations constructed out of them.

From the deficiency in conscious attention, in recent memory, and in learning (new conditioning) which results from their bilateral ablation or injury, we made the inference that the prefrontal areas constitute the more highly specialized agency for selecting the details of the external scene to which to attend and therefore for discriminating among them by way of recognition of likeness and differences, or homophony. If so, the defect in recent memory would be explained, by our subsequent examination of mnemic phenomena, as a lack of homophonous ecphory due to failure to file the recent impression with its fellows. In turn that led us to relate the prefrontal areas to the process of establishing new conditioned stimuli, as if they acted as a sort of catalytic agent in the original endowment of a sensorimotor impression with the current emotion.[20]

Finally,[21] we suggested the possibility that what we are calling the volitional process may be similar to, or even the beginning of, the processes of conditioning and learning, and we stated that this pos-

[18] See Appendix II, Section G 4.   [19] See Appendix II, Section H 1.
[20] See Appendix II, Section G 4.   [21] See p. 317 ff.

sibility "will give rise, further in our discussion, to consideration of its possible implications."

Let us now draw these several threads together into a skein, if not into a neatly woven fabric. We have concluded that the essence of the volitional process is probably the concentration of conscious attention and the maintenance of some particular content unchanged within the focus of that attention. We have also concluded that the point of access of the current emotion to the cortex is at the locus of consciousness—probably the left cingular gyrus in the right-handed. If so, does it not seem likely that the emotional endowment of the details of conscious experience, in process of being laid down as engrams, takes place at that point, and that the quantity of endowment of each engram, for any given intensity of emotion, is, first, proportionate to the then degree of concentration of conscious attention and, second, to the proximity to the focus of that attention in which the detail of experience appears. That interpretation would make of the volitional process the initiating agency in the investing of a sensation, or its engram, with the current emotion which we have supposed to be the essence of conditioning. After discriminated and homophonous experiences had been repeated often enough, there would be sufficient emotional endowment in the accumulating series so that, on recognition and revival, a new experience alone could direct conscious attention, without the intervention of the volitional process—direct it in the same way that occurs with something new which is intrinsically exciting because of its novelty (i.e., "investigatory reflex" or our alert). That interpretation would also presume that, in the absence of a current emotion—because it did not exist or was shut out of consciousness—or after the process of unconditioning had divested the current sensations and their revived engrams of emotional content, the volitional process could take place with little or no emotional interference or significance. Since, in fact, memories, when not revived by a current homophonous sensation, appear to be weak in their emotional effects, and since it is just such memories that we have assumed as the chief content of consciousness during volition, it might well prove true that the volitional process would more usually be free from emotion, though, at times, it also served as the initiating agency for emotional conditioning. This dual function would also explain the many parallelisms between the establishment of volitional behavior and the establishment of emotionally conditioned behavior.

This argument carries us back around the circle. When one pursues two independent lines of investigation, from different starting points and at different levels, and ends up with two entities, the names of which are different, the provenances of which are different, but which in other respects appear to be identical, it is natural to examine the question whether or not one has been dealing in both cases with one and the same thing. We have already found reason to think that the prefrontal areas have a special function in new emotional conditioning —act as some sort of catalytic agent therein. But is not the part we have just assigned, in that connection, even so tentatively, to the volitional process precisely that of a catalytic agent? Does not this convergence or identification of the two functions suggest that the prefrontal areas may have some very specific relation to, or function in, the volitional process? Throughout our examination of the latter we always left open the possibility that there might be some source for the secondary neural energy that is apparently available to the cortex, other than the stream of awakeness—some source whose energy gives rise to specific patterns, not merely to tonicity. However, even if the energy itself consisted of the diffuse excitation to which the stream of awakeness appears to give rise, it seemed necessary to suppose some agency capable of concentrating it and thereby making it effective. We considered the possibility that this agency is the content of consciousness itself— chiefly the memory-system—and that its faculty in this respect is a volitional analogue to emotional "interest." But in this respect, too, we left open the alternative possibility that there is another agency, external to consciousness, which concentrates either its own specific excitation, or the non-specific energy of awakeness. Presumably this agency, too, would require some faculty analogous to emotional "interest"—some system of valences that determined the distribution of its effect. We have now merely to suggest the second possibility, alternative to the one previously set forth, that the prefrontal areas are either both the energizing and the concentrating agency in the volitional process or that they are the latter only.

There is no use trying to determine the issue between the previous possibility and this new one. Nor is it necessary, for our purposes, to do so. All we do care to accomplish is to set forward the alternative as a potential claimant to one or both functions. The prefrontal areas appear to have a private source of excitation, arising also in the hypothalamus, but more temperate than the emotional stream, and elaborated and refined. They could, then, constitute the proximate source of secondary neural energy of response, and this would take the form of specific and highly selective excitations adding their strength to the weak excitation of particular memories and thus building up a supraliminal force. Or these areas could, on the other hand, be chiefly the means of concentrating the stream of awakeness because of some faculty analogous to emotional "interest." There is a pretty symmetry in supposing that the cortical analogue of the hypothalamus is its educated rival as well as mentor, and that the functions of the two parallel each other, though at different levels; the one would control secondary, the other primary, energy of response; the one would endow memory and sensation with its own refined value-system, the other with the "interest" arising directly from organismic interests; the one would produce the volitional process and volitional behavior, the other emotion and emotional behavior; the meeting point of the two, and their point of conflict, would be the locus of consciousness, where, then, not two only, but, as already suggested, three confluent streams would meet. But symmetry is not proof. The only value of the suggestion is its suggestiveness. It leaves open the door to further study; it invites the assemblage and consideration of new evidence; but it also enlarges the horizon and identifies a particular sector, within the new but beyond the old horizon, as being especially worthy of investigation.

D. ANALYTICAL SCHEME OF FUTURE COMPARED WITH PRESENT WANTS

1. GENERAL CONTRAST

It is useful to have an hypothesis, however purely hypothetical it is, which is consonant with our knowledge of the nervous system, with our observations of behavior and with our introspections. We cannot prove it; we cannot argue from it; all we can say is that it is plausible so far as we now know. But, if it is internally consistent (i.e., does not work both ways) and externally consistent (i.e., fits the three orders of fact—neurophysiology, behavior, and introspection), it helps us to *organize* our present knowledge and serves as a scaffolding in which to insert modifications as our knowledge enlarges, until, when it is repaired beyond recognition, a new hypothesis emerges or is substituted. We may now recapitulate the hypothesis developed in this and the previous chapter.

Identification of future wants as phenomena of conscious memory accounts for the fact that the list of future wants duplicates that of present wants;[1] that future wants are organized into a duplicate of the order of priority of present wants; that each future want is less potent than its corresponding present want; and that the behavior to which future wants give rise does not include the appropriate consummatory reactions. Identification of future wants as phenomena of the volitional process accounts for the fact that they occur (are ecphorized) in the absence of the corresponding present want or of a stimulus conditioned to that want; and that, in spite of their intrinsic weakness, they are capable of initiating behavior and even of competing with present wants. Identification of the sense of effort with the volitional process accounts for the fact that behavior in response to future wants stops when adequate provision is made; that a limitation is set upon it in terms of duration of the precurrent reactions; and that a further limitation is set upon it in terms of the interval between the precurrent and the ultimate consummatory reactions.

In order to summarize our results at this stage in our investigation, we shall now set up a systematic contrast between future and present wants in the several aspects and characteristics in which we have examined the two.

a. Present wants, if actual, are due to variations or tendencies away from homeostasis in the body which, if integrated activities are required for restoration of homeostasis, set up excitation (or depression) in the old brain; if surrogate, only the latter condition occurs. Future wants consist of conscious memories in the new brain, arising from the past experiences of present wants, and have no other existence or origin.

b. Present wants lead to behavior that has been divided into two parts, precurrent and consummatory. Only the latter includes the process of satisfaction of the want. Future wants produce precurrent reactions only and therefore involve no satisfactions. When, at the end of an interval—perhaps a long interval—the appropriate consumma-

---

[1] Because we have limited our consideration of present wants to those as to which we have physiological evidence, we are evading the question whether all wants are somatic in origin—that is, conversely, whether there are some that are purely cerebral. If there are, we would assume that they are future wants corresponding to no present want. It would then be difficult, if not impossible, to account for their origin under our hypothesis, unless we supposed them to be compound constructions in the memory-system of which only the parts had been experienced.

tory reactions take place it is because the corresponding present want has recurred.[2]

c. The determination of prepotence among present wants, at the level of integrated behavior, is prompt; only a single want, even among members of a constellation, can become prepotent there at one moment; and the mode of hypothalamic excitation so set up cannot be diverted to an objective inappropriate to the satisfaction of that single want.[3] The determination of dominance among future wants entails delay and cortical conflict; since that involves and permits the conjunction of many "allied" wants—that is, members of a constellation whose types of behavior are not "antagonistic"—it is possible for a whole constellation to be present in consciousness along with the major (dominant) want; the major objective will then be fixed by the "prepotent" want, but the behavior may be modified to include more or less of the minor objectives of the lesser members of the constellation.[4]

d. Present wants are involuntary phenomena, and the complete gamut of their chains of cause and effect may be wholly unconscious, except as these effects cause emotions or sensations which invade consciousness. Future wants have no existence except in consciousness and have no effects other than voluntary (volitional) effects, including

[2] We have already (Chapter 3) found it difficult to identify the consummatory reaction in many cases. This is particularly true of wants of prevention. But our distinction here applies quite sharply and definitely to these wants. When the object or condition which would produce such a want is present but not yet effective, in all probability it results in a surrogate present want. That, in turn, may result in behavior (precurrent) which prevents the actual want by leading to the *immediate* avoidance of the object or condition that would produce it. Consummation consists in this prevention or in the cessation of the surrogate want. When the object or condition is not present, but is only remembered, a future want may arise which leads to similar behavior (precurrent). But then the behavior leads to the *future* avoidance of the object or condition, and consummation does not occur until the avoidance actually occurs. If one raises his umbrella when it rains, he is driven by a present want; if he takes it with him because it may rain, he is driven by a future want—and only a contingent one at that.

[3] Healy *et al.* (*185, 248*) quote Jung (*Two Essays on Analytical Psychology*) to the effect that, "It does not lie in our power to transfer disposable energy at pleasure to a rationally chosen subject." As to primary neural energy we agree. And "sublimation" is not really an exception. In the first place, they also quote Ernest Jones, who says, "Experience teaches us that there is a considerable stereotypy in the forms that sublimation of a given tendency takes." In the second place, they say that sublimation of infantile sexual aims—which are, in Freud's phrase, "inhibited in their aim" (*zielgehemmte*)—constitutes an exchange for interests or modes which are *psychically related* only.

[4] This point, implicit in certain previous conclusions, will be fully developed as we proceed.

in the latter habitual actions over which volition exercises only strategic control.

e. Under our definition we have classed as present wants all causes capable of producing excitement or depression (emotional states) in the hypothalamus. Therefore, all present wants and only present wants can give rise to primary neural energy of response. Conversely, future wants are defined as causes capable, in the volitional process, of giving rise to (or utilizing or concentrating) that inferential entity which we have named secondary neural energy of response.

f. Since we have confined the term "emotion" to primary energy in its various phases—emotional state, emotion or emotional experience, and emotional behavior—we are assuming that present wants are all, and are the only, emotional phenomena. Conversely, future wants are themselves non-emotional, do not give rise to new emotional experiences, and the behavior they cause is non-emotional behavior.[5]

g. The generation of primary energy of response is not attended with any sense of effort. Therefore, present wants and all behavior, in so far as this is energized by primary energy, are effortless. The generation (or concentration) of secondary energy of response carries with it a sense of effort ("strain"). Therefore, future wants, their conflicts in consciousness either among themselves or with emotion, and the voluntary behavior to which they give rise are all effortful. In so far as this behavior is composed of habitual actions it is little or not at all effortful except in its strategic phases. But even such behavior may become effortful if, in its course, conflicts with emotions, including that of fatigue, arise anew.

h. The present want automatically arouses primary energy which produces behavior that may satisfy the want. The process lays down

---

[5] This flat dichotomy will be elaborated in the next subsection where we begin to combine our two hitherto almost wholly separate categories in mixed behavior—that is, as the two components in behavior already established in the third chapter.

So far as behavior is concerned, the dichotomy is not too flat; so far as conscious experience is concerned, it probably is. We have said that memories become endowed with emotion. If the total homophonous endowment is sufficient to produce a replica in the hypothalamus—that is, to become prepotent there—a present want arises; if it is not, only a future want can exist. In both cases, there may be experience of emotion —in the one, a newly felt emotion, in the other, the memory of emotion as part of a sensation or other impression. But the criterion of behavior proves which occurs. If a present want is produced, a consummatory reaction is indicated; if only a future want is produced, there will be no consummatory reaction. Our young piano-player, still learning his scales, stops when his hour is up; once become accomplished, he may practice his scales first, but that leads, before the end, to some playing for enjoyment.

a memory; but the memory is the experience of the want, not that of the production or expenditure of primary energy. That memory becomes a future want. It, too, gives rise, with the aid of secondary energy, to behavior. That process, as well, lays down a memory; but here the memory relates, not to the want but to the sense of effort involved in the generation (or concentration) of secondary energy involved in the behavior. Thus, the behavior induced by present wants offers no opposition to those wants either in experience or in memory; but the behavior induced by future wants, when experienced, produces in memory an opposition which is thereafter balanced against the want, permitting or preventing a repetition of the behavior. This we have called a process of calculation conducted by insight.

i. Present wants alone give rise to the subcortical component in behavior. Future wants do not alone give rise to the cortical component; for, so far as the cortex is concerned, it is more or less *subject to* present wants via the emotional stream. On the other hand, the cortex is autonomous with reference to future wants. In so far as the cortex is furnished from outside with the energy of present wants, behavior may result merely from a "release" of that energy. Its own energy it must mobilize; and that process tires far more quickly.

2. COMPETITION AND CO-OPERATION BETWEEN PRESENT AND FUTURE WANTS

Since our ultimate purpose in this study is analysis we shall find it more useful as we proceed to treat the behavior generated by present and by future wants, respectively, as if they were separate phenomena. It will appear that, in economic life, the latter looms up as the major element in precurrent reactions even though it may be regarded as the less important element, since it includes no consummation. However, among normal adult men, it is probably unusual to have a pure case of either type of behavior. Or, rather, most behavior, and perhaps all behavior for a part of the time it is going on, contains a mixture of the two components.[6] Only at the two extremes does one or the other

[6] It is necessary to make it clear, here, that we do not mean that more than one present want can be prepotent at one time, or that more than one future want can be dominant as a result of the resolution of cortical conflict. What we do mean is that there may be, and usually are, at the same time a prepotent present want and a dominant future want. Moreover, while the prepotent present want excludes all other present wants for the time, the dominant future want may have many "allied" future wants supporting, amending, and directing the behavior which is their resultant, however much the dominant future want alone has determined the strategic objective. An excellent report on

type exist alone. On the one hand, at the height of the orgasm, say, only the present want is operative and the whole cortical apparatus is swamped under a tidal wave of emotion. On the other hand, there are times of pure drudgery when, with not even an overtone of "interest," one goes through with a task that one has set oneself. Then emotion is non-existent, or completely excluded from consciousness, and the future want is acting in its purest form. Nevertheless, when, in between these two extremes, a present and one or more future wants are combining in energizing and directing behavior, the objective is always fixed by one or the other, the prepotent present want or the dominant future want. For that reason and on that basis we can analytically divide behavior into the two classes, though, in each, observation suggests that usually the other cause of behavior is participating in some degree.

For the purpose of reconciling our analysis with our observations, once and for all, so that from now on we can ignore these complications, we will, at this point, consider briefly the various forms which are taken by competition and co-operation between present and future wants. The following statement may not exhaust the possibilities, but it includes all the cases of mixed motivation that we have unearthed in our previous examination.

When the prepotent present want is determining the objective of behavior:

a. There may be a "release" of the present want through the total withdrawal of cortical inhibition and without cortical guidance of the excitation. The result is emotional behavior which, nevertheless, is in a sense voluntary if the "consent" to the "release" is a result of the volitional process.

b. There may be a "release" of the present want through selective withdrawal of cortical inhibition and with cortical guidance or even reinforcement of the excitation. The energizing is then chiefly done by the present want and the behavior is, to that extent, involuntary. The cortex is then said to be acting as the "servant" of the drive (emotion, or present want). But, since, for even selective inhibition and of course for any reinforcement, positive cortical excitation somewhere is necessary, such behavior is always partially energized by future wants,

---

the varied effects of reinforcement by "allied" reflexes, even at the simplest level, is contained in Sherrington, 375, Lectures V and VI. If such amendments occur at that level how much more are they to be expected at the highest level.

and that energy as well as all the form of the behavior, are the effects of the volitional process and, as such, voluntary.

c. The emotional energy of the present want may flag, if consummation is too long delayed. If, then, the corresponding future want is aroused, there is a blending of the two, as we have noted. The future comes to the aid of the present want in energizing the behavior. This may merely supplement the weakening primary energy; or it may wholly replace it if, in the process, the present want loses prepotence by interference. For then the future want may suppress the succeeding present want and bring things to the point at which consummation is possible. If, then, the present want can regain prepotence, it can conclude the procedure with consummation.[7]

When the dominant future want is determining the objective of behavior:

d. It is possible that one or more ancillary present wants, themselves to be satisfied by some features of the precurrent reactions produced by the future want, may become prepotent at different stages or moments in the process and help to energize the behavior. When they do so, the effortful character of the behavior is reduced, less secondary energy is required, certain emotional signs appear,[8] and there may

[7] We have classed imposed wants as present wants. But we cannot be sure that, after habituation to the taught behavior, the *domesticated* animal or man may not, in part, be driven by corresponding future wants—that is, by memories, arousing the volitional process and leading to effortful behavior. If so, domestication has spread the effectiveness of the future want system in the human and animal world. At least, it has done so when the ultimate motivation is imposed, even if it has not put it on a self-starting basis. We shall have occasion to refer to this possibility in a later chapter (Chapter 9), where it will seem necessary to distinguish between spirited (emotional) responses, such as that of a horse to "giddap," and the patient continuous exertions which are difficult to distinguish from those of men when they are voluntarily "working" toward some distant and self-imposed objective.

Another occasion in which it is difficult to establish a line of distinction is when suggestion, persuasion, etc., enter. Are the actual motivations thus aroused imposed present wants, or are they future wants?

[8] We assume that this is the explanation of the appearance of "zest," etc., in purely volitional and therefore intrinsically effortful behavior directed by a future want. But, we cannot go further than this obviously necessary allowance for the appearance of ancillary wants. We cannot agree that a future want is also itself an emotional phenomenon or that it arouses, as conditioned current stimuli may do, an emotional state (replica).

Rignano (and others) makes all motivation "affective." For instance, he says (345, 164): "Further, intelligence, by the ever increasing power which it confers of foreseeing internal psychic events, gives rise to a whole series of new affectivities, which express themselves as desires to prevent the eventual disappointment of future affectivities. Thus, for instance, the fear of future hunger gives rise, even in a satiated man, to an 'affectivity' directed towards the preservation and retention in his own possession of stored food, and, as a consequence, to the general 'sentiment of property,' and to a thousand other desires which civilized man experiences, and which develop in him in

even be concurrent emotional experiences, though usually of a mild order.

Thus, we see that the two systems only co-operate when the dominant or prepotent member of each concurs with the other in the type of behavior to be produced. Even then, one or the other is always determining. To this extent, then, the two systems are always competitive; and, at all other times, they are completely competitive. That is, when the prepotent present want and the dominant future want are "antagonistic," instead of being "allied" in the sense used above, one or the other completely excludes its competitor. The prepotent emotion may then be suppressed so completely that it does not even invade consciousness; or it may only be inhibited as to all motor outlet, subcortical or cortical. In either case the result may be inactivity—no behavior—or it may be a concurrent activity, "antagonistic" to the present want and produced by the future want. On the other hand, the energy of the present want may be so great that it submerges the whole future want system, puts all cortical inhibitory mechanisms out of action and overflows in the form of completely emotional behavior.

When we construe this whole process of competition and co-operation between the two systems in terms that we have used before at several points, we define all the negative or inhibitory effects upon the present want system produced by the future want system and its volitional reinforcer as "self-restraint"; and we define all the positive or excitatory effects of the future want system which produce conflict between future wants or which energize (including positive guidance) motor or other peripheral effects of any kind as "self-constraint." [9] This is an important distinction for us, for upon it we shall chiefly base another distinction that will arise in our later examination of human

---

such an intense degree: the envy of riches, the greediness of lucre, and other similar sentiments."

This is pure mythology, without basis in fact. It is hardly necessary to attempt to review here all the evidence, neurological, observational and introspective, which we have cited against such a construction. Perhaps it is only necessary to remind the reader of our plowing farmer, cited at the beginning of Chapter 5. To ascribe his behavior as due to "fear of future hunger" is to do away with all distinctions and to lump every cause together in one single omnium gatherum. If that is fear, what is not fear?

[9] The terms "restraint" and "constraint" were used, in our discussion of the creation of rage, to indicate the prevention of movement and the compulsion to movement by some external force. The antithesis here is an analogous one; but, here, the force is internal. Roughly speaking, "self-restraint" means forcing oneself not to do something one wants to do, and "self-constraint" means forcing oneself to do something one does not want to do. In both, the wanting is understood to mean only the emotion or drive which is, or expresses, a present want. See Chapter 9, Section A 1.

behavior in the field of production. There is no reason to suppose that, at any time, the quantity of secondary energy of response required for self-restraint and that required for self-constraint are concordant. While inhibition is probably only a by-product of excitation, the distribution of the inhibition is of course always dependent on the nature and channel as well, perhaps, as on the pattern of the excitation. Thus the positive activities of self-constraint do not necessarily supply the negative or inhibitory effects involved in self-restraint; nor is the excitation presumably producing the inhibition involved in self-restraint necessarily used, or even available for use, in the positive activities.

However, the distinction reaches still further. At the stage when future wants are competing with a present want in conflicts in consciousness, no behavior—no positive effect—is as yet taking place. Therefore, the inhibition of the present want at that stage is pure self-restraint and nothing more. If, as a result of the conflict, some future want has won, and it begins to produce behavior, something we call decision has taken place. The present want which was a participant in the conflict seems to be no longer a contender—at least in consciousness. Perhaps the inhibitory by-product of the activity itself continues to suppress it. We do not know. At any rate, during the course of the behavior, all of the volitional effort seems to be devoted to self-constraint. In so far as the component actions or their succession is not habitual, cortical conflict (excitatory or positive volitional effort) must continue. And this whether it has immediate overt consequences or not. But, in the course of the resulting behavior, if that is prolonged, other conflicts arise. Newly aroused emotions and particularly the gradual accumulation of fatigue attempt to interrupt and always finally succeed in doing so. These then seem to require renewed self-restraint (negative) even while self-constraint (positive) is still going on. Is the self-restraint at that stage purely a by-product of the self-constraint, or does it appear as a separate or even superimposed force? Again we do not know. But, since the two are then indistinguishable, we shall treat such incidental self-restraint as a part of the self-constraining process so long as the latter holds the field.

While the decision between a future and a present want is being made, the volitional process and its secondary energy necessary to inhibit the present want and to resolve the conflict between future wants involve effort. Once the decision is made, both these occasions for effort seem to terminate. Their quantity has then been fixed. They may be remembered (probably *in toto*, as being indistinguishable); but, if they are, they are remembered as being incidental to the conflict only. Thereafter, whether the decision involved a course of action or one of inaction, the volitional process and its secondary energy also involve effort in varying degrees for the duration of the course of action or for the interval of the course of inaction. The quantity of that effort is not fixed until the course is completed. Then it, too, may be remembered; but, if it is, it is remembered as being incidental, not to the period of preliminary conflict prior to decision, but to the period thereafter, during which the course of action or inaction was persisted in. Thus, for every volitional process involved in a conflict between a present and a future want which results in behavior produced by the future want—action or inaction—there must be two separate memories of effort, if there are any. These two memories are quantitatively in large part unrelated to each other and, if they participate in future conflicts, each will have its effect quite independently of the other. The first memory resulted from self-restraint, including an indistinguishable component of self-constraint; the second resulted from self-constraint, including such indistinguishable self-restraint as occured during those periods in which the inhibition incidental to the activity going on was insufficient to prevent interruption, so that some extra effort had to be superimposed. The first memory is measured chiefly by the intensity of the conflict produced by the present want during the period before the conflict is resolved—before decision; the second is measured chiefly by the duration of the activity or by the interval between the activity and final consummation.

Therefore, this distinction between self-restraint and self-constraint is necessary for another reason. Each time a volitional course of action of a certain type is deliberated upon, decision must be made anew—that is, the effort involved in the preliminary conflict is a current experience each time. Under those circumstances there is no reason to suppose that the memory of effort laid down in the course of the conflict on previous occasions is a factor at all. For it would merely be a weak duplicate of the current experience. On the other hand the memory of effort involved in the course of action or inaction is certainly a factor in the conflict, for that part of the effort has not yet begun to be experienced again. Only the memory of the previous experience can come into play at all. And we have found it necessary to assume that it is such memories of effort—duration or interval—

which act as the immediate limitations on behavior in response to future wants.

On these grounds we propose to establish a convention for use in our further analysis. Self-restraint is measured by the quantity of secondary energy and its accompanying effort required to repress a present want prior to, or during stoppage of, a course of action. Self-constraint is measured by the quantity of secondary energy and its accompanying effort required to arrive at a decision between, or as to any, future wants, plus all the secondary energy required, during the subsequent course of action, to carry it through to its conclusion. Since, during the preliminary conflict, the effort either of self-restraint or of self-constraint is being experienced, the memories of such past experiences are not active factors. But, during that period, the memory of the experience of effort during the course of action on previous occasions, since that is not yet being experienced, does enter as a contending factor and as a deterrent, to the extent of its force, to decision in favor of the course of action.

3. SCHEMATIC STATEMENT

Since our hypothetical scheme of future wants in respect of their relations among themselves and to present wants has been built up only step by step through our examination of the several categories of available evidence, it will clarify the exposition if, at this point, the details are brought together in schematic form. The elaboration of this scheme, with particular reference to the behavior of civilized man, is reserved for Part II.

Effective Occurrence. We are assuming that future wants become actual only when homophonous engrams of them are revived in conscious memory. Such revivals seem to be only slightly due to the ordinary ecphoric influences, which, in this case, would be occurrence of an homophonous experience (the corresponding present want), appearance of a conditioned stimulus (homophony), or the revival of an engram-complex of which the future want constitutes one compotent (association). Instead, the chief occasion for the revival of future wants seems to be "voluntary ecphory," whatever that is. The revival of future wants occurs largely as a result of the deliberate furnishing of a scene which is projected into the counterfeit future, and usually as a result of the deliberate projection of the subject himself into such a scene. From this position he can look about him, backward and forward along the time-scale, and nevertheless retain a particular contrast to the present—that is, to the immediate "expected" future and the most recent past.

Domination and Order of Priority. These correspond to prepotence and the order of priority among present wants. Dominance, and therefore the order of priority among future wants, depends upon the relative intensity of the memories, or of the whole homophonous series of memories. This, in turn, depends on the intensity of the several experiences of the corresponding present wants as the memories were laid down; and that, in turn, reflected their effective intensity at the normal maximum (i.e., average intensity at peak). Therefore, the order of priority of future wants is based upon the order of the corresponding present wants, respectively, which they duplicate. As memories, however, each future want has a much lower intensity than its corresponding present want—the actual experience.

Constellations. Future wants, duplicating the list of present wants, are organized into the same groups, or constellations, the basis of which is a single and joint system of reactions in the consummatory part of the process. There are two differences, however. Present wants, even members of the same constellation, are mutually exclusive; only one can be prepotent at one time in determining and energizing the precurrent or the consummatory reactions. Future wants, on the contrary, can coexist in consciousness. In fact, when they are "allied," as are members of the same constellation, they tend to coexist. On the other hand, future wants produce no consummatory reactions, although it is the joint consummatory reaction that is the link connecting the members of a constellation. The effect of this linkage—restricted to mnemonic association—and of this concurrence may be to produce modified or complicated precurrent reactions or even several different parallel precurrent reactions combined in a course of action, so that the whole is directed toward provision for each of the members of the constellation in proportion to its intensity.

Limitations on Behavior. This has turned out to be a complex system. It is the product of three limiting influences, independent of each other, which operate in triplicate in such a way that the particular precurrent reactions that result and the order in which they occur are the residue after all three have had their successive effects.

The first influence is what we have called duration effort. The quantity of duration effort that will be submitted to in the aggregate is itself limited by interruption—that is, by the recurrence of present wants or the accumulation of fatigue which intermittently put a stop to the volitional process of which it is a concomitant. The quantity (duration) of it available within that limit is one of the bases of what we have called capacity—though capacity is usually measured by the effects of the actions rather than by their duration.[10] Duration effort, being a deterrent, stops volitional action when adequate provision is reached; it tends toward the economy of energy in the task of securing such adequate provision; and, as we shall see later, it may, when the quantity required of it, thus fixed, is measured against the relative intensity of the future wants, determine an order of preference among those wants which is different from the order of priority in which they would otherwise be effective.

The second limiting influence is what we have called interval effort. The extent to which this is itself limited in the aggregate seems to vary widely from person to person, as we shall note in Part II, and we are too ignorant of its nature to attempt to suggest a basis for it. Since the several successive instances of each future want are projected at regular or irregular intervals along the time-scale, no two instances of any want have the same degree of futurity (date). For each of these instances interval effort is added to the duration effort involved. Its quantity is proportionate both to the duration effort and to the interval from the present to the date of the instance. This increment will necessarily suffice, at some point in the series of instances of each want, to exclude those of any greater degree of futurity. If, however, duration effort incurred *now* offers the prospect of being less than duration effort incurred at the date of the future instance, by an amount greater than the increment of interval effort to that date, this limitation is ineffective and we have the phenomenon called future labor-saving.

The third limiting influence is based on the rule to which the last-mentioned situation is the exception. Ordinarily the quantity of duration effort that will be required at the date of the future instance is the same as that required *now*. Since duration effort *now* has added to it the increment of interval effort, while duration effort *then* has no such increment, the tendency of our final influence is to nullify the effect of the whole system—that is, to prevent all behavior in response to future

[10] Capacity with regard to future and present wants are thus, immediately, complements of each other—that is, together they foot up to twenty-four hours a day so far as time is concerned.

wants. But this influence works selectively, as we shall see in Part II. For, when the subject voluntarily projects himself into the future scene, if it appears that duration effort will be impossible, ineffective, or unavailable at the date of the future instance, or even if it appears that it will be sufficiently greater then, this third limiting influence may cease to operate. When that happens, the pattern of behavior disclosed through the apertures left by its withdrawal is seen to be one determined by the relative intensity of future wants subjected only to the first two limiting influences.

7

MEANS AND THEIR ESTIMATION

A. ON METHOD

WE HAVE NOW COMPLETED, so far as we found it possible to do so, our restatement of the nature and operation of human wants and their satisfying in terms of the new behavioristic and physiological categories. From the data, we have constructed two analytical schemes or hypothetical systems—one for present wants and one for derived, or future, wants—consisting, at bottom, of two sets of forces and of two complex organic mechanisms through which these forces come into play. Henceforth our task will be to analyze the relations of these systems with the external world—the environment. For that we shall have to rely wholly on the data furnished by the observation of human behavior. But, in the course of this analysis, we shall find not only that our analytical schemes are further confirmed—because alternatives that might exist or that have been supposed to exist fail to account for the observed behavior—but also we shall find it possible to infer from that behavior certain additional details about the operations of the forces and mechanisms themselves, details which have not been disclosed by the chiefly intra-organic approach.

Our method of procedure is necessarily from the simple to the complex—that is, we are considering each of the several influences at play in succession and only then including its effects—so that we build up step by step the synthesis that finally conforms to and, in considerable part, explains reality. For this reason we are deferring, in this and the succeeding chapter, consideration of most of the different effects of, and the conflict between, the present and the future want systems. This omission must be borne constantly in mind. Our basis here will be the present want system. We shall bring in, incidentally, certain features and aspects of the future want system—more especially those correspondences that result from the fact that the future is derived from the present system, but also certain divergences between them that are based on differences already discovered in our previous studies of the two. Nevertheless, consideration of the relations of future wants to means at this stage will not stand on its own feet. It will be much modified as we proceed, to include the effect of the other influences.

B. QUALITATIVE RELATIONS OF MEANS TO WANTS [1]

I. THE THREE TYPES OF MEANS

In economic terminology the process of satisfying wants is accomplished by "means." [2] And these means are deemed to be, for the greater part, objects (or conditions) external to the person (i.e., commodities or goods), and, for the lesser part, acts of other persons (i.e., services). Since, in the preceding analysis, we have considered the processes of satisfying wants only so far as they consist of systems of reactions of the organism itself, it becomes necessary to reconcile these two views.

In the first place, let us identify these external objects and acts of others and their relation to wants in terms of the organic process described in our previous analysis. There we usually referred to external stimuli as if they were more or less discrete entities. Modern psychology utilizes the plausible supposition that, in some unknown way, the sensory receptive apparatus of organisms automatically organizes these separate stimuli into patterns (*Gestalten*). As these patterns become clear-cut and integrated, because they are experienced as a whole and thus lay down a series of homophonous memories which are the basis of recognition, they establish upon the stage of consciousness the *dramatis personae* of acts and objects in the environment. Thereafter sufficiently indicative stimuli (crucial parts of these finally integrated patterns) no longer stand by themselves. They are capable of ecphorizing the whole engram. So, too, can other patterns associated with the first in some one of the engram-complexes in which both were included. Thus the organism comes to impute and project the engram of the whole habitual pattern into the environment, and acts *as if* the object or act existed externally to it whether it is present or absent.

---

[1] We are using, here, the antithesis between "qualitative" and "quantitative" in its purely scientific sense. We do not mean by "qualitative" "degree of excellence"; we refer only to relationships due to differences of kind or character.

[2] Considering the consuming process only, Schumpeter says (*364*, 44), "the ultimate pair of data in economics" are "wants and the means for their satisfaction." As to the sufficiency of this statement, see below, Part II.

Now (1) if there exists an internal want in the organism, and if a stimulus or pattern of stimuli is interpreted as a sign that some imputed object or act is present in the environment, and if conditioning has taught that this imputed object or act can serve to get rid of the want, the system of reactions takes the form of *seeking* the object or act. In fact, when the want exists and conditioning has taken place, mere revived memories of the conditioned objects or acts may come to cause such seeking even when external stimuli do not yet signal their presence. If (2) there exists in the organism a quasi-external want which is actually being caused by stimuli from an object or act in the environment, the unconditioned behavior resulting may lead to *withdrawal* (from the source of the stimuli) and thus to getting rid of the want. Thereafter, by conditioning, that want may come to be imputed in the same way to all similar acts or objects, and signals of their presence may lead to conditioned withdrawal before such stimuli are received from them as will cause the actual want. If this occurs before the actual quasi-external want is produced, we say the behavior is generated by a central replica acting as surrogate for the want itself. The behavior—withdrawal—may be the same in both these cases; yet it has been customary to call it *avoidance* in the second case only. In Chapter 4 we agreed that, for the sake of clarity, we would apply the term "avoidance" only when viewing the behavior from the standpoint of external objects. As such it constitutes the antithesis to "seeking." From the standpoint of all actual wants, even including surrogate wants in respect of themselves, behavior is directed toward "getting rid of" the wants. In this aspect, all present wants are "wants to be got rid of." But, among present wants, surrogates, and surrogates only, lead to behavior directed toward "preventing" the corresponding actual want. Thus actual quasi-external wants are both "wants to be got rid of" and "wants to be prevented." By reason of the fact that the apparatus concerned is so much more elaborate and efficient, the part played by future "wants to be prevented" is very much more extensive. In fact, a large part of the future-want system is concerned with the future avoidance of objects (or conditions) and acts which would, if they were not provided against, cause quasi-external present wants. And here a further complication enters; for, in the case of future wants at least, it is possible that an organism should seek one object or condition as a means of avoiding another that would cause a quasi-external present want. For the rest the future want system always leads to "seeking." Whether, in connection with future wants, acts of others occupy a place alongside objects (and conditions), as they do with present wants, we shall consider later.[3]

Along these lines the usual economic category of "means" for the satisfaction of wants, construed in terms of our physiological analysis, would embrace all those external objects and acts of others which the person has learned are necessary or helpful in getting rid of his present wants, or his wants that will become present ones in the future, or in preventing other wants, present or to come, which would be apt to arise in the absence of these "objects or acts." This raises the second issue between the customary economic treatment and our previous analysis, which requires reconciliation. In this definition, as it stands, "means" are somewhat arbitrarily limited so as to exclude the reactions of the person himself.[4] Nevertheless, we have already found it evident that these latter are always an essential part, and sometimes the whole, of the process of satisfying wants. If, then, we are to submit to scientific investigation the relations of given men to a given environment in the process of satisfying their wants, we cannot possibly exclude all the individual's own reactions from the category of means. Therefore, in the second place, it becomes necessary to establish, as clearly as is possible at this stage of our analysis, the different part played in the process of satisfying wants by each of these three different kinds of means, as well as the relationship that exists between them.

We have frequently referred to Sherrington's distinction, within the class "reactions of self," between those which he calls consummatory and those which he calls precurrent. The line of demarcation is hazy; nevertheless the distinction is of some value. Now it is evident that the acts of others which themselves constitute means for the satisfactions of one's wants are objectively identical with the precurrent reactions of oneself, and are, for the most part, limited to substitution for such precurrent reactions. This for the reason that, normally and generally, one must perform one's own consummatory reactions.[5] It is

[3] This raises a question of definition which it is necessary to recognize, though hardly necessary to settle. Cannot another person be an object? We speak of the "object of one's affections." This shows that it is impossible to draw a hard and fast line between external objects and acts of others. The terms are set up for purposes of inclusion, not for purposes of classification.

[4] This customary limitation is largely accidental. It is due to the fact, I think, that, while economics has often described its field as "wants and their satisfaction," it has actually grown up as an investigation of exchanges.

[5] This is, of course, subject to many abnormal exceptions, such as artificial breathing, induction of food per rectum, etc. Also what will naturally be treated as consumma-

also evident that the part played by external objects or conditions in the satisfying of wants is an inactive one; that is, there is always required, in addition to such objects, at least a consummatory reaction to introduce them into the process.[6] Since in both these cases the means, in the usual sense, is at one remove from the final fact of satisfying a want, because there is always required also the intervention of a consummatory reaction of self, it will be analytically convenient to exclude such consummatory reactions from the category of means in the cases of reactions of self as well. Thus the term "means" is restricted by us to cover only precurrent reactions of self, similar actions of others, and external objects (or conditions) when they are, or may be, conducive to the satisfaction of wants. In all cases it will be understood that a consummatory reaction of self is necessary to complete the process, however or wherever in the chain of behavior the line of demarcation is drawn between that and the precurrent reactions. This is by no means a complete analysis of these various steps or incidents in the process; but it will serve our purposes so long as we confine ourselves to the aspect we are now considering, the part they play in the satisfying of wants.

The third reconciliation required is not so much with what has gone before as it is with the economic field to which we are limiting ourselves. Strictly speaking, acts of others as means to oneself may be considered to be beyond the pale of a direct economy. But this limitation that we are placing upon our scope is purely for analytical purposes—to simplify the problem. Therefore, it is better, for the sake of making our basic categories complete as we go along, to recognize this type of means and to deal with it so far as it abuts on our present subject matter. The inducement which procures such acts is definitely excluded from our present consideration. However, we have already been obliged to mention symbiosis and the difficultly differentiated imposed wants. Acts of others induced by symbiosis serve to satisfy wants of those others as well as wants of self. Acts of others induced by wants imposed on them by self seem also to satisfy wants of both parties, though the imposed want is an artifact. Finally, and not readily

---

tory reactions among infants, invalids, and the very rich are a more limited portion of the final members of the series, than for the healthy adult who "waits on" himself.

[6] The consummatory reaction, in the case of "wants to be prevented," is, as we have noted, often difficult to identify. It can only be defined as freedom from the object (or condition) or act to be avoided, and it is only due to a means when that means is the cause of the prevention of the want. See also p. 401, below.

distinguishable from these two cases, we have acts of others induced by exchange. But, in the last analysis, this resolves itself into an indirect procurement of the means for satisfying one's own wants by one's own acts. It is only this last process that we are deliberately excluding from further consideration in our examination of the abstraction we call a direct economy.

It may aid the reader to visualize the way we are viewing the relation of means to present wants if we now examine briefly the way our previous classification of the recurrence or occurrence of wants relates to this tripartite division of means and the separation of consummatory reactions.

I. Continuous Wants as Tendencies (non-interfering)
  a. Taking in (breathing) requires means as objects (atmospheric oxygen) but usually no means as precurrent reactions of self, acts of others or other objects (apparatus).
  b. Giving off
    1. Carbon dioxide (breathing) requires no means as objects, nor, usually, any other means.
    2. Heat (temperature regulation) requires means as external conditions (objects). It may also require them as apparatus (objects) and as acts of self (e.g., fanning) or of others (e.g., the same).
       In a sense these means are also preventive of actual wants (variations; see below).
II. Continuous Wants as States (interfering, but irregularly occurring)
  Requirements of means the same as under I.
III. Recurring (storage)
  a. Taking in (eating and drinking) requires means as objects (food and drink) and usually also precurrent reactions of self or acts of others to procure same.
  b. Giving off (defecation, micturition, etc.) requires no external means [7] nor precurrent reactions.[8]
IV. Sporadic (external relations other than taking in or giving off)
  a. Actual; require no means except for the cure of external injury.
  b. Surrogate; require any and all types of means.

We must note that consummatory reactions are necessary in all these cases, alone or in addition to means. In classes I, II, and III these consummatory reactions are readily identified; in IVa, they are often

[7] The means which are provided, in civilized society, in connection with these purposes are not means for the satisfaction of these wants. Instead they are means for the satisfaction of various wants for cleanliness, hygiene, etc. See under conglomerate means, below.
[8] Unless the postural reactions are regarded as precurrent.

difficult to identify; in IVb, they can only be imputed.[9] Nevertheless, we must assume their existence for all classes. What we have called "wants of prevention," if they are present wants, are all, strictly, of class IVb. As noted above, we shall find that the "want of prevention" is the most general type of future want, as well as of those present wants which lie beyond the range embraced in our physiological study. The satisfaction of such wants may be regarded either as the prevention of the actual want or, when the surrogate present want occurs, as the cessation of the replica (e.g., relief from fear). In so far as these actual or surrogate wants are prevented or corrected by a nearly simultaneous reaction (e.g., withdrawal), that is clearly consummatory. But when they are protected against by the future provision of means of any of the three types, so that not even the replica occurs, what, we may ask, is the consummatory reaction? Our expressions for the behavior through which we gain the benefit of such protective means for preventing wants take the general form of "enjoyment" of the means rather than that of prevention of the want. We speak of "dwelling" in houses, of being "cooled" or "warmed" by some agency, of "wearing" clothes, etc. By the very fact that we also need terms for the opposites of these forms of behavior, we indicate that these processes of enjoyment—these consummatory reactions—are never continuous. While the protective measures we take in the form of actions are only made available when the want threatens, those in the form of objects, once obtained, may be continuously available. Nevertheless, even then, it must be that the wants are not themselves continuous, but are, at most, irregularly occurring and, at least, sporadic; for, if they were continuous, we would avail ourselves of these objects continuously. Instead we "go outdoors," we alternate between being "cooled" and "warmed," we "undress," etc. Thus we are justified in calling the wants of prevention sporadic, or at least irregularly occurring, in spite of the fact that the means in the form of objects which we use for preventing them are most usually continuous in their availability when once procured. Since such provision is usually the result of a future want, but the consummatory reaction is exclusively the result of a present want, it becomes necessary for us to set up as the ultimate objective the satisfaction (consummatory reaction) of a present want that is prevented (i.e., never exists). While this sounds illogical, it is clearly the logic of the facts. Thus adequate analysis excludes from

[9] See note 6, above.

the category of means all consummatory reactions—all of the reactions of self involved in the actual satisfying of the want—and leaves as means only those actions of self and others which precede and are preparatory to satisfaction, together with objects (or conditions) whose effect, concurrent with the process of satisfying, is to get rid of or to prevent the want.

In dealing with present wants only, we have heretofore come to the conclusion that the process of satisfying a want, if started, usually reaches satiety. Exceptionally, it may stop short of that point for any one of three reasons: (1) interference by another prepotent want; (2) failure of the reactions initiated by the major want of a constellation also to satisfy some minor member; (3) insufficiency of an external condition (i.e., means as object or act of others). These three causes of incomplete satisfaction relate differently to the three kinds of means. The first cause, interference, results solely from a cessation of the means of the first type—precurrent reactions of self—or of the consummatory reaction, and argues no insufficiency elsewhere. The second cause, though it incidentally implies a deficiency in the constituents or "qualities" (serving the minor wants) of means of the last two types—acts of others and objects—actually results solely from a cessation of the consummatory reaction of the major want. Only in the third case is the direct cause a deficiency in means of the last two types—acts of others and objects—and only here is the premature ending of the reaction purely a consequence of them. In the first two cases it is evident that incomplete satisfaction is due entirely to the competition between wants, for it only occurs because of the entry of a more prepotent want or constellation, or because the major want of a constellation holds the field. In the third case, alone, can it be said that incomplete satisfaction is not purely an incident of the priority of other wants. Even there, as we shall conclude in a later chapter, though exhaustion of external conditions appears as the proximate cause, it is not usually ultimately responsible.[10]

It should be recalled that even the operation of these causes does not appear necessarily to leave the wants merely at a reduced level of intensity in all cases. Many satisfactions are on an all or none basis. For instance, the reaction of escape must either satisfy the want completely or not at all. It either succeeds or it fails; there is no middle

---

[10] It is ultimately due to the order of preference—i.e., the allocation and limitation of effort.

ground. To some extent this is also true of the sex act and of excretory functions. Carrying the process to its conclusion once is necessary to any satisfaction at all. What prevents satiation is the cutting off of repetitions or continuations. On the other hand, in the feeding constellation, we saw that premature cessation, while it may leave the constituent wants—either major or minor—partially satisfied, in the sense that the full quota which will prevent their recurrence for a customary period has not been ingested, does not leave the wants at an intensity part way down from the customary maximum to zero. Instead, any considerable amount of the constituent necessary for each want apparently results in complete disappearance of the want pro tem. Finally, if we have regard to behavior over a considerable period of time, we note that there is little reason to admit that these influences will produce the phenomenon of lasting incomplete satisfaction. Over such a period interference will not be apt to recur regularly at each reappearance of the interrupted want at prepotent intensity; therefore, sooner or later that want will be satiated. Similarly, incidental failure will be made good at some time if the minor want left unsatisfied has sufficient intensity ever to become itself prepotent, especially if its intensity can rise above its customary maximum by reason of the cumulative effect of repeated deficiencies in its satisfaction.[11] So, too, if external conditions prove insufficient during one process, the intensity of the want will either remain unchanged, in which case more of the necessary condition will be sought immediately; or the intensity will be somewhat reduced, in which case more of the condition will be sought as soon as that level, or the rise during the interval, re-establishes prepotence; or, finally, the intensity will fall to zero but rise again to prepotence sooner than usual, in which case more of the condition will again be sought.

It would follow from this that, in the long run, the final determinant of the number of present wants satisfied would depend upon the capacity to secure or provide means, rather than upon the interferences, etc., which appeared as the proximate determinants when wants alone were being considered. Under any one set of institutional and technical conditions this capacity reaches only to a certain point along the series of wants in their order of priority. Our thesis is that all wants within that reach are usually completely satisfied as they recur or occur during some considerable period of time; all wants beyond that reach are

[11] For example, salt hunger.

left completely unsatisfied. There are two exceptions, as follows: (1) It may be that minor members of a constellation, whose own intensities never arrive at prepotence because they are beyond the limit of capacity, nevertheless are incidentally partly satisfied during the reactions of some major want in their constellation; (2) it may be that a sufficiency of external conditions requisite for some included want is not available and cannot be made so—probably a rare case. In this way the limit of capacity must needs be related to time; for, so far as present wants are concerned, this limit is only set by the fact that, during the period taken, the wants that are included are supposed to occur or recur in such a way that one of them is always prepotent. Since the field would always be held by one of these, wants of a less intensity would be perpetually excluded. The capacity to provide means of all three kinds is then the crux of the matter. Therefore it will be one of our chief concerns as we proceed with our analysis.[12]

2. MEANS IN RELATION TO CONSTELLATIONS OF WANTS

The general failure to recognize the arrangement of the great majority of wants in constellations has led economists to establish two distinctions or relations among means which have, as a matter of fact, almost wholly to do with wants. The first distinction is to attribute to a single means the possibility of qualitative as well as quantitative differences in its capacity to satisfy a single want. While the composition of the usually compound means may vary in such a way that its content of the constituent, or active principle, or attribute, which serves to satisfy the major want of a constellation is quantitatively more or less, this is only superficially a qualitative difference. Actually, as we shall see shortly, it serves as the basis for determining the quantity of the means requisite for satiation of the major want. And the great bulk of variations in quality, so-called, consist in the presence in various degrees (or absence) of constituents or attributes which will serve incidentally toward the satisfaction of particular minor wants of a

[12] At this point we are not ready to take up the operation of this limit in detail. But, to avoid possible misunderstanding, we cannot leave one point unnoted here. Some wants can only be got rid of as and when they occur or recur. Others, in so far as they are due to environmental causes, can be prevented, not only by currently provided means "during the period taken" (above), but perhaps for a long period ahead by a single piece of "protective" means. That is, they can operate as future wants. Thus the effect of an inoculation or of building a house may carry far beyond such a period. This complication we shall consider fully in a later chapter.

constellation.[13] So-called qualitative differences in a means are therefore, for the most part, actually differences in the number of wants
which the means serves to satisfy and in the degree to which the quantity of the whole means requisite for satiation of the major want happens to contain the particular constituents or attributes which will also
satisfy the minor wants of a constellation.[14] The second doubtful relation is to assemble, as if they constituted a conglomerate of means to
the satisfaction of a single want, what really constitute a group of
means each more or less specific for the satisfaction of one of the different members of a constellation of wants.[15] So-called "complementary"
means, while physically separate, are, with perhaps a few exceptions,
of no different order than the various constitutents or attributes of a
single compound means mentioned above. They are means applied
jointly in a single process (system of reactions), but they serve each
their single or several separate member wants. And their conjoint application is not indispensable—a *sine qua non*—but merely enables the
process to serve for the satisfaction of a larger number of member
wants.[16]

Analyzed in this way it becomes evident that the individual constituents or attributes of a compound means, or the individual elements

[13] Of course most natural phenomena are compounds in this sense. As they exist in
nature they are rarely pure. Thus all animal and vegetable foods contain numerous
constituents several of which may serve as means to the satisfaction of different wants
in the constellation we call "eating."

[14] Menger, who, as usual, analyzes this feature more thoroughly than his fellow dis-
coverers of marginal utility, ignores all differences except as they reflect on *Werth*. To
him (*296*, 115–116) mere differences of kind or species among the means, if they are
indifferent in suitability (*Tauglichkeit*), are not, economically considered, differences
in quality. Quality differences are only of two kinds: when like quantities of means
produce (1) different quantities of satisfaction; (2) different qualities of satisfaction.
To us his different kinds or species are not mere different qualities simply because they
may be applicable to a single want; they are to be treated as different means altogether;
his first qualitative difference is to us a quantitative difference in the salient constituent;
and his second is to us suitability for separate component wants.

[15] This error of analysis has already been referred to on p. 184.

[16] Pareto discusses this supposed interdependence of means at some length (*317*, 252 ff.),
but chiefly by way of evasion of the issue. Menger perhaps (as Böhm-Bawerk says, *38*,
170) introduced the term "complementary," but only in connection with his "goods of
higher orders" (i.e., means of production). Böhm-Bawerk himself (*ibid.*, Chap. IX)
confines his discussion to production goods. His example of "right and left hand gloves"
is not an example of complementary goods, but a case where two of the same—though
asymmetrical—items are necessary for the complete satisfaction of the want of warm
hands and for any satisfaction of the want of being well-dressed. As means, a pair of
gloves is analogous to a pair of trousers. Personally I have been unable to find any unequivocal example of two really different and independent objects, both of which are
indispensable to the direct satisfaction of a single want by either. Always they turn out

in a set of so-called "complementary" means, come to be susceptible of distinguishing treatment by the organism, as if each were a means appropriate for a single want. Since, in the case of present wants, only one can be prepotent at a time—and that usually the major one—the effect of constituents or attributes capable of satisfying minor wants of the constellation in varying degrees is purely incidental. Behavior is directed only by the major want. But, as we have seen, all the members of a constellation of future wants can join in directing the complex of behavior constituting future provision. In that way the deliberate "planning" of a congeries of means for the joint satisfaction of a constellation of wants leads to the inclusion of means for the satisfaction of the minor wants as far down the order of priority as the capacity of the organism to control external means makes possible. But such deliberate "planning," or any assemblage of the separate elements of such a conglomerate, can only be conceived to take place in connection with provision for future wants.

These general statements as to so-called qualitative differences in single means and as to "complementary means," while they are the necessary inferences from and applications of our previous analysis, are so contrary to the habits of thought to which economists have become inured that it seems best to support them by some illustrations. These will also serve to expand the previously limited basis of our category of constellations and to include some important examples which

---

to be means of producing some third thing which is itself the direct means. Complementarity certainly applies to such intermediate means.

The notion of complementarity of direct means strikes me as a failure of analysis due to approaching the subject from the standpoint of means instead of that of wants. When analyzed, such examples turn out to be compound means or conglomerates of means (see text) which serve in a single process toward the satisfying of several members of a constellation; or they turn out to be parts of a complex means without any of which it will not serve a want at all. Examples of the latter kind are met with frequently in the literature as illustrations of complementarity. We may give one example. To satisfy the want for transportation one may wish an automobile. The essentials for that purpose are a great complex including the motor, the chassis, gasoline and oil. The first two essentials themselves include many parts. Without any of these parts one has no transportation. True, their period of replacement is different—the number of installments into which they divide as a durable means (see below, Section D 1). Nevertheless, each, or its replacement, is required to continue the whole as a serviceable means. The body, in its various details, and the tires, chiefly, are for comfort—a different want. The radio is for still a different want, etc. It is also true that one does not purchase tires if he has no automobile. Neither does a woman purchase beauty in a gown if she purchases no gown. But that is no more than to say that if the major want of the constellation is not provided for, neither are the minor ones.

we should have in mind as we proceed. As we have already noted, it has been customary in economics and other social sciences to treat certain wants as "desires" for conglomerate objects (or even acts) such as "air" or "food" (or "service"). Our analysis has already demonstrated that such wants are not simple, integrated things. On the contrary, each is a group of entirely independent wants whose only connection is the fact that they may be satisfied in a joint consummatory process. The point we are now making, though it concerns the means rather than the wants, is exactly similar. Neither are these conglomerate objects or acts simple or integrated things. And, in the same way, the only connection that unifies these conglomerates is that they may serve jointly in a single process for the satisfaction of a number of independent wants. Thus the principle that unifies both constellations of wants and conglomerate objects (or acts) is that they have, or pertain to, a single process of satisfaction. Such processes we have hitherto called systems of reactions. Now we must limit the process to the consummatory reaction. The conglomerateness is only characteristic of the means—that is, external objects or precurrent reactions of self or others—for the consummatory reaction of self is the very criterion according to which they are grouped, just as it is also the criterion by which wants are grouped in constellations. For this reason clarity demands that both constellations and their conglomerate means should be analyzed, not in terms of wants or means, but according to—and named for—the system of consummatory reactions which unifies them. All this applies with equal force to the slightly different notion of "qualitative" differences in a single means, which are in reality separate constituents or attributes independently serving separate wants. In this way, in reality, we do away with conglomerate objects (food), qualitative differences (flavor, beauty), and "complementary" means (coffee and sugar, cups and saucers). We come to treat each element as a separate means for a separate want, though we may group them as conglomerates or compounds according to the process in which they may serve jointly.

To indicate the scope of the system of constellations and the character of the conglomerate external means—or attributes of compound means—which serve them, we give a few tentative analyses of some of the fundamental systems. Since these extend beyond our physiological basis we are merely guessing as to the nature of many of the component wants.

CONSTELLATIONS

Name (Consummatory Reaction)	Component Wants or Groups of Wants	Means
1. Eating	Hungers or appetites for each of various constituents necessary for nutrition	These several constituents
	Disliked (disagreeable) taste or odors (prevented)	Acts removing such constituents (cleaning) or avoiding of acts causing them (burning)
	Ennui (prevented)	Variety in form of constituents and in ways of preparation
	Distaste (ocular) (prevented)	Ways and means of "appetizing" appearance
	Disliked activity (prevented)	Activity-saving equipment and service
	Disliked ugliness (prevented)	Aesthetic factor in service and surroundings
	Disliked unconventionality (prevented)	Formalistic factors in service and surroundings
2. Dressing	Temperature variation (prevented)	Means of avoiding excessive warmth or cold
	Discomfort from external causes (prevented)	Means of protection from elements, insects, etc.
	Discomfort from clothing (prevented)	Means which do not cause such discomfort
	Disliked activity (prevented)	Activity-saving clothing and service
	(Also all components of 4 and 5 below)	
3. Dwelling (for lack of a better word)	All of the components of 2, and of 4 and 5 (below)	

(In the remainder of the list we shall use any term which suggests the nature of the want, without attempting to analyze it into physiological terms.)

4. Cleansing	Disease (prevented)	Filth (avoiding or getting rid of), water, etc. (seeking)

CONSTELLATIONS (Cont.)

Name (Consummatory Reaction)	Component Wants or Groups of Wants	Means
	Discomfort (prevented)	As above, plus anointing oil, etc.
	Ugliness (prevented)	Soaps which produce "the skin you love to touch," etc.
	Inconvenience (prevented)	Equipment and service—tubs, vacuum cleaners, etc.
5. Decorating	Ugliness (prevented)	Ugly ways and means (avoiding) Beautiful ways and means (seeking)
	Non-conformity (prevented)	Unconventional ways and means (avoiding) Stylish ways and means (seeking)
	Insignificance (prevented)	Unenviable ways and means (avoiding) Enviable ways and means (seeking)

This very sketchy analysis is intended to be merely suggestive. All it shows, and all it is intended to show, is the independence which exists among the various component wants in each constellation and among the various objects or acts in each conglomerate, or the various attributes in each means.[17] It also shows that the unifying principle in each constellation and its conglomerate is a system of reactions which consists of the consummatory elements therein.[18] Having made the

[17] Nor is there any necessary validity in the order, either within or among the constellations. We are not arguing the point of the typical or general order of priority.

[18] While his terminology is purely descriptive, not analytical, and while he deals indiscriminately with conglomerates of means and compound means, the principle which J. B. Clark sought to establish (80, 213–217) seems to be closer to this analysis of ours than is any other readily to be found in the literature. If one converts his different "qualities" into different kinds, as we do, one gets much the same results as ours.

Somewhat approaching this method of analysis is, for instance, Pareto's reference to "subsistances" (317, 411). One element is "les moyens de se préserver des intempéries," including clothing, shelter, and, "pour les pays froids, le combustible de chauffage." The wants to preserve oneself from inclemencies belong in our constellations 2 and 3, above.

We may cite Fisher's list (142, 165) as typical of the classification by conglomerates of external means. He includes, as "the main sorts of enjoyable objective services," services of nourishment, housing and warming, clothing and personal adornment, personal attendance, amusement, instruction, recreation, and gratification of vanity. To be sure,

point, it is not necessary to labor it. Some of the minor members of each constellation may be practically regarded as more or less by-wants or overtones of the major members; and some of the elements in each conglomerate may be practically regarded as more or less qualitative differences in the external means. Nevertheless, analytically, they must be separated. The number of layers between the food and the ground [19] does not concern the man who is suffering real hunger; nor, if a man is shivering with cold, is he deterred from donning an overcoat because it is ragged. However, that statement of fact with regard to present wants must not include the implication that the satisfaction of the minor wants of a constellation is always entirely incidental to that of the prepotent member. These illustrations of conglomerates of means have made it even more clear that the process of conditioning may make it possible for man, when he is driven by future wants, deliberately to plan a conglomerate of means for the satisfaction of a constellation in such a way that provision is definitely made for minor wants as well as for the major want. Nevertheless, even then, the limit of capacity fixes the point in the order of priority at which such consideration of minor wants shall cease. And, if any wants which lie beyond that point are satisfied at all, it is not because they were considered in the plan, but only because the compound means happened to contain attributes which incidentally accomplished that result.

C. QUANTITATIVE RELATIONS OF MEANS TO WANTS

I. OBJECTIVE AND SUBJECTIVE MEASUREMENT OF MEANS

We have now established, by qualitative analysis, the three fundamental economic categories—or entities: wants; the process of satisfying them—consummatory reactions; and the means by which they are satisfied—precurrent reactions of self, actions (similar) of others and objects. We have also established the basis for treating the first two as magnitudes—that is, for their quantitative analysis. As magnitudes, present wants have been found to have but one dimension, intensity. In terms of this dimension they are comparable among them-

---

the last four seem to be hung together on the pegs of groups of somewhat vague wants.

Of Dunlap's nine desires (see p. 174) four are classed by the unifying behavior, three by objects (two of which are conglomerates) and two by terms for states of social relationship.

[19] See *Evaluation of Wants*, p. 244.

selves at any moment by reason of the mechanism for determining prepotence. And, by comparison over a period of time, they may be ranged in an order of priority according to the comparative intensity they customarily attain before, and in, securing prepotence—their capacity for "interference." As a magnitude, the process of satisfaction is also measured in the same terms—that is, in terms of the reduction of intensity it accomplishes. We have found reason to believe that this magnitude is usually equal to the entire reduction of the maximum intensity of the want to zero, and that it takes place almost wholly at the end of the process, the point of satiation. As magnitudes, future wants have also been found to have but one dimension, intensity. They, too, are comparable among themselves in the course of cortical conflict in which their dominance is determined. Their corresponding order of priority, which presumably duplicates that of present wants from which they are derived, is even more evident because they can be revived and reviewed in memory in rapid succession. However, there is no magnitude corresponding to the process of satisfaction in the case of future wants; for, as we have seen, the behavior produced stops short of the consummatory reactions that are necessary for all satisfaction. In fact, this is one of the chief bases for distinguishing future from present wants. As we proceed, we shall arrive at a definition of that which takes the place of this magnitude for the scheme of future wants.[1] Let us now examine the basis for treating means as magnitudes and try to determine the quantitative relation that exists between means, wants and satisfactions.

The first way in which the magnitudes, means, are identified and measured has been suggested at the beginning of this chapter. It is as the imputed source of stimuli—objectively, as we say. The pattern of stimuli derived from the presence of a means of satisfaction continues as long as the object or act is present. During the continuing experience each imputed source is identified as an unchanging (or comparatively so) individual item. The intensity of "interest" may change; but that does not affect the external stimuli at their source.[2] During the experience an engram is being laid down. As the experience is repeated, each being homophonous with preceding ones, the engrams of the earlier experiences are ecphorized and recognition of the ex-

---

[1] Hitherto, it has been merely referred to as "adequate provision."
[2] A loaf of bread does not appear objectively different to us when we are hungry than when we are replete.

perienced pattern takes place—both recognition of similarity and that of any dissimilarity within the limits of homophony. In this process individual objects or acts are grouped in classes or varieties when the individual phenomena, occurring simultaneously or successively, are indifferent (homophonous) among themselves, in essential (salient) respects. Among these essential respects are those which constitute what we call magnitude. Any one of these respects may be the basis of homophony among phenomena as to which, in other respects, there is recognition of differences; or, among phenomena classified together by reason of homophony in other respects, relative magnitude may constitute the basis of recognition of differences. Comparisons of magnitude—recognition of differences in these respects—are made along several different lines. Indifferent phenomena, if they are individually of the same magnitude in the chosen respect or if their individual magnitude is ignored, are counted; those of individually different magnitude in terms of the chosen respect are compared among themselves or with other phenomena in terms of that respect. The term "respect," in this connection, refers to the particular kinds of attribute or characteristic that the several phenomena have in common, which we call dimensions. For such comparisons two conditions are necessary. In the first place, the two or more phenomena must have one or more dimensions in common—that is, they must be commensurable. In the second place, for comparisons beyond those of more or less or approximate equality, precise measurement is necessary. This requires what we call a unit—that is, an object or process which is always of uniform magnitude in that dimension. Thereafter, the magnitude of each phenomenon, measured in terms of such unit, is stated in terms of number, which expresses the arithmetical relation of the measured continuum in that dimension to the unit of that dimension—that is, the process is reduced to the first method again, and the number of as-if-separated parts of which the continuum is thus conceived to be composed are counted.[3] Or the continuum may be counted as unity, for some purposes, and measured in terms of as-if-separated parts (units) for other purposes.[4]

All such objective measurement consists, then, in the comparison of external phenomena among themselves in terms of attributes or char-

[3] Thus the continuum of a period of time, a roll of dry goods, a bag of flour, or a barrel of wine is measured in terms of as-if-separate minutes, yards, pounds, or gallons.
[4] Thus a house may be measured, as to size, in terms of square feet of floor space. Nevertheless, after it is built, it is a unit.

acteristics which they have in common. When it is applied to means for the satisfaction of wants it is applied in the same way as to any other external phenomena. It takes no account whatever of the relation of those means to wants; nor is it affected by any such relation. The fundamental terms in which it is made—chiefly the physical dimensions, mass, length, and time—have no bearing upon the capacity of different means to satisfy different wants. The only bearing these terms have is this: If the capacity to satisfy a single want is distributed with absolute uniformity throughout a single continuum or several continua, then portions of the single or several continua which are equal in terms of any one of the objective dimensions will have equal capacity. But this is merely tautology, for the definition of "absolute uniformity" requires that it be true.

The second way in which the magnitudes, means, are identified and measured by men is in their relation to the satisfying of their wants. The general process of establishing quantitative relations between wants and means has usually been called in economic literature "subjective valuation," and the particular relation so established in any specific case has been called "subjective value." We have no objection to these terms. They can be converted to our use provided we are permitted to define them to suit ourselves. But, in doing so, it must be recognized that we may be taking liberties in a field that has almost been pre-empted by marginal utility theory in its various forms. Therefore, in order to place our own findings on a basis which will make them comparable to these other forms we shall develop them in the form of a scheme of subjective valuation. At the same time, in order to avoid confusion or the imputation of our own theses to others, it will prove necessary as we proceed to adopt a distinguishing terminology wherever differences in thesis are of the essence of the matter.

The term "subjective" has not appeared frequently in our previous investigations. But it may be a convenient one. Though we continue ourselves to take the objective point of view throughout—that is, we confine ourselves to the examination of the behavior of others and refuse as conclusive evidence our own unconfirmed inner experiences—it has been, and will of course continue to be, necessary to admit the existence of such inner experiences. On this basis we impute two different aspects of experience to the human beings that we study—their objective, or outer, experiences and their subjective, or inner, experiences. The sensory system is chiefly engaged in producing the outer experiences; the emotional and the mnemonic-volitional systems are wholly engaged in producing inner experiences. Means as external data (even if they are acts of self in relation to the environment) have, so far as the human being is concerned, only external existence; and wants, as internal data, have only internal existence. If so, means can only be viewed by the person as objective phenomena, and wants, if they are experienced in consciousness at all, can only be experienced as subjective phenomena.[5] The relation between means and wants, so far as the person experiencing both is concerned, is, therefore, necessarily a relation between an internal and an external experience, and the term subjective value can be stretched to cover this relation, whether it is conscious or not [6]—that is, it can be used to mean the reflection or the projection of the internal relatum upon the external one.

The subject of the identification of specific means to the satisfaction of specific wants has already been fully covered in our discussions of the process of conditioning, of which it constitutes so large a part. True, we have not been using the term "means" in that connection; but it should not be necessary to go over the ground again merely to introduce that term in place of the precurrent reactions or external objects and conditions to which we have previously been referring. On the other hand, the question of quantitative relation has not been considered at all. We have introduced the element of "interest" which we construed to be an endowment of sensorimotor processes (impressions) and of memories with a specific emotional content (i.e., a want). This, it appears, has a definite relation with the conditioning process —that is, the identification of means. But we have no grounds for assuming that it is quantitatively precise, either from the standpoint of the want or from that of the means. Therefore, while such a thesis should not be discarded as impossible, we shall have to rely on other approaches to the question.

Fundamentally, the question resolves itself into this: What magnitude upon the want side can be related to what magnitude upon the means side so that the two necessarily correspond and the means can be presumed to have conferred upon it that certain subjective value which only arises from the want? This is a more uncertain process

[5] And here we meet our first difficulty with the term. For "subjective" usually connotes consciousness; and we have seen that present wants may or may not involve consciousness.
[6] It is not worth while to make an issue of this since so large a part of the estimation of means is necessarily conscious, being volitional.

than objective measurement, not only because one magnitude is "subjective" instead of both being "objective," but also because the magnitude of only one of the relata, the means, is constant or comparatively so.[7] If the other relatum is taken to be the intensity of the want, that is a continuously changing magnitude whose only definite "size" is its customary maximum; if the other relatum is taken to be the satisfying of the want, that consists in a quantity of change in the magnitude of the want (reduction in its intensity). Thus, though we find that a means is, objectively, a constant, a want is a variable, and its satisfaction is one of the variations of the variable.

2. FULL MEASURES, PART MEASURES, AND OTHER SUBJECTIVE MEASURES OF MEANS

In order to arrive at some definite magnitude upon the want side that might serve as the basis of subjective valuation let us consider first the easier of these two possibilities. We have concluded that there must be a considerable degree of uniformity in the intensity at which each present want arrives before its rising latent intensity becomes effective and gives it prepotence. This we have called its customary or normal maximum. There can be no question that an organism that normally carries through the reactions to which it is driven by its prepotent want until that want is satiated will soon learn what is the full measure of a particular means necessary to complete the process—that is, the measure of a means that will reduce the intensity of the want from its normal maximum to satiety, or even, if that is different, the measure that may be necessary to avoid the recurrence of the want at prepotent intensity for a convenient period. This is the result of experience. But experiences leave memories. Therefore we may identify this quantity of means that we are here calling a "full measure" with the quantity we called "adequate provision" for a single instance of a future want. The second is, of course, derived from the first, just as the future want is derived from the present one. And the second is, therefore, of the same size as the first.

Here we find a definite and fairly uniform magnitude upon the want side and an equally uniform magnitude upon the means side that cor-

[7] The term measure, when applied to "subjective" measurement of wants and means, should not be understood as signifying the counting of units in the same way as is done with objective measurement. Apparently subjective measurement is confined to comparisons of more or less or approximate equality. As Mises puts it (*300*, 114), "Judgments of value do not measure; they arrange, they grade."

respond with each other. In the simplest case—food—both exist as experiences at the commencement of the process; the want is being felt and the full measure of means is being seen. At the end of the process both have ceased to exist as experiences, and their disappearance has been correlated because of the identification of the means. We have a right to say, then, that the measure of their relation is the reflection of the full intensity of the want at its normal maximum—or the corresponding reduction—upon the full measure of means. But present wants at their normal maxima are ranged in an order of priority. Then the full measures of means for all wants will come to be ranged in a similar order in respect of this relation between the two. The order will be one only of more-or-less, until and unless the intensity of wants and therefore their reflection upon means can be reduced to terms of units and counted. This, then, is capable of constituting a basis for, or one of the influences leading to, subjective valuation. If this were the only influence at work, the resulting ordinal arrangement (which we shall call the order of preference), exercised among full measures of each means and over a period long enough fully to realize the potential order of priority among present wants, would duplicate the order of priority of the wants.[8] And, since we have

[8] At this point we are introducing a new analytical tool, the order of preference among means for the satisfaction of wants. We do this because we are arriving at the point where the ordinal arrangement in which wants (or segments of wants) are satisfied may not follow the order of priority of wants. That is, in certain of our alternative schemes the order of preference and the order of priority may be the same; in others they will not; in fact they may be independent of each other.

The actual order of preference is a category of reality. It must conform to observation. Therefore the several orders we shall set up are only "virtual" orders—the order that would exist if only the particular cause (criterion of subjective valuation) assumed for the order were operative.

The most precise concept for this analytical tool, the order of preference, is a series of choices the ordinal arrangement of which is defined by conceptually extending the range of capacity step by step from zero until it reaches some limit actually imposed upon aggregate means. That is, at each step only those means are chosen which are indifferent among themselves and preferable to all others.

Hitherto, we have used the term choice only with reference to deliberate choice. Deliberate choices, since they involve conflicts in consciousness and the volitional process, can only be made among future wants or between future and present wants. No change in previous usage is involved so far as choices and orders of preference are dictated only by future wants. But, though that composes most of the process and though we shall confine our study largely to such choices, we must admit certain exceptions here. That is, it will be convenient to include as choices everything that goes to determine the behavior from which we construct the order of preference.

Deliberate choices are voluntary. In the orders of preference we are also including involuntary choices such as choices between present wants and those in which a present supersedes a future want.

concluded that the order of priority among future wants is the same as among present wants, and that adequate provisions for them are the same as full measures for present wants, the virtual order of preference among future provisions, if we disregard the question of the effect of futurity—an extraneous factor—would be identical with that among full measures for present wants. As we proceed we shall develop this as one of our hypotheses as to the virtual order of preference among means and therefore among satisfactions. Combined with its modified form, to be stated next, it is the only hypothesis that we can derive from our own study of present and future wants.

A modified form of this scheme is within the possibilities and should therefore be included as an alternative to, or combined with, the preceding one to cover certain cases. In our discussion of the phenomenon of incomplete satisfaction, the only type of failure to satisfy present wants that is directly related to estimation of means is the third—insufficiency of means. However, among future wants, all members of a constellation can co-operate in a program for the provision of a conglomerate or a compound means; therefore it is possible that the experience of incomplete satisfaction of minor members of the constellation due to the second type of failure to satisfy may survive in memory—that is, it may do so if it ever reached consciousness. Thus we have found two cases already, and we shall find more, in which a portion of means less than a full measure—a *part measure*—may become associated with incomplete satisfaction. It is evident that the phenomenon of incomplete satisfaction must result in what we shall call *segmentation*. It must involve, at the least, the division of the want and its process of satisfying into a part that is satisfied—the portion of the process carried out—and a part that is unsatisfied—the portion of the process not carried out. But segmentation may be more complex than that. It is possible that the want and its process may be divided into several stages or degrees of satisfaction. Thus there may be two or more segments.

Now it is clear that, under our supposition of the tendency to satiation, a virtual order of preference, based on the influence of wants only, would not include part measures of means unless it had to. That is, preference would always be for complete satisfactions, even of the minor wants of a constellation if they came within the limit of capacity. Part measures would never be chosen unless no more could be obtained—i.e., an insufficiency of external condition. If the intensity of a want remains approximately at a level during a complete satisfaction, it must also do so during the initial stage—the first partial satisfaction. If so, it seems that we would have to assume that the full intensity of the want at its normal maximum would be reflected upon the first part measure of means, just as it is upon the full measure. On the other hand, the correspondence between the full measure and the want is based on the experience that the full measure will reduce the want from its normal maximum to satiety. Here, by definition, satiety is not achieved. If the tendency is toward satiation, then satiation must be preferred to incomplete satisfaction. All that we can say at this point is that half a loaf is better than none, though a whole loaf would be better still. But, if the relative intensity of the want governs the virtual order of preference, we would have to assume that such a compulsory initial part measure would enter the virtual order of preference at the same point at which a full measure would enter.

Under the same supposition, it follows that a virtual order of preference based on the influence of wants only, in which segmentation could only occur by reason of insufficiency of external condition, would include only the first part measure—i.e., only the first segment would be considered. Therefore, to elaborate this modification of our scheme—to deal with comparisons of part measures of different size or of several part measures—necessarily involves the introduction of influences other than wants. Only such other influences could account for segmentation which is not compulsory, which may not be confined to the first segment, and in which the size of the part measure is not externally fixed. Since all the intervening analysis is necessary for the treatment of the whole subject of segmentation, we will have to reserve that until Part IV.[9] However, it is well to have this modification of our hypothesis in mind from the start.

Other hypotheses and schemes with regard to subjective valuation have been developed. In the following chapter and its appendix we shall undertake to sift out from the more important of them the possibilities that seem to be worthy of attention, and to examine and develop them in detail along lines parallel and therefore comparable to our own. At this point it will suffice merely to give warning that this will be our procedure.

[9] See Chapter 13, Section F.

3. OBJECTIVE MEASUREMENT OF FULL AND PART MEASURES

Considering, for the present, only our own hypothesis and what it implies, it is clear that once the quantity of any means required for a full measure, or for a regular part measure, has been determined, it becomes readily susceptible to the more elaborate and precise forms of objective measurement.[10] Since most of the schemes with regard to subjective valuation have played fast and loose with this relation of subjective to objective measurement, it is necessary that we restate at the beginning of our discussion the seemingly obvious and simple facts with regard to it. Let us see what can and what cannot be expected of this dual or combined method of measurement. Objective measurement, as we have seen, can be made and stated in a number of different terms. When means occur in separate but natural units of about the same size; or, if individual size is ignored, full or part measures, subjectively determined, may be restated in number of units (e.g., number of eggs or oranges). The resulting arithmetic expressions connote some definite, if not precise, relation between two different magnitudes of the same means. But they connote no other than the arithmetic relation between magnitudes of different means.[11] If a full measure of eggs is three, then a part measure of eggs consisting of one can be stated as one third of the full measure. It does not follow, however, that a full measure of cherries, being twelve, say, is four times as large as a full measure of eggs. When means are produced in separate units these units are artifacts. They may or may not be of the same size; and their size may or may not be ignored. Again, if they are of about the same size or if their size is ignored, they are counted. These arithmetic expressions have the same significance as with natural units—and no more. We see, then, that objective measurement by count of separate units of means has no meaning in this connection if it is applied to different means, and it only has meaning within limits if it is applied to a single means.

However, if the size of the natural or artificial separate unit varies

[10] Not all presently used objective measures were derived independently. Some, at least, are merely full measures. For instance, it is said that the standard wine bottle, holding something over 25 fluid ounces or one-fifth of a gallon, was originally made for use as a pitcher or decanter, and that its size was determined by what was considered the proper quantity of wine for one man at one sitting. Those were the days when men were men.

[11] That is, the comparison of six eggs and three oranges is not a comparison of magnitudes in any sense other than that it represents the fact that these natural phenomena happen to occur as discrete entities.

widely and is not ignored, then the size itself must be measured. Regarded from the standpoint of size, the separate unit then becomes a continuum. As such its magnitude is determined and stated in terms of the arbitrary units of some dimension—that is, as the number of as-if-separated parts of which the continuum is conceived to be composed. The fundamental physical dimensions being mass, length, and time, it is usual to select the units of one of these as the basis of such measurements. If the single means is physically homogeneous, the arithmetic relation between any two portions of it will usually be the same whichever of these dimensions and units are chosen. But among different means, or among the portions of a single means that are not homogeneous, this will only rarely be true, and then by chance.[12] Precisely the same procedure is required when a means occurs naturally, or is produced, as a continuum—that is, not separated at all into units which can be counted.[13] Again the numerical ratios between these portions of two different means marked off to be measured will be different in terms of each of the dimensions which they have in common.[14] The same will be true of a single means if it is not physically homogeneous.[15] Thus objective measurement of means as continua, in terms of any one common dimension, argues nothing as to the relation between their magnitudes in terms of any other common dimension if it is applied to different means, and it only does so within limits if it is applied to a single means.

Both separate units measured by count and as-if-separated arbitrary units of a continuum can be used, within these limitations, to state a magnitude in terms of multiples of such units. Or they can be used to state a magnitude in terms of fractions of such units. The degree of comminution possible depends upon the physical characters of the means. In general, the greater the degree of comminution the greater is the margin of error in the measurement. Moreover, there is always some physical limit below which accurate measurement of any comminuted means is impossible. But, subject to this limit, as to any two portions of a single means or of two means with a common dimension, the arithmetic ratio which stands for their relative magnitudes remains

[12] That is, two bolts of cloth of the same yardage do not necessarily weigh the same.
[13] For example, liquids or processes taking place over time.
[14] For instance, a gallon of liquid does not always weigh eight pounds.
[15] Eight pounds of water does not have the same volume (L^3) when frozen as when liquid (i.e., in its heterogeneous conditions). The end-slices of a loaf of fresh bread weigh less than slices from the middle, though of exactly the same volume, because they contain less moisture. Correspondingly, they contain more bread.

the same no matter into how many equal fractions each is divided, provided the number of equal fractions is the same in both cases.

Having applied all these various systems of measurement to the purpose of determining and stating the objective magnitudes of full measures or part measures of means, we may first note that this enables any organism, within its capacity for accurate objective measurement, to compare two different means for the satisfaction of a single want. If it finds that there is required, let us say, ten of the particular kind of objective units in which the first means is measured to complete a full measure (i.e., to accomplish satiation) and only five, perhaps different, units of the second, then, in this respect, 10 *a* units of the first equal 5 *b* units of the second. If, as frequently happens especially with provision for future wants, the means is objectively measured in large units, one of which serves for several complete satisfactions in series, the same comparison can be made in terms of fractions. Then ⅕ *a* unit of the first equals ⅒ *b* unit of the second, if an *a* unit of the first constitutes 5 full measures or adequate provisions while a *b* unit constitutes 10 such. Such measurement secures definiteness, since the magnitude of a full measure is thereby altered from a general impression of mass, length, or time to one that can be accurately reproduced, once experimental variations have settled on how much constitutes a full measure. All of this may apply equally to part measures, except that the particular magnitude involved there is apt to be much less precise and therefore much less definitely to be stated in terms of objective measures.

The second function such as objective measurement may perform is to enable the organism to make some comparisons of the effectiveness of a single means in accomplishing the satisfaction of two different wants to both of which it is appropriate but which constitute alternative uses. If the full measure for both uses is the same, it is obvious that the mechanism of prepotence and the order of priority which that establishes will, at least among future wants, lead to a choice that will assign the means first to that want whose normal maximum intensity is greater. If the full measures for the two uses are different, the choice is not so automatic or direct. At least, it is not if the relative intensities of wants are only determinable by the organism in terms of more or less, as we are supposing. Nevertheless, even then, if the full measure for the stronger want were much less than that for the larger (e.g., water for drinking *vs.* water for washing), there would be a tendency to provide first for the stronger want. On the other hand, objective measurement might teach that the same quantity of means that constitutes a full measure for the stronger want would serve for, say, five successive complete satisfactions of the weaker one (i.e., constitute five full measures). But, unless the organism were capable of adding together five separate experiences and of comparing their total to another single one, there would be no basis here for discrimination between the two uses. However, if extraneous conditions (limitations of quantity) are introduced that compel a choice between the two uses, and if it is assumed that experience had shown which choice yields the greater number of satisfied wants, we might conclude that the result would be the selection of a substitute means for the stronger want, if such were available, and the application of this means to the weaker, no other being available. Thus the organism might learn, in time, not to eat its own young.[16] Finally, if the objective quantities constituting full measures for both purposes were so nearly proportional to the comparative intensities of the two wants that no divergence could be discerned, it might be supposed that the organism would find a choice impossible—that the application of the means to one or the other purpose would be indifferent.

We have now developed two "subjective" magnitudes in connection with the process of satisfying wants. The first is the only—and only the—dimension of a want—its intensity. From this is derived, in the some dimension, the reduction in intensity that takes place from the normal maximum to satiety. The second subjective magnitude is only the dimension of some particular means for the satisfaction of that want —a full measure, as we call it. The full measure requisite for satiation may then be converted into terms of objective units of some kind. Each objective unit thereafter corresponds to the fraction of satiation—or the number of satiations—it will procure. Since the normal maximum intensity of the want is the only necessary datum for de-

---

16 Under these limiting conditions the result would not be due to pure subjective valuation. But it is well to mention the possibility at this point. Böhm-Bawerk (38, 163), assuming that the appraisal of the relative strength of wants can be exact, lays down the rule that "in the case of goods which allow of alternative uses . . . and therefore of furnishing different marginal utilities . . . the highest marginal utility is the standard." J. B. Clark, on the same assumption, is more careful. He says (80, 228) that "a thing of this kind is to be regarded as a bundle of distinct utilities, tied together by being embodied in a common material object." "The tests of the market measure these utilities separately." Only one is marginal. "The other utilities in the thing are intramarginal. They are higher utilities." All of which may be true if this measurement is within the capacity of men.

termining this full measure of the means, it is clear that this full measure of the means does not change in size when the intensity of want merely varies from its maximum. Nor is there any change in size in the fraction of satiation (or the number of satiations), procurable through the objective units of which it is composed. On the other hand, this full measure of a means has reference to that means only and to its relation to a single want only. It is stated in terms of the objective quantity of any particular means which, in the process of satisfying, corresponds to the reduction of the one-dimensional want from its normal maximum to zero. It is different for each of the various means applicable to a single want; and it is different for each single means as it may be applied to various wants. It follows that the quantity defined as a full measure of any means in no sense represents the magnitude of the want or any dimension of that magnitude.[17]

As a result of the foregoing analysis we may set up between two or more different external means, regarded solely with reference to their capacity to satisfy a single want, what we will call their *unweighted terms of substitution.* If, in terms of the above example, the objective quantity of means A required for satiation is 10 a units and that of means B is 5 b units, then $10a$ A $= 5b$ B. And the terms (as a ratio) are the same if 1 b B procures 10 complete satisfactions, while 1 a A procures only five. Now it must be noted that such an equation represents equality only in this single respect—that is, each of these magnitudes *corresponds to* a third, the complete satisfaction of the want which each accomplishes. Since, in the example, the dimensions in which the two quantities are measured and the units in which they are expressed are different, they are, in terms of their respective objective measurements, incommensurable. Yet this is all that is necessary for the purpose. Nothing whatever would be added in the way of

---

[17] This magnitude of means in respect of any one want—or a multiple of it to include such future provision as is provided—appears to be the same category as Walras's *"utilité extensive"*—the quantity demanded at the price of zero (*420*, 72 ff.). Ostensibly, he does not make the mistake of treating this as a dimension of a want, though, as to that, we raise a question in Appendix IV. It is therefore *"une grandeur susceptible de mesure"* (*ibid.*, 73). It is apparently also the same category as Menger's *"Bedarf"* (*296*, 32–45). I am inclined to agree with Stigler (*386*, 234) that Menger visualized thus the quantity necessary for a complete satisfaction, though he was not explicit about it and did not see its implications. But it is evident that the want also has a second dimension to Menger—its *"Umfang"* (see *296*, 162 and elsewhere). We shall have difficulty in discovering what that is. And to Jevons, Wicksteed, and the English school of marginal utility theory in general, extensity becomes indirectly one of the dimensions of pleasure or satisfaction. These difficulties also are fully discussed in Appendix IV.

definiteness by converting the expression to terms of the same dimension and unit for both means, if that were possible. The only result of that would be to change, probably, the numerical ratio. Nor can one deduce from this equation that $2a$ A $=$ $1b$ B; for that would only be true if, for any aliquot part of a complete satisfaction, the two were also substitutable for each other in this ratio. In fact, to be true, it would probably be necessary that a complete satisfaction could be attained by a mixture—$6a$ A $+$ $2b$ B, say. Neither of these secondary propositions is necessarily true because the primary proposition is true.

Since we are assuming, only tentatively and only at this stage of the analysis, that no other considerations affect this choice between substitutes, it is safer to refer to this first approximation as the "unweighted terms of substitution." For, on the face of it, there is here no possible basis for choice. Quite the opposite! The equation itself represents the fact that its two expressions are, in this respect, indifferent. On the other hand, since the full measure of means does not change in size when the want merely varies from its maximum, we are assuming permanently and throughout our analysis that these ratios between alternative means—their unweighted terms of substitution—are constants, so long as each of the means themselves remains "objectively" the same—in ways to be defined as we proceed—and so long as the experience of their relative capacity to satisfy the want remains "subjectively" the same.

After a qualitative analysis according to identity (an individual instance) or of kind (defined by the limits of indifference) we find, then, that means, unlike our two other entities, wants and the process of satisfying them, are magnitudes susceptible of measurement according to two entirely independent comparisons—that is, they have two kinds of dimension, one objective and the other subjective. The first kind is their number (count), or their size, in terms of number of some arbitrary unit (pound, yard, gallon, minute) which represents a physical relationship to some other object or process with the same dimension which is used as a standard unit. The relationship between different objects or processes, however, need not be the same in terms of their several objective dimensions if they have more than one of these in common. We have therefore to choose a single dimension in which to compare two means objectively. If coal and flour are both measured objectively by the pound, then, *in weight*, ten pounds of flour equal ten pounds of coal. All that means, in reality, is that 10 *a* units equal 10 *a* units, or that gravity acts on both quantities equally. This tells us nothing about these substances as means. Entirely independent of this is the subjective unit—their relationship to wants. The only basis we have so far found for this is the full measure necessary to a satisfaction—and possibly a part measure. This full measure we may take as the unit in this dimension. In this respect a full measure of meat is equivalent to a full measure of bread in satisfying the single want, hunger. Their unweighted terms of substitution are then *x* meat = *y* bread. If, now, in terms of their objective dimensions, *x* meat is 2 pounds and *y* bread is 1 loaf, then the unweighted terms of substitution, in terms of these objective units, are 2 pounds of meat equal 1 loaf of bread. But in no other respect are 2 pounds of meat and 1 loaf of bread equal. Even their objective dimensions are here entirely disparate, just as much so as are these, respectively, with their subjective dimensions.

D. THE BASES OF ESTIMATION

I. USEFULNESS

Implicit in all our discussion of the qualitative relations of means to wants has been the assumption that means may serve to satisfy wants. More explicitly we concluded, in the subsection on means in relation to constellations of wants, that this power to serve depends on some one (or more) of the attributes of the means; in fact it is the presence of that attribute which makes of the object or act a means. While such a specific attribute exists only in the object or act, its peculiarity among all the other attributes of the object or act is that it establishes such a relation with a want. This singling out is therefore also dependent upon some specific want. Having now refined down this relation to one between a specific attribute and a specific want, we need a term for it. Moreover, we need a term that does not carry with it the connotations of the various technical terms used in marginal utility analysis. For, in the gradual differentiation of these technical terms, none has survived which now corresponds precisely to this relation and to nothing else. Let us call this relation the *usefulness* of the attribute and, through the possession of the attribute, the usefulness of the means.[1]

[1] Menger's general term for this relation is *Tauglichkeit*. But, more specifically, "Nützlichkeit ist die Tauglichkeit eines Ding, der Befriedung menschlicher Bedürfnisse zu dienen" (*296*, 84). If recognized, it is for him the first general presupposition of the

So long as the means has this attribute and so long as the related want recurs at all, the relation continues and the means retains such usefulness. Any particular means may have usefulness through the possession of several of these attributes, and thus have independent relations to several wants. And this multiplicity may be of such nature that the application of the means to several wants can only occur alternatively; or it may be of such nature that the means can, in a single process, jointly serve several or all (a constellation).

This analysis of means into terms of the usefulness of their several constituent attributes enables us also to refine our methods for dealing with the quantitative relations of means to wants. If the attribute of the means which occasions the relation of usefulness is simple—or if, when part of a compound, it can be analyzed into simplicity—it can be measured objectively, directly, and independently of the measurement of the whole means.[2] Otherwise it is usual to measure merely the means itself in terms of some one of its objective dimensions and to make no quantitative statement of the attribute other than in terms of more or less. But this admits a possibility that we have not had to consider so long as we limited ourselves to the subjective and objective magnitude of the means as a whole—a possibility that we must now examine.

Obviously such over-all treatment covers only the simplest and commonest cases where the ability of an objectively homogeneous means to satisfy a want—its usefulness—varies with the objective magnitude of the means. To meet that condition it is necessary that each equal subdivision of the means possess the same quantity of the attribute which gives it usefulness as each other one possesses. Of such means it is convenient to say that in all parts of it the attribute exists in the

---

property of being a good (*Güterqualität*). *Brauchbarkeit* (used by others) is to him equivalent to *Nützlichkeit* (*ibid.*, 78, note). Our "attribute" he describes as "such properties of the thing as make it suitable to be placed in causal relationship with the satisfaction of this want" (*ibid.*, 3). Senior clearly distinguished between the attribute and the relation, though in a different terminology. He says (370, 7), "Utility, however, denotes no intrinsic quality in the things which we call useful; it merely expresses their relations to the pains and pleasures of mankind." Davenport says the same thing (107, 86). Mill (298, I, 537) called this capacity, "use." It is, of course, closely allied with the old "value in use." Even at the beginning of the development of marginal utility theory that was not clearly disinguished from "utility." Thus Walras (420, 21) uses the same term, *utile*, to define things that "correspond to some need and permit the satisfaction of it" as he does for his technical utility. As we shall see, the various terms for this last category convey quite different meanings than our usefulness.

[2] The calories in carbohydrates, or the protein content of flour can be measured objectively. They are usually stated, however, as rates—so much per objective unit of the means.

same *density*. The usefulness of any quantity of such means will be proportionate, then, to the product of the quantity of means into the density of attribute; and, for any given density, it will be proportionate to the magnitude of the means. We must now differentiate another class of cases having to do especially with those attributes of means which serve for the satisfaction of the minor wants of a constellation. Here the magnitude of the attribute is wholly independent of the magnitude of the means. True, the attribute does not and cannot exist apart from the means. Nevertheless, one cannot, in these cases, obtain more of the attribute by obtaining more of the means, but only by obtaining another means that contains more of the attribute. For instance, a woman's gown may satisfy several wants in the constellation "dressing" (above)—warmth, protection, comfort, beauty, etc. The attribute for each of these wants is different from that for each other. If, for the sake of the argument, we assume that the want of temperature regulation is the major want, we may assume that the gown is selected because it satisfies this want completely. It may not, then, satisfy the lesser members of the constellation completely. If, as to protection, it does not, that deficiency—at least in a man's opinion—could be corrected by more gown. But any deficiency as to comfort and beauty could not be so corrected. The wants for these attributes cannot be satisfied by more gown but only by a greater magnitude in the gown of the attributes that are regarded as comfortable and beautiful. Obviously, then, there is in such a case by itself no determinant of the quantity of means wanted.[3]

At first sight we may seem, here, to be smuggling in notions of quality under the rubric quantity. But that cannot be conceded. For these comparisons can always be stated in terms of "more" or "less" —more or less beautiful and more or less comfortable—and terms of more or less are quantitative, not qualitative. Thus we must conclude that in many cases, and usually when the usefulness is compound— that is, when the means contains several attributes each relating it to a different want—but also in some cases where the usefulness is simple, it is necessary to differentiate between those attributes which occur in proportion to the quantity of means and those which do not. In respect of the second type of attribute, increase of quantity of means

[3] The quantity of means wanted will be determined, in the case of compounds, by the prior want. In the case of simple usefulness the quantity is usually determined by the artificially fixed size of the separated objective unit—the kind we count (i.e., one gown).

does not increase satisfaction. That can only be procured by electing another means which has a greater magnitude of the desired attribute. Since we treat even a compound means separately in respect of each want it serves, and since we regard as different means any which have different densities of the appropriate attribute or different fixed quantities of such attribute, we can apply this characteristic of the attributes to the means that contain them. Thus means of the first type will be called means of proportional usefulness; those of the second type will be called means of fixed usefulness. One means can be both, but usually only in respect of its usefulness to different wants. It is in connection, particularly, with means of fixed usefulness that the modification of our first hypothesis is required, in order to cover incomplete satisfaction. These means constitute the most frequent reason why the part measure must often suffice for the minor wants of a constellation and thus the most frequent reason why only a segment of the want is satisfied.[4]

Having established this quantitative relation of usefulness in terms of the subjective full or part measures of means, let us see what effect this has upon the conversion of such subjective measures into terms of their objective magnitudes. Obviously it makes no difference so long as the subjective measures are considered only as a whole. The usefulness of a full measure is the same when the latter is stated instead, in one of its objective dimensions, as two pounds of meat, for instance. We can then say that each of two pounds of meat, as part of the full measure, has half the usefulness of the full measure. But we cannot infer from that that each has separately that quantity of usefulness. Alone it becomes a part measure. Its usefulness as such must be determined independently.[5] This becomes even more obvious in the case of means of fixed usefulness. If we could measure in a precise way the attribute—beauty, for instance—which gives rise to the use-

[4] It is convenient to continue to use the term part measure to cover any quantity of a means whose content of a fixed attribute is insufficient to satisfy the want it serves.
[5] This viewpoint is somewhat different from that of marginal utility theory. There it is any ordinally marginal unit that is critical; here it is every unit required for a full measure that is critical—or, in marginal terms, the ordinally last necessary to complete the quantity. If one wants to get upstairs, for instance, it does not matter how many times the first step is taken. Mere repetition of that will not get one upstairs. The first step is essential, of course, but no more so than all the other steps in the flight. If the objective is merely to get up, then the first step will get one up $\frac{1}{n^{th}}$ as much as will the whole flight. But getting upstairs and getting up seven inches are two different objectives, the satisfactions of which are incomparable.

fulness of a woman's gown as satisfaction of the want for beauty in the constellation "dressing," it would not follow that half the attribute would have half the usefulness—i.e., yield half the satisfaction. And we could certainly not assert that half the gown had, when separated from the other half, half the usefulness even in this respect.[6]

In most respects usefulness applies to adequate provision for an instance of future want on the same basis as to a full measure for a present one. The quantities of means and the quantities of usefulness are the same for both. We have already supposed and will later find considerable reason to believe that the usefulness of an adequate future provision is the same regardless of the futurity of the instance of future want for which this adequate provision is made. It follows that, if actual behavior does not show that such provisions are indifferent among themselves regardless of futurity, it must be due to some other influence than subjective valuation. However, two modifications are required when we apply the notion of usefulness to provision for future wants. The first is due to the different operation of the members of constellations when they act as present wants and when they act as future wants. We have seen that, since only the major present want of a constellation can be prepotent until it is satiated, any satisfying of the minor present wants is purely incidental. If so, only the usefulness of the means for this major want is considered. On the other hand, since future wants exist in consciousness as elements of the mnemonic-volitional system, the essence of which is conflict, or the simultaneous presence of a number of wants, the case is different here. To the extent that such conflicting wants are harmonized because they have a common system of reactions, they are allied, not antagonistic. Thus the decision which is the resultant of their co-operation comes to combine, in various degrees according to their intensity, the several attributes of a compound means or the several means composing a conglomerate which will yield at least some degree of satisfaction for all.

How does usefulness apply here? In so far as it applies to a con-

[6] As a footnote to this it may be worth while to hazard a guess as to the matter of terms of substitution between several means containing fixed quantities of the attribute serving a single want. Here the terms of substitution cannot be stated in the form of numbers of objective units of each means, for the quantity of attribute is not proportional to the quantity of means. If so, the means cannot be reduced to equality in a correspondence. No amount of the means that is half satisfactory will equal a means that is three-quarters or wholly satisfactory. Thus the choice is not between equivalents; it is between different degrees of incomplete satisfaction—and occasionally between one of these and complete satisfaction. As such, the several means are not, strictly speaking, substitutes for each other at all, though all may serve a single want.

glomerate of means each single means among which serves but one member, the case would be no different from other estimations of usefulness. The only combining is that of combining separate means that are separately estimated but are used in one process—one system of consummatory reactions. But when an individual means of a conglomerate, or any other individual means, is compound, because it contains attributes serving several wants, the case is different. The usefulness of each attribute is then measured separately. Does the final estimation of the means then equal the sum of the usefulness of all its attributes? We shall discuss this question more fully in the following chapter. Here we may say that we do not find it possible to settle this question at all definitely by observation—which is the only method available. In the commonest cases, summation seems not to occur. In some cases the usefulness seems to be cumulative, though apparently not precisely so. However, there is no reason to assume precision upon the basis of our premises. Even the difference between the intensities of the several wants seems to be measurable only in terms of more or less. How, then, can they be added? Also actual behavior often shows a choice of means in which the attribute serving some minor want is present only in a quantity insufficient for satiation. For that want the means is only a part measure. Presumably a full measure would have been preferred. But it was not chosen. Even more frequently the attribute is inadequate because it exists in fixed quantity. In order to obtain a larger part measure or a full measure it would have been necessary to choose another means altogether. Yet this one was chosen. We can probably assume that the usefulness, for a single want, of different quantities of a single means in which the attribute exists proportionally or of a different means in which it exists in fixed quantities can be compared with some considerable degree of accuracy. Whether or not that permits the more complicated comparison of the summated usefulness of quantities of two means for the same wants, one of which contains more of the attribute for one minor want and less of the attribute for another minor want in the same constellation than does the other, is a much more uncertain question. Perhaps comparisons of summated usefulness, when they occur, are much more rough and ready than those of usefulness as to a single want.[7]

[7] We did not complicate our consideration of unweighted terms of substitution, above, by introducing this elaboration. Nevertheless a word of explanation of the concept is necessary. A set of substitutes for the major want of a constellation may include, in various assortments, attributes fitting them to serve minor members. Thus, to use our

The second modification necessary when applying the notion of usefulness to provision for future wants concerns the types of means capable of being included therein. The essence of means, so far as future wants are concerned, is that their usefulness should persist, in whole or in part, from the time provision is made until the date of the instance of future want. Since by their nature all acts of self or others are ephemeral, it is clear that they cannot persist. Therefore, at first sight, they would seem to be excluded from future provision. That would leave objects as the only means which can be so included, and, among objects, it would leave only those which do actually last. Though these will constitute all our examples of future provision and our analysis will continue to be based on them exclusively, it is necessary to admit, here, that the distinction is not quite so sharp as it seems at first sight. Precurrent reactions, whether of self or others—though themselves ephemeral—may have somewhat permanent effects. The effects themselves cannot be thought of as objects, but they must be embodied in some object if they are to last. The object in which they are embodied may be the person himself. Thus the effects of learning (acts of self) and of teaching (acts of others)—existing as acquired skills—may endure.[8] To the individual in which they are embodied, such skills are in some sense future provision, in so far as they will themselves serve directly for the satisfaction of later wants; and they will enter as a factor to which we shall assign the name efficiency, in so far as they affect the relation between precurrent reactions applied to future provision and their effects, as we shall note in Part II.

If, now, we convert into terms of this relation between wants and means, now defined and refined as usefulness, our previously mentioned analytical tool, the virtual order of preference,[9] we see that, if

---

illustration in the next chapter, a constellation consisting of Wants C, F, H, and K may be offered the following substitutes (indicated by the corresponding letters): c, cf, cfh and cfhk; it is possible that ch, ck, cfk and chk might exist. All these compound means contain the attribute c. For the purpose of our analysis, means without c would have to be defined as for a different constellation—even if that were also "eating," for instance. Thus, to keep the record clear, a sherbet would have to be defined as "dessert," not "food."

[8] It is true that they do not exist independently of the person and therefore do not constitute what we shall call intermediate product, since product should not, if it is exactly defined, include human beings. It is also true that, in any indirect economy whose institutional arrangements are such that human beings cannot be the objects of property and therefore cannot be transferred, such skills do not constitute transferable property and therefore do not come within the strictly defined boundaries to which the term "capital" should be limited.

[9] See Section A, note 8, above.

such order reflected only the intensity of the several wants, declining through their order of priority, the corresponding virtual order of preference among means would be arranged according to the usefulness of full measures of the several means and would decline to the same degree through such order of preference.[10] Thus the process of subjective valuation has become for us a process only. We have not arrived at a method by which a certain subjective value can be assigned to one quantity of means independently of others. We have only arrived at a basis of comparison among all means—a basis that permits an ordering of them in terms of more or less usefulness. This can be, though in practice it has not always been, true of marginal utility analysis as well. In some applications that has required absolute quantities of subjective value, determinable before comparisons (and therefore choices) can be made.[11] But the fundamental distinction between ours and the method of marginal utility theory lies in the magnitudes of means to be compared. We offer a carefully defined and easily ascertainable magnitude as the basis of comparison. We shall have difficulty in finding any form of marginal utility theory in which this is done. And that will prove to be an invalidating flaw which, in most of them, cannot be corrected.

Quantitatively as well as qualitatively the relation of usefulness, once established, remains unchanged if the means remains unchanged. That is, so long as the means retains the same quantity of attribute and the want varies in intensity only through the same range—from its normal maximum to complete, or to some definite degree of incomplete, satisfaction—the magnitude of usefulness remains the same. Clearly this is the estimate or measure of a potential, a capacity, which only becomes actual when the means is applied to the satisfying of the want.

[10] It is not necessary to confuse this statement by introducing the question of incomplete satisfactions and the preferences among the corresponding part measures of means.
[11] Among early apostles of marginal utility theory, J. B. Clark (80, 380) clearly distinguishes between this ability of the person to compare at best roughly and the ability then to infer from his reactions more accurately. Others disclaim the possibility that an observer can measure changes in the intensity of a want, but tacitly assume that the person himself can do so, since the external effects which the economist does measure are assumed to be precise reflections of some exact internal measurement. See, for instance, Marshall (291, 15) and Jevons (224, 11). Again, many disclaim the possibility that an observer should compare the intensities of wants in two different persons. See, for instance, Jevons (224, 14) supported by his follower Wicksteed (440, 68 and 441, 146, 440, 488). As Pareto puts it (317, 265), there is "no bridge" between them. But another follower, of the "welfare" branch, was not so cautious. Edgeworth (133, 54, note 2) originally stated that "units of pleasure are to be equated irrespective of persons."

We shall have to consider next what happens to this potential—usefulness—when, after applying a means to the satisfying of a want, the process has involved a reduction in the quantity of attribute. That is a definite change in one of the two relata which presumably alters the relation between them. Thereafter, we shall proceed to consider all the changes that have been conceived to take place upon the side of the other relatum—the want—which have been supposed also to alter the relation. But, it should be noted here that, so far as concerns our own definition of the influence upon the want side that determines this potential, it is subject to none of these changes, as we shall see. Therefore, for our purposes, usefulness is a definite magnitude which gives us a firm basis for our further analysis.

Our conclusion is that it is this relation of potential usefulness, in terms of magnitude of fixed attribute only, or in terms of the product of density of attribute into quantity of means, which underlies and is the basis of all subjective estimation of means. While marginal utility theory has tended more and more to elide this continuing potential relation between a want and the appropriate attribute of a means, and has always failed to establish it as a magnitude which is subjectively measurable—if it has not denied this possibility [12]—we, on the contrary, find it indispensable to all explanation of the economic process. What we have done is to set up again, in somewhat different and at least more precise form, and as, within certain limits, a measurable magnitude, the category of usefulness, which bears a close relation to the old and discarded "use-value."

On the basis of the foregoing analysis it becomes possible, in a precise manner, to relate certain economic processes to the usefulness of means for the satisfaction of wants. In the first place we may define *consumption*—which we have derived from the category of consummatory reactions—in so far as it is concerned with means in the form of objects, to be the more or less gradual using-up of the attributes that give rise to the usefulness of a means, in the course of satisfying a want. By that statement we recognize that the attribute which makes of any object a means, is usually destroyed during the process, or suc-

[12] To set up even a roughly (subjectively) measurable magnitude, equivalent to the old "use-value," is, of course, also directly contradictory to the most precise of the classical economists. Ricardo says (Chap. XXXII) that one set of goods cannot be compared with another and that "value in use cannot be measured by any known standard." We only agree with him that "it is differently estimated by different persons."

cession of processes, of satisfying a want.[13] As the attribute disappears, obviously the relation of usefulness also disappears. In so far as consumption is concerned with means in the form of acts of self or others the definition is not quite so clear. Since an act is by its nature ephemeral, its attributes must always disappear as it is performed. It is used up as a means to the extent that its usefulness is availed of in the course of performance. For the rest, it merely disappears. On the other hand, the attributes of objects may be used up more or less gradually. When they are used up in a long series of successive processes, or in a prolonged continuous one, we arbitrarily but conveniently call them *durable* objects. When they last in use only through a single brief process,[14] or a short series, we call them *non-durable* objects.[15] It is more convenient and usually does no violence to the facts to regard any object capable of more than a single use, either durable or non-durable, as if it were used up in installments—that is, successive processes. In fact, the notion of installments of multiple-use objects fits better the facts of the recurrence and occurrence of wants, as heretofore analyzed, than does the idea of continuous use.[16] In this way the object comes to be treated as if it were composed of a number of parts, one of which disappears in the course of each process—each use.[17] While this is untrue of the physical existence of the object and

[13] Not, of course, always (e.g., jewels). It is a little strong, however, to say, as Cassel does (74, 13), "there is no such thing as consumption in the material sense. It is an economic conception." "Gloves, for instance, are worn out rather quickly, but their utility does not consist in their being worn out." It is true, as Marshall says (291, 64), "Often when he [man] is said to consume things, he does nothing more than to hold them for his use, while, as Senior says, they 'are destroyed by numerous gradual agents which we call collectively *time*' . . . but he uses them while time wastes them." Thus, we might regard consumption as the purely economic process of *using* which causes, or involves, the physical process of *using-up,* the latter being what we mean by the loss of the attribute. But, if this loss of attribute is not due to, or is not accompanied by, *using,* then the change is not due to consumption. That is the distinction we wish to establish in order to differentiate consumption from other losses of usefulness. On the other hand, if it were not for these physical changes, which are usually though variously inherent in the process of using, usefulness would continue forever and there would be no using-up. It is always and only a disadvantage that using involves destruction or using-up. As Senior puts it (370, 54), product "is produced for the purpose of being made use of. Its destruction is an incident to its use, not only not intended, but, as far as possible, avoided."

[14] The chief one-use objects are food, drink and fuel.

[15] For further discussion and more precise definition of these classifications see Chapter 10.

[16] See pp. 400–402.

[17] This viewpoint enables us to dispense with the separate entity "services of goods," which is only required when the "goods" themselves are regarded in their physical rather than their economic aspects. As Stigler points out (386, 232) Menger did not

is not even entirely true of its usefulness, it is the only way in which the successive uses can be equated among themselves and still sum up to the total.

In the single or successive process of using-up, the physical object may disappear altogether, or may change but slightly, or anything in between; it may be incorporated into the person, or it may stay where it was while the person moves on. That is not the point for economic analysis. The only point of interest is the using-up of usefulness for the want or wants to which the object is applied. Usefulness may remain for some of the other wants of a constellation (e.g., old-fashioned clothes) or for other wants (e.g., scrap). The quantity of using-up of usefulness is the quantity of consumption of means. In addition to this using-up, usefulness may disappear in other ways. We have already noted that the usefulness of acts of self and others may disappear in the course of performance without being used up—that is, without being consumed. The same thing may occur with objects. First the usefulness may disappear, without use, due to the destruction of the object, or due to the shrinkage or loss of the attribute which makes of it a means (spoilage, etc.). Second, it is possible for it to disappear, without use, due to a change in the other relatum, the want. But this is only a loss of usefulness, strictly speaking, if the want ceases to exist; and that is a most unusual event. What appears to be a change in the list of wants is, in reality, almost always a change in their order of priority (rare) or in the terms of substitution (frequent) among the various means appropriate to a particular want. The latter is not a change in the relatum, want, nor does it involve a loss of usefulness.

2. THE SIGNIFICANCE OF USEFULNESS

Subjective valuation has been the peculiar province, nay almost the discovery, of marginal utility theory. For that reason it becomes advisable for us to set up the hypothesis we have already presented in ways that parallel that, or those, of this theory in order that the similarities and the differences may become clear. The great progress in the analysis of subjective valuation which resulted from the simultaneous and independent original development of the several forms of the

---

make this distinction. Some of his followers have adopted it. Böhm-Bawerk, for instance (*38*, 339), finds that "the single service [our use] forms a smaller economical unit clearly distinguished from the good itself" which "is capable of obtaining a certain economical independence." The concept is, of course, general in the "mathematical school" and among those greatly influenced by that school.

theory, and from the work of succeeding investigators, has nevertheless left in its wake a considerable degree of confusion, not only in
terminology but in concepts as well.[18] It is difficult to present any one
form of the theory as *the* theory; and it is even more difficult to place
most of the several forms upon a basis which permits the application of
the necessary rules for dealing with magnitudes, according to the
theory of dimensions recognized in the physical sciences. However,
we shall attempt, in the rest of Part I and in Appendix IV, to sift out
from the several forms of the theory, the two which, subject to certain modifications, prove tenable on these grounds. Here we shall
only undertake to establish the single most radical point of contrast
between all forms of the theory, on the one hand, and the foregoing
analysis, on the other. That point concerns the definition and term
for the particular relation that subsists among and between the two
entities, wants and means, and their inter-operating process, the satisfying of wants by means. In this connection we will find it most helpful constantly to consider Menger, whose qualitative analysis of these
matters was much more thorough and precise than those of his more
mathematical contemporaries and their followers.[19]

As will become increasingly evident, the single magnitude in respect
of this particular relation that is covered by the term "usefulness," as
heretofore defined, suffices for the purposes of our own hypothesis.
Marginal utility theory has, I think, usually tacitly assumed—though
generally without analysis—the existence of this relation of usefulness.[20]
But, as we noted above, because of certain of its purposes and certain
of its assumptions, this magnitude has not sufficed for such theory. Instead, it has required, beside or instead of this one, the concept of another and far more fluctuating relation between wants and means.
According to this view the "subjective value" of a particular unit of
a particular means varies widely because, under different momentary
circumstances, there is conceded to it more or less of something which

[18] This, I think, has been largely due to an almost exclusive concern with the bearing of
this work on value theory, rather than on that of economic motivation.
[19] In startling contrast to the remarkable analysis of Menger and his extreme caution
in limiting himself to the boundaries of this analysis, appears the work of the man who
seems to me to be the original marginal utility theorist. Senior really assembled the raw
materials of utility theory when he summed up his ideas in defining intrinsic causes of
value (see *370*, 11–12 and *371*, 3–7). But he never developed these brilliant insights, nor
was he wholly consistent (systematic) with regard to them.
[20] See note 1, above.

goes by a medley of different names. Because we prefer not to identify the somewhat modified forms of marginal utility analysis, which we shall develop later, with any particular brand of that theory, we would like to avoid the use of any of the specific names for this something. But, since one of them serves our purposes particularly well, we will choose for it the name "significance." [21] To relate the two magnitudes to each other we shall define significance to be the significance of the usefulness—or the significant usefulness—of a particular unit of a means to a particular person at a particular moment in view of the then state of his wants, and in view of, or as a result of, his choices and limitations.[22] This definition implies that significance can be less than usefulness but cannot be more—which implication, I believe, does no violence to any form of marginal utility theory.[23]

The general concept may be stated to be this: As the quantity of means is increased, the significance of the successive increments de-

[21] The choice of the English word "significance" is obviously suggested by Wicksteed's usage. To him, as to us, significance pertains directly to a definite quantity of commodity or to his "service rendered by the commodity" (441, 43), which is our usefulness in its active aspect. Menger uses the same term (Bedeutung) to describe the recognized dependence of life or welfare, and thereby of the satisfaction of a want, upon the disposal over a good (296, 78 and 85). This dependence is strictly a relation between the satisfaction of a want and the disposal over a good (ibid., 106). But, in general, it first pertains to the satisfaction of a want and is then transferred or projected upon the good itself (ibid., 87). The term significance is colorless and unspoiled for technical use, while the popular term "utility" has been ruined for purposes of economic analysis by being used in the course of years for so many different or ill-defined purposes. For instance, the original "utilitarian," Bentham, used the term "utility" to mean the attribute, which is one of the relata of our usefulness (see "Introduction" to the Principles of Morals and Legislation, p. 3). Moreover the "utility of usefulness" would sound like hair splitting, though "the significance of usefulness" (or "significant usefulness") serves our purposes well. There have been frequent attempts to escape the use of the old and popular term "utility"; however, the difficulty for us is, as a few citations will show, that these economists are not agreed among themselves on what it is that is to be named. Fisher (142, 42) prefers the term "desirability," and Pigou (325, 23), "desiredness," because both conceive that the thing they wish to name is "intensity of desire" for an object. But desire, as such, does not relate to our scheme. To Pareto (317, 158-159) "ophelimity" is definitely a measure of pleasure; probably Jevons held this view of his degree of utility (see 224, 45 and 65), although at first (ibid., 38) utility is "the abstract quality whereby an object serves our purposes" (i.e., our usefulness); certainly Edgeworth did so (133, 61). Neither does a quantity of pleasure enter into our scheme. J. B. Clark's "effective utility," as he defines it (80, 376), and most of the older usages are synonymous with our usefulness, rather than our significance. Walras's usage of "utility" is so confused, as we shall see, that it cannot be said to have, for him, any definite meaning at all. We may be excused, I think, for again "sticking to Menger."
[22] The pseudo-mathematical term "coefficient of choice," which is sometimes used (e.g., Schumpeter, 364, 11), emphasizes this last feature.
[23] This was Mill's idea, I think, when he said (298, I, 537) "Value in use . . . is the extreme limit of value in exchange."

clines. It is clear that the equation of supply and demand, which assumes a decline of value, or price, as quantity supplied is increased,[24] is the fundamental concept underlying all early forms of marginal utility theory. It was from this source that the declining significance of means with increasing quantity was derived. Or, rather, it may be said that this generalization, derived from observation in the gross, received its first rational explanation on the demand side from the concept of declining significance. Now, as we shall note in Appendix IV, marginal utility theory did not distinguish at all, or at all clearly, between the three possible relationships to individual instances of single wants which are implied in the notion of declining significance. All treat roughly of "stocks," analyzed in terms of means rather than wants. However, in so far as this characteristic of declining significance is universal, it must be supposed to apply to three quite diverse situations. In other words, it requires three entirely independent assumptions:

a. That the intensity of a want, or other driving force, declines during a single satisfaction.[25]

b. That, for a means capable of alternative uses for different wants, its significance will be determined for an instance of the prior want up to satiation and that quantities superfluous for this satisfaction will have only the lesser significance derived from the subordinate want.[26]

c. That provisions for instances of future wants have less significance in proportion to, or as a result of, increasing degree of futurity.

In most of the literature these several assumptions are more or less mixed in a single conglomerate, the elements of which are often not distinguished. In our analysis, on the other hand, we are dealing separately with each of the three assumptions, as their nature requires. We are utilizing the first as the basis of two of our later hypotheses. But we are utilizing it on a wholly tentative basis, without acceptance or

---

[24] See, for instance, Mill's statement of it (*298*, I, 551).

[25] It is worth noting that J. B. Clark, for one, qualified this assumption very strongly. He said (*80*, 211), "The theory of value has not taken due account of the abruptness in the decline in the utility of an article, when successive units of it, wholly uniform in quality, are offered to one customer."

[26] We briefly stated the case of alternative uses on p. 421.

This assumption is here stated in its pure form in order to distinguish it completely from the first assumption (a). Occasionally it seems to occur in this pure form; but more often it is combined with assumption (a). That is, it is held that the initial increment of the means will be applied to the prior want until marginal significance is brought down to the initial level of the next want for which the means is susceptible of alternative use; etc. The end-result would then be equal marginal significance in all uses for which the supply sufficed.

rejection, subject to the proof or disproof which will be furnished by our final synthesis.[27] We are accepting the second without question in cases where it applies; for this is implicit in our order of priority of wants and in the virtual order of preference based on it.[28] We are reserving further consideration of the third assumption until Part II, where we shall find fairly well confirmed our conclusion in Chapter 6 that the apparent phenomenon is not due at all to subjective valuation, in its strict sense, but entirely to the influence of another factor, extraneous to the driving force of wants and therefore not related to the criterion according to which significance is gauged.[29]

While it is not always safe to impute the whole of this conglomerate assumption, nor even any definite one or more of its parts, to individual protagonists, the general statement is warranted that more or less of it is involved in every case. As a result, certain inconsistencies appear. It behooves us to examine, then, the more important conditions under which the significance of any quantity of means, as conceived in marginal utility theory, is less than its usefulness. These conditions may be divided into two groups. In the first group, significance becomes nil [30] for a particular person at a particular moment, with reference to a particular set of satisfactions. That is, this group presumes to deal only with the isolated effect of assumption (a) above. Some of the conditions in this group have been explicitly stated; some have only been implied or must be inferred. But to make our contrast complete, and because they are all necessary assumptions of the theory in all its forms, we must include them all. The first condition is usually made explicitly, but in various and somewhat indefinite terms and always as to an isolated example.[31] If, at the moment, the present want which the means

---

[27] It is true that our acceptance of partial satisfaction as an occasional phenomenon—more especially among minor wants—may seem to leave room for this assumption in our own scheme. Nevertheless, I believe the reader will agree that, so far as we are able to deal with partial satisfactions at all, they do not require the notion of declining significance.

[28] So far as demand for the particular means is concerned, the notion of reduced significance applies. But from the standpoint of our analysis, "In all cases like this, the second unit of the commodity is virtually a different thing from the first one" (J. B. Clark, *80*, 234).

[29] However, in view of the requirement that provision of means for future wants will not be made beyond the limit of futurity at which the means will lose its usefulness (i.e., no longer "keep"), it is necessary to suppose that means in excess of provisions within such a limit are always superfluous (i.e., have no present usefulness or significance).

[30] Or even a negative quantity, "disutility," etc.

[31] That is, it is implicit in all representations in which the curve of significance reaches zero at some point on the *x* axis.

serves is in abeyance or has been satisfied, such means has no significance for that instance of the want. As a corollary of that, if a particular unit of means is ordinally in excess of a full measure for an instance of present want or of an adequate provision for an instance of future want, it has no significance for such instances.[32] The mere attempt to define this condition shows that it cannot exist under the assumptions that we are entitled to import at this point. For, if future wants enter the picture at all, such a unit, in excess for these instances, ought to be significant as part of provision for some other instance of the future want.[33] Our analysis in Chapter 6 led us to suppose that innumerable instances of each future want extending into the indefinite future are, so far as they themselves are concerned, all equally operative in the present. Correspondingly, the number of adequate provisions required would then be unlimited. It is true that, out of deference to reality, we are already assuming that there is some such limitation. Nevertheless, our analysis in the preceding chapter led us to the conclusion that this is not due to the failure of such instances of future wants to be effective now—so that, therefore, the unit of means is deprived of significance—but, rather, that it is due to an opposing force which prevents the making of provision, leaving intact the future want and the significance it confers upon the unit of means.

The second condition is not made explicitly. In fact, it can only be inferred. But it necessarily follows from the assumption upon which the first condition is based. If a choice were made between two means appropriate to satisfying one want so that a full measure or adequate provision were made for the effective instance, the significance of the rejected means would be reduced to zero. For, being as superfluous as an excess of the chosen means under the first condition, it could not have significance if that excess did not. The difficulty with this condition is the same as with the preceding one, since it is indirectly dependent on that. A further difficulty, so far as subjective valuation

[32] The full measure or adequate provision may consist of 10 units, whereas this is the 11th. Hayek, in his introduction to Menger's *Grundsätze* (*296*, XV), suggests this view of the "edge" of a quantity—a marginal unit. Stigler uses the term ordinal in his article on Menger (*386*, 240). Apparently Menger's tables are the source of both suggestions. The marginal unit can only be identified mathematically, but not in time or in order. It is the unit which converts $n-1$ units into n units, or the reverse, where n units are required.
[33] That is, one cannot carry assumption (a), above, to its logical conclusion without excluding assumption (c).

standing on its own feet is concerned, is the one that we have already raised with our own unweighted terms of substitution. We recognized then that, without importing some other factor to govern choice, no choice between alternative means would be possible except in respect of minor wants of a constellation, the attributes serving which exist in fixed quantities in the means. For any two means serving the same want, in which the attribute yielding usefulness is proportional to the magnitude of the means, there must always be some quantity of the first that will yield the same degree of satisfaction yielded by any particular quantity of the second which is used as the basis for comparison. This will be true up to and including the quantities of each constituting a full measure. Such pairs of quantities are, by definition, indifferent.

The third condition has to do with that limitation that we are assuming under the name capacity. Usually this is imported into marginal utility analysis only in the form of a limitation on the available quantity of a particular means, rather than as a limitation on the available quantity of all means. In this way a factor is introduced which is extraneous to pure subjective valuation. But we can infer what would be the effect of a limitation on all means in terms of the general analysis. If a limitation on capacity exists, it involves a choice. Would it be possible that means might then be applied to the complete satisfaction of certain wants only, and that perhaps some wants would be excluded entirely? No! For, under such circumstances, if the first condition ever arose with reference to a want included—that is, if the significance of its means ever declined to zero—that would require, as a condition precedent, that the significance of the means for all the wants excluded had already declined to zero. Otherwise some of the latter means would have been preferred at some previous stage in the process of satisfaction.

The fourth condition follows from this. For, if our concept of capacity is an elastic one—such as we require for an analytical tool—we can contract it to the period during which means are being applied to a single want. Only one present want (disregarding constellations) can be satisfied at a time. That is the limit of capacity for the period required. For that period all other wants are excluded. If, with reference to that one want, the first condition could arise, so that one unit of its means would lose all significance, then, at that moment, the significance of the means for all wants excluded would also have had to decline to zero. Otherwise they would have been preferred at some previous stage in the process of satisfaction.

It may seem to the reader that in stating these four conditions—of which only the first is taken directly from marginal utility analysis and the others are inferred—we have merely set up straw men in order to knock them down. However, this seems to be the best way to expose the basic inconsistency in the notion of significance as an independent determinant of subjective valuation. We are tossed on the horns of a dilemma. Under the supposition of declining intensity during a satisfaction, either significance never declines to zero, because no want is ever completely satisfied, or, when any unit of one selected means loses all significance, all units of all means for all wants must already have lost all significance.

The second group of conditions include those under which significance is conceived merely to become less than its maximum—a maximum which is, in effect, our usefulness. These conditions are presented in the form of two schemes in which significance is graded down from its maximum to zero so that, at different particular moments and under different particular conditions, it may stand at any point along the scale between all and none. The first of these schemes is conceived to reflect the influence of what we are calling future wants. That is, it deals with the cases under assumption (c) above, as if these were isolated from the other influences. According to this, the present significance of a quantity of means declines at a somewhat uniform rate, toward and to zero, as the time at which the means will be applied recedes into the future—or, in our terminology, in proportion to the degree of futurity of each particular instance of the future want.[34] We have already found it necessary to concede that there is an influence that offers increasing opposition to provision for future wants in proportion to the length of the interval between the present and the date of the instance—its degree of futurity. But this is very different from supposing a diminution in the influence of the want. As to that we have concluded that instances of future wants diminish neither

---

[34] Perhaps this visualizes a more systematic treatment than has ever been accorded the subject in marginal utility analysis itself. But it seems fairly to represent the end-point toward which such treatments tend. See, for instance, Ely (*135, 140*).

Most of the originators failed to consider the effect of time in respect of future wants except as they included it as one of the elements diminishing the significance of successive increments of a stock of goods. We may cite Menger (*296, 32–38*). Marshall (*291, 93*) is even less explicit as to the time element. For Jevons's and Wicksteed's treatment, see note 35, below.

in vividness nor in intensity according to their futurity.[35] If either of these dimensions or any other related one, is responsible for conferring significance upon means, there is no reason to suppose that such significance varies with futurity. If so, then, whatever the elastic limitation on future provision is, it is not connected with subjective valuation, so long as that is held to rest on the determination of significance.

The second of these schemes has, in many cases, to be imputed. That is, in many cases, the first and second schemes seem to be merged. But, in others they are more or less distinct. In order, then, to deal with assumption (a) above as an isolated influence, we impute this scheme as at least a partial cause in all forms of marginal utility. We state it as the general thesis, which we brought up in the fourth chapter, to the effect that the intensity of a want declines gradually during the process of satisfaction until it would finally reach zero at satiety if the process were carried that far. Upon the basis of this thesis it is supposed that, whatever it may be that reflects significance upon the means, such influence would reflect less significance upon each successive equal increment of means used through the single process.[36] The ideas and names for the source of this reflection are, as we have already noted, various.[37] But, under all the various ideas and names, the thesis as to diminishing significance is uniform.

When we come to examine what actually happens under all of the sets of circumstances that we tried to include in the first group of conditions and under the first condition of the last group, we shall see

[35] Jevons (224, 71–74) admits this, in theory. If we were gifted with "perfect good sense and foresight," "all future wants, all future pleasures and pains, should act upon us with the same force as if they were present." But human minds are not so perfect. "A future feeling is always less influential than a present one" (ibid., 72). Nevertheless, his treatment diminishes the significance of future provision only according to the uncertainty that it will be needed, not in proportion to the time interval.

Wicksteed comes to the same conclusion, but more definitely. He says (441, 113): "The fact of remoteness or proximity [in time] should not, and within limits does not, in itself affect our estimates of the significance of things that are really of even and continuous importance to us. But very often remoteness involves uncertainty, so that we are not prepared to estimate a possible want in the remote future on the same terms as a certain want in the present or a highly probable one in the proximate future."

Nevertheless, the declining utility of expanding "stocks," as assumed by Menger, Walras, and others, must include this scheme as at least a part of the cause—alternative uses being the only other part.

[36] If the reader finds that this is not a satisfactory statement of what is sometimes called Gossen's law, I will refer him to the next chapter, where I discuss the various forms of the theory in greater detail and deal particularly with the notion that the successive increments of "pleasure" can be depicted as proportionate to the existing state of intensity, instead of to the reduction in intensity.

[37] See note 21, above.

that the notion of significance is unnecessary if our own hypothesis is accepted. All are readily explained in terms of our (under these conditions) fixed magnitude of the usefulness of a full or part measure of means, when that is combined with the other confluent influences—influences which we recognize as coming from outside the sphere of subjective valuation. The notion of significance as apart from usefulness is also unnecessary under all conditions so far as our own hypothesis, as previously developed, is concerned. And this because this hypothesis does not admit the last-named condition at all. It is predicated on the thesis that the intensity of want does not noticeably decline during the continuance of a single process of satisfaction, unless that process is interrupted, when it may perhaps assume some new position in the same or a later order of priority. Thus, if that were all there were to it—if it sufficed merely to present our own hypothesis —we need have made no mention of the matter of significance. But, in the first place, it is important, in considering this somewhat novel hypothesis of ours, to be able to relate, and so to compare, it to the general type of those which have held the field quite generally since marginal utility theory, in its various forms, became the vogue. And, in the second place, our thesis as to the maintenance of the intensity of a want throughout the process of satisfaction has not been proved. Probably it cannot be proved from physiological evidence. At least it cannot be, in the absence of an objective method of measuring the intensity of wants. It has merely been inferred from behavior, and this only in a very limited way. In the third place, we have to remember that our resuscitation of something of the nature of the old "use-value" to take the place of this mercurial entity, significance, may be regarded as an atavism. That is, to many it may seem that setting up again an "order of priority" as the chief scale among wants is merely to repeat what Böhm-Bawerk called the "mistake" of pre-marginal-utility value theory.[38] Our best procedure, therefore, will be to carry through, in our analysis, both alternatives; to compare at each stage the virtual orders of preference that would result by predicating either assumption; and, when we have combined these virtual orders with the effects of all other pertinent influences, to test each with reality. When we have done that it may turn out that we have proved our thesis as

[38] "By which scale shall we measure the importance of wants . . . the scale of kinds or the scale of concrete wants? When the older theory came to this dividing of the ways—the very first opportunity offered it of making a mistake—it chose the wrong way" (*38*, 142).

to the maintenance of intensity, so far as behavior can prove it. Thus we shall need the notion of significance—or significant usefulness—and shall continue to use the term as an analytical tool in connection with the hypotheses as to subjective valuation which we find it possible to sift out from the various forms of marginal utility theory.

In order further to clarify the relation between significance, on the one hand, as that will appear in the alternative hypotheses we shall develop, and, on the other, our own magnitude usefulness, it is necessary to consider the two special precipitations of significance that are crucial in these alternative hypotheses. The first is *marginal significance*,[39] or, more precisely, the significance of the marginal increment. As stated above,[40] the marginal increment of means is that one which comes ordinally last in any quantity considered—that one which converts n-1 units into n units, or the reverse. Two points require attention in this connection. In the first place, it should be noticed that this introduces, as the critical issue, the question of the size of the increment, since the distinction can only be made between two equal increments. But equal increments are usually defined in terms of objective units. Therefore, in this treatment, the arbitrary objective unit is apt to become of the essence of subjective measurement, as it is not in our treatment. Moreover, as we shall see, it has been customary to play fast and loose with these objective units, to impute to them a part which they are inherently incapable of playing. In the second place, it is obvious that this notion of a marginal increment is only needed if "it is supposed that whatever it may be that reflects significance upon the means would reflect less significance upon each successive increment of means used through the process"—to quote our own statement of Gossen's law, above. For what, we may ask, would be the marginal increment or unit under our hypothesis? All portions of a full measure of means contribute proportionately to making up the quantity required. Each is some fraction of the whole. And, if the intensity of the want is practically maintained at one level until satiation is reached, it is not

[39] This is, again, Wicksteed's term. Menger's nearest expression (*296*, 108) is "der Bedeutung, welche die wenigst wichtigen von den durch die verfügbare Gesammtquantität noch gesicherten und mit einer solchen Theilquantität herbeizuführenden Bedürfnissbefriedungen für das obige Subjekt haben." This is slightly inconvenient. *Grenznutzen* is Wieser's abbreviation, suggested by him in his *Ursprung des Werthes*, p. 128. Hence "marginal utility" (Wieser, *442*, 13, and Marshall, *291*, 93, note 1). Jevons's is "final utility"; Pareto's "elementary ophelimity": Walras's is "*rareté*," or "the intensity of the last want (*besoin*) satisfied"; Gossen's is "*Werth des letzten Atoms.*"
[40] See note 32, above.

possible to distinguish the effect of different portions, since none has any effect except as part of the whole. This is equally true of part measures. The only question remaining then would be whether each part measure, in turn, could be treated as marginal until the sum of them equaled a full measure. However, so far as spontaneous segmentation is concerned, the three reasons we have cited for the failure to satiate present wants and therefore the three chief occasions giving rise to part measures do not yield to such treatment. Different wants behave differently when the process of satisfaction is incomplete. Some seem to remain at the same intensity, some to find a new level, and some to disappear entirely for the time being. Further part measures would then have reflected upon them the same intensity, or less, or none at all. And, in the case of a means which suffices only for incomplete satisfaction for the reason that its attribute exists in fixed quantity, no more of that means will repair the deficiency. The notion of increment of means is there inapplicable. It is true, of course, that, once the magnitude of a full measure is objectively determined, a part measure will be seen to be less. In any choice between the two, the full measure will be preferred. Thus the satisfying of present wants and provision for future wants will always be made in terms of full measures, if that is possible. But we cannot say with any precision what will be the position of a part measure in the virtual order of preference, if only a part measure is available. And, if only that is available, the concept of the ordering and summation of several part measures is inapplicable. Hence, in terms of our analysis when restricted to pure subjective valuation, the notion of a marginal part measure has no meaning.[41]

The other special precipitation of significance, generally used in marginal utility theory, would be called, in our terminology, "total significance." [42] This might be assumed to be the sum of the several marginal significances of all the successively marginal units of which any quantity of means is composed. But it does not work out that way, as we shall demonstrate in Appendix IV. If it did, then, marginal significance being held to remain the same for each unit or increment

[41] The subject of a series of part measures is examined in Part IV (see Chapter 13, Section F).

[42] Again this is Wicksteed's term (441, 45). The Bedeutung of a Gesammtquantität is not, as we shall see in Appendix IV, an essential part of Menger's analysis. It is merely mentioned (see 296, 107 and elsewhere). Jevons's term is "total utility" (224, 45 and 49 ff.), which Marshall adopts (291, 93). Walras's is "effective utility" (420, 76) and Pareto's is "ophelimity" (317, 158).

regardless of the comminution of the unit or increment, total significance would be greater in proportion to the fineness of comminution; or total significance being held to remain the same regardless of the comminution of the unit or increment, marginal significance would be less in proportion to the fineness of comminution. Neither of these theorems holds good of marginal utility analysis. We shall have to defer the question as to what the actual relation between the two magnitudes is held to be. Here we can only say that total significance represents the significance of a quantity of means, generally coterminous with the whole available, or immediately available, supply, but also, with reference to the process of satisfying, the significance of that part of the means already consumed.[43] In the first place, we do not like this kind of quantitative analysis. It is based on perfectly vague and undefined quantities. But, in the second place, if we pin it down to something definite and apply it to our full measures or part measures of means, we do not need it. For then it does not differ from our magnitude, the usefulness of these quantities. Or rather, it does not differ unless the total significance of these quantities can be less than their usefulness either because they are not homogeneous within themselves in this respect or because some full measures of the same means may have less significance than others. Our definition precludes the first, and we shall find reason to believe that any appearance of the second is due to causes outside the sphere of subjective valuation. However, we will carry along the notion; for, in our analysis, we shall find marginal significance becoming merged into total significance, so that the latter becomes the only basic magnitude with reference to significance that survives. In this process it will come to represent for us the significance of any measurable quantity of means, and marginal significance will become merely the total significance of that one of all the successive measurable quantities which happens to be marginal.

---

[43] Wicksteed uses it of "supply" (*441*, 45), Marshall of "stock" (*291*, 93), Pareto of quantity possessed (*317*, 158), Walras of that (*420*, 103) or of quantity consumed (*ibid.*, 76), and Jevons applies it to a day's supply of the good (*224*, 45) or to a rate of supply (*ibid.*, 49 ff.). We see here what a conglomerate of the three assumptions, given above, appear in these several cases.

8

THREE HYPOTHESES AS TO
SUBJECTIVE VALUATION

A. SUBJECTIVE VALUATION—ITS STATUS AND REQUIREMENTS

IN THE preceding chapters we have elaborated from the deepest levels of causation at present available to us an hypothesis as to economic motivation. It is full of uncertainties and gaps, as well as being wholly tentative. Nevertheless, in its general outline it seems to interpret the facts correctly. In so far as it concerns the subject of Part I, wants and means, its chief bearing upon existing economic theory is its relation to subjective valuation. As noted above, subjective valuation has been the peculiar province, if not the invention, of what we are calling, for lack of any other generic term, marginal utility theory. At this level, then, our hypothesis has come into direct conflict with the general features of that theory. We shall therefore devote the remainder of Part I to the issues this conflict raises.

The present status of marginal utility theory is difficult to define because it is so diverse in different sectors. Perhaps, in terms of their present attitudes on this subject, economists can be divided roughly into three groups; those who continue to "believe" in more or less of the basic tenets of the theory; those who have evolved new modifications (reformations) in which they can continue to "believe"; and those who have become "unbelievers." Our hypothesis raises issues with regard to all three of these attitudes. The examination of these issues will be our task from this point on.

Let us first state our case against the "unbelievers." As Schultz said, "it has become fashionable for text book writers to belittle the role of utility in the analysis of price" because "so many economists have convinced themselves that the notion of utility is based on antiquated and erroneous psychology of human behavior, that it does not deal with measurable quantities and hence has no right of citizenship in a modern objective scientific treatment of economics." [1] This general attitude may be merely evasive or it may actually be "agnostic" as to this subject. It is purely evasive among those who contend that we can use the results of marginal utility analysis without answering the questions raised by the supposition of subjective valuation. Some regard the construct of a "felicific" or "hedonistic" calculus as merely a representation of the process of choosing, and do not feel it necessary—or possible—to look behind the choice to see what determines it. [2] Along such lines we arrive at the imputation of a wholly unanalyzed cause which, in careless hands, brings us perilously close to mere "word-magic." While the "agnostics" are on safer ground, in this respect, their attitude really implies that economics is either dealing with a class of phenomena whose causation cannot be inquired into by means of scientific method or that its basic phenomena lie outside the field of economic inquiry. Nor is the attitude, in either case, entirely consistent. It seems to be frequently overlooked that the preconceptions underlying the modern theory of demand rest on assumptions which were largely derived from, and which stand or fall with, certain of the chief tenets of marginal utility theory. General equilibrium theory is even more obviously and intimately involved. One cannot well retain these elements of one's stock of ideas or working tools and at the same time doubt or repudiate so essential a portion of their bases. It seems to me that, in either form, the position taken by the "unbelievers" is an untenable one. We must not be so easily put off.

Subjective valuation is the economic term for a process that is observable all the way along the biological scale from amoeba to man. That process is choice; and choice, as it shows in behavior, can cer-

---

[1] Schultz, 363, 95.

[2] Davenport (107, 100–101) regarded utility analysis as "nothing more than a schematic and very abstract account of this process of making these choices." Now alternatives, whether the choice is rational or irrational, are "weighed." Economics cannot deal scientifically with *weights* until it understands *weighing* (the operational concept) and *weight*. With this, I judge, Mrs. Robinson will disagree. She says (349, 214), "there is no part . . . of the analysis of value which requires a knowledge of the real nature of utility." That depends on what is meant by the "real nature." We do not know the "real nature," in one sense, of any force dealt with in physics. Yet none of those dealt with is merely an unanalyzed force. If economics is to be "a serious subject"—that is, if it is to be a science—it certainly cannot evade one of its chief problems. Sweezy, in arguing that empiricism must enter somewhere—at the statistical demand curve or further back—refers to "the economist who wants to be able to make general statements about the real world without first embarking on the laborious and often disappointing task of investigating its concrete properties" (388, 180). We cannot afford to be economists of this kind.

tainly be analyzed as the resultant of a set of conflicting forces, even if we have to impute purely hypothetical forces as the source of behavior. We do not need to know what these forces are in essence (e.g., the force of gravity); we do not need to concern ourselves with the question whether or how far they are conscious or unconscious, rational or irrational. But we must treat them in quantitative terms— that is, we must conceive and define them as magnitudes—and, once we have found some hypothetical scheme that fits the facts, we must be logically consistent in applying it. That is, however irrational may be the behavior, the imputed causation of it must be dealt with by economics in a strictly rational manner. From this viewpoint, the problem of subjective valuation is a problem in kinetics. It deals with the mainspring of economic behavior. It requires the analysis of the operational aspect of the want system—the forces that produce all economic activities. Therefore, however elusive, however difficult, however disappointing, it is a problem that must be grappled with if we are to have a science at all; it concerns the foundation upon which the whole science must rest—a foundation which is to economic behavior what physics is to the behavior of the universe. This being quite evidently the case, it seems to follow that it is impossible to justify a purely negative attitude toward the explanation of this phenomenon; and it is even more impossible to ignore the subject. Therefore, in full recognition of the essential nature of the questions involved, we proceed to concern ourselves with the specific difficulties in the various answers to them which have been presented by the members of that diversified group whose work has done so much to push back the frontiers of economic science in the last half-century or so. Thus we proceed to concern ourselves with the attitudes of the "believers" and the "reformers" rather than with that of the "unbelievers."

This can be done in a way that serves a larger purpose than mere negative criticism. By careful analysis it becomes possible to set up the requirements which any hypothesis on this subject must meet. We can then subject to these tests the various forms of marginal utility theory that we shall consider and thus perhaps discover whether they suffer from deeper defects than have already been noted—that is, whether or not certain of the assumptions on which they are based are untenable. Next, these requirements serve equally well for testing our own hypothesis. If, so far as we can now see, it meets them, that will furnish further corroboration and encourage further investigation. Finally, since our admittedly imperfect and incomplete hypothesis makes no pretense of being the last word on this subject, examination of the essential requirements should be of use in guiding future explorers in this field and, at least, in helping them to escape from some of the pitfalls into which past explorers have stumbled.

The several requirements which an hypothesis as to subjective valuation must meet are as follows:

1. The hypothesis must be self-contained and determinate in its results. In the theory of valuation as a whole, it may be useful to suggest a basis for subjective valuation which relies on some factor external to the subject, in order to determine what will be the choices. This cannot, however, supply a scheme for subjective valuation. It is necessarily true that subjective valuation must be capable of operating in the absence of immediate constraints or limitations on choice if, in determining choices, it is an autonomous factor at all. While many different forms of the theory have utilized such extraneous elements as given "terms of trade" or given combinations of quantities of means in connection with their schemes, of only one can it be said that it stands or falls on this count. That is, only one cannot be made determinate, in its present form, without introducing an extraneous determinant. Thus it will be unnecessary to deal with this requirement until we come to this one form.[3]

2. The hypothesis must rest on no assumption that can be shown to be fallacious. All forms of marginal utility theory, even the most recent, rest upon, or necessarily imply, the assumption that the intensity of a want—or any other supposed driving-force—declines during the process of satisfaction. Some forms also require the additional assumption that this decline takes place at a diminishing rate. If either assumption is unjustified, schemes resting upon it must be erroneous.[4]

3. Whether the force at play can be identified or not, it must be conceived in such a way as to relate it consistently to wants or to the process of satisfying them. The issue here is not the nature of the

[3] It is only of importance to our inquiry in the case of the systems based on indifference curves or surfaces. It seems to underlie Walras, and it constantly appears in Wicksteed. Nevertheless, both of these schemes can be used in ways that make them determinate. The "indifference" system is the only one that fails completely.

[4] That is, all forms require this to the extent that they include, in their usually conglomerate assumption already described (see pp. 437 ff.), differences of significance within a single satisfaction. I think it is fair to say that, while frequently not explicit, this assumption (a) is implicit in all of them.

psychological states or processes. It is the necessity of an ineluctable choice between the two possible types of magnitude related to processes —the static and the dynamic. Choices must be governed by one or the other. They cannot be attributed to both. Our application of this requirement will take the form of always consistently construing the subjective magnitude in each form of the theory to belong to one or the other of these types. Sometimes we shall try both alternatively. But we will not admit the use of both alternatives at once—a practice of which some forms of the theory appear to be suspect.[5]

4. The magnitude on the subjective side—the want—must be definable, though not necessarily identifiable. When it is supposed to be operating in deliberate choices it must be one that can reasonably be supposed to be recognized and judged by the subject.

5. The magnitude on the objective side—the means—must also be definable and capable of being judged by the subject.

Since the first requirement is only an issue in one instance and since we are making all the forms which we carry forward conform to the third, the only requirements to which we need to submit all schemes as to subjective valuation with which we shall deal are the second, fourth, and fifth. To that end we shall adopt the following procedure. We shall apply three tests to our own and to the other schemes of subjective valuation. The first test is that a scheme must not involve the comparison of magnitudes that are, by definition, immeasurable by themselves or incommensurable. The second test is that a scheme must not impute to the subject a capacity to perform mathematical calculations with regard to magnitudes that cannot be measured in terms of units, nor to judge subjective experiences in terms of several related magnitudes or dimensions, since either would require perfectly preposterous assumptions in respect of the psychic apparatus. The third test is this: The virtual orders of preference derived from the survivors of the first two tests will be combined with the virtual orders arising from the other and external influence, in order to determine which one produces a combined order that conforms to reality. Only

---

[5] That is, as we shall demonstrate, if the criterion of estimation is fixed in its magnitude by anything that occurs during phases of the process of satisfying (dynamic magnitude), then phases of all want-satisfactions that are equal in this respect will produce indifference among the corresponding quantities of means, regardless of the importance of the want or the then stage in its satisfaction. If the criterion of estimation is fixed in its magnitude by the state of the want or any related entity (static magnitude), at the several stages of satisfaction (including the initial one), then the quantities of means determined in the first way will not be indifferent.

this third test can prove or disprove the basic assumption of a decline of intensity (etc.) during satisfaction. Only this third test can finally prove or disprove any hypothesis.[6]

In general, we are assuming that there is not available, either to the subject or to us as observers, any precise unit of measurement for intensity of want or for any of the other subjective magnitudes introduced. So far we are in accord with Schultz's statement with regard to *measurable* quantities. In fact, this assumption seems to have arrived at so general an acceptance that it is probably unnecessary to inquire into the matter. On the other hand, we are assuming that all these different subjective entities are properly to be regarded as magnitudes, comparable in terms of more or less or approximate equality. This assumption seems to be a necessary one if choice is to be interpreted as the determination, by reason of their relative magnitudes, of a conflict of forces. Furthermore, when choices are deliberate (determined by the mnemonic-volitional process) we are assuming that the subject is also capable of judging the magnitude of the several conflicting subjective entities and in the same non-numerical terms. Thus we cannot join in rejecting any hypothesis merely on the grounds of immeasurability of magnitudes in terms of units if that hypothesis can be converted into one which only assumes comparability of such magnitudes.

Neither can we join in rejecting any of the hypotheses we deal with on the grounds that it "is based on antiquated and erroneous psychology of human behavior." These psychological theories and the hypotheses based on them have never been disproved. Pleasure, pain, desire, are names for introspectively discovered experiences whose existence we must admit on the same grounds upon which we admit consciousness, volition, effort. True, we lack knowledge of their neurological character and their precise workings and have therefore omitted them from consideration in our investigation in the previous chapters. But, in the future, that knowledge may be acquired; or other psychological entities, conceived to produce similar patterns of behavior, may come to take their places in hypotheses as to subjective valuation. All that we ask is that any such entities, derived from old or new psychologies, if they are to be used as bases for subjective valuation, shall meet the re-

[6] The method we are using to test this assumption (a, of the conglomerate) is an indirect one, and, as has been said before, cannot be completed until Part IV. However, a considerable part of this chapter and of Appendix IV must be devoted to establishing the proper basis for that test—that is, to discovering the actually possible varieties of determinate systems based on that assumption.

quirements stated above. Perhaps the old ones will serve, as well as any, as samples for our tests. Thus, while we shall in part be going over old ground, we shall, I believe, be going over it in a new way and one which may prove useful for future method.

In the first part of this chapter we shall set up the terms of the first test by way of applying it to the several chief types of criteria for subjective valuation. Then, in Appendix IV, we shall analyze the chief original presentations of marginal utility theory, together with the general scheme that has developed out of one of them.[7] In the course of doing so we shall submit to the first and second tests the several constructions we find it possible to place on these presentations. Some fail on the first test. Some on the second. Only two meet them both. But these two have to be modified in order to meet, respectively, the third and the first requirement named above. In the last part of this chapter we shall then set up the three hypotheses that seem to pass the first two tests. These will include our own, a second which develops directly from it, as a result of admitting the assumption of declining intensity during satisfaction, by the use of one construction of Menger's scheme, and a third, using the only other criterion we can find, on the same assumption, but modified in order to combine it with the scheme developed from Edgeworth's and Pareto's device of indifference curves and surfaces. The final test—the third—can only be applied in Part IV, where we bring together in a synthesis the several influences at play and thus secure a basis for comparing the completed hypotheses with reality.

B. THE MAGNITUDES AND THEIR GRAPHIC REPRESENTATION

I. THE THEORY OF DIMENSIONS

Our first test is based on the theory of dimensions as that has been developed in the physical sciences. This is, in fact, no more than the application of clear and consistent thinking to the treatment of magnitudes; but, without such application, entities cannot, for scientific purposes, be dealt with as magnitudes at all. As we proceeded with the working out of our own magnitudes in the previous chapter we were, at all times, applying this method. However, there was, there, no systematic statement of this theory, as it is called. Since the various

---

[7] The reader is advised to read the first two sections of this chapter before referring to Appendix IV.

forms of marginal utility theory have either ignored or have played fast and loose with the matter of the dimensions of the magnitudes involved, it becomes necessary, in order to make the defects clear, to establish in systematic form the data of the theory of dimensions. With certain elaborations of our own made necessary by the fact that the theory of dimensions has dealt only with precisely measurable magnitudes, their dimensions, and their units, these data may be analyzed into the following summary form.[1]

1. A "fundamental magnitude" is one that cannot be measured or stated in terms of any other magnitude. Therefore a fundamental magnitude can have but a single dimension—itself—though this dimension may be used more than once in measuring it. Thus volume has the dimensions L^3. The ultimate fundamental magnitudes or dimensions in the physical sciences are, as previously stated, mass (M), length (L), and duration, or time (T).

2. The numerical statement of a fundamental magnitude in terms of its dimension requires the establishment of an arbitrary unit.

3. Two fundamental magnitudes can only be related to each other:
   a. If they have a common dimension—each can then be numerically stated in terms of their common arbitrary unit, or they may be merely compared roughly in terms of more or less or approximate equality—[2]
   b. Or if there is some relation between them, other than a common dimension, which enables us to say that a certain quantity of the first *corresponds* to a certain quantity of the second —that these quantities are, in this non-mathematical sense, equal. This correspondence does not signify mathematical equality, since, having no common dimension, the magnitudes are incommensurable.

4. Such a relation or correspondence (3b) may be expressed in many ways; but all must include the name of the relation or corre-

[1] As the manuscript of this study was being made ready for the printer, I came across a remarkable article on measurement, provoked by the Final Report (1940) of the Committee of the B.A.A.S., representing Sections A and J, and written by S. S. Stevens of Harvard (103 *Science*, 1946, 677). I have made no amendments as a consequence of this article, since it seems to support the positions I have taken with reference to measurability of such magnitudes as are considered here, in particular. But, for a far more fundamental and far more competent treatment of the subject in this field, I refer the reader to Professor Stevens's article.
[2] This relation was referred to on pp. 411 to 412 as the basis for objective measurement.

spondence as well as statements of the two magnitudes so related. Usually the relation is one-directional—that is, it specifies which of the two magnitudes shall be the relate and which the correlate.[3] The most precise form of statement is as an equation which, however, signifies only a correspondence in terms of this relation, not mathematical equality. Thus the production (relation) of a 10-acre field (relate) = 100 bushels (correlate). Conversely, the land required for (relation) 100 bushels of crop (relate) = 10 acres (correlate).[4]

5. Such a relation, or correspondence, may then be conceived as itself a magnitude—a "derived magnitude." As such it becomes the expression of a rate, or ratio, between the two or more fundamental magnitudes, and as such, its mathematical character changes.[5] The dimensions of such a ratio are those of the fundamental magnitudes so related. The underlying concept of a derived magnitude is so many units of one magnitude per unit of the other. This is shown, in the

[3] Thus "I walked ten miles this afternoon" can be reduced either to the statement, "The distance traversed during my walk this afternoon = ten miles," or "The duration of my walking ten miles = all afternoon." Or, "I burned 100 tons of coal last winter" can either be stated, "My consumption of coal last winter = 100 tons," or "My consuming of 100 tons of coal = (or lasted) all winter." Thus the name of the correspondence must determine which is the relate and which the correlate. The period or scope of the correspondence (process or static relation) is defined in terms of the relate and its magnitude in terms of the correlate.

[4] The relata of any correspondence may be two (or more) entities, not treated as magnitudes. But this relation must be defined and they must be identified (e.g., this afternoon it rained). Or one of the entities may be treated as a magnitude (e.g., this afternoon it rained two inches). Or both may be treated as magnitudes (e.g., this afternoon it rained two inches in one hour). A correspondence of the type of these non-mathematical equalities must, first, deal with entities that are not only identified but also circumscribed or delimited—that is, conceived or stated in terms of their specific dimensions; second, it is usually necessary that at least one of the entities must be converted into a measured magnitude which must then be stated in terms of the arbitrary units of its dimension.

Two magnitudes with the same dimension can be roughly compared in terms of more or less or approximate equality in that dimension. They can be precisely compared only in terms of a numerical statement of the number of arbitrary units in that dimension which each measures. It follows that two relations, or correspondences, of the same kind can only be precisely compared if the entities so related are first converted into measured magnitudes. It is true that they can be roughly compared even if not precisely measured or susceptible of precise measurement; but only under certain conditions. Either (1) both relates or both correlates must be capable of being judged to be approximately equal, while the other pair are judged equal or different (more or less); or (2) the first relate must be judged to be less than the second and the first correlate more than the second, or vice versa; or (3) if the first relate and correlate are both larger or both smaller than the second ones, the difference between the relates must be very markedly greater or less than that between the correlates.

[5] This because the fundamental dimensions in which a correspondence is stated are one or more for each expression of an equation; those of a derived magnitude are two or more in a single expression.

theory of dimensions as, for instance, $\frac{L}{T}$, or better, LT^{-1}, the dimensional formula for velocity. Here the derived magnitude is no longer the relation, but is the *rate* of the relation; the relate has become the inverse dimension and the correlate has become the direct dimension. Correspondences are the raw materials (the data) out of which derived magnitudes are constructed, and the latter can only be based on correspondences. It serves no useful purpose to derive a rate from a correspondence unless the latter is measurable and measured in terms of arbitrary units in its dimensions.[6]

6. The dimensions of a derived magnitude, or rate, are usually among themselves incommensurable. Thus its numerical statement, which is frequently made in the form of a division of one magnitude by another incommensurable magnitude, must not be permitted to create any mathematical illusions.

7. Derived magnitudes may have several or many dimensions, combining different dimensions or the same ones more than once, directly as well as inversely. But all derived magnitudes have at least one direct and one inverse dimension. It is perhaps never useful, if it is even conceivable, to analyze a derived magnitude in terms only of two or more direct but different fundamental dimensions.[7]

[6] A fundamental magnitude may be a dynamic process (T) or a static entity (M or L). In dynamics all derived magnitudes are processes. When that process is other than time itself, time must enter at least once in the inverse dimension if the measurement of the process is to be the quantity of it that goes on over a period of time. Thus the correspondences upon which dynamic derived magnitudes are based (the non-mathematical equalities) are those of processes. Neither of these statements is necessarily true outside dynamics. That is, if a 10-foot board has a mass of 25 pounds, the correspondence is stated in the form; the weight of this 10-foot board = 25 pounds. If the weight per running foot is uniform, that can yield a derived magnitude, or rate: The rate of weight per running foot of this board is 2.5 pounds—that is, the rate of weight is ML^{-1}.

The elaborate kinds of derived magnitudes built up in dynamics may be illustrated in simple terms. If three badly trained bird dogs get up 24 quail in 40 seconds, that is a correspondence. The flushing by three dogs in 40 seconds = 24 birds. This correspondence can then be reduced to a rate, or derived magnitude, requiring three fundamental dimensions, (B) birds, (D) dogs, and (T) time. The units of the first two are natural separate units. The unit for the last may be the minute. The dimensional formula is then $BD^{-1}T^{-1}$, or birds flushed per bird dog per minute. And the example yields a derived magnitude, as follows: 12 birds per dog per minute, or per dog-minute. The last statement, dog-minute, does not mean that one is multiplying dogs by minutes; nor does the whole statement mean that one is dividing birds by dog-minutes; this because such operations are mathematically impossible.

[7] Expressions for units such as foot-pounds and kilowatt-hours suggest that incommensurables are being multiplied. But the foot-pound is a unit of work whose dimensions are ML^2T^{-2}; and a kilowatt-hour is a measure of energy whose dimensions are also ML^2T^{-2}. For further analysis of their nature, see Appendix IV, Section D 1. Also for discussion of an apparent exception, see supplementary statement on "The Erg-Second," at the end of this subsection.

8. To be comparable at all, a fundamental magnitude must be sufficiently large so that it may be judged objectively in terms of more or less or approximate equality with another magnitude having the same dimension. To be precisely measurable it must be sufficiently large so that, by the available technique, it can be stated in terms of its arbitrary unit to a degree of accuracy within some reasonable margin of error.

It follows that a relation or correspondence between two fundamental magnitudes with no common dimension is only measurable within the same limits.

9. In the same way, a derived magnitude can only be measured if the two or more fundamental magnitudes constituting its dimensions can themselves be measured, as above.[8]

10a. If the unit of a fundamental magnitude is made half as large, for instance, the numerical statement is doubled. But at some point in the process of continually subdividing the units, while there is no theoretical limit, they will become themselves immeasurable.

10b. If both units of a two-dimensional derived magnitude are made half as large, the numerical statement remains the same. That does not alter the fact that beyond some point in the subdivision of units, the magnitude is no longer measurable.

11a. If a fundamental magnitude is divided by two, for instance, the result is a fundamental magnitude half as large. Theoretically, this process of subdivision might be continued indefinitely. But, practically, the nether limit of measurability will be reached at some point.

11b. If both fundamental magnitudes composing a derived magnitude are divided by two, the derived magnitude remains of the same size.[9] Nevertheless, this does not alter the fact that, beyond some point in the process of subdivision, the magnitude will no longer be measurable.

[8] A fundamental magnitude, existing as a natural or artificial unit, is an absolute magnitude which can be gauged in terms of equality or more or less by comparison with some other magnitude with the same dimension. A derived magnitude, while only a relative magnitude, can also be roughly gauged in the same way (subject to the qualifications in note 4, above) provided its two fundamental magnitudes are natural or artificial separate units. But if two fundamental magnitudes are reduced to terms of the arbitrary units of a continuum, or can only be measured in this way, the derived magnitude can no longer be gauged. It must be calculated (i.e., it becomes a numerical statement).

[9] This points to the fact that the existence of a derived magnitude is inherently confined to a numerical value, though, of course, that value depends upon the units in which the fundamental magnitudes involved are stated.

12. Even if magnitudes are, or are as yet, incapable of precise measurement, their scientific treatment as magnitudes at all requires that their dimension or dimensions be defined and that their treatment should then consistently accord with, and be in terms of, the definitions so laid down. This remains equally true even if their fundamental dimension or dimensions are not reducible to units or even if they can only be defined as yet in terms of the entity itself (i.e., a new fundamental magnitude).

This matter of magnitudes, and the illustration of the application of the theory of dimensions to them, can best be demonstrated by mathematical notation. For our purposes the simplest form suffices —that is, graphic representation in geometrical form. This form has two advantages for us. It will be understood by more readers; and it has been the commoner form for marginal utility theory. Thus, by its use, we shall be able to show our own magnitudes in comparable form, and thus point the contrasts, while, at the same time, we are engaged in demonstrating graphically the defects which impair the validity of certain brands of that theory. As stated above, we shall sift out in this process all the constructions which seem to be legitimate under this first test. Only these will be considered in the text. In Appendix IV we shall apply this test—and the second one—to the several forms of marginal utility theory and will then combine the only elements that meet the requirements, though in a somewhat modified form, with certain constructions that we develop in the text.

It is advisable to remind the reader that we are admitting two alternative assumptions at this stage. The first is our own—that there is no considerable decline in the intensity of a want during a complete or incomplete satisfaction of the want. The second is that of marginal utility theory—that there is a gradual and continuous decline in the intensity of a want—or in any of the several psychological entities that are variously substituted for this—during the process of satisfaction.[10] When these two assumptions require different representation we shall give both.

The Erg-Second. It is highly presumptuous for me to question statements, on the matter of units with two direct dimensions only, made by so eminent a physicist as Eddington. Nevertheless, I find myself unable to

[10] The reader is reminded that this is part of the conglomerate assumption, more or less of which we have ascribed to all forms of marginal utility theory (see pp. 437 ff.). In our treatment we are separating out this part since it depends on wholly different factors from the other two parts.

accept them and must therefore defend my position. He says (*132*, 180) that "quantities such as energy, which we think of as existing at an instant, belong to three-dimensional space, and they need to be multiplied by a duration to give them a thickness before they can be put into the four-dimensional world." Thus for an erg, the unit of energy (and work), "the corresponding content of a region of space-time will be described as so many erg-seconds." And, by way of illustration, he says the "amount of humanity" in space-time is so many "man-years." That in itself suggests the stage of unanalyzed magnitudes.

The dimensions of an erg are ML^2T^{-2}. Therefore, those of an erg-second would be $ML^2T^{-2} \times T$, or ML^2T^{-1}. Such a dimensional formula indicates a magnitude that has the same relation to momentum that work (or energy) has to force. In terms of these concepts it would represent a certain momentum over a certain distance; or, more completely, a certain mass moving at a certain velocity for a certain distance. I am not competent to guess whether such a statement of the "atom of action," or quantum, is meaningful.

The dimensions of the erg (work or energy) are those of a process. A process can only take place over time. It cannot exist at an instant. Furthermore, in this case, time is of the essence in the measurement of the process; for the basis of the concept of the magnitude is acceleration; therefore, time enters twice in the inverse dimension. Obviously, then, this formula holds good only of kinetic energy. We may conceive potential energy as the capacity to do work, to produce or release kinetic energy. As long as it remains only potential it may be conceived as a state, not as a process. Then it may exist at an instant. It is conceived as what would occur over time *if* it became kinetic. But, if it does not become kinetic, it remains the same over time. To multiply it by time, then, is to change its actually unchanging value. In fact, it is to convert it into something else.

It seems possible that, if kinetic energy is a discontinuous, not a continuous process (see Chapter 14, Section B 1), it may be that its minimum step —the quantum—does not have the dimension of time at all. That step may consist of an instantaneous change of condition. If so, we would need a new dimensional formula for energy; perhaps one which expressed its quantum as a fundamental unit. Then, if the measure of the process were conceived to be the delivery of so much energy per unit of time, its formula would be QT^{-1}. For any definite time, the energy delivered would be $QT^{-1} \times T$, or Q. Such a fundamental unit would be equally appropriate for potential as for kinetic energy. For potential energy the formula would be Q; for kinetic energy it would be $q_1 - q_0$.

2. REPRESENTING A SINGLE WANT AND THE PROCESS OF SATISFYING IT

The first magnitude with which we are concerned is termed the intensity of a present want. We have already defined that term, so far as our own hypothesis is concerned. It is the force with which the want acts—its effective intensity. Usually that is directly felt, as emotion; when it is not, it may be judged by self-observation. We have been assuming that it is possible roughly to compare the intensities of the several wants, at least at their normal maxima. But we have also agreed that the intensity of a single want cannot be otherwise measured—that is, its only existence as a magnitude is relative, in terms of more or less than, or approximate equality to, other magnitudes with the same dimension. It is also evident that the notion of intensity involves the assumption that it is a static not a dynamic magnitude—the measure of a state, not that of a process.[11] Now it is well to make clear at once that, in the various forms of marginal utility theory, the corresponding entity is never quite the same as this and is often quite different. In certain forms the corresponding entity goes by a different name, though, like ours, it is a state which exists prior to the process of satisfaction, and which continues, as a state, during that process. Thus, on the supposition of declining intensity during satisfaction, we could relate such an entity to our own by regarding it as equivalent to the *remaining intensity* of the want at any particular stage in the process of satisfaction. As such, it would again be a static not a dynamic magnitude—the measure of a state, not that of a process. However, though the entities of this order that frequently appear in marginal utility are derived from the word "want," they are derived in a different sense of that word from the one we are using. Often, when it is said that we *feel* an intense want for something, the word "want" is being used in the sense of *desire*, wish, etc., or in its equally valid sense of *lack*. That is construed in two ways. The first construes the feeling as an impulse to action (conation); the second may assume the same feeling, but supposes that it is projected upon the object or act which would be obtainable as a result of the action. Thus, in both cases, when the intensity of want is construed as desire it is treated as if it were a feature of something which is a potential activity rather than of something which is a mere static condition. For our present purposes the first difference between this and our own entity is that it must be limited to what is felt in consciousness. However, that is a relatively unimportant difference here. What we shall be concerned with, here, is

[11] The definition of a static magnitude in mechanics is an equilibrated force. Being equilibrated there is no motion—only a tendency to motion (potential). Here motion would constitute the process. This shows that static magnitudes are not confined to the kind of static entities mentioned in note 6, above.

the question whether, if it is a static magnitude, it is legitimate to regard this entity as being directly related to the process of satisfaction, and thus to the means; or, on the other hand, whether, if it is regarded as a sort of hybrid combining the features of both a static and a dynamic magnitude, that is not the result of pure confusion of thought.[12] In other forms of the theory the corresponding entity, under several different names, is not a state that can exist prior to the process of satisfaction, or at any stage through it, but is only an experience that can be felt during it. That is, it is not a static but a dynamic magnitude. Our own analysis yields such an entity. It is the reduction of the intensity of the want at the end of the process. On the assumption of declining intensity, such an entity corresponds to the reduction accomplished through any phase in the process, however delimited. Though they may or may not be correlated with reduction of intensity, all other entities that are accompaniments of the process—that is, all psychological experiences such as relief from pain, pleasure, satisfaction, etc.—require the same treatment. All are dynamic magnitudes. It must be noted that such entities as these could not be projected upon the means except *pari passu* during the process of satisfaction. They do not consist of states that can be felt at a moment. They do not exist prior to the process. Nor can they be experienced except over a sufficient sector of the process to be appreciable. Therefore, any relation between such entities and means which treats them in terms of magnitudes can only be established after such a sector of the experience has passed; and there must be a definite chopping-off point in any such continuum. This means that the relation is altogether one established by past experience.[13]

Considering first only our own static magnitude intensity—includ-

---

[12] If the reader feels certain that the static magnitude, desire, can be itself projected upon the process and so upon the means, we only ask him to await our analysis of the way this comes about. It can only come about in two ways. One discards the static magnitude and substitutes a dynamic one—change. The other retains the static magnitude but eliminates means (or the process) as a related magnitude.

[13] We do not want to make too much of this distinction, for it will become increasingly obvious that preferences are generally exercised among provisions for future rather than present wants, and therefore on the basis of past experience. Nevertheless, it is worth noting that an entity of the first order can be apprehended directly as a momentary experience and its intensity judged, even if its effect, thereafter, is largely produced through the mnemonic-volitional system. On the other hand, an entity of the second order can only be apprehended indirectly through the mnemonic-volitional system, since it is an experience of considerable duration—far longer than the "specious present" or than the synchronous plus the acoluthic phase of a single stimulus—requiring to be "looked back on" in order that its magnitude can be judged.

ing, in so far as they are comparable, remaining intensity and such entities as desire—we may see that, as a magnitude, this seems to be analogous to the originally purely naïve sense-datum of temperature. Therefore, it is necessary for us to regard it as being, in the present state of our knowledge, at the same stage as was the category of temperature when that was merely a sensory datum. At that stage temperature was divided into heat and cold. Temperature was then an entity which could not be measured, but only felt.[14] It was felt, however, as more or less—and therefore as a magnitude—and its different degrees could be roughly compared. At that stage temperature was what we call a fundamental magnitude; that is, it could not be stated in terms of any other magnitude. Therefore, if it had been measurable, it would have had to be measured in terms of its own fundamental unit, just as length, mass, and time are measured, and not in terms of derived units, as it can be now. Most certainly it was not a rate or derived magnitude—a quantitative ratio between two or more fundamental magnitudes. Moreover, at that stage, temperature was one-dimensional —that is, it was not a composite even in terms of its own fundamental unit.[15] It was not comparable to an area or volume. Knowing nothing about this entity, intensity, except that we can feel it and observe its being felt, it is necessary, therefore, that we treat it in the same way that we treated temperature at the corresponding stage. It is a fundamental magnitude. It has therefore but one dimension. It is, in other words, its own dimension.[16]

[14] In the light of what has happened since with temperature how absurd it would seem to dismiss marginal utility theory as "mere hedonistic circle-squaring" merely because "utility" is as yet immeasurable! The phrase is quoted from Schultz (363, 119).

[15] Using the terms one-, two-, or three-dimensional in a discussion of dimensions is necessarily confusing, but cannot be avoided. The fundamental magnitude, space, is three-dimensional, but all three are in terms of one dimension (or unit), length. Unfortunately, the terminology does not discriminate between multiplicity in terms of one dimension and that in terms of several dimensions. But our context will always make the distinction clear.

[16] At this point it seems necessary, in order to meet the requirements we have set for ourselves, to attempt a definition of the magnitude, intensity of want, which will serve as a clear-cut concept to which we can be consistent. Obviously intensity cannot as yet be defined in terms of the physical concepts, force or energy. Physiologically, effective intensity of want appears to be a state of neural excitation or depression (plus or minus) in a circumscribed area—the hypothalamus. Since the area is circumscribed, the degree of excitation or depression seems to vary directly and proportionally with its quantity. Then intensity represents both degree and quantity of excitation or depression. Similarly temperature (degree) has been regarded as the quantity of heat per unit mass. We cannot push the analogy further; for, though we set an arbitrary zero on our thermometers, "below zero" does not indicate absence of heat; but depression seems to be, not only absence of excitation, but, in some way, its converse.

Heat is said to be fundamentally a form of energy and therefore "a mode of motion."

In the graphic representation of a single one-dimensional magnitude the most natural form to use is a line. This line may be placed vertically, horizontally, or at an angle. Our choice among these placements is usually governed by our mental representation of space. That is, something conceived as length is represented by a horizontal line; something conceived as height by a vertical line. We are accustomed still to represent temperature by a vertical line and to speak of high and low temperatures. But, of course, that has been the case only since we have visualized temperature in terms of the thermometer. And it might have ceased to be the case when the unit became a derived one. If the intensity of wants is, for the present, a fundamental and one-dimensional magnitude, then the given intensity of a single want may most readily be portrayed by a line. We judge from the terms used in connection with it—high, low, decline of, etc.—that this line is visualized as vertical. It is clear that there is not, and probably cannot be, any subjective unit of measurement of intensity. There is simply a rough sense of direction of change or difference and, therefore, of more or less or equality. So the term "degree of intensity" does not have the significance of a unit, as "degree of temperature" now has. Moreover, it is probable that, if the internal activities of the central nervous system could be observed in such a way as to make this process objectively evident and measurable, intensity of want would cease to be a fundamental magnitude and would be measured in derived units. Therefore, at present, it would be absurd to attach any significance to the absolute height of our vertical line; any height can be chosen to represent what we feel as the customary maximum intensity of a particular recurring want. We show this in Fig. 1.[17]

If, now, we introduce the consideration of changes in this magni-

---

Is excitation also a form of energy—a mode of motion? We do not know. Naturally we suspect that excitation is a process; but our ignorance of it compels us to treat it as a state. That is, it is probably a dynamic magnitude, though we know it only as a static magnitude.

If we could measure excitation as a process, we could derive from it a rate—i.e., the quantity of it that takes place in a unit of time. That we cannot do. True, we can detect changes in the degree or quantity of excitation. Such changes constitute a process; they can only take place over time. But these changes are not proportional to time; they do not, therefore, constitute a rate of which time is the inverse dimension. Instead, the process of change in intensity can be conceived only in the same fundamental and single dimension that is used for the degree or quantity of excitation. This dynamic magnitude has only the dimension i_1-i_0, just as the static magnitude has the dimension I.

[17] This also serves to represent the initial intensity of the want, or of desire, under the assumption of declining intensity.

tude, intensity—that is, if we combine the demonstration of the
dynamic with that of the static magnitude—we can use the same
method of representation. The process we call the recurrence of a want
—a change in the direction of rising intensity—is then represented by
a more or less gradual prolongation of the line upward from its base;
and the process we call the satisfying of a want—a change in the direction of declining intensity—as either a discontinuous or a continuous
contraction of the line downward upon its base. Or, for convenience,
we may keep the line intact, as a scale, and imagine the movement to
take place along it. Thus, on the assumption of declining intensity
during the process of satisfaction, we can continue to use this figure to
represent the remaining intensity of the want (or desire)—the static
magnitude—at any stage of the process. To
do that we merely conceive the then level of
intensity to be at some point below the maximum. Correspondingly, we can use the
amount of movement, so conceived, to represent a dynamic magnitude (process). The
reduction of intensity accomplished up to

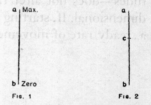

that stage then appears as the distance from the maximum down to that
point. And this can be construed just as well to indicate the magnitude
of any of the other experiences, pleasure, etc., attendant on the process
up to that stage. Thus, in Fig. 2, at the point *c*, *ac* represents the dynamic magnitude, reduction of intensity, and *cb* the static magnitude,
remaining intensity. Under our own assumption, there is no such intermediate point in the process of satisfaction. Instead, we imagine that,
at the point of satiation only, the intensity of the want drops from the
maximum to zero—i.e., from the top to the bottom of the line. However, under both assumptions, Fig. 2 serves better to show the recurrence of a want, for then, under both, intensity is conceived to be moving in the opposite direction (rising). Then *cb* would be taken to represent the present degree of intensity with relation to the maximum, *ab*.
All this could, of course, be just as readily shown on a horizontal line.

All these dynamic processes of change in, and these static differences
between, one-dimensional magnitudes can more conveniently be represented two-dimensionally, *if we safeguard ourselves by remembering
at all times that we are still dealing only with one-dimensional magnitudes.* We can do this in such a way that only one dimension of the
representation has meaning, and the other is merely used to facilitate

comparison of the magnitudes by showing them on parallel lines. Thus the eye can more readily compare their respective lengths. Instead of a succession of sections on a single line (like Fig. 2), we can place these sections parallel to each other and on the same base. Moreover, this is capable of much elaboration. For instance, if we wish to represent a single continuously diminishing one-dimensional magnitude, we can draw a completed or uncompleted right angle triangle. In this the altitude is the initial static magnitude, and other vertical lines (imagined) represent the successively diminishing static magnitudes at various stages. In fact, since we conceive the process to be continuous, we imagine an infinite number of vertical lines. But either of these forms of two-dimensional representation—of different or of changing magnitudes—does not alter the fact that the magnitude itself is only one-dimensional. If, starting at a given distance from a goal, I approach it at a steady rate of movement, the successive distances from my goal may

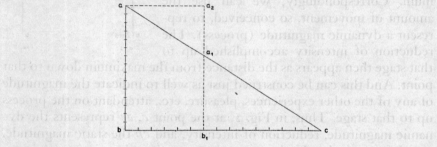

FIG. 3

be represented by a triangle, as in Fig. 3. This representation shows that, at any point in my progress, the distance from my goal is, say,

$a_1 b_1$. The ratio $\dfrac{a_1 b_1}{a\,b}$ shows the fraction of the whole distance remaining to be traversed; $ab - a_1 b_1$ (or $a_1 a_2$) shows the distance already traversed and therefore that expression divided by ab, $\dfrac{ab - a_1 b_1}{ab}$, shows the fraction of the whole distance already traversed. It happens that these expressions also correspond geometrically to $\dfrac{b_1 c}{bc}$ and $\dfrac{bb_1}{bc}$ respectively. But in no respect does bc represent another dimension of the magnitude; it is merely the second dimension of the diagram. The only dimension of the magnitude is shown vertically. True, if the two sides of the right angle triangle were equal, this single dimension would be represented by an equal number of equal units (sections of equal lengths) on both the altitude and the base. Nevertheless, in either case, it is clear that the area $bb_1 \dfrac{(ab + a_1b_1)}{2}$ has no meaning whatever. All this graph does is to show, in a more convenient way, the successive shortenings of a single dimension—distance.

When we apply this two-dimensional representation to the illustration of the changing magnitudes of intensity of want—or desire—(static), on the assumption of declining intensity of want, the remaining intensity of want, at any stage in the process, is shown, for instance, by a_1b_1, just as was the remaining distance from the goal above. And, when, on the same assumption, we use this to represent any portion of the process of satisfaction corresponding to a reduction in the intensity of the want (dynamic)—or the magnitude of any accompanying experiences—we see that such reduction is shown by $ab - a_1b_1$ (or a_1a_2), just as was the distance already traversed. But, again, for our own assumption, these representations do not serve. Instead we shall substitute a different one.

3. REPRESENTING THE RELATION OF A SINGLE MEANS TO ITS WANT

We can also use the one-dimensional method of representation to show two different dynamic magnitudes, each with its own dimension, which are in some way related through a common process—a correspondence of the kind suggested in Chapter 7, Section 2, and defined above. If, at the beginning of this relating process, both magnitudes have some maximum size as static magnitudes, each in its own dimension, and, at the end of the process, each is supposed to have arrived at zero, it is convenient to treat, and to represent, the quantity of change, the "length of the process" (dynamic magnitude), as the same in both cases. Thus the two magnitudes can be shown on a single line. But this does not mean that we are measuring the second magnitude in the—or a—dimension of the first, or vice versa. Each is measured strictly in its own dimension which may be incommensurable with that of the other. It means only that, in this particular instance, the two incommensurable dynamic magnitudes, or measures of process, have a relation of non-mathematical equality or correspondence.[18]

The graph (Fig. 4) represents both of two entirely independent

---

[18] Thus, if we are directed to eat an apple a day for ten days, we may relate these two magnitudes, apples and days. That does not mean that we give apples the dimension of time, or days the dimensions of apples. As we have said before, such an equality, or correspondence, is non-mathematical.

static magnitudes with different dimensions, and represents as of the same length the change in each (dynamic magnitudes) between the beginning and end of a process in which they are related. It could have been used, in our previous instance, to represent both distance traversed (motion) and the number of minutes required to reach the goal (time). Along the line, which can be either vertical or horizontal, and whose length merely represents the immeasurable static magnitude, maximum intensity of a want—and therefore the successive remaining intensities (static) and cumulative reductions of intensity (dynamic) on the way from maximum to zero, or complete satisfaction—it becomes possible to lay off, as equal fractions of the whole, the number of objective units of a means which are found requisite for such a complete satisfaction.[19] The total quantity of this means is that of a full measure as determined by experience. But the size of the objective unit in terms of which the quantity is measured, and therefore the number of units into which the quantity is subdivided, is arbitrary and may be varied. The number of units may be stated as n. It makes no difference, in this case, what size of unit is chosen so long as the number required is varied accordingly. *But, once the unit is chosen, it must remain of the same size; for then the numerical expression we are using has become the number of units, not the "quantity" of means.* The correspondence we are then expressing is that a complete satisfaction of the want (reduction of intensity from the maximum to zero) = 10 units of means (i.e., no longer merely a full measure). Since, in this case, the first static magnitude—maximum intensity—and therefore the dynamic magnitude—reduction of intensity—involved in a complete satisfaction, is not measurable in terms of any unit, even of itself, while, on the other hand, the second magnitude—the number of objective units of means—is so measurable, we can only say, on our own assumption, that, in this process, 10 units of means correspond to a complete satisfaction.

If we were to substitute, here, the assumption of declining intensity, it would be necessary to know that all the units of means, when consumed in succession, were not only equal among themselves objectively

FIG. 4

---

[19] The treatment of the measurement of means in this chapter is based on means as objects. It might be applied also, with due modifications, to means as acts of others or even as corresponding acts of self, provided there were no intervening objects (i.e., if both were limited to "services"). It excludes, however, acts of self which are part of the consummatory process. The reasons for these distinctions have been made clear in the last chapter.

but also equal in the reduction of intensity which each in turn accomplished, before we could calculate that each, in turn, accomplishes $\frac{1}{10}$ of a complete satisfaction. That is, an over-all correspondence between the whole want and the aggregate means does not suffice for that conclusion. Instead, we must be able to measure the correlate corresponding to each relate—each unit of means. Therefore, we must have a series of 10 correspondences, both factors in which are at least roughly measurable. That requires a capacity to discern, in the process, that the several units of means do reduce intensity by equal amounts. And that, in turn, requires an ability to compare the sizes of the successive reductions, without aid from the objective measurement of the means. Correspondingly, if it is quantity of pleasure or of satisfaction that we are concerned with, we would have to recognize the quantity associated with each unit of means. On the same assumption one might infer that, at any stage, the remaining intensity of the want would equal the initial intensity less the total of all successive reductions of intensity. But, here, such a calculation and such a capacity for measuring successive reductions would not be required. For, here, the static magnitude, remaining intensity, at any stage, could be directly judged, at least to the same extent that initial intensity could be judged.

However, when we thus undertake to depict some such correspondence between two otherwise independent processes (dynamic magnitudes), it becomes even more convenient to use two-dimensional representation. Going back to our example of motion, let us suppose that the altitude in Fig. 3 still represents distance traversed, but that the base bc now represents the number of minutes I am taking to reach my goal. As stated above, this could have been shown on the single vertical line in Fig. 4, in which the number of minutes would have been represented by the corresponding number of sections. However, two-dimensional representation, as in Fig. 3, brings out the fact that Fig. 4 might lead to unjustified conclusions. In Fig. 3, if we find that 15 minutes are required in the process and therefore divide the base, bc, into 15 equal sections, we cannot merely divide the altitude as well into 15 equal sections in order to find the distance traversed each minute. That would only be true if the distance traversed each minute were always the same; and we could only know that if the distance traversed each minute were measured. Given such measurement, we may also consider the case in which the distance traversed during each minute is found not to be the same. Let us suppose, for instance, that

distance traversed each minute grew steadily less because the ground
rose more and more steeply as I proceeded or because I grew progressively more weary. We could still have shown this one-dimensionally
(as in Fig. 4) by making the length of the sections decrease as we
descend along the vertical line.[20] But obviously it is again much clearer
to show this variation two-dimensionally; and, if the distance traversed
each minute is continuously less, we may even take the liberty of con-

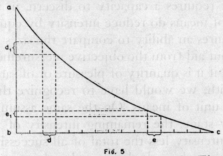

Fig. 5

verting the step-like figure into a curve, as in Fig. 5. This curve is
derived from the meeting points of the dotted lines, each pair of which
represents a single correspondence between two measured dynamic
magnitudes—the measured minute on the base and the measured distance traversed (motion) during that minute upon the altitude. For
instance, here, it shows that the proportion of the total distance traversed by the step d (as projected upon the altitude at d_1) is greater
than that traversed by e (as projected upon the altitude at e_1). Again,
however, the area subtended by the curve up to any point has no
meaning. It would always represent the number of minutes which
have already passed, multiplied by the distance still to be traversed. And
that does not make sense.

Now, if we convert the altitude, ab, in both Figs. 3 and 5, into terms
of intensity of want so that it represents both the static magnitude
(maximum intensity) and the dynamic magnitude (a complete satisfaction of a want) in their common dimension, and the base, bc, into
terms of the number of units of a means necessary completely to satisfy
that want (here 15), in its different dimension, we note that we must
draw different inferences, depending upon our assumptions. Under
our own assumption—maintenance of intensity—we would have to
ignore the hypotenuse of the triangle. Then the first diagram (Fig. 3),

[20] Then, however, we would have transferred the meaning of the sections from equal
minutes to unequal distances traversed each minute.

in terms of the altitude and the base, shows no more than that 15 units of the means equals a full measure and, therefore, that the whole 15 correspond, in this process, to the reduction of the intensity of the want from its normal maximum, ab, to zero (or b). The distinction expressed by Fig. 5 has no meaning under this assumption. Under the other assumption—declining intensity—the two figures have different meanings. Fig. 3, being a straight line curve which signifies a continuous and uniform decline of intensity—the same for each corresponding unit of means—shows that each equal section on ab corresponds to the same ordinal section on bc. But this can only represent reality if the reduction of intensity successively accomplished by each unit of means can be judged and is found to be the same as is that of each other unit—or $\frac{1}{15}$ of the whole. The question then arises how we are going to construe, in Fig. 3, the remaining intensity of the want, at any point (say a_1b_1). Is that to be construed as the measure of the dynamic process from that point on to satiation? Is it the measure of one of the magnitudes of a correspondence? If so, the correspondence, at that point, is between the remaining intensity of the want and the remaining units of means (b_1c) which, in this case, are 9 in number. It is evident, then, that, if we so construe remaining intensity, we are converting it to terms of reduction of intensity. That is, we are assuming, just as we did with our own maximum, or initial, intensity, that the difference at any point between the static magnitude and zero is a measure of the dynamic magnitude, or process, and therefore the basis for the derivation of a correspondence. So construed, all three magnitudes (maximum and remaining intensity and reduction of intensity) would be dynamic, would all be related to means in the same way, and would only differ in the particular portions of means to which they severally referred. On this construction, the remaining intensity could presumably be judged in the same terms as the initial (maximum) intensity—that is, in terms of more or less or equality. Its relation to the whole remaining means (9 units) would then be roughly determinable; and, if we were able to know that the effect of all units of means in reducing the intensity was the same, we could *infer* that the remaining intensity of the want, at a_1b_1, would be $\frac{9}{15}$ of the initial intensity, even though we cannot measure either initial or remaining intensity.

On the other hand, Fig. 5, being a concave curve which signifies a continuously diminishing rate of decline of intensity, shows each successive section on *ab*, corresponding to the ordinally same section on *bc*, to be smaller than the last, in spite of the fact that all sections on *bc* are of the same size. Just as in the case of distance traversed, the reduction in intensity accomplished by unit *d*, when projected upon the corresponding section of the altitude as d_1 is greater than is that of unit *e*, projected as e_1. But here, if precise measurement is impossible, one could only recognize the general trend toward less reduction of intensity for each successive unit of means. Precise comparison of non-contiguous phases such as d_1 and e_1 would be impossible. In Fig. 5 the remaining intensity of the want, at any point, construed as the measure of a dynamic process still to be accomplished, would again be related only to the remaining units of means at that point. But, then, we could no longer infer the fraction of the initial intensity which the remaining intensity represented by measuring the ratio of the remaining units of means to the total number. We could only infer that it is somewhat smaller than it would have been if the successive reductions in intensity had been judged to be equal. If, in Fig. 5, the curve had been shown as convex, that would have represented the fact that the rate of decline of intensity was assumed to be an increasing one. The relation between successive units of means in respect of the reduction of intensity of want to which they corresponded would then be reversed. Each would correspond, on *ab*, to a larger section than the last. Finally, it is well to remember that the two-dimensional representation in these two diagrams is merely for convenience and that it imposes none of its own characteristics upon the two one-dimensional magnitudes it represents. That is, area in the diagram has no meaning here.

Both these two-dimensional representations of the process of satisfying (Figs. 3 and 5) are designed principally to represent the assumption that the intensity of a want declines gradually during the course of a single satisfaction. Neither is necessary—in fact, neither is quite

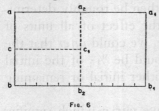

FIG. 6

fair to our own assumption. We should, therefore, append one diagram specifically designed to show our own concept of the process. In Fig. 6 the initial or maximum intensity of the want is shown as *ab*; the number of objective units of means required for a complete satisfaction (12) is shown along *bb₁*. The intensity of the want is conceived as remaining at the level

a (shown as aa_1) during the process and then, when the process ceases (is completed), as dropping from a_1 to b_1 ($=$ o). In other words the lines aa_1 and a_1b_1 represent in succession the course which the intensity is supposed to take during the process. Satiation, as a dynamic process, is thus represented by the two complete lines; while satiety, as a state, is represented as the point b_1, or any other point on the line bb_1, extended. The number of units of means on the base, bb_1, are only related in the aggregate to the process. Specific units have no sensible or measurable specific effect. They are merely required to make up the whole.

The proper physical analogy for this concept of the process would be the level of water in a siphon, rather than the level of mercury in a thermometer or the traversing of distance. In the latter cases, reduction in temperature corresponds to a gradual sinking in the tube and motion to the gradual accumulation of distance traversed. In the former case, the water rises gradually in the shorter leg as fast as it rises in the vessel in which this leg is immersed. As soon as this level reaches its maximum height (in the siphon) the water commences to flow. Thereafter, the height of water in the siphon remains at this maximum until the shorter leg is no longer immersed, because the water above this level in the vessel has been exhausted. This is purely an analogy—one among many in nature—which is suggested merely to aid the reader in conceiving this process on a basis which may be opposed to his preconceptions.[21]

It would contradict our own assumptions as to the several conditions so far considered under which only incomplete satisfactions of wants are achieved, were we to show a diagram representing successive satisfactions of several segments of a want. For under all of these conditions only the first part of the process is accomplished, or considered in the program; and, for the rest, the want remains unsatisfied on that occasion. When it again becomes prepotent, or again comes to be considered in a program, it will take some unpredictable position in this or a later order of priority, depending upon its then effective intensity. Except in the case of minor wants as to which progressive deficiencies raise the effective intensity above normal, that position could not be prior to the position its normal maximum intensity usually gives it, but might be anywhere further along in the order of priority. If, during the incomplete satisfaction, intensity is maintained as we

[21] Others are combustion, and the electromotive force of a cell.

suppose, the "shape" of a curve of incomplete satisfaction would be similar to that of a complete satisfaction as in Fig. 6. The reach along aa_1 would merely be cut short before a_1 was reached (say at a_2) representing the first segment of the satisfaction. The question then arises whether the height along ab would be the same as for a complete satisfaction. Doubtless the initial intensity would be the same in both cases. But if, for instance, only half a full measure of means were available, say bb_2, would we have to assume that the process of incomplete satisfaction would be shown by the lines aa_2 and a_2c_1 in succession, for instance, and that, at the instant the process was interfered with, or discontinued, the remaining intensity of the want should be conceived to be represented by c_1b_2, for instance? In that case $\dfrac{ac}{ab}$ would represent the portion of complete satisfaction achieved and ac would represent the reduction in the initial intensity of the want achieved by the corresponding part measure of the means, bb_2. We do not know whether or not this represents any of the facts. However, we will have to consider the question further in Part IV.

4. REPRESENTING THE USEFULNESS OF MEANS

What we have called the "usefulness" of a means is the quantitative relation between a specific want and a specific means, or its attribute. Viewed from one direction, as we said on p. 416, "the measure of their relation is the reflection of the full intensity of the want at its normal maximum—or the corresponding reduction—upon the full measure of means." Viewed from the other (and excluding part measures) the usefulness of any quantity of means is determined by the complete satisfaction of the want (or multiple satisfactions) to which it is appropriate, that a full measure of it will procure.[22] Usefulness is therefore based on a relation or correspondence between two incommensurable magnitudes of the kind we have just been considering. As such, it can only be stated in terms of the two incommensurable dimensions of its two relata. The expression for this correspondence would be: "The usefulness of a full measure of means equals a complete satisfaction of the want." That is, usefulness is the one-

[22] In this demonstration we are considering only those means whose usefulness is proportionate to the product of quantity of means into density of attribute. When the usefulness is fixed, because the quantity of attribute is fixed, it must be conceived as some definite and non-expansible portion of a complete satisfaction.

directional name of the relation; a full measure of means is the relate; and a complete satisfaction of the want is the correlate.

That suffices very nicely to establish, under our own assumption, the correspondence we need between the relate and the correlate in a common process. But it is time to recognize that the statements of the criterion for usefulness have been equivocal. We have not decided, or stated, which of the two magnitudes, the static or the dynamic, is determining. True, we may conceive them to be of the same size; but, here, we are considering a psychological process. Which of the two is appreciated in such a way that its magnitude is judged or determined? Either we feel and obey the state, or we feel and obey the quantity of process—not both. For our own hypothesis it might seem not to make much difference which we select, since we are assuming them to be of the same size. But, since, for other hypotheses, the results would be entirely different according to which criterion were chosen, we must be consistent and unequivocal with regard to our own. Furthermore, our whole physiological study has made it quite clear that we have regarded the determination of prepotence to depend on a conflict of forces, called intensity of wants, the resolution of which depends on their relative magnitude conceived in static terms. We shall therefore continue to assume for our own hypothesis that the static magnitude, initial or maximum intensity of the want, is the decisive one and that the dynamic magnitude, reduction from that point to zero, is only apprehended by way of fixing the correspondence, in the process of satisfying, with a full measure of means.

The simplest representation of usefulness is that shown in Fig. 4, the meaning of which we have discussed. Since the two sides of the equation are non-mathematically equal, both are shown as of the same length on the single line. The usefulness of means ab = the want ab. Or, since the means can be objectively measured and a full measure reduced to terms of its units (say 10), the representation of the magnitude of a full measure can be divided into 10 sections, one for each unit. That indicates only that the usefulness of 10 units of means ab = the want ab. As we have said before, it does not indicate that the usefulness of one unit of means $\dfrac{(ab)}{10}$ = $\frac{1}{10}$ of the want ab. We cannot know that since we cannot divide the want ab into tenths. All we can say is that the usefulness of one unit of means is, as part of the whole, one-tenth of the usefulness of the whole. This possible misrepresentation is obviated by the two-dimensional representation used in Fig. 6. There only the base, bb_1, is divided into sections; the altitude, ab, is represented only as a whole. There the exact character of the correspondence appears more clearly. The usefulness of 12 units of means, bb_1, = the initial intensity of the want, ab; and the correspondence is determined via the reduction of intensity from the maximum to zero, a_1b_1, which, in our case, is the same magnitude converted from static to dynamic terms. No correspondence is shown between any single unit of means and any quantity of reduction of intensity of want.[23]

We must again avoid giving the connotation of exactitude to the usefulness of a part measure of means, since we do not know very well how it is or can be estimated. But, if the supposition suggested on page 474 turned out to be true for certain cases, we might also use Fig. 6 to represent such usefulness. It is quite conceivable and seems to accord with some observations that, in planning future provision where only a part measure is available, the estimation of its usefulness is reduced in some rough proportion from that of the full measure.

[23] In order to make this quite clear an example may be useful. For this we take an analogy that is not quite analogous, because here the correlate is at least theoretically measurable, while in our case it is not. Let us suppose that we have a field from which is raised one wagon-load of hay. Then, in respect of the correspondence we call crop, or production, 1 field = 1 wagon-load of hay. The fundamental dimensions in which the two are stated are different—and they would still be different if they could be reduced to units and measured.

Let us suppose, now, that we have no means of measuring a wagon-load of hay; it is merely one load of a more or less regular size. But we can measure the field; it is 10 roods. Can we then say that the crop from 1 rood = $\frac{1}{10}$ wagon-load? We cannot; for, in the first place, we cannot measure the wagon-load and therefore cannot divide it into tenths; and, in the second place, we cannot measure the actual crop cut from each rood. It may well be that some rood in the field yields no hay while others vary widely in their yields.

Production, in this correspondence, is equivalent to usefulness in ours. It is the name of the correspondence. It is one-directional, so it is measured solely in terms of hay. It is expressed in the form of an equation between two fundamental magnitudes that correspond in a process. The production of one field, or 10 roods, = 1 wagon-load of hay. Of course a relation between two magnitudes is two-directional; but the names in the two directions are different. Usefulness is a characteristic of the relate, the means, just as production is a characteristic of the field, the relate. It is measured by the correlate in both cases. That is, we cannot say that the production of one wagon-load of hay is one field.

Usefulness can only be measured in terms of multiples of complete satisfactions for the simple reason that, like our wagon-load of hay, there is, according to our hypothesis, no other way of measuring it. It cannot be reduced to arbitrary objective units; it cannot even be divided into fractions of this natural separate unit.

Thus to say that the usefulness of $bb_2 = ac$, for instance, might not be far out of the way. We will see.

On the basis of the foregoing analysis, if we wish to represent diagrammatically the unweighted terms of substitution of two or more means for the satisfaction of a single want, we can do so in a very simple way—by drawing two parallel, horizontal lines of equal length. This is again two-dimensional representation of one-dimensional magnitudes, in which the second dimension of the representation has no meaning, and in which both of two different one-dimensional magnitudes, each with its own dimension, are shown, one on each of the single lines. The length of the two lines in Fig. 7, arbitrarily selected,

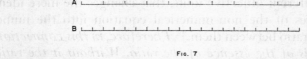

Fig. 7

represents the magnitude of a want—statically considered, its maximum intensity, and dynamically considered, the reduction of intensity from the maximum to zero (satiation). We cannot measure this magnitude; but we can assume that it is the same for both means. Since the usefulness of a full measure of both means equals complete satisfaction of the want, in the sense of this non-mathematical correspondence, it follows that the usefulness of a full measure of one means equals that of the other, in the same sense. When these non-mathematically equal full measures are each reduced to terms of their respective objective units and the number of units of each are indicated by sections on the line representing it, the two equal lines show the two means, of one of which (A) there is required 10 of its objective units and of the other (B) 20 of its different objective units, for complete satisfaction.[24] As noted in the previous chapter the terms of substitution are then, as to this want, A = 2B. It should be noted that this expression has no meaning whatever unless the objective units of the means are definitely determined and unchanging.[25] Moreover, we must recognize that the units in which the two means are measured, and in which their resulting one-dimensional quantities—as numerical values—are stated here, may be different and entirely unrelated to each other. The quan-

[24] All of the following is equally true if the usefulness of the means is equivalent to several complete satisfactions.
[25] It does not mean that the *quantity* required of B is twice as large as that of A. Subjectively the quantities are equal. In terms of weight, cubic contents, length, etc., etc., they may have all sorts of ratios, differing among themselves.

tity of one necessary to a complete satisfaction is subjectively equal
—or corresponds—to the quantity of the other necessary to a complete satisfaction. On this basis the terms of substitution are 1:1, and
we have learned nothing. Except in some such definite relation as this,
or that of weight, length, etc., we have no means of knowing what are
equal—or corresponding—quantities of two different means. And
these various possible equalities—or correspondences—may not coincide, or may not even be in constant proportion. Equal weights may
not be equal subjectively, etc. It is only the arbitrary division of two
such, in some respect non-mathematically equal—or corresponding
—quantities of different means each into a number of its own definite
and perhaps different objective units, that changes the mere identities
of the two sides of the non-numerical equation into the numerical
expression of a ratio between them.[26] *Therefore, in this connection, the
objective unit is of the essence of the ratio. Without it the ratio has
no definite meaning.*

5. REPRESENTING THE SIGNIFICANCE OF MEANS

We incorporated the term "significance" in our terminology chiefly
in order to distinguish the relation of wants to means when, under
the alternative hypothesis of declining intensity during satisfaction, it
is conceived that this relation or projection varies during the process of
satisfaction.[27] If we construe the remaining intensity of the want at
any stage to represent the dynamic magnitude, reduction of intensity
from that level to zero, we find no difference in the basis upon which
significance would be conferred upon the means by the remaining intensity of the want at any stage and that upon which it would be conferred by the reduction of intensity through any phase of the process.
The one would merely represent, always, the significance conferred
by that part of the whole process not yet accomplished, while the
other would represent the significance conferred by some part of the
process already accomplished. Any psychological entity such as desire
might well correspond to the former, so that its representation would
take the same form; and any psychological process such as pleasure

[26] If A stands for the quantity of means A which is subjectively equal to the quantity
B of B, then A = B. Only if A and B are defined as definite objective units can we say
A:B = 8:10; only then does there exist a numerical ratio between them.
[27] That is, we introduced the term to admit the first part (assumption *a*) of the conglomerate assumption which, to a greater or less extent of its all-inclusiveness, underlies
all marginal utility theory, in the broadest sense of that term (see pp. 437 ff.).

or satisfaction would be likely to correspond to, or to be capable of being shown in the same way as, the latter. Both types of entity would be dynamic magnitudes; the one would represent the disappearance of desire during the process, while the other would represent the accumulation of pleasure or satisfaction during the process. Obviously —though apparently this has not always been recognized—if they were so construed, that portion of the full measure of means which would have reflected upon it the remaining intensity of the want at any stage would be the whole portion remaining unused or unconsumed at that stage; and that portion upon which is projected any reduction in

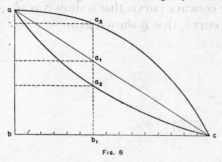

Fig. 8

the intensity of the want through any phase would be the portion which was used or consumed during that phase. For both possible projections of significance it is also necessary to consider the alternative possibilities (1) that the decline in intensity of the want takes place at a constant rate and (2) that it takes place at a changing rate, either diminishing or increasing. It is unnecessary to go into the complications of irregular rates of change.

Representations of significance can best be made in the two-dimensional form we used in Figs. 3 and 5. Considering first the reflection of significance by reason of remaining intensity of want at any stage— on the dynamic construction of the nature of the magnitude—we may show this in Fig. 8. There ab represents the initial intensity of the want and bc represents a full measure of means. The straight line curve, ac, shows a constant rate of decline in intensity; the concave curve, ac, shows a diminishing rate of decline; and the convex curve, ac, shows an increasing rate of decline. At the point b_1, the remaining intensity of the want stands at b_1a_1, on the first curve, at b_1a_2 on the second, and at b_1a_3 on the third. If, then, ab is conceived to determine the significance of the full measure of means, bc, it follows that the several different altitudes, b_1a_1, b_1a_2, and b_1a_3, determine, for each of the three curves respectively, the significance of the remaining means, b_1c.

If, now, the whole is not to be greater than its parts, it follows from this that, when we consider, alternatively, the reflection of significance by reason of reduction of intensity of want, we deal with the complements of these magnitudes. That is, the significance of the portion of means already consumed, bb_1, will be determined by the reduction of intensity accomplished during the phase of the process up to the point b_1. On the first curve, the straight line, that is shown as $ab - a_1b_1$; on the second, the concave curve, that is shown as $ab - a_2b_1$; and on the third, the convex curve, that is shown as $ab - a_3b_1$.

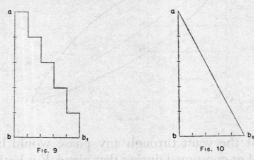

FIG. 9   FIG. 10

When we convert the dimension represented by the base in this diagram (Fig. 8) into terms of units of means, it is necessary to remind ourselves of what was said above in regard to keeping them fixed once their arbitrary size is determined. So far as representing the significance conferred by remaining intensity is concerned, dividing the base into 15 units makes no difference, provided the stage at which it is measured coincides with the end of the consumption of a whole unit. The only effect is to restate the quantity of means upon which the remaining intensity is reflected in terms of units. Thus we find that, at b_1, the several remaining intensities shown on the curves are reflected on the remaining 9 units of means. But as a representation of the significance conferred by reduction of intensity—assuming that can be at least roughly judged—the diagram no longer serves the purposes of clear demonstration—that is, it does so no better than did the successive sections along the altitude ab which we used on pp. 470–471. Instead, on the assumption of a continuous uniform rate of decline of intensity during the process and conceding that it is theoretically possible to assign to each objective unit of means its particular and in-dependent effect in the whole process, a clear form of representation could only be made as in Fig. 9. There, as each of the units of means (on bb_1) is applied, the intensity is supposed to decline by one step, which may then be projected on the scale shown along ab. Fig. 10 shows the same results, but as if the process were continuous *within* the units.

Now if we wish to represent this process in a way that will enable us still better to compare the successive reductions of intensity by each unit of means in order, we may separate this series of reductions —the heights of the successive steps along ab—and arrange them as vertical lines each placed at the end of its unit of means. This again uses a two-dimensional representation of the series of reductions, of which the second dimension has no meaning. So, in Fig. 11, at the end of each of the 5 units along the base, bb_1, rises a verti-cal line which represents the reduction of intensity ac-complished by that unit. All are equal because the rate of reduction per unit is constant. If the significance

Fig. 11

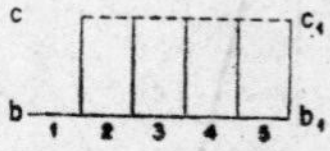

of a unit of means corresponds to its effect in reducing the intensity of a want, then the significance of each of these units is equal to that of every other, and the derived "curve of significance" of means becomes a horizontal line cc_1 parallel to the base and joining the tops of these vertical lines. But here the unit of the dimension of means enters as an essential element; for, here, there is no discon-tinuity in the process of satisfying, other than the end of the consump-tion of a unit of means, according to which to divide each part satisfac-tion from its successor. Thus the division is based only on the arbitrary selection of an objective unit. Nor does the fact that we have repre-sented the process as a continuous one in Fig. 10 alter this fact. If we made our units half the size, the reduction of intensity they would accomplish would be reduced to half as much, and so would their significance. Thus the height of the "curve of significance" depends upon the size of the unit chosen. If we made the units infinitesimal, the reduction of intensity they would accomplish would also become infinitesimal, and so would their significance. Then the "curve of sig-nificance" would correspond to the base itself. Since I know of no way of comparing the size of infinitesimal quantities, I should say such a representation would be mathematically meaningless. However, given measurable units of means and the capacity to measure the corresponding reduction of intensity of want, this curve (Fig. 11) does show the relative significance of successive units of means on the assumption of decline in intensity at a constant rate.

On the assumption of a diminishing rate of decline of intensity the curve representing this intensity would be the concave curve in Fig. 8. We redraw this in Fig. 12, changing the initial intensity to make the change in rate more marked in the diagram. This, in turn, results in the "curve of significance" given in Fig. 13. That shows a continuing diminution in the reduction of intensity accomplished by each successive unit in the series. Only this assumption results in a "curve of

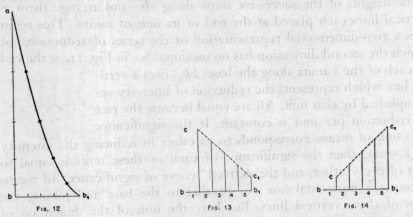

Fig. 12   Fig. 13   Fig. 14

significance," cc_1, which is negatively inclined. The assumption of an increasing rate of decline in intensity (a convex curve) results in a "curve of significance," such as that shown in Fig. 14, where the curve itself is positively inclined. Again, in both these "curves of significance" the unit of the dimension of means is essential and the slope of the curve depends entirely on the size of such unit chosen. With these, too, if reduced to infinitesimals, the curves cannot be shown as other than the base.

Thus we see that, if significance is a reflection of the reduction of intensity accomplished by a unit of means, a constant rate of reduction of intensity is represented, for the want, by a straight-line curve which is negatively inclined, and that the resulting "curve of significance" for the means is a straight line parallel to the base; we also see that a steadily diminishing rate of reduction of intensity is represented, for the want, by a concave curve which is negatively inclined, and that the resulting "curve of significance" for the means is a straight line negatively inclined; and we see that a steadily increasing rate of reduction of intensity is represented, for the want, by a convex curve which is negatively inclined, and that the resulting "curve of significance" for the means is a straight line positively inclined.

Several important conclusions arise from this diagrammatic analysis of the results of using the criterion of the comparative size of the successive reductions in intensity of want, or any psychological process accompanying that, as the determinant of the comparative significance of the corresponding successive objective units of means. In the first place, it shows us that the "curve of significance" of the successively applied equal units of means, if the rate of decline is constant or increasing, is wholly different from—though derived from and dependent on—the curve representing the decline of intensity during the satisfaction of a want. In the second place, it leads us away from the confusion of *remaining intensity* at the end of any stage of the process with *reduction of intensity* accomplished up to that stage, by segregating the latter, which, if the latter is the criterion of significance, is the only magnitude which has any bearing on the subject. In the third place, it compels us to deal only with finite objective magnitudes of means—the kinds of unit in terms of which we wish actually to compare means. For reduction to terms of infinitesimal quantities or increments would lower the "curves of significance," the dotted lines cc_1, in the case of all three of the figures (Figs. 11, 13 and 14), to the level of the base bb_1, and thus cease to have meaning. On the other hand, even if we avoid trying to deal in terms of infinitesimal quantities, another difficulty remains. Since we have frequently acknowledged that the selection of objective units by which to measure means is purely arbitrary, but nevertheless it will here determine the height and the shape of the "curve of significance," this seems to introduce, as a crucial factor, something which tends to render the results of the analysis equally arbitrary when it comes to comparing different means or different wants. In the fourth place, it shows us that, if the rate of decline in intensity is constant per unit of means, as in Fig. 11, the last unit (ordinally) has the same significance as the first. Thus one of the chief pieces of evidence advanced for the supposition that the intensity of want declines gradually during a single satisfaction—the supposed introspective observation that the "feeling" does so decline—might be reconciled with our observation that, nevertheless, the process is usually completed without interference, if we assumed the units of means to be large enough to have significance. For, in spite of this decline, *the last unit is then of equal significance with the first.* That might remove the conflict between this supposition and our observation, though it does nothing further positively to prove the supposition. But then the dependent theory of subjective value would fall to the ground, for then all units necessary to a single satisfaction would be of equal subjective value—there would be no difference between the marginal unit and any other. If the rate of decline in intensity is presumed to be an increasing one, then the "curve of significance" is precisely the opposite of the one usually shown in marginal utility theory. That, to be sure, would also tend to induce satiation. That, too, might help to reconcile our observations with the supposed introspective ones upon which marginal utility is based. Only if the rate of reduction of intensity is conceived as diminishing—and this, like the last, would be still more inaccessible to introspection and even further from confirmation by observation—is such a reconciliation not possible. For then the importance of successive units would diminish and the last small unit (or part of a larger one) would approach zero importance. On that slender thread the dependent theory of subjective value appears to hang if the criterion of significance is the reduction of intensity or any related psychological process.[28]

By means of this form of analysis we have also accomplished another result. We have shown that, if the remaining intensity of the want at any stage—shown by the various altitudes in our triangles—is construed as the measure of a dynamic magnitude, or part of the process of satisfying, the only correspondence with means that can be established for it is a correspondence with the whole quantity of means remaining unconsumed at that stage. Obviously such a construction divorces this magnitude entirely from any that has been represented in marginal utility theory. Furthermore, since, for our purposes, such a construction merely duplicates that based on reduction of intensity, it is of no use to us and we shall discard it. There remains

[28] By means of these successive forms of representation we have shown that the basic concept of marginal utility theory, if significance derives from anything that occurs during phases of the process, rests not only on the assumption that the intensity of the want declines during satisfaction but also that it declines at a continuously diminishing rate. That assumption can be represented by a derived curve, such as our "curves of significance" above, which does not depict the process of satisfaction and in which area has no meaning. Or, on the other hand, it can be depicted in another way next to be considered in which successive blocks of area come to have the same meaning as the successive altitudes in our curves.

for remaining intensity, as a criterion, only the possibility of construing it as a static rather than a dynamic magnitude. That possibility we shall explore. Its first and most puzzling difficulty is to find for it any relation with the process of satisfying and therefore any correspondence with means.

6. OTHER REPRESENTATIONS RELATING TO SIGNIFICANCE

There are two other ways of representing the several magnitudes concerned in this process, together with their relations—ways that have been commonly used in the presentation of marginal utility theory. In both, the dimensions of some of the magnitudes are different from our definitions, and the magnitudes are therefore different—though frequently the matter of dimensions is either ignored or confused. In both, unlike any of ours, the area in the diagram comes to have meaning. In the first, the two-dimensional area of the figure represents a magnitude—significance or what not—that is itself considered to be one-dimensional, and the one-dimensional base of the figure represents a magnitude—means, etc.—that is considered also to be one-dimensional. As a result of geometrical laws this permits the use of the altitude in the figure to represent a two-dimensional magnitude —the area divided by the base, $\frac{A \text{ (area)}}{B \text{ (base)}}$. As we have seen, such a dimensional formula is that of a derived magnitude, or rate. What the altitude stands for, then, is not significance, etc., but *rate* of significance, etc., per unit of means, etc. That is a different magnitude from the one we have been considering, although, like all derived magnitudes, it is built up from a correspondence, or equation, such as the one we have been using to demonstrate significance. We shall examine in Appendix IV the several illegitimate uses that have been made of this form of representation. In the second form of representation the two-dimensional area of the figure represents a magnitude—the entity causing significance—that is itself conceived to be two-dimensional. Again as a result of geometrical laws, this permits the use of the altitude and the base in the figure to represent the two dimensions of the area. This raises a number of questions which we also discuss in Appendix IV. What are these two dimensions of significance, or of that which lies back of and causes significance? How are they to be defined and measured or judged? If the base represents a dimension of significance, etc., how bring in the matter of means? Our conclusion in the appendix is that there is no answer to these questions and, for that reason, we dismiss the form of representation as fictitious.

However, the reader will have noted that the matter of rates has crept into the argument in the last few pages, where we considered the different possible kinds of rates of decline of intensity of wants—constant, diminishing, or increasing. Therefore, we cannot dismiss this subject without brief consideration at this point. The notion of such a rate of decline is that of a derived magnitude. It is a different treatment of the same relations between two magnitudes that we have dealt with as correspondences; in fact, it is a derivative of such correspondences. What do we mean by the rate of decline in the intensity of a want? If a want had two dimensions, we could speak of the rate of decline in the dimension, intensity, per unit of the other dimension. But since, so far as we know, it has not, we cannot speak of the rate of decline in terms of the want alone, because a rate requires two dimensions. What we have done, on the assumption of declining intensity during the process of satisfaction, is to speak of the rate of decline of intensity per equal portion or unit of means. In fact, that appears to be the only other dimension available upon which to construct a rate. In future, therefore, we shall confine ourselves to the consideration of such a rate. But even that rate will be found to involve certain difficulties.

Even so defined, would we gain anything by deriving such rates from our data and representing them? We have assumed them in our several curves—the straight line, the concave and the convex curves in Fig. 8, and the horizontal, negatively inclined, and positively inclined curves in Figs. 11, 13 and 14. But these curves represent the correspondences upon which the several rates, constant or changing, are based; they do not represent the rates themselves. That is a more difficult matter. The constant rate of decline, like velocity, has two dimensions—say IM^{-1}, where I is the dimension of intensity and M that of means.[29] But a changing rate of decline involves a series of

[29] Thus the rate of significance is a single expression in the form $\frac{I}{M}$, while significance as a correspondence was expressed by an equation whose dimensional formula was $M = I$. Here the relate of the correspondence has become the denominator (or inverse dimension) of the rate; and the correlate of the correspondence has become the numerator (or direct dimension) of the rate.

different rates of declines. Like acceleration, it has three dimensions, and is represented by IM^{-2}. That is, it is so much less or more decline in intensity per unit of means, per unit of means.[30] But, worse still, the changing rate would here have no bearing on our problem by itself; for it does not contain the decline in intensity per unit of means but only the change in that decline. Thus both rates would be required for any judgment. It would be necessary to know the rate of decline in intensity as well as the rate of diminution or increase in that decline. One cannot determine how much distance he will cover in the next hour merely by knowing the rate of positive or negative acceleration in his velocity; to know that requires also the base velocity at some point. Representation of such a compound basis for judgment is, therefore, a difficult matter. But that is not all. It would, if it were made, misrepresent reality. It is quite clear that neither of these rates can be apprehended by themselves. Even conceptually they can only be derived by calculations. Moreover they are superfluous. Why bother to calculate them, since it is evident that the only magnitudes that can possibly be felt and can therefore influence behavior, are the fundamental magnitudes and their correspondences from which these rates would have to be derived? [31]

7. REPRESENTING A SYSTEM OF WANTS

The two-dimensional (comparative) representation of a set of co-existing one-dimensional static magnitudes with a common dimension follows the same lines as the foregoing. Thus we may depict the order of priority of wants by a series of vertical lines gradually diminishing in height, as in Fig. 15. Here we have but the beginning of the series of wants pertaining to some individual; for the series is conceived to extend indefinitely. The intensity of each want is shown at its customary maximum; thus this is a representation of the *potential* order of priority, as we have called it; it represents the relative intensities only when and as the wants recur; and it shows the order in which they will be satisfied only in respect of provision for a sufficient

[30] So the dimensions of velocity are LT^{-1} and those of acceleration LT^{-2}.
[31] The character of the rate of decline—constant, diminishing, or increasing—can be inferred, without measurement, if the successive correspondences can be judged, but only then. That is, only if the reduction of intensity produced by successive units of means is judged to be approximately equal, can a constant rate be assumed; only if these reductions are diminishing, can a diminishing rate be assumed; and only if they are increasing, can an increasing rate be assumed. But if the sameness or the changes can be judged, what need of deriving a rate?

period to include the recurrence of all wants at their respective maxima.[32] But here we are comparing magnitudes which we cannot measure, since there is no unit in terms of which we can "count" them.
Therefore we are not able to show how much difference there is in
their respective sizes. As to that difference we have but two clues. The
difference between each adjoining pair of wants must be sufficient
to determine their position in the order; and the difference between
many of the more subordinate must often—or usually—be so slight
that we cannot perceive any great reduction in intensity of successive

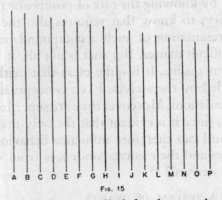

A B C D E F G H I J K L M N O P

Fɪɢ. 15

wants, at least after all the so-called fundamental wants are satisfied
and the person is endeavoring to expand his capacity to secure means
for the satisfaction of his less intense wants. Therefore, the difference
must be more than the *minimum sensibile* [33] and, nevertheless, at least
after the prior wants, of the order of smalls. It is what the mathemati-
cians call a "close order" but not a "continuous aggregate." [34] Much
the same problem confronted the early astronomers and, as is well
known, they made a first approximation to the measurement of stars
by arranging them in the order of their brightness (naïve sensuous
but objective measurement) and denoting the size of each (or of each
group) by its place in this series—the successive "orders of magni-

[32] It should be noted here, as well as in what follows, that we have to shift over to the
comparison of future wants, rather than the comparison of the felt intensities of present
wants; for it is impossible, according to our hypothesis, that the intensity of more than
one want can be felt at any one time. However, the order of priority is supposed to
be the same for both.

[33] Edgeworth (*133, 7*) suggests this psychological concept (Wundt's *ebenmerklich*),
but uses it in a somewhat different way.

[34] Therefore, incidentally, it cannot be represented by a curve, as were the successive
stages of reduction of the individual want on the assumption of declining intensity during satisfaction.

tude." In the same way we may say that Want A (in Fig. 15) is of the first order of magnitude, Want B of the second, etc. And we may do so in the knowledge that the difference in size between the first and the tenth orders of magnitude is more than nine times the *minimum sensibile*, though we cannot know how great it is. This representation of the order of priority is purely a static one. It is the "potential" order in terms of maxima. If the virtual order of preference among means followed the order of priority of wants and the intensity of the want were maintained throughout the process of satisfaction and then dropped to zero—both of which conditions are met by our own

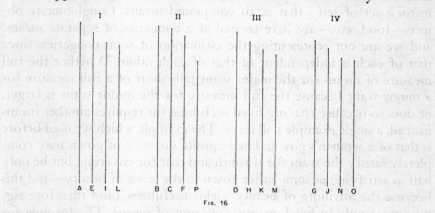

Fig. 16

assumptions as to subjective valuation—this mode of representation would also serve fairly well to show the system of processes of satisfaction for all wants. But we will perceive, as we proceed, that it cannot be used to represent the system of processes of satisfying upon the assumption of declining intensity, as was possible when we considered a single want alone. And we will find much difficulty in arriving at any diagrammatic representation of the whole system of processes under such a condition.

In the same mode we can represent the aggregations of allied wants which we have called constellations. Let us assign all the Wants A to P inclusive (Fig. 15), to their respective constellations, I to IV (Fig. 16). These constellations are arranged in the order of priority of their major wants. The difference between the magnitudes of the major want and the various minor wants of each constellation is now greater than that between successive wants in the order of priority. Thus, in constellation I, Want A is of the first order of magnitude, E of the fifth,

I of the ninth, and L of the twelfth. This representation is also purely of static facts and cannot be used for showing the processes.

Through these successive steps we have arrived at the point where we can represent the two possible forms that may be taken by the summation of the usefulness of a means serving several wants of a constellation. We may remind the reader that any summation of usefulness would be limited, according to our analysis, to those compound objects (or acts of others) which contain constituents or attributes giving them usefulness for several different wants of a constellation, so that the usefulness may be availed of in a joint process—consummatory act of self—that is, to compound means. Conglomerate objects—food, etc.—are here treated as a congeries of separate means, and we are not representing the estimation of such congeries, since that of each is independent of that of each other. Whether the full measure of means for the major want falls short of a full measure for a minor want because the full measure for the minor want is larger, or does so because (having fixed usefulness) it requires another means instead, a single example will serve. The example which we used before is that of a woman's gown. The requisite quantity of gown may completely satisfy the want for warmth and that for covering, but be only half as satisfying as some other gown to the sense of beauty—and this because the attribute of beauty yields usefulness (and therefore significance) only in fixed quantity per unit of means. The formula for the usefulness of such a full measure of means applicable to constellation II (Fig. 16), for instance, might be, $B + C + \frac{1}{2} D$. But this summation encounters the difficulty that it is an addition of immeasurable magnitudes. Thus the nearest approach to a mathematical statement which is possible is in the following form:

$$1 \ (2^D \ \text{O.M.}) + 1 \ (3^D \ \text{O.M.}) + \tfrac{1}{2} \ (16^{\text{th}} \ \text{O.M.})$$

Furthermore, we must recognize that, while such summation is theoretically possible and doubtless does occur, it can, at best, be only rough. According to our previous examination of the estimation of usefulness of part measures, when these are included, the summation would necessarily be even rougher.

In order not to beg the question of summation of usefulness, at this point, we are going to introduce its two possible forms, which we may call simultaneous and successive summation.[35] The formula given

<hr />

[35] This question was referred to and postponed in Chapter 7 (p. 430). It is dealt with more fully in Section D 2 below.

above in terms of orders of magnitude represents the aggregate use-fulness of a compound means for the several component wants of a constellation. This aggregate can only be recognized—summation can only take place—when these are future wants. For, unlike present wants, future wants can coexist. They can be "allied" during conflicts in consciousness. If simultaneous summation can take place, Wants C and D would add their estimations of usefulness to that of Want A at the place Want A occupies in the order of priority; if successive summation takes place, the process of addition would only occur by way of accumulation at the places, successively, which were occupied by Wants C and D in the order of priority. The different effects of these two procedures will be considered when we come to analyze the orders of preference.

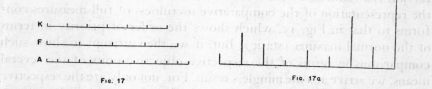

Fig. 17   Fig. 17a

Hitherto we have passed over the question of representing the com-parative usefulness of a single means for several wants which it may serve alternatively but not jointly, because we had not yet developed the idea of the order of magnitude of wants. To represent this we may (in Fig. 17) show, on parallel horizontal lines, the usefulness of full measures of this means for three such wants (A, F, and K). For complete satisfaction of A, 13 units are required; for that of F, 4 units; for that of K, 6 units. In order, then, to establish a ratio in which the different numbers of units of the means required to make up the differ-ent full measures is considered it is necessary to reduce the expressions for the means to a common denominator—that is, to terms of a single unit. Thus the expression for the ratio between the comparative use-fulness of a unit of the means for these several alternative uses takes the form: $\frac{1}{13}A : \frac{1}{4}F : \frac{1}{6}K$. But this expression presents the same diffi-culty as the summation of these magnitudes would, since A, F, and K are immeasurable. The lines representing A, F, and K are of the same extent horizontally in Fig. 17 as they are vertically in Fig. 15, for each represents the complete satisfaction of the respective want; that is, each equals the static measure of maximum intensity. But all we know of the relative size is that A is of the first order of magnitude, F of the sixth, and K of the eleventh. Therefore the comparative usefulness of a single unit of means which will serve for the satisfaction of several different wants (of different constellations) can only be expressed as $\frac{1}{13}$ (1st O.M.) : $\frac{1}{4}$ (6th O.M.) : $\frac{1}{6}$ (11th O.M.). This elaborate formula may seem to the reader to be the figment of an overheated imagination. Nevertheless, observation indicates that it represents approximately what men, and even higher animals, frequently do in the process of making their choices.

When we undertake to show comparisons of the usefulness of the several specific means for several different wants we may start with full measures of each as a basis. Obviously, since the subjective magnitude, a full measure, corresponds in each case to the subjective magnitude, a complete satisfaction (dynamic), and since complete satisfaction is a reduction of intensity from the normal maximum to zero, the representation of the comparative usefulness of full measures conforms to that in Fig. 15, which shows the order of priority in terms of the normal maxima (static). But, if we then attempt to show such comparisons in terms of the respective objective units of the several means, we arrive at a meaningless result. For, not only are the respective units quite arbitrary, but many magnitudes of means will be incommensurable, having different dimensions (pints, yards, etc.); and, even if some are commensurable or can be measured in the same unit, comparisons in these terms have no meaning in this connection. If we find that a ton of one means has more usefulness than a yard of another, we may have the general impression that it is partly due to the fact that a ton is larger than a yard. But, if we try to find a subdivision of a ton that is a unit of approximately the same "size" as a yard and will therefore serve as a basis for comparing the usefulness of the two means, we will run into difficulties and disagreements. Even if the two means can be measured in a common dimension, we will find the common denominator to be wholly specious as a basis of comparison. For instance, to compare the usefulness of carpeting and gingham we may find a common dimensional unit, the square yard. But, now, if we also compare their usefulness per pound, we will get a different ratio. Which is the proper basis for comparison?

The objective unit of measurement is, as we have already stated, always arbitrary. Those of different dimensions are incommensurable and therefore incomparable. Even for a single dimension the customary unit may, in one case, be a large one and, in others, a small subdivision of that. Thus, when the objective unit is introduced into a comparison of different means a purely factitious element enters. Depending on the unit chosen in each case, and even regardless of that, we should have an arrangement of means in order of usefulness which had no rhyme or reason. Such an order is represented in Fig. 17a, where the several successive vertical lines show what might happen to be the comparative usefulness of a unit of means for each of the first eight wants in their order in Fig. 15. A single unit of means for an unimportant want might show great usefulness; a single unit for a highly important want might show slight usefulness. Nor could we say that this was not due to the fact that the unit of the first was large while that of the second was small. That is, in each case, the usefulness of the unit of means would depend, on the one hand, upon the maximum intensity of the want it served, and, on the other, upon how large a fraction of a full measure it happened to represent. In the first respect, usefulness would be in direct proportion to the position of the want in the order of priority; in the second, it would be in inverse proportion to the number of units required for a complete satisfaction of the want.

At this point we are not going to discuss the representation of systems of wants and of their processes of satisfaction upon the assumption of declining intensity during the process; and, therefore, questions relating to the summation of significance for different wants or the comparative significance of different means will be postponed. This because it becomes necessary first to clarify our propositions with regard to the only two possible criteria for significance we have found —that of remaining intensity and that of reduction of intensity. We have noted that, as we have so far construed remaining intensity— that is, as a dynamic magnitude measuring the process of reduction of intensity from that level to zero—we have found it to be no different from reduction of intensity. On that basis we have, not two criteria, but a single one. There remains to be explored the possibility of treating remaining intensity as a static magnitude only, which might make of it a different and usable criterion. On the other hand, the results of our examination of reduction of intensity, so long as we measure the phase in terms of units of means, has turned that into an unusable criterion (completely arbitrary). Again, however, there remains a further possibility to explore—the possibility that we can find some other measure of phase that will not have the same objections. When we have conducted these further explorations we will have a better basis for dealing with these two possible criteria and will be able to use them in the course of our development of two of the virtual orders of preference.

The interested reader is now referred to Appendix IV, wherein we undertake to examine the several varieties of marginal utility theory in the light of the analysis of magnitudes, their dimensions and their representation, which we have now made in this chapter, and to explore the psychological assumptions implicit in each, in order to determine which of them, or what parts of them, meet the requirements of a rational and possible scheme. The rest of this chapter will then be devoted to the parallel and comparative development of the three criteria for the estimation of means which we find, in the text or in the Appendix, are able to meet the two tests we are imposing. From these we shall infer three different, and alternative, virtual orders of preference among means which will be carried forward to their final test in Part IV.

C. THREE POSSIBLE MAGNITUDES AS CRITERIA OF SUBJECTIVE VALUATION

I. DEFINITION OF THE CRITERIA AND THEIR PSYCHOLOGICAL SETTING

In the previous section of this chapter we promised ourselves the exploration of further possibilities that suggested themselves for making remaining intensity and reduction of intensity (or something analogous) serve as possible criteria for subjective valuation. In Appendix IV we found two criteria that passed both the tests. Neither conforms to the classical representation of marginal utility theory. Nor, in fact, does our working out in either case conform closely to its source. The first possibility was suggested by Menger's "significance" when that is construed to mean remaining intensity as a static magnitude. It was outlined in the Appendix. While this gives us no direct relation to means, it does at least provide us with an aspect of remaining intensity which is different from its aspect as a measure of process, and thus enables us to avoid mere duplication of the other criterion, reduction of intensity. The second possibility was suggested by the "indifference curves" of Pareto, Edgeworth, and Hicks. True, theirs is not a scheme of *pure* subjective valuation; nor does their chief inference and assumption—unlimited substitutability—seem to accord with reality. However, it gave us a key to another approach to the problem, which was also outlined in the Appendix, and which we shall incorporate with our own third criterion—reduction of intensity of want—and thus cure the latter of its most obvious and most debilitating defects—the arbitrary nature of objective units and another to be mentioned later. In the rest of Appendix IV we have considered the criteria utilized in all other brands of marginal utility theory. All these have been rejected either because they failed to pass our first test —that the magnitudes involved should be themselves measurable, even if only theoretically so—or because, when subjected to our second test—psychological possibility—they turned out to involve calculations with regard to magnitudes that cannot be measured—arithmetic applied to non-numerical magnitudes—or to involve the judgment of subjective experiences in terms of several related magnitudes or dimensions, and therefore required assumptions with regard to the capacity of the hedonic apparatus that we can only consider preposterous. This procedure, while it has seemed in part to be devoted to dealing with ghosts that are laid, has nevertheless served the purpose of illustrating the precise requirements that any scheme of subjective valuation must meet and, therefore, of preventing recourse to the revival of the older ideas in order to escape the indeterminateness of the indifference curve scheme as it stands today.

We now proceed to analyze and appraise the three possible hypothetical systems of pure subjective valuation which have seemed, after our investigation, to be susceptible of reduction to precise terms. For this purpose we will continue to exclude all extraneous influences, except the single one of some limitation on total means which is implicit in any consideration of the subject. Each of these surviving systems is based on its own hypothesis as to the virtual behavior of the organism in respect of subjective valuation and as to the organism's capacity (psychological) to compare the driving forces that are leading it to satisfy its wants. It may well be that we are not in position as yet to choose the most probable among these hypotheses. The truth might even be a mixture of them. At least, we are in position now to see clearly what each involves by way of psychological corollaries, and to what courses of virtual behavior each would lead, if operating as an isolated cause.

The three criteria we have now selected are based on different assumptions. On our own assumption that the intensity of a want is maintained approximately level throughout the process of satisfaction, there is but one possible criterion. That assumes that the normal maximum intensity of the want is reflected on the full measure of means, because both disappear in the course of a common process (i.e., a correspondence). Thus full measures of means for different wants have conferred upon them estimations of usefulness proportionate to the maxima of the several wants (static magnitudes). Or, it assumes in certain cases of incomplete satisfaction—but only in certain cases—that only a segment of the whole want may be reflected on a part measure of means. The usefulness of such part measures will then be estimated as less than that of a full measure, but how much less it is hard to say. On the assumption that the intensity of want declines during satisfaction there are a second and a third possible criterion.[1] The second supposes that the remaining intensity of the want (static magnitude) at each stage (including the stage before satisfaction begins) is the decisive factor. As yet we have not settled upon a way of relating this purely static magnitude to the process of satisfaction and therefore a way of relating Menger's "significance" of the want to our significance of the means. But it is already obvious that the only definitive relation that is inherent is one connecting the static magnitude at its several stages and the dynamic magnitudes during the phases between these stages. The third criterion under this assumption supposes that the reduction of intensity (dynamic magnitude)—or the quantity of pleasure or any other accompanying psychological process—that is accomplished through any phase of the satisfying, reflects upon the quantity of means consumed during that phase, so that the significance conferred upon any quantity of means, however divided off, depends only upon the quantity of process accomplished to which it corresponds, without regard to the maximum or remaining intensity of the want. According to this third criterion, if we assume the rate of decline of intensity—or of accompanying process—to be constant, successive equal quantities of means for each want would have equal significance. Since this is opposed to the assumption upon which this criterion is based, and for reasons that will appear as we proceed, we eliminate this possibility.[2] If, for this criterion, we assume an increasing

---

[1] This, we recall, is the assumption underlying all forms of marginal utility theory in so far as they deal with the satisfactions of single instances of wants (see pp. 437 ff.).
[2] Because, when we apply the subjective unit of means that we find it necessary to use for this criterion, we are left with no basis for choice among any means for any wants. All are indifferent among themselves. That can certainly not conform to reality. The use of the quantity of process per arbitrary objective unit as the ground of division has already, we think, been eliminated on the ground of absurd results.

rate of decline of intensity, etc., successive equal quantities of means for each want would have greater significance. This would lead to such a preposterous system of choices that we find it not worth following up.[3] These eliminations take the form of another assumption with regard to the third criterion—reduction of intensity. We shall assume, for this, not only that the intensity of want declines during satisfaction, but that it declines at a diminishing rate. Only on this basis can we develop a scheme whose resulting behavior would conform to a pattern different from those of the second and yet agree with the predictions of marginal utility theory that the criterion will confer less significance on each successive equal quantity consumed during a single satisfying.

While these criteria as stated sound specific, they are, as a matter of fact, very broad—almost all-inclusive. As already noted, the first two are alike—except in their assumptions—in that, at some stage in the process, either the initial state only, or that and any subsequent state, they depend on the state of the want—its actual or potential energy of response. Both representations are susceptible of being construed also to represent desire in so far as that is conceived to be a static magnitude; but only if it is conceded that desire, as reflected upon means, fails to discriminate between, and is not proportionate to, small differences in quantities of means.[4] On the other hand, the first and third criteria are alike in a different respect; for we have recognized that, under our own criterion, the quantity of means upon which usefulness is projected is determined in terms of the dynamic magnitude, reduction of intensity from its maximum to zero. Thus, in this respect, both criteria depend on a change in the state of the want during some phase. But only the third criterion measures significance in these same terms. Only there can the magnitude be conceived as simply as that—i.e., that the quantity of reduction of intensity during the phase determines the significance of the corresponding quantity of means consumed. For this reason the third criterion permits the inclusion, under the

[3] To assume that the criterion worked in this way would remind us of the procedure in the case of the child who, finding that he always enjoyed his first helping of ice cream more than his second and preferring "to keep the best till the last," decided always to take his second helping first. Here, too, though for the opposite reason, he would prefer the policy of taking his second helping first.
[4] If desire is conceived to disregard large differences in quantities so that it is as great for the first "little bit" as it is for the full measure, then it excludes our secondary hypothesis with regard to part measures. So conceived, desire would either act like a rate and, as such, become immeasurable, or it would act like the static magnitude, remaining intensity, that we are proceeding to develop.

same form, of almost any other feature of the process we can think of. It can be stated in the form of any accompanying experience, such as the quantity of pleasure or satisfaction derived during any phase. Moreover, the third criterion, unlike the first, can even include a kind of desire which is proportionate to the quantity of means if that desire is presumed to be declining through the process.[5] Thus, while we shall adhere to our terms for these criteria because those terms relate all three to a single analytical scheme and thus make clear the real distinctions between them, we shall nevertheless be free at all times to conceive the second and third alternatively in terms of any psychological entity we may prefer which, as a magnitude, would behave in the same way.[6]

Before proceeding it will be well for us to establish, quite definitely, the psychological requirements that underlie these three supposed criteria, together with the task each would set before our subjective measuring apparatus. We concede that all three are based on magnitudes that are conceivably capable of being judged by themselves. Thus they pass our first test, without question—a yes-or-no test which wrecked the criteria of several of the forms of marginal utility theory.[7] What we are doing now is to pass all three so far as the second test is concerned—psychological possibility. But now the reader is being asked to determine for himself their several passing marks on this test—

[5] That is, it can do so if desire takes the position in the scheme which we have assigned to reduction of intensity at a diminishing rate of decline of intensity. As then conceived it would not be a rate. It would be a feeling corresponding to a definite quantity of means, a feeling which steadily diminished in magnitude in terms of its only dimension, "intensity," just as we are supposing the several entities, pleasure, satisfaction, etc., to diminish in magnitude in terms of their several single dimensions.

[6] For the purpose of clarifying the necessary relation of these assumptions to any scheme of subjective valuation that might be proposed it is worth while to be explicit here.

a. If the criterion of choice is any dynamic magnitude (phase of a process), lessening significance of successive portions of means requires the assumption that the process slows down in terms of equal portions of means supplied (i.e., a diminishing rate of process, or of reduction of intensity).

b. If the criterion of choice is any static magnitude (stage of a process), lessening significance only requires the assumption that this magnitude contracts in process (i.e., a reduction of intensity without reference to rate).

For if, under (a), the process is at a constant rate, all portions of means will have the same significance; and if, under (b), the magnitude does not contract in process there will be no lessening of significance, and the only possible scheme will be of the order of our first hypothesis (discontinuity).

[7] Our analytical tool, the order of preference, reduces the comparison of all means, as we shall see, to terms of subjective units which are different for the three criteria. Thereafter, the ordinal arrangement in a series of choices does not involve or suppose a standard scale against which each quantity of means can be measured independently. It assumes that comparisons are limited to those of more or less or approximate equality among the quantities of means, so determined.

that is, to grade them according to probability, having only acknowledged that all are possible.

Let us consider first how these criteria would work among present wants. Our own psychological inquiry has resulted in the scheme of a potential order of priority among present wants. This was worked out in the fourth chapter. Here it is necessary to make its connotations more clear and explicit in certain respects. We do not suppose that all wants ever exist at their normal maxima at any one moment; but we do suppose that it is common, among men, for several or many wants to coexist at some level of latent intensity sufficient to overcome inertia and thus to compete among themselves for prepotence. Among present wants the order of priority therefore represents a sort of limit or norm towards which there is a general tendency. The more

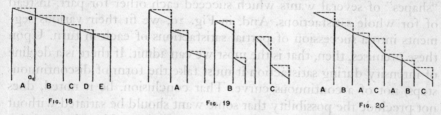

Fig. 18   Fig. 19   Fig. 20

nearly the actual situation approaches this norm, the more nearly will the following analysis represent the results of this competition. The several processes of satisfying different wants, if of different constellations and if all require integrated action, cannot be pursued simultaneously but only successively. Thus only one want can hold the field at a time and, during a period in which no prior wants occur or recur, each subordinate want can only begin to be satisfied when any prior one that has been prepotent has ceased to be satisfied. We may illustrate these successive processes of wants A, B, etc., in Fig. 18. Now, if one concedes that there is a tendency towards the coexistence of many present wants and that, nevertheless, prior wants are often satiated before any beginning is made toward satisfying subordinate wants, there is only one possible "shape" for the curve of Want A. We would then have to assume that the intensity of A, immediately before satiation is represented by the altitude aa_1, and that, at the point of satiety, it drops from that level to a_1, or zero. If that were not true, then, as soon as the decline in intensity of A brought its remaining intensity below the maximum of B (also aa_1), the process of satisfying A would be interrupted by the equally pressing tendency toward satisfying B. How-

ever, even if one does not admit that prior wants are ever satiated before lesser wants obtain any satisfaction at all—that is, if one assumes
a decline of intensity during the process of satisfaction—a second
difficulty remains. For, at the point aa^1 the process of A, if incompleted,
would not give place to that of B. Instead, both wants being of equal
intensity, the apparatus would be on a dead center. Neither would be
prepotent. Therefore, on the supposition of the coexistence of present
wants, the explanation of any succession of processes whatever,
whether or not prior wants are satiated, requires the assumption that
the "shape" of each curve includes discontinuous drops in intensity,
each sufficient to permit the intrusion of at least a considerable segment of the successor want. After that segment the first want might
resume prepotence. Thus, in Fig. 19, the solid lines show the possible
"shapes" of several wants which succeed each other for part, instead
of for whole satisfactions. And, in Fig. 20, we fit their various segments into a succession of partial satisfactions of each in turn. Upon
these premises, then, that is the most we can admit. If there is a decline
of intensity during satisfaction it must take the form of discontinuous
steps, not of a continuous curve. That conclusion, be it noted, does
not preclude the possibility that some want should be satiated without
the satiation of all. For instance, at the end of the fifth phase of the
succession shown in Fig. 20, A has been satiated, yet B and C have
only been partially satisfied, and others may not yet have been satisfied
at all.

    This graphic representation seems to support our previous conclu-
sion. Present wants are intermittent in time in respect of competing
for prepotence; but, to the extent that they coexist, their changes in
intensity during the process of satisfaction are discontinuous. They
must be. Otherwise only the first want could be satisfied and that to
the point only where its remaining intensity became equal to the initial
intensity of the next want. At that point there could be no choice, or
there would result merely a rapid interchange of prepotence. If several wants are coexistent, the assumption of discontinuous changes of
intensity is necessary to explain satiation, if that ever occurs. And it is
equally necessary to explain the intervention of a partial or complete
satisfaction of a subordinate want between two partial satisfactions of
a prior want, if that ever occurs. Therefore, on the supposition that
present wants usually coexist, there can be no want whose process
of satisfaction has any of the "shapes" shown in Fig. 21. Such con-

tinuous declines are impossible except for parts of the curve—that is, except through a phase in which the want is prepotent. Even then, such a phase may just as well be shown as a horizontal line, such as the broken lines in Figs. 18, 19 and 20, since we are then deprived of any means of knowing what "shape" it has.[8] The result is that, on our own assumptions, the curves indicating the "shape" of the changes in intensity of a want with respect to the process of satisfying must be in the form of a rectangle for each want (like Fig. 6) or in that of a succession of steps, each representing a segment of the want. And these two "shapes" indicate, respectively, that the intensity is approximately maintained throughout the whole process, or that it is maintained through each part of the process, though each part is at a lower level than the last.

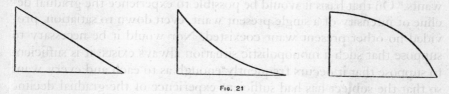

Fig. 21

As a matter of fact the latter "shape" may be consistent with our physiological interpretation; for, in that, we found that we must admit certain occasions when wants are not satiated. The occasions when this might be related to the "shape" of the satisfaction were "incidental failure" and insufficiency of requisite external conditions. In such cases only a segment of the want is satisfied, though for each the extent of the discontinuous drop in intensity at the end of the partial satisfaction seems to vary among different types of wants. Thus even our own hypothesis admits both these "shapes" and only asserts that the curves representing satisfactions are discontinuous rather than continuous. Furthermore, in connection with future wants we have already found evidence of what we may call "deliberate," as opposed to this "spontaneous," segmentation in the satisfaction of wants. Therefore, we will concede both forms in our further analysis, recognizing that our physiological scheme admits both and that both admit of satiation of some, if not all, wants that are satisfied at all. But, with regard to the second form, we will have to recognize that, so far as our observation

[8] Moreover, if the difference in the maximum intensity between one want and the next is very slight, then the prepotent want must show a considerable phase in which intensity remains practically horizontal in order that any effective segment of it should be satisfied before "interference" by the next in order would take place.

of spontaneous segmentation goes, only the first segment ever participates in the competition between wants—later ones would be merely
assumed—and that we do not know to what level intensity declines at
the end of such segment.

Under the first postulate we have now excluded, so far as present
wants are concerned, the continuous decline of intensity during satisfaction that constitutes the assumption necessary for our second
criterion, remaining intensity. As a result we have to see what new
or different postulate is required in order to admit this assumption.
All that we need to do, here, is to adopt as the norm or limit the opposite pole from that of the previous case. That is, we now suppose
a general tendency toward the existence of one present want only at
any one time—toward the absence of competition between present
wants.[9] On that basis it would be possible to experience the gradual decline of intensity of a single present want, even down to satiation, provided no other present want coexisted. Nor would it be necessary to
suppose that such a monopolistic situation always exists; it is sufficient
to suppose that it occurs frequently enough as to each and every want
so that the subject has had sufficient experience of the gradual decline
of intensity to zero in each case. On this postulate curves such as were
shown in Fig. 21 would represent what could at least be actually experienced. The third criterion—reduction of intensity, etc.—also
requires this new postulate, since, otherwise, it would be impossible
to have the experience of a diminishing rate of decline of intensity
or of quantity of pleasure after that rate had fallen below the highest
rate of the next competing want. We shall see presently what else the
third criterion requires.

Since we admit that these postulates represent no more than tendencies toward one or the other of the two poles and that even our
own does not assume that the potential order of priority is ever attained
in fact—that is, that there is ever a moment when all wants coexist at
their normal maxima—it is quite evident that the concept of an order
of preference among the satisfactions of present wants is an unreal concept. Under the second postulate the order in which satisfactions would
take place would tend to be the order in which they happened to occur

[9] It will be noted that these two postulates are not really mutually exclusive. Under
both there would be two poles—one, coexistence and competition, the other, single
existence and monopoly. The postulates differ only in that they suppose a greater
tendency toward one or the other pole and assume that the records of experience are
based primarily on one or the other condition.

or recur at levels of latent intensity sufficient to overcome inertia. Even under the first postulate—coexistence and competition—this purely temporal order would only be altered to the extent that the latent intensity of one want, in the course of its rise toward its maximum, happened to exceed at some point the latent or effective intensity of some other. It would all be a hit or miss matter without order or regularity. Thus we are compelled, in order to establish any positive basis for an order of preference at all, to transfer our attention to the field of future wants. Only in that field can we find evidence of any systematic and regular comparison between wants—of any choices not merely dictated by the impulses of the moment and, therefore, of anything like an order of preference which persists with a considerable degree of uniformity. Furthermore, as the more elaborate analysis of the program for future provision in Chapter 10 will disclose, examination of this field suffices for another reason.[10] Among men past the hand-to-mouth stage of existence, practically all means other than acts of self must always be provided in advance if they are to be available at all.[11] A realistic order of preference among means can then only be established in the field where alone the preferences are exhibited. The only difficulty we face in introducing the field of future wants at this stage of the argument is that we have not yet worked out the basis for discrimination between instances of a single want according to their degree of futurity. For that reason the reader will have to permit us to establish the temporary convention that, in what immediately follows, we are considering only choices between instances of future wants without regard to their degree of futurity—that is, as if we compared only a single instance of each want and treated all of them as being on a par so far as degree of futurity is concerned.[12]

So far as future wants are concerned we have recognized that the whole record of experience of all wants—and perhaps at all stages or during all phases of their satisfaction—may be present and in conflict in consciousness, and in the mnemonic-volitional apparatus, at one and the same time. It is true that we might well suppose that the only

[10] That is, it suffices for the examination of a direct economy to which we are now confining ourselves.
[11] Durant (*The Story of Civilization*, I, 5) makes this one of the two essentials of civilization. He says, "The civilized may be defined as literate providers."
[12] What we are actually doing, stated in terms of our analysis in Chapter 10, is to limit our consideration here to the program considered each producing day for the following consuming day (night). In this program, according to the convention, interval effort does not enter, or is not considered.

records there available would have arisen from actual experiences or from experiments with the memories of actual experiences (insight). That is, it is hard to believe that this system has raw materials upon which to work that are not derived from experience. But that requirement seems to have been already satisfied. Our two postulates, above, would make it possible that all three of our criteria had been matters of experience of the satisfaction of present wants. What then are the further requirements as to these records of experience—these conscious memories—in order that they may be regarded as measurable and measured or, better, as judged and compared magnitudes which are identifiable and sufficiently regular in size to permit systematic comparisons of some degree of permanence?

2. DEFINITION OF THE SCOPE OF THE CORRESPONDENCES AND THEIR ESTIMATION

The several correspondences must ultimately be based on the magnitudes of the respective criteria (experiences), on the one hand, and on those of corresponding quantities of means, on the other. Since the latter constitutes the relate, and since the relate defines the scope of the correspondence, the first requirement is that the whole quantity of means, or any part quantity that is to serve as the basis for a subordinate correspondence, must have boundaries that are fixed and easily recognizable. These boundaries may be fixed directly; but they may also be arrived at indirectly. Our own criterion readily meets this requirement. Maximum intensity before the beginning of the process and satiety at its end correspond to the presence of a full measure of means, before taking, and to the absence of such means, after taking.[13] These boundaries, the beginning and the end, are fixed, regular and easily recognizable. Intensity can be felt at the beginning; it has disappeared at the end. The boundaries of part measures of means are not so simple, especially when the attribute yielding usefulness exists in fixed quantity. However, we have agreed that this problem is one we are not going to attempt to solve as yet, if at all. Part measures, incomplete satisfactions, and segments of wants are magnitudes introduced into this study up to this point by way of admission of their existence under certain limiting circumstances. It remains possible that we shall find them beyond the reach of our present method.

[13] In the case of durable means we shall see, in Chapter 10, how this seems to be converted into terms of the disappearance of installments.

For the second criterion, remaining intensity, including the assumption of continuous decline, the matter of boundaries is less certain. Aside from the general feeling that intensity was declining, what points in the process could be selected that would form definite bases for comparisons of intensity? Continuous decline presupposes an infinite number of different levels in each case. The boundaries of the several phases which would serve as the determining point of a not too numerous series of stages might be fixed by the completion of the consumption of equal fractions of a full measure or even by that of whole objective units of the means. Such a basis would serve the purpose; and with this criterion it makes no difference that the number of subdivisions of means—portions or units—is entirely arbitrary or that they may be incomparable as between two different wants. For the only comparison required is between equal, greater, or less remaining intensities at different points in the process; and, these intensities would remain the same no matter into how many portions or units the intervening means consumed were divided. However, whether it were arrived at indirectly by comparing remaining intensities at the end of the consumption of arbitrary portions or units of means, or, on the other hand, it were arrived at directly, we shall find another natural definition of scope or boundary which is much simpler. It requires far fewer memories. And, the greater the number of subdivisions of means supposed, the more nearly would stages fixed in terms of means yield the same pattern of behavior as would stages fixed in these other terms.

For the third criterion—reduction of intensity, etc.—an insuperable objection is encountered if we try to divide the process of satisfaction into equal portions in order to compare the significance that would be conferred through the several phases. The division can be made in terms of equal quantities of means so long as it is used only for the comparison of different phases of a single want. But, as between different wants, that does not serve at all. As we have already noted several times, greater significance might then be ascribed to the fact that the unit or portion chosen was held to be larger for one than for the other. And, since different means are incommensurable, there exists no basis for finding equal quantities of each. Thus, here, direct fixation of boundaries in terms of means gives us no basis at all, and we will have to find some other definition for the scope of the correspondence.[14]

---

[14] We have seen how arbitrary would be "curves of significance" of means based on the significance per objective unit. The heights of the several curves for different means would depend primarily on the size of the objective unit of each. Comparisons of sig-

We turn, then, to the question of the second requirement in the hope that it may turn out to offer a way of also satisfying the first. Within the scope or boundaries of a correspondence set directly or indirectly in terms of the relates it is equally necessary, in order to treat the correspondence as one between determinate magnitudes, that one should be able to measure or, at least, to judge the relative size of the correlates. What different requirements do our three criteria set for us in this respect? What task does each place upon the subjective measuring apparatus? We have eliminated for all our criteria the requirement that measurement should be made in terms of precise units. That is too much to ask. There remains only the possibility of comparisons of each in terms of more or less or of approximate equality. The matter of such judgments applied to our own criterion has already been fully set forth. We simply assume that the order of priority among future wants (memories) corresponds to that among present wants, being derived from it. Thus all future wants can be compared, for they reflect the same relative differences that exist between the normal maxima of the present wants, though they exist at much lower levels of intensity. If so, the judgment of more or less would consist only in a rehearsal of previous experiences.

When we consider the second criterion the question becomes a more difficult one. We have already noted that, on the assumption of continuously declining intensity, every experience of satisfaction would consist of a near infinite number of intensities each less than the last. It seems impossible that all should be remembered. Aside from the general impression of decline that such an experience would leave, what, we may ask, would be the strategic specific intensities that might be remembered? If the strategic intensities were those felt at the end of each equal portion or objective unit of means and these subdivisions were small, the pattern of behavior would tend toward the same result as it would if the strategic intensities were, in the case of each want, confined to those at which its remaining intensity had declined to the level of the initial intensity of the next want in order, and so on down the order of priority.[15] Up to such a point the remaining intensity of

nificance based on fractions of a full measure would be equally indeterminate. For, if the chooser found that he preferred the first tenth of one means to the first tenth of another, nothing would prevent him from taking an eighth or a sixth of the second, instead.

[15] This, we will recall, is the basis of the order of preference that we developed, in Appendix IV, Section B, from our second construction of Menger's scheme.

each prior want would be felt as greater; at that point the intensity of both the prior and the next want in order would be felt as equal. This assumes a considerably more complex capacity for comparisons and a considerably larger furniture of memories than does our own criterion. Nevertheless, it assumes no more than is inevitable upon the assumption of declining intensity of want, if any remaining intensity— any other than the initial intensity—has an influence on behavior.[16] It is not precluded by the fact that, with present wants, such stages would put the apparatus on dead center. For here we are dealing with future wants. The next phases of satisfaction for both of two, or all of more, different wants would be included in a program of provision whenever, at such a stage, the remaining (or initial) intensities of these two or more wants were judged to be approximately equal. Furthermore, this furnishes us with a simpler system of boundaries for the correspondences than does the subdivision of means. The boundaries of the first correspondence are then fixed at the two stages delimiting the phase during which the initial intensity of the first want in order is declining to a remaining intensity equal to the initial intensity of the next want. During that phase a certain quantity of means is consumed (a part measure). That quantity can be measured objectively. It then enters indirectly as the relate of the correspondence. That quantity then has more significance, upon the second criterion, than does any other quantity of any means whatever. We do not need to know what quantity of significance it has. All we need to know is what we do know—that it has *more* significance. Similarly for the second pair of correspondences, the boundaries of which are the stages delimiting the second phase. That phase begins for the first want when its remaining intensity is equal to the initial intensity of the second, and, for the second, at its initial intensity. The two phases, being indifferent, proceed together to their common terminus, the stage at which the remaining intensity of both is judged equal to the initial intensity of the third want in order. Similarly the quantities of means (subjective units)

[16] We are not going to argue the psychological probabilities in this connection. The assumption is the least that we can make, if we are to admit the second criterion at all; and we wish to admit that criterion, for it is one of the two possible types of criterion on the assumption of declining intensity during satisfaction. True, it is difficult to see how the experiences of these several strategic intensities could have been acquired; and it is difficult to see how, in consciousness, the phases up to these several stages, in the case of each want, could have been so marked off. However, since we can, as yet, have no final psychological proof of any of our criteria and since we are going to submit this one, in the end, to the test of reality, we might as well adopt this as the most plausible form, or the least improbable form, of the second criterion.

required for each want during that phase can then be measured objectively, and become, respectively, the relates for these two correspondences. The significance of both, on this criterion, is the same. Again we do not know nor need to know precisely what it is. We only know it is the same for both and greater than that of any other quantity of means. Thus, down the whole order of priority of wants a successively increasing number of subjective units, definable as objective quantities, are all found, in turn, to have the same significance. And this process can be carried as far as capacity reaches.

It is necessary to recognize, of course, that the successive quantities of each means corresponding to the phases so delimited would all be of different size. Thus the scope of the several correspondences under this criterion would turn out to be an irregular series something like the following, for instance: 1.6 units of means for A, highest significance; 2.4 units of means for A and 1.8 units of means for B, of equal and next highest significance; 2.1 units of means for A, 1.6 units of means for B, and 5 units of means for C, of equal and third highest significance. This because the quantities of each means necessary to produce reductions of intensity down to the next strategic level would determine the scope of the several phases, and naturally these would vary as between successive pairs of wants. Again this imposes a considerable, though perhaps not impossible, strain on the memory.

In the second place, it now becomes evident that this second criterion of significance is a peculiar one. Like the others it is to be judged only in terms of more or less or approximate equality and thus is only a relative magnitude serving for comparisons. But, unlike the others, this one bears upon the process to which we are relating it only in these same terms. Even conceptually and even were it measurable, the remaining intensity, being a static magnitude, could not be used to measure the significance of the several portions of means; while conceptually, at least, that is altogether possible in the case of the two other criteria. The simple mathematical reason for this difference is that, since this criterion is a static magnitude, the sum of remaining intensities at all stages would be greater the greater the number of stages at which it is determined—or, to put it in its extreme form, the sum of the significance of the means when divided into parts would, on this basis, be greater than that of the whole.[17] Of course, this peculiarity

[17] To add up the several static magnitudes under this scheme in order to relate them to the whole process would be like adding up the successive readings of the thermometer during a drop in temperature in order to relate them to that process.

pertains to all static magnitudes when they are connected with processes —that is, with dynamic magnitudes. It is inherent in the fact that they are not measures of process but of states or of potentials.[18]

Under the third criterion we are supposing that the static magnitude, intensity of want, has no direct influence. The criterion for significance is now the dynamic magnitude, quantity of reduction of intensity or of experience of pleasure, satisfaction, etc., that has been accomplished during a phase in the process. Obviously it is impossible to give any quantitative character to such a determining factor until *after* it has been experienced. One could not measure the reduction of intensity accomplished by, or the pleasure derived from, the consumption of a quantity of means until the point is reached at which its consumption is completed. Since any appreciable consumption requires time, the whole experience would therefore have to have become a memory before it could become a judgeable magnitude. This imposes

[18] This, being the root of an illusion that seems to have pervaded much of marginal utility theory, is worthy of further examination. The static magnitude and the rate are the only two magnitudes that can remain comparatively unchanged through a process— that is, only these could behave as marginal significance is supposed to behave without regard to whether the quantities of means were a little larger or a little smaller. The rate is a measure of the process itself, which may gradually decline during the process. But, I think, we have already disposed of that as a possible criterion for significance. There remains to be disposed of the illusion with regard to the first. The static magnitude is not a measure of the process, though it, too, may gradually decline during the process. The only relation of such a magnitude to a process is that changes in it may be the cause or the result of a process, and that when it arrives at certain critical points the process may begin or may cease. Thus so long as the depth of water behind a dam is above a certain minimum, water will flow over the dam; at the minimum, it will cease to flow. So long as the steam pressure in a boiler is above a certain minimum, steam will blow off through the safety valve; at the minimum it will cease to blow off. If the successive measures of altitude along a road are each less than the last, your car may coast. When they become constant, the motion soon ceases. In the first two cases, the greater the excess over the minimum, the greater, other things being equal, will be the process; in the last case absolute altitude has no bearing whatever. But, in all three cases, the static magnitude has no definite relation to any quantity of process. In the first case, the flow depends chiefly on the length of the dam; in the second the blow-off depends chiefly on the size of the boiler; and in the third case the amount of motion depends chiefly on the distance between the successive altitudes. The reason that we cannot cite the theory of dimensions in support of any general rule for such relations is probably due to the fact that the physicist never conceives the magnitudes relating to the processes he studies in these naïve terms.

So, if we choose as our criterion a static magnitude, we choose one that operates only to determine choices during phases of the process that lie between critical points of the magnitude. We cannot derive a quantitative measure of the significance of means by this method; even conceptually that is impossible; but we can derive an order of preference; and that is our ultimate objective. Significance, here, is conceived in terms of alternatives and not at all in terms of absolute magnitudes or even absolute excesses over minima. There is, then, no pertinent magnitude to project upon means as a measure of its significance.

an almost impossible task on the apparatus if the direct criterion is the reduction of intensity itself. For that would require an ability to compare intensities of want at the two stages of a process of satisfaction that delimited the phase (stages which are separated by an interval of time), to judge the quantity of difference between these two intensities with sufficient accuracy to be able to compare the sizes of two such differences (reductions), and also to retain a memory of this magnitude in one experience in order to compare it with that in another experience which cannot occur simultaneously. However, the use of the type of criterion which seems to have been assumed in the development of the Edgeworth-Pareto scheme rescues us from this apparently insuperable difficulty. We worked out this modification in Appendix IV, Section E. It resolves itself into substituting a quantity of experience—a dynamic magnitude—in the place of a difference between two static magnitudes. When, in this way, we convert the criterion into terms of quantity of pleasure, satisfaction, etc., experienced during such phase, the task of judging and comparing its magnitudes seems to be not wholly impossible. At least we will assume for the sake of argument that it can be done.[19] We will even go so far as to assume that the several quantities of pleasure, etc., are proportionate to the corresponding quantities of reduction of intensity, even if the subject cannot know the fact. This for the sake of preserving the generality of the third criterion.

Having granted this much, let us see what we can find in the way of reasonable boundaries for the correspondences upon which such a criterion would be based. How delimit the phases? The stages used in the case of the second criterion are no longer available; for intensity of want is no longer a factor. The stages of completion of consumption of the several portions or units of means will not serve, as we noted

---

[19] This assumption is, nevertheless, a pretty hazardous one. We will recall that, for this criterion, we are using only the concave curve of a want—that is, a steadily diminishing rate of decline of intensity and so, presumably, of the quantity of any accompanying experience. Thus, if the phases were delimited by units of means, one would need to be able to compare not only the effect of one slice of bread with that of one mouthful of meat but the effect of each successive slice of bread with that of each other and with that of each successive mouthful of meat, each of which would always have a less effect from that of its predecessor in the ordinal arrangement. Hypotheses which rest on the presupposition that such subjective comparisons can be made, and then remembered, as to small units or small individual parts of whole experiences seem to border on the preposterous. At least, we can only consider this to be psychologically possible if comparison is confined to units of considerable size with considerable differences of effect. That is, the differences must be greater than the *minimum sensibile*.

above. At least they will not serve as between means for different wants. Yet the boundaries of the phase are here of the essence of the matter; for, here, the criterion itself being something that takes place between the beginning and the ending of the phase, as it was not before, these boundaries limit both relate and correlate. After many experiments the only boundaries I have found that produce a usable scheme are those which delimit a subjective unit, as previously described at the end of Section E, Appendix IV, and as there modified from the notion of indifference as worked out by Pareto and Edgeworth. The subjective unit is the smallest quantity of pleasure—or reduction of intensity—which can be compared to another quantity of pleasure and found to be equal to it within a reasonable margin of error. At the beginning of the process of satisfying of every want we suppose that there must be some quantity of consumption of means for each that yields such a uniform subjective unit of pleasure. If so, it will be possible to determine the number of objective units of each means that correspond initially to these several equal subjective units. Thus the boundaries of our several correspondences are fixed. What we have then done, in reality, is to reverse our correspondences. That is, we no longer attempt to find the different quantities of reduction of intensity or of pleasure (correlate) that correspond to the several equal quantities of means (relate). Instead, we find the different quantities of means (correlate) that correspond to equal quantities of reduction of intensity, etc. (relate).

This suffices for a start, and it is the only attack on the problem that I have found workable. But, used once for the start, we discard it. Or, rather, having found what minimum objective quantities of all means are indifferent when all wants are completely unsatisfied, we then reverse our correspondences back to their original form. We adopt these initially equivalent objective quantities of means to establish the boundaries of all subsequent correspondences—to limit the phases through which all subsequent experiences of pleasure, etc., are experienced. Thereafter, it is the so-determined objective quantities whose comparative significance is judged. True, it would be possible to continue the initial process—to find what were the next quantities of each means that were subjectively equivalent and so on. While such a method would be possible, its great complexity is against it and its anomalous results seem too far from reality. As stated in Appendix

IV we therefore eliminate it from the possibilities.[20] The result is that, after depending on the capacity to determine approximately equal quantities of pleasure at the start, we come to depend on the capacity to distinguish between more and less pleasure thereafter. From which it follows that, after the initially indifferent partial satisfactions have all been accomplished, there will always be a preference. The objective quantity of one means, so determined, will be found to yield more pleasure, etc., than will the independently determined objective quantity of some other, and so on continuously as far as capacity reaches.

On this basis the objective quantities of each means composing a subjective unit, once determined, would remain the same throughout. In contrast to the second criterion, this would impose a much lighter burden on the memory. On the other hand, when it came to remembering even the relative significance of all subsequent similar quantities of all means, the burden would be heavier. For, since there is no reason to suppose that the diminishing rate of decline of intensity would be the same for all wants, it would be necessary to compare and remember the significance—or the comparative significance—of each subsequent similar quantity of every means and thus to arrange them in an order of preference far more complex than that of the second criterion. The demonstration of that fact can best await the diagrammatic working out of the resulting virtual order of preference in the next section. This criterion, like the second, could be developed solely on the basis of more or less or equality. But, unlike the second, significance here would be reflected by a definite dynamic magnitude so that, conceptually at least, it would be an absolute quantity and could be used to establish a precise correspondence—and potentially a rate—between the relate and the correlate.

D. THE THREE VIRTUAL ORDERS OF PREFERENCE

1. AMONG MEANS SERVING SINGLE WANTS

When we first introduced the term "order of preference" in Chapter 7, we did so in order to establish the conceptual basis for a system of choices among specific quantities of various means—a basis which would permit us to use, alternatively, several different possible criteria for choice or preference and therefore to dissociate the choice among

---

[20] It will be recalled that such a scheme leads to the satisfying of wants in inverse order to their position in the order of priority (see Appendix IV, Section E, note 31).

means from the order of priority among wants or even, if necessary, to make the former entirely independent of the latter. Such a concept belongs in the categories of reality—that is, the actual order of preference must be an observable phenomenon. It follows that the several different possible criteria cannot all produce the actual order of preference. For this reason our method has been to develop for each of these criteria its *virtual* order of preference in order, when all are corrected for the common interfering factor which will be introduced later, to determine which virtual scheme conforms to the actual pattern and thereby which criterion is the actual one.[1]

This, as noted before, is the method of the exact sciences. In the exact sciences the term "virtual" means something different from the term "real." In order to analyze the part played by each factor in a complex, its virtual behavior must first be determined—that is, what it would do if left to itself—if it operated *in vacuo*. If this is done correctly for each, then, by combining the virtual behavior of all factors and taking account of the interaction of each on the other, the result will accord approximately with reality. For instance, Newton's first law reads, "Every body continues in its state of rest or of uniform motion in a straight line [or now, along a curvature of space] except as it is compelled by forces to change that state." The first part of this law states the innate tendency of a body—its virtual behavior. Actually a body never behaves in this manner; for the "exception" is the universal rule. That points to the basic difficulty in the use of this method—the discovery and isolation of those factors that are autonomous. Newton successfully uncovered one in this law. However, many factors are not autonomous. If the virtual behavior of any factor, when examined, is not determinate—that is, if when left to itself it may behave in any number of different ways—it is not autonomous and is therefore not one of the decisive factors in determining real behavior. Or, on the other hand, that may be proof that it has been improperly or incompletely analyzed (incompletely, in the sense that it must be a com-

[1] As previously noted, the virtual method is similar to that one, common in economic literature, usually called "*ceteris paribus*." Marshall stated that it was his method and described it well. He said, in the Preface to the 5th edition of the *Principles*, "This scientific method is a great deal older than science; it is the method by which, consciously or unconsciously, sensible men have dealt from time immemorial with every difficult problem of ordinary life."

We may remind the reader of our remarks in Chapter 5 (pp. 264-266) with respect to this virtual method, at a point where we were using it in reverse. Here, as then stated, we begin to use it directly.

pound or mixture of factors as yet unanalyzed). Many of the formulations of marginal utility theory which we have examined may be made determinate if an extraneous factor is introduced. This second factor may appear under the guise of what Wicksteed calls the "terms of trade"; or it may appear proximately as the limitation of quantities of particular means. But in either case, these rest, respectively, on some ultimate factor which determines the terms of trade or the various limitations of quantities of means. Now, if subjective valuation is one of the autonomous and decisive factors in human preferences it must be found to be determinate when examined on the virtual basis.[2] In the following, therefore, we shall consistently exclude all such extraneous considerations in order to confine ourselves to autonomous factors capable of development into determinate virtual schemes. The one exception we are making, in Part I, by way of departure from this strict limitation of our examination to wants and the process and means of satisfying them, as if this were an independent and self-contained system, is in respect of the vague and as yet unanalyzed notion of the limited capacity to provide aggregate means. This limit appears to be imposed from outside such a system, and therefore the analysis of its nature and virtual effects has naturally been deferred. But it has been allowed to creep in merely in order to avoid too great a departure from reality. We have not used it in any respect as an integral part of our analysis. And it will appear, as we proceed, that it has no influence on our virtual orders of preference other than to prevent them from extending to the complete satisfaction of all wants.

In setting up the schemes of our three virtual orders of preference we are, at the start and in order to simplify the presentation, going to limit ourselves by assuming that each means is only suitable to the satisfaction of a single want. This condition seems to exist to a considerable extent. It therefore requires examination for itself. Moreover, by first establishing such schemes we can more easily, thereafter, see what modifications are required to adapt them to conditions in which one compound means serves toward the satisfying of the several wants, major and minor, of a constellation.

Under this simplification it is clear that, as already noted,[3] our first criterion—usefulness conferred on full measures of means by the nor-

---

[2] It will be recalled that it was on this ground that we rejected the indifference curve system of Pareto, Edgeworth, and Hicks, in the form in which they have presented it, as a scheme of pure subjective valuation.

[3] See pp. 416–418.

mal maximum intensities of the wants via the reduction of such intensities from the maxima to zero—would produce a virtual order of preference precisely corresponding to the order of priority and extending along that order as far as capacity reached. That is, a full measure of means for the prior want would be preferred to all others; a full measure for the next want in order would be preferred over all remaining; and so on. All wants within the reach of capacity would be completely satisfied, with the possible exception noted below; and no wants beyond the reach of capacity would be satisfied at all, except incidentally as members of constellations. The exception is this. To the extent that "spontaneous" or "deliberate" part measures were considered—recalled or planned for—they might take positions in the order of preference subordinate to the normal positions of the corresponding wants in the order of priority. That would depend on whether a complete satisfaction of a subordinate want is actually preferred to a necessarily incomplete satisfaction of a prior want. As to this we have grave doubt, however automatically it would seem to follow from our analytical schemes. At any rate, we do not know and must therefore be vague.

The order of preference that would result from the second criterion —the static magnitude, remaining intensity of want, at the several stages of its decline—has also been outlined. It, too, would produce an order of preference influenced by the order of priority. But, since the quantity of means preferred for each prior want would only be that which sufficed to bring its intensity down to the level of the next want in order, the order of priority would only fix the stage at which the satisfying of each want in turn would begin to be included in the program. Between each pair of stages all wants included at all would be on a parity with each other. Therefore, whenever the limit of capacity was reached, all wants which had been satisfied at all would have been reduced to the same level of remaining intensity and all wants whose initial intensity was below that level would not have been satisfied at all. The primary determinant of each successive quantity of means for each want would be the extent of the difference between the intensity at the beginning and the end of each phase—that is, between each successive pair of strategic intensities, or stages of remaining intensity. This series would be irregular in size. The secondary determinant would be the rate of decline of intensity of the want. If that were a diminishing rate (that is, if each successive equal quantity of means

reduced the intensity by less than its predecessor), then, as compared
to the quantities set by the primary determinant alone, the quantities
required for each phase would be successively larger; if it were an increasing rate, successively smaller; and if a constant rate, the same.
But, since this secondary determinant would only go to modify an
irregular series, and since we are supposing the size of the successive
quantities required of each means to be learned directly by observation, we can ignore the question of changing rates of decline. The
same is true of different rates of decline among the several wants. The
different effects would be lost to notice among such irregular series
and could only be determined by a complex calculation that would
be redundant.

Though we assume that the magnitudes of the several wants are
the same for the third criterion as for the others—that is, that there
exists an order of priority arranged according to the quantity of total
reduction of intensity or total pleasure to be derived from a complete
satisfaction of each—the order of priority, as such, would have, on this
criterion, no direct influence on the order of preference. Instead, the
initial choice would include subjective units of means for each and
every want, made up of quantities which yielded in each case the same
reduction of intensity, or the same pleasure, as in every other. We have
assumed, for this criterion, that the rate of decline of intensity or of
quantity of pleasure per subsequent quantity, objectively the same
as the first, is a diminishing one. Even then, if the diminishing rates
were the same for all, there would be no choice among the several
quantities for the second phase of satisfaction of all wants. But, as a
matter of fact, uniform diminishing rates in terms of such subjective
units would be impossible. The very predicate that the initial quantities of reduction of intensity or of pleasure are equal, while the total
reduction of intensity or pleasure to be accomplished differ according
to the magnitude of the want—order of priority—makes it necessarily
true that the diminishing rate shall diminish more rapidly the "smaller"
the want. Fig. 22, which shows derived "curves of significance" of the
subjective units of means, similar to those we have used before, gives
us the basis for analyzing this effect. The effect of the initial indifferent set of subjective units of means for all the wants A to J, is shown
by the rectangle between the pair of broken lines rising from O and J,
etc. The average rate of effect for each member of the set is shown
by the altitude halfway between O and J, etc. Since this initial effect

is the same for all wants, all the lines representing the diminishing rate of effect for the several wants A to J must intersect at the peak of this first altitude, the base being common to all. After the initial choice—one subjective unit for every want—had been made, a preference would appear. The line representing the diminishing rate of effect for Want A—the "greatest" want—intersects the altitude of the second subjective unit, J to I, at the highest level. Following this out, the order of preference thereafter would be 2^DB, 2^DC, 2^DD, 2DE, 3DA, 2^DF,

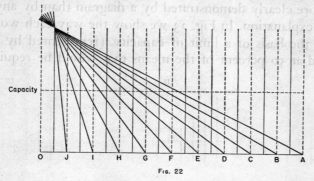

Fig. 22

3^DB, 3^DC, 2^DG, etc.[4] If capacity were exhausted at the level shown, the following percentage of the number of subjective units required for the complete satisfaction of the several wants would have been chosen:

A	B	C	D	E	F	G	H	I	J
50%	56%	50%	57%	50%	60%	50%	66⅔%	50%	100%

But the percentage of complete satisfaction, or the percentage of total pleasure to be derived from the complete satisfaction of each want, would be roughly as follows:

A	B	C	D	E	F	G	H	I	J
70%	80%	74%	81%	74%	84%	75%	88%	75%	100%

It is clear from this demonstration that the smaller the subjective unit in proportion to the magnitude of the "least" want, the more

[4] The effect of converting any of these lines into concave curves would be to defer preferences for them, while convex curves would signify earlier preferences—both as compared with straight lines. And the dividing line of the shift would be the point of tangency of the curve with a straight line curve parallel to this one. But, since a concave curve would subtend a smaller, and a convex curve a greater, aggregate of altitudes, they would represent, correspondingly, smaller and greater wants than are represented by straight line curves. Thus, our order of wants along the base would be destroyed. Convex wants would strike the base earlier than their position on account of size, and concave wants later.

nearly would the degree of satisfaction of every want continually be the same as that of every other.[5] But this uniformity would not result, as it did under the second criterion, in reduction of all to the same level of intensity at each successive stage. Instead, it would result in a reduction of all by the same proportion of their total intensity—or a yielding of the same percentage of the total pleasure to be derived in each case —through each phase.

Perhaps the difference between the operations of these three criteria can be more clearly demonstrated by a diagram than by any amount of verbal explanation. In Fig. 23 we show the way each would work out upon the basis of a limit of capacity (represented by a broken line) fixed at 50 percent of the means that would be required com-

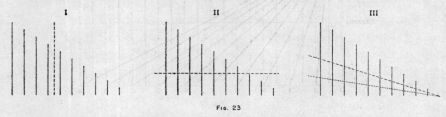

Fig. 23

pletely to satisfy all wants. In each figure, I, II, and III represent the first, second, and third hypotheses. The series of wants is shown by the series of vertical lines descending along the order of priority. Their comparison disregards the question as to whether the "size" of the want is measured by its maximum initial intensity or by the aggregate pleasure to be derived from its satiation. In each figure the vertical lines can also be read to mean the quantity of means required for a complete satisfaction of the want. In the first two figures the proportion of total means required, which is within capacity, is treated as if it were the same as the proportion of total intensity of wants satisfied by that capacity. In the third figure that cannot be done; for, as we have just seen, by reason of the declining rate of accrual of pleasure, while only 50 percent of total means required is available, that will produce 75 per-

[5] This is seen more clearly if one drops out of the list the smallest want shown, J. But the abstract proof is that, in so far as the tendency is realized to assign to each the same proportion of total subjective units required, the same proportion of total pleasure will be secured. Thus for 50% of total units the satisfaction will be 75% complete for all. For, regardless of the rate of decline, the area of any right-angled triangle to the left of an altitude halfway along the base is three quarters of the total area of the triangle.

This also signifies that the norm for this criterion would be to maintain a condition in which the rate of reduction of intensity or of pleasure would be the same for all wants, though there would be no experience of the rate itself.

cent of the total satisfaction to be derived. Therefore, in the third figure we show, by the broken line, the limit of capacity in proportion to the total means required and, by the dotted line, its limit in proportion to total satisfaction.

2. AMONG COMPOUND MEANS

We may now proceed to examine the question as to how far these three orders of preference among means serving each but a single want would have to be modified to include the cases where a single means serves several wants of a constellation. It is clear that any such modification could take but one form in the order of preference based on the first criterion. Either the means serving several wants would be moved forward in the order to a position preceding that conferred by the major want of the constellation; or it would not. Whether it were so moved or not would depend on whether the estimations of the usefulness of the means for the several wants were summated in a single choice (simultaneous summation) or, on the other hand, they affected choice only successively and independently of each other (successive summation). We may consider three different conditions.

a. As a basis for any deliberate choice we must assume that the several attributes of a single means, each serving a single want of a constellation, are distinguished and recognized, consciously or unconsciously (i.e., volitionally or emotionally). If they are not distinguished and recognized they cannot be judged, and we would have to assume that the only estimate of usefulness would be that for the major want, while the satisfaction of any minor want in the constellation would be purely incidental and unplanned. That is, we would have to assume that deliberate planning for future wants would, under such conditions, follow the same course that we have established for present wants forming a constellation. There would be no summation of either kind.

b. Probably the commonest cases are those in which there are several different means available for a constellation of wants each one of which is recognized to contain a different assortment of the attributes serving the various members of a constellation. These differences may be inherent in the natural materials or they may be produced differences.

For wants C, F, H, and K, being members of a constellation, there can be made available, let us say, four different means which, being designated by the attributes serving each want, are c, cf, cfh, $cfhk$.[6] If these wants summated simultaneously, Means cfh or $cfhk$ might well take precedence in the order of preference over a or b, the means for the single Want A and for the single Want B. That is, while all the wants served were subordinate to A and B, simultaneous summation of usefulness might place the joint means ahead of that one serving only A or that one serving only B. If the wants do not summate simultaneously, but merely summate successively, Means a and b will take precedence. As preferred means for the constellation, c might then follow, since the difference in usefulness between c and cf is only f, and Want F has not sufficient force to supersede Wants D and E, which are prior to it in the order of priority, and to assert its claims. After Wants D and E are provided (or planned) for, F will be considered. That will lead to the substitution of cf for c; and so on. Only if capacity reaches to Want K will $cfhk$ take the place of the other means available for the constellation. Thus we construe successive summation to affect choices made for the major wants of constellations, not by way of changing the order of preference from the order of priority, but by way of substitution of means more satisfying to each minor want, as it comes to have a voice in the matter, for means already selected without reference to their preferences.

While it is impossible to prove which of these two results actually takes place, I am inclined to think, on the basis of the evidence we shall furnish in Part IV, that the supposition of simultaneous summation, in such cases, is inconsistent with most observed behavior. If it occurred, there would probably be instances in which a compound means serving many members of some constellation of rather subordinate wants through its different attributes would take precedence over the means serving only one, but that a very important, want. Apparently that almost never occurs; or, rather, it almost never occurs merely by reason of unconstrained preference (pure subjective valuation).

We conclude that the safest hypothesis is that, under these particular most usual conditions, the wants forming a constellation do not summate simultaneously and therefore do not change the order of preference from the order of priority. Instead, the operation of a constel-

[6] This is the same as the illustration used on p. 430, note 7, where the subject was first introduced.

lation leads to a change in the means selected for the constellation as a whole as each member of it, in turn, comes to be considered and included in the expanding limit of capacity (successive summation). Until and unless it is so included, any satisfaction of a minor want is purely incidental.[7]

c. The cases in which simultaneous summation actually occurs seem to be limited to those in which one attribute of a means is recognized as serving for the satisfaction of a number of different members of a constellation of wants.[8] In such cases it appears that, there being no differentiation of the means serving more and more of the minor wants, all members tend to combine on the single means which serves them all. On that basis a constellation such as C F H K, in the foregoing illustration, may secure for its single means precedence over that for Want B, say.[9] At least our scheme should allow for this possibility.

It is doubtful that the existence of compound means would have any influence on the order of preference dictated by the second criterion. And this by reason of the apparent impossibility of summation. It will be recalled that the very basis of this criterion eliminates even the concept of an absolute magnitude for significance. Its applica-

[7] To convert this conclusion from observation into terms of our discussion of conflict in the mnemonic-volitional system in Chapter 6, Section B 3, we would have to suppose the following: If different means are available, containing more or less of the attributes serving different members of a constellation, each would have associated with it a different memory of effort. To the extent that a means serving more members also involves a more intense memory of effort, only the intensity of these additional members would be available to counteract the excess. This would serve to make the members of a constellation antagonistic rather than allied, until, with the expansion of capacity along the order of preference, they were, in turn, included. They would only become allied as each in turn was included. Again, if but one means is available and it is a question of its quantity—density of attribute proportionate to quantity—that quantity would be initially determined by the major want and only increased for the benefit of minor wants as and when they were included. On the other hand, with a means whose single attribute was fixed in quantity—not proportionate—and which served many members, these members might well summate simultaneously, particularly if the increased effort thus made available would increase the degree of satisfaction of all (see case c, below).
[8] This would obviously include cases where only the means as a whole is so recognized without distinction as to attributes.
[9] Among the peasant women of Eastern Europe, ceremonial national costumes assume great importance. Let us say that the attribute, beauty, is the essential one. But the beauty of such costumes serves other wants than the wearer's want of beauty. Upon this attribute also converge the wants for conformity, for the personal attention and admiration of other women, for social eminence and, finally, no doubt, on a large scale, for the attraction of the male (sex). Thus the great labor that has gone into these costumes —their *elaborateness*—while directed toward beauty, may well have caused deferment of the satisfaction of other wants which hold positions in the order of priority ahead of the want for beauty or any other of the above-mentioned wants, taken alone.

tion consists in a series of choices in which equals are combined and the greater is preferred to the less. But, without the concept of absolute magnitude how is it possible to determine whether or not two "lesses" exceed one greater? [10]

The compound means seems, at first, to present a difficulty in the case of the third criterion. If it is conceived that a single means can yield more pleasure, satisfaction, etc., when it serves toward the satisfying of several wants at the same time than if it serves only toward the satisfying of the major want of the constellation, it would follow that the subjective unit of a means would be smaller, if compound, than it would if simple. That is, the pleasure per objective unit being thus increased (by summation), the number of objective units would be less. The result would be that the initial subjective unit of any means that served a constellation of wants would yield a smaller percentage of total pleasure, satisfaction, etc., to each of these wants than would the subjective units of means serving but a single want to wants of approximately the same rank in the order, respectively. But since, as we showed above, the initial satisfaction would be a smaller proportion of complete satisfaction, in such cases, the rate of diminution of subsequent partial satisfactions would be lower. Therefore, the initial deficit would gradually be eliminated by subsequent choices, and the general trend would be toward an equal percentage of total satisfaction at all stages, just as with the unmodified order of preference. If it were conceived that the means would yield no more pleasure when serving several than when serving only the major want of the constellation, then, of course, the order of preference would be modified in a different way. The minor wants of a constellation would be satisfied upon purely an incidental basis. That is, the objective quantity of means necessary to make up an initially equal subjective unit would be determined for the major want of the constellation only. This quantity would be less than that required for a subjective unit for each of the minor wants in the constellation. The deficit would be greater the more subordinate the want. Nevertheless, since, under this supposition, the subjective unit would be larger than under the first supposition and since preference in subsequent choices would again be dictated by the slowest rate of decline—that of the major want of the

[10] It is no mere mathematical trick to say here that, if $+ 1 > - 1$, it is also greater than $- 1 + - 2$.

constellation—the trend would be toward progressively eliminating these deficits among the minor wants as the process proceeded.

E. SUMMARY

By way of clarification and final summary we may now contrast the characteristics and the implications of the three virtual orders of preference arising from the three alternative hypotheses that we have found to be within the reasonable bounds of possibility as bases for the subjective valuation of means.

1. THE MAGNITUDES UPON THE WANT SIDE

Our own hypothesis is based upon the supposition that intensity of want is the driving force, that it is maintained approximately level during a process of satisfying and that it declines to zero in a single step at satiation. Alternatively we admit the possibility that, under certain conditions, only a partial satisfaction would be planned for, and that the decline of intensity, though also in a single step, might not then reach zero. Under this hypothesis the only magnitudes that would require to be compared, among the several wants, are their respective normal maxima of intensity. And the only magnitudes that would require to be related to the process of satisfying are the ultimate reductions of intensity from these maxima to zero—or perhaps to some higher point in the case of incomplete satisfaction.

The second hypothesis is also based upon the supposition that the intensity of want is the driving force. But now it is supposed that this intensity declines gradually during the process of satisfying. The scheme is not affected by the question whether the rate of decline is constant, diminishing or increasing.[1] The magnitudes that would require to be compared among the wants are their several initial intensities and their remaining intensities at the point at which each in turn is reduced to the level of the initial intensity of the next want in order. At such points the two (or more) intensities would be recognized as equal

[1] As noted above, the rate of decline is probably indeterminate under this hypothesis. The fact that different quantities are required to bring each want down to the initial intensity of the next, and so on, might just as well be due to larger or smaller differences between the initial intensities of successive pairs of wants as to the fact that a certain quantity of reduction of intensity could, through successive phases, be produced by a smaller quantity, or only by a greater quantity, than through previous phases.

—or indifferent. These magnitudes have no relation to the process of satisfying except that the successive strategic points are reached only during that process.[2]

The third hypothesis is based on a different supposition. Instead of the intensity of the want, it supposes that the driving force is an experience which occurs *pari passu* with the process of satisfying—an experience of pleasure, satisfaction, or even of the reduction of intensity of want. It also assumes that this driving force diminishes per successive equal phase in the process—marked off by equal quantities of means consumed. That is equivalent to the supposition, under the second hypothesis, that the intensity of the want declines during the process of satisfying; but here there is added the supposition that it declines at a diminishing rate. The magnitudes that would require to be compared among the wants are, therefore, the quantities of pleasure, etc., derived during successive phases in the process of satisfying each. Since the means for different wants are incommensurable, the only common unit in which to compare such phases is what we have called the subjective unit—that is, the initial phase of satisfaction in which the quantity of pleasure, etc., experienced is the same for each want. But, since the process of satisfying is a continuous one, the only boundary for such a phase that could be marked off and remembered is the objective quantity of means consumed during that phase. Thereafter, these objective quantities, derived from the subjective unit, would become the required magnitudes related to the process of satisfying. And, thereafter, as the process proceeded, the successively diminishing quantities of pleasure, etc., derived from these objective quantities would serve as the magnitudes to be compared among the several wants.

2. THE MAGNITUDES UPON THE MEANS SIDE

Under the first hypothesis the subjective unit of means is uniquely determined as a full measure. The disappearance of the full measure, in the process of reducing the intensity of the want from its normal maximum to zero, would fix the boundaries of the correspondence between these two dynamic magnitudes. The place in the order of preference of a full measure of each means would be fixed by the static magnitude, the initial intensity, or order of magnitude, of its corresponding

---

[2] So most processes can only occur over time. Yet time is not necessarily a dimension of such processes (e.g., chemical reactions).

want. And the comparative usefulness of these full measures, each taken as a whole, would correspond to these initial intensities. That is, there could be no quantitative relation between usefulness and amount of means except in these lump-sum terms. The part measure of means would be indeterminate, except as it might be fixed as a full measure for the major want of the constellation. Its place in the order of preference would also be indeterminate; but we are supposing that there might be some sort of subordination of the satisfactions that are recognized to be incomplete.

The successive subjective units of means under the second hypothesis would be of irregularly different sizes. Each would be fixed, in turn, by the quantity required to reduce the initial or remaining intensity of the want to the level of the initial intensity of the next want in order. The placing of these irregular units in the order of preference would then be determined by the static magnitudes, initial or remaining intensity, of the several wants at the corresponding stages. These units would have, as a whole, significance more or less than, or equal to, each other. There could be no quantitative relation between significance and amount of means except in these irregular and lump sum terms.

Under the third hypothesis the subjective units of means, once determined, would remain of uniform size throughout the process. Each would be that quantity which would yield, at the start, an amount of reduction of intensity or pleasure, etc., that would be indifferent from the amount yielded by the initial subjective unit of every other means. In the order of preference the first units for all wants would be on a par and would therefore be chosen together regardless of the intensities of the several wants. Thereafter, the place in the order of preference of all subsequent units would be determined by comparison in terms of more or less. But, since all subsequent units are assumed to accomplish less reduction of intensity, or yield less pleasure, than the initial one, that one which showed the lowest rate of diminution would be chosen next, etc. While significance would be determined for each such subjective unit in these uniform but lump sum terms, the possibility seems not to be excluded that there might be a more refined quantitative relation between significance and amount of means within these units. We shall see.[3]

In respect of the relationship between the two magnitudes constitut-

[3] See p. 531, note 10, below.

ing the correspondence—wants and means—we may note that the first and second hypotheses are alike in making the static magnitude, intensity of want, the determinant of the order of preference. On the other hand, the first and third are alike in making the dynamic magnitude, reduction of intensity (or pleasure), the basis of the relation to the process of satisfaction and thus to the magnitude of means. Therefore, the first hypothesis occupies an intermediate position between the two opposite extremes occupied by the second and third. The criterion in the second hypothesis is unrelated to the process or to any dynamic magnitude; and that under the third hypothesis is not directly related to intensity of want or any other static magnitude. As a result, if the process of satisfaction were to stop at any point before satiation, the magnitudes which underlie the first and second hypotheses might be supposed to remain at least potentially as they were at that point; but the magnitude underlying the third hypothesis would necessarily disappear, since it is itself only an aspect of the process.

3. THE VIRTUAL ORDERS OF PREFERENCE IN RELATION TO THE ORDER OF PRIORITY, TO SATIATION, AND TO CAPACITY

Under the first hypothesis the virtual order of preference would, from beginning to end, follow precisely the order of priority, accomplishing the satiation of each want in turn until, at some point, capacity was exhausted. Then all wants subordinate to that limit would remain wholly unsatisfied except for incidental satisfaction. To the extent that there was "spontaneous" or "deliberate" incomplete satisfaction of some wants that have a position in the order of priority within the limit of capacity, it is to be supposed that the other segments of these same wants would have positions beyond the limits of capacity. To what extent segments of wants for which incomplete satisfaction was planned would be deferred in the order of priority to positions subordinate to the places occupied by their complete satisfactions is a question. We shall have something further to say on that in Part IV.

Under the second hypothesis the order of priority would only influence the order of preference in respect of the beginning of the satisfying of each want in turn. Thereafter it would cease to have any influence, and satisfying would proceed *pari passu* for all the wants that had, one by one, been included. At some point capacity would be exhausted. At that point all wants of an order of magnitude less than that of the last want whose satisfying had been begun would be excluded from all, even a beginning of, satisfaction. And, at that point, all wants whose satisfying had been partially accomplished would show remaining intensity (unsatisfied) approximately equal to the initial intensity of the first want excluded. Thus there could not be any want whose satisfying had reached satiation.

Under the third hypothesis the order of priority would have no influence whatever at the start. Instead, the process would begin at one and the same choice for all together. Thereafter, however, the influence of the order of priority would appear indirectly. Since the wants whose satisfaction involves greater total reduction of intensity (the more intense wants), or yields greater totals of pleasure, necessarily show the lower rates of diminution per subjective unit, successive choices would show cumulative pluralities for each want roughly proportionate to its rank in the order of priority—its order of magnitude. Conversely, since the subjective unit for each want yields a fraction of its total reduction of intensity or pleasure in inverse proportion to the rank of the want in the order of priority, the earlier phases of the process would show a greater degree of satisfying, the more subordinate the position of the want in that order. When the limit of capacity had been reached no wants would have been satiated and no wants would have been altogether excluded. Instead, all would have been satisfied to about the same degree. That does not mean that their remaining intensities would then be at a uniform level. It means that the proportion accomplished of the total process of satisfying—either in terms of reduction of intensity or of pleasure experienced—would be about the same for all. Since it is assumed that all are subject to a diminishing rate of reduction all would have been reduced to a level of intensity considerably less than half of their initial magnitudes, if, for instance, the limit of capacity had permitted the apportionment of half of a full measure of means to each.

Since, according to our concept of an order of preference, it consists essentially of a continually expanding limit of capacity, it follows that if, after the existing limit had been reached, there occurred an expansion of capacity, its effect would merely be to continue the process of the order of preference. Thus, under the first hypothesis, since further quantities of means for all wants previously included would be superfluous for these instances, such increments of capacity would be applied to procuring full measures of means for the next wants in the order of priority that had previously been excluded. Under the second hypothesis, increments of capacity would include an initial provision for the first want previously excluded, but perhaps for no more than the first. This because such an increment would also have to be spread over the indifferent phases of every want whose satisfaction had been partially accomplished within the previous limit. Under the third hypothesis, increments of capacity would include no more wants in the program, since all would have been included from the start. Instead, such increments would be applied to increase the degree of satisfaction—proportion of total pleasure—of every want from the point reached under the previous limit to a new and higher point which, within the limits set by the discontinuities of large subjective units, would be at an approximate level for all wants.

4. THE COMPARATIVE ESTIMATION OF OBJECTIVE UNITS AND THEIR MARGINALITY

Under all three hypotheses, the quantities of means to be estimated would first be determined as subjective units. Therefore, for all three, the measurement of these quantities in terms of objective units would be a subsequent procedure assumed to be performed for the sake of convenience in remembering and identifying them. Under the first and third hypotheses, these quantities, once determined, would remain always the same. For the first, one would know that the full measure of means for each want was made up of so many objective units; for the third, one could know how many objective units constituted the initially subjectively equivalent quantities of means for each of the different wants. But, under the second hypothesis, as we noted above, the matter would be more complicated. For then the successive subjective quantities of a means might each contain a somewhat different number of objective units from every other subjective quantity of the same means.

Under the first hypothesis we have said that the objective units composing a full measure would be estimated as a whole.[4] As a whole they would have usefulness proportionate to the order of magnitude of the want. For a single instance of the want an objective unit in excess of those composing a full measure would be superfluous. It might still be esteemed as useful, but only potentially so and with reference to some

[4] See Chapter 7, and particularly pp. 445–446.

other series of choices. It would not appear in this particular order of preference at all.[5] On the other hand, the shortage of one objective unit from the full measure would, of course, convert the latter into a part measure and therefore convert a complete into an incomplete satisfaction. If so, the difference between the two satisfactions would seem to hinge on the single unit short; that unit would seem to become marginal. However, let us for a moment take a realistic view of the order of preference. We assume that a full measure for Want A is preferred to a full measure for Want B. If, now, we abstract one objective unit from the full measure for Want A, we often find that the remaining part measure is still preferred over the full measure for Want B. Worse still, if we continue to abstract objective units we are apt to find that the preference remains the same. At some point in the process of abstraction it is possible that, in the case of not very pressing wants, the part measure will be relegated to a subordinate position in the order of preference. But, in the case of pressing wants, my observation is that such is never the outcome. In fact that seems to be conceded, though on a different thesis, by marginal utility theory.[6] Now, on the other hand, if we concede that satiation of Want A ever takes place, we must also assume that a full measure for Want A is preferred to a part measure for Want A. If the difference between them is so slight that both have the same position in the order of preference, how explain the fact that, if further means for Want A can be made available, the conversion of a part into a full measure will also take precedence over a full measure for Want B?[7] The only way to resolve this difficulty is to revert to our concept of the maintenance of the intensity of a want during the process of satisfaction. According to that concept the force acts throughout the process at the same level. The force itself is not related to the quantity of means. All or

[5] That is, being superfluous for this series of choices, its usefulness will depend on some other series—i.e., choices with reference to a set of instances of future wants with some different degree of futurity. This makes it clear that differences between parts of stocks for different dates depend on the effect of futurity. Having isolated that factor, we reserve examination of it to Part II.

It is of course true that means capable of alternative uses which are superfluous for a prior want may appear again in the order of preference when the subordinate want it serves is reached. As noted in Chapter 7, that signifies only that a full measure for the second purpose will have usefulness, as compared to its usefulness for the first purpose, in proportion to the maximum intensities of the two wants.

[6] The thesis there is that, the smaller the quantity, the greater the marginal significance.

[7] According to the view of any form of marginal utility theory that accepts assumption (a) in the conglomerate referred to on pp. 437 ff., this not only does not take place but could not. That is the fundamental question of fact that is in dispute.

any part of a full measure for Want A may well be preferred to a full measure for Want B because the intensity of A is greater than that of B throughout its satisfying. The concept of marginality is here wholly inapplicable.[8]

Under the second hypothesis the objective units composing each successive subjective unit of means would also be estimated as a whole. As a whole the objective units composing each successive subjective unit would have less significance than those composing the subjective units already preferred and more significance than those composing subjective units not yet chosen. As a whole they would have significance equal to that of the objective units composing subjective units of other means that were chosen along with them. Objective units composing subjective units of every means which were excluded by the limitation of capacity would nevertheless continue to have significance, even for the immediate series of choices. Their significance would merely be inadequate to cause their inclusion.[9] Again, as under

[8] If we should attempt to apply the concept of marginality to such a curve of wants as was shown in Fig. 6—our own hypothesis—the derived "curve of significance" on the basis of reduction of intensity in the completed process, analogous to Fig. 11, would show a series of objective units of means of no "height" (no reduction of intensity) and then a final one of the full "height" of the want. But this would be absurd. One cannot attribute the cumulative effect of a series of units to the final unit alone. We can only say, as we have said before, that the usefulness of a unit of means, while necessarily equal only to the fraction it represents of the usefulness of a full measure, is estimated only as part of a whole.

The only realistic scheme is that of segmentation, which we have already outlined. If, normally, the intensity is maintained or nearly maintained throughout a single complete satisfaction and then drops sharply, the necessary means for such want will be viewed as a whole. But if, abnormally, this satisfaction is prematurely ended ("spontaneous" segmentation) for any of the reasons previously discussed, the remaining intensity will either stand at the same level or will at once find a new one. If the response was escape, intensity would not decline because one almost escaped. If it was eating, intensity would decline markedly, if briefly. If it was protecting oneself from the elements, though one was not satisfied with incomplete protection, still partial protection would be deemed somewhat better than none. In this way we reconcile the two schemes. The means needed for the whole of a satisfaction will be regarded as an aggregate *if possible*. If something beyond the purview of choice prevents the attainment of such whole satisfaction, it may turn out, in some cases, that so great a part of the whole reduction of intensity as our first scheme shows did not depend on the final unit. Or, in other cases, it may turn out that the estimate was correct (e.g., escape). So the "shape" of the satisfying of the want in expectation and its "shape" in partial realization might or might not be different. The question remains, then, to what extent experience of partial satisfactions leads to "deliberate" segmentation. That question we shall undertake to explore in Part IV, though we seem to lack any positive data bearing upon it.

[9] They would still be "desired," but means for other wants would have been "desired" more. Thus, as soon as one introduces the notion of a limit of capacity, the first group of conditions detailed at the end of Chapter 7 are shown to become impossible. Then all the conclusions arrived at with reference to "non-economic goods" become inconsistent with the scheme upon which their explanation has been supposed to rest.

the first hypothesis, the concept of marginality would be inapplicable to the objective units composing a single subjective unit. All would be on a par in respect of significance. But here one could apply the concept of marginality to the whole groups of objective units composing subjective units. That is, in a succession of choices, each subjective unit in turn would, as a whole, become marginal.

All these latter statements also apply in exactly the same way under the third hypothesis. Again the several objective units composing a subjective unit could not be distinguished in their estimation. But this time that would be because, by definition, the subjective unit is the smallest quantity whose reduction of intensity or yield of pleasure can be at all precisely compared with that of others.[10] Again objective units composing a subjective unit excluded by the limit of capacity would still have significance, even for the immediate series of choices— they would merely have insufficient significance.[11] And again the concept of marginality could not be applied within the subjective units but only to each subjective unit as a whole in the succession of choices.

It must be borne in mind that, at best, none of these orders of preference is more than a virtual system. In other words, it is quite evident, after our careful analysis, that none of these three hypotheses, when it is carried to its logical conclusion, corresponds precisely to reality. Human beings do not behave, when they make their choices, in precisely any one of these three ways. Since these are the only hypotheses we have discovered, based on the consideration of wants alone, which have seemed to be internally consistent and logically possible, the conclusion is suggested that, as a matter of fact, choices are constrained by an extraneous influence which we have not yet considered. It will be well, then, to leave unsolved the problem as to which of these surviving hypotheses we shall select, and to return to this question later, when we have examined the various possible extraneous influences, in the hope that, by combining one of these pieces of "pure" analysis with the complementary ones which we may develop, we shall find a parallelogram or polygon of forces the virtual effects of which do

[10] This, in spite of the fact that the third criterion relates to the process—the dynamic magnitude—while the second does not, so that a larger objective unit should have more significance than a smaller one, while both have the same significance if within a single subjective unit under the second criterion. For, under the third criterion, by definition, no difference in significance between a larger or smaller objective unit within a subjective unit could be distinguished.

[11] They would be in the same condition described in note 9, above.

conform to, and explain, reality. This suspension of judgment is wiser in any case, because it is always within the possibilities that the development of the virtual behavior of other factors, which may be decisive elements in the whole pattern, will disclose a basis upon which to correct or complete the analysis of virtual behavior on these hypotheses in such a way as to make that one, now seemingly most unreal, approach closest to reality. Finally, it is certain that our present knowledge of psychology is not sufficiently assured to enable us to discard any of these three hypotheses, however improbable it seems, on the ground that it is psychologically impossible. It will only be possible to do that on the ground that its virtual results, even when modified by those of all other factors we find at play, fail to conform to the observed facts. That is our third test, which will be applied in Part IV.

Part II

"REAL COSTS"

9

WORKING AND ITS RESULT—PRODUCT

REDUCED to its simplest terms the classical formula for economic activity reads "wants-efforts-satisfactions." [1] There is peculiar merit in this formula. For, if economic life had been studied in these terms of process rather than in those of static physical objects, much that is false or illusory or beside the point might have been avoided.[2] In these terms that which lies between wants and their satisfactions is not a mass of differentiated physical "factors," but solely *human efforts*. Yet economic analysis has not been pursued in these terms.[3]

Before we can adopt such a formula, however, as a basis for our further analysis, it is necessary, first, to determine what is meant by the term "effort" and, second, to reconcile or relate this formula to the one we have developed in Part I—wants-means-satisfactions.

A. THE PLACE OF EFFORT IN THE SCHEME

1. THE EFFORTFUL *vs.* THE EFFORTLESS

When we undertake to determine exactly what is meant by "effort," in economic dynamics, we face certain difficulties; and these in part due to the fact that effort is usually defined in terms of pain-pleasure psychology and in part because the concept usually lacks precision.

---

[1] As given by Bastiat (*26, 65*). To Menger (*296, 252*), the direct *Deckung des Bedarfes* is the *Endziel;* but, like many others, he substitutes *Gewalt über die Mittel* (*ibid., 69*) for efforts. Böhm-Bawerk corrects him, at least as to production, when he says (*38, 17*), that the "end and aim" is "the making of things with which to satisfy our wants" (i.e., making, not merely having, as if the having were automatic). The simple picture presented by this formula is only true of what we call a "direct" economy. But since, in this study, we are examining only a direct economy we shall reserve discussion of that point until some later time.

[2] As Johan Åkerman puts it (*7, 121*), "*Periods of specified activity* are thus to be regarded as the atoms of econometric synthesis"—and, we may add, of the previous economic analysis.

[3] It is to me a curious fact that Pareto, who expresses this formula so purely—"Nous étudierons les actions logiques, répétées en grand nombre, qu'exécutent les hommes pour se procurer les choses qui satisfont leurs goûts" (*317, 145*)—should nevertheless have constructed his analysis in terms of things rather than processes—even to reifying persons (*capitaux personnels*).

In Adam Smith's terms the notion is equivalent to "toil and trouble"; to Hearn, "effort, as the very term seems to imply, is more or less troublesome"; to Jevons it is "any painful exertion of body or mind." [1] However, in all these and other views or definitions it is clear that effort is not the mere expenditure of physical or mental energy; rather it seems to be a psychical quality ("toil," "trouble" or "pain") which accompanies some behavior and is absent from other behavior, so that it differentiates behavior into two classes—the effortful and the effortless. True, all muscular activities are conceived to require, or consist of, the expenditure of physical energy; and this connotes external resistance, otherwise no energy would be needed. That issue will be dealt with in Chapter 11. But it is clear that it is not such external resistance that is conceived to convert activities into the effortful kind; for such external resistance opposes all activities alike. Moreover, such external resistance could not account for the effortful quality of mental activities, since, by definition, these consist of excitations which do not produce overt effects in relation to the external world. Therefore, in this usage, effort must be conceived to be due to an internal, not to an external, factor.

We are warranted, I think, in ignoring the hedonism and in identifying the effort here referred to with the effort we analyzed in Chapter 6.[2] As such it is distinguished from muscular exertion, and its effortful quality is conferred upon it, not by external resistance, but by the sense of effort that accompanies it.[3] Furthermore, since the sense of effort may be attendant on thinking (conflict in consciousness) as well as on doing (consequent activities), and since it may also be attendant on inactivity (self-restraint) as well as on activity (self-constraint), it is clear that either our term "behavior" must be stretched to include conflicts in consciousness without overt effects (including self-restraint) or we must adopt a new term to cover all cortical activities of which the sense of effort is a concomitant. Since, in psychology, the term "behavior" has been given a scientific connotation of objectivity (observable actions) it will therefore be convenient to use the economic

[1] Smith, *381*, I, 32; Hearn, *186*, 24; Jevons, *224*, 168. The first two are cited by Jevons.
[2] It will be recalled that, to us, the sense of effort—and the memories it establishes—is chiefly a merely inferred force or resistance necessarily imputed in order to account for the observable limitations on behavior in response to future wants. We identified this dynamic magnitude with the introspectively derived sense of effort, largely because William James's analysis of the latter seemed to fit it so neatly into the pattern prescribed by our inferences.
[3] See especially p. 345.

term "effort" or "efforts" to cover all cortical activities which involve the sense of effort, whether these have overt effects or not. Hereafter we shall use the word to designate such cortical activities.

It will be well now to remind ourselves of the dichotomy, established in Chapter 6, between the effortful and the effortless. The effortless consists of all activities in so far as they are energized by primary neural energy of response and of all bodily inactivities in so far as they are permitted by an absence of all energizing. That includes the whole of the subcortical component of behavior examined in Chapter 3. It includes the whole emotional system—emotional state (hypothalamic), including replicas, emotional reaction (motor and autonomic) and emotion, or emotional experience (cortical). It is, therefore, the present want system—including surrogates—in its entirety. The effortful consists of all activities in so far as they are energized by secondary neural energy of response, and of all inactivities (self-restraint) produced by secondary energy. In turn, that includes the whole cortical component of behavior. It includes the whole mnemonic-volitional system—conflicts in consciousness between conscious memories and between them and emotions, together with the resulting repression of emotions or the resulting motor actions, all of which are non-emotional. It is, therefore, the future want system in its entirety.[4] However, as we have noted in Chapter 6, Section D 2, although these two systems are in competition with each other, they may also co-operate. In fact, it happens that a large part of the time the dominant future want and the prepotent present want are not antagonistic to each other. Then either the former voluntarily directs the energy of the latter toward the involuntary objectives, or the latter involuntarily supplements the energy of the former by deriving satisfaction from the voluntary precurrent reactions. In our further examination of the forms which economic efforts take we shall classify them, or these two components of them, according to this dichotomy, though recognizing that there is often a mixture.

A further dichotomy, already elaborated from this one,[5] will be required as we proceed. The competition between the mnemonic-volitional system and the emotional system has two aspects. In so far as the secondary energy of the former is required for, and devoted to,

---

[4] It is worthy of note that this feature of the distinction coincides well with Jevons, though ours is unrelated to his hedonism. To him, one of the requisites of effort is that it is "undergone partly or wholly with a view to future good" (see *224*, 168).

[5] See pp. 388 to 391.

the inhibition of the emotional system its effect is negative. We have
called that self-restraint. In so far as this secondary energy is required
for, and devoted to, conflicts in consciousness between memories only
and to the motor execution of the decisions reached by the resolution
of such conflicts, it appears only in its excitatory aspect and its effect
is positive. We have called that self-constraint.[6] While inhibition is
probably a by-product of excitation so that secondary energy may
always evince both these aspects, nevertheless it is clear that, during
all processes of thinking and doing, one or the other aspect is always
predominant. Two antagonistic courses of activity cannot be pursued
simultaneously. One or the other must be chosen. Deliberate choice is
the function of the mnemonic-volitional system. Moreover, for any
course of activity of considerable duration that choice must be effective
for a period of time. Thus we find it essential to distinguish the effort
involved in the preliminary decision between the two systems—the
secondary energy of the mnemonic-volitional system inhibiting the
primary energy of the present want system (self-restraint)—from the
effort involved in the subsequent thinking or doing, when secondary
energy is devoted primarily to excitation of these processes. This for
two reasons. The former produces no overt effects; results stem from
the latter processes only. Secondly, the former is measured wholly
by the intensity of competition offered by the present want system,
while the latter is measured only by the intensity and duration of the
effort involved in the thinking and doing.[7] And this intensity and duration, in turn, are, as we shall see, largely dependent on external data
(minus the effect of habit). We shall try to preserve this distinction
between the effort involved in self-restraint, or overcoming competing
present wants, and that which is required for the thinking and doing
(self-constraint). And this without denying that the two phases may
alternate or even mix; for courses of action decided upon may be interrupted or terminated by present wants before they are completed,
and occasional emotions may require temporary revivals of self-restraint
during the process.

[6] The distinction is commonly and naïvely expressed as not doing what one "wants"
to do, on the one hand, and doing what one does not "want" to do, on the other.
[7] See p. 391. The measure of self-restraint is the quantity of secondary energy with
its accompanying sense of effort that is required to repress a present want prior to a
course of action or during a stoppage of it. The measure of self-constraint is the quantity of such energy and effort that is required to arrive at a decision between future
wants or as to any future want (thinking), plus all that is involved in the subsequent
course of action (doing).

With this scheme in mind it becomes necessary to clarify, for the reader, the way it fits into our entire system of energetics. In Part I we dealt with present wants only as forces; but when we introduced future wants we found it necessary to treat them not only as, in themselves, forces—reinforced by volition—but as inherently opposed by internal resistances taking the form of the sense of effort. Thus, in Part II, where we are examining the effortful, we are dealing with an energetic system in which the force of wants (future) is countered by internal resistances to their provision. We must assume, then, that only when the want is strong enough to enable it to overcome these resistances will provision be made.

However, the introduction of such internal resistances does not complete the picture. We conceive the human organism to dwell in its habitat—the natural environment. The original economic forces are the wants of this organism. His present wants energize internal activities. Some of these lead also to external activities—behavior, strictly speaking. Opposed to the resulting external activities is the system of natural resistances arising in the environment (which we shall examine in Part III). In order to overcome these resistances, physical exertion (muscular) may be necessary. The force of the present wants directly causes this exertion. Thus, under such conditions, the energetic formula reads, the force of present wants *vs.* external resistances. Internal activities, energized by present wants, which do not lead to external activities of course meet no external resistances. Nor is there inherent in the present want system any internal resistance to such purely internal activities—at least so far as consciousness is concerned. The future want system interposes, in tandem, two other elements into this series. These are interposed in such a way that, at the point of contact, so to speak, between the present want system and the effector relations with the environment, volitional effort intrudes. Behind it lies its incitor, the future want system—again an original source of economic forces. But volitional effort has two faces. Its face opposes the forces of future wants with a kind of internal resistance—the sense of effort. Its obverse is, on the other hand, itself force. This latter force can be directed either way, or both ways at the point of contact. That is, it can be directed against the present want system so that it sets up internal resistance to that system (self-restraint). In that event, it opposes a resistance to a force with static results. Or it can be directed outwardly into external activities with dynamic results.

When that occurs, it, too, meets the system of natural (external) resistances and must overcome them with physical exertion. But then future wants are only the indirect cause of the exertion. The formula is the force of future wants *vs.* the internal resistance to effort ←——volition——→ the external force of effort *vs.* the external resistances of the environment.

While this system of forces and resistances may be conceived as analogous to a physical (mechanical) system, it cannot be construed in physical terms. That would not be economically realistic. When present wants lead only to internal activities no external resistance is encountered. But future wants, as defined, and the internal activities to which they give rise, usually have reference to external activities, ultimately if not immediately. Therefore, the solely internal activities that they set up may play a part in the external activities. Thus we have to include in our scheme the effortful internal activities (mental) along with the effortful external activities (physical) as a part of the system of energizing effortful behavior—and that whether the mental activities are preliminary or concurrent, so long as they are auxiliary. And this inclusion takes our whole concept of forces and resistances out of the purely mechanical sphere into the economic.

2. PRODUCTION *vs.* CONSUMPTION

The next step necessary is to reconcile and relate the new formula, wants-efforts-satisfactions, to the one used in Part I, wants-means-satisfactions. Since they differ only in respect of their second expressions, let us commence by considering what, if any, relation effort, or the dichotomy, effortful *vs.* effortless, has with the three types of means as classified in Chapter 7. Among reactions of self—whether activity or inactivity—those which are consummatory are concurrent with the existence of the present want as well as with the process of satisfying, and are therefore effortless; those we have called precurrent may be effortless, if their precurrence is one merely of order of procedure, or even if they temporally precede the consummatory, but then only during the interval of time in which the present want to which they are appropriate is actually prepotent and in so far as it yields sufficient energy of response by itself. Other precurrent reactions of self are effortful behavior (effort), for, in so far as they are not energized by present wants (primary), they must be energized by future wants (secondary). When we consider the second type of means, acts of others, from this standpoint, we are immediately in difficulties; for then it is obvious that such acts can only be effort to those others who perform them; and to the recipient to whom they constitute means they have no existence in the aspect of effort at all. And this Janus-faced character of means becomes even more evident in the third type, objects; for objects, while they seem to be means to the person whose wants they are satisfying, do not intrinsically constitute effort to anyone. They are something of a quite different order.

It is apparent, then, that our two provisional formulae, wants-means-satisfactions and wants-efforts-satisfactions are, in respect of their second expressions, viewing the single process from opposite angles. The first views the process from the standpoint of the satisfying of wants. From that angle means are regarded as "given"; they are assumed to be readily available and suitable for use; and, whether they consist of acts (precurrent) of self, or of others (services), or of objects, they are treated as if they only required consummatory reactions or effortless precurrent reactions by the recipient. And, of these last, the consummatory reactions are themselves the process of satisfying the want as well as that of using the means. In this aspect means are judged by their usefulness.

In the second formula, on the other hand, means are not "given." Instead, they are viewed from the standpoint of the effort involved in providing them—that is, in bringing them to a point at which only a consummatory reaction, or at least effortless behavior, will be required to use them. To the extent that the means consist of "services," the providing of them would consist in performing precurrent acts of self or others. But the second formula considers only those acts of self which are effortful. Therefore it could include only those precurrent acts of self that are energized by secondary energy because they constitute provision for future wants. But since an act cannot endure after it is concluded, it cannot constitute provision for the future. Therefore such "services" of self do not appear in our second formula.[8] Acts of others, to the extent that they do not incidentally constitute satisfactions (consummatory reactions) to these others as well, must

[8] We discussed briefly in Chapter 7 the possibility of permanent effects in oneself of such acts (e.g., learning). By this route one might introduce such acts of self into our second formula—treating the person as the object means.

necessarily be effort, but not effort to self.[9] Here, by definition, the acts and the use are simultaneous ("services" of others).[10] Since we are confining ourselves to the consideration of a direct economy we omit this type of means from present consideration, merely registering the fact of its existence for future examination. To the extent that means are objects, the providing of them consists in making them available and suitable for use—that is, ready for consummatory reactions, or effortless behavior, with respect to them. But here the effort and the satisfying, the providing and the use, are not simultaneous. That is, the only effortful precurrent reaction is one which is involved in providing for a future want. The satisfying, or use, only occurs later when the expected instance of the want materializes—when the present want recurs. For this reason, in the latter case, it has been customary to consider the effort involved as if it were stored up or embodied in the object until the latter is used. This is a convenient convention which relegates the object as means to the condition of a lay figure, a mere depository in which effort is stored and out of which usefulness is taken. But we must not let this convention confuse us into thinking that it is also true that usefulness is that which is put in and effort that which is taken out.[11] As a matter of bookkeeping we consider the effort to be "spent" only as and when the usefulness is used up; that is, we charge it off when the results toward which it was directed are finally accomplished. But that is only bookkeeping. The effort was made in the providing not in the using. Conversely, while the object, before the act of providing was performed, may have had little usefulness and ultimate usefulness may have been the result of effort, there is no necessary quantitative rela-

[9] We are postponing the discussion of symbiosis and imposed wants. And, in this study of a direct economy, we do not propose to deal at all with mutuality and its inducements or incentives.

[10] "Services" are generally made to include a good many effects on objects which are more or less lasting and therefore constitute provision for future, as well as satisfaction of present, wants (e.g., cutting hair or grass). But they also include strictly ephemeral effects (e.g., fanning).

[11] By way of explanation of the position we are going to take throughout the following pages, it is well to state here our view of the appearance and disappearance of usefulness. It is safer to think of usefulness as something that appears only at the end of the process of production, when the product has become suitable and available—i.e., ready. This because, if the means require production, usefulness does not exist in nature except as a latent, potential, or partial magnitude. On the other hand, this is also because we must not think of usefulness as appearing *pari passu* with the expenditure of effort; first, because the product is not strictly usable at all until it is ready; and, second, because there is no real proportionality between usefulness and effort. Effort is aimed at usefulness. But it may fail altogether.

tion whatever between the effort and the resulting or pre-existing usefulness. The two aspects of the object, as of the acts, are of wholly different orders. In the second aspect means are judged by the effort which has been expended upon them in order to make them suitable or available; and the only means so viewed are acts of others (as effort by these others) and objects (as "stores" of effort by self or others).[12]

If now we try to combine these two aspects of means into a single formula, we find it is impossible. Rather we must proceed from this point with two formulae. In the first of these, means either consist of effortless behavior by self or others, or of objects—that is, of all three types of means—the provision of which did not require effort by anyone and which can be immediately used by effortless behavior. In this formula the behavior is limited to consummatory reactions which, in effect, themselves constitute the process of satisfying; to effortless precurrent reactions of self, which practically accompany or just precede the consummatory reactions; and to acts of others, which do not constitute effort for them since they incidentally also satisfy wants of these others.[13] Thus the first formula reads, present wants-effortless behavior using means-satisfactions. In the second formula, which covers all cases in which the providing of means involves effort, we have future wants leading to efforts, and these in turn providing means. And, since the only means that can be provided now for future wants are means of the third type, this formula is, in effect, restricted to means as objects. Thus the second formula reads, future wants-effortful behavior providing means.

The first formula is that of consumption. It describes and delimits consumption. It views the economic process in that aspect only. The second formula is that of production. It describes and delimits production and views the economic process in that aspect only. However, this stark division requires two modifications to bring the analytical rubrics into conformity with the psychical dichotomies. In the first place, as noted before, the systems of present and future wants frequently co-operate. When present wants require the reinforcement of future wants—usually in energizing precurrent, but occasionally even in energizing consummatory, reactions[14]—or when ancillary

[12] In those varieties of means of the first two types, where the effect of effort is stored up in the recipient (typically learning and being taught), the same caution must be observed.

[13] Chiefly symbiosis. The status of imposed wants is somewhat different.

[14] For example, one may have to force himself to eat when, on account of illness, he may have no "stomach" for the food.

present wants relieve or eliminate the effort involved in precurrent reactions directed toward provision for future wants, the process simultaneously partakes in some degree of both consumption and production. In the second place, since it is to be assumed that all "production is in order to consumption," we must allow for the successive combination of the two formulae in practically all cases where production takes place at all. In terms of our analytical entities this means that it is presupposed that, when provision is made for an instance of future want, the anticipated present want will materialize on or about that date. Then, at the end of an interval, the effortless process will follow the effortful process. For this successive combination the formula would read, future wants-effortful behavior providing means-present wants-effortless behavior using *provided* means-satisfactions. This recognizes and separates the two aspects of the Janus-faced means; but it is limited to means as objects.[15]

This combined formula represents the whole course of the kind of economic behavior that we study. For, as we shall see, consumption not preceded by production is usually, or almost wholly, excluded from the purview of economics. Therefore, we shall hereafter refer to consumption which, according to the first formula, stands alone, as "direct consumption," thus differentiating it from the general type of consumption studied, for which means as objects must be provided in advance.[16] But the separation of, and the distinction between, the two formulae, or the two parts of the combined formula, is important, and we shall have occasion, as we proceed, to use it as the criterion for a number of our classifications. Moreover, it will be convenient to ignore the blending of the two fundamental criteria in which the future want system contributes something during consumption and the

[15] It will be noted that, in the combined formula, the word "provided" has been inserted in the formula for consumption. On this see below.

[16] As we have previously noted, as soon as man's production and technology reaches a certain early stage—beyond that of hand-to-mouth—practically all his wants are provided for, if they require provision, in advance—that is, as future wants. The results are that the present-want system is almost wholly relegated to consumption, and that practically all production is a result of the future want system.

Our system of economic energetics seems to me to clarify an issue which has caused considerable confusion in the past. "Goods" available for direct consumption, as we call it, constituted, in classical economics, a part of the rubric "free goods," or noneconomic goods. Our distinction is based neither on the fact that they are plentiful, not scarce, nor on the fact that they are unappropriated, perhaps because not worth appropriating. It is based solely on the fundamental physiological basis. Are they ready and available for use in such a way that they require no provision—no production? The typical means capable of direct consumption is the fresh air, when we are out of doors and not too near a chemical plant.

present want system contributes something during production. For, having recognized the blending, we choose to denominate each process according to the factor that is uppermost in it. Thus we obtain a clear-cut division that yields a usable classification of behavior.

In the formula for consumption means are treated as "given"—that is, either they do not need to be provided by effort or the fact that they have been is ignored—and they are viewed in the aspect of usefulness; in the formula for production means do need to be provided; but since the providing then becomes the essential consideration, the means themselves are treated merely as the inert medium through which efforts accomplish the eventual satisfying of wants, and they are viewed in the aspect of the effort involved. Thus, in both formulae, we escape the physical viewpoint and adopt the economic one.[17] And we appear to take the position that efforts are the sole way of providing means that are not "given." As such, products in their aspect as physical objects as well as "land" and "capital" in the same aspect, disappear from our scheme. And we confine ourselves to elaborating the analysis of production in terms of efforts—whose present categories, we shall find, are neither sufficiently explicit nor adequately analyzed for our purposes.

In the scheme of economic energetics which these two separate formulae set forth, we have two rival forces conflicting with each other; the one, set in motion by that one among present wants which attains prepotence, may overcome, or may be restrained from outlet by, the other, set in motion by future wants. Or, if such a future want lends its support to a present want the second force may reinforce the first, and vice versa. True, in both cases present wants are the ultimate origin, since only from these develop future wants; and in both cases satisfaction is presumably the end-result. Nevertheless, we may say that, in so far as the energetics of the first formula is effective, wants are short-circuited almost directly into the satisfying behavior; in so far as the energetics of the second formula is effective the process is roundabout. It is the latter process with which we are particularly concerned.[18] In so far as the two forces conflict, the objectives of both

[17] Cassel (75, 10) makes somewhat the same point. He says, "we must always let the *economic* point of view be decisive. . . . This rule has not always been observed. Particularly, a *technical* way of looking upon production and distribution in their successive stages has been adopted with the result that the formation of economic concepts has been thwarted."
[18] Statements of energetics are frequently made which confuse or amalgamate these two forces. The following (Mises, 300, 113), for instance, is only strictly true of the

cannot be pursued at the same time. Our quantitative analysis of their operation in a direct economy will therefore rest largely on their inherently competitive nature. The roundabout process is described by the combined formula. In so far as means as objects cannot be made available and suitable without production, consumption of such means cannot occur unless preceded by production. To that extent production must prevail in the competition. On the other hand, in so far as means as objects, or any other means, can be made available and suitable without production, the process described in the first formula may prevail in the competition with that described in the second. Thus the competition may be construed ultimately to be between consumption under the first formula alone (direct consumption) and consumption under the combined formula.[19]

In terms of our analysis, then, we may make the following summary statements relating each of our economic categories to that one of our psychological categories which is uppermost in the causation of the process—determining the objective. Production is identifiable with

_____

direct operation of the first force: "Action arises only from needs, from dissatisfaction. It is purposive striving towards something. Its ultimate end is always to get rid of a condition which is conceived to be deficient." Or, as Galton puts it (*Inquiries into Human Faculty*, p. 18), "We are goaded into activity by the conditions and struggle of life. They afford stimuli which oppress and worry the weakly, who complain and bewail, and it may be succumb to them, but which the energetic man welcomes with a good-humored shrug, and is better for in the end." On the other hand, the operation of the second force, into which a time interval usually enters, is well stated by Davenport (*107*, 124): "Man is the beginning and end of productive effort. The creation of utility is purposed by him for his consumption. He puts forth effort that he may enjoy its rewards. The economic cycle begins and ends in him. He works that he may live." He was evidently thinking in terms of our direct economy, for this statement is not precisely true of an economy of "enterprise." Or, in somewhat different terms, but still better, is the way Marshall puts it (*291*, 140): "While demand is based on the desire to obtain commodities, supply depends on the overcoming of the unwillingness to undergo 'discommodities.'" And, again (*ibid.*, 324) he speaks of "two opposing sets of forces, those which impel man to economic efforts and sacrifices, and those which hold him back." These statements, it will be noted, apply equally well to direct and to indirect economies, whereas those quoted above (note 1) from Menger and Böhm-Bawerk and the one quoted here from Davenport hold good only for direct economies.

Marshall's use of the term "discommodities," which to Jevons signified "ashes and sewage" (*224*, 58), illustrates the unfortunate confusion in economic terminology. But by "discommodities" Marshall meant our "efforts," for he proceeds to define them as "labour, and the sacrifice in putting off consumption." As to this, see below.

[19] These formulae do not cover the case of acts of others, either in the form of "services" or in the form of providing objects, which involve effort. For, then, provision for satisfaction of the wants of self cannot possibly be effective as an objective. The future wants of self cannot energize the efforts of others. That, however, is a problem which we do not need to consider in a direct economy. Acts of others have only been included here to provide a complete basis for the consideration of all means in an indirect economy, which we hope to examine in the future.

the activities we have defined as effort. On the other hand, consumption is to be identified with the activities we have defined as the satisfying of wants. Consumption is equivalent to the operation of primary energy of response, while production only takes place at all when secondary energy of response is in operation. Production is limited to providing means for future wants, or for the wants of others. Consumption is limited to the satisfying of present wants. Production is effortful behavior; consumption is effortless behavior.[20]

In order to make the results of all our preceding analysis fully usable as we proceed to examine the rest of the economic process, we must now convert them from the status of a cross-section of events, in terms of which we have worked them out, into the status of a continuous flow of events, as they appear in economic life. These events—future wants, estimations of means, efforts and provision of means, present wants, satisfactions—are intermittent. Nevertheless, period by period, the process repeats itself and may therefore be regarded as irregularly continuous. There is an irregular but continual recurrence of present wants, and an irregular but continual addition of provision for the future, as the present becomes the past and immediate provision is consumed or lost; as a result of current experience, estimations of usefulness are continually being revised; and as a result, chiefly, of changes in terms of substitution, due especially to knowledge of new means,[21] and of changes in capacity to provide, but also to some extent of changes in the order of priority of wants, programs for future provision of means are continually altered. Thus we acquire a dynamic picture for which it is difficult to find a physical analogy. In a sense it is a flow; but it is a flow continually changing in detail, both in constituents and in direction.

The continual execution of the individual's program for provision [22]

[20] A somewhat different energetics, which makes this same distinction but which takes a more physical view of the process, is given in the picturesque statement of J. B. Clark (*80*, 24): "Man making wealth and wealth making man constitute the whole economic operation. Humanity takes the active and aggressive attitude in the former part of the process, and it takes the passive and recipient attitude in the latter part."

[21] Not only general knowledge, but also among particular individuals. Hence, in an indirect economy, appears the factor, knowledge of what the market affords, and the effect of increasing that knowledge by advertising ("educating the consumer").

[22] Menger's delightfully all-embracing term is *Vorsorge*, which, in his usage, seems to combine all three of its meanings. It covers "providence" as well as the present sense of our originally synonymous terms, "foresight" and "provision," from the Germanic and Latin, respectively. Thus (*296*, 34), in view of caring for the future, Menger's *Bedarf* becomes "that quantity of goods which is necessary to the satisfaction of his wants during that period over which his *Vorsorge* [foresight or providence (care for provid-

against a continuously "oncoming" future is the point of contact of
the system of wants with the rest of the economic process. In the
usual economic terminology, which we may apply even to a direct
economy, the rest of the process is concerned with "supply"; at this
point of contact there is expressed the system of "demand." Out of
the system of supply and into that of demand there is flowing a continuous stream of means as objects which, when they arrive in the
latter, more or less gradually disappear or yield up their usefulness.
The ultimate force, we may call it, which draws these means into the
demand system—the force which occasions the flow—is the intensity
of present wants. But the proximate force is the system of future
wants, derived from them and proportionate to present wants in intensity, though at a lower level. And the moment, or point, at which
this proximate force is actually brought to bear is that at which these
future wants are anticipated by carrying into execution the program
of provision for them.

Since it is necessary for the sake of reasonable simplicity and will
do no injury to our experiment with the others, we shall limit ourselves in Part II to our own hypothesis as to the virtual order of preference. Moreover, we shall, in this chapter, ignore the effects of different degrees of futurity. Under these two conventions we shall assume
that each individual's program of provision would extend itself along
the order of priority of his wants as far as his capacity to provide will
reach. His distribution of means among them would be such that he
would provide for the satiation of a prior want before he would provide at all for the next subordinate one (except incidentally). Thus
he would follow the order of magnitude of the wants rather than
seek the goal of reduction of all to an equal intensity or the satisfaction
of all in the same proportion. And, though his program is conceived
to deal only with future wants, we will treat it as if it dealt only with
one set of recurrences or occurrences of an equal degree of futurity.

---

ing) or provision (actual providing)] extends." But it should be said that, to Menger,
this *Bedarf* is not simply quantitative; it is an assortment. He frequently refers to the
collectivity (*Gesammtheit*), which (*ibid.*, 30), as "the mirrored picture of his wants,"
exists as "an articulated whole which cannot be diminished or increased in any essential
part without affecting the realization of the joint purpose [*Gesammtzweck*—life and
welfare] which it serves." I cannot find in reality evidence supporting this view. Nevertheless, as Stigler notes, in his article on Menger (*386*, 240), "this mode of analysis [in
the form of "an individual's budget policy for that period"] properly avoids the unrealistic, misleading 'dinner-table' examples . . . used by Jevons and, for that matter,
most modern texts."

One further prefatory remark. While we have recognized that the occurrence of present wants, their competition, or even the comparison by the individual of their relative intensity, and the resulting selective satisfaction of them may constitute what is called an irrational process, it is clear, on the other hand, that the estimation of the usefulness of a means, the estimation of the quantity of effort involved in providing it, as well as the planning of a program of provision for future wants, are all so-called rational processes. These rational processes consist of, and result in, more or less successful estimates. A wrong estimate is not irrational; it is merely incorrect. Only the absence of estimating—a continual yielding to the impulse of the moment— could be called irrational.[23]

B. WORKING AS EFFORT

1. THE DISTINCTION OF WORKING FROM LEISURE

As a first approximation we have let "effort" stand for all effortful activities, mental or physical, that human beings carry on, or need to carry on, in order to provide means for the satisfaction of their future wants. Even after we have analyzed this effort into its constituent parts we shall find it convenient to continue to use this customary generic term for the aggregate of productive activity. But, in the usual economic analysis, human effort for economic purposes is divided into two classes or types—variously named—which are, in common parlance, called "working and saving." We shall now proceed, in this and the following chapter, to examine in turn the nature, characteristics, and economic function of each of these two types of effort. In this chapter we deal only with the first type—working. Since we have already identified the entities called economic effort with the psychological entities we examined in Chapter 6, it is well to state, then, that we are now identifying only duration effort, as we called it there, with working. The other form of effort will be dealt with in the next chapter.

What is commonly meant by the term "working"? Since I regard

[23] Menger (*296*, 121–122) makes somewhat but not quite the same distinction. To him "significance" is not merely the result of an estimate which may be wrong. It is rather the underlying fact which is estimated. It is, to him, the quantity of reduction in the intensity of a want which *will* result, rather than the present estimate of that reduction. But only the latter is an actual force in economic life; so we cannot agree.

While we also cannot agree with F. R. Macaulay's identification of *rationality* with *correctness*, he gives an interesting discussion of estimating (see *278*, Introduction).

semantics as probably the most fertile of the still largely unexplored fields available for objective psychological research, I may be excused for introducing first a bit of evidence from that field. In Chapter 5, Section A, we attempted to discriminate between behavior specimens from the animal world that were evidently energized by present wants and those that must be energized by what we then called "non-present" wants. We found there a number of border-line cases. While it furnishes us with no evidence on the question whether these doubtful cases are responses to present or to future wants, it is worth while to cite one anthropomorphic intuition—an attribution of themselves to the animal—for the sake of the acute, if wholly naïve, discrimination it exhibits in defining the two types of behavior we assigned to "non-present" wants wherever they appear in the animal world. All of the animals who evidence these types of behavior, and, in fact, many of those who perform the border-line types, are called, in common parlance, "workers," "busy," "industrious," etc. The sterile females or neuters among the social insects, who perform all that is done of these activities, are the "workers." All their fellows perform only what we have called consummatory reactions—that is, responses to present wants. The so-called working season of the "busy" bee and the wasp is the summer season only. The worker wasp works about sixteen hours a day on the day shift and, if she has not died from exhaustion during the season, dies from cold at the end of it. The worker bee works about thirteen hours a day, also on the day shift, but often survives the winter. The "industrious" beaver's activities are always described by observers as work. His working year is about twelve weeks; he is always on the night shift; and the Indians say that one who is "lazy" is exiled from the community.[1] Aside from the social insects and the beaver these terms are never, so far as I know, applied to wild life. Though he is undoubtedly nearest to man in general intelligence, the monkey "does not do any 'work.'" In fact, he is "incapable of working."[2]

On the other hand the term "work" is applied to draught animals, oxen and horses, and would be appropriate to the ants' slaves and beasts of burden. But to the ants' pets or sporting animals (and ours) it is never applied—at least, in this sense. Hunting dogs, foxhounds, hunting horses, race horses, riding horses, are evidently not conceived to

[1] See Appendix III, Section A.
[2] Quoted by H. Klüver (239) from (Mrs.) N. Kohts (25, J. de Psychol., 1928).

work. A driven horse is working. One that is running away is not held to be working. Does a shepherd dog work; or an eskimo dog, when drawing a sledge? What is the differentiating characteristic that guides man in imputing to some of these animals his experience of working and to others not? In dealing with that question we find it necessary to divide it into two parts. The first part is concerned only with wild-life, and then only when the working appears to be voluntary—where the animal appears to work of his own accord. The second part is concerned with domesticated life where, because the animal (or man) may be "made" to work, it is to that extent involuntary. Reserving this second part for examination later in this section, let us consider here only the first part of the question. We shall find, I think, that the naïve criterion conforms to, and confirms, the one we built up in the two chapters on future wants. Common usage includes under "working" all activities that are assumed to be effortful. The only activities among animals so construed are those that we have found good reason to believe are instigated by future wants.[3]

It is, of course, not necessary to set up a verbal definition of what we mean by "working" in economic analysis. All that is necessary is to differentiate it from certain activities, or behavior, which we defi-nitely cannot and do not mean to include in it—which, in fact, we mean to contrast with it.[4] Our analysis of effort, to which "working" belongs, gives us the basis for these exclusions. Our tentative term, in Chapter 6, "duration effort," defined the kind which we now char-acterize as working. But what we need to do now is to carry through the distinction which we have based on difference in causation into easily recognizable and objective categories of activity or inactivity. Considering first activities only, let us start with a global whole, such as "all exertion of body or mind." [5] Then we may proceed to strip off from this *omnium gatherum* those activities which the purpose of our analysis requires that we distinguish from working, at least as sharply as that turns out to be possible. In the first place, our analysis of effort

---

[3] That is, it appears that the imputation is partly made because the activities are con-tinuous and long-sustained (i.e., effortful); it is partly made because the individual does not do them for himself or himself only but for the young or the whole group (i.e., al-truistic); but it is chiefly, I think, because they consist of precurrent reactions not ac-companied by or soon followed by consummatory (i.e., future wants).

[4] In the words of Henry George (*169*, 44–45), "All we are trying to do, all that is neces-sary to do, is to fix, as it were, the metes and bounds of a term that in the main is well apprehended—to make definite, that is, sharp and clear on its verges, a common idea."

[5] Jevons, *224*, 168.

and our definition of future wants makes it evident that all consummatory reactions such as breathing and eating are activities of consumption, rather than of production.[6] Therefore all consummatory reactions are to be excluded from working. In the second place, to the extent that precurrent reactions are engendered by emotional drive because, and to the extent that, they constitute responses to present wants, they may be carried on for their own sake (i.e., yield their own satisfaction). Examples are the activities energized by euphoria and the preliminary activities energized by sex. This type of precurrent reaction must also be excluded from working. But is it also to be called consuming? A term to distinguish it seems necessary. We may call it playing.[7] But, in many cases, we find it difficult to distinguish between consummatory and precurrent reactions. Is not playing as a result of euphoria itself consummatory? Therefore, a more usable basis for the distinction between consuming and playing would seem to be the part played in the process by means (other than acts of self). As an activity we shall reserve the term "consuming" for processes depending chiefly on the use of means as objects (or, in an indirect economy, of acts of others). As an activity we shall reserve the term "playing" for processes depending chiefly on acts of self. But we must recognize that here again we may have mixtures. "Playing" games involving apparatus and "playing" the piano require the use of means. Where the means are incidental and the satisfying is derived less from the use than from the activity, we may call the activity playing.

While it is possible to make a clear-cut distinction between the activities of consuming, as defined, and those of working, it is not possible to do so as between playing and working. We have already introduced the class of ancillary wants—present wants which are them-

---

[6] This does not define consumption. For, as we have seen, the process of satisfying wants includes the prevention of many, as well as the getting rid of others. In the case of prevention there may be no precisely consummatory reaction and certainly no activity. For instance, having provided means to protect ourselves from the elements—preventing this state of discomfort—there ensues no consummatory reaction or activity. Consuming such a means involves no reaction or activity whatever. It is non-activity (like dwelling, wearing, etc.). See below.

[7] I set no store by the choice of this word to name non-working activities and certainly do not intend anything derogatory by it. It is not "invidious," as Veblen would *say;* nor is it intended to be invidious, as Veblen would *mean.* I use it because it seems to be the most general term. Children play in their playground. Even adults are now being provided with national playgrounds. All games, all musical instruments, and most compositions are played. At the theater the play is played. The term continues to connote its origin even when, in indirect economies, the players have lost their amateur standing. This term seems also to be the generic one in biological literature.

selves satisfied by the precurrent reactions of other wants. Thus, as cited before, hunting may come to be energized by an ancillary present want after it ceases to be the means through which hunger is appeased.[8] To the extent that they remain effortless, such activities are to be regarded as playing, not as working. In spite of their origin they become themselves, in effect, consummatory, or nearly simultaneous precurrent, reactions (satisfactions), and are therefore not efforts. This suggests that the distinction between playing and working is one between components rather than between forms of activity; for many activities have behind them a certain quantity of emotional drive, and yet not sufficient to lead to their being carried on for their own sake. We may regard this insufficient drive, where it exists, as the playing element involved in some varieties or stages of working, and may suppose that it is widely different among different persons as to each variety or stage.[9] If activity is induced by emotional drive of sufficient strength to lead to its being carried on for its own sake, we will call it playing;[10] if not, we will call it working, with or without some element of playing in it.[11] After this stripping off we are left with a

[8] Another instance is knitting for amusement, where the playing involves incidentally the production of a means to the satisfaction of some other want.

[9] We have already associated this element of behavior with certain kinds of wants, e.g., "instinct of workmanship," love of power, the "half-artistic joy in technically perfecting the productive apparatus" (Schumpeter, 364, 13). McDougall says (284, 116), "nor can any hard and fast line be drawn between work and play." The playing element includes "desire of increased skill, the pleasure of make-believe, the pleasure of being a cause," and usually includes the desire to emulate or excel.

In order, it seems to me, to demonstrate that an economy cannot depend on this element in working to provide its necessary means, Mises undertakes to analyze such an element out of existence (see 300, 163–173). But this extreme is neither necessary for his argument, nor is it realistic. To a various but usually small extent all working, up to some limit in duration, is an end in itself. Nevertheless, not much working would be done if this were its own sole reward.

Veblen, who supported the other view, nevertheless agreed that his "instinct of workmanship" yields ground somewhat readily, "under pressure," "in competition with the other, more elemental instinctive proclivities" (413, 34). Nor did it seem to him to be concerned so much with getting results as with the way of going about the getting of results (ibid., 31 and 34). In this view the playing element of work might be a detriment to its effectiveness.

If we undertook to refine this analysis somewhat further we would find it necessary to distinguish the satisfactions derived from making, or having made, from those derived from doing. Most of the former appeal to that unknown psychological entity, the "ego." The latter may be purely sensuous.

[10] Disregarding the fact that secondary energy of response may be required to direct the primary to its goal, and even that, in certain cases, secondary may be required to reinforce primary energy when the latter flags.

[11] This general distinction between working and playing, based on our physiological approach, is ventured in spite of the common defeatist attitude on such problems, exemplified, for instance, by Knight. He says (242, 25): "The positivist might well ponder

definition of the activity called working as all activity other than consuming and playing.

This brings us to the second part of our initial question as to the
imputation of working to animals. If domesticated animals (and human
slaves) are sometimes conceived to be working and sometimes not, can
the distinction there also be based on whether their behavior is a response to future wants, and so effortful, or in response to present
wants and so effortless? This introduces what we have called imposed
wants. It is a question which does not concern us in examining a direct
economy only.[12] But, in order to have the best basis possible for deal-

---

the fact that no objective definition can be given of 'work' and 'play,' fundamental as
the concepts are in any discussion of economics or of conduct in general."

At any rate, it is well to recognize that we have already, in the above, discriminated
a mass of activities which still seem to cause confusion in economics. J. M. Clark states
that "the necessary maintenance of labor is even more clearly an overhead cost" (83,
361). We have not yet discussed overhead costs. But we may assume that they have to
do with production. It is equally clear to us, therefore, that "the necessary maintenance
of labor[ers]" is a part of consumption, not of production. Economics has escaped
from what Böhm-Bawerk called (38, 67 and 69) "the frequently and justly criticised
tendency of the English school to look upon the labourer ["not as members of the civil
society in whose interest industry and commerce are carried on but"] as a machine of
production, and to consider his wage simply as an element of the costs of production—
a deduction from the national income and not a part of it." Are we now to go back, in
the name of "humanity," to the same scientific error and the same practical confusion
that was discarded, at least partly by reason of its "inhumanity"?

More recently, in a discussion of "disguised unemployment" (350, 236) Mrs. Robinson has attempted to make the distinction between occupation (our "other activities")
and employment (our "working") hinge on the degree of "productivity." But no such
distinction is possible. When we wash or dress it is always the same thing. But it may
be either working or playing. If we hurry through it to get it *done* as quickly as possible
it is probably working. To some women, who do not hurry through it, it seems to be
playing. When others do it for us, it may be working for them (nurses, valets, etc.).
When our mothers first did it for us it was certainly playing for them. In neither case
is there a difference in "productivity."

For the analysis of a direct economy, where a person provides his own means, these
distinctions suffice. But, since, later, we hope to consider also indirect economies, it is
well at this point to raise a further question. Among our kinds of means we have included acts of others. We must now add to that the possibility that certain "means"
may be objects which embody effects due to the acts of others. From the standpoint of
these others, such acts, if they are not playing, are working. But here we find that,
in the indirect economies which have actually existed, much of such working would
not be included in the economic category of production. The activities of the housewife, of the Good Samaritan, of Peter the Hermit are not (or were not) playing in our
sense. Neither are they called production. We shall consider that question further when
we begin to deal with indirect economies.

[12] In a direct economy we limit ourselves to efforts toward the satisfaction of own
wants. Thus we suppose all the initiative to come from within the person. This also
neglects suggestion and persuasion, which are important causes of behavior in an indirect (social) economy. Nor are these easy to differentiate from imposed wants. When
the parent or the calculating master proceeds by arousing the wants we call ambition

ing with it in an indirect economy while we are still considering the behavior of organisms in general, we may, in passing, outline it here. Apparently man, in applying the term working to these cases, discriminates between the animal that is driven and the animal that is only *released*. In the latter case the objective and its drive is supplied —or largely supplied—by the animal itself. Management then consists chiefly in imposed restraint. We can safely follow this and assign the behavior to the animal's own present want. In such cases he is not said to be working, in this sense; neither is he working, according to our definition. On the other hand, when he is driven, the question is far more difficult. "Breaking" the animal is done with bit and bridle, saddle or cart—and the whip. In the language of conditioning he is punished when he does not do what the trainer wishes. That is, the present want producing pain is imposed on him. He learns that, to put a stop to that want, he must do what is wished (reinforcement). In this way he learns to prevent the want. Thereafter, having become conditioned to the signals—the whip, etc.—he avoids them. The sight or sound of them becomes enough. A replica of the present want (fear), produced by these conditioned stimuli, substitutes itself for the actual want as an energizer, most of the time. All this is clearly response to present wants or surrogates and is therefore, within the terms of our definition, not working. Nevertheless, at least after the animal has become thoroughly broken, so that he performs the activity under direction with but little threatening via conditioned stimuli, men have always called the activity working; in fact, this has been the star example of working, particularly when the wants have been imposed on other men (slaves). Are we to assume that, under such training, a future want system (memory and volition) gradually develops and takes over from the present want system so that the behavior becomes effortful? Or are we to assume that our distinction as to cause is not entirely valid and that the real distinction comes, in the course of time and at least in these cases, to be based, on the one hand, on the own "wish" and, on the other hand, on the "will," whether the latter is one's own or that of some other and imposed? But perhaps these alternatives are actually one and the same thing. If, as was suggested in Chapter 6, volition is a development from parental in-

---

or love of eminence, honors, praise, etc., are these instigations education or are they imposed wants? Only by knowing whether the motive of the instigator is "ulterior" (i.e., selfish) or not can we determine that question.

fluence and, at first, does not stand on its own feet, is it not possible that the "will" is itself an outgrowth of that of the master, whoever he be? Along this line we could construe behavior in response to imposed wants, after it had become habitual and had ceased to be energized for the most part by the present want system, to be energized by a somewhat infantile future want system and so to become effortful behavior, or working.

This solution of the difficulty, while it is only a guess, is somewhat supported by another consideration. We have already found it difficult sharply to distinguish the behavior resulting from imposed wants from that which is called symbiosis—mutual back-scratching. The domestic animal is watered, fed, housed and generally cared for. So was the slave. He is *provided for,* but on condition. There is always some mutuality. This mutuality seems to grow in its influence, over time and at least among the more docile. At what point must we say that behavior becomes no longer a response to an imposed want and converts itself into a response to the trained animal's or man's own future wants which are thus provided for by indirection? [13] If so, has the energizing not then come to be furnished by a future want system that has come into being through education? May we say that imposed wants are present wants, so long as the subjected one remains wild or refractory, but that they tend to develop, in time, into future wants to the extent that subjection to the will of another or the recognition of mutuality develops a less or more self-standing mnemonic-volitional system? [14] We will have to leave it at that.

What we have said so far might seem to apply chiefly, or only, to physical and not at all, or not appropriately, to mental activities—i.e., to "exertions" of "body" but not to those of "mind." Our physiological psychology regards both as activities of the central nervous system which, so far as the expenditure of nervous energy is concerned, may not differ widely. Again it is not possible to distinguish the two, since mental (cortical) activity may accompany physical (muscular). Nevertheless, the dichotomy is again convenient if the term mental

---

[13] Such mutuality blends in with the "rewards" of the conditioning process. But we have assumed that conditioning can only be procured by rewards when these rewards constitute the reinforcement of a present want actually then effective. Mutuality may depend on provision for future wants. Hence it is not reward, as technically defined; nevertheless, as we suggested in Chapter 6, volition and conditioning may be closely allied in nature and only differ in the absence of emotional reaction in the former.

[14] The difference between the two would then lie in the degree of spontaneity—a particularly difficult quality to judge except in the simplest cases.

activity is restricted to that subliminal neural process that we have defined as deliberation and which usually precedes or occurs in the absence of—though it may at times accompany—overt behavior. One type of consuming is of this order. The "enjoyment" of many kinds of means, objects or acts of others, may involve mental activity or emotional experience induced by a present want and yet show no overt signs that could be construed as either consummatory or precurrent reactions. If these passive experiences involve the use of means, as do light reading, the theater, etc., we may include the mental activity in our category of consuming. Also we find one type of playing which is of this order. At its least intensity it may take the form of revery or "daydreaming"; at higher intensities it may become "inspiration," which is nevertheless energized only by a present want and its emotion. It consists of mental activity for its own sake and, by definition, does not depend chiefly on the use of means.[15]

Again, from these two forms of mental activity we distinguish that which constitutes working. In general the conflict in consciousness energized by secondary nervous energy of response at the behest of the future want system is always to be deemed working. The exercise of insight with its subliminal experiments, the marshaling of all memories bearing on the subject (voluntary ecphory), comparisons and estimations, the transportation of oneself to some point in the counterfeit future in order to develop a program, these are usually conducted for, and always by, the future want system and are therefore to be regarded as constituting the forms of mental activity that working takes. True, such mental activity is not always confined to a preparatory period.[16] It may accompany physical activity as well; in fact, to the extent that the actions have not become habitual, it must do so. Nevertheless, it then becomes impossible to distinguish the mental from the physical activity except when the former becomes so intense that the latter must pause and make way for it.[17]

[15] Or, if we wish to stretch the notion of acts of self, it might be said to involve only this type of means.

[16] It is, for instance, when we "think out" a problem and come to a decision for later execution. Then we may be conscious of expending much mental effort.

[17] In passing we may say that the same situation exists with playing. While "daydreaming" is purely mental and certain forms of exercise are purely physical, the two are often combined (e.g., chess or bridge).

Effort sufficient to maintain motor action is, of course, continuous and intense, to the extent that the action is not habitual. It is required for concurrent or parallel conflicts in consciousness—thinking or mental working—and for the volitional concentration of attention. But the line cannot be drawn sharply. Speaking and listening, writing

As in the case of the physical activities it is not possible to draw a hard and fast line between mental activities that constitute playing and those that constitute working. In part, this is due to the fact that, since there is no overt behavior, the only evidence is introspective; and this is not to be trusted, for mild emotional drives and accustomed mnemonic-volitional processes may be almost indistinguishable to the subject. In part, it is due to the fact that the two may intermix. That is, in purely mental as well as in chiefly physical activities, emotional drive may have the co-operation (direction and support) of mnemonic-volitional processes; or ancillary present wants may satisfy themselves and therefore help to energize mental activity initiated and principally directed in the interest of future wants. But, in general, if the objective is determined by a present want, we shall call the process playing; if it is determined by a future want we shall call it working with some element of playing in it.

As to the two kinds of working—physical and mental activity—it must be clear that the expenditure of mechanical energy by the muscular system upon the environment is not the criterion for the category and actually has little or no bearing upon the quantity of effort involved. In the first place, working in the form of mental activity expends, per se, no mechanical energy whatever upon the environment. Nevertheless, it may involve effort to the same extent as does physical activity. In fact, the very difference between the physical activity when it is breaking new paths and when it has become habitual indicates that the mental part of the activity (the strictly cortical process) is the chief factor in all effort. In the second place, the mechanical energy put forth in playing is quite generally equal to or greater than that put forth in working, though it may usually be briefer. That does not make working out of it. Thus our category of working has little or nothing to do with that of physics (mechanics). We are not suggesting its measurement in foot-pounds.[18] Both physical

and reading, though they involve motor activity of the small and the postural muscles, are chiefly mental activities. Thus we generally treat them as mental working, when they are chiefly energized by volitional effort.

[18] What we are saying, therefore, has no relation to a common viewpoint of physiologists. As T. H. Huxley expressed the latter (210, 304): "The amount of mechanical work a man does may be determined with no great difficulty, whether we calculate it as work done in walking or in turning some machine or in some other effort which results in overcoming a resistance. This work is measured in terms of the [external] resistance overcome, or weight lifted, multiplied by the height through which it is raised. . . . A good day's work is about 150,000 kilogramme-metres."

and mental working are for us effort solely because they are energized by secondary neural energy of response and are therefore accompanied by the sense of effort. The difference is that physical working involves physical (muscular) relations with the environment; mental working does not.[19] In practice, most working is a mixture of the two components in complementary proportions, varying in its composition from nearly zero to nearly 100 percent of either.[20]

Intimately connected with these three categories of physical and mental activity, consuming, playing, and working, are two other types of behavior, if they can be called such, which do not constitute "exertions of body and mind" (activity) at all. The first of these forms the remainder of the category "consuming." It is the non-active state of receiving the benefit of the prevention of present wants. Since the term prevention argues that this is due to means, in the absence of which the wants would have occurred (protection), it must be the result of past provision—that is, production, effort, working. But, strictly speaking, no consummatory reaction is involved therein. Nor is mental activity involved. The recipient is passive. Literally, our combined formula would then have to read, future wants-efforts pro-

[19] For our future analysis of a direct economy this separation serves. According to this criterion volitional conscious attention to the environment is mental, not physical, even though muscular adaptation (postural) is required. The criterion would have to be slightly modified if, in an indirect economy, the processes of social communication, listening, speaking, reading, and writing are to be treated, as they usually are, as mental working. Then what Hughlings Jackson called the "small muscles" would need to be excepted from the muscular relations.

[20] It is well to emphasize again that the line we are drawing between working and playing does not accord with the institutional distinction in a complex society (indirect economy). There, many forms of activity called working would be largely or even wholly what we define as playing. Since the activities we define as playing satisfy only certain wants, the isolated man cannot play all the time. Some time is required to provide for the satisfaction of his other wants. But, in an indirect economy, in so far as his playing satisfies other men's wants so that they are willing to provide for his other wants, he may occupy his so-called "working time" with activities that are, to him, largely or even wholly playing. Nevertheless, to the extent that he thus "plays" for the indirect purpose of satisfying his other wants, the satisfaction of his want for playing is not its own sole purpose, and the future-want system doubtless contributes a considerable part to the energizing of the activity. It is also true that, in such an economy, the amateur may play for the satisfying of other wants such as prestige, loyalty to a group, or pure competitiveness (emulation). In this way the compounding may become very complex. Institutionally, however, in both cases, the distinction is usually made on the basis of the professional or amateur status of the player—that is, on the basis of a money inducement. That is not our criterion here. From our standpoint a considerable portion, if not all, of the housewife's functioning is not in behalf of present wants and is, therefore, working. On the other hand, a considerable portion of the painter's, the singer's, the golf professional's and even the businessman's (on the higher rungs) is in behalf of present wants and is therefore the component of playing.

viding means-no present wants. The second type of behavior also constitutes an inactivity which can also hardly be described as a consummatory reaction. But here no means are directly involved and the present want does occur. In fact the want itself may be said to be the result of the expenditure of effort—and of other activities. In the course of all activities the organism runs down as a generator of energy, because it consumes its ready supplies of fuel and because it accumulates waste products of the combustion of this fuel. The want we have called fatigue is a shortage of coal and an accumulation of ashes. Also, acting as a safety contrivance to prevent waste of energy or overfatigue, there is the fatigue of attention, involuntary or voluntary —a loss of "interest" or its correspondent—which we call ennui or boredom. But this last we do not construe as itself a want. Rather it is an insufficiency in the energy of response to other wants, present or future, when that energy has not been adequately supplemented by effort. Nevertheless, the behavior produced both by the present want, fatigue, and by this loss of energy, ennui, when not compensated, may be called "resting." Interpreted in its other aspect, resting includes all inactivities, both physical and mental, which are due to absence of energizing by either primary or secondary neural energy of response.

The only form of inactivity that is effortful is the one we have noted before, self-restraint (i.e., the volitional repression of a present want). We will have to let that stand outside our present categories since it cannot be construed to belong with any of those which are effortless and, at the same time, can hardly be included with working.[21] As a productive factor it is waste effort. Therefore, after stripping off the effortless kinds in this third class, "inactivities," there remains nothing. Nevertheless, we should note the relationship of working to these two inactivities. Since the passive reception of the benefit of the prevention of present wants, though itself an inactivity, does not exclude simultaneous activity, this form of consumption may accompany working.[22] On the other hand, since resting obviously does preclude simultaneous activity, resting and working are incompatibles.

While all of our categories overlap or mix with each other to a cer-

21 It is possible that this anomalous form is also represented, in part, by the kind of effort we shall discuss in the following chapter. However, I do not think we now know enough about that kind of effort to say.
22 For instance, the worker in a heated factory is enjoying the prevention of his want, the excessive loss of bodily heat, while he works.

tain extent we have found it possible to divide the whole into these several parts by giving to each part the name of its chief component. For certain purposes, particularly when we are considering the allocation of time to competing uses, it will be helpful to lump together the several non-working or effortless categories—the activities, consuming of both sorts (physical and mental) and playing of both sorts (physical and mental) together with the inactivity, resting—and to adopt one term for the aggregate. We shall call this *leisure*, emphasizing particularly the fact that it represents an allocation of time. In this aggregate we shall include all passive consuming (inactivity) of the third kind that takes place during leisure.[23] In the last analysis, our distinction between the activities which are regarded as leisure (effortless behavior), on the one hand, and, on the other, the activities which are regarded as working (effortful behavior) is that the former are assumed to be energized by primary neural energy of response while the latter are assumed to be energized by secondary energy. Since the sense of effort is only associated with the operation of this secondary energy we may also use the criterion, "effort," as the basis for distinguishing working from leisure. Leisure time is occupied with those "exertions of body and mind" which constitute consummatory reactions with regard to, or other consuming of, means, or which constitute emotionally driven reactions not involving the consumption of means (playing), or of those inactivities which involve no "exertions of body and mind" (resting), or of mixtures of them. This second criterion permits us to include such inactivities as are effortless (i.e., excluding self-restraint) and thus to present a dichotomy; activity or inactivity produced by present wants is leisure; activity (mental or physical) produced by future wants is working.[24]

In our original physiological analysis of present wants we found that systems of reactions associated with different constellations of wants are conflicting, in the sense that they cannot be carried on at the same time. When these same systems are analyzed, as above, in terms of the component elements of leisure, on the one hand—that is, as the ele-

---

[23] However, since passive consuming does not preclude working, we cannot make the category a part of our antithesis. It may be on either side.
[24] Inactivity produced by future wants consists of the other form of effort (self-restraint) which we shall take up later.

We have treated fatigue as a present want. Yet, unlike all the others, it does not incite primary energy. Rather the opposite. Nevertheless, the inactivity it induces is effortless. This anomaly should always be borne in mind in any formula dividing wants between present and future according to the source of energizing.

ments resting, the three kinds of consuming, and the two kinds of playing—and, on the other hand, of working, this non-miscibility is no longer quite true.[25] But, on the whole, there must be a division of time between working, on the one hand, and what we call leisure, on the other. Leisure time is the non-working time assigned to the activities called consuming and playing and to the non-activity called resting—or bodily re-creation.[26] Thus all expenditure of effort in the form of working has an alternative (or competitor), in respect of the appropriation of time, in what we have called leisure—that is, other activities not requiring effort, and inactivity.

We may say that working is that kind of activity (or component of activity) which does not constitute in itself the satisfying of a want and which therefore requires to induce it the prospect of adequate provision—and the ultimate satisfaction to be obtained thereby—in order to offset the component effort.[27] Thus we see that there are two good reasons for not working. One is that working requires effort. The other is that its tempting alternative, leisure, is always beckoning.[28] Thus working also requires self-restraint. It is clear, then, that working will only be carried on when the expected provision for future wants is backed by sufficient force to exceed the sum of the effort and the alternative which can be had without effort. If the effort itself is measured against the force available to the future wants, then, in order that working should be carried on, this force must exceed the effort by an amount greater than the force exerted by those wants whose satisfactions can be secured without effort.[29] On the other hand, it is

[25] That does not signify that the two analyses contradict each other. Not at all. It only means that leisure has been divided by other criteria into reactions involving or not involving the use of means and non-reactions, while working consists of activities in so far as they are not energized by present wants, but by future wants; and these can, as we have seen, co-operate with a single present want.

[26] The classical economists regarded all such activities as "unproductive." In fact they made the mistake of including therein the working of others if it only conduced to the service of the consumer or to his play. Even so recent and "modern" an economist as Veblen preserves this distinction (see *411*, *58*). If "services conduce to . . . physical efficiency and comfort . . . they are to be accounted productive work." Other "employment" (*sic*) is "performance of leisure." And see note 11, above, for the difficulties into which this unfortunate use of the term "employment" leads.

[27] Marshall's definition of "*labour*" (*291*, *65*) deals only with the positive element and depends wholly on the indirectness of the satisfaction. Jevons includes most of ours (*224*, *168–169*); and Hearn, whom Jevons quotes, includes roughly all of ours (*186*, *24–25*).

[28] Senior (*371*, *66*) also gave these two reasons as "antagonist principles to the acquisition of wealth." The first he called indolence (dislike of labor) and the second idleness (desire of amusement). Typical of the "moral judgment" period of English economics!

[29] Jevons seems to have seen only the necessity of some net surplus, not that it must ex-

also necessary to note that all the satisfactions to be obtained as a result of working, except those which are derived from the component element of playing in the process itself, exist only in the form of expectations during the time that the process of working continues —that is, they relate only to future wants. In order to realize these prospective satisfactions in experience it is necessary to stop working and begin consuming. That is, leisure is also the period when the result of working is enjoyed. Conforming roughly to general practice we may set up an analytical convention under which, in each twenty-four hours, the working-day is conceived to precede the consuming-day—or night. Under this convention, we shall conceive that, during each working-day, effort is expended in providing means which will be used in the satisfying of wants during the succeeding consuming-day. Since all these wants exist only as future wants during the working-day, all the activities connected with providing the means involve effort. If the effort is confined to working, then all means produced each working-day are consumed in the succeeding consuming-day.[30] Of course this convention can be applied only to the provision of means in the form of objects—that is, embodied effort. But that constitutes the only type of means that can be provided in advance.[31]

---

ceed a certain size (*224*, 177–178 and 234). Even Mises adopts this error of omission from Jevons (*300*, 166). J. B. Clark ignored the surplus. To him (*81*, 317) there is merely "a social line where work and its fruits are subjective equivalents." To Knight (*240*, 63) this one is at least the "most crucial" of the two. Wicksteed saw and distinguished the two deterrents and lumped them together in his "reserve price" (*441*, 327). As usual Menger makes a very complete and balanced qualitative analysis of these matters (*296*, 149, note 1). and J. M. Clark (*83*, 359–361) makes an exact statement of them for a modern indirect economy.

[30] That is, under this convention we are excluding, as we shall see in Chapter 10, what we called interval effort in Chapter 6. This is a largely arbitrary exclusion, since interval effort begins as soon as duration effort is concluded on each measure of means. Nevertheless it will be found to conform to the usual treatment of the data. We have already been using this convention where we have excluded consideration of the degree of futurity of instances of future wants.

[31] The reader can adjust the notion of the consuming day by introducing whatever elements and quantities of working therein he sees fit, provided none of these include activities so far as they are energized by present wants or inactivities permitted by the absence of all energizing.

All the economies, past and present, with which we are familiar have stood at various stages in the general process of conversion from the domestic to the industrial (or exchange) form. In the domestic form, or portion, it is more difficult to divide production from consumption, working from leisure. The housewife and the domestic servant are the most anomalous actors on this stage if we confine production to the industrial and commercial (extra-domestic) sphere. If we do this, however, we get no criterion usable in a science. If we do this, the character of much manufacture would have changed in my lifetime. If we do this, we accept statistical availability as the basis for our scientific classifications.

We must have scientific categories capable of application to any economy at any

2. THE LIMITATION OF WORKING

Recognition of these two reasons for not working brings us to a conclusion somewhat different from that of the usual analysis. Let us first work out, in terms of our hypothesis as to limiting mechanisms with regard to the expenditure of effort, as developed in Chapter 6, Section B 3, the scheme of energetics which seems to govern the duration of working—or, more precisely, since it is always diurnally intermittent, the working-day. This leads us to suppose a program for each working-day, worked out in advance—a plan developed by the person as a result of projecting himself into the counterfeit future. It must be understood that we are not attempting to state, in terms of quantity of sense of effort incurred, the magnitude of a day's working. Duration effort—working—appears to have two dimensions, intensity and duration. We can measure its duration; we cannot measure its intensity. In fact, we can only determine the influence of intensity in a relative way and at certain strategic points. Distribution of working over the several adequate provisions for different future wants may be, and probably usually is, made largely in terms of duration, assuming average intensity.[32] Here we shall assume to start with, subject to modification later, that the order of priority of the future wants of equal futurity governs, since the intensity of each want determines its relative capacity to mobilize secondary energy. It would govern without other influence if the duration effort required for adequate provision of each were the same as for each other.[33] For, as we have noted before,[34] the memory of the sense of effort involved in the activity required to make adequate provision is conceived to oppose —be compared with—each future want. Since we have not yet come to consider the influences which cause differences in the duration of

time. The foregoing division between working (production) and leisure (consumption) seems to serve that purpose as well as any.

[32] There will be, of course, specially disagreeable and difficult tasks, as well as specially agreeable and easy ones. There will be many which have become so habitual that they require little effort. We cannot take account of these complexities. Moreover, though they may influence the distribution of working among future wants, they will not have much influence on the duration of working on the average day.

[33] This concerns what are called the "coefficients of production" which we shall deal with later.

[34] See p. 354, Supposition 14. This is an inherently necessary supposition, since it is quite obviously what most people are constantly doing. The magnitude of memories of the sense of effort seems to be governed chiefly by the duration of the effort and only occasionally by its variation from normal intensity.

effort required for the different adequate provisions, we shall disregard them here, as we did with our virtual orders of preference. Thus we shall assume, at this stage, that they all require the same duration of working and therefore that any future want whose capacity to arouse secondary energy is sufficient to induce this duration of effort of average intensity will be included, and all whose capacity is deficient for this will be excluded.

On the other hand, this question of sufficiency or deficiency will be determined at a single strategic point, or several of them, for the whole aggregate of the day's program. And that point (or those points), in turn, will be determined by the influences which supplement secondary energy, or make more effortful its generation, and those which oppose it. And this is true, even if we abstract all differences between the several tasks. Thus, even if we can legitimately, or do arbitrarily, ignore intensity of effort in different tasks and confine ourselves to its duration, in the matter of the distribution of the whole working-time over the various adequate provisions, we come back to intensity as the determining factor in limiting the working-day. The dimension "duration" alone may determine the distribution of time; but the dimension "intensity" is the critical factor in determining the aggregate duration to be distributed—that is, the initiation of the working-day, the occasions and extent of interruptions *en passant*, and its termination.

Our energetic scheme works out, then, in terms of three major factors: (1) the differing capacity of future wants to mobilize secondary energy and thus produce effortful activity or repress the primary energy behind effortless behavior; (2) the requirements for such secondary energy to initiate and maintain the activity, in view of supplements to it and of obstacles to its generation; (3) the requirements for such secondary energy to compete with and overcome primary energy. As to the first factor (1), we conceive an ordinal arrangement of future wants, in their order of priority, thus evidencing a gradually but steadily declining capacity to mobilize secondary energy. This arrangement is not temporal. Dominant wants are not necessarily provided for first; nor is the least potent want the last one covered in the day's program. So far as the program is concerned all wants are considered together in advance. So far as execution is concerned they come in any convenient order. This factor determines the potential rate of supply of secondary energy along its range. It may be looked at as the invitation to provision for future wants—the inducement to effort. The rate of demand for such secondary energy is represented by the two other factors.

The second factor (2) represents the average intensity of working effort required in the form of self-constraint—that is, the requirement of such energy for the activities, when it is neither supplemented nor detracted from. From this basic requirement there is to be deducted (2a) the contribution made by the playing element (auxiliary primary energy).[35] Ignoring the complexity in this factor by reason of the variation as between different tasks, we may assume a gradual decline in this contribution as the working-day proceeds, and, as a result, a rise in the secondary energy required. To this basic requirement there is to be added (2b) the increase of secondary energy necessitated by boredom or ennui. In so far as that is merely the loss of emotional "interest" it is wholly a reduction of the playing element (2a). But frequently maintenance of the volitional kind of conscious attention, not identical with the emotional, calls for increased secondary energy. This is particularly the case with routine and repetition which cannot be left to habit. Ennui is also likely to increase the demand as the working-day proceeds. To this basic requirement there is also to be added (2c) the increase of secondary energy needed to overcome the effects of fatigue. While, as noted before, fatigue is a present want, it does not supply primary energy and therefore does not compete with secondary.[36] Quite the contrary. It saps primary energy and therefore reduces the auxiliary (2a). It also increases the effort involved in the generation of secondary energy.[37] Fatigue follows a somewhat irregular but perfectly certain crescendo during the working-day, and therefore constitutes an inevitable increase in the demand for secondary energy as the day proceeds. At some point, if the working-day has not been ended for other reasons before that time, the requirement of secondary energy to overcome fatigue will always rise beyond the capacity of the marginal future want to mobilize it, and working will cease; the working-day will end and leisure, at least in the form of resting, will commence.

[35] Edgeworth wanted to treat this as negative fatigue or pain of work (see *133*, 66). But it is poor analysis to lump unlikes together. The playing element may exist even with fatigue or pain (e.g., athletics).
[36] Moreover, we must remember to include all the debits and credits of the alternative chosen on one side of the formula, and leave only those of the alternative rejected on the other. Fatigue is here a consequence of working, not an independent present want.
[37] For a more exact statement of this, see supposition 19, p. 357.

The third factor (3) represents the variable intensity of secondary energy required for self-restraint. It is measured by the intensity of primary energy which secondary energy is called upon to repress and succeeds in repressing.[38] In so far as primary energy is inhibited incidentally in the course of activity this factor may be regarded as latent. The element of self-restraint does not then appear. Nevertheless, it is probably even then potential.[39] When primary energy succeeds in penetrating to consciousness as emotion—as a present want —this factor becomes active, and specifically inhibitory secondary energy in the form of self-restraint is then required. The chief occasions when this is apt to occur are of three kinds: (3a) At the start, when the program is being planned and before activity has commenced, we conceive the preliminary conflict in consciousness to take place. Then the competition of present wants, at least those demanding playing, is at the full. If the program is to be initiated at all, sufficient secondary energy is then required to overcome this exhibition of primary energy. During the working-day there are times when other present wants recur (3b), either regularly, as hunger and thirst, or irregularly, as watching a circus parade.[40] Then, either active self-restraint is called for or, without it or in spite of it, there is a temporary interruption in the activity. In the latter event, working ceases as well, and there may be no self-restraint at the moment. Such occasions for self-restraint, or such interruptions, tend to occur the more readily at times when habit has reduced excitatory effort and hence its by-product of inhibition, when voluntary attention flags due to boredom or ennui and, in so far as that is different, when the supplementary play element is weak or missing. Under normal conditions the third

[38] There are, of course, no "coefficients of production" (see note 32, above) for leisure. Primary energy expresses itself only in the intensity of the prepotent present want. Nevertheless, we have to recognize that the processes of satisfying present wants require time.

[39] Once the decision is made—the conflict resolved—in favor of working, the force of the present wants that are in competition may be driven from consciousness. At least, we know, as a matter of observation, that when the course of activity has been begun it is usually completed, subject to interruptions and, at least sometimes, for the reason that it has then become impossible at once to go back and elect the rejected alternative —leisure.

[40] My use of this illustration here and in Chapter 6 is due to personal observation. My former business office was on the ground floor of a main street in a medium-sized city. When the annual circus parade turned up I always saw a hundred or more men and women, from the legal minimum up to the oldsters, rise from their desks and throng around the windows. When the parade had passed they seeped slowly back to work, with much conversation and laughter.

kind of occasion (3c) usually supervenes. If we were to ignore the influence of fatigue and other elements causing a rising requirement of intensity of self-constraint, there would always come a time when the competition of leisure exerted greater force than was available for further provision for future wants. That is due to the fact that, as we have said, "leisure is also the period when the result of working is enjoyed." There is no sense in future provision unless time is taken to consume it. That requires leisure. Thus, even in the absence of fatigue, the working-day will normally be terminated at some time for this reason. However, the actual energetic situation on this occasion is very complex. It may also occur that, in the absence of fatigue, or ignoring it, when provision has been completed for prior wants the next in order has insufficient capacity to provide the self-restraint necessary to overcome the competition of primary energy and thus to continue working. On the other hand, admitting fatigue, we have to recognize that it saps primary energy (and therefore the competition provided by present wants demanding activity) and also increases the demand for secondary energy. In this respect it affects the three elements of leisure differently. It diminishes the force of those present wants to be satisfied by playing, even to the point of eliminating them altogether. If fatigue is great, it may also diminish the force of those present wants to be satisfied by consuming. Thus the increase of fatigue reduces the competition of such present wants and reduces the requirement of secondary energy for self-restraint. The only element of leisure upon which fatigue has the opposite effect is resting. But resting is an inactivity. It is the satisfaction of the present want "fatigue," itself. That present want does not present itself as primary energy requiring self-restraint to repress it. Rather it presents itself as a loss of primary energy as well as a demand for increased self-constraint to continue activity in spite of it. For this reason fatigue and its satisfaction, resting, have been treated as an influence on the second factor in our energetic scheme. They do not belong with the third factor at all.[41]

[41] In terms of the usual analysis, the beginning of leisure is supposed to seem more inviting as the working-day proceeds. But this assumption may be based on either one of two reasons. The first involves a question of observation. As a matter of experience, when effort has caused great fatigue, the initial leisure is hardly enjoyable at all; consuming and playing become impossible; and rest only becomes pleasant after relaxation has taken place and the aches and pains have been washed away. On the other hand, as Pigou points out (325, 462), "physiology teaches that, after a certain period of work of given intensity, the body requires a certain interval of rest in order to return to its

What we infer is that, in this complex, under normal conditions fatigue is not permitted to rise to the point where it puts an end to the working-day of and by itself. Instead, and before it has risen to the level where it has much diminished the force of the present wants whose satisfaction is playing or consuming, either the force of the future want ordinally next to be provided for turns out to be insufficient to instigate the effort involved in further self-constraint—or self-restraint—or present wants have a way of rearing their heads as the day goes on so that neither incidental nor specific inhibition suffices to overcome them any longer. Something of this order seems to constitute the third occasion for self-restraint. When it arises, the capacity for self-restraint sooner or later becomes inadequate and therefore self-restraint ceases, because leisure is chosen. That ends the working-day.

Thus we see that, according to our scheme of energetics, there are two alternative interruptions to working whose effects are sufficiently lasting to put a stop to the working-day and start the consuming-day. The first is due to the insufficiency of self-constraint to counteract fatigue and maintain the effort. When that is the chief cause of the interruption then, in proportion to the degree of fatigue at the critical point, the consuming-day (or the earlier portions of it) will be given over to resting. Consuming as activity will be reduced and playing may well be eliminated entirely, since the drive to both is primary energy and fatigue has reduced that at the same rate it has increased the effort involved in generating secondary energy. The second alternative interruption is due to the insufficiency of self-restraint to counteract present wants other than fatigue and thus to maintain the working. This may be due to the lesser force of ordinally subordinate

initial state, and that this interval grows more rapidly than the period of work." Thus at least the necessary duration of resting, if not the initial satisfaction, increases as fatigue increases.

As to the use of leisure for consumption, J. M. Clark suggests that it is of little advantage until working has "provided for the necessities of physical existence and a reasonable stock of energy"—the latter presumably for working as well as playing (83, 364). And, on the other hand, Pigou argues, for the workers, that "every extra hour worked lessens the opportunity for enjoying whatever purchases their wages may enable them to make." These comments show clearly what we assert in the text, that the three uses of leisure, resting, playing, and consuming, do not respond in the same way in respect of the quantity of initial satisfaction procured by leisure, as its beginning is postponed, and that any analysis of the changes in the "first satisfaction" would be very complicated.

The other reason is a question of analysis. It may involve a failure to discriminate the elements of the alternative chosen from those of the alternative rejected, as described in the text. It is not true when the invitation is to rest. It is only true when the invitation is to play or consume.

future wants or it may be due to some sort of bobbing-up of present wants in general. When this is the chief cause, the consuming-day (or the earlier portions of it) will be given over, not to resting, but to consuming and playing. That may well continue until primary energy is sapped by fatigue as a result of activities that it has itself energized.

The ending of the working-day—and thus the major influence which fixes the quantity of working—as determined by either of these conjunctures omits one essential factor which we must now recognize though we are not yet ready to deal with it. We have assumed that the first factor, capacity to mobilize secondary energy, declines along the order of priority of future wants. Thus the measure of this capacity at any moment depends upon which future want is then dominant. Even if we ignore differences in the duration of working required for adequate provision for these several wants—treat them tentatively as the same—there remains the question how long each of these uniform periods must be. If adequate provision requires a long time for each, then after a certain number of hours the capacity for mobilizing secondary energy would still stand at a higher level than it would if only a short time were required. The pattern of requirements for secondary energy remaining the same, the working-day will then tend to be of longer duration the longer the time required for each adequate provision. But this extension will only result from the net effect, not the gross effect; for the longer the working-day the greater the requirements for secondary energy in one form or the other.

Such a physiologically determined working-day, or limitation on working, is only the underlying system of causation. It may well be operative only when the individual himself decides the question, as of course he must do in a direct economy. Even then we must recognize the existence of a diurnal rhythm among the mature [42] which tends to limit the working-day to the daylight hours. This has become reinforced by something of a convention. Also we must note that this scheme represents a highly evolved combination of energizers whose full force only appears in economies which have passed out of the hand-to-mouth stage altogether and among individuals who have attained a highly effective mnemonic-volitional system. In many economies observable today which approach the abstraction, a direct econ-

[42] See Appendix II.

omy, the matter of the working-day is at a very undeveloped level. On the other hand, in an indirect economy this influence is only one of those governing the length of the working-day and is even by itself apt to be effective only as a representation of the average of individual limits. The more highly organized an indirect economy becomes, the more widely spread becomes a conventional or even legal working-day which is not derived from this individualist formula, though it is apt to reflect a general or average conformity to it. Then the duration may be imposed without regard to the individual; or it may be conventionalized as a rough approximation to the average of individual limits; or, finally, it may be fixed by law, though, then, it is usually fixed only as to the maximum that can be imposed, not as to the minimum that will be required. However, under the conditions we are examining in this study, when these are fully developed and self-dependent, the physiological scheme probably represents not only the experience of a working-day but also the planned program for it. This because the latter is wholly based on the former and therefore doubtless comes rather faithfully to duplicate it. While this energetic scheme is an elaborate one, it nevertheless appears to represent reality. All we are really saying is that, while working, the capacity for effort always exceeds the requirements, and that temporary or final cessation is always due either to a decline in capacity below these requirements or to a rise of one or the other requirement which lifts the sum of them above capacity. That sounds reasonable.[43]

Having now worked out this scheme in terms derived from our study in Chapter 6—namely, in terms of a set of forces—future wants as mnemonic-volitional phenomena, opposed by the resistance of the sense of effort in its two aspects, self-constraint and self-restraint—we shall henceforth find it more usable if we rearrange it, or translate these same factors into other terms, in order to bring into sharper relief the facts of choice. On the one side we range the factors concerned with the alternative elected; on the other, the factors concerned with the alternative rejected. When working is going on, leisure is not being enjoyed; when leisure commences, working has stopped. These are mutually exclusive alternatives. Moreover, working is effortful be-

[43] It does not seem necessary to review here the correspondence between this scheme of the limitation of working and the scheme as to the limitations on effort (other than the influence of futurity) which we worked out in Chapter 6. While stated in different terms, this scheme is derived from the earlier one. The reader can check the correspondences for himself.

havior; leisure is effortless behavior. When working is going on, there is a "real cost" because working is effortful; [44] there is also a "sacrifice" because the costless (effortless) alternative has been rejected.[45] Hitherto, we have, in a sense, included in one rubric, effort, both the self-constraint which makes working effortful and the self-restraint which is necessitated by the competition of the costless alternative. Here-

[44] We are using this common economic expression, "real cost," in its usual precise sense. That will be made clear by enclosing it in quotation marks. It is the quantity of effort expended or required per unit of product. As such, it does not duplicate but only complements the rest of our set of technical terms for the magnitudes involved, as will appear in due course.

"Labour was the first price" (Adam Smith, *381*, I, 32) in the sense that, in a direct economy, working is what is given—and, in a day-to-day economy, all that is given —in order to get. Walras thought this theory—perhaps the original form of the so-called "labor theory of value"—had not been effectively refuted, and undertook to do it himself (*420*, 165 ff.). He did not succeed, because what he was shooting at was a straw man. To say that the "real cost" of a product—the "price" in that sense—is the effort (both kinds) required to produce it, is not to say that its "value" arises from or is conferred by this effort. Such statements (Marx, for instance) were merely misunderstandings of this theory. Its "value" arises from, or is conferred by, its usefulness in satisfying wants; and that in turn is what warrants its cost, the effort which must be expended in order to get it. The fact that this cost has come, institutionally, to be expressed in money does not alter the situation. It merely makes it necessary to distinguish the true cost as the "real cost." Marx's whole theory, by which he treats the part of the "real cost" arising from working and the whole "value" as identical, and uses the term "value" to cover both, is, of course, wholly erroneous and a gross piece of muddy thinking. Neither does the fact that money "value" tends to settle around money cost prove that money cost and money "value" are identical, nor that money "value" is determined by money cost. But that does make it necessary for us to distinguish subjective value from money value. For, while the latter cannot rise higher than the former, the former is usually above the latter. This bit of heterodoxy will be developed in our final synthesis.

[45] We are not using this term, "sacrifice," in quite its usual economic sense. To us the sacrifice is not any rejected course of action, as it is in its most familiar use (opportunity cost), but only the rejected objectives or reactions of competing present wants.

As we shall point out later (Chapter 12) the theory of opportunity costs, while it considers chiefly alternatives both of which involve effort, assumes the effort as given. Actually the basic formula for the inducement to effort must be conceived as Future Want — Effort > Sacrifice. That is, when the sacrifice consists of effortless behavior it has no minus expression. Therefore, in substance, Future Want > Effort + Sacrifice.

In effect, what we are saying is that the competition between working and leisure— between the behavior produced by future wants and that produced by present wants —is not merely one between future and present wants, nor like that among present wants only. Instead, it is also a competition between impulsive effortless activities or inactivities and volitional or effortful activities. Among present wants both the winner and the loser (the sacrifice in the sense of opportunity cost) are costless alternatives. Among future wants both the winner and the loser (again the sacrifice in the sense of opportunity cost) are costful alternatives. But the basic competition that regulates the quantity of working and therefore of production is the competition between future and present wants. To the extent that working occurs it is a victory of a costful alternative over a costless one.

after, we wish to include, as working effort and therefore as "real cost" in working, only the secondary energy expended in the thinking and doing which we call working; and we wish to distinguish from that altogether, as sacrifice, either the primary energy which opposes the working or the secondary energy required to prevent it from doing so.

There are three good reasons for this rearrangement. The first is that there is no objective basis whatever for conceiving the extent of self-restraint required. On the other hand, it is easy to conceive leisure objectively. Even if we cannot measure the intensity of present wants, we at least know what they are and how forceful they can be. We know that, at the start and all during the working-day, the alternative, leisure, is open. Potentially, at least, these forceful present wants are continual competitors and must be overcome if they are to remain the rejected alternative. Yet it may be that, except at the start and when they produce interruptions, these primary energizers are inhibited entirely incidentally—that is, the inhibition is a by-product of the excitation we are calling self-constraint. To that extent no extra effort is required for self-restraint. Nevertheless, these present wants are always there as competitors. So, to do full justice to them as competitors, it is better to separate out the sacrifice—the rejected alternative—and to assume that it is always as great as the intensity of the present wants that are being curbed. The only thing we have to be careful about is not to count this form of resistance twice, once as the competing but rejected alternative, and again as the effort of self-restraint involved in the elected alternative.

The second reason for separating out effort as self-constraint, and treating that as the only "real cost" of working, is that only that is associated with the activities which produce future provision. The need for self-restraint is wholly a handicap on such activities. True, it may make them more effortful; it may even make them longer than would otherwise be necessary. But the added effortfulness, or the added time required, do not increase the future provision. They represent lost energy.

Finally, this rearrangement emphasizes the fact that a choice *is* made; that it is usually a continuing rather than a vacillating choice, except for normal interruptions; and that therefore, for rather large blocks of time, the force behind the elected alternative, after deduction of the resistance presented by working, must exceed the force behind the rejected alternative. That is, in our revised terminology, Future Wants — Working as Effort > Sacrifice.

It is not easy to depict this complex scheme in a diagram. Nevertheless, we will attempt a rough portrayal.[46] In Fig. 24 the magnitude (intensity) of each successive hour of required working effort—the second factor—is shown by the altitude of the broken curve cd or cd_1 above the base ab. At the start this is ca. After the first hour, with the

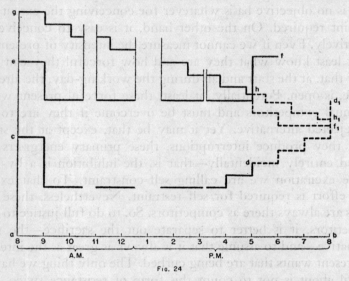

Fig. 24

aid of habit or of the element of playing, this requirement declines.[47] At the end of the eighth hour it begins to rise due to fatigue. By the end of the ninth hour it has risen to d. There, if the working-day is to be ended by a bobbing-up of present wants at 5 P.M., working

[46] This particular diagram does not pretend to be typical of the process; it is merely a possible sample.

[47] It is important to note that the playing element in working is a deduction from the effort requirement of working. It does not belong with its fellow present wants upon the sacrifice side. Working and its accompaniment of playing is what is done (the alternative chosen); sacrifice is what is not done (the alternative rejected). It appears to me that, at times, constructions dealing with opportunity cost do not keep this distinction clearly in mind.

It is of course possible that activities instigated by future wants may, at times, have sufficient emotional drive to eliminate the need of effort. Then working becomes playing and our curve cd should drop to the base ab, carrying the curve ef down with it by the same decline.

We have not tried to include the effect of boredom or ennui. This would cause the curve cd to rise somewhat and, to maintain the same differential, would affect the curve ef by the same amount.

effort will cease at d. If not, accruing fatigue will cause the require-ment to continue to rise until, at d_1 or 8 P.M., the working-day is ended by excessive fatigue.

The magnitudes of present wants requiring activity measure the sacrifice. These magnitudes—the third factor—are shown for each successive hour, or part, by the altitude of the broken curve, ef, or ef_1, above the curve cd or cd_1. Thus the altitude of ef, or ef_1, above the base is the sum of effort proper plus sacrifice, measured in terms of intensity. We are here treating the magnitude of sacrifice as if it continued the same, except for the temporary interruptions, whether active, as at the start, or latent. In other words, we are not attempt-ing to represent its actual magnitude except at the several strategic points. During the three temporary interruptions—from 10:30 to 11:00 A.M., from 12:30 to 1:30 P.M. and for a few minutes after 3 P.M.— present wants exceed the capacity for self-restraint. During those periods, then, there is no working effort. This is shown by gaps in the curve cd. If the working-day is to be ended by a bobbing-up of present wants at 5 P.M., it is because the curve rises to f, in spite of the dimin-ishing effect upon it of the first hour of accrued fatigue. If it is not to be so ended, the effect of present wants generating primary energy continues to shrink more rapidly, until at f_1 it is very slight. But at f_1 the rise of the requirement for working effort to d_1, on account of fatigue, puts a stop to the working-day, even if, because of the diminu-tion of primary energy, leisure will for a time take the form only of resting, not of playing or consuming—that is, even if, by that time, the sacrifice and its corresponding requirement of self-restraint have become very small.

The capacity of future wants to generate secondary energy—the first factor—is shown as a section of the order of priority on the broken curve gh or gh_1. Each provision is treated as if it required one hour's working. If a half-hour's working sufficed, the curve would be steeper; if two hours' working were necessary, the curve would be less steep. When the foregoing temporary interruptions occur, the lost time on any provision has only been deferred and is made up after resumption. The decline of capacity for effort from g to h or h_1 is not a temporal order; it is entirely ordinal. Nevertheless, so far as the program is concerned, at each critical point this capacity will be measured by the relative force of the particular want for which, after that quantity of working has been performed, provision is to be included or excluded by adding or not adding an increment of working.[48] If the working-day is to be ended by a bobbing-up of present wants at 5 P.M., it is because the intensity of effort plus sacrifice at f becomes greater than the capacity for effort of the least future want in the series gh at h.[49] If not, the working-day ends at 8 P.M. because, by reason of the increase of fatigue and in spite of the decrease of sacrifice, the intensity of effort plus sacrifice, rises to d_1 which is greater than the capacity for effort of the least future want in the series gh_1 at h_1.[50]

It is evident that the conjunctures at h or at h_1 have nothing to do with determining the direction in which the working has been applied prior to that point, except that they make certain that such working will, at no time during the working period, be applied to any provision for a future want which has a capacity to generate effort less than the altitude at h or at h_1.[51] The allocation of these total working hours, within that limit, to provision for different future wants would be wholly determined, so far as we can see at the present stage of our analysis, by the order of priority of wants. The only effect of the conjuncture at h or h_1 is to limit the duration of the working; that is, the total number of working hours. It is at once evident that

[48] That is, we are adding to the unreal assumption that all provisions require the same working-time, the real assumption that there is no tendency (or almost none) to apply the most effortful hours to the most important wants and the least effortful to the least important. If anything, the opposite would usually be the case (except in emergencies), since there might be a tendency to attend to the most important matters first.

[49] If what we have called the bobbing-up of present wants toward the end of the working-day is in reality a reasoned conclusion that the time has arrived to enjoy the fruits of working, as suggested under our third occasion for self-restraint above, then it would have to be construed, in the diagram, as a sharp drop in curve gh after h, rather than as a sharp rise in curve ef at f, as shown.

[50] As noted before, the level of h or h_1 is dependent on the time required for each provision, being higher if that time is long and lower if that time is short. Thus this scheme is not definitive until the determinants of duration of working per adequate provision have been developed and inserted in it.

[51] As noted before, a distaste might exist for some special forms of working which were only part of the day's program. But, while this would change the shape of our curve cd at some point, it would have no effect on the result unless it were postponed till the end of the working-day and thus caused it to be terminated sooner than otherwise.

In other words, the two elements which oppose provision for future wants—effort and sacrifice—are summated, and it is reasonable to assume that their sum is greatest toward the end of the day, except for temporary interruptions; so that becomes the crucial point. If distaste exists for the form of work which constitutes the whole day's program, then, of course, the curve of effort, cd, is higher throughout. This is, I think, a preferable treatment to that of Fisher (*142, 172*), who seems to assume that the driving force can be less than the resistance (capacity less than requirement). Under those conditions, in a direct economy, working of that kind would not have taken place.

this limitation on working hours turns out to be one of the factors constituting that entity which we have previously dealt with as "the limited capacity to provide means." [52] This analysis shows that, so far as this factor is concerned, it is not a limitation of capacity at all.[53] It is rather a point at which, in the process of choice (conflict in consciousness), the mnemonic-volitional system (future wants) is faced with a sense of effort, required for self-constraint (working) or self-restraint (sacrifice) or both, that overbalances it (exceeds its capacity), so that thereafter the choice will naturally favor not working.[54] Or, if the choice is not made during actual experience but in terms of memories which are a result of that and with reference to a planned program, the limitation on working will be set in advance as the conclusion of that program.

At this point we require some clarification of the notion of capacity and of this limitation upon it. The net number of hours included in the working-day, after deducting time out for the temporary interruptions, represents the total working effort available during that day for allocation among provisions of means for future wants. Thus, in respect of this factor, that fixes the limitation. But capacity is usually measured in terms of product, and only in those terms can it be related to number of wants provided for. Therefore, capacity itself depends upon another factor—i.e., the relation between quantity of working and quantity of product—a factor to which we are devoting a large portion of Part III. In turn, as noted above, that relation indirectly reacts upon the length of the working-day in some degree.[55]

[52] As we proceed through Parts II and III we will develop the other two factors limiting capacity. Together they determine the quantity of means that can be produced within the time set by this factor—the limitation of working—and only influence this factor indirectly by reason of the greater or less capacity to mobilize secondary energy on the part of the future wants that come ordinally toward the end of the program.

[53] Walras, and the scarcity school in general, in order to fit working (*travail*) into their scheme, make it valuable because it is "limited in quantity," and therefore "rare" (*420, 165*). In that kind of analysis a man's wife is valuable to him because he chooses to have only one, and that choice gives her the very highest degree of rarity—uniqueness.

In order to enjoy the satisfactions the means for which we work to obtain, it is necessary, as we have already noted, first to stop working. The limitation of quantity of working is therefore, in part, due to the fact that it is generally impossible to produce and consume at the same time. Is this unfortunate lack of ambidextrousness a source of the value of working?

[54] On the principle of "I could not love thee, dear, so much." This points, I think, to the impossibility of using the notion of "seller's reserve" as one of the competing satisfactions in the one-sided system of marginal utility analysis; cf. Wicksteed particularly, but also Walras. [55] See note 52, above.

Also we must remember that capacity covers provision for future wants only. This because, in a developed economy past the hand-to-mouth stage, precurrent reactions directed by present wants, if they procure means, do so only for direct consumption, as we have called it; and, if they do not, they are construed as playing. Thus, from the standpoint of the wants, such means are not provided—they are found or utilized on the spot; and, from the standpoint of the activities, procuring the means does not involve working. For this reason capacity itself does not cover such means and its limitation in respect of the working factor is not affected by such occupations, except through their competition.

At this stage in our analysis we are not ready to examine the way in which the global total of working, so determined, is allocated among the various kinds of means. The only determinant we have so far developed is the order of priority as expressed in the virtual order of preference. And that is wholly tentative, as yet. But one conclusion is already clear. Within the edge or margin of this quantity of working, by reason of the fact that gh or gh_1, the curve representing capacity for effort, and ef or ef_1, that representing the sum of the effort and sacrifice, do not converge until h or h_1, there is left a more or less wide gap between them prior to one of those points; therefore, until one of these points is reached, there must have existed a considerable unused capacity for effort.[56] If this were the only kind of effort, or where this is the only kind of effort actually expended—i.e., where working is for the following consuming-day only—this gap would represent the analogue in a direct economy of what has been called the "consumer's surplus." [57] For two reasons we are not prepared to accept this interpretation; though neither are we in a position to deny it. In the first place, that would require the identification of this unused capacity as a differential between "satisfaction" and "dissatisfaction." In turn, that

[56] We recall that, in Chapter 6, we supposed the capacity for effort to be proportionate to the intensity of the future want—though much greater—but that only the effort required, up to this point, is actually generated.
[57] Fisher wants to call this surplus "net income" (*142*, 171). If we were to accept the notion that the essential factor is this surplus—the net of "satisfactions" over "dissatisfactions" or the gross of alternative "satisfactions" which involve no "dissatisfactions"—we would be compelled, as Pigou points out (*325*, 467), to substitute for the classical ideal of maximization of production the actual ideal of maximization of this surplus. He calls attention (*ibid.*, 85) to the fact that any extension of work beyond the point where such a surplus exists—his "satisfactions in excess of dissatisfactions"—lessens "economic welfare." To that, of course, we can subscribe even on our own interpretation of the facts. But such a contingency would be impossible in a direct economy. It is only possible when the working-day is imposed.

would require the identification of our capacity for effort with "satisfaction." But future wants, which provide this capacity, do not include satisfaction, since they are defined as wants which only generate behavior stopping short of consummatory reactions. Moreover, the energizing of the future want itself is weak; its chief source of energy is the volitional effort that it can mobilize. But there is no "satisfaction" in volitional effort. Quite the contrary. It is itself effortful, and is therefore, if it can be described in these terms, a "dissatisfaction." Thus we have no reason for accepting this treatment of the curve gh as one representing "satisfaction," and some reason for confining ourselves to our own interpretation of its meaning. In the second place, our scheme requires no such motive as the supposed "maximization of the consumer's surplus." In Chapter 6 we elaborated our hypothesis partly upon the evidence that effortful behavior (unlike effortless behavior) is economized (minimized) on its own account. If so, it is not necessary to suppose that the gap is produced for its own sake. Instead it seems to be purely incidental—a by-product of the fact that the least possible effort is always used, and that only when the least possible effort becomes greater than the capacity for it, does it cease to be made (i.e., the gap closes). We read the gap to represent an economizing of effort. As such it is not net "satisfaction," nor even "satisfaction" at all. In the vague terms of this hedonistic psychology, it is merely a lessening of "dissatisfaction." [58] We conclude that we can only construe the gap between these curves, so long as it exists, to be the unplanned and perhaps unconsidered result of the motive of minimizing effort, not the result of the "maximizing of the consumer's surplus."

In connection with this question we must reiterate that we do not suppose that comparisons are made between the effort involved in a specific period of working during the day and any expected satisfaction to be derived from the particular means upon which that working happens to be expended, so that the order of allocation of working is from the greatest difference to the smallest difference between these two magnitudes. Instead, we suppose—tentatively at this stage of our investigation—that the ordinal, though not the temporal, order of allocation of working is according to the order of priority of wants, and that the only points at which the issue arises is at the points of con-

[58] Mathematically speaking, of course, a diminution of the minus factor in an equation has the same effect as an increase in the plus factor. But mathematics and observational science are two very different matters.

vergence—temporary interruptions during the day and the final one at the end. Because of this ordinal arrangement, at least for the planning of programs, it is probable that the most effortful hour will always be compared with the provision back of which is the least capacity for effort, and that this pair will provide the final issue. The rest of the time we assume that working merely does not require the full intensity of effort that could be mobilized if it were needed.

This analysis demonstrates the fact that complete provision for all future wants, even for the following consuming-day only, is merely a conceptual limit. It makes it evident that, with the competition of leisure, all these wants could not be provided for unless both of the following conditions were met: (1) It would be necessary that the final quantity of means necessary for an adequate provision for the most subordinate future want included would still afford greater prospective usefulness, or significance, than the satisfaction of the first present want to be given the benefit of leisure. (2) Or it would be necessary that all wants requiring working for their provision could be provided for in a neutral phase of working-time during which working was playing—i.e., during the period when the curve of working effort practically coincides with its base ab in Fig. 24.[59] Obviously the first of these conditions could never subsist if wants were subject to the decline of intensity during a single satisfaction which is assumed by two of the three hypotheses as to the virtual order of preference which we developed in the previous chapter, if this decline were reflected in the potency of the future want as well. For, on that assumption, the final satisfaction would be very small.[60] Nor would it be probable under our own hypothesis; for then it would be necessary that the least future want, or segment, to be satisfied by means requiring effort was of greater intensity than the want for leisure. But this, as well as the alternative of these necessary conditions (2) is inconsistent with our supposition that the order of priority of wants extends indefinitely; for, obviously, this phase of working can hardly be supposed also to extend indefinitely. Therefore, under any of the several possibilities as to the virtual order of preference in providing for future wants, it must be supposed that the choice of the alternative, leisure, will put a stop

[59] See note 47, above.
[60] Either because the remaining intensity, toward the end, was very small, or because the diminishing rate of pleasure (or diminishing rate of reduction of intensity) had arrived at the point where a very small quantity of pleasure would be derived.

to the making of provision for such wants as can only be provided for by working long before they are all satiated.[61]

C. WORKING IN QUANTITATIVE TERMS

1. THE THREE ASPECTS OF WORKING AND THEIR RESPECTIVE MAGNITUDES

In the foregoing we have succeeded in differentiating two of the three aspects of working. But the first and foremost aspect—the *sine qua non*—though implicit in what we have been saying, has not yet been differentiated, defined, and described. This first aspect is the *effect* of working. That is a quantitative relation between the working and the providing of means toward which it is directed. We then treat as the second aspect of working the effort involved. And this has no direct quantitative bearing on the effect.[1] It is merely one of the factors determining the duration of working that will be performed per worker per day—in accordance with the foregoing analysis.[2] That leaves, as the third aspect of working, the leisure sacrificed. This, too, has no bearing on the effect. Again it is merely another of the factors already discussed that determine the duration of working. The first aspect, effect, is impersonal and non-psychological. It is an almost technical relationship of "cause and effect," which we shall call "contribution." The second aspect is a personal and psychological one. It is that which makes of working what we are calling a "real cost." The third aspect is also personal and psychological. It is the alternative, leisure, which must be forgone while working. It is this which makes

---

[61] Cassel, the arch-exponent of scarcity theory, regards wants as unlimited. But activities are "economic" only when "conducted under the condition that the possible satisfaction of wants is limited" (74, 7). This accords approximately with Walras (420, 22 and elsewhere). Scarcity theory arises from treating means as the ultimate factor and not going behind them to the expenditure of effort and the sacrifice of leisure by which most of them must be obtained. When that is done the limitation is seen to be no more due to scarcity than it is when the satisfaction of any want is preferred to that of another. If I prefer loafing to working my shortage in the results of working is not due to scarcity.

[1] Effort relates to working not to its effect. Working may involve toil or travail, pain or weariness, force or energy. The effect has no more to do with these than has mass, length, or time. Nevertheless, since the quantity of working performed over a period of time will be stated as work, according to our system of magnitudes, the magnitude of effort involved in working over a period of time becomes related, in this indirect fashion and in what might be a wholly irregular ratio, to the magnitude of work.

[2] And yet Jevons considered this, as "pain," to be "the all-important element in Economics" (224, 204). How one-sided!

of working a sacrifice. The scientific treatment of economic data requires that these three aspects of working be kept as separate in analysis
as they are in fact, for frequently only one of the three has any bearing on a particular issue.

These three aspects of working are also separate and independent
as magnitudes. As between different persons the effect per hour "at
work" may vary widely. But this magnitude is more or less objectively
measurable and can therefore conceivably be reduced to terms of a
standard unit. Conversely, the duration of working, and therefore
the quantity of effort in terms of its dimension, duration, in order to
produce the same effect, will vary in the opposite direction. As between different persons the intensity of effort involved in working
may also vary widely. So too may the sacrifice. Moreover, for the same
person at different times the effect per hour, and therefore the hours
required for a certain quantity of effect, may differ; the intensity of
effort of his working may vary widely; and it is quite possible that
the sacrifice may do so as well. Nevertheless, these last two are not
objectively measurable. As a result there is no uniformity in the ratio,
effect:effort:sacrifice, between different persons or with the same
person at different times.[3] We note that one man seems to be making
harder "work" of a job than another; even that he tires more quickly;
that this varies with each at different times; and that the indolent obviously value leisure more highly than do the industrious. But the
only definite bearing of these variations in respect of the latter two
aspects is on the determination of the working-day, when this depends
on choice. And in this determination the effectiveness of the working—
the aspect of its effect—also enters, as we have seen. For the greater
the effect, other things being equal, the greater the quantity of provision to be procured by a certain amount of working-time. Through
this connection we begin to introduce at the thin end of the wedge
what will prove, as we develop it, to be the missing and essential factor
in determining the duration of working.

Bearing these considerations in mind we shall have to use these magnitudes in our further analysis in a careful way. In the aspect of contri-

[3] Edgeworth (*133*, 33) notes the "familiar circumstance" that "the *disutility* of (common) labour (labour subjectively estimated) does not increase in proportion to *work
done* (labour objectively estimated)." We take no stock in the unit of pain or sacrifice
which Cairnes seems to have developed from Adam Smith. Nevertheless, we may make
a rough comparison by deductive methods. The voluntary working of those who have
incomes derived without working, which is not always diminished even by the imposition of discipline, shows that, to some, the effort and sacrifice are less than to others.

bution to (effect on) produced means we shall undertake to develop working as a measurable magnitude capable of being standardized in a direct economy in terms of uniform objective units of effect produced per hour. In the aspect of "real cost"—that is, as one of the two forms which human effort takes in economic activity—we shall treat working as a magnitude which, in its dimension "duration" is the reciprocal of that—namely as the number of hours of working required to produce a certain quantity of effect—but, on the other hand, one which, in its dimension "intensity" cannot be stated in terms of uniform objective units, but which is, nevertheless, at each moment and for each individual, of some definite size which, at critical points, plays a part in determining the quantity of working.[4] And since, for each person, the marginal unit of working, which involves the greatest intensity of effort, must be chargeable indiscriminately against any and all of the provisions made during the working-day, we must conceive each of his units of working as if it involved this greatest intensity, though recognizing at the same time that, during the day, considerably less than his capacity for effort may have been utilized.[5] Because this magnitude, working effort, has the dimension "duration" and because we are thus conceiving the dimension "intensity" as if it were throughout at its critical level, we may conventionally treat the magnitude "working effort" as if it varied only in the dimension of time. And this permits us to say that the magnitude of working conducted over a period of time involves also a proportionate magnitude of effort which represents the "real cost" aspect of that work. Having arrived at that convention, which assimilates the magnitude of the first two aspects of working, we might as well go the rest of the way so far as the magnitude "real cost" is concerned. While recognizing that, for a given quantity of effect, the duration of working by one person may differ from that by another, or by himself at other times, we shall adopt the notion of a standard effect per hour of working. This alters nothing in dealing with a direct economy. But it will prove a convenient simplification

[4] This statement glozes over a difficulty which, fortunately, we do not need even to face. As between two persons, and perhaps as between two different times or conditions for one person, we do not know whether it is the effort involved in a given task which differs, or whether the effort involved is the same and only the capacity for effort differs. Actually, that question is impossible to answer.

[5] Hobson's view that working which is enjoyed—playing—is not a "real cost" (*Law of Three Rents*) is tenable. All we are saying is that, for analytical purposes, since the mass of available working always involves a mass of effort (even if not evenly distributed) and since effort is a "real cost," it is necessary to treat all working as a "real cost."

in dealing with an indirect economy. Thus "real cost" in this kind of effort becomes the number of standard hours of working required per unit of produced means.[6] In the aspect of sacrifice we shall treat working in the same terms in which we treat the intensity of wants. That is, we shall regard the sacrifice per period of working to be equal to the aggregate intensity of the several present wants that might have been satisfied by leisure during an equal period. But, though this serves conceptually, it gives a speciously quantitative impression. For the intensities of present wants can probably not be summed except in the roughest way.[7] Therefore, the sacrifice involved in any quantity of working will have to be treated as an area which is immeasurable (merely below the critical level) up to some definite boundary beyond which critical point the alternative, leisure, is chosen. At that point the magnitude only becomes measurable in the sense that we know that, there, leisure plus effort equals capacity to generate effort. That is, it then becomes comparable in terms of more or less, or of equality. Even at that point we cannot think of it in terms of "size," since the fact that the left side of the equation is then greater than the right may be due to an increase in either of its two expressions just as well as to a decrease in that of the right side.[8]

[6] Or, stated in the original psychological terms, we recognize that effortful activity varies in the intensity of the accompanying sense of effort. But, since we cannot determine the magnitude in this dimension upon a quantitative basis, except at certain critical points, we are converting the term effort to the use of expressing the magnitude in terms of its dimension duration, only. Thus a quantity of effort, as working, will stand for the duration of the effortful behavior, not for the magnitude of the attribute that makes it effortful.

[7] This was our conclusion in Part I. Nevertheless, something of the kind obviously takes place when a "day off" is evaluated. For then, though the leisure of that day, at the time the program is decided upon, may consist as yet of future wants only—at least non-present ones—the invitation to leisure is presented by a compound of several wants, not by a single prepotent present want.

[8] This system does not fit in with Davenport's—to me entirely unsatisfactory—notion of opportunity costs. He himself admitted (*107*, 61) his questionable use of the term "cost." We are restricting the term "sacrifice" to the alternative of working—i.e., not working—since our order of preference takes the place of the "sacrifice" of alternative product. Nevertheless, that restriction makes no difference when we come to dealing with the defect in the notion of opportunity cost. We limit the term "sacrifice" to the designation of the opportunity open but forgone, or the best extra-marginal alternative —in our case, leisure. And we reserve the term "cost" for something that is not forgone, but is actually, on the contrary, the necessary concomitant of (the disadvantage inherent in) the alternative opportunity which is chosen. Starting with this more realistic view, the cost of any satisfaction remains throughout the effort necessary to attain it, and cannot, by hook or crook, be construed as some other alternative which is forgone—not even the effect of an alternative application of the effort. From Davenport's

The only direct relation between working and the satisfying of wants is via the effect of the working. Since it is this relation which we are particularly engaged in studying we must always measure working, as a magnitude, in terms of effect; that is, we must state it in its objective terms. It is only through this objective relation that the subjective comparisons can be made between the memories of the effort involved and the future wants to be provided for, or between these two, when fortified by volition, and the force of the present wants that can be satisfied without working (leisure—the sacrifice). In turn, the only influence of these indirect subjective comparisons is to set a limit to the duration of working, or to eliminate provision for those wants as to which the magnitude of the effort involved in the working (duration) exceeds the magnitude of the future want (both as memories). In connection with our combined formula, future wants-effortful behavior providing means-present wants-effortless behavior using provided means-satisfactions, then, working effort will always be treated as a magnitude in terms of its objective aspect, effect, and its other aspects will remain, for the most part, qualitative connotations, which we recognize to be present in a greater or less degree.[9]

---

viewpoint, and others', what is expended to gain satisfactions—effort—becomes a costless and given mass (or an automatic flow) so that the only "cost" of the alternative chosen is the alternative not chosen. As an analytic implement for dealing with economic energetics that is hopeless, because it omits one of the vital factors. It is not the alternative sacrificed that results in economic product. Only effort results in product. For the complete statement of our rebuttal of this view, see Chapter 12.

[9] This is essential in the treatment of both direct and indirect economies. We shall see, in the last chapter of Part III, how essential it is for the direct; and no one has stated more explicitly than Hicks—nor more nearly in terms of our own analysis—how essential it is for the indirect. He says (194, 90): "It is the actual service [effect] performed by the labourer which is bought and sold, not the sacrifice he endures in order to perform that service, or the effort he expends in doing it."

Intra-marginal effort and sacrifice of the individual have no influence on working except to make of it something which must be induced. In the direct economy the difference between quantities of effort and sacrifice within the margin and at the margin is merged in the general differential between requirements of effort (plus sacrifice) and capacity for effort; in the indirect economy this special surplus might theoretically be distinguished; but, since it would remain to the worker, instead of going to the consumer, it would not appear in the general system of economic relationships which we study. As a matter of fact both surpluses are wholly imaginary, and are the results of an analytical scheme, not of observation. Both should be construed as economies of will-power and not in crude hedonistic terms. We do not appreciate reduced requirements of effort as if they were "pleasure" or "satisfaction" or what not. The relation thereto is wholly indirect; reductions in the requirements of effort per unit of product may enable more "satisfactions," but only because it permits more provisions for the same quantity of working.

2. TERMINOLOGY AND DIMENSIONS

The common economic term for this type of effort has been "labor." This term will not serve our purpose. In the first place it has been spoiled, even in its technical use, because it has been applied indiscriminately to the persons (laborers) who make the effort and to the effort itself. Used in the phrase "land, labor and capital," it obviously stands with physical objects for a class of persons—and often a limited class at that.[10] In the second place, we shall find it easier to attach special technical senses to, and for this purpose to vary the forms of, that other equally familiar word which we have been casually using up to this point. Therefore, for this kind of effort, in the objective aspect of its contribution with which we shall be chiefly concerned as we proceed, let us adopt the form "working," as the nearest approach in English to a verbal noun,[11] the better to indicate that we mean by it the dynamic process of expending this kind of effort and producing this kind of effect; the form "work" to indicate the *effect* of this kind of effort;[12] and the form "worker" to cover any person

[10] Thus the term has acquired the sense of one kind of working only (largely physical) and that by far the less contributive kind.

[11] The name of an action; the *nomen actionis* of the grammarians.

[12] This is no fine-spun analytical distinction. It lies at the very foundation of economic life. Without it the management of economic enterprise in a modern economy would be operating entirely in the dark. As every employer knows, there is no necessary quantitative relation between working time and effect produced or even the force delivered. Therefore we will have to reduce this variable to terms of a constant, a standard unit of work and a standard rate of working.

Engels, in an editor's addition to note 1, Vol. I, p. 14, of Marx's *Capital* (294) makes the distinction between "work" and "labour." To him the first means the same as it does to us; but the second is our "working," though particularly in the aspect of sacrifice. Marx himself made the distinction clear, if more metaphysical. He says (*ibid.*, I, 170), "While the labourer is at work, his labour constantly undergoes a transformation: from being motion, it becomes an object without motion; from being the labourer working, it becomes the thing produced" (not quite that; rather the effect produced).

In order to make this necessary distinction clear we must examine the nature of the process, working. Since it is harder to visualize the effect of mental working, we will take as an example the application of physical force. The effect of human force may be to change the form or location of certain objects. This change may result in making the objects useful—or more useful. But in practice no one of these succeeding steps necessarily follows upon the preceding one, and rarely in any two series are the quantitative relations identical. Moreover, the measurement at each step is according to a different scale from that of the others. Hardly any two men produce the same effect with the same force or effort. Hardly any two equal effects embody exactly the same usefulness, if the material is destined for different products, or if, for the same product, the effect is applied at different stages, or is applied by different techniques, or under different natural conditions. The practical task of organizing and operating production finds its chief difficulties in these three unruly and undependable sequences. And it is these which undermine any "labor theory of value" in its crude form, because that treats the conversion of working into "value" as direct, automatic, and quantitatively exact.

who performs this type of effort. The first and the last of these forms are clear without further explanation; the second is not. "Work" is often used as another name for the process "working." [13] In physics, a force is said to *do work*. But the measure of the process in physics is, nevertheless, only the effect. Therefore, it is also used there in the sense we have chosen. This *double entendre* causes little or no confusion in physics; for, in general, work is expressed as the measured quantity of effect in terms of foot-pounds or ergs, etc. (that is, as the effect of a unit of force operating over a unit of distance). In our usage, then, "work" will be a quantity of effect of "working"—corresponding somewhat to the usage of number of "ergs" in physics. It is hardly necessary, however, to point out that our effect (work) cannot be measured in ergs. Working includes mental as well as physical activity; even its effect cannot be measured in ordinary physical units. It is heterogeneous; it is largely a conceptual entity. Yet we shall find some basis for treating it as measurable in economic rather than physical terms. At any rate, it is clear that effect is the magnitude of something accomplished, or an estimate of something to be accomplished. It is not the process of accomplishing it. For the latter we reserve the term "working." Finally we may note that, just as in physics, any useful *objective* measure of the magnitude "working" (the process) must relate it to its effect, "work" (that which has been accomplished by working).[14] Working, we may say, is a dynamic magnitude; work is a static one.

Proceeding from this definition of entities, and in default of any physical unit as a basis of measurement, we must attribute to work but a single dimension, W. It will be convenient to adopt as our unit of work that quantity which some standard worker can perform in one hour.[15] But such a form of unit does not include the time dimension.

[13] Thus "at work," "go to work," etc.
[14] While this distinction is not made clear in physics, it is implicit in the units of work and of power. Thus our magnitude "working" corresponds more nearly to the physical magnitude, "power," than it does to "work." It is clear, I think, that there is no other way of measuring working. One cannot measure a process by elapsed time, but only by how much of the process happens in the elapsed time. How absurd it would be to measure motion by the hour. You have moved four hours; I have moved two hours; ergo, you have moved twice as much as I. Yet that has been the tendency with working. It would be simple and easy if working could be measured by that objective standard, the clock. Unfortunately the objective measurement in terms of effect is much more difficult.
[15] The reader may object that such a unit can only be established for one kind of work and that different kinds of work are hardly comparable in such terms. Such an objection does not hold in the examination of a direct economy to which we are now confining ourselves. For then, there being but a single worker (analytically), the units of

The light year is a unit of this form. It has but one dimension, distance or length, and does not include that of time. If, then, we make the unit of working correspond, it is necessary, since, as a magnitude, working is a rate—the rate at which work accrues in the passage of time—that the unit should have two dimensions, work directly, and time inversely. Thus the unit of working would be the performing of the standard quantity of work in one hour (i.e., 1 W per hr.) which would conform to the dimensional formula WT^{-1}. It is of the utmost importance to keep in mind this distinction between the two magnitudes, working and work. Work is treated as a fundamental magnitude; working as a derived one. The rate, working, is, so to speak, a magnitude which can exist in a cross-section of time.[16]

The quantity of work produced by working over any period depends of course, in the first place, upon its effectiveness (skill, etc.).[17]

_____

different kinds of work would be what this worker could perform in an hour. In other words all work is made in this respect homogeneous and therefore commensurable by the assumption of a single worker. Let us suspend judgment as to whether different kinds of work can be made commensurable in an indirect economy. That is a problem which we hope ultimately to tackle.

Since we are ignoring, at this stage of our analysis, the factor of technique, we need only say here that we assume a single technique in each of such comparisons of performance as we are considering here.

[16] Three points with regard to these dimensional formulae may require further explanation. The dimensions of a quantity of process taking place over time do not include the dimension time if the process can be measured objectively—e.g., distance traversed as a measure of motion. A statement of this point, with direct reference to the mechanical concept of work, but in terms apt for our purpose, is found in Ganot's *Physics* (p. 49): "It is also to be noted that no direct reference to *time* enters the conception of a quantity of work; if we want to know how much work a labourer has done, we do not ask how long he has been at work, but what he has done—for instance, how many bricks he has carried, and to what height; and our estimate of the total amount of work is the same whether the man has spent hours or days doing it."

We may, however, choose as a unit for such a process the quantity of it which takes place in a unit of time under standard conditions. So the light year, which has only the dimension L, serves as an astronomical unit of distance.

Having adopted such a standard unit, and thus having implied that the rate of the process varies over time, it becomes necessary to use the standard unit of the process in the formula for the rate. That is, the rate of the process then becomes some multiple of the quantity of it which takes place in a unit of time under standard conditions, per unit of time.

[17] Jevons wanted to measure the "intensity of labour by the amount of physical force undergone in a certain time" (*224*, 204). That, of course, is entirely inconsistent with including "mental exertion," as he did (*ibid.*, 168). Marshall discusses the application of human "power" as if, in his time, it were still an important element in working (see *291*, 193). How little importance remains to it with the introduction of natural power! Physical energy of man has a cheap competitor in nature; mental energy has no competitor in nature. Human working now has almost nothing to do with the output of human "power."

By effectiveness or efficiency we mean only the rate at which personal mental and

This we have recognized in adopting the unit of standard work. Greater or less efficiency would be stated as multiples or fractions of the unit of working—that is, of the quantity of work delivered per hour. It depends, in the second place, on the number of workers. The sum of the working of three workers might be $0.5 + 1 + 1.5$ units of work per hour, or $3 \ WT^{-1}$. We may speak of working going on at such and such a rate. Thus 10 workers, working at the standard rate, $= 10$ units of working; one worker, working at double the standard rate, $= 2$ units of working. But as soon as we say that this goes on for 10 hours or 2 hours (i.e., as soon as we multiply it by a number of time units) the resulting magnitude is work, not working. For $10 \ WT^{-1} \times 10 \ T = 100 \ W$, or $2 \ WT^{-1} \times 2 \ T = 4 \ W$. Thus the only multiples of units of working that remains units of working are multiples in terms of number of workers or of super- (or sub-) standard working. Multiples in terms of time convert working into work.[18]

In the preceding subsection we found it practically impossible to measure the effortful aspect of working and work in terms other than those used for the effect aspect—namely standard hours. Therefore, in default of any other, we shall assume that the dimensions of working and work as "real costs" are also WT^{-1} and W respectively. The effort and the effect are inseparable, even if they would not have the same magnitudes were they measurable independently of each other. When, then, we refer to a product as having a "real cost" of 10 W we are thinking of the magnitude as representing the effort of this kind embodied in the product. When we refer to a worker as having contributed 10 W to a product we are thinking of the magnitude as representing the effect of this kind embodied in the product.

D. PRODUCT—THE RESULT OF WORKING

From the obdurately physical viewpoint, which still persists in economic analysis, the results of working are "goods" and "services"—more or less enduring material objects and ephemeral acts. In vain

---

physical energy is delivered and the inverse of the degree to which it is wasted. Again these have to do only with external effects.

[18] Pigou says, "It is well known that the ordinary factors of production are two-dimensional, in the sense that a unit of any of them can only be expressed as a quantity of stuff multiplied by a quantity of time" (*325*, 772). "Stuff" indicates the physical view. This "well-known" fact is not true of work or working, nor, for that matter, of any magnitudes I am aware of other than space. For working, the unit is something "*divided*," not "multiplied," by a quantity of time. Jevons made the same—his usual—mistake in assigning these dimensions (see *224*, 170).

has it been frequently pointed out, as to the first, that man creates nothing physical except babies; that his working has its physical effect only in the transformation and the transportation of matter, the rearrangement of the relative position of parts of a whole or the moving of the whole.[1] That generalization is accepted; but then, with entire inconsistency, these results of working continue to be conceived nevertheless as an aggregate of material objects and nothing more. The traits of matter are of great concern to technology, and thus indirectly to economics; they are often of importance in the art of consuming; but otherwise the chief chains in the economic process have almost nothing to do with them.[2] In order, therefore, to continue to carry on our purely economic analysis we will attempt to reduce to terms of process the stages which intervene between what we have called working and the final satisfying of wants.

As one of the two kinds of effort which occupy the second position in our second formula (production) we have distinguished working from the activities and inactivities of leisure—consuming, playing, resting. Working is seen to be a process, the measure of which is its effect, work, per unit of time. As such, it has replaced in part our earlier analytical tool, means. And we have noted that effort, including working, constitutes the method of providing means. From this it appears that the result of such effort is not means, but the *providing* of means.[3] That being the case, it is clear that the effect of working is, as well, entirely confined to the corresponding accomplishment, *provision*. Work (effect) is the constructing of a house, or the raising of a bushel

[1] See, for instance, Marshall, *291, 63*, and Senior, *370, 51*. To add to the large collection of such comments, from an unusual source, it may be worth while to quote the late Mr. Justice Holmes. He says (*Collected Legal Papers*, p. 281): "All that a man contributes to the world is the intelligence which directs a change in the place of matter. A man does not create the thing he handles or the force he exerts [nowadays]. The force could be got cheaper if the directing intelligence were not needed. The whole progress of the world in a material way is to put the need of intelligence further back [in the process]."

[2] The study of materials and their suitability for different purposes, the study of their treatment and fabrication, is a part of technology; and technology is intimately related to economics. But this is not the economic aspect of technology; it is rather the chemical or physical aspect. Economics is concerned only with that aspect of technology which appears as the ratio of input of effort to output of usefulness or satisfaction.

[3] It would have been more appropriate, in view of the common reification of the term means, if we had chosen the other of the pair of terms, "ways and means." "Ways of satisfying wants" expresses the facts exactly. Senior (*370, 51*) defines this aspect of production as "an alteration in the condition of the existing particles of matter." That is too narrow. But he does say that "this alteration is a product" (i.e., the alteration, not the matter).

of grain, not the house or the grain. It is not a measure of substance but a measure of process accomplished, and the physical substance is a mere carrier or medium. In the analysis of a direct economy this essential distinction is not clearly exposed; in that of an indirect economy it will stand out as vital.

In the first section of this chapter we also introduced the twin terms of customary economic terminology, production and consumption. We have already tentatively defined production, or producing, as the process of expending effort in providing means for the eventual satisfaction of wants.[4] This will turn out to be much broader than the usual coverage of the word.[5] But we can pare it down if that becomes necessary. At least, this definition already excludes consuming, playing, and resting. The result of this process, production, is called product. Interpreted in the previous terms product is, then, not the means, but the providing done on means—their *provision*. Or, again, product is not a house, but the having constructed a house. At first sight, then, we seem to have two terms—work and product—to convey a single concept. However, even in common usage that is not true. The two concepts are distinct, though related; and, as magnitudes, they may differ, though each exhibits certain tendencies to assimilate the other to it. In accordance with our practice of utilizing existing terms so far as possible we shall, therefore, attempt to come at the sense of "product" as a technical term in economics and merely to define it as precisely as possible in such a way as to differentiate it from, and at the same time show its relations to, "work." The first difference has to do with the classifications within the two categories. The classes of work consist of different kinds of work, each of which constitutes some one part of the effect composing the entire result; on the other hand, the classes of product are the different kinds of entire result. Thus product, or a quantity of product, is the term for the conglomerate result of working, and views this result in the aspect of a single or a compound produced means; but work is the term for the several specific effects of working which, when conjoined, go to make up this product.[6]

[4] In its final form, the definition of production, at the end of Chapter 10, will exhibit one minor amendment to this version, at least so far as indirect economies are concerned.
[5] Because we are not yet ready to establish, for an indirect economy, the criterion of differentiation between economic and non-economic means. In the direct economy all means which require effort because they require provision may be considered as economic and those which do not as non-economic.
[6] The less concretized is our thinking about these magnitudes, the better. Too much visualizing keeps us from analyzing. But what we need is operational concepts—that

If this is so, is it possible to relate the magnitude of product to that of the work that has gone to make it up? We can measure quantities of work of the same kind in their common dimension, even when they are performed by different persons or at different times or places. But product may be a composite of different kinds of work. Are the several specific effects of working commensurable among themselves? If not, they cannot be summated. Product composed of heterogeneous work and therefore itself, in this aspect, heterogeneous, could not then be measured in terms of work. However, this is not a question which we can, or need to, examine while we are considering a direct economy only. For, to a single individual, while some kinds of working or working at some times may involve more effort or more sacrifice than other kinds or at other times there is no possible way to measure the comparative effectiveness of the various kinds of work except in terms of the time he finds each should take. That is, his work must seem homogeneous to him, in the aspect of effect, for he has no external standard with which to compare it. Therefore, he can summate quantities of different kinds of work put into single products and can compare these sums as between different products. In this way, then, the magnitude of product can be assimilated to the magnitude of the work it represents.

On the other hand, in the objective aspect, or in the aspect as means to the satisfaction of wants and in terms of usefulness, two quantities of product which are strictly indifferent are treated as equal.[7] But the two may represent different quantities (aggregates) of work according as the two lots of product have come through one or another channel of production. In either of the first two aspects what we call *uniform* product can be, and is, measured as a magnitude in terms of some arbitrary objective unit, even if it consists of lots among which the composition in terms of the quantity of each or all of several different kinds of work varies. This makes it necessary to distinguish, on the one hand, the magnitude represented by the aggregate of the work

is, concepts derived from the percepts that are germane to our purpose, rather than from the merely naïve percept, "looks."

[7] At first the use of the term "objective" in this connection may seem to be erroneous. Is not the equivalence we intend by the term "indifference" rather a subjective equivalence? But, on second thought, I think the reader will agree that the criterion by which we classify products is an objective one—units, which vary among themselves only in "unnoticeable" ways; while subjective equivalence means equal usefulness, and may exist between two objectively *different* products.

(effect) which has gone into the product (and which may and usually does vary as between different lots of a single product defined by the limits of indifference) and, on the other hand, the magnitude of the product itself, in its objective or subjective aspect. All objectively or subjectively equal quantities of a single product, so defined, must be conceived as of equal magnitude; nevertheless, they are usually unequal quantities as aggregates of work. Thus we differentiate the magnitude product from the magnitude work. True, product is the result of work; though only the entire result. Nevertheless, we have to treat it quantitatively in somewhat different terms. We have to measure it as a certain number of objectively indifferent units. The way these divergences are reconciled will be dealt with at the end of Chapter 12.[8] But it is clear that they must be reconciled. For the objective units in which different products are measured are apt to be different and incommensurable, and, from the standpoint of usefulness, any mass of heterogeneous product cannot be summated. That has already been demonstrated in Part I. Thus the only common denominator in which to measure (or conceive the magnitude of) such a mass is in terms of work. To do that, one among the different lots of each uniform product must be chosen as standard, and all lots must then be measured in terms of the work which the standard lot represents. Only thus can we measure, or even conceive, all product as a magnitude. Here the assimilation is complex. First, the magnitude as work is made uniform in order to assimilate it to the equal magnitudes of product. Then, in turn, the latter are assimilated to the standard magnitude of work.

Still a third differentiation appears. The magnitude of product must also be conceived to vary according to the stage it has reached in the process up to the point at which it is suitable and immediately available for use. Perhaps in the aspect of usefulness it may have no magnitude until that point is reached. Nevertheless, it already exists as product. Before that point is reached it is merely less produced and therefore merely a smaller magnitude as product. We can only use as a scale for measuring the magnitude of product, during this stage, the proportion of the total work required that has already been applied. Thus, in

[8] There we consider differences in work required per unit of product both for the reason that the natural conditions (resistances) in the several channels of production differ and for the reason that different techniques are used. In Part II we are ignoring these differences.

this case, the magnitude of product is assimilated to the magnitude of work.[9]

Since these distinctions and definitions will enable us to use the common terms as technical terms—that is, as terms with a perfectly precise meaning—we will briefly restate the whole series in their order. Working embraces all activities and all components of activities that are not playing or consuming. The two latter include all responses energized by, or to the extent they are energized by, present wants. Consuming, as an activity, includes the consumption of means that were provided in advance when the wants were future wants. Direct consuming covers the consumption of means that do not require to be provided in advance—i.e., those which are so ready and available that the precurrent reactions of present wants or even consummatory reactions alone suffice to procure them. Working, as one of the two forms of economic effort, is related to the providing of means only in respect of its effect, work. As a magnitude we can measure working, in its aspect of effort, only in terms of one of its dimensions, namely duration. But, because this duration is not, among different persons or at different times, proportionate to the effect, because the effect can be measured objectively, and because the measure of a process cannot be exactly stated in terms of duration only, we convert working into a standardized process—i.e., so much effect per hour. Thereafter working, which may be more or less intense and effective than the standard, is reduced from its uncorrected actual duration to its corrected duration as a quantity of standard process.

Production consists of the application of the effect of working (work) to the provision—making suitable and available—of means for future wants—that is, to produced means or product. Means which do not require to be produced because they are already suitable and available for direct consumption are not product. While any one product, or produced means, is the entire result of the application of successive amounts of work, we treat it as a somewhat independent magnitude because it is also capable of being measured in its other aspects. It can be measured objectively in terms of the appropriate arbitrary units for each indifferent means. Then its magnitude as a conglomerate of work, due to the fact that the sum of the work put in

---

[9] This is only true with regard to a single technique. The comparison of magnitudes of two lots of uniform product, at the same stage in the process, but produced by different techniques and therefore requiring different quantities of work, presents a complex problem.

on it will vary under different conditions, will vary from this. It can be measured subjectively, but with less certainty, in terms of its usefulness. How far that can be carried and how independent of objective measurement it can be made has already been demonstrated in Chapter 7.

Finally, the contribution made to any product in the form of working effort is measured in terms of the quantity of standard work incorporated in it. Conversely the "real cost" of the product, in the form of working effort, is this same quantity. Thus among different lots of a single product the "real cost" will vary according as the contribution has had to be greater or less on account of conditions. But these conditions do not include variable efficiency of working. That is eliminated by reduction of work to standard terms.

The economic process is subject to much leakage. The quantity of effort—working—of a single worker may not be commensurate with the effect—work; equal quantities of work applied to a single product may not result in equal quantities of product; sometimes working does not result in product at all—it is wasted; frequently equal quantities of means of the same kind, to which have been applied equal quantities of work, do not turn out to have equal usefulness—i.e., are not subjectively indifferent; sometimes a certain lot may have none.[10] There is a complete absence of necessary proportionality in these several aspects or at these successive stages. Between different workers and different products the lack of proportionality is even more notable. As between two workers the same effort—working—results in widely different effect—work; the same amounts of work performed on two different products result in widely different objective amounts of product; and these objective amounts of different products have almost nothing to do with their comparative usefulness. Therefore, it is absolutely necessary for us to distinguish sharply between these several magnitudes and to take account of the shrinkage and disproportionality at or between the several steps or phases in which they are determined. At this stage of our analysis these distinctions may seem somewhat finespun. Nevertheless, they will turn out to constitute an important part of the basis of all realistic economic analysis.

[10] We have already illustrated the first two forms of leakage. Sisyphus is a good illustration of the third. This book may turn out to be an illustration of the last. And some, at least, of the contents of the "bargain basement" proves it. We cannot follow Jevons (*224, 170*) in considering but three quantities, "the amount of painful exertion, the amount of produce, and the amount of utility gained." So simple a formula merely serves as a starting-point and requires much refinement.

In passing, one other point needs to be made. The term means has already been made broad enough to include precurrent reactions of self and acts of others as well as material objects. Thus we might include in product the results of working, both when these are embodied—i.e., take the form of some change in external matter—and when they constitute means in and of themselves—i.e., consists of acts without such separate effect. However, so far as precurrent reactions of self are concerned, if they constitute means in and of themselves, they cannot be product (produced means). For the effect is then ephemeral, so that it cannot constitute providing for future wants. As such it cannot be work and the reactions cannot be working. Then they must be playing or consuming, not producing.[11] So far as acts of others are concerned, they do not appear in the analysis of a direct economy. Nevertheless, when we come to examine an indirect economy, they will appear to constitute a very considerable portion of total product, so that we must continue to allow for this exception. Naturally, when we speak of product here, being concerned with a direct economy only and therefore with product in the form of objects, we will have in mind the material objects which embody and are the present locus of the work. But the aspect of these objects to which the term will chiefly refer will be their content of the effect of effort, rather than their material form or even, usually, their usefulness.[12] When we come also to deal with acts of others, we can usually only think of product as happening *en passant*.

For the sake of clarity it is also necessary to choose now a single definite set of terms out of the confusion of tongues in order to describe the various stages and categories of product. While working is being done upon it, and work is accumulating in it, we will speak of *product in process;* at the end of this process it becomes *finished product.* This distinction does not always apply (in an indirect economy) to product not embodied, which is sometimes viewed as being finished *pari passu.*[13]

[11] We must remind the reader that these components can be mixed—e.g., playing in the form of knitting results in the provision of an object means for a future want. Whether or not that is working and production or playing depends, then, on whether the product is incidental or is the prime objective. We also recall the fact that learning (and being taught), while no object means are produced, may nevertheless be working, and in some respects the permanent effects resemble product.

[12] Pareto, for instance, distinguishes only between the two latter. To him (317, 303) products are material because they manifest themselves objectively, but immaterial in the aspect of "the effect they are destined to produce" (nearly "usefulness").

[13] It does apply to haircuts. But perhaps a haircut belongs among embodied products. It does not apply to the fanning of an oriental potentate.

In this connection we must note that what we called above a *uniform* product is not uniform at the various stages in the succession of processes by which it is prepared for consumption (i.e., it does not remain uniform while it is product in process). During that time it may seem to be not one but many different economic results. Nevertheless, the naïve view, which identifies the physical substance—or its separate, not yet aggregated parts—as the product in process, is the most convenient, provided we bear in mind that this substance is, economically, merely a carrier and locus of the effect, work, and of other effort. According to its ultimate destination we shall distinguish product as *final* or *intermediate*. Final product is the provision made of ways and means directly capable of satisfying wants—whether the effort is embodied in material form or, in an indirect economy, not so embodied. Intermediate product is product which is not to be, or cannot be, consumed, but which is to be used, immediately or mediately, in the production of final product. This, then, must all be in material form (including therein all physical manifestations). We will deal with that subject in Part III: In Chapter 7 we also distinguished between *durable* and *non-durable* means, and noted that this classification applied only to means in the form of objects. Since the terms "product" and "means" refer to the same thing in its two aspects, and since product is a subclass of means, this distinction also applies to product. But it should be noted that, just as this distinction denotes nothing as to the physical "hardness" of the means, but only an arbitrary line between long and short periods during which its usefulness is to be used up, so too it denotes nothing as to the character of the production which went into the product. There is no inherent difference between the production of durable and that of non-durable product. Quantity of working has nothing to do with making product durable.[14]

Finally, we must bear in mind that working—as an element of production—even when its effect is embodied in an object, may or may not alter the physical condition of the object. That is not its function. It may merely move the object as is; it may even only discover it. Working is aimed toward—though it may not succeed in—contributing the attributes, or to the availability of the attributes, which occasion the usefulness of the object.[15] If it does not do so, it is wasted;

[14] Somebody—I think somebody of the modern Austrian school—to the contrary notwithstanding. Thus "roundaboutness" and "durability" have been treated as if they had some quantitative relation to each other.

[15] Usually the material itself is not usable per se. Then the production contributes all

if it does, then it constitutes one of the two elements of the "real cost" of this usefulness. If the usefulness of the object is already complete and it is available without the intervention of working, then the object does not represent product. If it is consumed at all, it is, as we say, *directly* consumed.[16]

---

the usefulness; e.g., metals, textile fibers, etc. Cruder foods and drinks, fuel and other sources of power have potential usefulness, as is, and the contribution of production consists in making it available or actual—adding to it, in that sense.

[16] Marshall says (*291*, 64) that "*Consumption* may be regarded as negative production." That statement is neither wholly true nor safe when it is true. Ordinary breathing is direct consumption without production. And what is taken out of product in consumption of produced means is not really the same thing and not quantitatively proportionate to what was put in. We call the result of successful working, in objective product, an addition to its usefulness, though the result really consists of physical changes in form and in position, or in less tangible changes in its relation to us, which are aimed at that. Moreover, as we have seen, it is not really the enjoyment of this usefulness which takes it out of the product. That is the result of the physical changes which accompany the process of using. Because of its picturesque nature and because it well represents a "sticky" view among economists, I am tempted to recall Henry George's phrase (*169*, 40). He says that wealth is "labor impressed upon matter in such a way as to store up, as the heat of the sun is stored up in coal, the power of human labor to minister to human desires." Very pretty; a sort of law of conservation of energy for economics; but one which has validity only very "figuratively speaking."

The "obdurately physical viewpoint" is well exemplified, in this connection, by Stigler's comments on "The Economics of Carl Menger" (*386*, 233, note 7). He says: "Menger saw what on occasion some of our modern theorists have failed to see; that where there is only one productive factor and one product that factor must be economically identical with its product, for no change could have taken place in the factor in the absence of another factor. Where this heroic construction is assumed it is nonsense to speak of costs, returns, or distribution." If the factor is regarded as an *inactive* physical object, yes; if it is regarded as an activity, such as effort, no. The product of effort is not effort; the consumption of product is not the consumption of effort. Therefore, this "heroic construction" cannot apply to the "factors of production," as we are proceeding to analyze them, at all.

10

RETAINING AND THE JOINT RESULT—
EXTANT PRODUCT

THE SECOND of the two classes or types of human effort for economic ends was referred to in the previous chapter as "saving." The analysis of this entity—or these entities—is perhaps at present one of the chief problems of economic analysis; for, in spite of the progress that has been made in clarifying the various aspects and characteristics, great confusion still remains; so much so that, as we shall see later, long controversies are carried on in which the respective parties are talking about different entities or aspects, though they are calling them by the same name. At least a part of the difficulty, therefore, lies in the terminology, to which we shall have to give careful attention.[1]

A. THE FUNCTION IN GENERAL

1. THE THREE ASPECTS

Let us begin by inquiring how economics has usually regarded this second economic process concerned with the providing of means, a process which is said to involve effort and which can therefore be regarded as itself a kind of effort. In terms of the ordinary economic concepts—production and consumption, as we have now defined them—this second occasion for effort is most commonly conceived to consist in postponing consumption for some time after production has taken place.[2] Of course such postponing is only possible with the type of means we have called objects. This process seems, then, to concern itself only with one of the three types of means. Viewed in a more pre-

---

[1] Also some part, as Pareto says (317, 305-306) is due to the fact that "no one, or almost no one, studies the question of transformations in time with a mind completely freed from *parti pris*. Each one knows, even before having studied the question, in what way it should be solved, and he speaks like an advocate of the case which he is charged to defend." We shall try to be among his exceptions.

[2] It is also sometimes conceived to be forgoing consumption altogether, except, perhaps, for the annual "return" on the production.

cise way, if consumption of this kind of means is taken to be—in the definition given in the seventh chapter—"the more or less gradual using-up of the usefulness of a means in the course of satisfying a want," then this process seems to be non-consumption; that is, it is the complementary *not-using-up* of product which occurs before it is put to use and continues at a diminishing rate until the gradual using-up is completed. As such it appears entirely negative—what the lawyers call a "non-happening" or "forbearance." [3] But it may be viewed on its positive side as well. When product is not-used-up it is *kept* or *retained*. So stated, keeping or retaining product becomes the alternative to using it up. And this statement is preferable because there can be no advantage in mere not-using-up per se, while there may be an advantage in keeping or retaining for future use. For that reason, and because that is the objective and measurable aspect, we prefer to identify the process by its positive, not by its negative side.

So construed, this entity becomes symmetrical with working and is seen also to have three aspects. We saw that the process "working" has its almost mechanical aspect, namely its effect, work; so, too, the process "keeping or retaining" has its similar aspect, its effect, which is that the product persists as an economic entity. That is the performance which constitutes the "contribution" aspect of both processes. We saw that working also has a more personal and psychological aspect, the "effort" involved, which makes of it a "real cost." Judging by its usual economic classification as a form of effort, which we shall consider presently, keeping or retaining appears also to involve effort and would therefore also, in this respect, constitute a "real cost." Finally, working was seen to have a third aspect, also personal and psychological—the fact that, while working, the alternative, leisure, has to be forgone. In that aspect working is a "sacrifice." Keeping or retaining apparently also has its alternative, which is using-up or consumption. In that aspect—its negative side—it, too, involves a "sacrifice." [4] It is true that

[3] "A contract is a promise. . . ." "A promise is an undertaking . . . either that something shall happen, or that something shall not happen, in the future." (*Restatement of the Law of Contracts*, American Law Institute, pp. 17 and 19.) This fits the sense of "forbearance," as used by Commons (*92*, 74 ff. and 128, and *93*, 19 and 88). Though contract and "transactions" do not seem to be the same categories that we are discussing they will be found to be closely related. And the distinctions between "happening" or "non-happening," and between "performance" and "forbearance," are even closer to ours between the effort and effect aspects and the sacrifice aspect of working and of retaining.
[4] We are again distinguishing the aspect of performance which we call "contribution" from the aspect of the effort involved in this performance, which we call "real

in the case of keeping or retaining, the second and third aspects seem, at first sight, to be more nearly identical than they are in the case of working. The effort of working is inherent in the process, and is independent of, or in addition to, the sacrifices involved in refraining from leisure. The effort of keeping or retaining, on the other hand, appears to consist almost wholly in refraining from consumption.[5] Nevertheless, it is well to keep these two aspects separate. The effort is the accompaniment of the one alternative chosen, while the sacrifice is the fact that the other alternative is not chosen. Moreover, further analysis may prove to distinguish them still more sharply.

2. TERMINOLOGY

At this point it will be well to pause and consider the matter of terminology. The first term we used, "saving," will not do. It has a strong connotation of a money economy. We are not at present analyzing a money economy, but a direct one. When we come later to deal with the indirect—usually a money economy—we shall find that the process of saving is far removed from the quasi-physical process we are now examining, and it will be a question whether there is even an exact correspondence between the two processes at their respective levels, or in their respective media.[6] To identify the two entities now would beg that question. Therefore, we reserve the term "saving" for future use. Another term, "not-using-up," is not only impossibly awkward but, though exact, it represents the negative aspect exclusively. The same is true of "postponing" or "deferring" (e.g., con-

---

cost," and in turn from the aspect of the "sacrifice" involved in not doing something else.

A further word about this terminology. Unfortunately the term "cost" has come to have an almost ineradicable connotation of money cost, or of exchanges between individuals in the course of various processes which take place in terms of money (at least as to one side), and are only to be converted into "real" terms by the application of an index number of purchasing power. "Real costs," as used in this analysis, have nothing to do with money or exchanges. "Real costs," here, are the reactions or actions of human beings which involve effort and which are necessary to, and result in, product and extant product.

[5] That is, they would seem to be one and the same thing, if the sacrifice is measured by not using up the product retained. But, as we shall see, this is not the usual form that the sacrifice takes.

[6] This is the recently mooted question whether "saving" and "investment" should be defined in economic analysis in such a way that they constitute magnitudes which are automatically equal, or, instead, in such a way that variations in either merely set up tendencies to bring the other into agreement with it. In either case there is the further question how far such a relationship will hold true of investment as a "real" magnitude instead of a "money-value" magnitude.

sumption). The word "waiting," which Marshall proposed and which
has come into somewhat general use, is subject to a similar objection.
It will turn out to be too partial. Moreover, it seems too definitely to
settle the question of the temporary duration of the process. Nor is it
any longer used in its transitive form.[7] Finally, the original name of
this process, which Senior was the first to establish as an entity and
which he called "abstinence," is not only wholly and merely a name
for the sacrifice involved, but has been so belabored by that school of
economics which still believes the economic earth is flat that its use as
a colorless and scientific term is no longer possible.[8] We may fall back
on one of the two common words we used to describe the positive
side of the process—"keeping" or "retaining." Of these two the latter

[7] One can no longer "wait" a product. Actually Macvane proposed the term and
Marshall adopted it as a sort of rear-guard action to permit the retreat of Senior's "abstinence" (see *291*, 233). Cassel used both terms—"waiting" and "abstinence"—in the
Nature and Necessity of Interest, in which he seems to me to have been on the road to
an analysis in terms of process. But, in the *Theory*, where he seems to have discarded
that in favor of a concrete notion of capital, he uses "saving" and "waiting." In this he
is perhaps typical.

"Waiting" seems not to be a good term for a process which may continue indefinitely.
On the other hand, Knight's claim (*240*, 371), that the process "must be permanent and
not a mere matter of waiting" (derived no doubt from J. B. Clark, whose concept we
will discuss later) is absolutely contrary to fact and a most singular illusion. Nevertheless, the term "waiting" also begs that question too much.

[8] As to the first point, Senior did, however, (*370*, 60) also include the aspect that ab-
staining is "among the most painful exertions of the human will" (our effort). And he
treated the "desire for expenditure" (consumption) as an "antagonist principle to the
preservation, and consequently to the accumulation of wealth" (*371*, I, 66). His entity is
one of the three agencies of production (*ibid.*, 59). Therefore, it must be either the
agent or the process; it cannot be what is not done, the sacrifice. Also he did not construe keeping final product for own use ("unproductive use") as "abstinence" (*370*, 58
and *371*, I, 197-198). Not only do we not make such a distinction; we do not admit its
existence.

This is another case where we owe much to Senior's insight. If his unpublished papers
had been available, it is possible that Lassalle's (and also, as I recall it, Rodbertus's) barb
—emotionally effective but theoretically untenable—would never have been shot.
There (*371*, I, 199-207) he enlarges on this and other matters which are mere unsys-
tematized hints in the *Outline*, and makes another distinction which we shall have to use
later. However, it is true that the word "abstinence" has a "moral complexion," as Cassel put it (*74*, 184), slightly tainted with alcoholic associations since the subsequent pro-
hibition movement. And that is undesirable in a scientific term.

As to the second point: the fact that Marxian economics denies or ignores the existence of the second form of human effort seems to me to put it in the same class with
Wilbur Glenn Voliva's physical geography. Such an omission precludes the possibility
of understanding *any* economic system whatever; and, for that reason, the work of
this school cannot be taken seriously as a contribution to the scientific analysis of the
subject. It must be apparent to any reader of *Das Kapital* that Marx thought he had discovered in the economic synthesis a vacuum which he terms "surplus value." Actually
this "vacuum" corresponded to his own "blind spot." Then, curiously enough, he named
his book after the particular part of the process which he appears to have been wholly
unable to see.

seems preferable on account of its wider range of forms. It is color-less and therefore scientific; it is a verbal noun of the form nearest, in English, to a noun of action, like working; it is transitive and therefore connotes retaining *something*—the active and chief, or "contribution," aspect of the process; it has a noun of agency which is usable, "re-tainer"; it has an alternative verbal noun, "retention," with the sense of the past participle, which will be useful, though we will find its ap-plication to be limited to one aspect only. With the exception of the last, convenient forms are available which are parallel to those of the verb "work."

The two economic occasions for effort are, in this terminology, working and retaining. Since both involve effort and are the only activities which do so, we shall use "effort" as the collective term for the two. Both are processes. He who carries on the first is a worker; he who carries on the second is a retainer. The effect of the first is work. The "real cost" of the first, in the sense of effort performed, is also work. The use of the term retention in connection with the second will correspond with work, but only in the aspect of "real cost." It should be understood, however, that we are not merely treating the terms "retaining" and "retention" as new names for old and general economic concepts or categories. They are, rather, names for entities which have been almost, but never quite, distinguished from their con-comitants. Just as we measured working by what is *being* accomplished, without regard to the effort or the sacrifice involved, so now we can measure retaining by what is *being* accomplished only. In both cases the quantity of effort and the quantity of sacrifice involved in any quantity of accomplishment may vary widely; neither has any neces-sary proportion to the effect. The entities called "waiting" and "ab-stinence," since these are names associated only with the effort and the sacrifice, and do not relate to the effect, are therefore not quite the same magnitudes as those to which our terms refer.[9]

[9] As to other terms and entities which are related, see the last part of this chapter. Böhm-Bawerk remarks the necessity of dissociating the sacrifice from the effect; "whether there is sacrifice and moral desert in it or not is all the same to the result" (*38*, 120). That is the point we are making. It is absurd to talk about "sacrifice objectively meas-ured" as "manual work done," "commodity manufactured," and "capital abstained from," the way Edgeworth does (*133*, 34). The sacrifice is the alternative forgone. And that, having been forgone, can have no objective effect. Nor can it be subjectively measured in the sense of comparison between persons, as Davenport points out (*107*, 353). Nevertheless, to deny the existence of any concomitant "genuine sacrifice," as Keynes seems to do (*237*, 376), or to say, as Davenport does (*107*, 353), that "abstinence is in no case a fact of pain" (while, to him, working may be), is to blind oneself to the

3. THE MAGNITUDES AND THEIR DIMENSIONS

When we come to examine these two entities, retaining and reten-tion, as magnitudes, we run into considerable difficulties. It is clear that, from the objective viewpoint, the cross-section of the process—the magnitude of the retaining being done at any moment, in terms of its effect—is the quantity of product then being retained. The greater the aggregate of product being retained the greater the retaining being done. Nothing but product is retained or needs to be retained. For, by definition, means that are not product are available and suitable (i.e., ready to hand) and can, therefore, be availed of by the precur-rent, or even only by the consummatory, reactions to present wants that we call direct consuming. Now we have regarded product, as a magnitude, to be the result of a congeries of several kinds of work— the only form of "real cost" we have as yet considered; and we have recognized that, while each kind of work is measurable in its own terms, the different kinds may be incommensurable among themselves and therefore impossible of summation. That offers a problem which we have not yet tried to solve because, for the reason given in the previous chapter, it does not appear in a direct economy. We will post-pone its consideration, and merely assume here that it is soluble and that product, as a compound of different kinds of work, is a measurable magnitude in an indirect economy, as it certainly would seem to be in a direct one. On the other hand, we have seen that product also repre-sents usefulness. It is Janus-faced. And, as we noted at the end of the previous chapter, the two faces may not be of the same size—the use-fulness of two lots even of a single product may not be proportionate to the work embodied in them. If we treat the magnitude of product in the same way that we did that of means—that is, regard a quantity of any product as a number of separate objective units or unit parts of a mass which are objectively indifferent among themselves and which are subjectively estimated to have the same usefulness—it would be necessary to admit that, over a period of time, or even at one and the same time, different units of a single product may not represent the same quantity of work. Which of the two possibly different magni-tudes of product is the dimension of retaining? It might be supposed

---

realities. If non-consumption is no sacrifice, then consumption is no advantage and there is no purpose whatever in economic activity. And, while forgoing "pleasure" may not be "pain," I should imagine most hedonists would have agreed that it is something very like it.

that the size of the sacrifice depends on the quantity of usefulness not being used. On the other hand, this sacrifice may turn out not to be measured by the product that is being retained, but rather by some other product not made at all. Also we are undertaking to measure the effect of retaining in objective terms and not in subjective terms, just as we did with working. Finally, since one cannot add together magnitudes with different dimensions, it would be quite impossible ever to summate the effort of both kinds which had gone into a product—to state its combined "real costs"—if we were to measure the two forms of effort in different and entirely unrelated terms, one in terms of work and the other in terms of usefulness. Therefore, we shall choose to relate the magnitude of the retaining being done, in its aspect of effect, to the magnitude of the "real cost" embodied in the product, not to that of the usefulness of the product, though we have found it necessary to modify that practice in two respects in order to permit certain influences of the magnitude usefulness to come to bear. All this, being interpreted, means that nothing but "real cost" is retained or needs to be retained. The "real cost" of product measures the retaining that is done on it. While we have agreed that work is heterogeneous and that, therefore, the measurement of a compound of it may be a difficult problem outside a direct economy, nevertheless it is clear that retaining is entirely homogeneous, in its aspect of effect. It is a quantity of uniform process, regardless of the variation in the effort or sacrifice involved, with no qualitative differences—even such as may be resolved into quantitative differences.

Retaining of product, viewed as a process going on over time and in terms of its effect, is a larger or smaller quantity according only as the quantity of product, so defined, that is being currently retained is larger or smaller. Therefore, retaining, in the aspect of effect, has but one dimension, which we may tentatively call P (or, subject to adjustments, W). Now it should be noted that this is an unusual, though not unique, form in which to measure a process. It uses a static, not a dynamic, dimension; it uses a fundamental dimension, not a derived one (a rate) as is customary with processes. Nevertheless, it is the only one available. And this because, though the process in this aspect is one that goes on over time, it does not change its size nor accumulate by reason of the mere passage of time.[10] It would necessarily follow from

[10] In the words of a statistician, in another connection, time is here related "merely as an observational cross section; not as an independent variable." My notes attribute this to J. Dean (113).

this formula for retaining, as effect, that retention, viewed as the quantity of effect of this process accomplished during a period of time, would have to have two dimensions, that of the process, P, and that of time, T. But in this case T would enter as a direct dimension; for the longer the time (or the unit of time) as well as the greater the product, the greater the magnitude of retention, as effect. Therefore the dimensional formula for retention, in this aspect, would have to be PT. Now, as we have several times noted in previous chapters, such a dimensional formula is an anomaly, if not a monstrosity.[11] Moreover, if this process in this aspect does not change its size or accumulate with the passage of time, such a dimensional formula would belie the facts. We conclude, then, that it will be impossible to measure the effect of a quantity of this process accomplished in the same static terms that we can readily use for measuring the rate of the process.[12] It will be some solace for this rebuff to find that we need no such magnitude anyway. It is difficult, if not impossible, to conceive. It is certainly impossible to measure. For a single product a rough approximation of it would consist in the average of the various magnitudes of the product, taken at unit intervals during its life, multiplied by its life in terms of the same time units. For an aggregate whose lives coincided it would be the sum of these

[11] Or, perhaps we should say that they represent naïvely analyzed magnitudes. Thus a foot-pound sounds like a ton-mile. It sounds as if its dimensions were ML. But they are not. And a ton-mile is an unanalyzed magnitude. One might say, for instance, that a substance varies in mass in proportion both to its density and its volume. Therefore, its dimensions would be DV. But the analyzed dimensions of D are MV^{-1}. Then $M = MV^{-1} \times V$, or M.

[12] Thus we see again that Pigou's general statement to the effect that "the ordinary factors of production are two-dimensional" (*325, 772*) is also wrong in this case. Furthermore, the "factor" must be either the agent or the process; it cannot be the effect, even though we may measure the process in terms of its effect. And neither this agency nor this process is two-dimensional, in his sense. If we choose to measure quantity of product in terms of money value, it would be even more incorrect to measure the process, "capital disposal," as Cassel does, in year-pounds (MT; *74, 199*), or "waiting," as Pigou does, in year-value-units (*325, 161*, note 1). Jevons made the same mistake (*224, 229*). His "*amount of capital invested*" is the same magnitude as our "retaining," or, more exactly, our "extant product," to be defined later; his "*amount of investment of capital*" is this anomalous magnitude, PT: "The first is a quantity of one dimension only —the quantity of capital; the second is a quantity of two dimensions, namely, the quantity of capital, and the length of time during which it remains invested."

Fisher has it better, but still not right. He says (*142, 52*): "A fund is fully specified by one magnitude only; a flow requires two—the *amount* of flow and the *duration* of flow. From these a third follows—the *rate* of flow or the quotient of the amount divided by the duration." The rate is correctly stated. But the amount is not independent of the duration. It is proportionate to it—that is, it is the rate multiplied by the duration. The magnitudes necessary to specify a continuing flow are its rate and its duration. The amount is sufficient by itself, if the flow is a completed past event. But then it has become a fund.

first. For an aggregate whose lives did not coincide it would be the sum of those portions of the first magnitudes that were lived within the period chosen. Without defining the period in terms of time units, so that both beginning and end had uniform and fixed dates, the magnitude would be undefined. Moreover, when these complicated measurements were achieved we would have learned nothing. Since this conceptual impasse is the source of one of the chief aberrations in present-day capital theory, we will undertake to make clear in the last section of this chapter what misconceptions underlie the errors.[13]

[13] An illustration of this dimensional quandary purely in the form of a somewhat close analogy may be helpful. A flood is a process. It consists, primarily, in the entry of more water into a watershed than is currently being drawn off from that watershed. In other words it is the difference between two flows—a flow in and a flow out. The convenient and usual method of measuring it, however, is in quite other terms. It is stated in terms of the height in feet and inches to which the water rises at some critical point in the flow—the flood-mark. Now this is not a measure of process (dynamic) nor even a measure of volume (static); it is a static measure representing the cross-section of the process—in this case in only one of its dimensions. Nevertheless, it serves the purpose of measuring changes in the degree of the flood because it registers, fairly accurately, the excess of the rate of inflow over the rate of outflow. In that respect it is analogous to our magnitude, the effect of retaining being performed.

In a sense, however, the "height" of the flood is a measure of rate; for it is proportional to the rate of flow at the critical point. And this rate, in turn, changes in proportion to, and thus reflects, the ratio between the rates of inflow and of outflow. Nevertheless, this measure is not stated in the dimensional formula of a rate—a derived magnitude. It is a one-dimensional measure in terms of the dimensional formula, L. If the rate were stated as a derived magnitude, it would need to take the form of a rate of flow—so many gallons per minute—that is, L^3T^{-1}. The quantity of flow in any certain length of time—the amount of the flood—would then be so many gallons—i.e. $L^3T^{-1} \times T = L^3$. Now, while not impossible, this would be very difficult of calculation. At any particular moment the whole quantity of flood, in these terms, would be the number of gallons of water in the watershed in excess of its usual contents. That could only be calculated by determining the excess over normal of the average width and depth (cross-section) of all confluent streams and then by multiplying that by the weighted average length of these streams up to the critical point. Or, during the whole life of the flood, its measure could be taken in the number of gallons of water, in excess of normal, which had passed the critical point. This could be approximated by measuring the excess flow for each hour and summating these quantities for the whole life of the flood. But then the measure of the flood would be the quantity of process accomplished in terms of gallons—a one-dimensional fundamental unit—and time would not appear.

On the other hand, when the "height" of the flood is used as a measure of the rate, no such conversion into terms of quantity of process accomplished is possible. For then the quantity of flow in any certain length of time, at the rate L, would become LT. That is a meaningless formula in the theory of dimensions. It is foot-hours. It would, of course, be possible to measure the flood in terms of the number of hours during which the water stood above normal. But that would be a measure of duration only, not of quantity of flood—of T, not of LT. True, by calculating the number of gallons per minute of flow added for each rise in the "height" of the flood by one foot and then multiplying it by the certain length of time, one would estimate the quantity of flow for that time. But that procedure would consist in the conversion of the dimensional formula LT into something else.

The definition of the magnitudes, retaining and retention, in their two other aspects—that of "real cost" and that of sacrifice—eludes us at this stage of our analysis; first, for the reason that we have not yet identified either the effort or the sacrifice involved; and, second, because we are therefore unable to determine their dimensions in such a way as to relate them to the rest of our magnitudes.

B. LIMITATION OF RETAINING THROUGH THE INFLUENCE OF FUTURITY

1. RETAINING AND RETENTION AS EFFORT—ANALYTICAL AND CONVENTIONAL

The second aspect of retaining, and the only one that includes retention, is that of "real cost." In order to incorporate it in a more nearly full-length portrait of the place retaining and retention occupy in the scheme of "real costs," we must now relate to these entities, in their aspect of effort, the sketch we made of the influence of futurity as a limitation on provision for future wants (Chapter 6, Section B 4). There we found it necessary to impute a resistance to making such provision which is analytically separable from the resistance due to the effort involved in working—duration effort. It cannot be precisely the same form of resistance, because, after the working effort is concluded, it extends during a time when there is no further working effort. We called it interval effort in order to distinguish it from duration effort and in order to indicate that it only accrues, as a separable magnitude, during the interval between the application of duration effort and the date of the instance of the future want for which provision is made.

The fact that we have given this factor, or influence, the name interval effort should not be taken to mean too much. We might have called it "the influence of futurity." For, as to the nature of this kind of effort our ideas are, as already noted, very dim; there is no physiological identification whatever to guide us; our psychological introspections are vague about it; and the only objective knowledge we have in regard to it are its effects.[1] But the effects prove the existence of

---

[1] Because of these uncertainties it does not seem worth while even to set up an hypothesis as to the psychological character of interval effort. On its face it would appear to be of the order of inactivity, rather than activity, and therefore a kind of self-restraint rather than self-constraint—inhibitory rather than excitatory. But, as we have noted before, the only time when self-restraint (inhibition) is demonstrable is before the decision is made and action commenced. Thereafter, except for interruptions, it subsides

some limiting influence other than those we had previously dealt with in Chapter 6; they submit to certain sorts of treatment in terms of magnitude from which the characteristics of the influence can be inferred; and therefore a hypothetical entity of this order must be imputed. On the other hand, there is some reason to identify this entity with effort of the more demonstrable variety. Like duration effort, interval effort acts as a deterrent to future provision; like that, its quantitative relations show that it constitutes a resistance to, rather than a diminution of the force of, future wants; like that it derives from experience, but thereafter has its chief effect in the memory-system. Furthermore, the dimensions of interval effort, as nearly as we can determine them, seem to relate it intimately to duration effort—that is, one of the dimensions of the resistance it offers is proportionate to the duration effort already made. It is not proportionate to the force of the want it opposes.[2]

Having identified working in the aspect of effort with what we previously called duration effort, we may now likewise identify retaining in the aspect of effort with the corresponding entity, interval effort. In doing so, since our previous analysis construes interval effort to be the expression of the influence of futurity, we come now to construe the "real cost" aspect of retaining as the limitation upon the quantity or period of retaining which is exercised by the influence of futurity. But, as soon as we complete these identifications, we find that, although the distinction between duration effort and interval effort seems at first sight to be logical and analytically satisfactory, it does not serve to distinguish our two forms of effort—working and retaining. In our analysis of effort in general at the beginning of the previous chapter, we suggested that the most probable hypothesis to explain the observed and felt difference between activities (self-constraint) or inactivities (self-restraint) which are effortful and those which are not is that the former are energized by secondary energy of

---

into the undemonstrable condition of a by-product of excitation. That is true of working; and we shall find that it is equally true of retaining. In fact, with retaining, the choice once made is usually irretrievable, except gradually with the passage of time—as we shall see. If so, it is hard to see the necessity of continuing self-restraint in view of the absence of an alternative. Nevertheless, the effort certainly continues, for it is out of that continuing experience that its effect as a memory arises and becomes effective in advance. We will have to leave this dilemma unsolved.

[2] This particular point, as to which we made a summary statement on pp. 365–367 (Chapter 6) is more fully analyzed in Appendix V, Section A, where we deal with the more usual recent explanation of the influence of futurity—"time-discount" or "time perspective"—which is a thesis that does not withstand analysis.

response (mnemonic-volitional system) while the latter are energized by primary energy of response (emotional system). This follows from the fact that the former are concerned only with future wants, and therefore involve no consummatory reaction, while the latter are concerned with present wants which always include a consummatory reaction if possible. Now it is evident that this criterion obliterates the distinction between the two kinds of effort —duration and interval. In other words, working, by the very fact that the criterion for distinguishing it from other activities is that it is not directed toward present satisfaction, necessarily also involves production in advance of consumption. Thus, under our definition of working, what makes it effortful is the fact that it includes simultaneous retaining—activity in advance of the existence of the want as a present want.[3] Nor have I been able to discover any other criterion by which we can distinguish working from playing or consuming— effortful from effortless behavior—that does not at the same time include retaining with working and therefore automatically define retaining as effortful behavior. It follows that, to deny that retaining is effort would be to deny that working is effort, and economic life would come to be viewed as one grand game played for the "fun" of it.[4]

Nevertheless, the distinction between the two kinds of effort is a useful one, though it is entirely concerned with a change in the process which only appears with the passage of time. During the first phase of the process the very fact that the activity can be defined as working is a result of the fact that it involves concurrent retaining. But then, after the stage in the process is reached at which the working is finished, the effortful character is associated with retaining alone and no longer with working and retaining combined. At that stage, the working having been done, it comes to be at least theoretically possible to use the product at once instead of deferring consumption still further. If that is not done, it must be because retaining is continued. Looked at

[3] Essentially, that confusion also underlies the analytical distinction between duration and interval effort. For duration effort can only take place over time. If so, does not interval effort necessarily commence at the beginning of the period of duration effort even if it may be regarded as a separate entity only after the end of this period?

[4] This points to the absurdity of the distinction between "earned" and "unearned" income. I find it made even more specific by Bowley (*The Change in the Distribution of the National Income*, Oxford, 1920, p. 7), who refers to "the income of individuals, whether it arises from ownership or effort" (i.e., retaining in its proprietary aspect is *contrasted* with, not included as, effort).

in another way, it is clear that the effort involved in working in order to provide two equal products may well be the same for both, while that involved in deferring the consumption of one of these products longer than that of the other is necessarily greater for the first. That is, the effort involved in the required quantity of working does not vary after the stage of completion of the product is passed, merely because the deferment of consumption is prolonged. Thereafter, the effort occasioned by deferment becomes a separate element to which we give the name retaining.

However, for the purposes of our analysis, we shall find it more useful to establish the dividing line at a somewhat different point, based on the convention we have already adopted with reference to the working-day. Since the producing must, by the nature of things, precede the consuming of the product, and since it has become customary that the whole working-day should precede the whole consuming-day (with minor exceptions) we shall not treat the product accumulated during the working-day by way of provision for the following consuming-day (or night) as being the subject of retaining. During the current working- and consuming-days there is no choice involved as to whether to retain or not; nor was there a choice, at the time of planning, as to the product still to be produced. Necessarily the provision cannot be consumed before it is produced, and conventionally it is not consumed until the working-day is over. On this basis we shall establish an analytical convention according to which we shall assign, as the critical stage in the process which distinguishes the two kinds of effort, the end of the consuming-day which follows each working-day. If consumption is completed within this period, the retaining involved will be ignored and all the effort will be assigned to working; if consumption is deferred beyond that time, all further effort will be assigned to retaining. Where the working required for any product exceeds what can be allocated from a single working-day, retaining of each of these installments will be conceived to begin the next day after it has been made; where the product is not used up in the consuming-day following its completion—whether it required time in one or several working-days—retaining of the unused installments will also be conceived to begin the next day. In terms of degree of futurity of future wants—that is, in the terms in which we first established this convention—the future wants whose instances are dated as of the following consuming-day will be regarded as having a degree of futurity of zero. Our base line for measuring the effect of the influence of futurity will therefore be the following morning after production.

We are going to distinguish the instances of future wants which are projected only to the following consuming-day as *current* wants. Under our convention, establishing the next morning as the base line for retaining, provisions for these wants involve no retaining. The term future wants, under this convention, will still be used to indicate instances with more than zero futurity. But this must not lead us into error. Current wants must not be confused with present wants. They are not. As to the entire programs for working-days or their execution, we are still dealing only with future wants. Those dated as of the following consuming-day are merely given a degree of futurity of zero so as to differentiate the functions necessary in a day-to-day economy from those required for a long-range economy. Thus we consign to the program for the following consuming-day—current wants—a single order of priority of future wants, a single virtual order of preference and a single selection of provisions. This program must include all wants that are to be satisfied at all, if, as is usually the case, they must be provided for in advance. All other parts of the program deal with provision for instances of future wants whose degree of futurity is greater than zero and for which provision must intrude in this single order of priority and of preference if it is to be made at all. It follows from this not arbitrary discrimination that retaining is only required when the product produced in the working-day, or days, exceeds, or has exceeded, the product consumed in the following consuming-day, or days; or, to reverse the fixed point, when there is consumed each twenty-four hours less than is, or has previously been, produced.

Now that we have definitively differentiated the retaining which accompanies all working—and is included in it as "real cost"—from the retaining that is done after the working or any installment of it is concluded, so that we have separated retaining from working as a "real cost," it becomes necessary for us to modify our concept of the magnitude of product being retained and therefore of the quantity of retaining being done on it. Our previous definition of the magnitude of product being retained, as the measure of the retaining being done, based it primarily on the accumulated "real cost" of working embodied in the product, subject to adjustments when that "real cost" of different lots of uniform product varies and to adjustments for loss of usefulness. Now, if retaining is a "real cost" as well as working, this magnitude of product must include the accumulated retaining that becomes incorporated in the product after the product is completed as well as the accumulated working up to the time of completion—that is, it must include retention as a "real cost" as well as work, both being the magnitudes of the effort involved in the process accomplished upon such product. But, as soon as we undertake to do that, we see that retaining as a "real cost" is a very different magnitude from retaining in terms of effect. Primary, or "simple" retaining, as effect, can be measured in terms of P, treated as a quantity of W. Thus it can be stated as the retaining of 10 standard units of work—the effect of working 10 standard hours. But, the "real cost" of retaining measures retaining in a different aspect. The "real cost" of retaining 10 standard units of work is but a minute fraction of the "real cost" of these 10 standard units of work.[5] This minute fraction is the constant, K, already introduced in Chapter 6. Thus when we include the "real cost" of the retaining already done—retention—in the magnitude of the product as a measure of the retaining being done, we add but a minute fraction per time unit to the magnitude of the product. For any short period the increment is therefore so small as to be negligible. When the period is long enough to justify it we must, however, convert "simple" retaining into "compound" retaining, according to which the magnitude of retaining, as effect, becomes the sum of the "real costs" of both kinds, work and retention, which has already been embodied in the product. As we proceed we shall find it possible to establish a somewhat definite quantitative relation between the effort involved in retaining and the effort involved in working by establishing a somewhat definite value for the constant, K—so much so that it will become possible roughly to add the two "real costs" together for the purpose of establishing the combined "real costs" of the product. By this means, too, we find it possible to state the magnitude of retaining as a "real cost" in the proper dimensional formula of a rate—that is, in such a way that it becomes the performance of a unit quantity of retention per unit of time. For, having established the unit quantity of retention as a fairly definite magnitude in relation to a unit quantity of work, we can use that as the measure of the rate. By this means we

---

[5] In fact, the "real cost" of retaining 1 hour's work for 1 hour in a modern economy is probably, as we shall note below, of the order of 1/175,200 of the "real cost" represented by the hour's work.

have introduced the magnitude retention, in the aspect of "real cost," in a way that could not be done, when it was considered in the aspect of effect. For this reason, when we refer hereafter to retention we shall always mean a quantity of "real cost"—or, more precisely, a quantity of the process accomplished in its aspect of "real cost." It will have no reference to the effect aspect of retaining. Moreover, now that we have identified retaining, in its aspect of effort, and all retention with what we were tentatively calling interval effort, we shall abandon that inconvenient special term and shall consider it implicit in the terms for this one of our two economic functions when we are regarding it as a "real cost."

In order to clarify these difficult statements let us now convert them into terms of suitable dimensional formulae. We have said that the magnitude of retaining being performed, in the aspect of effect, is the magnitude of the product being retained (cross-section of the process). The magnitude of retaining being performed, in the aspect of "real cost," is the rate at which this form of effort is being made. The magnitude of the retention ("real cost") which has been performed on any product is this rate (or its average over the term) multiplied by the time over which the retaining has been done. The "simple" dimensional formula for retaining, as effect, is therefore P in terms of "real cost" adjusted—that is W. Since, in the previous chapter, we found it possible to use the unit W for working performed (work), both in the aspect of effect and of "real cost"—through the device of a standard hour of working—the dimensional formula for work, in both aspects, is W. Then working, in both aspects, is WT^{-1}. But because, in its two aspects, retaining is not measured in the same terms, it will be necessary to distinguish the dimensional formulae of the two aspects. Let R_e stand for retaining in its aspect of effect, R_i stand for retention in its aspect of "real cost" and R_iT^{-1} for retaining in its aspect of "real cost." Under the primary or "simple" measure of retaining, as effect, its measure is P or W. That is, $R_e = P$, or $R_e = W$. But the "compound" measure of retaining, as effect, is different. Then, since retaining as effect, as we noted above, is measured by the whole "real cost" retained—the retention performed subsequently as well as the work performed originally—the corrected magnitude of R_e becomes $W + R_i$ (adjusted); the magnitude of retaining, as "real cost," R_iT^{-1}, then becomes the above-mentioned minute fraction of $W + R_i$ (adjusted) per T—that is $(W + R_i)KT^{-1}$. In both these formulae

$R_i = WK$. For any period of time, T, $R_i T^{-1}$ accrues and becomes $R_i T^{-1} \times T$ or R_i (retention). Such an increment of R_i increases the magnitude of R_e and also, but subject a second time to the constant —the minute fraction—the magnitude of $R_i T^{-1}$. Then, since this increment of R_i has the dimensional formula WK, we can substitute the latter. $R_e = W + WK$, $R_i T^{-1} = (W + WK)KT^{-1}$, and $R_i = (W + WK)K$. The difference between measuring R_e in terms of W alone, as before, or in terms of $W + R_i$, is very slight, if the constant K is a small fraction and the period of retaining is short. This being the case, it will be simpler to proceed with our examples on the basis of the formula for "simple" retaining, and only to introduce the corrected formula, or "compound" retaining, as a complication to be borne in mind. The realism and scientific utility of this way of viewing these entities will, I think, become apparent as we proceed with our analysis. After all it is no more than a precise and unequivocal version of the way they have always been viewed.

With these magnitudes and their dimensions clearly in mind, it becomes evident that we conceive retaining, like working, to be a process carried on *from outside of*, but *on*, a product. Retention we conceive, like work, to be embodied in the product itself.[6] While product is in process and work is accruing in it, after the following consuming-day the quantity of retaining being currently performed increases *pari passu* with the accumulation of the work and the retention already performed. Both have been stored up and both must be retained from then on. When the product is finished—no more work added—only the retention performed continues to accumulate. Thereafter, as the product begins to be used up, the quantity of retaining being currently performed is, according to the convention previously alluded to, conceived to decrease *pari passu* in proportion as the product is used up; nevertheless, the retention continues to accumulate, though at a decreasing rate, as this new but decreasing retaining continues to be embodied in the product. The retention embodied up to any point is then a function of these successively increasing and decreasing rates at which retaining is being performed and of the time elapsed between the beginning of working and that point, up to the completion of the using-up. Obviously at the moment when it is completely used up there is no product left to embody the accrued retention. But the same

---

[6] But, just as worker, working, work and that which embodies it are separate entities, so are retainer, retaining, retention and that which embodies it.

is true of the work which was embodied. Both are conceived to have disappeared; the work perhaps long after it was concluded; the retention only just as it was concluded. We will elaborate the analysis of these relationships and this disappearance at a later point. This summary outline is furnished here only for the purpose of making it clear what we regard these entities to be and how we conceive them to behave.

2. THE INFLUENCE OF RETAINING AS EFFORT—"SIMPLE"

In order to clarify the influence of futurity, through the effort of retaining, in limiting provision for future wants—that is, as a limitation on the retaining done—it is necessary for us to establish a simplified situation in which we eliminate all interfering factors and thus isolate the effects of this one alone. To that end, we will, in the first place, lay the scene at the time a plan or program is being considered. Probably no retaining is ever initiated except as the result of such a plan. We have inferred that the faculty involved in such planning is the ability of a man (or an organism) "voluntarily" to project himself to a definite place along the time-scale into the counterfeit future and to furnish that position with appropriate details in the form of associated memories of past experiences—here future wants and memories of the two kinds of effort. This program is analogous to that already outlined for a day's working; but, whereas the latter may be confined to consideration of future wants dated as of the following consuming-day only (current wants), our base line for retaining means that this program necessarily involves a longer view ahead. In fact, at this first stage of our analysis, it involved the indefinite future without limit. Thus there are two differences between the respective programs. The first has to do with the dates of the instances of wants considered. The program for a working-day, as previously considered, covered only current wants; this program may permit a mixture of future with current wants. The influence of futurity, according to our convention, does not enter so far as provision is made for current wants only. We therefore isolate this influence when we discover its effect upon the capacity of future wants to intrude into the program. The other difference has to do with the scope of the programs. A program for a day's working may be confined to provision for current wants. Or it may include provisions for some future wants. However, a program of provisions for future wants may cover several or many days' working; a program of provision for current wants, only, can reach no further than one day's working. In the second place, we are going to continue our entirely arbitrary assumption that provision for each instance of a future want requires one hour's working. This in order to study the influence of futurity by itself.[7] But, even for this purpose, we will find it necessary on occasion to alter this assumption and to introduce, with due notice, variations in "real cost" per adequate provision when these variations arise from certain special causes—labor-saving and retaining itself. Finally, for the sake of simplicity, we will regard the unit of decision to be a full day's supply, even if, in the case of recurring wants, that may include several adequate provisions or full measures.[8]

In the setting described we may now undertake a graphic representation of the way retention as an anticipated "real cost" limits the quantity of retaining that is undertaken. We will first analyze it on the "simple" basis and can then adapt that to the "compound" basis with a slight modification.[9] The standpoint from which the program is considered is the present, and the influences at work are therefore wholly memories of past experience, some taking the form of orders of priority of future wants repeated at various degrees of futurity, some the form of current wants in their single order of priority, some the form of memories of uniform quantities of working effort per day's provision (our arbitrary assumption) and some the form of memories of variable quantities of retaining effort.

In Fig. 25 we give a graphic representation of this formula in its simplest form. Projected along the time-scale for 90 days ahead are successive instances of a future want, *ae*, and the quantity of work required to provide for it for one day, *ce*. At each date the instance

[7] There is another reason for our arbitrary assumption at this point. It will be our thesis in the following chapters that the quantity of "real cost" of work required for an adequate provision is imposed and governed primarily by the environment subject to two other intervening variables. But, though the environment has some influence in determining the "real cost" of retention required on some of the occasions we shall shortly analyze, this "real cost" is, on certain occasions, determined only by the influences we are here considering—i.e., it is a matter of choice. Thus this is the place to study retention cost; while variations in work cost must be deferred.
[8] The reader should regard the analysis in this chapter as a first approximation only. It is too simple and too precise. It is an instance of the virtual method. In Part IV, where we introduce the other chief variables, we shall find it necessary to modify in certain important respects the scheme developed here.
[9] That is, at this stage, we measure the retaining, in one of its dimensions, only by the work being retained and not, as we shall in the next subsection, by the work plus the accrued retention being retained.

of the want is shown as of the same force as the current instance, *ab* being parallel to the base *ef;* and at each date the resistance offered by the work, if done *then,* is shown to be the same as for the current working-day, *cd* being also parallel to the base *ef.* The rising solid line *cb,* superimposed upon the broken line *cd* (representing work), shows the rate of accrual of retaining as effort. The altitude between the solid line *cb,* and the broken line *cd,* at any point, shows accrued retaining as effort at that point—that is, the quantity of retention

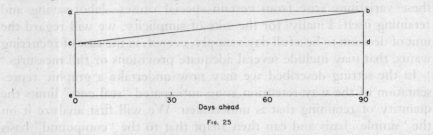

Fig. 25

which would have to be added to the work, if done now, as compared to the work alone, if done then. Thus the total of the two efforts, or resistances, for provision made now, at any point along the time-scale, is the altitude between the rising solid line *cb* and the base *ef.* Considering the matter from the viewpoint of the present, the total of these resistances, *bd + df,* equals the force of the want, *bf,* at 90 days ahead. Provision would not be made now for that date or for any date beyond it. On the other hand, also from the viewpoint of the present, the total of these resistances, altitude to *cb,* is greater than that of work resistance alone, altitude to *cd,* for any intervening date as well. Therefore, if no other influences entered, provision would not be made now for any date ahead. That is the impasse to which reference was made on pp. 371–372. The influence of futurity, standing alone, would negative all present provision for future wants. Here, then, we have, in their simplest form, the two limitations established by retaining as effort. If the alternative of working then is open and equal, retaining as effort prevents any future provision now. Even if the alternative is not open, retaining as effort prevents any future provision now for a date at or beyond 90 days. If work then is not equal, but is less, whether or not provision will be made now for a date less than 90 days ahead will depend on whether the diminution of work is sufficient to off-set the increment of retention—that is, whether *ce* is less than *df* by more than *bd.*

At once we must put the reader on notice that this diagram distorts reality. The constant K is here shown as if it were ⅕, if the unit of time is taken as 30 days, or ⅟₁₅₀, if it is one day. Actually, as we shall work it out later, the constant in a developed and civilized economy is less than a thousandth part of that figure. Obviously, such a minute constant would be too small to show on any diagram. Hence all our diagrams illustrating this influence must be severely discounted. The foreshortening necessary throws the proportions all out of scale. Upon the basis of the usual constant of the present day in this country, the exclusion of future provision, which we show here as beginning for 90 days ahead, would only begin at about 20 years ahead. On the other hand, the assumption of one hour's work per day's provision is also quite artificial. However, we are examining now a direct economy which starts from scratch—no retaining. For such a case this degree of foreshortening may not be so much of an exaggeration.

This obvious difference between our constant, as shown here, and reality raises two other questions. The first question is whether or not the line *cb* should be a straight line—that is, whether we are dealing here with a constant or with a variable. So far as "simple" retaining goes—retaining of work only—we are going to assume that we are dealing with a constant, but only on account of complete lack of knowledge of anything to the contrary. It is, of course, not impossible that the fraction increases with the distance of projection, or that it does so, at least, beyond some distant point. The second question is whether differences in make-up or circumstances between individuals cause them to have different constants. To this the answer seems certainly to be yes. In fact, our two cases above—the modern and the primitive economy—affirm that. This question must be disentangled from another. It is quite possible that there are, among different persons, decided variations in the faculty of placing oneself in the counterfeit future and of peopling it with future wants, by association and voluntary recall, and of calculating contingencies. That does not concern the constant. The question here is affected only by variations among different people in the matter of effort. Now we cannot tell, as between two different persons, whether the fact that the first provides only for a less distant future than the second indicates that the sense of effort involved is for him more intense, or, instead, that it indicates merely that his capacity or his willingness for volitional effort is less. That is, we do not know whether the magnitude of effort in the individual case is determined in its negative or in its positive aspect. But, as to that, the same uncertainty exists also in the case of working effort. And it is equally indeterminate there. We might as well admit that, since we do not know what effort is, we cannot measure it. However, whichever is the determinant, there appear to be differences in the constant between different persons. Admitting this, we may regard our graphs as representing only a sample individual and may proceed on the assumption that, for any one person, the effort involved in retaining one unit of work for one unit of time is always the same no matter for what want the provision is made and no matter for how far in the future this provision is intended. In this respect the effort of

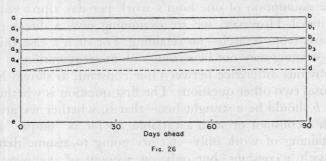

Fig. 26

retaining seems to be different from that of working where, we believe, the effort increases during the working-day and perhaps differs for different tasks.

So much for the limiting effect of the effort on retaining and retention under the simplest conditions, when related to a single future want only, and to a provision for that want which always involves the same amount of work. Let us now add the first complication, variation in the force of the want. Since we are proceeding upon the hypothesis that all instances of each future want have the same force as the current instance, this variation can only be introduced by substituting for the single future want a section of the whole series of orders of priority of the future want system. In order to examine the effect of this variable by itself, we will continue to treat full day's provisions for all these wants as if they involved a uniform amount of work. In Fig. 26 we show a section of the series of orders of priority of future wants in its relation to a uniform quantity of work and therefore to a uniform rate of accrual of retention. Now the altitudes of the lines, ab, a_1b_1, a_2b_2, a_3b_3, and a_4b_4 above the base, ef, show the force of five different future wants, A, B, C, D and E, as projected up to 90 days ahead. Each evinces the same force for any date shown. The altitude to the broken line cd represents the effort involved in each day's provision. It is the same for all five wants and, for each, it is the same for all dates. Again, at any point, the altitude between the solid line cb_2 and the broken line cd shows the accrued retaining as effort (retention as "real cost") up to that point. Thus, again, the altitude from the base ef to the solid line cb_2 represents, at any point, the total effort involved in provision now for an instance at that point along the time-scale. This alters the conclusions shown in the previous figure only in one respect. Even if the alternative of work *then* instead of *now* is not open, the influence of futurity alone will, according to this exaggerated constant, exclude provision now for Want E for more than 30 days ahead, for Want D for more than 60 days ahead, for Want C for more than 90 days ahead. Likewise for Wants B and A at 120 days and 150 days, respectively, if we extrapolate from the diagram. This demonstrates that, work being equal, the influence of futurity, even if the alternative of provision then is not open, tends to curtail the interval as we proceed along (down) any particular order of priority of future wants. If other influences lead to their being made at all, provision will be made further in advance for prior wants than for subordinate ones.

Finally, let us represent the effect of variation in the other variable, amount of work per day's provision. That is, let us momentarily abandon our assumption. Fig. 27 shows everything as before except that we have but one want, whose force at all dates is the altitude of ab above the base ef, and except that we have three alternative quantities of work per day's provision, whose resistance equals the altitude of cd, c_1d_1, and c_2d_2, respectively, above the base ef. Now our formula for the accrual of resistance on account of "simple" retaining as effort is WKT^{-1}. Using numerical values solely for purposes of representation and not as reflecting reality, let us give W for the altitude ce, as $7\frac{1}{2}$, for the altitude c_1e, as 5 and for the altitude c_2e, as $2\frac{1}{2}$. Since, if the unit of time is a day, our constant is here shown as $\frac{1}{150}$, and since it is the same for all, R_1 (or accrued retention) will equal $1\frac{1}{2}$ in 90 days for c_2e, 3 in 90 days for c_1e, and will have equaled $2\frac{1}{2}$ in 50 days for ce. Again extrapolating to bring the point out, if any provision is made, the limit for ce is 50 days ahead, for c_1e 150 days ahead, and for c_2e 450 days ahead. The ratio between the time limits is therefore

1:3:9, though the ratio between the quantities of work involved is only 3:2:1. From this we conclude that a reduction in the quantity of "real cost" in the form of work involved in a day's provision for any future want results in a more than proportional extension of the interval before the influence of futurity precludes further provision now, even if the alternative of provision then is not open.

This last diagram represents the conclusion reached on p. 366 that "each activity, in turn, which offers a resistance less by a uniform amount than its predecessor, extends its reach by a greater distance along the time-scale than did its predecessor." That conclusion was

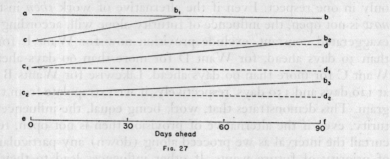

Days ahead

Fig. 27

there presented without proof, which was promised in Part II; but it was used as the chief argument for identifying the influence of futurity with increases in resistances rather than decreases of forces. Absolute proof is not possible. But, in Appendix V, Section A, we do what we can along that line. First, we cite evidence from observation that seems to support our interpretation of the energetics of this system; second, we undertake to show that the chief alternative interpretation is untenable since it would lead to a program quite contrary to reality. The reader who questions the foregoing conclusion is therefore referred to Appendix V.

3. THE INFLUENCE OF RETAINING AS EFFORT—"COMPOUND"

This analysis will enable us to make still clearer the difference between the magnitudes of the two aspects of retaining—its effect and its "real cost," or effort. The quantity of "simple" retaining being done, as effect, is measured in terms of a static magnitude, the quantity of work being retained. Since we regard product as a compound of work, that is much the same as saying that such retaining is measured in terms of the quantity of product being retained, provided the necessary adjustments are made on account of the slightly different concepts for these two magnitudes. On that basis, and except for these adjustments, the quantity of retaining being done on any product would not change after the work incorporated in it had been finished.[10] Now we have already noted that the other aspect of retaining, the effort involved in it or its magnitude as a "real cost," is much smaller than its magnitude as effect. If we take as the unit of the effect of retaining 1 W—that is, 1 hour's standard work—then retaining 150 W would equal 150 units of retaining as effect. But, according even to the exaggerated constant used in the previous section—$\frac{1}{150}$ per day—the magnitude of the "real cost" involved in that amount of retaining would be 150 W × $\frac{1}{150}$ per day, or an amount of effort per day to retain 150 units of work which was equal only to one hour's working effort (i.e., 1W). Thus to perform 150 units of retaining for one day involves—on the basis of this constant—a quantity of effort equal to one hour's working effort. At the end of one day the accrued retention would represent that quantity of effort; at the end of 150 days accrued retention would represent 150 times that quantity of effort; at that point the retention as effort would be equal to the work as effort, and the aggregate of the two forms of "real cost" would be twice the original "real cost" in work only. On the basis of a "civilized" constant, that doubling up might not occur for twenty years; for our example of a direct economy the doubling would probably take place somewhere in between these two extremes.

Now we have to consider the question whether real life confirms this "compound" accrual of the "real cost" of retaining and therefore, at any moment, the consequent "real cost" of retention already performed, and therefore, between any two moments, an increase in the quantity of retaining being currently performed. That resolves itself into the question whether, in actuality, work alone measures the quantity of retaining being done or whether that measure is, instead, the accrued "real cost" of both kinds. If it is the latter, then our assumption above that we were dealing with a constant fraction would have to be altered. Or, rather, while a constant may represent the facts for "simple" retaining, conversion to terms of "compound" retaining would, by adding the magnitude of accrued retention discontinuously or continuously, alter our straight line projection in

[10] That is, it would not do so until the product began to be used up. The effect of that process will be examined later.

the diagrams. The alteration would take the form of changes of direction up from the base, if the increment were included discontinuously, and the form of a concave curve,[11] if the increment were included continuously.

There are two difficulties in testing such a question by appeal to reality. The first is that the alteration to allow for "compounding" would be almost imperceptible under conditions at present observable. That becomes clear when one considers the diminutive rate at which retaining as a "real cost" accrues. Even with our exaggerated constant the direction of the solid line cb in Fig. 25, if the increment were included discontinuously every 30 days, would veer upwards at 30 days ahead by only $\frac{1}{150}$ part of the angle bcd. The second difficulty is that this phenomenon occurs very rarely in such a condition of isolation that it can be examined by itself. Usually products of a sufficiently long life to offer the necessary perspective for such a test as this do not remain of the same "size." That is, as we noted in the last chapter, such products are almost always in use and thus begin to diminish in "size" for other reasons from a date shortly after they were produced. Obviously, such a major contraction in magnitude would conceal any tendency toward such a very minor expansion in magnitude as would be produced by "compounding." [12]

However, it is probably safer to conclude that a slight correction should be made in our dimensional formula in order to cover "compounding." That is the same as saying that we should regard the magnitude of retaining as effect to be measured by the total "real cost" of the product retained—subject to the aforementioned adjustments—rather than by the work incorporated only. If so, as we noted above, the effort involved in retaining is not precisely at the rate of WKT^{-1}; instead it is $(W + R_i)KT^{-1}$—or, since $R_i = WK$, it is $(W + WK)KT^{-1}$. Then accrued retention at any point, as a measure of effort of this kind incorporated in the product, would be stated in terms of the dimensional formula $(W + R_i)K$—or, since $R_i = WK$,

---

[11] Concave, in the sense we use it, means curving up.
[12] At present I can see no way in which this question can be settled by comparing with reality the pattern which the several possible formulae produce. In our day, the constant of those whose constant counts in economic life is usually so small a fraction that the difference between the patterns these formulae would produce becomes minute. In so far as we can fit any of them to reality we seem to be able to fit one as well as the other. Moreover, here and now so many other factors enter into the picture (risk, "liquidity preference," etc.) that we cannot disengage the effect of the calculation of effort from the rest and determine exactly how it works.

as $(W + WK)K.$[13] In turn, we shall conceive of the influence of futurity as being represented by a rising curve of very slight concavity, projected from the present, rather than by a rising straight line.

C. OCCASIONS FOR RETAINING

In the previous section we established the limitation upon retaining by reason of the effort involved—or, what is the same thing under our construction, the limitation set by the influence of futurity. Considering only "simple" retaining, since the margin of error on account of omitting "compound" retaining is very slight, we found that the effect of this supplement to the initial resistance, involved in the work alone, operates differently under different conditions. If (1) it is expected that the same quantity of working can furnish the provision when the instance of the future want shall become current—i.e., for the next night—then the increment of resistance to making the provision now, by reason of the effort of retaining during the interval, will prevent any provision now. The line of least resistance will be to wait until the time comes. "Sufficient unto the day is the evil thereof." If (2) it is expected that working when the instance of the want shall become current cannot, for some reason, furnish the provision, the alternative of the line of least resistance is not offered. The choice, then, is now or never. But, even at that, the effect of the effort of retaining sets a limit to the futurity of an instance that will be provided for now. If the aggregate of the effort of working now plus that of retaining during the interval is greater than the force of the particular future want, provision will not be made now. That means that, for each want, the influence of futurity sets a limit at some point along the time-scale beyond which provision will not be made under any condition. If (3) it is expected that by doing the work now, in whole or in part, the aggregate of work then and now will be less than its quantity if all done then, and by more than the increment of resistance offered by retaining the work done now during the interval, the influence of futurity will be overcome and the choice will be now and easier as against then and harder. Thus we may say briefly that the influence of futurity shuts out all provision for future wants when the alternative of postponing provision until the instance becomes cur-

---

[13] The mathematical, as opposed to the dimensional, formulae for such a magnitude as our total effort, when computed discontinuously or continuously, are given by Fisher (*142*, 357–362).

rent is open and equal. That brings us to a point where it becomes necessary to examine in a systematic way the occasions when retaining *is* done—that is, the exceptions to the general rule due to the several conditions under which the alternative is not open or equal. It is these exceptions, the reader will recall, that sufficiently handicap the line of least resistance so that it is no longer such. It is these exceptions, and only these, that occasion retaining at all. It is with reference to these that we used the analogy, in Chapter 6, of the organist, without whom the apparatus does not play—the final factor that negatives the negativing of the influence of futurity and releases the mechanism of the future want system.[1]

The nature of these exceptions—the only occasions for retaining—brings out the fact that there is no advantage in mere future provision as such. No benefit is obtained by building up a stock which is to be kept unused forever. Its only reason for being is that it will be used at some future time. Therefore, in spite of certain abnormalities of motivation and in contradiction to psychologists and biologists who think they have found an "acquisitive instinct," we assert that, in general, future provision is never made unless it is expected that, upon some definite future occasion, it will be needed and cannot then be provided or cannot then be provided so easily.[2] The operation of conscious memory with reference to the counterfeit future is to project against the screen a pattern derived from the past. The operation of insight leads to the alteration of this pattern in so far as it rearranges its details and thus anticipates the probable exceptions to the rule.

1. THE TWO CONTINGENCIES

The exceptions noted above are grouped into two classes, occasions when the working cannot be done then and occasions when working now, or working now and then, is sufficiently less than working only then. But, when we come to examine the occasions when working cannot be done then, we find that they, in turn, fall naturally into two sub-groups which we shall term contingencies and technical necessities. Let us first consider the contingencies. In Chapter 5 we distinguished between recurrent future wants, which can be dated at times certain because they are regular in their appearance, and contingent wants, which occur fortuitously and can therefore only be

---

[1] See pp. 372–373.
[2] For a brief discussion of the so-called "acquisitive instinct" see Appendix V, Section B.

dated at times uncertain, or according to the frequency with which they occur over a period. Within the period in which a contingent want is expected to occur once, its date may be fixed at the beginning or at the middle (average) of the period. The contingencies we are now dealing with relate to the working, not to the wants; but it will be analytically helpful to divide them into kinds, according as the instances considered are of recurrent or contingent wants.

a. The first type of contingency is this—that, at some date or dates within the future envisaged, all or part of the working being done to provide for current wants will have to be discontinued. In an economy entirely dependent on its own current working—a direct economy—any untoward event (accident, illness, weather) which prevents or reduces the working-day will also, in the absence of future provision, put a stop to, or reduce, all consuming other than direct consumption. For this reason, contingencies of the first type bear upon provisions for all wants that are being provided for currently. That, in turn, limits their effects to regularly (daily) recurring wants, the only kind that can be provided for currently. It is at once evident that this type of contingency embraces the special case of provision made during the working-day for the following consuming-day, or night— that is, for current wants. Working and leisure cannot be concurrent and, therefore, working will not be done during the consuming-day. This fact, together with the technical necessity that the working be done beforehand, precludes working when the wants become present wants. However, we have agreed to accept the convention that such providing does not involve retaining. Therefore, while admitting that it is in essence a special case of the same type, we will confine ourselves to treating this contingency only when the instances have a degree of futurity greater than zero.

The only proof that such a contingency may occur—that is, that it actually exists in the present, in the legal sense—is that such occasions have sporadically occurred in the past. Experience reminds one that then, if no provision had been made, one went without. On the other hand, it also tells one that, if provision had been made, it was used up when the occasion arrived. If, then, such occasions are expected to repeat themselves at regular or irregular intervals, it will become the practice to anticipate such repetition by replacing each future provision as and when it is used up. This matter of replacement will be considered in due course. It may mean that, if the contingency is conceived to be likely to occur *at any time*, provision is maintained at all times—that is, that a permanent stock on hand comes to be established from which, on occasion, a part is used and as soon as possible replaced. If, on the other hand, the expected contingency does not arise, future provision against it is only to be justified by a certain law of probability—the supposition that, nevertheless, it *might* occur. Independent, then, of actual experience there is insight, in obedience to which a potential takes the place of a prospect, and the sense of security is gratified. This is almost a separate want in itself. On the other hand, continued failure of the contingency to appear may lull one into a sense of security even in the absence of future provision. Therefore, both directly, on account of the revision downward of the probability of occurrence, and indirectly, on account of the fading of the sense of insecurity, decreases or eliminations of future provision are likely to be made when the expected contingency does not arise with some frequency. We arrive at the conclusion that the estimation of this contingency (inability to work) is an actuarial matter.

b. The second type of contingency is this: during some period within the future envisaged, an irregularly occurring want may occur without warning. Since we have to assume that only the regularly recurring wants would be provided for during each working-day for each following consuming-day (i.e., as current wants), such irregular wants could never be provided for at all except by means of future provision (i.e., as future wants). This absence of current provision for all future wants which we have called contingent wants converts this contingency into one dealing with the occurrence of the want rather than with the occurrence of inability to provide for it. However, as we suggested in Chapter 5, that merely redirects the whole of the actuarial calculation described above from the question whether working then will, for some reason, be impossible to the question whether the sporadic want is likely to occur during the period envisaged. The practice with regard to replacement or the maintenance of a permanent stock on hand will be directed by the same considerations as for the first type of contingency.[3] But the fundamental difference between the two types is that the first concerns all wants cur-

---

[3] In a modern economy one of the closest approaches to the conditions of a direct economy is a camping trip. When one plans his supplies for such a trip he includes provision for such contingent future wants as he believes likely to occur during the period; but he excludes many very important provisions for such wants as he believes not likely to occur.

rently provided for while the second concerns always and only a single want or constellation.

2. THE THREE TECHNICAL NECESSITIES

a. The first technical necessity is imposed by a characteristic of natural processes. It may be that some natural material or power necessary for a certain product, and available in the present, will cease to be available within the future envisaged. This is the usual condition with regard to growing things as well as some others. We will denominate such processes, by their common characteristic, as *intermittent* natural processes. To take a most primitive instance, let us suppose that the seed of wild grain is the much preferred material with which to satisfy the prior want, hunger. That seed must be gathered during the period between the time it ripens and the time it falls and germinates.

The opportunity will not occur again for a year. As a result, this is a case in which, except for a few days each year, the issue is between future provision or none at all. After the season, current provision will be impossible. Thus the occasion when the provision cannot be made currently is not a contingency; it is a certainty; and experience soon teaches precisely when, along the time-scale, it begins and ends. The actuarial feature has practically disappeared. Unlike the first type of contingency, but like the second, this technical necessity relates to but one want, not to the whole gamut. Or, more exactly, it may relate to one perhaps compound means which may serve for more or less of the members of a constellation. Unlike both types of contingency, this occasion for retaining is a long one, usually much longer than the period during which the provision for it can be made. And unlike them, this occasion is not dated at some single day or brief period along the time-scale and is not separated from the present by an interval. Rather, it begins at the end of the season and may be continuous thereafter until the beginning of the next season.

b. The second technical necessity is due to the nature of what we call *durable* objects (means or product).[4] Since we conventionally

---

[4] In Chapter 7 we defined as durable all means which lasted in use through more than one brief but continuous process. Also we pointed out that the term referred to an economic, not a physical, characteristic. Here it is well to reiterate that the term does not mean hard *vs.* soft, nor even lasting *vs.* perishable. It means only long usability *vs.* brief

define a durable as a product which is used up in installments and since this implies use for more than one day, it necessarily follows that a durable is future provision as to all its installments beyond the first. Certain wants can only be satisfied by products which come in this category; others are usually or preferably served by such products. Again, we have a condition under which the issue is between future provision or none at all. Current provision by itself cannot, by definition, be a durable.[5] Again the occasion is a certainty, not a contingency, so no actuarial estimates are involved; the issue concerns a single want only, or at most the several members of a constellation; and again, unlike the contingencies, this occasion stretches over time from the completion of the durable through to the end of its life. Even if the want does not recur daily, nevertheless retaining must continue until the last installment is used or loses its usefulness.

It is possible that the making of a durable which would last many days could be fitted into the program for one working-day. But usually it is spread over many days for the reason that it requires much work. Furthermore, in order to abstract from the effect of various quantities of work per provision, we are using the assumption that each day's provision for any want requires one hour of work. Hence, in our examples, as many hours of work will be required for a durable as there are installments in its life. If the number of hours in a single working-day are insufficient, or if all these hours are not made available under the program for provision for a single want, the durable

---

usability. The scaffolding or concrete forms used in building are physically durable and yet economically almost non-durable. Coal is hard and very lasting, but it is *the* type of the non-durable.

Upon the effort side there is no economic difference between durable and non-durable products other than that the former always require retaining and the latter may not.

Because it has devoted its efforts to dealing directly with the whole mass of objective data of an economy, the National Bureau of Economic Research has been faced with the necessity of deciding in which class to place every individual product. In two recent studies by the Bureau the authors have distinguished between durables (life in use of more than two or three years), semi-durables (of "intermediate service life") and perishables or transient goods (of service life less than six months or "momentary"). See Simon Kuznets, *Commodity Flow and Capital Formation* (National Bureau of Economic Research, 1938), I, 6, and Charles A. Bliss, *The Structure of Manufacturing Production* (National Bureau of Economic Research, 1939), p. 42, note 21. These seem valid and useful criteria of classification for the purpose. For our purely analytical purposes we may distinguish merely between the product of which one physically undivided unit represents more than one day's use, and that which does not. The fact that the usual "commercial package" contains more than one day's supply does not make the product a durable in our sense. It merely indicates that some "future provision" is customary.   [5] Cf. Cassel, 74, 190-192.

cannot be made in one day. Then the durable proves to be the occasion for retaining, as well, in another respect. The whole of the working-time required must be applied in advance of any of the uses of the produce, because the product must be finished before it is usable at all. And during this period of incubation each day's work must be retained, also, up to the time of the first day's use. That, in turn, means that even the first day's installment requires retaining. No current provision is possible at all. Whereas, under the first technical necessity current provision is possible during the season, here, if the working requires more than one day, it is impossible at any time. On the other hand, whereas, there, each day's future provision may be made for its own sake only and independently of all others, here all installments of future provision are bound together in one product; none can be made without all, subject to choice as to durability—that is, as to the reach of the furthest provision.

c. Partaking of the nature of a durable in most respects, though in itself quite distinct, is what may be called long-process product—the third of our technical necessities. By this term we mean to cover all non-durable products which, by the nature of the process or conditions of their production, require that working be done on them for more than our conventional day in advance. The chief types of such a class which might be found in a direct economy are: (a) products whose process of production must include and therefore await an intermittent natural process which takes its own time; (b) products whose process of production includes considerable transportation. Type (a) may have first appeared when stages were introduced in advance of the purely harvesting process described as our first technical necessity, by reason of inserting the intermittent working processes called sowing, plowing, cultivation, etc. When that was done it became necessary to await the conclusion of the natural process of growth before the results of this advance working could be had. In the interval perhaps little or no further working was required on this particular provision. All processes such as growth, fermentation, curing, or seasoning (of wood) take time and therefore belong in this class.[6] The

---

[6] It is essential to distinguish between the enhancement of usefulness which takes place, over time, by reason of a natural process, and the purely permissive human function of retaining which is requisite to it. Retaining does not enhance usefulness; it keeps products as they are. But in a limited number of instances, means "improve" over a period. If, then—but only if—working was required in the early stages of the process, retaining is required in the interval before the process completes itself. The natural process itself is costless; but the requisite retaining is a "real cost." The analogy of biological growth

second type appeared when it became advantageous or necessary to go to a distance (included as working) in order to secure a material or ingredient which was essential to the preferred means of satisfying some want within the limit of capacity. Such a condition could only exist, under our limiting assumption of one hour's work for each day's provision, if it remained possible, by transporting several days' supply at one time, to complete some number of days' provision, as a lot, in an equal number of hours' working, including that required for the going and returning. However, even without that assumption, whenever transportation itself required more than one day, or whenever transportation plus the rest of the production process did so, this condition would arise.[7]

Adhering to our assumption that each day's provision requires one hour's working, it is clear that long-process products have much the same characteristics as durables. Technical conditions preclude the enjoyment of the result in the form of current provision—that is, immediately. The first day's provision is therefore necessarily deferred. If the want is a sporadic one whose occurrence is of the kind envisaged as a contingency of type two, this may make no difference, though it will often be impossible to prepare one day's provision at a time by applying successive fractions of the hour over the period during which the want is in abeyance. But, if the want is a regularly recurring one, this will make a difference; then these same technical conditions frequently demand that the long process should produce, as one lot, a block of provisions none of which will be available until all are finished. The only exception to that is the case of a continuous process which, once started, requires one hour a day of working and results continually, beginning some time later, in an output of one provision per day. However, both cases are of the same order as a durable, since the second, as we shall see shortly, has the same pattern as a durable after that has begun to be continuously replaced.

In all cases, then, the long-process product resembles the durable when that, as is usual, requires work applied over more than one day. That is, it imposes the necessity of retaining the successive increments

---

is generally a false one when applied as an explanation of the advantages of future provisions of all kinds. It applies only occasionally and to one kind.

[7] Moreover, such transportation would usually involve several products or their materials at once, with different future dates. When the farmer goes to town he has a "list." Even in primitive times the errand was probably not a single one and the degree of futurity by no means uniform.

of intermittent or daily prior work before the first day's provision becomes available. Moreover, with the rare exceptions noted above, it also resembles the durable in that it involves the necessity of a block of future provisions which, though they are not physically inseparable as with a durable, will be introduced into the program as a whole or not at all. Thus, with these exceptions, long-process product also involves retaining of the unused future provisions after completion. Like durables, this occasion is a certainty, not a contingency, so no actuarial estimates are involved; it concerns provision for a single want, or constellation, only; it stretches over time from the beginning of the work to the date of the last provision included, whether or not the want is a daily recurring one, or, at the other extreme, fortuitous in its occurrence.

3. THE TWO TECHNICAL OPTIONS

The most important occasions for retaining—and in a modern economy the occasions which account for the greater part of it—are wholly due to certain options given by technical conditions, in which the element of future provision in and of itself is entirely incidental to the chief purpose.[8] In order to examine these options we must abandon our assumption that the "coefficients of production" are the same for all products—that, in our example, one hour of working is required for one day's provision of each and every want. And this because the essence of these options consists in the fact that technical opportunities exist which offer, at the price of some working now and therefore of initiated and continued retaining, an economizing of working then and now, in the aggregate. We may call these two types of option large-batch processes and indirect processes. While, in actual historical development, it may well be that both these technical opportunities for economizing working have developed chiefly in connection with what is called the "division of labor," they are not intrinsically nor necessarily among the economizings which can only be availed of by many workers each specializing concurrently on a different part of a single process. Rather, these particular economizings are also available, within narrower limits, to an individual worker through the same scheme applied successively instead of concurrently. They are therefore appropriately discussed in connection with a direct economy in which there is no exchange.

[8] We shall fully discuss the characteristics of these options in Chapter 12.

a. When the technical possibility exists of economizing working by reason of a large-batch process, the reduction in working is due to the fact that a large batch of product (many days' provision) can be carried simultaneously through each of the successive steps of a process of production with a smaller expenditure of working-time than is required if each small part of the batch (each day's provision) is put through the complete process by itself. If, for instance, there are ten steps in a process, one hour may be required to put one day's provision through these ten steps to completion. On the other hand, if the first hour is devoted to the first step only, the second to the second step only, etc., it may be possible to put through a batch of 20 days' provisions in exactly the same total of working time. The result is that, like the durable requiring more than one day and like the long-process product, none of the product is finished until the full 10 hours have been applied. The whole output arrives at the end. Then, before it is completed and, thereafter, until it is used up, this large batch requires retaining. Obviously, the retaining is not done for the sake of future provision per se. On the contrary, the retaining offers an increment of resistance which must be offset, nay more than offset, by a decrement in the total working required.

b. The second type of technical option is offered by those processes which involve the production of what we have previously called intermediate product which is itself then, and only, used in the production of final product.[9] It exists when, by producing first an intermediate product and using it thereafter in producing final product, the total quantity of working required will be reduced. The more typical instance arises when this intermediate product is itself a durable, such as a tool or machine. Therefore, in our subsequent illustrations, we will examine that particular instance only. The intermediate product which is used up in one day follows the same lines as the durable in that it has to be produced beforehand, but differs in the fact that each day's supply may be produced only one day beforehand. However, the nature of the intermediate durable product is usually such as to require working-time during more than one day, so that, again in this case, the benefit does not begin until the process of producing it is

[9] We may remind the reader that, in the previous chapter, we defined intermediate product, whether finished or unfinished, to be such product as does not itself become physically a part of final product. Unfinished final product—product in process—or its as yet uncombined parts, is not intermediate. This is a naïve but useful distinction.

completed. Therefore, again, retaining is required from the beginning of the work to the time of use of the last installment. As in the case of the first type of technical option, the retaining is not done for the purpose of securing future provision; it is done, instead, for the resulting reduction of working-time—the hours released—or, as we shall see, for the sake of the additional wants that can thereafter be satisfied by application of some of the hours released. The intermediate product, upon which the retaining is performed, is wholly incidental, because it has itself no usefulness as future provision. At most it may be regarded as a store of future working-time economized.[10] It merely happens that, technically, in order to free working-hours, it is necessary first to produce product which is not consumed currently—is never actually itself consumed at all—and that involves retaining. However, in this respect, one must note this difference between the two technical options. While in neither is the product which is retained wanted as future provision for itself, in the former case it does constitute such—it is eventually consumed—while in the latter case it does not—it is not and cannot be consumed.

In this case it is evident that the quantity of retaining required must be stated in terms of the effect of the number of hours' working applied to the intermediate product—that is, the work which the product represents. For this product, the machine, cannot be conceived as a number of days' provision at all. Even in the aspect of its use—its using up—it is merely a kind of substitute for working-hours. It is purely "instrumental," as we say, and has itself no usefulness at all in our technical sense. If it cannot be conceived as a number of days' provision, how relate it, or the retaining done on it, to the magnitude of wants? Its direct relation is to working effort, not to future wants. If that is true of this occasion for retaining, it suggests that this does not work differently from the others, but is merely the purest case, and therefore that the quantity of retaining performed in all cases is to be measured by the work retained and not in terms of the quantity of product as an embodiment of usefulness. On that construction, this occasion for retaining confirms our choice of a dimension for retaining in its aspect of effort.[11]

[10] Those who separate the "services" of durables from the "durable goods" themselves make this statement true of all durables. See, for instance, Cassel, (74, 190). For us it is only true of durable *intermediate* product.

[11] In fact, the impossibility of fitting this particular form of retaining into the scheme I

4. GENERAL CONSIDERATIONS

The foregoing analysis of the several reasons for retaining seems to include all those which are basic and which could appear in a direct economy.[12] Many actual cases are combinations of two or more of these basic reasons; they should be resolved into their constituents. That is, it is well to keep the constituents separate for analytical purposes even if they are frequently or usually combined. The commonest combination is that of a durable with something else—e.g., with future provision for a contingency of the second type or, as intermediate product, with the second technical option. In some cases the durability of a durable may be decided on the basis of the first type of technical option, as if a large number of installments were treated as a large batch. It is also usual that long-process products are made in large batches for the purpose of work-economizing, and therefore combine the attributes of both. There are instances where the second technical option seems to be adopted because, by means of intermediate product, objectives can be reached that cannot otherwise be reached at all.[13] While, at first sight, these appear almost to constitute an occasion by themselves which would not, therefore, be judged purely on the work-economizing basis, that is obviously only true if regard is had exclusively to the immediate product. The end-result of these, like that of the other cases, is to satisfy some want to a greater

first used, as described in Appendix V, Section A, was one of the reasons for giving up the notion of time perspective, etc., which is supposed to diminish the force of future wants, and developing that of interval effort as an increment upon duration effort. When, in a scientific exploration, one finds a recalcitrant datum, it is that which compels an hypothesis which does fit. The old saw, "The exception proves the rule," unfortunately does not apply to the construction of scientific hypotheses. There one has no hypothesis if there is an exception. For scientific purposes we must adopt Sherlock Holmes's correction of the old saw and always proceed on the assumption that "the exception disproves the rule" (see *The Sign of the Four*).

[12] It is evident that the chief modern reason for retaining—namely, to turn the savings over to others to use in return for income—cannot occur in a direct economy. But these occasions do describe the types of "investment" even in an indirect economy. Thus they represent the *occasions* for which savings are *demanded*.

[13] For instance, a tree cannot be felled at all without a tool; non-vocal music cannot be produced without an instrument. But the alternate result in both cases is the better satisfaction of a want which can also be satisfied without these means. Aniline dyes and electric power are work-economizing products—final or intermediate—which substitute for natural dyes and human power. However, the first makes possible acetanilide, and the second makes possible powerful electric furnaces with otherwise unattainable temperatures. Nevertheless both are, in the last analysis, substitute methods of arriving at ultimate purposes which existed, or can be construed to have existed, before they were discovered.

extent with the same working, or to the same extent with less work-ing.[14]

In Chapter 12 we shall analyze intermediate product more fully and also from a different angle—that is, from the viewpoint of the causes that make it advantageous (work-economizing). All of the five or six types there considered are of advantage only because they afford op-portunities to economize in the working-hours required for a given result. The type in which that feature is least obvious should perhaps be mentioned here lest the reader conclude that, in selecting the tool or machine as our only example at this point, we have omitted another important occasion for retaining. We may call this other type *storage facilities,* including therein housing of natural or working processes. In so far as the latter are durable product intended for the prevention of certain wants of the worker while he works, they are, of course, not intermediate product at all, strictly speaking. At first sight, stor-age facilities appear to be purposed for the prevention of loss of product, during or after production. That is true, of course; but it is not the ultimate purpose. If, without storage facilities, some of the product will be lost (spoilage, etc.) from time to time, and perhaps in time all of it will be lost, the working-time per provision that is ultimately usable will be at a higher rate than if loss can be prevented. Therefore, this rate can be reduced by storing in such a way that most of the provisions are ultimately usable. Even then, storage facilities —durable intermediate product—will not be provided unless the working they require will be more than offset by the working that will be economized by preserving product otherwise lost.

The order in which the several occasions have been named has no significance other than analytical. It may be guessed that the order of their historical development was different. Perhaps the first technical necessity was the first occasion for retaining; perhaps the durable fol-lowed next; but it is possible, so far as the women's working was con-cerned, that contingencies of the first type were recognized at an early stage. If man had descended from the carnivora (along the lines sug-gested by Clarence Day), it is hard to see when, if ever, the recog-nition of these occasions for retaining would have arisen. But it is equally true that there is no evidence of such recognition in the cog-

---

[14] To the extent that they satisfy the want better but at the expense of more working—eliminating our arbitrary assumption of one hour's work per provision—we can only consider them when we come to treat of variable "real costs."

nates of those strains from which he did descend—even the anthropoids. If, on the other hand, he had come from the rodents or the social insects, he would have become differentiated from lines in which the tradition of retaining was probably already very ancient. The various types of behavior in response to future wants among beavers, which we noted in Chapter 5, demonstrate their recognition of several of the foregoing occasions. The beavers' winter food-supply is a response to the first technical necessity. The lodge is a durable; so is the dam; but some of the latter may also show signs of recognition of a contingency of the second type—the control of flood waters. Surely the technical option of large-batch production is utilized in the harvesting process, and that of intermediate product in the slides and tunnels and particularly in the systems of canals and dams to permit easier transportation and traveling. Similar recognition is obvious among some of the social insects in their winter stocks and their fairly durable residences. If we can believe the testimony, two species of ants recognize the occasion of long-processes. Certainly the roads of leaf-cutting ants must be construed as labor-saving intermediate product.

D. LIMITATION OF RETAINING THROUGH COMPETITION WITH CURRENT WANTS

When, and only when, the foregoing occasions for retaining exist and are recognized, will the question of undertaking it—of making future provision—arise. For, under all other conditions, it is easier to let the future take care of itself. With these exceptions, the resistance offered by doing the working then or doing it now are equal; but to the resistance of working now is added that of retaining during the interval, so that working then is always the line of least total resistance. But, even in the case of these exceptions, the resistance to retaining still exercises an influence—the influence of futurity. It still sets a limit to the degree of futurity that will be considered in a program, as far as the contingencies and the technical necessities are concerned, and it sets a minimum upon the economizing of working that must be offered, as far as the technical options are concerned. If the total resistance on account of working now and retaining for the interval is greater than the force of the future want, provision for the first two kinds of occasions—the contingencies and the technical necessities—will not be made. Or, if the total resistance offered by working now and retaining for the interval is greater than the reduction of resistance offered by the economizing of working then, the technical options will not be availed of.

However, upon these occasions and within these limitations of futurity, still another factor enters which has a bearing upon the decisions that are made with reference to the program of provision for future wants. That factor is the competition offered by current wants for the working-time available. The future want system, when limited to instances with a degree of futurity greater than a day, does not operate in a vacuum. It is in direct competition with current wants. This is because, for any working now, either for provision for current or for future wants, only the current working-day, as we analyzed it in the previous chapter, is available. It is true that future wants are handicapped in this competition, as we have already seen. They involve retaining; current wants do not. But, in all other respects, the two seem to meet on a par. The force of the wants is the same; the resistance on account of working per provision should be the same—under our arbitrary assumption. Let us then, for the sake of setting up the terms of this competition in its clearest and most contrasting form, treat the handicap from which only future wants suffer—accrued resistance to provision for them on account of the retention involved—as if it were a deduction from their force rather than an addition to the resistance against them. That leaves working as the only resistance and it is opposed equally to the force of current wants and to the net force of future wants.

This competition of current wants (which do not involve retaining) with future wants (which do involve it) introduces into our analysis the aspect of sacrifice involved in retaining—the third of its three aspects. To the extent that a future want succeeds in this competition it may do so by displacing provision for a current want by causing a *forgoing* of such provision. But it may also have another effect. Therefore, this competition is not a simple affair which can be stated in the form of a rule. Rather, because it is the final meeting-point of all the factors occasioning or limiting retaining, it is a highly complex matter which requires to be worked out in detail for each type of occasion and under varying sets of conditions. Only in this way is it possible to determine what sacrifices are involved in retaining, which sacrifices will be made and which will not, and therefore to disentangle, from the other influences at play, the influence of the sacrifice aspect of retaining upon the quantity of it that will be undertaken.

Such a detailed analysis has been worked out in Appendix V, Section C. The interested reader is referred to that Appendix for the grounds upon which the following summary conclusions are based.

In order to demonstrate this competition between future and current wants, we conceive the system of future wants in the form of a series of instances of each want with differing degrees of futurity. From the force of each instance we deduct the specific resistance on account of the retention its provision requires. Thus the net force of the successive instances becomes less as we proceed along the time-scale. The order of priority is reproduced at each degree of futurity and, under our limiting assumption, the differences between the net forces of all wants in any single order of priority remain the same all across the time-scale. Against this system we now juxtapose the system which determines the length of the working-day, as developed in the previous chapter.[1] When we do that, it at once becomes clear that what is involved in future provisions is not merely a forgoing of certain current provisions, which lose out in the competition, but also a possible extension of the limitation on the working-day. It is true that future provisions involve the effort of retaining, while current provisions do not. But even after we have deducted this increment of resistance from the force of the instances of future wants which the expected occasions permit to compete, those high in the order of priority are likely still to exert more force than minor current wants are able to exert. As a result, such future provisions are then inserted in the current order of preference ahead of the minor current wants. Their net force being greater than the gross force of the current wants displaced, the curve *gh* in Fig. 24 is, to that extent, raised and elongated at its further end. That has the effect of postponing its meeting-point with the curve of working (working effort and working sacrifice) and thus of lengthening the working-day. Obviously, for any definite quantity of future provision thus given preference, the greater the increase of working-hours induced the fewer current provisions will need to be forgone. Conceivably, extra working-hours might care for the whole future provision leaving current provision unaffected. But actually this will be impossible. For no current provisions will be made for wants whose force is less than the now increased resistance offered on account of working effort and working sacrifice by the new last hour of working. Therefore, what occurs is a maintenance of balance

[1] This juxtaposition is shown in Fig. 60, Appendix V, Section C, where the details are elaborated.

between these two—these forces and resistances—though at a higher level for both than if future provision had not intruded. That excludes current wants whose force is less than the higher level of resistances, while, at the same time, it includes those future wants whose greater force induces longer hours.

The way that double effect works out, as is demonstrated in the appendix, may multiply the number of working-hours available for future provision. In order to increase the number of working-hours it is necessary that the force of the marginal want, future or current, to be included in the program should rise until it has a net force greater than the heightened resistance offered by the last working-hour to be newly added. In other words, the "ante" is raised. But that effect can only be produced by future wants sufficiently high in the order of priority and involving sufficiently short retaining to meet that test. When they do meet it, extra working-hours are induced. But that, in turn, has the effect of displacing all current wants whose force is now inadequate to meet the test. Then the working-time hitherto applied to provision for such current wants is also available for future provisions—that is, the intruding future wants have made available to themselves that time as well. Thus, in a simple case where the last working-hour is just induced by the least current want, a future want capable of inducing an extra hour's working will, at the same time that it does so, exclude the least current want, and thus have available two hours per day for its provision.

Upon the three assumptions, (1) that there is an order of priority—declining maximum intensities—among future wants of the same degree of futurity as well as among current wants, (2) that there is an increase in the working effort required, and perhaps also in the intensity of the wants to be satisfied by leisure (working sacrifice), as working-hours are prolonged, and (3) that the expectation of occasions interpolates some provision for future wants into the order of current wants in spite of their handicap—and it seems to me that these assumptions are quite inescapable—the only conclusion one can arrive at with reference to the establishment of a limit to retaining by reason of the sacrifice involved for future provision of this type is that it is not an independent process which is self-determined. Instead, the initiation of retaining may have as one prerequisite an increase in the quantity of working over and above what would be carried on in the absence of future provision—at least it will have that effect in any case in which the net force behind any future provision is greater than the resistance of the previous last working-hour. That will constitute one factor in the limitation of the quantity of retaining. The other prerequisite for the initiation of retaining is a diversion of working from current provision for subordinate wants to future provision for prior wants, and thus a curtailment of current consumption. The continuance of this retaining, after it has been initiated, until the occasion arrives, is without alternative, as we have demonstrated in the appendix, except in the one case of provision for a contingency of the first type. In that one case such a continuance has as its prerequisite that there continues to be forgone either a reduction of working-time for as long as the future provision would make possible if it were used now, or a temporary expansion of consumption to subordinate wants by the use of hours of working so released.

Thus, while it is being accumulated—and, in this one case, also while it is being continued—future provision may involve more working as well as less consuming in the present than would otherwise be the case. The change that the incursion of such an occasion brings about is a change in the order of preference away from that of a single order of priority of wants—an intrusion of future wants into the current program—and the effect of this change is the same in all but two respects as any other change in the order of wants. The first respect is that this particular change involves also retaining; and the second is that, once these future wants are provided for, the order of preference among the wants returns to its former state. By reason of the combination of these two effects a certain volume of retaining for future provision does not usually evidence merely the fact that, in the past, there was reduction of current consumption. Instead it is usually also a sign of extra working in the past. And, in the special case of the first contingency, the fact that this retaining continues over a period (i.e., that the provision is continued until the occasion arrives) indicates that more working is currently being done than would be temporarily necessary, as well as the fact that less consuming is being done than would be temporarily possible, if this future provision were consumed now. In the case of none of the other occasions, does this alternative exist. It is more accurate, then, to regard the process which appears as the initiation of retaining (accumulation) to consist both of the expansion of producing and of the concomitant contraction of consuming; and, in the one case where the alternative continues, to regard that which appears as continuance of retaining (maintenance of accumulation) to consist both of the non-contraction of producing and the concomitant non-expansion of consuming in so far as the using-up of the future provision would make that possible.

We may now recall the fact that we originally distinguished between effort and sacrifice on the ground that the former is associated with the alternative chosen while the latter is the fact of not having chosen the other alternative—that the effort involved in working, for instance, is something positive which occurs while the process is carried on, while the sacrifice is merely the not-having-done something else. In the light of that definition it is clear that the extra working induced by a program of future provision is not any part of the sacrifice due to retaining, for it is associated with the alternative chosen. Furthermore, in so far as it constitutes one of the factors in the limitation of the quantity of retaining it is of precisely the same order as when it is involved in working for current provision only. The only difference is that, here, we are dealing with an order of preference which is modified from a single order of priority of wants by reason of the fact that the expectancy of the occasion has inserted some future provisions of higher priority ahead of some current provisions of lower priority. The sacrifice involved in retaining is therefore confined to the surrender of a certain amount of current consumption. That is, exactly as with working, the sacrifice consists of the forgoing of the less potent alternative. It is measured by the current consumption forgone during the time accumulation is taking place, and, in one case, by the additional potential consumption forgone during the time the retaining is continued. Since the latter is merely a continuation, and should not be counted twice, it is evident that the sacrifice is made altogether in advance, at the time the program is adopted and the provisions are accumulated. It is therefore made, as to each day's program, before the retaining begins, not while it is carried on.

The inducement necessary to procure this sacrifice is a quantity of future provisions which, subject to a deduction for the retaining required, have behind them forces just greater than has the current consumption forgone. When this inducement appears just sufficient, retaining will be initiated; and, in the case of the first contingency, so long as it continues to appear just sufficient, retaining will be continued. The sacrifice is measured by the lesser alternative rejected; the inducement to make it is the just greater alternative preferred. Since this sacrifice is just compensated there cannot be any resistance to making it. There could hardly be resistance to forgoing the poorer of two alternatives and choosing the better. In fact, this sacrifice appears to be of exactly the same kind that appears in the case of all preferences among wants. So, too, in the order of preference among satisfactions for present wants, or in the order of preference among provisions for current wants, the greater is always preferred to the less, and the less is sacrificed. That makes this sacrifice appear to be of a somewhat different kind than the sacrifice involved in working—the sacrifice of an actual satisfaction of present wants. In the case of working the sacrifice involves self-restraint, whether or not that is incidental to the self-constraint—that is, whether or not the inhibition is reciprocal to excitation producing activity or not. Here the sacrifice seems to involve neither self-restraint nor self-constraint.[2] It is merely the suppression of the weaker of two contestants for dominance in the mnemonic-volitional process. Moreover, because every current provision forgone is just better than equalized by some future provision preferred, it is clear that there is no surplus either intramarginal or at the margin so far as this sacrifice goes.[3] The only surplus which appears at all is the intramarginal difference between the lesser degree of working effort and working sacrifice involved in working before the limit is reached, on the one hand, and, on the other, the greater than marginal importance of all but the least of the intermixed current and future provisions that are included and to which that working is applied. But this surplus, though enhanced by the lengthening of the working-day, is of precisely the same order as the one we found in the case of working and is therefore assignable wholly to working and not at all to retaining.

Having distinguished the joint or alternative effects of these two factors in limiting the quantity of retaining that is undertaken, we must point out two implications of the foregoing oversimple contrast. The first is that the very elasticity of the limitation of the working-day reduces the retaining sacrifice involved in the program. For it may lead to the application of extra hours of working and thus make unnecessary

---

[2] We cannot conceive of its involving self-restraint, since the current wants forgone, being a part of the future want system, represent no primary energy of response.

[3] If the difference between the current provisions for wants, in their order of priority, is considerable—if the order of wants is sharply stepped down—then a slight surplus might be considered to develop by as much as the importance of the preferred future provision was more than "just greater" than the current provision displaced.

the forgoing of an equivalent quantity of current provisions. The second qualification is this. As we show in Appendix V, Section C, wherever hours of working are applied to a program of future provision over more than one day and involve more than one provision for one want, a complication enters. Then, if the number of provisions can be varied at will, since those for lesser wants or further instances will be deferred and will have less net force, the number of hours of working and the number of current provisions forgone may decline from day to day. On the other hand, if the number of provisions is fixed, as it is apt to be in the case of durables and the two technical options, so that the opportunities are offered on an all or none basis, the fact that the first day's future provision cannot be had until all are completed will probably lead to a maintenance of the original schedule throughout the period of accumulation.

At this point we may combine our conclusions with regard to the effects of all factors concerned upon the quantity and period of retaining. The question of whether retaining will be initiated at all is, at any time, determined by the expectation of an occasion involving an instance of one or more future wants of sufficient force, after deduction of the resistance offered by the intervening retaining required, to compete for the last hour of working with the least current want included in the current day's program. Within these limits, the quantity of retaining which will be initiated and the period for which it will be undertaken [4] (subject to the condition below) are dependent variables which vary *directly* with:

1. a. The extent to which the framework of the time-scale is filled in with contingencies; or
   b. The extent to which technical necessities compel retaining in order to satisfy certain wants at all, either future only, or both current and future; or
   c. The extent to which technical options exist affording an opportunity to gain a considerable net advantage in the economizing of working-time by producing in large batches or by means of intermediate product.
2. The intensity of the particular future wants concerned.

[4] The quantity and the period are, under our simplifying assumption, the same magnitude, so far as the period of use is concerned. That is, 20 days' provision lasts 20 days. With varying "coefficients of production," however, they would not need to be the same. And, even in our illustrations, the period may vary before accumulation is complete according to the number of hours per day that will be assigned to the provision.

The dependent variables vary *inversely* with:

1. The rate of accrual of retaining as effort;
2. a. The steepness of the curve of working effort, plus
   b. The steepness of the curve of working sacrifice (first hour of leisure);
3. The intensity of the particular current wants for which provision will have to be forgone.

Thus the chief effects of the new factors introduced when we consider the competition of future with current wants prove to be selective, not general. True, these factors (2a, 2b, and 3 above) do set nether limits to the future wants that can obtain provision now; but they do that also to the order of priority among current wants. Their selective effect is to determine which future wants will be permitted to intrude and, when permitted, how rapidly they will be provided for—that is, what will be the period of accumulation.

The period of accumulation will not always be governed merely in the interests of reducing the influence of the inverse factors to the minimum. Sometimes it will be the result of what we have called, in Appendix V, the principle of the greatest net advantage—a principle which includes abbreviating the period of accumulation, even at the cost of more extra hours of working and more current forgoing, if by that means the period of retaining can be sufficiently shortened to overcompensate. This principle applies only where no provision can be had except as future provision (durables and some long processes) and to the two work-economizers.

In Appendix V we have examined separately the question of replacement.[5] There we have found that replacement always involves a new decision. Each of the occasions for retaining is likely to be a repeated or continuous affair, appearing along the time-scale at regular or irregular intervals for as long a time into the counterfeit future as is envisaged. Although provision will at first be made for one occasion only, or for a limited period of use only, similar occasions will appear even now, projected to a time after the first future provision will have been used up. If the effect of the rate of accrual of retaining as effort is not so great as to preclude consideration of such further provision, the question of replacement will arise as soon as the period of accumulation for this first provision is finished. When it arises it will be dealt with differently according to the character of the particular occasion, and

[5] See Appendix V, Section C 4.

it will usually be dealt with differently than on the original occasion. The reason for the latter difference is this. By thus taking time by the forelock, a longer period is available over which to spread the current forgoing and the extra hours, if any, so that fewer current wants will require to be forgone daily and fewer extra hours worked daily, and the former will involve lesser sacrifices and the latter lesser efforts and sacrifices. The details are worked out in Appendix V.

The effect of replacements upon the quantity of retaining performed also varies according to the occasion. Since, in the case of the first type of contingency no part of the first provision is used until the contingency arises, if a second provision is commenced immediately upon the completion of the first, retaining will tend to rise to double its original quantity and in the event to decline again to that quantity. Or, if the second provision is not commenced until the first contingency is past, retaining will tend to decline to zero after the first occurrence of the contingency and thereafter to rise only day by day to its limit when the new provision is completed. In the second type of contingency, usually, and in the first type of technical necessity, always, there will merely be a single or a gradual decline to zero and then a subsequent rise on the same basis as when initiated. The same will be true of many long processes (at least in a direct economy). In the case of durables, the rest of long processes and the two work economizers, if the setting remains the same and the rate of accrual of retaining effort is low enough, the replacement will be commenced as soon as the first provision is completed. But it will be commenced at the rate of producing each day a quantity of provision equal to that used up each day. Thus, when the first provision is used up, the second will just be completed and ready.[6] In these cases, retaining tends to continue at the same level once it is initiated—each day's subtraction from the original being compensated by an equal addition to the replacement.

Isolation of the question of replacement makes it obvious that to continue retaining at the same level while the accumulation is being used up regularly or erratically, or at any level above the remainder of the original provision, involves the constant initiation of new retaining to counterbalance disappearance. While this may not increase the total, it is, in every other respect, to be construed as a decision on a par with the original one. Therefore, we may say that, in all cases, the regular

[6] That is, it will do so on our simplifying assumption.

or occasional replacement necessary to maintain a constant quantity of retaining intact, when the product is regularly or irregularly used, involves exactly the same kind of sacrifice, though perhaps of less important current wants, as that which was involved in the original initiation of the retaining. In all instances where it is possible to replace the product used up with little or no extra working—and this is probably impossible only in future provision for technical necessities of the first type and in some long processes—most of what is involved in the replacement—unlike the original provision—is current consumption forgone.

If the setting changes—if, for instance, the rate of accrual of retaining as effort rises markedly, or the occasions cease to be considered—the quantity of retaining tends to change (to diminish) but not in the same way for all its forms. Future provision of the first type would then be consumed at once, and prior to the arrival of the contingency. Provision for a contingency of the second type can only be consumed when the contingency actually arises; that for all the others only at the rate of one day's provision or use per day. But in all cases, alike, the change in the setting may put an end to all replacements. Repetition of the sacrifice may then not be made. From this it is evident that, so far as the initial quantity of retaining is concerned, the decision is irrevocable, except in the first case—future provision for a contingency of the first type. In all the others revocability exists as to the replacements only. Therefore, with this one exception, unless the product retained is wasted, the quantity of retaining, once established, can only decline as, and in so far as, these inherent limitations on the speed of using up permit. The original sacrifice has been made. Except as noted, it cannot be unmade; and the opportunity to change one's mind exists only as to the replacement. But, until the replacement is started, the opportunity always continues as to that.

E. CERTAIN COROLLARIES AND COMMENTS

Now that we have brought to a head, in examining their joint results, the effects of all our separately analyzed factors which bear upon the quantity and period of retaining, several incidental observations with regard to the completed picture may be appropriate.

The first and most important is the intimate relation disclosed between working and retaining—at least in a direct economy. As soon as one considers the competition of future wants (involving retaining) with current wants, one finds again that the two functions cannot be completely distinguished, one from the other. In subsection B 1 above, we noted that working, since by definition it is directed toward the provision of means for the satisfaction of future wants only, must involve retaining until those future wants become present wants. And it was only because we found it convenient to separate the combined performance of both functions from the performance of retaining only that we adopted the convention whereby the retaining included with working for the next consuming-day (or night) would be treated as the criterion which makes the activity effortful, and that retaining, as a separate function, would be treated as if it began only the next morning. Only for that reason did we distinguish between the future wants of the following consuming-day (current wants) and those with a degree of futurity greater than this arbitrarily fixed zero (future wants). But, now, we have found that a program of strictly future provision, as well, mixes the two. For, if that future provision will not or cannot be made without extra working, then retaining and working are again inextricably bound up together. Finally, they are coupled again under another condition. Economizing of future working involves retaining; and, in fact, this retaining is not done for the purpose of future provision at all, but solely to permit the economizing of working.

In certain respects we find the position at which we have arrived to be at variance with some features of the usual economic analysis of this subject—new or old. One point seems clear. It is apparent that the customary treatment of this complex matter is altogether insufficient. We have found that, at the time the program is adopted, it is not based upon a straightforward "discounting of the future" (the equivalent of our retaining as effort) and upon the quantity of sacrifice of current provision involved, which are the only factors usually considered. We have found, instead, a complex operation within a framework that includes those factors but which involves an actuarial estimate of contingencies and an appraisal of the other types of occasion. Thereafter, this modifies the limit of working, or is itself modified by the inelasticity of this limit. Thus the "discounting of the future," or anything resembling it, turns out to be only one of the factors governing the quantity of retaining for future provision—and that not the chief one—while the matter of sacrifice turns out to be purely incidental, being the lesser alternative rejected.

Two other issues arise as a result of our analysis of the replacement process. The first concerns the revocability of retaining. Those who have come to regard the sacrifice involved in retaining—the current consumption forgone—as the chief factor, and thus largely to overlook the aspect of retaining as effort and the effect that has in limiting the futurity of provision, have treated "saving," as they call it, as if it were an act done once and for all when the program is adopted and put into effect—that is, when accumulation is complete. This treatment loses sight of the fact that retaining is a continuing performance which must be continuously maintained during the life of the provision; that, in turn, means that the memory of the effort the retaining involves acts in the present as a deterrent to all future provision in proportion to the degree of futurity of its average or even its furthest uses; and that, in turn, means that it is never sufficient that, at the start, to-be-realized advantages should merely balance current disadvantages (forgoing current consumption or extra working). Such a view also overlooks the very considerable degree to which the initial—or, in one case, the continuing—sacrifice is revocable. As to provision for a contingency of the first type, the sacrifice is always and continuously revocable; as to all other occasions, so far as the original provision is concerned, it is not. But, for all occasions alike, the sacrifice must be repeated, and is therefore subject to a new decision, if, as, and when, replacements are to be made. Since replacements will be made, in most cases, continuously, the program is continuously revocable, although the length of time required to revoke it completely will be the same as that required for complete using-up. Revocation will also involve the waste of any partly finished replacement, after that has been started. The so-called permanence of "saving" is therefore a most dangerous illusion.

All opportunities to choose between mutually exclusive alternatives offer an option. The chooser *can* choose the less preferable. He usually *does* choose the more preferable. But conditions may change and make the more the less preferable. The fact that one alternative is steadily preferable and that this is the one usually chosen does not in any way eliminate either the existence of alternatives or the necessity of choice. So, in this case, there always exists an alternative to the initiating of new retaining for replacements; and therefore there is always a choice. The fact that the choice is almost always made in one way, under our institutional system, neither means that it has to be so made nor that it can be made without a decision. True, the decision may consist in adopting a rule; but the rule is backed by nothing more than the decider's authority over himself. To deny the possibility of non-replacement of retained product as it is used up, or even to blink the fact that this replacement is entirely optional, merely because replacement—new retaining—is usually preferable and therefore, as a matter of course, usually preferred, is as absurd as it would be to deny the existence of a consumer's choice between two alternatives merely because one was usually preferable or because the consumer usually preferred it.

Another almost equally popular error arises from the replacement process. If retaining is continuously maintained at a practically unvarying level, by reason of currently replacing what is currently consumed or used up, it becomes easy to slip into the error of thinking of the daily replacement as if it were that which is daily used up, and thus to overlook the essential part in the process which is played by retaining.[1] Nothing could be more fallacious; for, if it actually were the daily replacement which is used up daily, then no retaining would be necessary and no such effort or sacrifice need to have been incurred at all. Or, on the other hand, if account is taken only of the current position, then replacement becomes quite unnecessary, since the maturing future provision of that day furnishes the current provision without benefit of the replacement. In that light, replacement can only be regarded as a new sacrifice involving new effort for a new future provision which would be placed at the further end of the series. Though this error is a common one, our previous analysis has sufficiently demonstrated how little the daily replacement of the daily use has to do with obtaining any of the advantages offered by these occasions for retaining, and

[1] An example of this not uncommon error is to be found in Schumpeter (*364*, 38). But, to a certain extent, J. B. Clark, and Knight, after him, have slipped into the same confusion. See J. B. Clark (*80*, Chap. *IX*) and Knight (*241*, 404-405), as well as the latter's recent series of articles disputing the Austrian "period of production" concept. It has seemed to me that Knight, in refuting Hayek and others, has succeeded in saving economic theory from the frying-pan only to dump it into the fire; and that quite unnecessarily.

However, it should be said that the concept of *capital* as against *capital-goods*, which Clark proposed and which Knight seems to have adopted, is the nearest approach I know of to our entity "retaining." Only, failing to see that the former consists of *continuing performance*, they attach to it a quality of permanence which it does not—or may not—have. Looking only at the original sacrifice—"abstinence"—they conclude that it is an act done once for all. See especially Clark (*80*, 134 and 139). His failure to analyze it as a process, instead of a sort of super-entity ("abstract quantum," *ibid.*, 119) like the German "state," seems to me to have been the cause of the famous dispute with Böhm-Bawerk (see *39* and *82*).

that retaining is the *sine qua non*—the sole method—for obtaining any of them.

In classical theory, it used to be assumed that future provision of the general order covered under our contingency of the first type—a stock of consumables—was the original and enabling condition precedent for all other accumulations; that, when retaining was to take any other form, this sort of future provision was the prerequisite; and that, during the time such other to-be-retained product was being made, the economy would consume its future provision of this kind. Doubt has already been cast on this assumption since it has been realized that, in a modern economy at least, current provision arises from a constant flow and not from a stock which is occasionally consumed and thus temporarily ceases to exist.[2] But, if any authority remains for this ancient supposition, our analysis should make it clear that there is no warrant for it. The making of a sufficient provision to enable nearly full consumption to continue during the accumulation of durables, long-process products, large batches, or intermediate products, would double the total quantity of extra working and current forgoing as compared to the quantity required when the accumulation of these durables, etc., is carried on without such future provision. To the extent that the two periods of accumulation overlapped, the effort and the sacrifices would necessarily be of far higher intensity than those required when the usual principle of greatest net advantages is followed. To the extent that the accumulation of the future provision preceded that of the durables, etc., this preliminary step would succeed only in placing the ultimate benefits eventually to be secured from the durables, etc., further in the future, and therefore subjecting them to a greater deduction on account of the retaining involved. It is quite impossible that such a choice would ever be made. It is true that, during any period of extra working and forgoing for other purposes, that part of any existing future provision for a contingency of the first type which would not be provided under the temporarily extended

---

[2] Nevertheless this notion persisted with Jevons (*224*, 223–224 and 226) and, more remarkable still, seems to have been implicit in the viewpoint of the founder of modern capital theory, Böhm-Bawerk (see *38*, 93–94). Even Knight seems to take this position (see *240*, 322–323) in spite of the fact that J. B. Clark had exposed its fallacy. As Cassel points out (*75*, 13) this is the basis of the wage-fund theory, traced to Adam Smith (Book II, Intro.). Actually the producers' stock of consumable product in a modern economy is not deliberate future provision at all. It is a result of irregularity of demand, time taken in physical distribution, technical necessities of the first type and of large-batch economizings in mass distribution.

working limit would not seem worth retaining. Perhaps it would be used, while it lasted, and then replaced later. But only to this limited extent would future provision, as such, aid in the process of initiating retaining for other purposes, and then only because it was temporarily not itself worth retaining.

In our examination of the determination of the quantity of retaining that will be done we have now succeeded in finding only two conditions in which all the retaining done is not marginal, in the sense that the total resistances are just less than the total forces. Therefore, with these exceptions, there can never be said to be intramarginal retaining —retaining done with a difference, or surplus, between the resistances and forces. It is true of course that a quantity of retaining undertaken in response to one setting may become temporarily intramarginal in respect of a new setting and remain so until all quantities have been adapted to this new setting. But that sort of movement of dynamic equilibrium (process of change) is usually not included in the concept of marginality. The two conditions which constitute the exceptions apply only to retaining for the exercise of the two technical options. There, as we have noted, the retaining is always intramarginal to some degree and may be so to a considerable degree. And this because the options themselves constitute an irregular and discontinuous series in respect of the time-saving they make possible, and because the economizing must at all times be sufficient, after deducting all the sacrifice and effort involved in the retaining called for, to overcome the inertia and risk involved in the change of method.

It is this intramarginality of the effort or of the sacrifice, or of both, involved in retaining for the purpose of exercising the technical options that makes less exact than is desirable the determination of the quantities of working and retaining that are equivalent in respect of the effort involved—the basis on which they can be summated or are interchangeable. For these options are the only instances where retaining is done directly to economize working and therefore the only ones where an exact determination could be made of the length of time the product of one hour's working will be retained in order to economize one hour's working—that is, the number of units of retention which are equal in this aspect to one unit of work. Nevertheless, the net gain is not so large at its minimum that it prevents us from making rough estimates of this ratio. Therefore, we shall hereafter treat the unit of retention as if it were convertible into the unit of work, on some basis, and will therefore assume that the two "real costs" can be roughly summated.

While it does not apply to a direct economy in which there can be, by definition, no exchange, it is well to make a generalization here for later application to an indirect economy where exchange is possible. And this lest a certain restriction which we have established above should lead the unwary into an error. In an indirect economy the fact that retaining once initiated, apart from replacements and with the exception of that for a contingency of the first type, is irrevocable—that the sacrifice once made cannot be unmade—is true only for the economy as a whole.[3] As to all groups or individuals within the economy it is then untrue to the extent that exchanges are possible—i.e., liquidity exists. Therefore, as to groups or individuals in an indirect economy, in this particular respect future provision for contingencies of the first type is characteristic of retaining on all occasions. All programs are revocable and all involve continuing sacrifice to the extent that the product retained can be exchanged for product which can be consumed now.

Again, while it has no special meaning in a direct economy where the worker and retainer are one, it is important to recognize now, also for future reference in the analysis of an indirect economy, where retaining may be separated from working, that the last of our occasions for retaining—that of intermediate product—is the typical one which shows the character of inducement that must offer itself in order to stimulate voluntary retaining where retaining is an economic function performed by some for others; for this is the only case where retaining is devoted to product which in itself has no usefulness to the retainer so that the advantages must be external to it—must take the form of release from hours of working or the satisfaction of more wants, or some of each. In all other cases the product which is retained itself represents—though only indirectly in the case of large batches —the provision for future wants which balance the effort and sacrifice. And these provisions can only benefit him—and thus offset his effort and sacrifice—if the worker-retainer himself consumes them or their equivalent on their occasion or little by little. Therefore, in all other cases than that of intermediate product, the effort and sacrifice would never be made by him if he did not expect to consume the product

---

[3] We may remind the reader that all of our analysis of a direct economy is true of *any* self-sufficient economy as a whole.

or its equivalent himself. But, in the case of intermediate product, it makes no difference to the retainer whether he uses it himself or not, provided it is he who realizes the prospective advantages.[4] Since the successive uses of the machines represent in themselves no future provision whatever, the whole of the advantages consists in the working-time it economizes. It is this, and this only, which goes to offset the effort and sacrifice.

In a direct economy, to the study of which we are now confining ourselves, the application of effort must be made in advance of securing any means requiring effortful behavior, and it must be made specifically to certain means. Thus the program is all for specific future wants, though perhaps only for the following consuming-day. In an indirect economy, in which some scheme for the distribution of product is inherent, if that scheme permits any choice at all, it must involve "generalized purchasing power" (i.e., money or its functional equivalent). Under such circumstances the program of the individual does not need to confine itself to future wants. He does not need always to collect the means in advance. So far as he alone is concerned, he can secure them almost instantaneously and with little trouble (precurrent reactions of self). Then present wants may enter into direct competition with future wants and not merely put a limit on the program of provision for future (including current) wants as a whole, as in the direct economy.

[4] Let us suppose, for instance, a pair of direct economies in contact with each other and thus jointly composing, at least potentially, an indirect economy; that Economy A is retaining a machine by reason of the fact that it has exercised the technical option and has expended extra working and forgoing, while Economy B has not done this. Now (on the terms used in Appendix V, Section C), if an arrangement were made between the two by which Economy B took over the operation of the machine, it could, in the two hours per day it was previously using to produce current provisions for the two wants which the machine subserved, produce its own and provisions for Economy A as well. Thus A would be relieved, by reason of having made the machine, not only of half the time devoted to these two wants but of the whole of it. This example makes clear the utter absurdity of the Marxian doctrine of "surplus-value," a surplus which is conceived to be confiscated by the retainer of the machine. For it was the action of Economy A and not that of Economy B which created this "surplus-value," and it is Economy A which has sustained the whole effort and sacrifice of doing so. When B is enabled to make four provisions instead of two in two hours per day on condition that it gives the extra ones to A, B is no worse off and no better off than it was before. But since B has sustained no part of the "real cost" there is no reason why it should be better off. However, since A will be better off by reason of this deal than it would be if it used the machine itself, it is likely that it will agree to divide this additional advantage with B. Then, by this concession, B makes a net gain which is at absolutely no "real cost" to itself and which it did nothing whatever to make possible. That is the usual working out of technological progress in an economy of private capitalism.

But, though this difference exists, and though we shall adhere to our limitation of the program to future wants for the sake of analytical consistency, the difference is not so great as it might seem. In a civilized economy practically every adult, and most children who have any generalized purchasing power, have a program. For they have commitments, and their purchasing power is received in lump sums periodically so that each lump sum must last until the next receipt. The difference in procedure appears then chiefly in the degree to which this program is permitted to be upset by present wants. Among the foresighted and thrifty, program and expenditure practically coincide. Among the happy-go-lucky they do not. The rest of the difference is accounted for by the amount which both may deliberately set aside in their programs for impulsive expenditure for present wants as they arise.

Thus, in an indirect economy with generalized purchasing power, the competition of present wants with future wants is practically limited to departures from plan and to unassigned allowance for present wants within the plan. With due allowance for these two exceptions our analysis is therefore also applicable to indirect economies. The essence of these exceptions is that they are unplanned as to distribution, if not as to aggregate amount. They are still explicable, however, by our scheme. Present wants are much stronger than their future counterparts, except as the latter are reinforced by the volitional process. The first exception above assumes that the volitional process is quiescent or inadequate at the moment. The second exception assumes that a block of purchasing power has been exempted from the operation of the volitional process. However, as to these exceptions, it must be recognized that present wants do not occur in their order of priority. Except as several, or many, or all present wants coexist, the order of priority has no effect, and then only as to the order among those which do coexist. Thus, under both exceptions, the competition is offered at any moment only by the prepotent present want at that moment. Therefore, the accident of occurrence or recurrence may have as much to do with the result as does the order of priority.

Even in a direct economy, where the competition of present wants (not current) is confined to their effect in interrupting or limiting the working-day, there is room, of course, for a wide difference in the capacity for effort of both kinds among different persons. So far as the effort involved in retaining is concerned this means that the rate of accrual of retaining effort varies. But it is probable that, in no case, is the apparatus involved in the entire complex process so stupid as to work as if there were no limitation by reason of futurity, or so blind as to work as if that limit stood at the point we have called the zero. Rather it seems to be, generally speaking, a delicately adjusted affair for preserving a balance between future and current provision in respect of the effort and sacrifice to be incurred and the ultimate satisfactions or economizings to be achieved. Perhaps, in fact, the chief difference we observe among men as compared with the capitalistic animals we have cited is that their calculations of the several occasions, of what is and what is not worth while, are more highly developed.[5] For surely ants, bees, and beavers are greater and more intense workers, even for future provision, than are most men.

It may seem to the reader that, in the foregoing, we have imputed altogether too much exactitude to the operation of this complicated apparatus in connection with determining the quantity and period of retaining. But I think this is not so. Let us look into the question. It is true that, in the earlier chapters, we expressed doubt as to the capacity of the human animal to measure subjective magnitudes with any such accuracy as is demanded by much of marginal utility theory. But we did admit, there, that it is necessary to suppose that man is capable, at least, of comparing these magnitudes and of determining, in a rough way, when two are equal or which of two is greater. No more than that capacity is demanded here. The complexity is, of course, increased by the addition of a vast series of orders of priority of future wants each with a different degree of futurity. On the other hand, there is an offset to that complexity. The comparison of present satisfactions may be—perhaps usually is—a mere matter of impulse, of purely irrational actions. This we have assumed in our hypothesis as to the mechanism for determining prepotence among present wants. The comparison of future satisfactions (of current or future wants) is, on the contrary, es-

[5] One of the clearest illustrations of this, and one that approaches the conditions of a direct economy, is the program for equipment and supplies to be taken on a camping trip—an illustration we have already used. We rely on "direct consumption" for the drinking water. We rely on playing or working when the time comes for our camp fire. But, as to the things that cannot be made available in the wilderness, we discriminate carefully between those necessities, comforts and luxuries that are "worth the trouble" and those which are not. The order of priority of our future wants is an abbreviated one; some contingencies of the second type are provided for; others are calculated as not likely to arise. True, the resistance which sets these limitations is chiefly the effort of transportation, not the effort of retaining. But, in this instance, the former works out in somewhat the same way that the latter would.

sentially what is called rational. For, to be effective, sustained action is required, and sustained action, in turn, is likely to be dictated by "rational" considerations. The effect of the mnemonic-volitional process can be damaged or distorted but cannot be furthered by "irrational impulses"; for it is, by its very nature, deliberate and calculating. Action which has not these characteristics is not dictated by the mnemonic-volitional system.

Nevertheless the process of furnishing the counterfeit future is also, by its nature, of the order of estimates. It is not itself experience; it is a kind of "preview" of those past experiences which have been projected against this screen. However, that does not affect our thesis; for we are examining the springs of action, not its consequences. An estimate may turn out to be wrong. Doubtless there occur many disappointments as well as occasional pleasant surprises. Nevertheless, the estimate had its effect when it was made; and the effect was exactly the same (except in respect of the satisfactions eventually derived) as if it had been right. Behavior dictated by the mnemonic-volitional process results wholly from the estimate. There is no existential reality in the present which we can call the future. Therefore, there is no criterion—scientific or otherwise—by which the correctness of an estimate of the future can be judged at the time. Judgment is rendered in the event, by hindsight. And by that time the action is history. Therefore, what we are interested in analyzing is what *would be* the "rational action," given any system of forces and any system of resistances. This does not argue that action *would be* entirely "rational," nor that estimates *would be* entirely correct. It admits that there are other factors at play, such as errors, misapprehensions, impulses, etc. But these are interferences. It follows that we not only can but must analyze these mnemonic-volitional forces and resistances *in vacuo*. For they can only account for that part of the result that conforms precisely to what they would accomplish in the absence of interference. Finally, the process which involves retaining differs, in this respect, only in degree from that involved in all other choices—those among future wants, among means, and even among the different directions in which working can be applied for current provision. All these are based on estimates, as well.

It would be a mistake, however, to leave the impression that we think that the process we have examined in this chapter has always been the only cause of retaining of future provision, of durables, of the product of long processes, of large batches, and of intermediate product. It is doubtless true that many advances in these respects have been accidentally stumbled upon in the course of human progress—the result of "seasonal unemployment," of "playing," of slavery, of robbery, etc. It is perhaps even true that the practice of retaining has developed largely as a result of the actual experience of benefits conferred by these chance advances in the past. Nevertheless, today, the system we have set forth has doubtless become the chief determinant of the quantity of retaining done, and I am convinced that it is no exaggeration of reality to assume the highly flexible but nevertheless precise system of judgment which our analysis has outlined.

Doubtless there are still minor exceptions to the operation of this system. We sometimes—usually in our spare time—take time by the forelock and do today what could equally well be done tomorrow. And, sometimes, we put off until tomorrow what could be much more easily or better done today. But the chief exceptions relate to certain classes or certain increments of means. To complete our picture, to sharpen its confines, it will be well here briefly to mention these exceptions. The following classes of means, or means under the following conditions, are not retained.

1. "Non-economic Goods." Any means that it is expected will always be available when wanted for what we have called "direct consumption" (i.e., consumption with no prior production) is never retained. Sometimes under special conditions the same object (air or water), has to be produced (artificial ventilation or municipal water supply). Under these conditions the object becomes product—an "economic good"—and, in some cases, also becomes the object of retaining after work has been done on providing it.

2. Product. Means requiring to be produced and therefore only available for current wants, at the soonest, may still not be subject to retaining. Of these the chief types are:

a. Product that will not "keep." By definition, such means, to be product, must be capable of "keeping" until the following consuming-day. But if they will spoil, etc., after that, they cannot be retained.

b. Product which requires too much retaining for reasons inherent in its nature. Under this rubric we may include provisions of any kind which will not be needed for so long a time that the influence of futurity shuts them out. But the chief case is product requiring too great, not too long, retaining. Storage facilities constitute a kind of intermediate product different from the example which we considered in connection with the second technical option—the machine or tool —but which we discussed in Section C, of this chapter. However, they, too, are not themselves provision for a want. Even though the working necessary for storage facilities could be equalized, and thus justified, by the working economized through preserving otherwise lost product, the quantity or period of retaining required for such storage facilities might, when it is also assessed against such economizing, be deemed to make the retaining effort not worth while. If so, the product itself cannot be stored and therefore cannot be retained.

c. Superfluous product. Any surplus of product, found or made, beyond a full measure required for any instance of a future want provided for—or the sum of the full measures for a series of instances— and thus constituting unintended potential provision, may be reserved, or it may be rejected. If it is rejected, it is obviously not the subject of retaining. If it is reserved, the future provision rests on a different ground from those described under our occasions. It represents an unplanned work-economizer. The usefulness of the product is recognized, even though it be superfluous as far as the program is concerned. And, though it would not have been made as a result of planning, it exists and it can take the place of a current provision sometime. If it were not reserved, the working already done on it would be wasted. By reserving it, that otherwise wasted hour will save one hour in the future. Here retaining, as an overt act, seems to be performed; but, as a "real cost," it probably is not considered at all (apart from storage facilities). Therefore, it is preferable to regard such superfluous product as not being the subject of retaining.

F. COMPARATIVE SUMMARY OF THE TWO ECONOMIC FUNCTIONS

Failure to distinguish between the three aspects of each of the human functions which constitute the process of production is responsible for much of the existing confusion in regard to this subject—and especially in "capital" theory. The result is that statements are constantly made as to the whole which are true only of one aspect.[1] In order that the reader may carry forward the results of this analysis of these aspects it may be well to emphasize them again. Product, the provision of produced means, its appearance and its continued existence, is due solely

[1] For some examples, see supplementary statement on "Capital Theory," at the end of this subsection.

to two forms of what we have called, generically, human effort. These two forms are working and retaining. From the standpoint of contribution—that is, the causative relation between processes and results—the first form of effort results in objectively measurable quantities of production—a flow—and the second results in a part of this production, also objectively measurable, remaining not used up as product—a stock. This aspect is the only one that requires to be considered when we regard production solely from the standpoint of demand—as the means for the satisfaction of wants. In that aspect it is the objective quantities of product, flowing or remaining, to which usefulness is subjectively attributed. But the fact that production is the result of what we have called, generically "effort" imports two other aspects.

Let us consider the third aspect before the second. It is what we have defined as sacrifice. In order that the required working and retaining be done it is necessary that leisure and current consumption, respectively, should to some extent be forgone. These, then, are the alternatives in the two cases which are not adopted. Therefore, they cannot be the cause of the result, but are merely permissive factors. There are, however, important differences as well as correspondences between working and retaining in these respects. In the case of working mere non-leisure does not result in product, nor, therefore, in the provision for future wants, for these require produced means; in the case of retaining mere non-consumption today does result in more remaining product, but it does not necessarily result in any advantages. True, both constitute sacrifices; but the sacrifices may be purely negative.[2] In the case of working, the sacrifice of the alternative is continuous during working-time; then it stops. In the case of retaining, the sacrifice is all made (except in one case) at the time each element of the retaining is commenced. Then it, too, stops. But, since this commencement of successive elements may be stretched over many days, the sacrifice for the whole provision is, like that of working, made piecemeal during the period when accumulation is occurring and, thereafter, again piecemeal, as replacements are made. In both cases, sacrifice is the result of a choice, and it is therefore being made at all times during which the alternative is wholly or partly open. With retaining, except in the case of future provision for the first type of contingency, the choice becomes irrevocable for each part of the program as executed; but it only remains irrevocable until the provision is used up. For then the

[2] We may illustrate the distinction by the analogy of military drill. Leisure = "at rest"; non-working and non-leisure = "attention"; working = "forward march."

question of replacement, if it has been deferred so long, compels a new choice.

Finally, the second aspect is the specific effort involved in working and retaining. It is this effort which composes the only positive element and therefore what we have called the "real cost" of the process. The effort and the sacrifice involved in working occur simultaneously, though in varying proportion, and may therefore be summated at any moment of the working-day. In fact, it is probable that they cannot be entirely distinguished, except analytically, nor their quantities separately estimated with any accuracy. In the case of retaining the positive aspect—effort—is obviously separable in a qualitative way from the negative one—the sacrifice—for our analysis has indicated that it is performed at a different time, not simultaneously, as with working. The sacrifice wholly precedes the making of the effort as to each portion of the program, except only in the case of the first contingency. Therefore, the two aspects can, in this case, be readily distinguished and their quantities separately estimated. Again, whereas the effort involved in working, for any definite curve of working effort, changes in rate from perhaps zero to a gradually increasing intensity as the working-time increases, the effort per time unit involved in retaining, is, for any particular rate of accrual, a uniform quantity regardless of duration. To induce the working-day, the force of the wants being provided must at all times be in excess of the sum of current working and the current sacrifice of leisure—in fact, the force of the least want must just exceed the maximum (last hour) of these latter. To induce retaining of any particular provision, the force of the want must not only be sufficient to insert itself in the working-day at the cost of the sacrifice of current consumption or of extra hours of working, or both, but it must also be sufficient to offset the influence of futurity—the rate of accrual of retaining multiplied by the period of retaining required. A further important point to emphasize is that retaining is not only a continuing process from the standpoint of contribution (effect); it is also continuing from the standpoint of effort ("real cost"). That is, the function human beings perform in retaining involves effort, and therefore "real cost," from the time the process of retaining begins until it ends. The sacrifice is made once, at the time when and to the extent that a choice becomes irrevocable. The effort continues—and is calculated in advance—during the entire interval between the beginning of working and the final using-up.

We have seen that the influence of the last two aspects of working and retaining—as effort and as sacrifice—is exercised by way of limitation on the quantity of working and retaining done. Only the first aspect constitutes the relation between efforts and satisfactions. There is no necessary equivalence between the ratios of the quantities of objective work and retention represented in two products, or even two lots of product, and the ratios of the quantities of effort or of sacrifice involved in each, respectively. Objective results are one thing; subjective "costs" and "sacrifices" are quite another and largely independent matter.[3]

---

[3] In a direct economy all kinds of work would be related to each other in terms of the hours of working required for them; for there would be no other basis of comparison. So much objective effect of this kind requires so much time; so much of that a different time, etc. An independent observer of several direct economies could compare these results and discover that the ratio of effect per hour at different processes was different for Economy A and for Economy B, etc. He could even determine an average, or standard for each process. And that will turn out to be the way in which different kinds of work are related in an indirect economy, in which the problem first arises. This qualitative difference in the effect, or contribution, aspect of working does not appear, primarily, in the case of retaining. All retaining is, by its nature, uniform in its effect. The qualitative differences in work do, however, affect secondarily the measurement of retaining, since this is measured chiefly in terms of the work retained. Again, however, this problem would only appear in an indirect economy.

In a direct economy the effort and sacrifice at different periods of the working-day would be roughly comparable as more or less. Also some kinds of working would be felt as involving more effort than others. But the appraisal of effort plus sacrifice per hour of working, or per unit of work, would only be critical at the limit. It would only affect the total quantity of working, not its application. Therefore, it has no meaning to assign any definite quantity of effort and sacrifice to a unit of work—to relate the subjective to the objective magnitudes. And here an independent observer could make no comparison as between several economies. He could only observe the different limits, which might just as well be due to variation in the intensity of wants. The same would be true of the effort and sacrifice involved in retaining. They are not inherently greater for one purpose than for another; they may or may not become greater as the quantity of retaining done expands—that depends on the rapidity of execution of the program. The quantity of retaining done depends, in the last analysis, on a preference for product requiring retaining over product not requiring it—a preference which must be sufficient to overcome the influence of futurity. Moreover, this being the case, it would be clearly impossible for an observer to compare retaining in these aspects as between two or more direct economies.

Finally, in a direct economy, it is impossible exactly to relate the effort involved in retaining to that involved in working—to measure them against each other as "real costs." Always at least one of the alternatives between which a choice is made constitutes a mixture, of which the proportion of each constituent is indeterminable, or, in the one case cited on p. 653 where there is a direct comparison of retaining with hours of working economized, the requisite net gain comes in to make the comparisons inexact. Nevertheless, we assume a roughly estimable ratio. And we are justified in doing this for analytical purposes, since, in an indirect economy, where the two functions come to be performed by different persons, they do then become comparable in these aspects, though even then only at the limit for each and through the medium of a generalized potential means for the satisfaction of wants.

By reason of the fact that we have used the inductive method in arriving at our analysis, in these two chapters, of the two human economic functions in production, there remains one point which may require restatement and emphasis in order that the reader may have it quite clearly in mind. In presenting the various kinds and occasions of choices we have set up contrasts between different assortments out of the whole mélange of forces and resistances. Sometimes the expression on one side or the other has been an arithmetic sum—two resistances; sometimes it has been an algebraic sum—a force minus a resistance. Now, for our future use, it is necessary to make it clear that the "real costs" of product include only the effort of working and of retaining that have gone into that product. Sacrifices—the sacrifice aspect of working or retaining—are in no respect a part of the "real costs." Neither, except as they may influence the working or retaining required, do the nature and quantity of product have any bearing on "real costs." And, finally, the nature and the timing of wants have no direct influence in determining what the "real costs" of provision for them will be.

The most lucid way in which to make this point clear is by means of some simple formulae. The simplest case is one between two wants, one of which stands higher in the order of priority than the other. That may be shown as $A > B$. Without introducing further factors we may say that the alternative A will be preferred over the alternative B. Then B becomes the sacrifice involved in choosing A. But, as soon as "real costs" are included, the problem of choice becomes more complex. Let us give "work as effort" our usual designation of W and "retention as effort" that of R_i. Whatever of these two are involved in provision for A or B constitute resistances to, or deductions from, the force which A or B offers. The competition between the two alternatives is determined then by the net forces remaining after such deductions.[4] That is, if A is still to be preferred, it can only be because $A - (W + R_i) > B - (W + R_i)$. If $(W + R_i)$ presents the same resistance to both—as in our examples—then, because $A > B$, A will be preferred even with "real costs" considered. After the choice is

[4] At this point this is the simpler way to think of it. In Part IV, where we bring in different "real costs," we find it preferable to use the ratio $\dfrac{A}{W + R_i}$. But, here, with the assumption of equal costs, the order of surpluses and the order of ratios would be the same. And the reason for rejecting the notion of surplus requires considerable explanation.

made and the working and retaining are begun, the necessary $W + R_i$ in the second expression drops out. This is because no "real cost" is incurred for B. The working and retaining is done for A and all that remains of the lesser expression is the sacrifice, B—the alternative rejected. We have already precisely defined the extent to which the sacrifice does remain, or recur, both for working and for retaining.

If one of the alternatives, say B, is a current want while the other, A, is a future want, then B involves no R_i. R_i, in the expression for B, is zero. Or, $A — (W + R_i) > B — W$. Then B alone stands for the kind of sacrifice of current consumption which we have described as the element of sacrifice in retaining. Obviously neither B, nor $B — W$, is any part of the "real cost" of A. That "real cost" is the $W + R_i$ associated with A, as given. B is merely the rejected alternative, and the working that would have been involved in it (the W associated with B) and which was presented as a resistance to it at the time the program was formulated, never occurs at all. If, however, the same choice also involves extra hours of working for A, the future want, then its W becomes a greater resistance than the W required for B. Let us call the hour that could be used for either—the last present hour—W_1; let us call the extra hour that can only be induced by A, W_2. Then, if A is preferred, it is because $A — (W_2 + R_i) > B — W_1$. A similar complication appears when the provision for A, let us say, involves a longer period of retaining (*cet. par.*) than that for B. The additional retaining may then be designated as R_{i2}. If A is still preferred, it is because $A — (W + R_{i1} + R_{i2}) > B — (W + R_{i1})$.

A mixture of these two varieties of formulae best conveys the choice that is frequently presented between a costless alternative and one that involves "real cost." Such is the competition between future wants involving working, or both working and retaining, on one hand, and leisure, on the other. Let A stand again for a future want and B, this time, for the prepotent present want that is the spearhead of the competition offered by leisure. Such a situation means that, if A is to be preferred as a current want, $A — W > B$; or, if A is a future want, $A — (W + R_i) > B$.

All this merely makes more explicit what we have said several times before. "Real cost" is something that actually occurs as an accompaniment of the alternative that is preferred; sacrifice is the alternative rejected and therefore something that either does not occur at all (is merely estimated) or which is presented only as an impulse or memory to be repressed. At the time the choice is made—in advance—"real cost," as anticipated or estimated effort, may appear on both sides of the formula, on one side only, or on neither side—the last in choices between costless alternatives. But the "real cost" that appeared at that time on the side of the rejected alternative is a "real cost" that is not incurred—never becomes actual. Only the "real cost" of the preferred alternative is converted from an anticipation or estimate into a fact of experience. And only the two forms of effort are "real costs," whether in expectation or in experience.

In our future considerations we will, in general, refer to the two human functions in connection with production by the collective term "contribution" when we are considering them in the aspect of their effect only, and by the term "real costs" when we are thinking of them in the aspect of effort. But when we are considering the inducement to such contributions we will also have to refer to the aspect sacrifice (at least the rejection of the choice of *effortless* alternatives) since this diminishes the effectiveness of the inducement. However, as a matter of convenience, on account of our formula (future wants-efforts providing means), we will also continue to use the collective term "effort" for both working and retaining without specific reference to any of the three aspects.[5]

Capital Theory.—After making some attempt to annotate the foregoing analysis completely in order to relate it to the various current forms of capital theory, for the purpose of pointing out its correspondences and differences, I have given up the task simply for the reason that such notes would need to be far more voluminous than the text. But one comment remains necessary. Any reader who has followed this analysis in only a superficial way might conclude that it is, to a large extent, merely a restatement in different form of Böhm-Bawerk's theory of capital—that theory which, with its various elaborations, has so generally held the field since he proposed it. It is true that the foregoing analysis is based on his theory and that the factors entering it are much the same. If I had to define the difference it would be that we have taken apart his analysis and recombined the same factors in a different way, and with the factors of working, so that our results are very considerably different. In the main these differences are along four lines.

1. We have separated the economic function, retaining, and its accom-

---

[5] This terminological difficulty is frequent in many sciences, where a single term has both a broad and a narrow sense. "Iron ore" is the generic term for minerals containing iron. Though it is the iron content that gives it the name, we do not mean by "a ton of iron ore" minerals containing a ton of iron.

plishment, retention, from the physical objects retained. Analysis like his, in purely physical terms only, necessarily comes to a dead end.

2. We have shown the way in which retaining and working are indissolubly intertwined, and have also differentiated between the sacrifice involved in retaining (anterior) and its effort (current).

3. We have discriminated, as he failed to do, between those of his factors which are deterrents to future provision—for itself or incidental—and therefore to retaining, and those factors which induce it; between the "abstinence" and the "waiting" (sacrifice and effort), on the one hand, which tend to prevent a supply of retaining, and the several particular kinds of advantage which tend to create a demand for it and, therefore, in a direct economy, to induce it.

4. Finally we have corrected his false assumption of "the greater fruitfulness of lengthy methods of production" (*38, 273*) (in which we may include our large batches). His assumption that "the lengthier the production method employed the greater the quantity of products that can be obtained," which is at the basis of the whole notion of degrees of "roundaboutness" and the length of the "period of production," excludes technical possibilities which are "capital-saving," and is, in any case, based on an erroneous criterion. Technical options follow no such regular pattern. And the correct statement is that "lengthy" methods of production are not adopted unless they result in sufficiently "greater fruitfulness."

However, not all modern capital theory is pure Böhm-Bawerk. For that reason it seems desirable to go a little further in order to justify our reference to the "existing confusion" in capital theory and our ascribing it to the failure to keep the several aspects separate.

The worst cases arise when quantity of retaining is identified with the use or "services" of the product retained. Thus, to Pigou (*325, 161,* note 1), the unit of waiting is "the use of a given quantity of resources . . . for a given time." So, too, Pareto says (*317, 309*) "la transformation dans le temps consiste dans cet usage." As well make the unit of working the consumption of a given quantity of product in a given time. Because we relate phenomena in a chain of cause and effect we are not warranted in treating all the members of the whole series as identical.

However, the origin of the error of the greatest practical significance is perhaps to be ascribed to Senior. In the *Outline* (*370, 182*), and adopted by Carey (*70, 301*) he says that "the distinction of profit from rent ceases as soon as capital, from which a given revenue arises, has become, whether by gift or inheritance, the property of a person to whose abstinence and exertions it did not owe its creation." "The constructor of a canal has profits —his heir has rent, because it is *the gift of fortune* and *not the result of sacrifice*." This curiously extreme position errs in three vital respects. First, it personalizes economic functions; second, it confuses proprietary arrangements with economic functions; third, it is blind to any but the single sacrifice aspect of retaining—"abstinence"—erroneously assumes that is made once and for all, and omits all consideration of the continuing effort.

Whether independently, or from this source, J. B. Clark continued and fortified this last error, and I take it that Knight is following in his footsteps. Clark looked only at the initial choice—the sacrifice—which he called "abstinence." Apparently he assumed that this sacrifice is entirely irrevocable, that replacements are, "in a sense, automatic" (see *80*, 134). Apparently, too, Knight follows him in this, since, "in the aggregate an excess of present consumption over current production is, of course, impossible" (*240*, 135). True, Clark does admit (*80*, 156) that the "capitalist" can treat his "capital" as a reserve and, in case of need, live on it. And perhaps Knight's difficulty is due to belief in some imaginary constraint that prevents aggregate "capital" from declining, though it permits individual "capitalists" to sell out to each other and spend their fortunes.

But this is not all. For, by the most extraordinary piece of intellectual legerdemain, Clark completely—or almost completely—eliminates our effort—his "waiting." He does this by eliminating the Austrian "period of production"—our life in production and use—so that the current use corresponds to the current replacement and the whole of retained product is disregarded. See, on this, his Chapter XX (*80*) on the synchronizing of production and consumption. See, also, his "wood-lot" example (*ibid.*, 131–132). Apparently Knight follows him here, too, for he wants to "exorcise" the usual notion of "waiting." See "Issues in the Economics of Stationary States" (*241*, 403) as well as his debate with the Austrians cited hereafter. Thus apparently for Clark, at least, "waiting" is limited to the purely technical, and inconsequential, variety we have referred to above—waiting during the period of accumulation for the first use to be ready. On this see Clark (*80*, 311).

The result of all this confusion of aspects is not only that "abstinence"— sacrifice—is confined to the initiation of retaining, and all that is involved in continuing (future provision) or replacing is overlooked (see, specifically, Clark, *80*, 13), but that the element of "waiting"—effort—is completely elided.

It strikes me that this is one of the most dangerous illusions in economics. It makes plausible the conclusion that, if you remove the inducement to continue existing retaining and to replace what is used up, you do not thereby destroy rapidly all existing "capital" as well as put a stop to "capital formation." This, of course, unless you replace the incentive which induces voluntary retaining by compelling involuntary retaining. And there is evidence that this illusion, so widely prevalent, has recently been having just such a result. A reference to Kuznets's *Commodity Flow and Capital Formation* (*247*, I, 479 and 495) suggests that the net decline in private real capital (deflated prices) in the United States during the years 1931–1935 inclusive was not far from 30 billions of dollars. And this reduction is almost wholly confined to failure to replace durables. If the reduction in quantity—or life—of "perishables" and "semi-durables" in the hands of consumers were also taken account of, the figures might be even more astounding.

G. EXTANT PRODUCT—THE RESULT OF
WORKING AND RETAINING

1. THE ENTITY AND ITS CHARACTERISTICS

Perhaps the most difficult and treacherous concept in the entire field of economic analysis is the one with which we will now attempt to deal. We have regarded product as the result of working; the symmetrical entity in the case of retaining may be called *extant* product.[1] As to this latter, the fact that it is product is due entirely to working, while the fact that it is extant is due entirely to retaining.[2] The respective effects of the two processes, working and retaining, are therefore completely discrete; one is in no way a substitute for the other. It is quite impossible that working should cause product to remain extant;[3] it is equally impossible that retaining should cause product to come into existence. Therefore, while the entity, "product," is the result of working only, the entity, "extant product," is the compound result of working and of retaining and cannot occur at all without the co-operation of both.[4]

Strictly speaking, if we are accurately to visualize the operation of

---

[1] By definition, according to our convention, this is limited to product which remains in existence at the end of the "following consuming-day."

This is approximately Adam Smith's category "stock." We have not adopted his term because (1) it is no longer used in economic literature and its trade use refers to product in process, or finished, in the hands of the producing organization; (2) even with Smith it had a curious *double entendre*—mixing static and dynamic magnitudes; (3) it included money *qua* money; (4) it is not definitive (stock of what?).

Extant product is not the same thing as capital in any of the various economic meanings of the latter.

[2] That is, having been produced, the fact that it remains extant is due to the fact that it is not yet used up; and that, in turn, is the negative side of our definition of retaining.

The convention which conceives as part of final product that instalment of intermediate product which has been used in its production seems somewhat to modify this statement; for then retaining the intermediate product helped to make possible the production of the final product, even if the latter, like telephone service, is incapable of remaining extant. We will discuss that point in the twelfth chapter.

[3] The physical indestructibility, comparatively speaking, of certain materials is due neither to working nor to retaining. On the other hand, the difference between economically long-lived and economically short-lived product is not due to anything in the quality or quantity of working. That is of the same order for both.

[4] Because of what we have called the "irrevocability" of the decision to initiate retaining, which exists in most cases, Böhm-Bawerk concluded that his equivalent of retaining is "not among the *means* of production, but among the *motives* of production—the motives that decide the direction of production" (*38*, 123). A similar failure to distinguish between an action and the motive which gives rise to it would also class working with the "motives." For, if we are going to ignore the element of effort, the only distinction between working and other human activities is in their *direction*—the kind of satisfactions sought.

the two human functions in the economic process of production, we must conceive the effect of working—product—as a flow passing into consumption the next night. Working, alone, results in a day-to-day economy. Analytically, we might almost go so far as to say that the effect of working is production, not product—a process, not a mass. Thus, strictly construed, any continuing existence as product beyond the next consuming-day is due to retaining. At least, we must see that what distinguishes extant product is not that it is the result of working. That is true of all the product that has been made from the beginning of time, the great bulk of which no longer exists.[5] The distinguishing characteristic of extant product is that it still exists because it has been and is now being retained. To retaining alone is due the development away from a day-to-day economy. The fact of extant product, as distinguished from other past product, is solely the consequence of a second form of human effort which is as certainly effortful as is the first form.[6]

We conceive this entity, "extant product," as a global whole, the collectivity of all products existing at any moment;[7] and we view it in the aspect of the past working (work) and the past retaining (retention) that has been embodied in it and has not yet been charged off. That is, while we recognize that it exists in material form, the physical

[5] While the failure to note this obvious distinction lies at the root of the popular "capital is past labor" fallacy (so is past consumption), it is surprising to find the same error in the scientific world. Nevertheless one frequently does so. For example Aftalion (5, 156–157) says "Lorsqu'on embrasse le procès entier de production, on ne voit en oeuvre d'un bout à l'autre de ce procès que le travail et la terre." "Capital" is merely the "ancien produit" of both and there is no "facteur spécial comme le capital." Böhm-Bawerk (38, 97) refuted the notion that "capital is no element" since it "springs from the co-operation of nature and labour." Nevertheless the physical view clings on. Since "labour" itself springs from the co-operation of men and women, Adam and Eve and Nature become, in that view, the only "factors" of production. As to nature as a "factor," see the next chapter.

[6] Except for the differences in terminology and those between "extant product" and "stock" or "capital," these statements are no more and no different than what Adam Smith said a hundred and fifty years ago. But the "faithful" have often wandered from the true faith in the meantime. He said (381, I, 314) that "the whole annual produce, if we except the spontaneous production of the earth" is "the effect of labour." On the other hand, "Parsimony, and not industry, is the immediate cause of the increase of capital. Industry, indeed, provides the subject which parsimony accumulates. But whatever industry might acquire, if parsimony did not save and store up, the capital would never be greater" (ibid., I, 320).

[7] The collective mass we call "extant product"; the individual items, "an extant product" (sing.) or "extant products" (plur.). The individual items have, in this aspect, but two features in common, (a) that they were produced and (b) that they now exist economically (i.e., have some remaining life in use). Needless to say this entity has no time dimension such as Pigou (325, 159) attributes to "capital."

aspect is not germane to economic analysis. For that purpose we view it in its economic aspect only—or, at present, only in this one of its two economic aspects (the "real cost" aspect). In this aspect, then, extant product represents the excess of production over consumption to date.[8] Its existence necessarily connotes the fact that—however vague and immeasurable these two magnitudes are—the total satisfaction of wants cannot have been as great as it would have been if no extant product now remained.[9] This statement is a first approximation and is subject to much refinement as we proceed. The first qualification we need to make is a minor one, necessary merely for consistency in our analysis. Consumption, here, must be defined as we have defined it—that is, as consumption of product only. It should not include the direct consuming of means which require no working (i.e., no production).[10] The second qualification is necessary in order to embrace all the stages of the process along which extant product may be distributed. From the beginning of the time when material enters the process of production, working is being done upon it and work accumulating in it. If, according to our convention, the product is not

[8] Among the early American definitions of "capital" is one in these exact terms. See Tucker (*409*, 51). This form practically coincides with Mill (*298*, I, 103). In other treatments it is more nearly synonymous with that vague and ill-defined entity "wealth," which, as Ely points out (*136*, I, 22), has been used to cover the flow as well as the stock and which usually includes much beside product.

It is interesting to the observer of the circuitous routes by which economics has arrived at some of its fundamental "truths" to note the extent to which this entity was at one time treated as an end in itself. The moral connotation of economic "abstinence" is derived from the early concept of "wealth" (economic well-being) as a stock of product. Progress consisted in increasing "wealth." Any economic activity which did not further this increase was "unproductive." Davenport makes the same point very nicely (*107*, 123). The purpose of an economy was not to increase its consumption but rather its extant product. True, in itself, the fact of extant product, which can only exist by reason of a deficit in consumption under production, seems to deny that consumption is the sole goal. Hence the error. But the act of retaining (not-using) has no virtue in itself any more than has the act of working. The truth lies in the paradox that the greater the extant product—if rightly planned—the greater *becomes* consumption. Thus it is in fact a means of ultimately increasing consumption. To perceive that point requires dynamic rather than the merely static thinking of the founders. Yet the original confusion of "wealth," in its proper sense, with extant product instead of with consumption, doubtless increased our "wealth" (well-being) besides laying the basis of our present scientific understanding.

[9] And this regardless of greater "productivity" due to the existence of extant product; for if, at this moment, all extant products had just been used up, consumption would have been greater than it has been.

[10] Needless to say, neither does it include what Marshall (*291*, 67) and others have called "productive consumption"——i.e., "the use of wealth in the production of further wealth." Again the physical rather than the economic viewpoint! Economically speaking that is merely a transfer from one form of product (intermediate) to another (intermediate or final). It is not consumption at all.

finished and used up in the consuming-day following its producing-day, retaining then begins to be done upon it and retention to accumulate in it. Thereafter it grows to a maximum size, in this aspect, usually upon the commencement of use. As it proceeds to be used up, the accumulated effort disappears (or is charged off), installment by installment.[11] Nevertheless, retaining continues to be required for the unused installments and retention to accumulate therein. Thus, along the series of installments, the quantity of disappearance from each grows somewhat greater than the fraction of the original maximum which each of the successive installments represents. The magnitude of each constituent extant product which goes to make up our global whole is determined by its place in this pattern; and extant product is the sum of these magnitudes.[12] The pattern of life of the constituent products also reminds us of the fact that this global whole is, over a period of time, a perpetual succession.[13] That is, the products constituting it come and go, while the collective entity may continue indefinitely. In the third place, since we have not included the using-up of intermediate product as a part of consumption, we must find some way to make an adjustment by which this using-up is transferred into the product which is, or is to be, consumed, and thereby into consumption. This pattern, in the fourth place, makes it clear that extant product cannot include that character of product which we call "services" —product not embodied in material form. But these, since they must be consumed as they are produced, if at all, necessarily constitute simultaneously a part of both members of our formula, production and consumption, and therefore no part of their difference. The only production which can be part of this difference is production which takes a material shape, since only this can remain extant. A fifth qualification arises from an inherent inconsistency in our two viewpoints of product, to which we have already alluded. Two objectively equal lots

[11] We may remind the reader of our analysis of using-up in Chapter 7. To some extent this "disappearance" is only a valid and valuable convention (depreciation). While they may not disappear in a physical sense, nor even show their wear and tear, it is true, economically speaking, that there remains of products at any time only that portion which is not used up. Physical substance is not produced; neither is it consumed, though it may incidentally change form in the process of consumption.

[12] These changes are presented more fully in subsection 3, below.

[13] E. A. Saliers (359, 3) makes the statement that "With the exception of land [which we exclude], but a very small percentage of the wealth extant in 1800 is still intact and useful."

This perpetual succession is of the same order as that of population and can be thought of in the same terms. Similarly, J. B. Clark (81, 303) said "Laborers are perishable, but social labor is continuous."

of product which are also indifferent subjectively may nevertheless have involved different quantities of working or of retaining or of both. If we conceive the magnitude of extant product in terms of the "real cost" embodied in them, these two lots are of different size. If we conceive the magnitude objectively or in terms of usefulness, they are of the same size. This raises the question of "differentials," which we shall examine in Chapter 12. At this point we may say, however, that it is analytically convenient to follow the usual practice of an indirect economy. Up to the point of putting into final use, the two lots are conceived in terms of their different "real costs"; thereafter, they are conceived in terms of the higher of the two "real costs" or of their usefulness, whichever is lower. Finally, we have already brought out the point, of which we will remind ourselves later, that there are certain characters of change that may take place in the usefulness of products, while they remain extant, which are in no way due either to working and retaining or to consuming—using-up. But these, too, may have to be regarded as changes in the magnitude of particular extant products and thus have an effect on the size of the global whole.[14]

Since extant product has all the characteristics of other product, in addition to its own special one, it is obvious that it may be classified in the same ways. Thus we have the distinction between durable product, which is necessarily a part of extant product, and non-durable product, which may or may not be according to whether provision is made more than a day in advance, or not;[15] we have the distinction between final and intermediate extant product, according as to whether the product constitutes a direct or only an indirect means of satisfying wants; we have the distinction between product in process and finished product; and, as to the latter, we have the distinction between finished product in reserve and finished product in use (the last can be durable only, if non-durable is defined as single use). Finally, though the distinction is not applicable in a direct economy, we may have extant

[14] There is not only loss of product after production, but, for precision, it would be necessary to determine, as we pointed out in the previous chapter, what constitutes standard working. That includes the problem of defining waste or excessive working effort.

[15] This distinction, in practice, does not need to be as fine as that. We may use the dichotomy, long-lived *vs.* short-lived (in use). Walras's use of this criterion to divide "*capitaux*" from "*revenus*" was bad analysis, as I think is now generally agreed. Even Pareto seemed to dislike it (see *317, 293*). But then most of Walras's *qualitative* analysis was bad. The disorderly confusion of his categories is best shown in the summary on p. 182 (*420*). It is his *quantitative* work which first gave outline to the great synthesis.

product both in the consuming and in the producing organizations.[16] These four dichotomies overlay each other. Each is wholly independent of the other. Both classes of each pair may include members of either class of any of the other pairs.[17]

This apparently simple category, or analytical entity, is a most useful one. In the first place, since it is defined as product, it can include nothing which is not product.[18] That disposes, in a precise way, of the various other heterogeneous entities such as raw natural resources, raw land, human beings, which are so often included—it prevents flavoring the entity to taste. It also clears up the question of what it is we are talking about. Here we are not referring to sums of money value, accounting rubrics, proprietary categories, material objects as such, subjective magnitudes or any of the multifarious other phenomena which are frequently—nay usually—confused with this one. Again, since this entity consists of product, distinguishable only by reason of the fact that it is extant, it cannot be supposed to have any other special characteristics which are not attributable to all product as such. That deprives us of the possibility of attaching to it such special attributes as a mysterious capacity for growth, the power of coming into existence of and by itself or of causing other product to do so, the faculty of immortality, etc.[19] It is, in fact, a very comfortable, matter-of-fact en-

[16] See also the supplementary statement on "The Rubric Capital," at the end of this subsection.

[17] Pareto's classification (see 317, 437–438) is a good example of the confusion which results from attempting one classification according to three or four conflicting sets of criteria. His "savings" are roughly equivalent to our "extant product." They become "savings-capital" and are no longer "savings" if they are non-durables in the hands of the producing organization which are destined to be exchanged for work. They are "transformed" (mirabile dictu) into "capital," and cease to exist in either of the two previous forms, when they (?) are exchanged (?) for work, cattle, and machinery. In the second case their destination becomes determining; in the third the physical objects disappear from view and the proprietary interest becomes determining.

[18] It is limited to what is produced and excludes what grows, or occurs, or exists independently of man's intervention as a producer. This is of vital importance in exact analysis. It precludes, for instance, Menger's difficulty (see 296, 133, note 1). He cannot admit the Güterqualität of Enthaltsamkeit because much Capital exists only "durch blosse Occupation." That is, by making a wrong (too-inclusive) classification, he misses the essential characteristic of a large portion of his data.

[19] If J. B. Clark had clearly analyzed the major portion of his concept of "pure capital" as being a process, and then had treated the rest of that concept and his "capital-goods" both as a global mass (extant product) and as individual extant products, the misunderstanding of his position by Böhm-Bawerk, already referred to, would probably never have occurred. There is nothing mysterious or abstract about a continuing objective process; neither is there about a collectivity which constitutes a "perpetual succession." The body is said to renew itself every seven years. That does not make of it an abstraction. Neither is the continuous giving off of heat by the sun, which makes life on earth continuously possible, in any respect an abstraction.

tity which leaves no room for poetic imagination and may therefore be reasonably counted upon to remain the same—to remain unspoiled by the blandishments of the literary.

The Rubric Capital.—Böhm-Bawerk, following the classical school, includes in his rubric "Social Capital" only the extant product in the hands of the producing organization. He also includes money, which except as it is produced metal we would have to exclude, and excludes certain improvements "completely incorporated with the land," which we cannot exclude. (See *38, 65–66.*)

It is particularly objectionable now to retain the old distinction between extant product "used to produce more wealth" and the rest—which tends to confine it to extant product in the hands of producers—at a period in our development when we are actually directing a major part of our total retaining to, and therefore putting much of our extant product in the form of, durable final product for several or joint consumption.

When we come to treat of indirect economies, and particularly of those highly organized ones in which the consuming organization is separate and distinct from the producing organization proper, we may find it necessary to distinguish the production still carried on in the former from that carried on in the latter. Along these lines we would need also to distinguish product in the hands of these consuming organizations from that in the hands of the producing organizations proper. Thus, in the possession of the consuming organization, we would find the following classes of the total extant product:

a. All future provision of finished non-durable final product (finished in the economic sense that it has been finally distributed by the producing to the consuming organization).

b. All finished durable final product (finished in the same sense).

c. Considerable quantities of finished intermediate product both durable and nondurable (kitchen equipment, fuel, etc.).

d. Small quantities of unfinished final product in process of production in the consuming organization.

Even for product in the hands of producing organizations proper we shall not use the term "capital." In its usage in economics the term has been thoroughly spoiled for scientific purposes. Therein it has meant indiscriminately all or part of retained product (plus extras according to taste), all or part of the quantity of retaining being done (conceived as an abstract entity—Clark, etc.—or as a sum of money value—McLeod, etc.—but never as a function being performed) as well as the retainers (the persons who are *doing* it).

It seems to me that nothing is to be gained by disputing any longer as to the meaning of, or the content of the category to be designated by, the term "capital." The only solution is to define, as we have tried to do, classes of extant product and to give to each a specific classificatory name—ours or any others preferred.

We shall reserve the term "capital" for an entity, to be examined later, which is so named in business and legal usage. This entity is (strictly) the sum of the final (personal) dominant interests in a fund (or, as an aggregate, in all funds) and is usually stated in terms of money value according to some conventional basis of valuation. The term is also loosely used of intermediate (impersonal) dominant interests as well (which results in duplication if included in an aggregate). On this see the author's *Institution of Property* (*313*, 469–481). Or, for the same result, in accounting terms, see Littleton (*270*, 183 ff.).

2. RELATIONS OF THIS MAGNITUDE TO THE TWO FUNCTIONS

Our interest in this entity at the present stage of the analysis is in one of its economic aspects only. In that aspect, such constituent extant product represents, at any moment, a definite quantity of work and of retention—that which has been put in to date less that which has disappeared (been charged off) to date.[20] The sum of these individual quantities, put in and remaining, is the measure of the quantity of retaining now being done, and therefore of the function which is making this extant product possible. As long as the global whole continues, the retaining must continue; or, in the obverse and—except for loss (waste) and gain—in the proper causal order, if aggregate current retaining changes, the quantity of extant product must change correspondingly. If the aggregate retaining does not change, but nevertheless extant product is being used up, it is only because new retaining is taking the place of the old; that is, because equivalent retaining is being initiated for one purpose as fast as its quantity declines for some other, or because it is being initiated for replacement as fast as it ceases because of using-up. The purposes and the products may constantly change, but the total may nevertheless remain the same. In accordance with our analysis of retaining, the quantity now, at any moment, required to carry the global whole of extant product represents approximately the past effort of working incurred when each portion of it was produced. Also it represents the past effort of retaining—the retention accumulated in each of its constituents. It also probably represents a

[20] Since it is work and retention that are being retained, their disappearance necessarily reduces the quantity of retaining required.

The reader should perhaps be put on notice that we are building up an alternative way of rendering commensurable an objectively incommensurable congeries of different products. One way—the usual one—is in terms of comparative significance or usefulness; this way is in terms of comparative contribution of human effort in both forms. Thus we are not accepting the mathematical school's conclusion that there is only one means of commensuration—"*en numéraire*" (see, for instance, Pareto, *317*, 424).

higher intensity of working effort (per unit of work) on account of the extra working-hours which were, in the past and in spots at least, necessary to build it up to its present magnitude. That is, while extant product involves no more working than did consumed product, it has usually involved, in a direct economy, working of a greater degree of effort in the past by the *retainer*.[21] That, however, though it needs to be remembered, does not alter the magnitude of retaining. For, we recall, the magnitude depends on the quantity of work represented, and the quantity of work, as effect, has been standardized without reference to the intensity of effort involved. If we view the mass as continuing, so that we take account of the passage of time, we see that, in order to maintain the same magnitude, there is also constantly required new and current working because of all new retaining that is taking the place of the old (replacements). And, from this same viewpoint, we see that the quantity of effort which is being expended currently upon the unchanged magnitude continues at an unchanged rate. There is nothing mysterious or abstract about all this. The same mass, at a moment, represents the past sacrifice of leisure as well as the effort of working; and, as it continues through time, both this kind of sacrifice and this kind of effort are also required to maintain it by replacement, etc.

The supposition that, once established, a mass of extant product requires no further sacrifice or effort to maintain it is, as has been said, one of the most dangerous illusions that is prevalent in economic theory. In the mass the effort of retaining may be continuous; in detail it is always and only incurred for relatively near-by provision for certain specific wants or for the economizing of working. Looked at in the mass, the sacrifice seems all to have been made when extant product was increasing to its present dimensions; but, in detail, new sacrifices have to be made as fast as the future provisions that warranted the old are used. This view of a continuous process which is nevertheless, in detail, continually beginning and ending, leads us to the concepts of gross and net initiation of retaining (new retaining). That portion of the gross new retaining which goes only to offset disappearance of extant product in use (using-up or waste) does not increase the total retaining done, though it involves new sacrifices and new working effort. Therefore, if the net of the new retaining initiated is a positive

[21] In an indirect economy, where worker and retainer may be different persons, this higher degree of effort is put in by the retainer *only*, to initiate the retaining, not by the worker who may make the product retained.

quantity, the total retaining done (the quantity of extant product) increases; if it is a negative quantity, the total decreases. Or, in other terms, in the first case extant product increases; in the second, it decreases. A striking analogy exists to illustrate this point. All viable nature is the result of the process of growth. "The indispensable condition of growth is that income be greater than expenditure. A variable amount of the food-income is used to meet the everyday expenses of living; the surplus is available for growth; and this must be understood as including, besides increase in size, that imperceptible growth which brings about the replacement of worn-out cells by fresh ones." [22]

The notion of wealth and the more limited one of "capital" have become so permeated with the concept of property [23] that it is necessary for us to take some pains to prevent our somewhat similar category, extant product, from being so contaminated by mere contagion. It is obvious, of course, that, just as the working which goes into a product must be performed by some worker, so must the retaining be performed by some retainer. Because these constitute the human economic functions both can only be performed by individual human beings. Nevertheless, in the complex indirect economies which we hope later to examine, there is no necessity that the worker should ever see or come in physical contact in any way with the product in which his work is incorporated; nor is there any necessity that the person who is doing the retaining should have the retained product in his possession. True, no society can exist economically without some tacit or formal proprietary system. But there is an enormous variety of actual and potential systems, some of which show the greatest complexity of indirect relations between the ultimate worker and retainer and the extant product. In a direct economy, to which we now confine ourselves, there need be no overt system, since the usual definition of property is "relations . . . between persons . . . with reference to 'things.' " [24] Nevertheless, in order that there should be extant product,

---

[22] Thomson and Geddes, *395*, I, 15. The "biological analogy" has been under attack in the social sciences ever since Spencer first used it; but when the *economic* analogy begins to be used in the biological sciences it appears that there must be something to it.
[23] Menger's *Verfugung* up to Weber's *Verfugungsgewalt* make property of the essence of the matter. Walras distinguished between *de facto* and *de jure* appropriation (*420*, 38). Neverthless appropriation is a prerequisite (*ibid.*, 23). So is it with Fisher ("dominion," *142*, 328), and even Davenport (*107*, 132 and 211, including note 1), to cite but a few. Worse still is the French application of proprietary categories (legal)—for example, Walras's and Pareto's "*capitaux fonciers*" (*immobiliers*) and "*capitaux mobiliers*" (see Walras, *420*, 180–181, and Pareto, *317*, 435–437).
[24] See the author's *Institution of Property* (*313*, 290).

retaining must have been initiated and continued. That is a condition imposed by the nature of things, not by human relations. The economic function and its effect are wholly independent of any particular proprietary system and must be examined apart from such social arrangements.

Toward the close of the seventh chapter we examined the various forms of loss of usefulness and its significance other than those resulting from consumption. Obviously these can hardly occur except with extant product, for almost all such changes require some interval of time. It is now necessary to reconcile disappearance in respect of that aspect of product—that which is to be taken out—with our analysis of its other aspect—that which has been put in. While it is pure convention to regard work and retention as disappearing from product *pari passu* with its using-up in consumption, the convention seems legitimate. Since the sacrifice and effort have been made for the purpose of making provision for a want or of economizing working, when and as these purposes are accomplished and the benefits balance off the "cost," it seems reasonable to regard both as things of the past—equalized and thus neutralized. If, however, usefulness disappears for any of the other reasons cited, whether due to mistaken estimates, or to later changes in the want-satisfaction system, or to physical spoilage, etc., the work and retention incorporated in the extant product cannot be so balanced off. Nevertheless, since, economically speaking, the prospective benefits have wholly or partly disappeared, the effort might as well be forgotten. The entity which occupies the place of consumption in these cases is what we call "economic waste." But, here, that which was put in is the same as that which is taken out. The waste is a waste of the effort and the sacrifice themselves. And here the change in quantity of retaining to be currently done thereafter is initiated by a contraction in extant product in its aspect of usefulness which does not arise by the voluntary act of the retainer, as does the contraction which occurs by reason of use.[25]

25 That is, we consider that retaining can be performed only on that which has economic existence. When product ceases to have economic existence, in whole or in part, because of disappearance of usefulness by reason of such loss, the whole or the part can no longer be the subject of retaining, any more than it can after it is used up. There remains the question whether the retaining which was expected to be done thereafter constitutes, because of its influence on the program, any part of the waste even though, according to our convention, it is not performed. It does not. Its only effect was that it reduced the sacrifice from what it might have been, to the extent of the overestimation of the quantity of retention above that which was, in the event, actually to be performed. The waste is entirely that of the working plus the retention performed to date.

It has become customary for us to think of economic waste as if it were inherently at the cost of the retainer. And this, because, under the institutions with which we are most familiar, this is its usual incidence. But that is not inherently necessary. In a direct economy the worker and the retainer are one and the same. The waste of work is *qua* worker and that of retention is *qua* retainer. Under other institutions and in an indirect economy, arrangements would be quite conceivable which would provide that all loss on account of waste would fall on the workers. But whoever bears the loss, it is always, in any form of economy, a waste for which there is no compensation whatever. No part of an economy can gain from waste at the cost of any other part.

On the other side of the ledger we have to consider the possibility that there may be gains of usefulness while product remains extant, other than those which are due to production (i.e., to the effects of working and retaining). And again, as in the case of losses, these may arise from physical or from economic causes. Corresponding to physical destruction, spoilage, etc., we have various natural processes such as growth, chemical change, etc. Some of these may occur without the intervention of man, and all of them may be conceived separately from the direct effects of man's intervention.[26] Nevertheless, when we come to examine these processes in the succeeding chapters we shall find that only the variable effect of man's intervention counts in the economic scheme. And we shall come to the conclusion that the magnitude of all these particular accretions of usefulness, occurring while product is extant, corresponds, unless it is wholly irregular and unexpected, to some magnitude of human effort which deliberately provides the opportunity for its occurrence.[27] In respect of increases in usefulness due to a change in the want-satisfaction system while the product is extant, the situation is somewhat different. In this category may be in-

[26] The favorite example, the "working" of wine, takes place, to be sure, without the *working* of man. But it cannot take place without the *retaining* of man; though the latter is only a permissive, not a causative, agent. See, on this, the remarks on p. 631, note 6.

[27] Here we can take the physical (classical) view and regard the accretion of usefulness from such processes as a part of the "bounty of nature." Or we can take the economic view, disregard the fact that the same processes may occur in "wild" nature, and conceive those which occur in "tame" nature to be like other accretions of usefulness in the course of production. The latter view is preferable, because the only justification for the working and retaining performed in these cases is the estimated accretion of usefulness which arises as a result of the natural process. For instance, tilling has no possible other justification.

cluded both *unexpected* increases, even when due to natural causes (above), as well as those due to underestimates in general. In all these cases we have, during the period the product is extant, an unforeseen accretion in usefulness over and above the quantity which appeared sufficient to justify the sacrifice and effort when the program was initiated. Such increments do not alter the magnitude of the product in the aspect of that which has been put in ("real cost"); they only alter it in its other aspect (usefulness). But we easily recognize this excess since it is of exactly the same order as the surplus from working which we have already examined. It is merely another unnecessary, but this time also an *unforeseen*, surplus or gain. While it is of the opposite sign from economic waste—positive instead of negative—it is not its exact antithesis. But for practical purposes we may regard it as such.

As in the case of economic waste, there is no inherent reason to assign such unforeseen surplus to retaining. Under some institutional systems that is its incidence; under others it might be included with the surplus from working. In a direct economy the two surpluses are indistinguishable. Only, from an analytical standpoint, we must see that such unexpected surpluses usually manifest themselves during intervals between the periods of working while retaining only is continuing, or at the end of the process after working is completed. And, from a practical standpoint, it would appear that, if the loss from economic waste and the gain from unexpected surplus are to be divided on other than a per capita basis, both should be divided on the same principle. The one should go to offset the other.

We have treated product, in its economic aspect, as solely the result of working, and have divided it, first, into "services," so-called, and those other results which, so to speak, consist of a compound of matter and a fleeting human act, treated with a fixative.[28] This latter type of result we have divided again into the class which is consumed (or lost) at once—in the conventional period—and that which remains extant. To the extent and for the time that this second class of product remains extant, it does so because, and only because, it is continuously retained. From this way of viewing the phenomena there

---

[28] As Senior put it, so nicely (370, 52), "In each case there is, of course, an act and a result; but in the one case our attention is called principally to the act, in the other to the result."

arises a certain analytical difficulty which must be faced. If product can be completed without the intervention of retaining—and we have recognized that this is the characteristic of a day-to-day economy— we seem to imply that the process of production lasts only so long as working is being applied. But that form of effort we have called retaining continues from the beginning of working to the end of using-up —if more than a "day." Is not that, too, a part of production? As a matter of fact the dilemma is largely a matter of terminology. In the aspect of their usefulness, the necessary changes in the form or place of material objects is only accomplished by working. The only effect of retaining is to keep product the same. If we wish to look at production in this aspect, we must define production of material product as such changes; then we cannot include that part of the process which takes place after these changes are effected, even though, thereafter, retaining continues to be done. If, on the other hand, we wish to view production in the aspect of the "real costs" involved, we must define production as the expenditure of effort upon the provision of means to the satisfaction of wants; in that case we must include the period of retaining, even after such changes are completed. In examining an indirect economy the process of production for any product is usually conceived to last as long as that product is in the hands of the producing organization. But there are two exceptions to this. The first extends such period when the producing organization continues to do the retaining for the consuming organization. The second terminates such period when finished product goes into use in the producing organization as intermediate product—at least it does so as to the intermediate product itself. In the case of a direct economy it does perhaps less violence to our preconceived notions to define the process of production as completed when the product is ready for consumption or use, even though we recognize that human effort continues to be applied to it, after that, until it is used up or its usefulness is lost. Exact terminology, however, would require two terms, one for the first phase only and the other for the two phases together. Without attempting a revision of current terms, we shall treat the process of *production* as if it stopped when the actions which result in "services" or in the transformation or transportation of material objects are finished. That is our name for the first phase only. The two phases together constitute the process of *contribution*, and the latter overlaps the process of consumption.

3. THE LIFE CYCLE OF AN EXTANT PRODUCT

Our analysis to this point has presented product in two economic aspects, that of the means of satisfying wants and that of the result of human effort. These two are definite and distinct. In the conventional economic dichotomy, the one envisages product from the side of demand, the other from the side of supply. Having treated the two aspects successively, and to that extent separately, there may be some risk that the reader will retain an impression that the "shape" of the life cycle of a product in these two aspects is the same. It is well, then, to call attention to the difference between the two. In the aspect of "real cost," of effort expended, the life cycle of a product has the "shape" shown in I, Fig. 28. During the period of time represented by

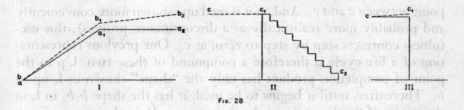

Fig. 28

the horizontal distance from a to a_1, working is being done and work is accumulating in the product. The altitude at a_1 represents the total work embodied in the product. Therefore, the ratio of the altitude to the horizontal distance traversed represents the rate at which work has accrued—that is, the quantity of working that has been continuously performed during the period. Or that rate (working) might be represented by the rise along the line aa_1 per unit period on the base. Therefore, again, the rate is proportional to the angle of inclination of aa_1, if the latter is a straight line. When working is finished, the quantity of work remains constant, as shown from a_1 to a_2. From the initiation of the working (if more than one day), retaining commences. Thereafter retention accumulates. We have agreed to measure retaining by the quantity of product retained, viewed in its aspect of effort. Therefore, the quantity of "simple" retaining involved at any point between a and a_1 is represented by the altitude at that point. As we have seen, it is possible for human beings roughly to compare the effort involved in a unit of work with that in a unit of retention. It is then possible to summate the two forms of effort by converting the unit of retention into terms of units of work.[29] This additional accumulation of effort in the form of retention—when reduced to a common term—is indicated by the altitude from aa_1 up to the broken line which rises from b to b_1 until the product is finished. Since it is necessary, secondarily, to retain the accrued retention as well as the work embodied, the quantity of "compound" retaining currently required until the product is finished is, then, the altitude to b b_1 at any point.[30] From this point, so long as the product is retained (not used up or lost) retention, unlike work, continues to accumulate as from b_1 to b_2 with the result that the retaining required increases constantly, though slightly.

On the other hand, in the aspect of usefulness, the life cycle of a product has the "shape" shown in II, Fig. 28. Therein it has no usefulness until it is finished. Then its usefulness is the altitude to any point between c and c_1. And, as it is used up (shown more conveniently and probably more realistically as a discontinuous process), this usefulness contracts step by step to zero, at c_2. Our previous representation of a life cycle is therefore a compound of these two. Up to the point of completion product has only the "shape" shown in I, up to b_1. Thereafter, until it begins to be used, it has the shape b_1b_2 in I, in the aspect of "real cost," and the shape c c_1 in II, in the aspect of usefulness. When it begins to be used, its "shape," in the aspect of "real cost," must be made to conform to II, because of the disappearance of the result of effort. Conventionally, we do this by adding the retention that will accumulate by reason of the decreasing retaining which will be done from c_1 to c_2 in II, to the total effort accrued at b_2 and then dividing the sum by the number of steps (installments). Thus we "charge off" effort as "real cost" at a uniform rate per installment, though we recognize that the last installment has required more retention than the first. This latter point, the accumulation of retention during use, is shown in III. Since the using-up of one installment per unit of time during 10 units of time gives an average life in use,

[29] If we take the unit of retention to be the retaining for one hour of the effect of one standard hour's working then, at 5% per annum, the unit of retention is equivalent, in terms of effort, to $1 / 175200$ of a unit of work. Ordinarily, however, it is more convenient to consider the unit of retention (R_1) as the retaining of the product of 1 hour's working for 1 day. Then $1 R_1 = \dfrac{1}{7300} W$. Conversely, in this relation, which is the same in both cases, the effort involved in one hour's standard work is equal to that of the "simple" retention involved in retaining that product for 20 years.

[30] To be precise, the retaining and retention, on a compound basis, are very slightly higher than this, for this only accrues "simple" retention.

per installment, of 5 units of time, retaining at the rate shown at b_2 in I must be carried on for an average of 5 units of time. But, since the continuance of such retaining for 5 units of time involves, secondarily, the accrual of retaining itself as a "real cost," accrued retention will increase the retaining done. When this increment is reduced to common terms of effort, that becomes the broken line $c\ c_1$. Thus, the "real cost" of working and retaining per installment here will conventionally be one-tenth of the altitude from the base to c_1.

From this we see that, in the aspect of usefulness, a product has no magnitude until it is complete, remains of the same size until it is in use, and then declines (or is conceived to decline) step by step until it is used up. On the other hand, in the aspect of "real cost," there is an accumulation of the cost of working as long as that continues and of the cost of retaining until the end of the using-up. Finally, from the standpoint of effect—the aspect of contribution—while the magnitude of a product may seem to increase as a result of working, it is difficult to conceive of its increasing as a mere consequence of retaining. Rather that seems only to preserve it intact. The effect of all past retaining seems always to have disappeared. In this aspect its effect is essential but not cumulative; it is like the heat of the sun.[31] Failure to distinguish the different changes in magnitude of product which occur in these three aspects causes a confusion which leads to many difficulties in economic investigation.

While this analysis actually fits in with what we have said and shall say about the magnitude, product, it may be necessary to reintroduce the reconciliations in order that the reader may not be confused. We have said that aggregate product is measured in terms of the work and retention incorporated therein—its "real costs." In the individual case adjustments downward from this magnitude are made for using-up or loss of usefulness. As between two equal lots of a

[31] This may be worth elucidating. The effect of working (work) accumulates (presumably) in the product as it is performed. After working two hours there is more product than after working one. The effect of retaining does not accumulate; it merely continues. After retaining two years there is no more product than after retaining one year. But the "real cost" of retaining accrues in the product in exactly the same way as does the "real cost" of working. Retaining for two years represents twice the retention, and therefore twice the effort, that retaining for one year does, just as working for two hours represents twice the effort that working for one does. Thus the effort (and "real cost") of retaining is proportionate to retention performed, not to retaining, just as that of working is roughly proportionate to work performed.

This points to the unsatisfactory nature of the American concept of "time utility"—Pareto's "transformation dans le temps" (317, 305 ff.). There is no regular and inherent growth of product over time.

single product—objectively and subjectively indifferent—whose "real costs" are different—different channels or techniques—such differences are eliminated in measuring the product. This is done on various bases, as we shall see. But the objective and subjective viewpoints can have no other influences than these on product as a magnitude—can assimilate its magnitude in "real cost" to their own magnitudes in no other respect. And, even when these adjustments are made, product continues to be defined as a magnitude in terms of a compound of work and of retention. On the other hand, different products are objectively incommensurable as we saw in Chapter 8; and their usefulness, while comparable, is also incommensurable in terms of any unit. Therefore, a mass of different products cannot be summated and become an aggregate magnitude in either the objective or the subjective aspects. But, in the aspect of "real costs" such an aggregate is not only conceivable; it is measurable. It is measured in terms of the effect of a standard working-hour and, through that, in terms of the "real cost" of work and of retention. Thus "real cost" remains the only dimension, or dimensions, of product in terms of which quantities consisting of aggregates of different products can be conceived or stated.

4. THE QUESTION OF THE LIFE OF EXTANT PRODUCT AS A WHOLE

It is now possible to perceive the way in which these several related entities and their magnitudes must be conceived—the only way in which they can be conceived.[32] As stated at the beginning of this section and now confirmed, we have to visualize retaining, in its aspect of effect, as a process which continues over time but is not measured by time. As a magnitude it can only be measured by the quantity of extant product being currently retained. The whole setting determines this quantity. Thereafter, if the setting remains the same, the quantity of retaining tends to remain the same except for, and to allow for,

---

[32] *En passant* we should emphasize that, while these entities are closely related, they are not identical and should be thought of differently. Essentially, the differences are those between processes and masses. Working and retaining are processes. Work and retention are masses. A part of the former and all of the latter are embodied in material objects (product). Product is a mass which may not endure (almost a process) or which may endure (extant product). Masses remain or disappear; processes continue or stop. The measure of masses is in terms of static dimensions (volume, weight, etc.); the measure of processes is in terms of dynamic dimensions (flow, etc.). At times the latter can only be measured as cross sections (static magnitudes) like retaining (head of water, etc.). But, usually, they are measured as masses per unit of time, like working (gallons per minute, etc.).

erratic consumption.[33] If now, no changes occur and therefore the magnitude of retaining being performed, and of extant product, remains of the same size, it is because of the exact correspondence of the two members of each of two pairs of independent comparisons. First, it is because, for the new retaining which is initiated for replacements, etc., that part of the setting which arises from estimates of future wants, future efforts, and sacrifices in which the replacements are judged reproduces, so far as net effects are concerned, the setting that existed originally when the installment of extant product that is being currently used was decided upon. Second, it is because experience of actual occasions now is justifying the original estimate of occasions— which constitutes the rest of the setting. When these correspondences exist the whole tends to remain the same, because what is taken out each day is balanced by what is put in each day. Nevertheless, what is taken out each day represents a small, and perhaps a very small, part of the aggregate which has been put in from the beginning.

This continuous process began at some time certain. But it may never end. It may be continuous. To the extent that it is continuous as to the aggregate, the notion of a time dimension for retaining, as effect, and for extant product is inapplicable. We might say that so much retaining is being done per hour—put our measurement in the form of a rate per unit of time—but that would add nothing to the statement that so much retaining is being done currently, or that there is such and such a quantity of extant product. The time dimension is redundant. The only dimension that has any bearing on these magnitudes is the quantity of product that is being retained. That being the case, it is evident, as we have said before, that our entity, retention—or the quantity of retaining accomplished—does not appear at all in the aspect of effect. What use is there in determining the quantity of retaining, as effect, accomplished? [34] How can we say how many days or years

[33] The analysis which lies behind Cassel's somewhat descriptive statements (74, 134-142) seems to me to accord exactly with this conceptual model of ours, and to be free, as is usual with him, from the one-sidedness or oversights which characterize most of the other analyses of this process.

[34] Thus, we measure the rate of the process, retaining, both as effect—in terms of the total "real cost" of product retained that remains not charged off—and as effort or "real cost"—in terms of the "real cost" of *doing* such retaining. But we measure the quantity of process accomplished, retention, only as effort or "real cost"—in terms of the "real cost" of *having done* such retaining. As effect, the dimensional formula for retaining is $R_e = W + R_1$. As "real cost" it is $R_1 T^{-1} = (W + R_1)KT^{-1}$, where K represents a very small fraction. The dimensional formula for retention, as "real cost," is $R_1 = (W + R_1)KT^{-1} \times T$, or $(W + R_1)K$.

this process, as an aggregate has continued? Each day or year it would represent just that much more of retaining accomplished. It would be continuously piling up as time moves. For each economy the accrued retaining accomplished to date would be the average amount of retaining it has done since the beginning of the process, multiplied by the number of days or years since it was begun.[35]

An analogy may aid us here. In its physical aspect the magnitude of a primeval forest can only be reckoned in physical units—say board feet. If conditions remain the same, the number of board feet in that forest may remain approximately the same for hundreds, even thousands, of years. The forest is a result of the phenomenon of growth. Yet, as a whole, it no longer grows. If we introduce the element of time and undertake to say how old the forest is, we must assign as its age the entire span of years since it first began to grow. And, in this sense, it grows one year older each year, though it grows no larger. But in no other respect does the element of time have meaning in connec-

---

As effect, retaining has no time dimension (inversely). It is measured in terms of a static magnitude. As "real cost" it has such a dimension. It is a dynamic magnitude of the derived order—a rate. That permits its conversion into a static and fundamental magnitude by including time as a direct dimension as well. And that gives us the quantity of process accomplished, as "real cost." But the quantity of process accomplished, as effect, would be $R_eT = (W + R_i)T$—a meaningless formula.

[35] Since this is the core of the current dispute between the Austrians, as represented by Hayek and others, and Knight, and since it lies at the root of the Austrian notion of "roundaboutness" and "period of production" or "investment," it is well to follow this question through in terms of our entities.

It may also be well to remind the reader that Jevons is as responsible as anyone else for the "period of production" notion (see 224, 228–229). He identifies the "use of capital" with the lengthening of the "average interval between the moment when labour is exerted and its result or purpose accomplished." And he quite erroneously deduced therefrom that "the same capital will serve for twice as much industry if it be absorbed or invested for only half the time"—a common delusion among the Austrians also. As well say that the same "labor" will serve for twice as much industry if it be employed for only half the time. What is this magnitude "industry," we may ask? It can only be output. That converts the statement into the first form given in the supplementary statement on "Roundaboutness," at the end of this section. In that case, as we shall see, the "life" of the extant product does not enter into the formula.

The above statements apply, of course, to retaining and its accomplishment in the aspect of effect only. As "real costs" of individual products, both retaining and retention are essential to our analysis. Retaining is the rate at which this "real cost" is accruing; retention is the quantity of this "real cost" that has accrued. In use, as we have seen, these "real costs" are gradually charged off. Thus, for each product, it is possible to estimate the magnitude of retention accrued and not yet charged off. If that can be done for each product, their sum would represent the total retention for all products —that is, for extant product. But what bearing would that have on economic analysis? On the same basis it would be possible to estimate the aggregate quantity of work embodied in extant product, less the portion charged off. What meaning would that have? The magnitude of extant product includes both.

tion with the forest. On the other hand, when we come to deal with the individual trees, time is of the essence of the matter. For each tree is constantly growing; that is, it is becoming larger at a certain rate per unit of time. Its age, then, determines its size. The forest is constituted of trees which are continually growing larger. Nevertheless the forest remains of the same size. And that for the reason that the average age, or, if you will, the statistical pattern of the number of trees at each age, remains always the same. Now, if we conceive the forest also to be growing larger, it may be doing so for either of two reasons; the number of trees may increase, or the same number of trees may live (and grow) longer. In the latter case the average age increases; in the former, if the increment all starts at one moment, the average age is reduced until the increment is of the average age, and is increased thereafter until the increment dies; but, if the increment appears gradually over a life, then, while it is in process of being added, the average age is reduced, and when the whole increment has been added, the average age returns to the previous point.

Now it might be possible to measure the size of the forest by multiplying the average age by the rate of growth and then by the number of trees. But this seems a very roundabout way of coming at the total size, as compared with measuring the number of board feet. It is also possible to conceive changes in the size of the forest in terms of changes of average age, if this is the only change (i.e., the second of the above causes of change). But it is not possible to do so if the change in the average age is due to an increase in the number of trees. For then, though the average age decreases for a time, the size of the forest has increased. And, in either case, it is much simpler to conceive of changes in the size of the forest as consisting of changes in the number of existing board feet. Still less is it possible to do what the Austrian school has attempted to do; that is, to say that, at a given rate of growth, the size of the forest is governed by its *average* age. It is governed by its *aggregate* age, it is true. Thus we might say that the magnitude of the forest is 10,000 tree-year's growth at the rate of 10 board feet per year. But it would be somewhat simpler to say that it is 100,000 board feet.

This analogy illustrates the difficulty with the Austrian conception of "period of production," or "investment," when applied to the aggregate, in that it leads to confusion between producing more product in advance of consumption by the same interval and producing the same quantity of product in advance of consumption by a longer interval.[36] In the former case the quantity of retaining being done is increased. In the latter, it is not. In the former, the average life of total product being retained is not increased—only the aggregate life of product being retained is increased. In the latter case both are increased.[37]

Following out this analogy we see that the concept of retaining as effect—the quantity of process occurring at a moment, or the rate,—is useful, as an analytical entity, both in application to the aggregate product retained (extant product) and to any individual product retained. It is a measure of the function being performed upon the whole or upon the parts. But, on the contrary, the concept of retention—past performance of the process—is only useful as a measure of "real cost" —that is, as a means of allocating the quantity of function that has been performed upon a specific individual product, which necessarily has a definite and limited "life," and from which retention, like work, is continually disappearing as the product is used up. As to the aggregate (extant product)—a perpetual succession—retaining as effect is measured by that aggregate; as to the aggregate, the notion of retaining as effect, already accomplished, has no meaning; for as to the aggregate, we may "wait" forever. But, in their aspect of "real cost," and as to individual products, retention is a record of the past; retaining is current performance. Then retention has no dimension of time; retaining as "real cost" has the dimension of time, but it is an inverse dimension.

It is essential, if the science of economics is to be further developed, that the analysis and classification of the entities we have been examining in this and the last chapters should be more exact and explicit than they have been. In this respect, at least, the foregoing "qualitative" analysis moves in the right direction; but it makes no claim to be definitive; the process of improving our "analytical tools," so-called, is one which, it is to be hoped, will never end. The refinements and distinctions suggested here do not, in the main, impair the accepted theory of capital—if there can be said to be such a theory. They do necessi-

---

[36] For a further discussion, see supplementary statement on "Roundaboutness," at the end of this section.

[37] It is clear that our Future Provision A (Appendix V, Section C 1) would represent the same quantity of current retaining, as "real cost" being incurred, whether it were produced for 30 days in advance or for 60 days in advance. But, in the latter case, it would represent, at the end, twice the retention, as "real cost," that it did in the former.

tate the substitution of several exact entities and terms for one vague and general one; they qualify many too broad generalizations; they alter some conclusions.

Roundaboutness.—The Austrian school seems to have a very *roundabout*, or worse, way of conceiving what they call "roundaboutness."

The essence of "capitalistic" production, so-called, centers chiefly about the second of our two types of technical option—intermediate product. It would be natural to assume that it is this to which the expression "roundaboutness" refers. Its measure, then, depends first on the degree to which such options exist and are exercised in proportion to the aggregate of production. It is related, then, in some way to the quantity of intermediate product. The question arises whether the degree of "roundaboutness" is conceived to be (1) the ratio of the average of extant intermediate product existing during a period to total final product for that period, or (2) the ratio of the installment of intermediate product used up during a period to the total final product for that period after deducting this installment, or (3) the "period of production" (or investment), that is, the aggregate age of all constituents, including the installment, of final product for the period. If it is the first, then, roughly, the ratio is the average amount of retaining, as effect, performed per annum to the amount of work performed per annum, and the "life" of the extant product does not enter into the formula. If it is the second, then it is the ratio between the amount of effort applied indirectly to final product and the amount of effort applied directly. But there again the "life" of the extant product does not immediately enter into the formula. If it is the third, then it varies with the ratio of the installment to total product, times the age of that installment. In the first interpretation two economies would be equally "roundabout" because the annual final product of both and the extant intermediate product of both were the same, in spite of the fact that the intermediate product of the first was being used up (and replaced) at double the rate of the second. In the second interpretation the first economy might be conceived to be twice as "roundabout" as the second since the proportion of indirect effort was twice as great, in spite of the fact that the extant intermediate product of both was the same. And this is directly contrary to what the Austrians would say of it. In the third interpretation, since the size of the installment used by the first economy was twice as great as that of the second, but, as a result, the "life" of this installment was only half as great, the first economy would be $\frac{1}{2} \times 2$ times as "roundabout" as the second—in other words, equally so. But that arrives at the same result as the first interpretation by a circuitous and unnecessarily complicated route.

I do not think the question of these interpretations is an important one—it is a mere matter of terminology. But posing it clearly serves one useful purpose. It shows the root of the difficulty which confronts the Austrian notion of "roundaboutness," in that this notion attempts either to combine, into one, two incompatible ratios—that of "capital" use to "labor" use, and that of indirect application of effort to direct application—or it introduces, as if it were an essential feature, the time element which necessarily cancels itself out and disappears. The fact is that the fundamental characteristic of "roundaboutness" seems to be not temporal but, so to speak, economically spatial. It is the indirect application of effort to final product. On the other hand, the fundamental characteristic of "capitalistic" production seems to be the use of retaining as well as working because of the exercise of technical options requiring intermediate product. In neither does the dimension of time enter, and the criteria for measuring the two characteristics are entirely independent of each other.

On this subject see, of course, the whole series of articles in Knight *vs.* Hayek. But see also, particularly, Cassel, 75, 15–22. The latter concludes that instead of the "period of production," "a more natural and reliable measure of the importance of capital in the social economy could be obtained simply by calculating the quotient between the capital and the income of the economy." This, though broader, is along the lines of (1) above.